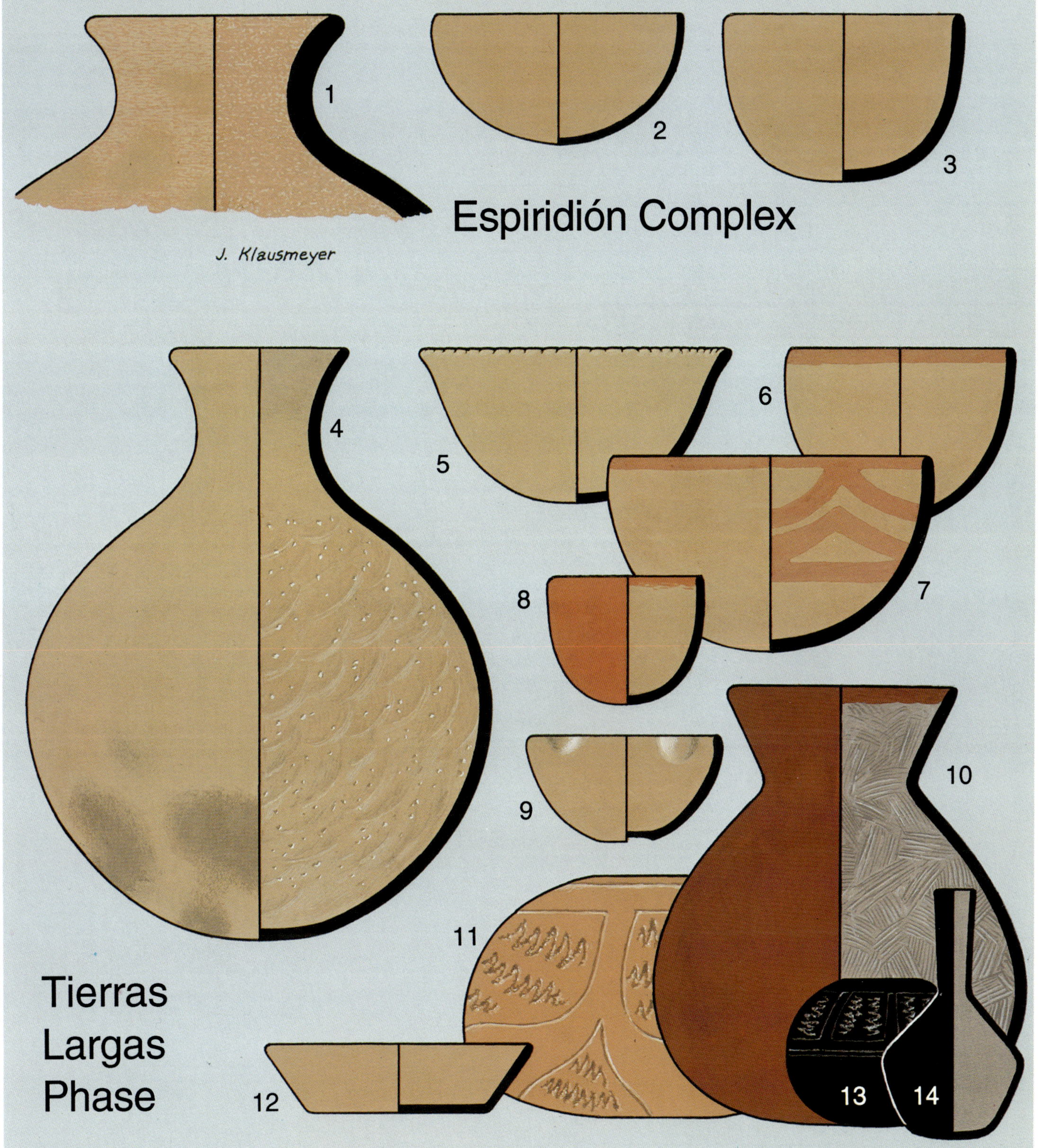

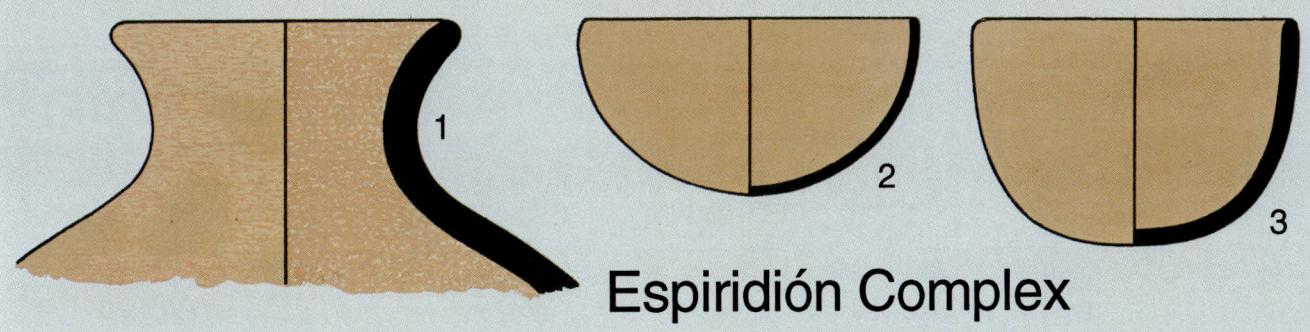

1
2
3
Espiridión Complex
J. Klausmeyer
4
5
6
7
8
9
10
11
12
13
14
Tierras
Largas
Phase

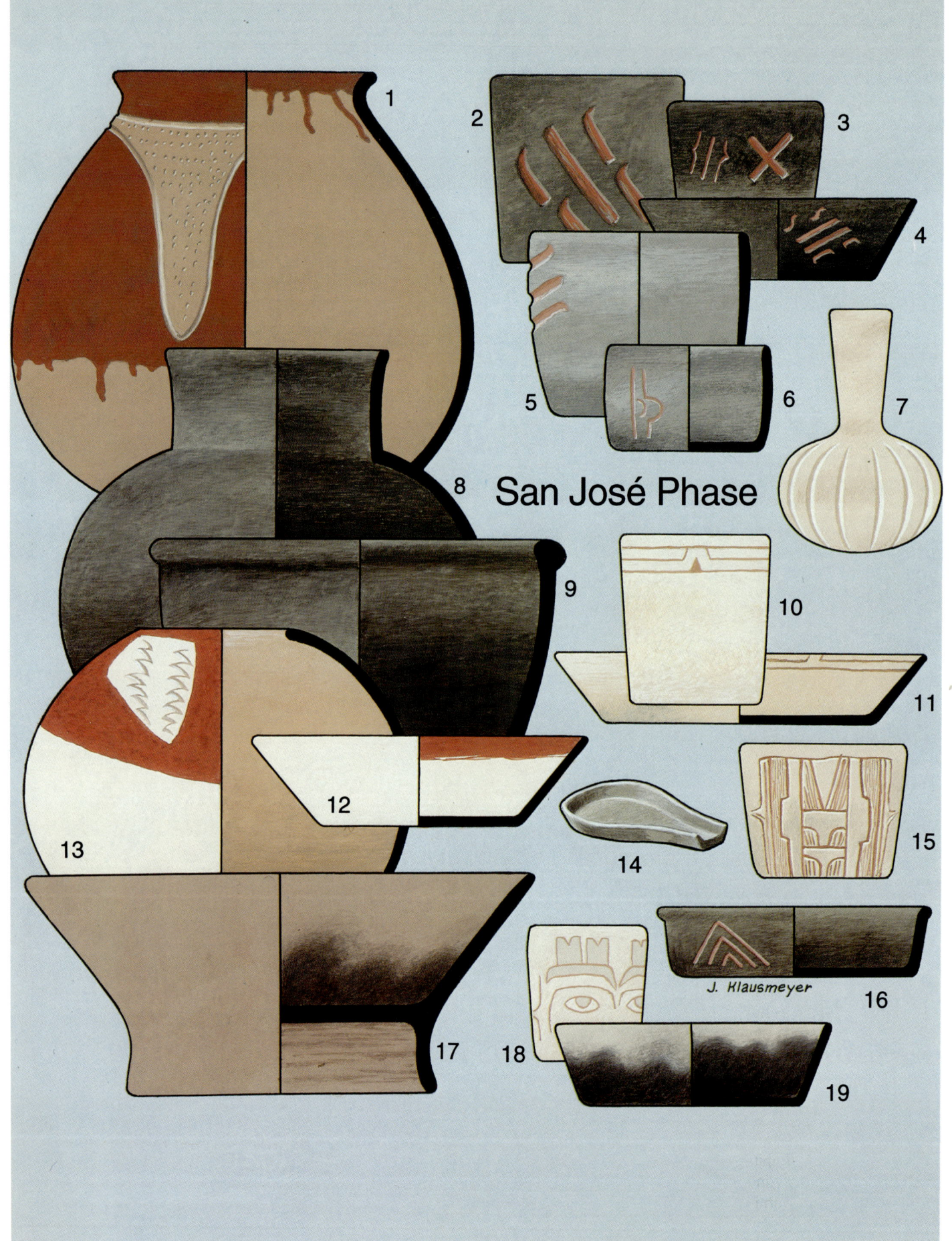

Frontispiece B. Vessels representative of the San José phase. *1*, Fidencio Coarse jar with zone of sloppy jabs. *2, 3*, Leandro Gray cylinders with excised motifs. *4*, Leandro Gray outleaned-wall bowl with excised fire-serpent. *5, 6*, Delfina Fine Gray cylinders with excised motifs. (Red pigment has been rubbed into the excisions of *2–6*.) *7*, Atoyac Yellow-white fluted bottle. *8*, Leandro Gray jar with vertical neck. *9*, Leandro Gray bolstered-rim bowl. *10*, Atoyac Yellow-white cylinder with incised double-line break. *11*, Atoyac Yellow-white outleaned-wall bowl with incised double-line break. *12*, San José Red-on-White outleaned-wall bowl. *13*, San José Red-on-White tecomate with zoned rocker stamping. *14*, Leandro Gray spouted tray. *15*, Atoyac Yellow-white cylinder with incised stylized were-jaguar. *16*, Leandro Gray bolstered rim bowl with outside left rough and excised. (Red pigment has been rubbed into the motifs of *15–16*.) *17*, Lupita Heavy Plain charcoal brazier (burned through use). *18*, Atoyac Yellow-white cylinder with incised realistic were-jaguar, featuring color contrast between matte and burnished areas. *19*, San José Black-and-White outleaned-wall bowl.

PREHISTORY AND HUMAN ECOLOGY OF THE VALLEY OF OAXACA

Kent V. Flannery and Joyce Marcus
General Editors

Volume 1 *The Use of Land and Water Resources in the Past and Present Valley of Oaxaca, Mexico*, by Anne V. T. Kirkby. Memoirs of the Museum of Anthropology, University of Michigan, No. 5. 1973.

Volume 2 *Sociopolitical Aspects of Canal Irrigation in the Valley of Oaxaca,* by Susan H. Lees. Memoirs of the Museum of Anthropology, University of Michigan, No. 6. 1973.

Volume 3 *Formative Mesoamerican Exchange Networks with Special Reference to the Valley of Oaxaca,* by Jane W. Pires-Ferreira. Memoirs of the Museum of Anthropology, University of Michigan, No. 7. 1975.

Volume 4 *Fábrica San José and Middle Formative Society in the Valley of Oaxaca,* by Robert D. Drennan. Memoirs of the Museum of Anthropology, University of Michigan, No. 8. 1975.

Volume 5 Part 1. *The Vegetational History of the Oaxaca Valley,* by C. Earle Smith, Jr. Part 2. *Zapotec Plant Knowledge: Classification, Uses and Communication about Plants in Mitla, Oaxaca, Mexico,* by Ellen Messer. Memoirs of the Museum of Anthropology, University of Michigan, No. 10. 1978.

Volume 6 *Excavations at Santo Domingo Tomaltepec: Evolution of a Formative Commmunity in the Valley of Oaxaca, Mexico,* by Michael E. Whalen. Memoirs of the Museum of Anthropology, University of Michigan, No. 12. 1981.

Volume 7 *Monte Albán's Hinterland, Part 1: The Prehispanic Settlement Patterns of the Central and Southern Parts of the Valley of Oaxaca, Mexico,* by Richard E. Blanton, Stephen Kowalewski, Gary Feinman, and Jill Appel. Memoirs of the Museum of Anthropology, University of Michigan, No. 15. 1982.

Volume 8 *Chipped Stone Tools in Formative Oaxaca, Mexico: Their Procurement, Production and Use,* by William J. Parry. Memoirs of the Museum of Anthropology, University of Michigan, No. 20. 1987.

Volume 9 *Agricultural Intensification and Prehistoric Health in the Valley of Oaxaca, Mexico,* by Denise C. Hodges. Memoirs of the Museum of Anthropology, University of Michigan, No. 22. 1989.

Volume 10 *Early Formative Pottery of the Valley of Oaxaca,* by Kent V. Flannery and Joyce Marcus, with technical ceramic analysis by William O. Payne. Memoirs of the Museum of Anthropology, University of Michigan, No. 27. 1994.

Related Volumes

Flannery, Kent V.
  1986 *Guilá Naquitz: Archaic Foraging and Early Agriculture in Oaxaca, Mexico.* New York: Academic Press.

Kowalewski, Stephen A., Gary M. Feinman, Laura Finsten, Richard E. Blanton, and Linda M. Nicholas
  1989 *Monte Albán's Hinterland, Part II: Prehispanic Settlement Patterns in Tlacolula, Etla, and Ocotlán, the Valley of Oaxaca, Mexico.* Memoirs of the Museum of Anthropology, University of Michigan, No. 23 (2 volumes).

MEMOIRS OF THE MUSEUM OF ANTHROPOLOGY
UNIVERSITY OF MICHIGAN
NUMBER 27

PREHISTORY AND HUMAN ECOLOGY
OF THE VALLEY OF OAXACA

Kent V. Flannery and Joyce Marcus
General Editors

Volume 10

Early Formative Pottery of the Valley of Oaxaca

by Kent V. Flannery and Joyce Marcus
with technical ceramic analysis
by William O. Payne

ANN ARBOR
1994

© 1994 by The Regents of The University of Michigan
The Museum of Anthropology
All rights reserved

Printed in the United States of America

ISBN 0-915703-34-3

The University of Michigan Museum of Anthropology currently publishes three monograph series: Anthropological Papers, Memoirs, and Technical Reports. We have over seventy titles in print. For a complete catalog, write to Museum of Anthropology Publications, 4009 Museums Building, Ann Arbor, MI 48109–1079, or call (313) 764-0485.

Library of Congress Cataloging-in-Publication Data

Flannery, Kent V.
    Early formative pottery of the Valley of Oaxaca / by Kent
V. Flannery and Joyce Marcus ; with technical ceramic analysis by
William O. Payne.
      p. cm.—(Prehistory and human ecology of the Valley of
Oaxaca ; v. 10) (Memoirs of the Museum of Anthropology,
University of Michigan ; no. 27)
    Summary in Spanish
    Includes bibliographical references.
    ISBN 0-915703-34-3 (acid-free : pbk.)
    1. Indians of Mexico—Mexico—Oaxaca Valley—Pottery. 2. Indians
of Mexico—Mexico—Oaxaca Valley—Antiquities. 3. Oaxaca Valley
(Mexico)—Antiquities. 4. Pottery, Prehistoric—Mexico—Oaxaca
Valley. 5. Mexico—Antiquities. I. Marcus, Joyce. II. Title.
III. Series. IV. Series: Memoirs of the Museum of Anthropology,
University of Michigan ; no. 27.
GN2.M52 no. 27
[F1219.1.O11]
306 s—dc20
[972'.7401]   93–6452
                                                                              CIP

The Paper used in this publication meets the requirements of ANSI Standard Z39.48–1984 (Permanence of Paper)

for

Gareth W. Lowe

who has seen more Early Formative pottery
than all the rest of us put together

Contents

List of Tables xv
List of Illustrations xv
Acknowledgments xxiii

CHAPTER 1.	INTRODUCTION 1
CHAPTER 2.	THE RAW MATERIALS AND POTTERY-MAKING TECHNIQUES OF EARLY FORMATIVE OAXACA: AN INTRODUCTION, by William O. Payne 7
	Geologic Origins 7
	Beneficiation of Materials 9
	Forming Techniques 9
	Decoration of Wares 12
	Drying Practice 12
	Firing of Wares 12
	Cooling and Drawing of Ware 13
	Functions of Early Formative Pottery 13
	Glossary of Ceramic Terms 16
CHAPTER 3.	STUDIES OF TRADITIONAL POTTERY MAKING IN THE VALLEY OF OAXACA, 1955–1973 21
	San Marcos 21
	Coyotepec 21
	Ocotlán 22
	Atzompa 22
	Pottery Making at Atzompa 24
CHAPTER 4.	SITE FORMATION PROCESSES AND THE QUALITY OF SHERD COLLECTIONS 25
	The Incorporation of Sherds into Households 25
	Small Middens Near Houses 28
	Sherds in the Dooryards of Household Units 28
	Bell-Shaped Pits in Dooryards 28
	Community and Barrio Middens 29
	Samples from Public Buildings 31
	Arroyos and Slopewash 33
	How Formative Villages Grew 34
	Summary 36
CHAPTER 5.	SYNCHRONIC AND DIACHRONIC VARIATION IN CERAMICS 39
	Summary 39
CHAPTER 6.	TYPES AND SHERD COUNTS: SOME METHODOLOGICAL QUESTIONS 41
	The Order of Data Presentation 41
	Honk if You Like Undecorated Body Sherds 42
	An Adequate Sample of What? 42
	Our Choice of Ceramic Typology 43
CHAPTER 7.	THE ESPIRIDIÓN COMPLEX 45
	Purrón-Espiridión Comparisons 45
	The Origins of Pottery Making in Oaxaca 47
	Bottle Gourds as Prototypes in Other Regions 47
	Pottery Types of the Espiridión Complex 50
	Purrón Plain 50
	Espiridión Thin 51
	Tierras Largas Burnished Plain 52
	A Possible Figurine or Miniature Mask 52

CHAPTER 8.	THE TIERRAS LARGAS PHASE	55
	Tierras Largas Burnished Plain	56
	Tierras Largas Unburnished Plain	65
	General Category: Early Highland Red-on-Buff Painted Wares	66
	Avelina Red-on-Buff	69
	Clementina Fine Red-on-Buff	75
	Matadamas Red	83
	Matadamas Orange	87
	Ocós Black	93
CHAPTER 9.	THE TRANSITION FROM ESPIRIDION COMPLEX TO TIERRAS LARGAS PHASE: MIDDEN STRATIGRAPHY	103
	The Threshing Floor Sector	103
	Bedrock	103
	Zone H	103
	Zone G2	106
	The G2-G1 Boundary	106
	Zone G1	107
	The G1-F Boundary	107
	Zone F	107
	House 18	107
	Conclusion	107
CHAPTER 10.	A SAMPLE OF TIERRAS LARGAS PHASE HOUSEHOLDS	113
	Household Unit LTL-1, Area B, Tierras Largas	113
	Household Unit LTL-3, Area C, Tierras Largas	113
	Feature 100 at Tierras Largas	113
	Feature 65, Area B, San José Mogote	119
	Summary	120
	Appendix to Chapter 10	121
CHAPTER 11.	DATING TIERRAS LARGAS PHASE PUBLIC BUILDINGS	123
	Structure 3	123
	Structure 5	126
	Structure 6	128
CHAPTER 12.	THE SAN JOSE PHASE	135
	"Earth" and "Sky" in the Symbolism of the San José Phase	136
	An Inventory of Free-Standing Motifs	140
	The Origins of the "Double-Line-Break" Motif	140
	An Inventory of Double-Line-Breaks	140
	Pottery Types of the San José Phase	149
	Fidencio Coarse	149
	Leandro Gray	157
	Atoyac Yellow-white	180
	San José Red-on-White	221
	Lupita Heavy Plain	233
	Hybrid Type: Atoyac Yellow-White Outside, Matadamas Orange Inside	252
	San José Black-and-White	252
	Xochiltepec White	254
	Delfina Fine Gray	259
	San José Specular Red	268
	La Mina White	272
	Coatepec White-rimmed Black	274
	Delia White	277
	Other Foreign Pottery Types	280
	Paloma Negative	286
	Cesto White	286
	Madera Brown?	286
	Guamuchal Brushed	286
	Synchronic Variation in Foreign Types	286
CHAPTER 13.	THE TRANSITION FROM TIERRAS LARGAS PHASE TO SAN JOSE PHASE: MIDDEN STRATIGRAPHY	287
	Features in Bedrock	287
	Zone G	292
	Zone F	292
	Zone E	292
	Selected Features from Zone E	292
	Zone D2	293
	Later Stratigraphic Levels	293

CHAPTER 14.	CHRONOLOGICAL VARIATION DURING THE SAN JOSE PHASE: HOUSEHOLD SEQUENCES IN TWO RESIDENTIAL WARDS	301
	Area A: Four Households and a Midden	301
	Summary of Area A	305
	Eight Houses from Area C, San José Mogote	305
	Features Related to the Area C Houses	316
	Summary of Area C	317
	House 14, Area C	325
CHAPTER 15.	SYNCHRONIC VARIATION 1: DIFFERENCES BETWEEN A HIGH-STATUS HOUSEHOLD AND A LOW-STATUS HOUSEHOLD	329
	House 13, San José Mogote	329
	Houses 16–17, San José Mogote	333
	Evidence for High Status	333
	Conclusion	339
CHAPTER 16.	SYNCHRONIC VARIATION 2: DIFFERENCES BETWEEN RESIDENTIAL WARDS AT THE SAME VILLAGE	343
	Household Units C4-C1, Area A	343
	Houses 16–17, Area B	344
	Conclusion	348
CHAPTER 17.	SYNCHRONIC VARIATION 3: DIFFERENCES BETWEEN VILLAGES 30 KM APART	349
	Midden Stratigraphy of Operation A at Abasolo	350
	House 1 of Abasolo	355
CHAPTER 18.	DATING SAN JOSE PHASE PUBLIC BUILDINGS	357
	Structure 7, Area C	357
	Structure 16, Area A	362
	Structures 1 and 2, Area A	367
	Conclusion	371
CHAPTER 19.	CERAMIC CROSSTIES AND EARLY FORMATIVE RADIOCARBON DATES	373
	Problems with Radiocarbon Dating	373
	The Espiridión Complex	374
	The Tierras Largas Phase	375
	The San José Phase	376
	Ties with the Basin of Mexico	376
	Contrasts with Morelos	379
	Ties with Southern Puebla	379
	Ties with the Gulf Coast	381
	Relations to the South	381
	The San José/Guadalupe Transition in the Etla Region	383
	Conclusion	384
CHAPTER 20.	THE OLMEC AND THE VALLEY OF OAXACA: A REVISION	385
	How Our Ideas Have Changed	387
	A Revised Model for 1994	389
	Suggestions for the Future	389
CHAPTER 21.	RESUMEN EN ESPAÑOL, por Sonia Guillén	391
Bibliography		395

TABLES

9.1	Sherds from the Threshing Floor Sector of Area C, San José Mogote	110
10.1	Sherds from Household Unit LTL-1, Area B, Tierras Largas	114
10.2	Sherds from Household Unit LTL-3, Area C, Tierras Largas	116
11.1	Sherds from Debris Lying on the Floor of Structure 6 after its Abandonment	133
12.1	"Double-Line-Break" Motifs on Atoyac Yellow-White vessels	148
13.1	Sherds from the Control Section of the Area C Master Profile, San José Mogote	297
14.1	Sherds from Midden Levels (D3-D1) and Household Units (C4-C1), Area A, San José Mogote	307
14.2	Sherds from Eight Houses in Area C, San José Mogote	321
16.1	Occurrence of Sherds with Pyne's Motifs 1–18 in Household Units C4-C1, Area A, San José Mogote	344
17.1	Sherds from the Lower Strata of Operation A, San Sebastián Abasolo	352

ILLUSTRATIONS

1.1	Map of the Valley of Oaxaca, showing Early Formative sites and present-day communities mentioned in the text	2
1.2	Chronology chart of Oaxaca and seven other regions of Mesoamerica	3
2.1	A hypothetical geological cross-section of the Valley of Oaxaca, showing rock formations and soil deposits relevant to pottery making	9
2.2	Raw materials used for pottery making in ancient and modern Oaxaca	10
2.3	Use of a *platillo* or potter's bat by a Formative potter in the Valley of Oaxaca	12
2.4	Two pats of unfired clay body from House 9, Area C, San José Mogote (San José phase)	13
2.5	Probable potter's bats from the San José phase (Lupita Heavy Plain ware)	14
2.6	Fragment of lightly baked clay mold, apparently for making hemispherical bowls with pinched-in sides	15
2.7	Lightly baked clay mold, probably for making flat-based bowls with vertical walls like those in Atoyac Yellow-white and Leandro Gray	15
2.8	Quartz pebbles used for burnishing pottery in prehispanic Oaxaca	16
2.9	Arroyo near San Marcos Tlapazola whose banks are a source of gray or yellowish-gray soil	17
2.10	Above-ground "kiln" in a dooryard at San Marcos Tlapazola	18
2.11	Another view of the same above-ground "kiln" at San Marcos Tlapazola, with its load of new griddles and potter's bats	19
3.1	Geological map of the area between San José Mogote and Oaxaca City	23
4.1	Idealized drawing of a large Formative village in the Valley of Oaxaca, showing the kinds of proveniences from which our sherd samples were drawn	26
4.2	House 14, Area C, San José Mogote, seen in cross-section in the east profile of Square S18E	27
4.3	Feature 130 from Tierras Largas, an example of a large bell-shaped pit whose walls had begun to collapse	30
4.4	Feature 159 from Tierras Largas, an example of a small bell-shaped pit	30
4.5	Feature 31 of San José Mogote, a bell-shaped pit and its associated backdirt, found while cutting the Area C Master Profile at a point far south of the squares shown in Fig. 9.2	31
4.6	Artist's reconstruction of a typical public building of the Tierras Largas and/or Early San José phase	32
4.7	Artist's sketch of what a public building like the one shown in Fig. 4.6 looks like after having been razed to make way for a new one	34
4.8	Profile drawing of Area A, Barrio del Rosario Huitzo (lower levels only)	35
4.9	A portion of the western Area B profile at San José Mogote, not far from its intersection with the Area C profile	37
7.1	Pottery of the Purrón complex from the Tehuacán Valley	46
7.2	Vessel shapes of the Purrón and Espiridión complexes: possible prototypes for the (a) tecomate, (b) hemispherical bowl, and (c) jar, all achieved by cross-sectioning gourds	48
7.3	Two vessels that may shed some light on the origins of pottery in Oaxaca	49
7.4	Are they gourd bowls or pottery vessels?	50
7.5	Purrón Plain pottery from House 20, Zone H, Area C, San José Mogote	52
7.6	Espiridión Thin pottery from House 20, Zone H, Area C, San José Mogote	52
7.7	Tierras Largas Burnished Plain pottery from House 20, Zone H, Area C, San José Mogote	53
7.8	Tierras Largas Burnished Plain pottery from House 20, Zone H, Area C, San José Mogote	53
7.9	Tierras Largas Burnished Plain pottery from House 20, Zone H, Area C, San José Mogote	54
7.10	Puma or jaguar face modeled in lightly fired clay	54
8.1	Tierras Largas Burnished Plain jar, Vessel 2 of Feature 57-A, Tierras Largas	58
8.2	Tierras Largas Burnished Plain jar, Vessel 2 of Feature 57-A, Tierras Largas	59
8.3	Tierras Largas Burnished Plain jar rims and shoulders from features at Tierras Largas	60

8.4	Interior of Tierras Largas Burnished Plain jar, showing "pocked" surface treatment	61
8.5	Interior of Tierras Largas Burnished Plain jar, showing "wiped" surface treatment	62
8.6	Tierras Largas Burnished Plain hemispherical bowls from Tierras Largas and San José Mogote	63
8.7	Tierras Largas Burnished Plain hemispherical bowls from Tierras Largas and San José Mogote	64
8.8	Tierras Largas Burnished Plain hemispherical bowl with slightly flaring rim from Feature 40, Tierras Largas	66
8.9	Top and side views of Tierras Largas Burnished Plain hemispherical bowl with notches cut on rim from Feature 40, Tierras Largas	67
8.10	Tierras Largas Burnished Plain flat-based bowls from Tierras Largas and San José Mogote	68
8.11	Two sherds from Tierras Largas Burnished Plain bowls with thickened rim, grooved on top of the rim, and decorated on the exterior with zoned rocker stamping from Area D, Tierras Largas	68
8.12	Tierras Largas Burnished Plain vessels from Tierras Largas and San José Mogote	69
8.13	Tierras Largas Burnished Plain tecomate rim with zoned dentate stamping, Household Unit C1, Area A, San José Mogote	69
8.14	Sherds from Tierras Largas Burnished Plain bowls with thickened, incurved rims decorated with incised "rim ticking" from Feature 116, Area B, Tierras Largas	70
8.15	Sherd from Tierras Largas Burnished Plain bowl with eccentric rim, decorated on the exterior with rocker stamping	70
8.16	Tierras Largas Burnished Plain body sherds with plastic decoration, all from Tierras Largas	71
8.17	Tierras Largas Burnished Plain body sherds with plastic decoration	72
8.18	Tierras Largas Burnished Plain sherd, possibly from a bottle	72
8.19	Tierras Largas Burnished Plain body sherds with "micro" rocker stamping from Area D, Tierras Largas	72
8.20	Tierras Largas Unburnished Plain bowls from Tierras Largas and San José Mogote	73
8.21	Possible Tierras Largas Unburnished Plain body sherd from Area B, Tierras Largas	73
8.22	Avelina Red-on-Buff jars, tecomates, and minor vessel forms from Tierras Largas and San José Mogote	75
8.23	Avelina Red-on-Buff hemispherical bowls from Tierras Largas and San José Mogote	76
8.24	Reconstruction drawings of Avelina Red-on-Buff hemispherical bowls from Tierras Largas	77
8.25	Reconstruction drawings of Avelina Red-on-Buff hemispherical bowls from Tierras Largas	78
8.26	Reconstruction drawings of Avelina Red-on-Buff hemispherical bowls from Tierras Largas	79
8.27	Avelina Red-on-Buff hemispherical bowl with red band at rim outside, geometric design (horizontal stripes) inside	80
8.28	Three rim sherds from an unusual Avelina Red-on-Buff bowl with slightly restricted orifice	80
8.29	Overhead view of a badly weathered Avelina Red-on-Buff tecomate from Feature 116, Tierras Largas	81
8.30	Clementina Fine Red-on-Buff hemispherical bowls	84
8.31	Clementina Fine Red-on-Buff hemispherical bowls from Tierras Largas and San José Mogote	85
8.32	Clementina Fine Red-on-Buff hemispherical bowl, slipped specular red and completely burnished on the outside	86
8.33	Clementina Fine Red-on-Buff hemispherical bowl with pinched-in sides, all red outside, from Tierras Largas, Test Square 2851	86
8.34	Clementina Fine Red-on-Buff vessels from Feature 142, Household Unit LTL-1, Area B, Tierras Largas	87
8.35	Rim sherd from neck of Clementina Fine Red-on-Buff bottle, red band at rim inside, all red outside from Feature 142, Household Unit LTL-1, Area B, Tierras Largas	87
8.36	Unusual Clementina Fine Red-on-Buff double vessel from Feature 142, Household Unit LTL-1, Area B, Tierras Largas	88
8.37	Matadamas Red jar neck from Feature 73, Tierras Largas	89
8.38	Matadamas Red vessels from Tierras Largas and San José Mogote	90
8.39	Matadamas Red tecomate from Household Unit C1, Area A, San José Mogote	91
8.40	Matadamas Red body sherds with zoned interrupted rocker stamping from Area B, Tierras Largas	91
8.41	Matadamas Orange jar rims and bodies from Tierras Largas and San José Mogote	91
8.42	Matadamas Orange hemispherical bowls from Tierras Largas and San José Mogote	94
8.43	Matadamas Orange vessels from Tierras Largas and San José Mogote	95
8.44	Matadamas Orange tecomate with false rocker stamping in zones, from Feature 116-west, Area B, Tierras Largas	95
8.45	Matadamas Orange tecomate rims with plastic decoration	97
8.46	Matadamas Orange tecomate with plain band at rim followed by a band of interrupted rocker stamping, from Features 134 and 135, Area B, Tierras Largas	97
8.47	Matadamas Orange tecomate rims with plastic decoration, all from Tierras Largas	98
8.48	Matadamas Orange tecomate body sherds with plastic decoration, all from Area D of Tierras Largas	98
8.49	Matadamas Orange tecomate body sherd with shallow grooves outlining zones of punctation	99
8.50	Ocós Black, Oaxaca Variety bottle sherds from Area A, San José Mogote	99
8.51	Ocós Black, Ocós Variety sherds from San José Mogote, Area C, Zone G	99
8.52	Ocós Black, Ocós Variety sherds from the floor of Structure 6, Area C, San José Mogote	100
8.53	Ocós Black, Ocós Variety tecomate sherds from the floor of Structure 6, Area C, San José Mogote	100
8.54	Ocós Black, Oaxaca Variety cylinders and outleaned-wall bowls from Area A of San José Mogote	101

9.1	Simplified map of San José Mogote	104
9.2	Master grid of squares for Area C, San José Mogote	105
9.3	South profile of the Threshing Floor Sector, Area C	106
9.4	South profile of Square S18L of the Threshing Floor Sector	108
10.1	Plan view of Household Unit LTL-1 from Tierras Largas	117
10.2	Artist's reconstruction of Household Unit LTL-1, Tierras Largas, as it might have looked late in the Tierras Largas phase	117
10.3	Feature 86, a bell-shaped pit associated with Household Unit LTL-1 at Tierras Largas	118
10.4	Feature 142, a bell-shaped pit associated with Household Unit LTL-1 at Tierras Largas	118
10.5	Plan view of Household Unit LTL-3 from Tierras Largas	119
10.6	Feature 65 of San José Mogote, the lower part of a bell-shaped pit excavated into bedrock near the Area B Master Profile	119
11.1	Plan view of Structure 3 at San José Mogote, a Tierras Largas phase public building	124
11.2	Simplified cross-section of the collapsed remains of Structure 3, San José Mogote, as it appeared between Squares S21 and S25 of the Master Profile of Area C	125
11.3	Working in Square S25A of the Area C Master Profile	125
11.4	Simplified cross-section of the collapsed remains of Structure 5, San José Mogote, as it appeared between Squares S28 and S32 of the Master Profile of Area C	127
11.5	Plan view of Structure 6 at San José Mogote, a Tierras Largas phase public building	129
11.6	Plastered pits containing powdered lime, found in Tierras Largas phase buildings in Area C, San José Mogote	130
11.7	The western side of Structure 6's recessed floor	131
11.8	Structure 6, Area C, San José Mogote (view from the east)	132
12.1	Representations of the fire-serpent (Sky) in the Formative art of the Basin of Mexico	137
12.2	The derivation of the most common fire-serpent (Sky) and were-jaguar (Earth) motifs used in the San José phase	138
12.3	A rim sherd from an Atoyac Yellow-white cylindrical bowl with a relatively realistic incised were-jaguar motif on the exterior, from cleaning profile at the level of the San José phase deposits, Area C, San José Mogote	139
12.4	Reconstruction drawings of vessels from the fill of Structure 1, San José Mogote	139
12.5	Variants of Pyne's Motif 1 (fire-serpent), Valley of Oaxaca	141
12.6	Variants of Pyne's Motifs 1 and 2 (fire-serpent), Valley of Oaxaca	141
12.7	Variants of Pyne's Motifs 3, 4, and 5, Valley of Oaxaca	142
12.8	Variants of Pyne's Motifs 6 and 7, Valley of Oaxaca	142
12.9	Variants of Pyne's Motif 8 (were-jaguar), Valley of Oaxaca	143
12.10	Variants of Pyne's Motifs 9 and 10 (were-jaguar), Valley of Oaxaca	143
12.11	Variants of Pyne's Motif 11, Valley of Oaxaca	144
12.12	Variants of Pyne's Motif 12, Valley of Oaxaca	144
12.13	Variants of Pyne's Motif 14 (Earth), Valley of Oaxaca	145
12.14	Variants of Pyne's Motifs 15 and 16, Valley of Oaxaca	145
12.15	Variants of Pyne's Motif 17, Valley of Oaxaca	146
12.16	Variants of Pyne's Motifs 17 and 18, Valley of Oaxaca	146
12.17	Atoyac Yellow-white outleaned-wall bowl sherd from Zone C, Area C, San José Mogote (San José phase)	147
12.18	Rim sherd from an Atoyac Yellow-white cylinder found in Zone D, Area C, San José Mogote (San José phase)	147
12.19	Plog's design elements 1 to 44, Atoyac Yellow-white pottery	150
12.20	Plog's design elements 45 to 92, Atoyac Yellow-white pottery	151
12.21	Plog's design elements 93 to 143, Atoyac Yellow-white pottery	152
12.22	The 41 most common double-line-break design elements on Canoas White pottery of the Tehuacán Valley	153
12.23	Fidencio Coarse jar necks from San José Mogote and Barrio del Rosario Huitzo	155
12.24	Fidencio Coarse jar necks from San José Mogote, Tierras Largas, and Barrio del Rosario Huitzo	156
12.25	Fidencio Coarse jar shoulders with zoned, neat, punctation-like jabs, all from Area A of San José Mogote (San José phase)	157
12.26	Fidencio Coarse jar shoulders with paired jabs, all from Area A, San José Mogote (San José phase)	158
12.27	Fidencio Coarse jar shoulders with paired, stepped jabs, Household Unit C3, Area A, San José Mogote (San José phase)	159
12.28	Fidencio Coarse jar shoulders with zoned areas of sloppy jabs, all from Area A of San José Mogote (San José phase)	160
12.29	Fidencio Coarse body sherds from jars or tecomates with plastic decoration, all from Area A of San José Mogote (San José phase)	160
12.30	Fidencio Coarse tecomate with punctation and incising in zones, drab red wash outside zones, from above Feature 151, Area C, Tierras Largas	161
12.31	Reconstruction drawing of same Fidencio Coarse tecomate seen in Fig. 12.30	162
12.32	Fidencio Coarse tecomates from Tierras Largas, San José Mogote, and Barrio del Rosario Huitzo	163
12.33	Varieties of Fidencio Coarse hemispherical bowls from the site of Tierras Largas	164
12.34	Leandro Gray bottle sherds from San José Mogote and Tierras Largas	166
12.35	Leandro Gray bottle neck found while cutting the profile, Area C, San José Mogote	167
12.36	Leandro Gray bowls with flat bases and outleaned walls, from San José Mogote and Huitzo	168

12.37	Leandro Gray bowls with flat base and outleaned walls, undecorated, from San José Mogote and Huitzo	169
12.38	Leandro Gray bowls with flat bases and outleaned walls, excised	170
12.39	Top view of reconstructed Leandro Gray bowl with flat base and outleaned walls, showing interior decoration	171
12.40	Close-up of Leandro Gray bowl shown reconstructed in Fig. 12.39	172
12.41	Leandro Gray bowl with flat base and outleaned walls, excised on the interior with an elaborate version of Pyne's Motif 1, from Burial 20, Tierras Largas (San José phase)	173
12.42	Leandro Gray cylinders or bowls with nearly vertical walls, undecorated, from San José Mogote and Huitzo	174
12.43	Leandro Gray cylinders or bowls with nearly vertical walls, excised, from San José Mogote and Tierras Largas	175
12.44	Leandro Gray cylinders or bowls with nearly vertical walls, excised, all from Area A of San José Mogote (San José phase)	176
12.45	Leandro Gray cylinders, excised	177
12.46	Leandro Gray cylinders or bowls with nearly vertical walls, excised, all from Area A, San José Mogote	178
12.47	Leandro Gray cylinder with stylized were-jaguar (Earth) motif that combines excising and fine-line hachure	179
12.48	Rim sherd from Leandro Gray cylinder with incising and fine-line hachure on the outside, from Household Unit C4, Area A, San José Mogote (San José phase)	180
12.49	Leandro Gray cylinders from Burial 4, Area A, San Sebastián Abasolo (San José phase)	181
12.50	Leandro Gray cylinders with variants of the fire-serpent motif found with Burial 4 at San Sebastián Abasolo (San José phase)	182
12.51	Leandro Gray bowls from Burial 1, Area A, San Sebastián Abasolo (San José phase)	183
12.52	Vessel 1 from Burial 1, San Sebastián Abasolo (San José phase)	184
12.53	Leandro Gray bowl with nearly vertical walls, excised with Pyne's Motif 1 (fire-serpent)	184
12.54	Leandro Gray cylinders with excised designs, both from Area A of San José Mogote (San José phase)	185
12.55	Rim sherds from Leandro Gray cylinders with variants of Pyne's Motif 1 excised on the outside, both from Area A of San José Mogote (San José phase)	186
12.56	Rim sherds from Leandro Gray cylinders with Pyne's Motif 1 excised on the outside	186
12.57	Rim sherds from Leandro Gray cylinders with designs of only local distribution, excised on the outside	187
12.58	Occasionally, San José potters decorated the exterior of Leandro Gray bowls whose walls leaned outward more than 10%, treating them as if they were cylinders	188
12.59	Leandro Gray tecomates from San José Mogote (all San José phase)	189
12.60	Vessels 1 and 2 from Burial 2, San Sebastián Abasolo (San José phase)	190
12.61	Leandro Gray tecomate rim with a plain rim band outlined by incising, a perforation for suspension, and a body divided into zones decorated with what appears to be interrupted dentate stamping	191
12.62	Leandro Gray tecomate rims from Area B of Tierras Largas (San José phase)	191
12.63	Leandro Gray body sherd with "micro" rocker stamping, from Household Unit C4, Area A, San José Mogote (San José phase)	192
12.64	Leandro Gray body sherd with dentate stamping, Zone D2 midden, Area A, San José Mogote (San José phase)	192
12.65	Leandro Gray bowls from San José Mogote and Huitzo, ranging from hemispherical to incurved-rim in shape	193
12.66	Sherd from Leandro Gray bowl with incurved rim, decorated on the outside by excising and three-dimensional modeling	194
12.67	Leandro Gray bowls with bolstered rim, undecorated, all from Area A of San José Mogote (San José phase)	194
12.68	Leandro Gray bowls with bolstered rim, decorated on the outside, all from Area A of San José Mogote (San José phase)	195
12.69	Leandro Gray jar necks and shoulders from Area A, San José Mogote (San José phase)	196
12.70	Leandro Gray vessels from San José Mogote and Barrio del Rosario Huitzo	197
12.71	Leandro Gray spouted trays from San José Mogote and Tierras Largas	198
12.72	Top and side views of broken Leandro Gray spouted tray, Tierras Largas, Feature 150 (San José phase)	199
12.73	Top view and three-quarter view of the broken spout from a Leandro Gray spouted tray, from Area C, San José Mogote (San José phase)	199
12.74	Leandro Gray vessels from San José Mogote (San José phase)	200
12.75	Leandro Gray vessels from San José Mogote and Barrio del Rosario Huitzo	201
12.76	Sherd from a Leandro Gray effigy vessel, House 16, Area B, San José Mogote	201
12.77	Leandro Gray sherds showing a variety of decorative techniques	202
12.78	Leandro Gray bowls from San José Mogote and Barrio del Rosario Huitzo	203
12.79	Some of the earliest vessel forms to appear in Atoyac Yellow-white	206
12.80	Atoyac Yellow-white bowls with flat base and outleaned or outcurved walls, from San José Mogote, Tierras Largas, and Barrio del Rosario Huitzo	207
12.81	Atoyac Yellow-white bowls with flat bases and outleaned or outcurved walls, from San José Mogote and Barrio del Rosario Huitzo	208
12.82	Atoyac Yellow-white bowls with outleaned walls and interior incising, from San José Mogote and Barrio del Rosario Huitzo	209

12.83	Atoyac Yellow-white cylinders (bowls with nearly vertical walls), undecorated, from San José Mogote and Barrio del Rosario Huitzo.	210
12.84	Vessel 7, Square C13, House 1, Area A, Tierras Largas (San José phase), an Atoyac Yellow-white cylinder	211
12.85	Vessel 2 of Burial 4, Area A, Tierras Largas (San José phase), an Atoyac Yellow-white cylinder with somewhat eroded slip	211
12.86	Vessel 3 of Burial 4, Area A, Tierras Largas (San José phase), an Atoyac Yellow-white cylinder with charcoal gray firing clouds	212
12.87	Vessel 1 of Burial 12, San José Mogote (San José phase), an Atoyac Yellow-white cylinder with three parallel incised lines just below the rim	213
12.88	Atoyac Yellow-white cylinder from House 16, Area B, San José Mogote (late San José phase)	213
12.89	Vessel 6, Square C13, House 1, Area A, Tierras Largas (San José phase), an Atoyac Yellow-white cylinder, incised on the exterior with Pyne's Motif 10 (were-jaguar) in fine-line hachure	214
12.90	Atoyac Yellow-white cylinders (bowls with nearly vertical walls), decorated, from San José Mogote and Barrio del Rosario Huitzo	215
12.91	Atoyac Yellow-white tecomates and incurved-rim bowls from San José Mogote and Barrio del Rosario Huitzo	216
12.92	Atoyac Yellow-white tecomate rims with plastic decoration, all from Area A of San José Mogote	217
12.93	Atoyac Yellow-white tecomate sherds with plastic decoration, all from the San José phase	218
12.94	Atoyac Yellow-white tecomate body sherd from Zone D1 midden, Area A, San José Mogote (San José phase)	219
12.95	Atoyac Yellow-white tecomate body sherds from Zones D1 and D2 of the Area A midden, San José Mogote (San José phase)	220
12.96	Body sherds from Atoyac Yellow-white tecomates with zoned rocker stamping, both from Area A, San José Mogote (San José phase)	221
12.97	Atoyac Yellow-white tecomate body sherds with interrupted rocker stamping, Area A, San José Mogote (San José phase)	222
12.98	Atoyac Yellow-white tecomate body sherds with plastic decoration, all from San José Mogote (San José phase)	223
12.99	Atoyac Yellow-white bowls with bolstered rim from San José Mogote and Barrio del Rosario Huitzo	224
12.100	Atoyac Yellow-white jar necks from San José Mogote and Barrio del Rosario Huitzo	225
12.101	Miscellaneous vessel forms in Atoyac Yellow-white	226
12.102	Atoyac Yellow-white vessels which, because of the traces of pigment found in them, are suspected of having been used as pigment dishes during the San José phase at San José Mogote	228
12.103	Atoyac Yellow-white ceramics with three-dimensional sculpturing	229
12.104	San José Red-on-White vessels, all from San José Mogote	230
12.105	San José Red-on-White tecomate from puddled adobe cap of Stage I, Structure 1, Area A, San José Mogote (San José phase)	231
12.106	San José Red-on-White tecomate from puddled adobe cap of Stage I, Structure 1, Area A, San José Mogote (San José phase)	231
12.107	San José Red-on-White tecomate rim from Household Unit C3, Area A, San José Mogote (San José phase)	232
12.108	San José Red-on-White tecomate body sherds with rocker stamping in several styles	233
12.109	San José Red-on-White tecomate body sherd with rocker stamping in a white zone, from Household Unit C4, Area A, San José Mogote (San José phase)	234
12.110	San José Red-on-White tecomate body sherd with interrupted rocker stamping in zone, from straightening profile at level of San José phase deposits, Area C, San José Mogote	234
12.111	San José Red-on-White tecomate body sherds with interrupted rocker stamping in white zones, from Zone D2 midden, Area A, San José Mogote (San José phase)	234
12.112	San José Red-on-White jar necks and shoulders, all from Area A at San José Mogote (San José phase)	235
12.113	San José Red-on-White bowls from San José Mogote and Barrio del Rosario Huitzo	236
12.114	San José Red-on-White bowls from Area A of San José Mogote (San José phase)	237
12.115	Lupita Heavy Plain tecomates from Area A at San José Mogote (San José phase)	238
12.116	Lupita Heavy Plain tecomates from Area A, San José Mogote (San José phase)	239
12.117	Lupita Heavy Plain tecomate sherds with plastic decoration, from straightening the profile at the level of the San José phase deposits in Area C, San José Mogote	239
12.118	Sherds from Lupita Heavy Plain tecomates with spaced pairs of jabs, all from Household Unit C3, Area A, San José Mogote (San José phase)	240
12.119	Lupita Heavy Plain tecomate body sherds decorated with sloppy jabs in zones, from Household Unit C3, Area A, San José Mogote (San José phase)	240
12.120	Lupita Heavy Plain tecomates with plastic decoration, both from Area A, San José Mogote (San José phase)	241
12.121	Lupita Heavy Plain tecomate body sherds, showing several styles of rocker stamping	243
12.122	Lupita Heavy Plain tecomate body sherds with interrupted rocker stamping in zones	244
12.123	Lupita Heavy Plain bowls and *platillos* (probable potter's bats) from San José Mogote and Tierras Largas	245
12.124	Lupita Heavy Plain charcoal brazier or potstand from below House 6, Area C, San José Mogote (San José phase)	246
12.125	Lupita Heavy Plain charcoal braziers or potstands from San José Mogote and Barrio del Rosario Huitzo	247

12.126	Lupita Heavy Plain charcoal braziers or potstands from San José Mogote and Barrio del Rosario Huitzo	248
12.127	Vessel 8, Square C13, House 1, Area A, Tierras Largas (San José phase), a Lupita Heavy Plain charcoal brazier or potstand	249
12.128	Fragment of Lupita Heavy Plain charcoal brazier or potstand with mat-impressed floor, from Barrio del Rosario Huitzo, Area C, cleaning profile at level of Guadalupe-phase deposits	249
12.129	Lupita Heavy Plain charcoal brazier or potstand, from San José Mogote, Mound 1, Zone C, overburden above Structure 19	250
12.130	Unusual Lupita Heavy Plain vessels from Area A, San José Mogote (San José phase)	251
12.131	Vessels combining Atoyac Yellow-white and Matadamas Orange slips, from San José Mogote and Tierras Largas	251
12.132	San José Black-and-White cylinders or bowls with nearly vertical walls, all from Area A, San José Mogote (San José phase)	255
12.133	Rim sherd from San José Black-and-White cylinder with deep carving on the exterior	256
12.134	San José Black-and-White low cylinder with deep excising; motifs include the St. Andrew's cross (Pyne's Motif 7) and "music bracket" (Pyne's Motif 11)	256
12.135	San José Black-and-White bowls, all from Area A, San José Mogote (San José phase)	257
12.136	Fragment of effigy vessel in San José Black-and-White, from House 1, Tierras Largas (San José phase)	258
12.137	Xochiltepec White bottle sherds from San José Mogote, Area C, Zone G (Tierras Largas phase)	260
12.138	Xochiltepec White sherd from the shoulder of a carinated bottle	260
12.139	Xochiltepec White vessels from San José Mogote and Barrio del Rosario Huitzo	261
12.140	Sherd from unusual tecomate or incurved-rim bowl that appears to be a Xochiltepec White vessel covered with red paint, then decorated with post-firing scraping and incising	262
12.141	Delfina Fine Gray cylinder rim with excised design, found at Las Canoas in the Tehuacán Valley, an Early Santa María phase site	262
12.142	Delfina Fine Gray cylinders or bowls with nearly vertical walls, all from Area A of San José Mogote (San José phase)	264
12.143	Delfina Fine Gray cylinder from the Zone D midden, Area A, San José Mogote (San José phase)	265
12.144	Sherd from Delfina Fine Gray cylinder, decorated on the outside with "music brackets" and fine-line hachure from Household Unit C2, Area A, San José Mogote (San José phase)	267
12.145	Delfina Fine Gray cylinder sherds found while straightening profile of Area C, San José Mogote, at the level of the San José phase deposits	267
12.146	Delfina Fine Gray bowls, all from San José Mogote (San José phase)	268
12.147	Delfina Fine Gray vessels from San José Mogote (San José phase)	269
12.148	Sherd from Delfina Fine Gray bolstered rim bowl, excised on the outside with a fire-serpent design, from cutting profile at level of San José phase deposits in Area C of San José Mogote	270
12.149	San José Specular Red vessels, all from San José Mogote (San José phase)	273
12.150	San José Specular Red sherds from San José Mogote, Area C, found while cleaning profile at the level of the San José phase deposits	274
12.151	Unusual tecomate rim sherd, tentatively classified as San José Specular Red from Feature 41, Area C, San José Mogote (San José phase)	274
12.152	La Mina White vessels, all from Area A of San José Mogote (San José phase)	275
12.153	Coatepec White-rimmed Black bowls from San José Mogote, Tierras Largas, and Barrio del Rosario Huitzo	278
12.154	Coatepec White-rimmed Black outleaned-wall bowl rims from San José Mogote (San José phase)	279
12.155	Delia White vessels from Tierras Largas, San José Mogote, and Barrio del Rosario Huitzo	280
12.156	Delia White beaker from Feature 58, Tierras Largas (Guadalupe phase)	281
12.157	Delia White hemispherical bowl from Burial 14, Area C, San José Mogote (late San José phase)	282
12.158	Reconstruction drawing of incised hemispherical bowl in Delia White from Burial 14, Area C, San José Mogote	282
12.159	Paloma Negative sherds from Tlapacoya-Zohapilco, Basin of Mexico, and Area A of San José Mogote	283
12.160	Fragments of probable Cesto White bowl with sunburst "grater bowl" design incised on the interior of the base, Vessel 6 from House 16, Area B, San José Mogote	284
12.161	Guamuchal Brushed tecomate sherds from Area C, San José Mogote (San José phase)	285
13.1	East profile of Squares S15-S20 of the Control Section, Area C Master Profile, San José Mogote	288
13.2	East profile of Squares S20-S25 of the Control Section, Area C Master Profile, San José Mogote	289
13.3	East profile of Squares S25-S29 of the Control Section, Area C Master Profile, San José Mogote	290
13.4	East profile of Squares S29-S33 of the Control Section, Area C Master Profile, San José Mogote	291
13.5	Feature 22, a pit dug into bedrock, Area C, San José Mogote (late Tierras Largas phase)	294
13.6	Feature 23, a pit dug into bedrock, Area C, San José Mogote (late Tierras Largas phase)	294
13.7	Tlatilco-style roller stamp from Zone C, Area C, San José Mogote (San José phase)	295
13.8	San José phase objects with variants of the "paw-wing" motif, both from Area C, San José Mogote	295
13.9	"Yuguito" of fine-grained black stone (San José phase) from Square S2, Area C Master Profile, San José Mogote	295
14.1	South and west profiles of Area A, San José Mogote, showing the stratigraphic relationship of Household Units C4-C1 and the Zone D midden	302
14.2	Plan of Household Unit C3, Area A, San José Mogote	304
14.3	Cross-section of Feature 2, Household Unit C3, a bell-shaped pit used as an earth oven	305

14.4	Plan of Household Unit C2, Area A, San José Mogote	306
14.5	Feature 32, a pit associated with House 6 of Area C, San José Mogote	313
14.6	View of the floor of House 2, Area C, San José Mogote, a San José phase residence	314
14.7	Plan of House 2, Area C, San José Mogote, showing objects piece-plotted on the floor	315
14.8	Artist's reconstruction of House 2, Area C, San José Mogote	316
14.9	Plan of House 4, Area C, San José Mogote	318
14.10	Cross-section of Feature 35, a subfloor depression in House 4, Area C, San José Mogote	320
14.11	Plan of House 14, Area C, San José Mogote	327
15.1	Plan of House 13, Mound 1, San José Mogote (San José phase)	330
15.2	Artist's reconstruction of House 13	331
15.3	A 5-m section of the Area B profile, San José Mogote	334
15.4	Plan view of bedrock in Area B of San José Mogote, showing postholes, rain-runoff canals, a cistern (Feature 58), and a burial (Burial 18)	335
15.5	Artist's reconstruction of House 17 and its attached shed or lean-to, "House 16"	336
15.6	Plan view of Houses 16 and 17, Area B, San José Mogote (San José phase)	340
16.1	Excised Leandro Gray sherds from Household Units C4-C1, Area A, San José Mogote (San José phase), showing variants of the fire-serpent	344
16.2	Excised Delfina Fine Gray and Atoyac Yellow-white sherds from Household Units C4-C1, Area A, San José Mogote (San José phase), showing variants of the fire-serpent	345
16.3	Incised design elements on Atoyac Yellow-white vessels from Household Units C4-C1, Area A, San José Mogote (San José phase)	346
16.4	Decorated Leandro Gray and Delfina Fine Gray sherds from House 16, Area B, San José Mogote (San José phase)	346
16.5	Incised design elements or larger motifs on Atoyac Yellow-white vessels from House 16, Area B, San José Mogote (San José phase)	347
17.1	The south profile of Operation A at San Sebastián Abasolo	351
18.1	Partial plan of Structure 7, Area C, San José Mogote, a San José phase public building	358
18.2	The northeast corner of Structure 7, San José Mogote, a San José phase public building	359
18.3	The northeast corner of Structure 7, San José Mogote, a San José phase public building seen from the south, showing the recessed floor, the vertical faces of the north and east walls, and several postmolds	360
18.4	Cross-section drawing of the surviving remnant of Structure 7, San José Mogote, showing the various layers of construction	361
18.5	Plan view of Structure 16, Area A, San José Mogote, a one-room building on a puddled adobe platform surrounded by a sand floor	363
18.6	Two workmen expose the nearly vertical west face of the puddled adobe platform supporting Structure 16	364
18.7	Plan view of Structures 1 and 2, Area A, San José Mogote (San José phase)	365
18.8	Artist's reconstruction of Structures 1 and 2, San José Mogote, as they might have looked late in the San José phase	366
18.9	Monuments 1 and 2, two carved stones associated with Structure 2, San José Mogote	367
18.10	The south stairway of Structure 2 (see Fig. 18.7 for location)	368
18.11	Structure 1 as it appeared when initially discovered (view from the southeast)	369
19.1	Double- and triple-line-break motifs on Cesto White and Pilli White vessels from Tlapacoya-Zohapilco, Basin of Mexico	378
19.2	Portion of Cesto White bowl from Tlapacoya-Zohapilco, Basin of Mexico	379
19.3	Double- and triple-line-break motifs on Amatzinac White pottery from Chalcatzingo, Morelos	380
20.1	Depictions of Earth, or the were-jaguar, on white-slipped vessels from Tlapacoya, Basin of Mexico	389

ACKNOWLEDGMENTS

The pottery analyzed in this volume was excavated during the course of the University of Michigan project "The Prehistory and Human Ecology of the Valley of Oaxaca." That project was supported by four grants from the National Science Foundation to Flannery: GS-1616 (1967), GS-2121 (1968), GS-42568 (1974), and BNS-7805829 (1978). Those grants enabled Flannery and Marcus to excavate at San José Mogote, Barrio del Rosario Huitzo, San Sebastián Abasolo, and San Pedro y San Pablo Mitla; GS-2121 was also used to support Marcus Winter's dissertation work at Tierras Largas. Additional excavation of Formative villages was made possible by NSF doctoral dissertation improvement grants to Robert D. Drennan for work at Fábrica San José in 1972 (GS-32066), and to Michael E. Whalen for excavations at Tomaltepec in 1974 (GS-40325). That support is greatly appreciated.

All the above work was done under permits issued to Flannery by Mexico's Instituto Nacional de Antropología e Historia. We are very grateful to the many Mexican officials who made our research possible, and would like to single out the late Ignacio Bernal, José Luis Lorenzo, the late Guillermo Bonfil, and Enrique Florescano for taking a special interest in our project.

Once in the field, we were greatly helped by officials of the Centro Regional de Oaxaca (INAH), especially Manuel Esparza and Lorenzo Gamio. The staff of the Centro Regional, and especially Angeles Romero, Nelly Robles, and Roberto Zárate, were very supportive of our work, and we thank all of them.

A great number of graduate and undergraduate students, many of whom are now professional archaeologists, worked on our Oaxaca project. During the pottery analysis seasons of 1968 and 1970, Flannery was assisted (in alphabetical order) by Suzanne K. Fish, Susan H. Lees, Kathryn Blair Vaughn, Jane C. Wheeler, and Marcus C. Winter, all of whom participated in the sorting of sherds, the drawing of rim profiles, and the drafting of preliminary type descriptions. During this period, Sue-Ann Florin undertook the task of determining Munsell color ranges of sherds.

New excavations at San José Mogote from 1974 to 1980 produced so much additional material that it was necessary for Marcus to reanalyze all the Tierras Largas material and to rewrite the type descriptions; she also defined the newly discovered Espiridión Complex. Meanwhile, Drennan's work at Fábrica San José, and especially his multidimensional scaling program for Guadalupe and Rosario phase attributes (Drennan 1976a, 1976b), made it necessary for Flannery and Marcus to reanalyze those two phases and rewrite the relevant type descriptions.

During this same period, Nanette Pyne (1976) undertook a study of free-standing pan-Mesoamerican motifs on San José phase pottery, and Stephen Plog (1976) analyzed "double-line-break" design elements on San José and Guadalupe phase pottery. Thus, while the final analyses in this volume were our responsibility, we owe a great debt to all the archaeologists mentioned above.

All the sherds we recovered were washed and numbered by our workers Pablo García, Eligio Martínez, Ernesto Martínez, Juan Martínez, Felix Sosa, and Rodolfo Sosa, all of Mitla, and Armando Jiménez and Isaac Jiménez, of San José Mogote. They also counted hundreds of thousands of undecorated body sherds which we had separated by type.

Rim profiles were drawn in the field by Flannery, Marcus, Fish, Lees, and Vaughn, and drafted for publication by Werner Riedl. Whole or restorable vessels were drawn by a series of artists, including Kay Clahassey, Nancy Hansen, John Klausmeyer, Rubén Méndez, Susan Payne, and Margaret Van Bolt. All photographs were taken either by Chris L. Moser (1967–1974) or Marcus (1975–1981). The negatives were printed by Charles M. Hastings, John Clark, and S. O. Kim. We are particularly indebted to Moser for his expert photography, both in the field and in the darkroom; he worked hard to bring out such textural attributes as pitting, brushing, burnishing, and rocker stamping.

This volume also features profile drawings, plan drawings, and reconstruction drawings of buildings by Kay Clahassey, John Klausmeyer, and David W. Reynolds.

The list of fellow archaeologists who helped us in the field is so long that we greatly fear we may have left someone out. John Paddock, who first encouraged us to work in Oaxaca, provided great moral support. So did the late Cecil R. Welte, who helped us find many important sites. Ignacio Bernal—the original discoverer of such sites as San José Mogote, Barrio del Rosario Huitzo, Tierras Largas, and San Sebastián Abasolo—encouraged us in every way possible. So did our colleagues Richard Blanton, Gary Feinman, Laura Finsten, Stephen Kowalewski, Linda Nicholas, and Dudley Varner, all of whom discovered new Formative sites while we were working at San José Mogote.

Colleagues working in other areas of Mesoamerica either visited our excavations or gave us valuable insight into our ceramic crossties with their regions. Christine Niederberger loaned us sherds from Tlapacoya-Zohapilco and borrowed some of ours for thin-sectioning. Richard S. MacNeish confirmed our identifications of Purrón Plain and Coatepec White-rimmed Black. David Grove visited us and identified our possible Morelos sherds. Ronald Spores let us examine his Early Formative material from Yucuita and Etlatongo. Michael D. Coe allowed us to analyze a number of San Lorenzo sherds that turned out to have been made on Oaxaca clays. Robert and Judith Zeitlin helped us establish our ties to the Isthmus of Tehuantepec. Gareth W. Lowe, to whom this book is dedicated, allowed us to analyze Delfina Fine Gray sherds that had reached Aquiles Serdán in Chiapas. Tom Lee and Pierre Agrinier showed us Early Formative collections when we visited the New World Archaeological Foundation headquarters in Chiapas. At Copán, William L. Fash showed us his burial vessels from the Gordon Complex, material clearly related to our San José phase material.

Thanks also to our colleagues Dick Adams, Will Andrews, Mike Blake, Rich Blanton, John Clark, Dick Drennan, Gary Feinman, Susan Gillespie, David Grove, Norman Hammond, John Henderson, Frank Hole, Mike Love, Tricia McAnany, Linda Nicholas, Steve Plog, Elsa Redmond, Jerry Sabloff, Bob Sharer, Charles Spencer, Ron Spores, and Henry Wright for frequently asking, "How is the pottery volume coming along?" They kept us going.

Finally, we acknowledge our immense debt to William O. Payne, the author of Chapter 2 and the *de facto* coauthor of every pottery description in this volume. Without his patient search for the sources of ceramic raw materials, his microscopic examination of hundreds of sherds, and his simulation of most of our Formative types, this study would be immeasurably poorer.

Chapter 1

Introduction

There is, for me, a fascination attached to the observation of ancient pottery in Mesoamerica which I lack words to describe adequately.

Gareth W. Lowe
[in Green and Lowe 1967:vi]

The Valley of Oaxaca lies in the southern highlands of Mexico between 16°40'-17°20' N and 96°15'-96°55' W. It is drained by two rivers—the upper Río Atoyac, which flows from north to south, and its tributary the Río Salado or Tlacolula, which flows westward to join the Atoyac near the modern city of Oaxaca. The valley is shaped like a "Y," or three-pointed star, whose center is Oaxaca City and whose southern limit is defined by the Ayoquesco gorge, where the Atoyac River leaves the valley on its way to the Pacific Ocean. The climate is semiarid, with 500 to 700 mm of annual rainfall, confined largely to the summer months. The valley-floor elevation averages 1550 m.

As revealed by settlement pattern surveys (Kowalewski et al. 1989), the Valley of Oaxaca has a relatively high density of villages of the Early Formative and Middle Formative periods. During the mid-1960s, interest in cultures of this period was very high among Mesoamerican archaeologists (Flannery [ed.] 1976). From 1966 to 1981, almost without interruption, one or both of the authors of this volume worked at Formative villages within the valley. Among the sites excavated were San José Mogote, Barrio del Rosario Huitzo, San Sebastián Abasolo, and San Pedro y San Pablo Mitla. During that same period, three other early villages were excavated by archaeologists affiliated with our project. These villages were Tierras Largas (Winter 1972), Fábrica San José (Drennan 1976a), and Santo Domingo Tomaltepec (Whalen 1981). Those sites are shown in Figure 1.1.

In this volume we begin the task of describing the pottery from Early Formative proveniences at San José Mogote, Tierras Largas, Huitzo, and Abasolo. In a later volume we will describe the Middle Formative pottery from these and other sites. We should begin at the outset by making it clear that much of this study was completed by 1970. New excavations at San José Mogote between 1974 and 1978 did make it necessary to revise a great deal of our earlier work, but even those revisions antedated the publication of such recent works on ceramic analysis as Rice (1987) and Sinopoli (1991). Our work, therefore, was done too long ago for us to benefit from their insights. We did benefit from earlier works by Sabloff and Smith (1969, 1972); Gifford (1960, 1976); Smith, Willey, and Gifford (1960); Willey, Culbert, and Adams (1967); and others (see Chapter 6).

Our goals in writing this book were several. Some of those goals, of course, were obvious: to fix our Early Formative sites in time and space by linking our ceramics to those of neighboring areas, and to show our pottery to our colleagues by illustrating as much of it as we could. In the course of doing this, we also hoped to learn how Formative Oaxaca pottery was made, where the potters got their raw materials, and how vessels were used within the household.

Beyond the obvious, there were other goals. One was to base our ceramic sequence not on arbitrary levels within excavation trenches, but on real cultural units—houses, features, middens, public buildings, and so forth. That goal has been largely realized, although some cultural units were so thick that we arbitrarily divided them into thinner subunits.

Another goal was to understand better the sources of ceramic variation. Was all variation between Formative sherd collections chronological? We discovered that it was not. There were differences in ceramics between high-status and low-status households, between residential wards within large villages, and between villages in different parts of the valley. All those synchronic differences are dealt with in Chapters 15–17.

1

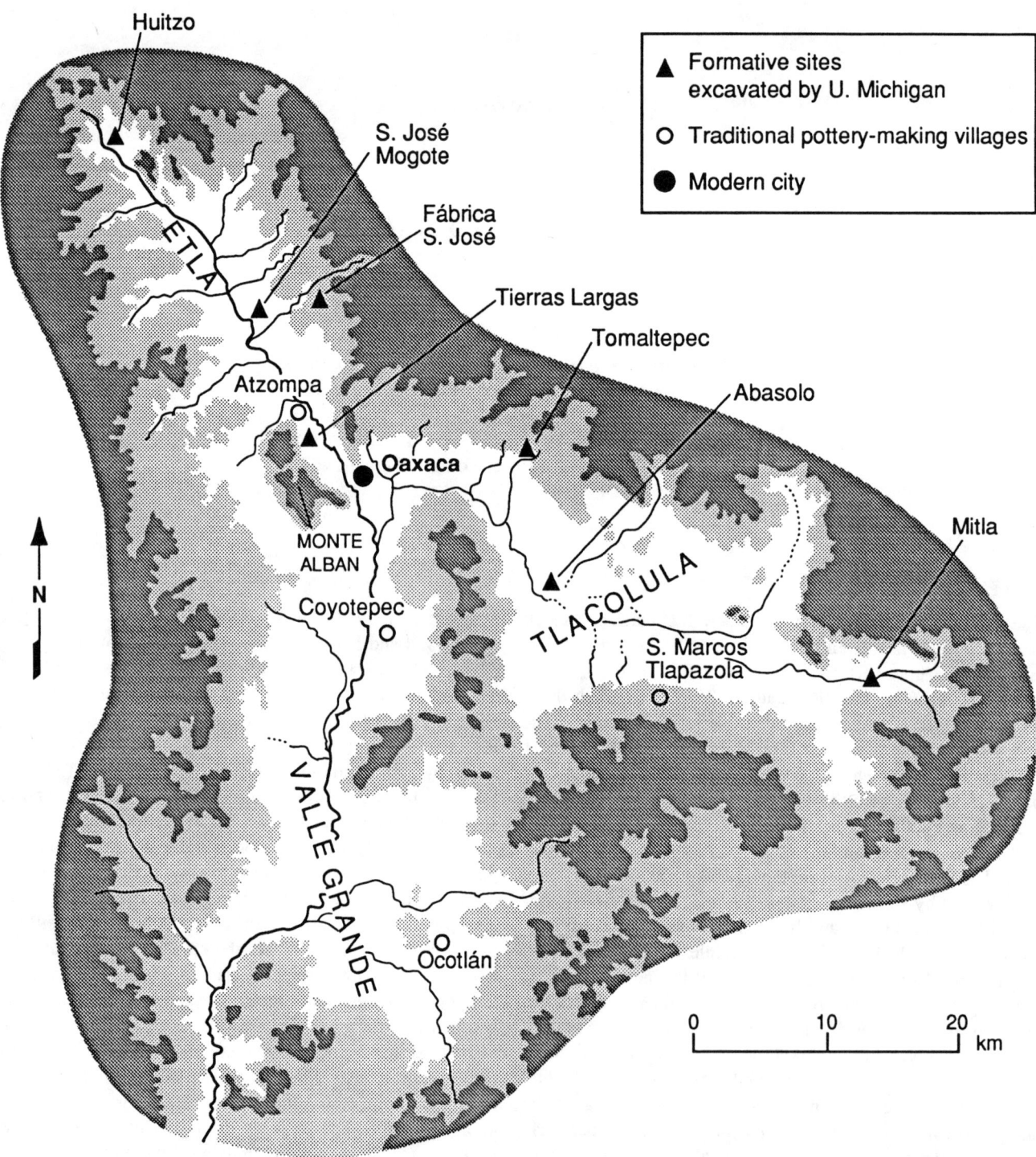

Figure 1.1. Map of the Valley of Oaxaca, showing Early Formative sites and present-day communities mentioned in the text. Heavy stipple indicates mountainous areas; light stipple indicates piedmont. White areas represent the valley floor.

Still another goal was to reverse two recent trends in chronologies based on Mesoamerican pottery—increased reliance on radiocarbon dates and decreased reliance on shared ceramic attributes. In order to make it impossible for us to use radiocarbon dates as a crutch, we do not even discuss them until Chapter 19. All correlations of our Early Formative deposits with such contemporaneous sites as Tlatilco and Tlapacoya-Zohapilco in the Basin of Mexico, Chalcatzingo in Morelos, Ajalpan and Las Canoas in the Tehuacán Valley, San Lorenzo on the Gulf Coast, Laguna Zope in the Isthmus of Tehuantepec, Chiapa de Corzo in the Grijalva Depression, and La Victoria and Salinas La Blanca on the Guatemalan Coast are based on ceramic crossties rather than absolute dates (see Fig. 1.2).

Because of our desire to correlate our Early Formative pottery with that from the sites mentioned above, we have chosen to divide our ceramics into standard binomial types ("Leandro Gray," "Matadamas Red") similar to those used by most of our colleagues working on Formative Mesoamerica. As explained in more detail in Chapter 6, each of our types is defined on the basis of attributes such as clay body, color, surface treatment, vessel form and decoration, attributes that coincide in time as well as space. Obviously, it is the *cultural attributes* such as vessel form, surface color, and decoration that most closely link us to neighboring regions, while the *geological attributes* such as clay body, aplastic material, and parent rock formation are largely imposed by the geology of the Valley of Oaxaca (see Rice 1987:275). From time to time we see the same "type" being made on two different clay bodies, one native to the Valley of Oaxaca and one foreign. In such cases it is clear that we are dealing with a "cultural type" or "mental template" spanning several regions, with geological differences imposed by the available raw materials. Our solution to this problem is to propose only one "type" ("Ocós Black," "Xochiltepec White"), within which there are several "varieties" based on the raw materials used.

While *attributes* play a large role in our type definitions, categories such as *ware* and *mode* do not. We use "ware" purely in the vernacular sense, to refer to a product of the potter's craft (e.g., "white ware," "white-rimmed black ware"). As for modes, Rouse (1960:313) defines those as "certain attributes the analyst judges to reflect communitywide standards for manufacturing and using" ancient pottery, or "any standard, concept, or custom which governs the behavior of artisans of a community, which they hand down from generation to generation." While we refer to various "traditions" of Formative pottery making in Oaxaca that were probably handed down from generation to generation, "modes" per se do not figure prominently in our type definitions. Long-term Oaxaca "traditions" that began in the Early Formative include the use of press-molds for pottery making, and a great fondness for gray ware.

We had very little trouble recognizing the pottery types our colleagues in neighboring regions had already defined. Our biggest complaint is that they have created too many type names for the same ware. We have white-slipped ware that is *culturally* the same in the Basin of Mexico, Puebla, Morelos, Tehuacán, Oaxaca, Tehuantepec, Chiapas, and Guatemala, but it is variously called Pilli White, Altica White, Cesto White, Amatzinac White, Vergel White-to-buff, Burrero Cream, Conchas White-to-Buff, and dozens of other names mainly because it is *geologically* different. To draw an analogy from the field of biology, the situation we have would be comparable to zoologists' having all species and no genera. What zoologists do to avoid confusion is to have conferences at which many colleagues get together and decide on overarching generic terms that acknowledge the similarity of related species. Formative archaeologists need to do something similar before there are too many pottery type names to remember.

The Format for This Study

In this volume we discuss three phases or ceramic complexes with Early Formative pottery (see Frontispiece). These are the Espiridión complex (Chapter 7), the Tierras Largas phase (Chapter 8), and the San José phase (Chapter 12). The format is generally as follows. First, we describe the pottery types for a given phase and illustrate as many examples as we can. We then select the best stratigraphic units available for quantifying the pottery of that phase—not only the number of sherds of each type, but also the number of attributes within a type. Where possible we pick a series of stratigraphic levels that show the way sherd frequencies change as one phase gives way to another. We then select a series of houses (or household units) from that phase and list the sherd collection from each by type and attribute. Next, for those phases with public buildings, we show how the public buildings were dated with sherd collections once the phases had been defined (Chapters 11 and 18).

Later, toward the end of the volume, we deal with the issue of synchronic variation in ceramics by comparing low-status vs. high-status households; villages located 30 km apart in different arms of the valley; and residential wards featuring different pan-Mesoamerican motifs, such as the "fire-serpent" and "were-jaguar." We go on to compare our ceramics to those of other Early Formative sites, evaluating the radiocarbon dates associated with our ceramics and proposing an absolute chronology for our phases (Chapter 19). The volume ends with a reevaluation of what the term "Olmec" means in the light of our data and other recent studies of the Formative. Chapter 20—the one in which that reevaluation takes place—is the only chapter in the volume (besides this one) in which the term "Olmec" appears. As the reader will see, there are reasons for our avoidance of that term.

What We Learned from William O. Payne

We have been fortunate in this study to have had the guidance of William O. Payne, a professional ceramicist and former professor at Orange Coast College in Costa Mesa, California. Payne, a veteran of excavations at Zacatenco in the Basin of Mexico and Yagul and Lambityeco in the Valley of Oaxaca, has long had an interest in Precolumbian pottery making. Payne not only exam-

	TLAPACOYA-ZOHAPILCO	CHALCA-TZINGO	TEHUACÁN VALLEY	VALLEY OF OAXACA	SAN LORENZO	LAGUNA ZOPE	CENTRAL CHIAPAS	CHIAPAS COAST
MIDDLE FORMATIVE	TETELPAN	CANTERA	STA. MARÍA	GUADALUPE	NACASTE	RÍOS	DILI	CONCHAS
EARLY FORMATIVE	MANANTIAL							JOCOTAL
	AYOTLA	BARRANCA	LATE AJALPAN	SAN JOSÉ	SAN LORENZO	GOLFO	PAC	CUADROS
					CHICHARRAS		COTORRA	CHERLA
	NEVADA	AMATE	EARLY AJALPAN	TIERRAS LARGAS	BAJÍO	LAGUNITA	OCÓS	OCÓS
					OJOCHI			LOCONA
			PURRÓN	ESPIRIDIÓN				BARRA
LATE PRECERAMIC								

Figure 1.2. Chronology chart showing roughly equivalent phases in the Valley of Oaxaca and seven other regions of Mesoamerica. Correlations are based on shared ceramic attributes, not radiocarbon dates (see Chapter 19).

ined all our Formative pottery types under the microscope, he also was able to simulate most of them, using clays from the Valley of Oaxaca and an electric kiln provided by our colleague John Paddock.

We entered the Valley of Oaxaca with a lot of misconceptions about Formative pottery making. We imagined that potters traveled to some mysterious place that only they knew about, where they collected "paste"; this "paste" was then mixed with "temper" (from some equally mysterious source), and pots were made by "coiling" as they were in the Southwestern U.S. Some of them, we deduced from their surface appearance, had been "stick polished."

Payne laid to rest all these myths. The first thing he made clear to us was that archaeologists make ancient pottery making much more complicated than it really was. No Early Formative potter in Oaxaca, he explained, ever had to walk more than 5 km from his village to get the basic clays from which the most common pottery types were made. The key to most Early Formative pottery was the western piedmont of the Valley of Oaxaca, where Precambrian metamorphics (predominantly gneiss) run for 70 km, from Huitzo in the north to Ayoquesco in the south. Almost any arroyo in that piedmont was a potential source of "clay body," a term Payne considered preferable to "paste." Moreover, it was usually not necessary to add "temper" to the clay from that piedmont; the clay already contained enough aplastic material, so much in fact that some would have had to be removed rather than added. To be sure, some of our early types were made on finer clays than those of the piedmont, but those finer clays were from the alluvium of the Atoyac River and its major tributaries and would have been readily available to any village. If aplastic material had been added to those finer clays, it would have been available in the piedmont as "grog," a term preferred by Payne to "temper."

According to Payne, much of our Early Formative pottery had been press-molded, not "coiled"; in fact, even the ceramics built up by hand had been made with concentric rings of clay rather than coils. And none of our pottery was "stick-polished," because you can't polish pottery with a stick. Rather, our pottery was "burnished" with a quartz pebble. (No Early Formative pottery was, in fact, polished, since polishing must be done with an abrasive powder.)

One day we showed Payne a white-slipped bowl with two

parallel incised lines at the rim, belonging to the type we have called Atoyac Yellow-white (Chapter 12). Payne got in his vehicle and set off for the Pan-American Highway. Near Tlacochahuaya in the eastern valley he stopped at a road cut to get some clay body. In the mountains above Mitla he found a fossil hot spring that had produced white kaolin clay. On the way home, he cut the spine off the end of a maguey leaf. After soaking and decanting the clay, he press-molded a new bowl over an Early Formative vessel, slipped it with white kaolin from the fossil hot spring, and incised it with the maguey thorn. After firing at 720° C in an electric kiln, it was indistinguishable from prehistoric Atoyac Yellow-white. Payne further convinced us that the firing temperature of each of our types was probably a more meaningful statistic than the hardness on the Mohs scale traditionally used by archaeologists. After all, Early Formative pottery occupies a relatively narrow range of the Mohs scale.

In Chapter 2, Payne has provided us with a very useful account of the geological raw materials used by the Formative potters of the Valley of Oaxaca, the techniques used for forming pots, and the fuels and methods used for firing it. But Payne's influence extends beyond that chapter; every one of our pottery type descriptions incorporates his analyses of how a particular type was made. His role was to define the *geological* attributes of each type; ours was to define the *cultural* attributes, based on the work of our colleagues in neighboring areas.

The Pottery Type Descriptions

Each of our pottery type descriptions begins with Payne's analysis of the clay body, the source of any wash or slip, the surface treatment, and the firing temperature as determined by simulation. We have provided assessments of the color of the clay body (both sherd core and surface), the color of any slip or paint, and the range of firing clouds, using the Munsell Soil Color Charts which are in common use in archaeology (Munsell Color Company 1954). We have substituted "firing temperature" for "hardness."

For the various vessel forms within each type, we have provided verbal descriptions, photographs, line drawings, and dimensions such as height, diameter, and wall thickness. Since we were also concerned with the function of each vessel form, we have measured the volume as well; that measurement helped us to decide if a given vessel was for an individual serving, a whole family's meal, or major storage. Volumes were taken by filling whole or restorable vessels with sesame seed, then pouring the seed into a graduated cylinder marked in milliliters or cubic centimeters. As a guide for this study, we had ethnologist Teresa Graedon's measurement of Zapotec family meals at Santo Tomás Mazaltepec, not far west of San José Mogote. Graedon (pers. comm.) found that one adult male could drink 800 milliliters of atole (maize gruel) at one meal, while an adult female could drink about 600 milliliters. Thus, a 600–800 ml vessel was probably one adult's portion. We have used this as a rule of thumb to interpret the function of Formative vessels.

Finally, the designs with which each vessel was decorated were studied. We were fortunate in having two preliminary works already available to us. One was Nanette Pyne's (1976) study of free-standing motifs on San José phase pottery. The other was Stephen Plog's (1976) study of "double-line-break" design elements incised on Atoyac Yellow-white pottery of the San José and Guadalupe phases. We have built on, and added to, both those studies in this volume.

We have illustrated as many sherds and restorable vessels as possible. Some of our illustrations were prepared by Werner Riedl, an Austrian engineer and draftsman. Readers of his illustrations should not spend time looking for the letter *i* in his alphabetical labels, since it is not European custom to use it (it is considered too similar to a *j*). Some of our other illustrations, prepared by American artists, do contain the letter *i*.

We have tried in this volume to do something we wish our colleagues would do more often: we have given the exact provenience for every sherd we illustrate. This makes for extremely long captions, but we think it is worth it. Indeed, we hope it starts a trend.

Special Topics for Consideration

In addition to defining pottery types and phases, discussing stratigraphy and giving the provenience of every illustrated sherd, we spend time in this volume on several topics we consider to be important but often insufficiently considered in most pottery volumes. One, of course, is the distinction between synchronic and diachronic variation in ceramics, discussed at greater length in Chapters 15–17.

Another special topic is the quality of sherd collections, which we discuss at length in Chapter 4. Most archaeologists working on Early Formative sites in Mesoamerica have done a good job of describing and illustrating their pottery types. What they have often not done is to convince us that their sherd samples come from a meaningful context. All too often the sherds have been picked out of building fill, or collected from arbitrary levels whose actual nature is unknown.

We believe that only a small percentage of any Formative site—perhaps no more than 20 percent—is primary deposit. In some sites, 80 percent of the matrix is earth that has been moved at least once, maybe twice, maybe even three times. The more often sherds are moved, the smaller the individual sherd becomes, the greater the sherd count, and the higher the number of sherds per kilogram (Marcus 1982, and in preparation). Often the deposits that are richest in actual numbers of sherds are the least reliable in terms of defining a time period. Often the deposits that are poorest for showing chronological variation are the best for showing synchronic variation, and vice versa. Thus a ceramic study is no better than the stratigraphy and archaeological context from which the sherds came.

In this volume, the pottery type descriptions are no better than those produced by any number of Formative archaeologists. Indeed, we have drawn on the work of many of our colleagues, and consciously modeled our descriptions on theirs so that the interregional crossties will be clear. However, we have tried to be much more explicit about the contexts from which our sherds came than they usually are.

In Chapter 4 we discuss the differences among middens, houses, household units, features, public buildings, slopewash, and arroyo fill in terms of the quality of sherd collections. In subsequent chapters we take pains to make clear whether our sherds come from middens, features, house floors, dooryards, or public buildings. Each of those contexts is treated separately, and the problems each presents are made explicit. We believe that if everyone did this whenever he or she presented a ceramic study, a number of diachronic and synchronic problems in Early Formative archaeology could be cleared up. Those problems, we suspect, are not the result of bad type descriptions but of bad sherd collections. Our study is certainly not entirely free of such problems, but by giving the provenience of every illustrated sherd and the context of every sherd collection we use, we hope to make it easier for our colleagues to resolve any problems inherent in our work.

Chapter 2

The Raw Materials and Pottery-Making Techniques of Early Formative Oaxaca: An Introduction

by William O. Payne

During the decade of the 1970s, in collaboration with the archaeologists of the University of Michigan project, I undertook a study of the Formative pottery of the Valley of Oaxaca. My goals were two-fold. First, I hoped to trace all raw materials used by Formative potters to their places of geological origin. Second, I hoped to identify manufacturing techniques used in the production of Formative pottery.

For the most part, these goals were realized. All the common pottery types of the Oaxaca Formative were made with clay bodies, slips, and pigments found in and around the valley. Most of these raw materials are available over so wide an area that potters would rarely have had to walk more than five kilometers from their village to obtain them. There are minor local variations in the ingredients from site to site, but this is to be expected given the geologic origin of the clay minerals and nonplastic inclusions. Despite this variation, it is usually not possible to determine whether certain types came from pottery centers in one part of the valley and were transported to other parts of the valley, because the same contributing soils and mineral deposits are of such widespread occurrence. The occasional pottery types imported into the valley stand out because of their anomalous raw materials.

In general terms, it seems relatively clear how Oaxaca's earliest pottery was produced. Traces of manufacture can be found on many of the whole or restorable vessels. Many of the techniques used in the Formative have survived in one or another of the villages which still make traditional pottery in the Valley of Oaxaca (see Chapter 3). Others are techniques widespread among Native American potters in Mexico and the western United States.

Geologic Origins

The bedrock geology of the Valley of Oaxaca is the product of several ancient developmental stages (Lorenzo 1960; Michael Kirkby, unpublished studies, 1966–1968). The oldest stage consists of Precambrian metamorphic rocks, predominantly gneiss and schist. While such rocks are often so altered that one cannot determine what they consisted of before metamorphosis, Oaxaca's basal complex gives every evidence of having been igneous material of the granite–granodiorite–diorite group. Not only are there dikes of pegmatite, granite, and diorite still to be found in the area, but also the minerals in the Precambrian gneiss are ones that are common to crystalline rocks like granite and diorite.

A second major stage in the geologic development of the valley was the laying down of Cretaceous limestones. These calcareous rocks are exposed primarily in the western part of the valley, for example at Monte Albán. They also outcrop at places like San Lorenzo Etla and Rancho Matadamas, where they provided veins of chert and chalcedony for making ancient chipped stone tools (Whalen 1986).

A third major stage in the valley's development saw the deposition of Miocene volcanic tuffs, or ignimbrites. These were flows of molten volcanic ash which probably smoldered for years, like those which gave Alaska's "Valley of Ten Thousand Smokes" its nickname. Such ignimbrites are primarily exposed in the eastern part of the Valley of Oaxaca, from Tlacolula to Mitla, where they sometimes form cliffs and mesas at places like Yagul, Caballito Blanco, and the Mitla Fortress (Kirkby, Whyte, and Flannery 1986).

Finally, during the Pleistocene and Recent epochs, considerable alluvium was laid down on the floor of the Valley of Oaxaca by the Atoyac River and its tributaries. This alluviation—accompanied by changes of river course and interrupted by periods of downcutting—has reworked the erosion products of all earlier rock formations and altered the grain size.

Figure 2.1 shows a hypothetical cross-section of the Valley of Oaxaca. It is not intended to represent any one place in the valley, but rather to show the typical relationships of the formations from which ceramic raw materials came.

One whole group of Early Formative pottery types, from Tierras Largas Burnished Plain and Fidencio Coarse to Atoyac Yellow-white and Leandro Gray, was dependent on the disintegration of the Precambrian gneisses and schists which form the valley's basal complex. The clay bodies from which these types were made are *residual clays*, that is, ones which formed *in situ* above the parent rock formations as the result of weathering and decomposition (Fig. 2.2*b, c*). What the Early Formative potters evidently did was to go to places where gullies were eroding headward into the piedmont gneiss. My study of buried soil profiles in these arroyos and headward cutbacks in the foothills of the valley reveals much layering and intermingling of decomposition products. In the cross-sections of piedmont arroyos one finds yellow-brown to red-brown soils which were the ones preferred by early potters. These soils can be used virtually as found, except for simple refining. They already contain all the nonplastic material needed, in the form of metamorphosed crystalline minerals; no "temper" needs to be added to them, and in fact what the Early Formative potters did was to remove the larger aplastics by sieving or winnowing. The plastic component of these soils, which is quite variable, is the result of the disintegration of feldspars in the gneiss, and results in various kaolinite clay minerals. The combination of these kaolinites and ever-present iron oxides, together with the leaching out of the calcium minerals, has resulted in clay bodies that acquire sufficient hardness at reasonably low temperatures. Nonplastic inclusions, which average about half of the clay body, vary in size from visibly coarse in thicker wares like Fidencio Coarse to very fine in the thinnest and most delicate examples of Clementina Fine Red-on-Buff.

Some of the other clay minerals and ingredients used during the Early Formative come from the Miocene volcanic tuffs. These ignimbrites are subject to rapid erosion and break down easily into plastic clays of the montmorillonite group. Deposits of hydrothermal clays are found at the sites of ancient hot springs, where the rocks have completely broken down into a highly plastic, but complex, clay mineral that is a combination of montmorillonites and kaolinites (Michael Kirkby, pers. comm.). Material in these altered ignimbrites, or in the feldspar dikes within them, can become so iron-free that it forms a white or off-white kaolin. Such material was used as the engobe, or slip, seen on Atoyac Yellow-white pottery (Fig. 2.2*e*).

Another group of pottery types, including Delfina Fine Gray, Socorro Fine Gray of the Rosario phase, and some of the later Monte Albán I gray wares, was made not with residual piedmont clays but with valley floor alluvial clays. These *transported clays*, which have often been carried considerable distances from their parent material, are finer in texture (Fig. 2.2*a*). And because the alluvium of the valley floor is a mixture of materials washed down from a variety of parent rock formations, such clays include not only the crystalline minerals typical of the Precambrian gneisses and schists, but also minerals from the Tertiary ignimbrites or Mesozoic limestones. In general, these finer alluvial clays were used to make serving vessels, while the coarser piedmont clays, with their greater resistance to thermal shock, were used to make cooking vessels.

The colorants used on Early Formative pottery consist almost entirely of iron oxides. These oxides are most plentiful in the Precambrian gneiss, which is also rich in minerals such as magnetite, hematite, biotite mica, and other raw materials used by Formative villagers. Pods of *barro colorado* (used as the red wash on Fidencio Coarse) and veins of hematite or limonite (used as the red stain or paint on Avelina Red-on-Buff) occur in the complex gneisses (Fig. 2.2*d*). Some occurrences are completely oxidized, while others still contain visible crystals of unoxidized hematite. The latter pigment, called "specular hematite," was used on many examples of Clementina Fine Red-on-Buff. Some iron oxides appear yellowish or orange on Early Formative wares (e.g., Matadamas Orange), but most of these ceramics will turn red if heated to a sufficiently high temperature.

In some parts of the valley, pegmatite dikes intruding into the Cretaceous limestones have decomposed into a coarse kaolinite product. At the present time this kaolinite is being used occasionally by some of the potters at Santa María Atzompa (see Chapter 3). It would be difficult, if not impossible, to distinguish this material from a similar kaolinite originating in the ancient gneisses once it had been made into ceramics. Such material occurs in colors ranging from very dark red through orange and yellow to almost white.

Some valley floor alluvials, used in great quantities at the present time by potters in the villages of San Bartolo Coyotepec and Santa María Atzompa, are a product of the disintegrated volcanic tuffs and the finer sediments from the gneisses. These soils settled in low, swampy parts of the valley as a result of slow-moving waters, and in many areas became covered with thick vegetation. Continuous coverage by such plants over a period of time results in the deoxygenation of the underlying sediments, causing the red iron oxides to turn black. The present-day potters use the older, underlying strata of these fine-grained sediments, which because of their age have acquired greater plasticity. Furthermore, such clays tend to become lighter in color after firing than do the more recent deposits. (Mining of these lower strata has unfortunately resulted in the death by cave-in of several inexperienced diggers.) Firings of wares made from these clay bodies have been observed locally as high as 900° C (around 1650° F) without distortion or blistering.

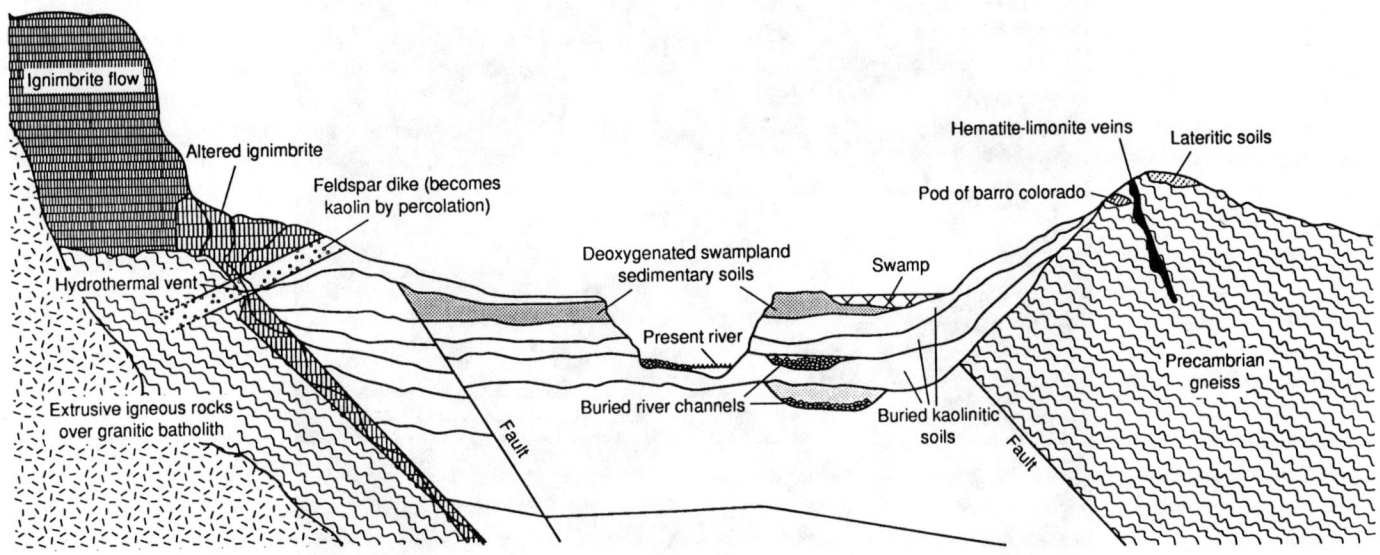

Figure 2.1. A hypothetical geological cross-section of the Valley of Oaxaca, showing the rock formations and soil deposits relevant to pottery making. This section is not intended to represent a particular place in the valley, but rather to show typical relationships among the formations from which ceramic raw materials came.

Beneficiation of Materials

Many of the exposed soil profiles in the Oaxaca piedmont show great disintegration of parent rock material at lower depths, indicating considerable age. These lower deposits, exposed by stream or gully downcutting, consist of finely divided particles of the decomposition products of the Precambrian gneiss, and appear under the binocular microscope to be identical to many clay bodies used by Early Formative potters.

How accessible were these sources to Early Formative villagers? It should be stressed that Precambrian gneiss is exposed in the western piedmont of the Valley of Oaxaca for 70 kilometers, from Huitzo in the north to Ayoquezco in the south. However, not all Early Formative villagers were located near a profile where the better, more deeply buried material was exposed. In such cases, it appears that the higher layers of the soil profile could—if sieved, winnowed, or decanted—result in a clay body that was virtually as good as that found at lower levels.

My experiments with winnowing of such soils showed that it can produce clay bodies grading from very coarse to very fine, roughly approximating the range of clay bodies seen in Early Formative pottery. Whether winnowing was the technique used in the Early Formative is not known, but the method is still in use among the Pueblo Indians of the Southwest U.S. and the Cocopai and Paipai of Baja California. In traditional pottery-making villages of the Valley of Oaxaca today, the clay body is usually sieved through homemade screens of twigs and slender branches.

Decanting may also have been used by Formative potters, although it is difficult to prove. In this technique, the clay is allowed to stand in water until the heavier, larger particles have settled to the bottom; then the lighter material is poured off.

At any rate, the need to "age," or increase the plasticity of, some clay bodies is well known among Native American potters. My experiments with local Valley of Oaxaca materials show that clay bodies from the upper, or less desirable, layers of exposed piedmont profiles can be improved for working purposes by being allowed to stand for several days in a wet environment before wedging (kneading) and forming into ware. Atzompa potters do this with some of their less well aged clay bodies today (see Chapter 3).

Iron oxide colorants were evidently ground on stone metates, mixed with water, and used from small bowls. We know this because traces of red pigment remain on many metates and manos at Early Formative sites, as well as on the ceramic category "spouted trays or pigment dishes" (see Chapter 12). These spouted trays, only slightly larger than a standard ashtray, clearly appear to have been used to hold and pour liquid red pigment.

There was usually enough clay mineral in the local Oaxaca colorant samples to form a bond with the still-damp pottery vessel to which it was applied. My experiments with local hematite sources (e.g., Fig. 2.2d) resulted in a decorative red stain identical to that used on Early Formative wares like Avelina Red-on-Buff and San José Red-on-White.

Forming Techniques

Two principal techniques of forming pottery are evident in Early Formative ceramics from Oaxaca. In one technique, a new vessel is formed by press-molding clay over a previously made pot (or a gourd vessel). In the other technique, the potter begins by taking a lump of clay and pounding it into a disc or concavity which becomes the base of the new vessel. Concentric rings of

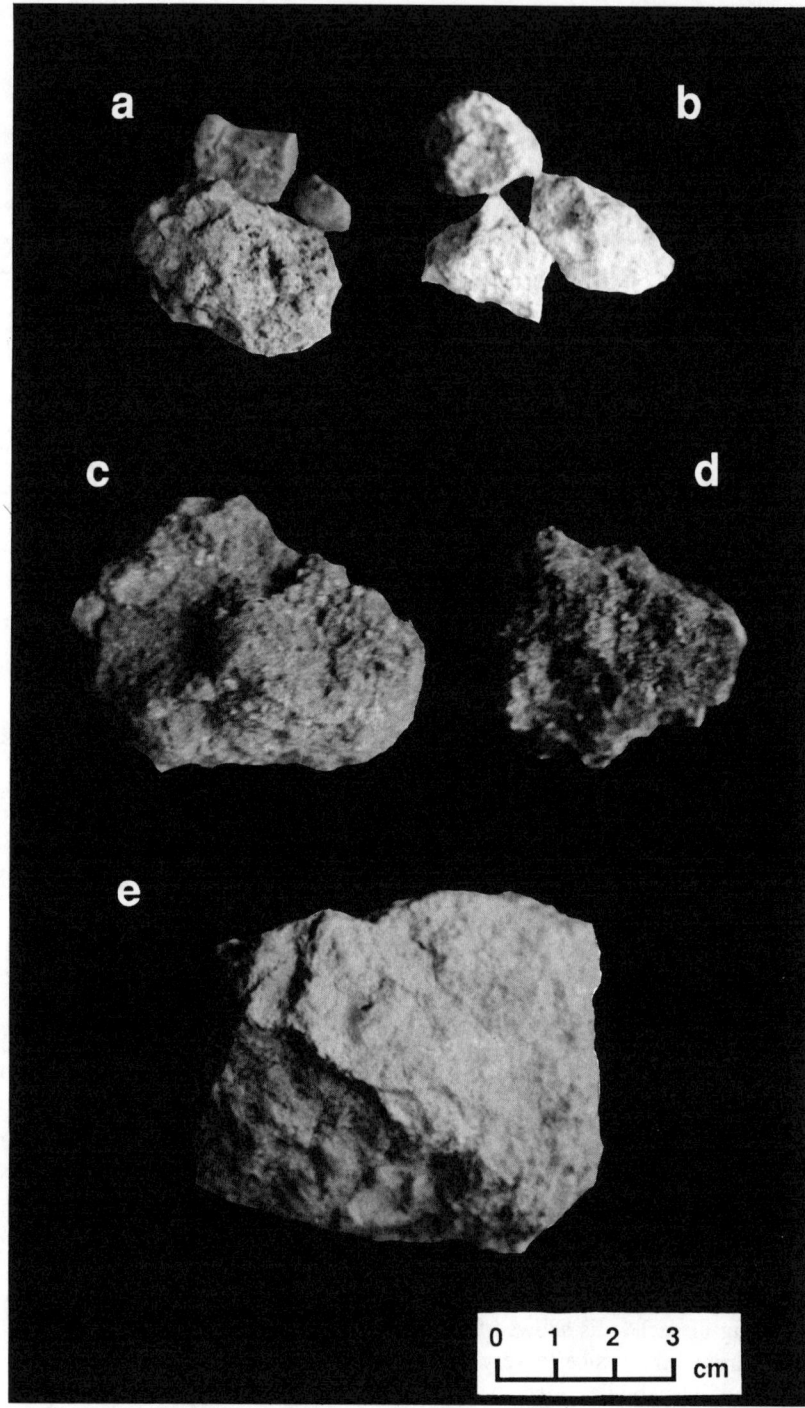

Figure 2.2. Raw materials used for pottery making in ancient and modern Oaxaca. *a, barro liso,* a transported alluvial clay from the Cacaotepec area that is used by Atzompa potters today. The clay is from an old alluvium, buried under more recent deposits. *b, barro áspero,* a residual piedmont clay that has formed above Precambrian gneiss at Sta. Catarina Montaño. The Atzompa potters use this as grog, mixing it with *barro liso. c,* residual piedmont clay from near Tlacochahuaya in the Tlacolula region. This clay, the product of weathered Precambrian gneiss, can be used to simulate the clay body of Atoyac Yellow-white, Fidencio Coarse, or Leandro Gray. *d,* hematite-bearing red clay from Abuelo, a hamlet between Atzompa and San Pedro Ixtlahuaca. This clay can be used to simulate the nonspecular red stain or slip on Avelina Red-on-Buff. *e,* white kaolin clay from the Nochixtlán Valley, Oaxaca. This clay can be used to simulate the engobe on Atoyac Yellow-white.

clay (not coils) are then added to the disc or concavity in order to build up the sides of the vessel (and the neck, if it is a jar). In the course of forming the vessel the maker may place it on a "potter's bat," a kind of tournette or shallow saucer which rotates as the potter works (Fig. 2.3). These two techniques—press-molding and concentric rings—could even be combined when making a large vessel such as a storage jar. The lower half might be press-molded over a previous jar set upside down, after which the upper half could be built up by adding concentric rings (see Chapter 8).

The concentric ring method is the most common one seen today in villages such as Santa María Atzompa, San Bartolo Coyotepec, and San Marcos Tlapazola. The potter begins with a pat of clay body on a potter's bat of fired ware either made for the purpose or salvaged from a broken pot. Usually the bat is dusted with wood ash or dry clay powder, which serves as a separator to prevent the new vessel from sticking to the bat. The wall of the new vessel may be started by pinching up the edge of the pat of clay, or by adding a concentric ring of clay body to the edge. Successive concentric rings are then smeared together smoothly, either with a worked sherd, a shell, or most commonly a piece of gourd. More care in smoothing and scraping is given to the surfaces of the piece which are to be burnished than to those which are to be left unburnished. Use of the concentric ring forming method may usually be detected by holding a prehistoric sample horizontally toward a strong light source. Horizontal ridges are evident in many of the Formative specimens I examined.

Evidence for this method of vessel forming comes from House 9 of Area C at San José Mogote, a residence of the San José phase. The evidence consists of two pats of unfired clay body, such as that used for Fidencio Coarse. One pat (Fig. 2.4, left) is unused. The other (Fig. 2.4, right) has been punched into the concave shape usually used as the base of a small jar; because the jar was never finished, no concentric rings of clay have been added to this concave "pre-form." These pats of clay clearly indicate that the occupants of House 9 made Fidencio Coarse jars by the pat and concentric ring method.

In addition to this evidence from House 9 of San José Mogote, several Early and Middle Formative deposits produced shallow, saucerlike vessels that appear to be potter's bats (Fig. 2.5). Such bats appear to have been used from late San José phase times onward.

Evidence for the press-molding technique also comes from San José Mogote. A fragment of what appears to be a lightly baked clay mold for making oval bowls with pinched-in sides was found just south of Structure 6 in Area C of San José Mogote (Fig. 2.6); this provenience dates to the late Tierras Largas phase. A second, more complete mold comes from Feature 62B of House 16 in Area B of San José Mogote (Fig. 2.7); this provenience dates to the San José phase. This second artifact appears to be a lightly baked clay mold for making cylindrical bowls like those seen in Atoyac Yellow-white and Leandro Gray. The clay used for the mold resembles that from the "La Casahuatera" locality near San Lorenzo Cacaotepec, and is similar to that used for the *crema* wares of Monte Albán I. There is a burned hole in one end of the mold, possibly the result of accidental burning of a wooden handle used to hold molded vessels near a fire so as to speed up drying. Since Feature 62B was a hearth in a lean-to associated with House 17 (see Chapter 15), this scenario is not unrealistic.

Many of the flat-based bowls with outleaned walls, and flat-based cylinders with vertical or nearly vertical walls, made during the San José phase appear to have been press-molded. In addition, if some hemispherical bowls of the Espiridión Complex and the Tierras Largas phase were press-molded over gourds (see Chapter 7), this technique may be as old as pottery making itself in the Valley of Oaxaca.

Press-molding is done by laying previously flattened slabs of clay body over a gourd or a previous vessel, often using wood ash or dry clay powder to prevent the two vessels from sticking together. The side of the new vessel laid against the mold will sometimes appear flat and smooth, without evidence of scraping or manual smoothing. Of course, later burnishing can destroy this evidence of molding.

It appears that during the Tierras Largas and San José phases, the basal portions of large jars were press-molded over the inverted bases of previous jars. The upper portion and the neck were then built up by adding concentric rings (see the Tierras Largas Burnished Plain jar in Fig. 8.2 of Chapter 8).

Tools used in forming or finishing (in addition to those mentioned above) included scrapers made from sherds or pieces of gourds whose edges had been blunted by grinding, and patches of deer hide used for smoothing wet clay. Some vessels might also have been scraped smooth with pieces of split river cane. I was able to duplicate the smoothing of Early Formative rims by holding a wet piece of deer hide between the fingers while the vessel was rotated. It was also shown by experimentation that surface finish could be improved prior to burnishing by smearing it with a wet piece of hide to bring more clay mineral to the surface.

Burnishing is a pottery technique often misunderstood by archaeologists. They confuse it with polishing, which is incorrect, since polishing involves the use of an abrasive. One even hears streaky burnishing referred to as "stick polishing," which is an oxymoron, since pottery is harder than a stick and cannot be polished or burnished by it. Early Formative pottery was burnished with quartz pebbles, many of which were found in the Oaxaca excavations (Fig. 2.8); streaky burnishing results from uneven burnishing with the rounded tip of a burnishing pebble, or a pebble with an irregular projection.

The purpose of burnishing is to reduce the porosity of the vessel surface, thus reducing absorption or evaporation of moisture in the contents and making the pot easier to clean. Some of the finest burnishing was done on wares containing relatively large nonplastics, and some wares (such as Leandro Gray) were double-burnished—once when leather-hard and once when completely dry. Moving a quartz pebble over the surface of the clay brings finer particles to the surface and closes the pores.

Figure 2.3. Use of a *platillo* or potter's bat by a Formative potter in the Valley of Oaxaca (reconstruction drawing by John Klausmeyer, based on a photo by Shepard 1963: Frontispiece). The potter forms a new vessel on the *platillo*, rotating the latter slowly on an inverted jar.

Decoration of Wares

Several techniques of decoration were used on Early Formative pottery. Plastic decoration—such as incising, excising, or stamping—might simply be applied to the clay body. In other cases, the clay body might be covered with a colored coating. Such coats could vary from a simple iron oxide paint or stain, to a wash of *barro colorado,* to an actual slip or engobe in which a mineral colorant was added to a watery solution of clay. The most common slips were red (iron oxide plus reddish clay) or white (finely decanted kaolin clay poured over the vessel).

Some wares, while wet or damp, were impressed with fingernails, comb-like dentate tools, or curved objects which could be "rocked" back and forth. In other cases, a sharp object such as a maguey spine could be used to incise lines on the vessel. Where this incising penetrates a slip of one color to reveal an underlying clay body of another color, it approaches the kind of incising known as *sgraffito* (see Glossary). Some of the most spectacular plastic decoration, however, took the form of *raspada,* or excising, where areas of the leather-hard surface were carved out with a slat of cane or an obsidian blade. Often, incising and excising were combined.

Excellent examples of *sgraffito* are seen on Atoyac Yellow-white bowls. A locally available off-white, hydrothermal, kaolin–montmorillonite slip was applied by pouring into and over the vessel, or by application with some sort of swab or soft brush such as animal fur. After nearly dry ware was burnished, a thorn or sharp stick was dragged at a steep angle below the rim to form the characteristic "double-line-break" motif. This incising revealed the brown clay body color below the off-white slipped surface. This was the true *sgraffito* technique. In Avelina Red-on-Buff bowls, stains of iron oxide were painted on rims with some sort of delicate brush, then burnished to a high gloss. Possible brushes could have been animal fur, animal tails, or perhaps a tied cluster of hair. Stains were applied with a fine brush if an unlined application was desired.

Drying Practice

Part of a potter's success depends not only on his or her knowledge of clay bodies, but also on their drying characteristics. Wares today in the Valley of Oaxaca are made indoors, and preliminary drying for one or two days is done within a house or shelter. The pots are not inverted until the rims are nearly dry; this avoids edge-cracking. Since most of the clay bodies are "open" (i.e., they contain ample amounts of nonplastics), they dry readily and evenly. The dried wares have a surprisingly high dry strength, and will survive rough handling and stacking in depth for firing. Conditions in the Valley of Oaxaca are excellent for the rapid drying of pottery.

Firing of Wares

No kilns have so far been recovered in any of Oaxaca's Early Formative sites, or in contemporary sites from other areas of Mesoamerica. Since kilns are known from later sites in the area (e.g., Whalen 1981; Winter and Payne 1976; Flannery and Marcus 1983b:299), this absence of early kilns probably means that Early Formative villagers fired pots above ground, as do the potters of San Marcos Tlapazola in the Tlacolula arm of the Valley of Oaxaca today (Figs. 2.9–2.11).

At San Marcos Tlapazola, fuel of dried maguey leaves or organ cactus stems is piled on the ground out in the open, in an unroofed but fenced-in dooryard or *solar*. Large sherds from old vessels are placed on the fuel, and the pots to be fired are in turn placed on the sherds. The pots are then covered with more sherds, and more fuel is piled on the whole heap. The last step in building such an above-ground "kiln" is the placement of a ring of large ollas around, and close to, the unfired pots and fuel pile. Gaps are filled in with fuel, and the fire is then ignited on the downwind portion of this mound of material. As the burn continues, more fuel is added to keep a relatively even heat in the mound. Burning continues until a dull red glow is seen in the new vessels under the sherds. I recorded a temperature of 700° C after

Figure 2.4. Two pats of unfired clay body from House 9, Area C, San José Mogote (San José phase). *Left,* unused pat from Square S15B. *Right,* a pat that has been punched into a concave shape to serve as the base for a small jar (found in Square S17B). The clay body in both cases appears to be the residual piedmont clay used for Fidencio Coarse (see Chapter 12). From their small size, it would appear that these pats were for miniature vessels, perhaps burial offerings.

only 53 minutes during one firing. As there was no smothering of the kiln, and the fuel was allowed to burn completely in the open air, the pots oxidized a rich red; the protecting sherds prevented all but a few fire smudges.

Fuels observed in use by potters in the Valley of Oaxaca today vary from annual shrubs to oak, pine, manzanita, and mesquite branches. However, only when potters desire higher temperatures than those achieved in Precolumbian times do they resort to the use of dense woods from the latter trees. For most purposes, annual shrubs, maguey leaves, and organ cactus stems are adequate.

Cooling and Drawing of Ware

There is no advantage in drawing recently fired wares from a hot kiln. It is only anxiety that compels a potter to draw the ware before it has cooled. Some potters feel they *must* know whether the firing was successful or not. Modern-day potters at San Marcos Tlapazola pick their newly fired vessels from the kiln almost immediately with hooks made from long sticks. These sticks are dipped in water to avoid igniting on any surviving hot coals. (In one such kiln opening I observed at San Marcos, not so much as a single vessel had cracked in a load of just under 200 pieces.) After the vessels have been drawn from the kiln, they are brushed off with a wad of maguey fiber to remove the ash.

Our description of firing at San Marcos may explain why no Early Formative kilns have been found in Oaxaca. Above-ground firing results only in a large area of fine ash and some refired sherds among those which were piled around the new vessels. Formative sites are full of ash and refired sherds, but it would be difficult to prove that they had resulted from the manufacture of pottery. Even "kiln wasters" might be rare in Early Formative sites, if the potters were as successful as those in San Marcos Tlapazola.

An interesting question is how Early Formative potters produced "smudged" wares such as San José Black-and-White, or reduced-fired gray wares such as Leandro Gray. Some suggestions as to how those wares were produced can be found in the type descriptions (Chapter 12). Above-ground firing, such as that done at San Marcos Tlapazola, usually produces oxidized (buff, red, or brown) pottery. However, the burning mound can be "smothered" toward the end of the firing by covering it with dirt, ash, or some other material. This would result in reduced (gray or black) pottery and would also probably be archaeologically undetectable.

Functions of Early Formative Pottery

Most archaeological reports refer only to "storage vessels," "cooking pots," or "serving dishes." While Espiridión and Tierras Largas phase vessels had a relatively limited range of shapes, San José phase vessels show tremendous diversity. We have already mentioned the possible pigment dishes and potter's bats of that phase, and the pottery type descriptions will make it clear that there were charcoal braziers, tecomates for storage, large jars for cooking, and smaller bowls for individual servings of food. There also seem to have been chipped sherds that served as pot lids. However, archaeologists should also consider the

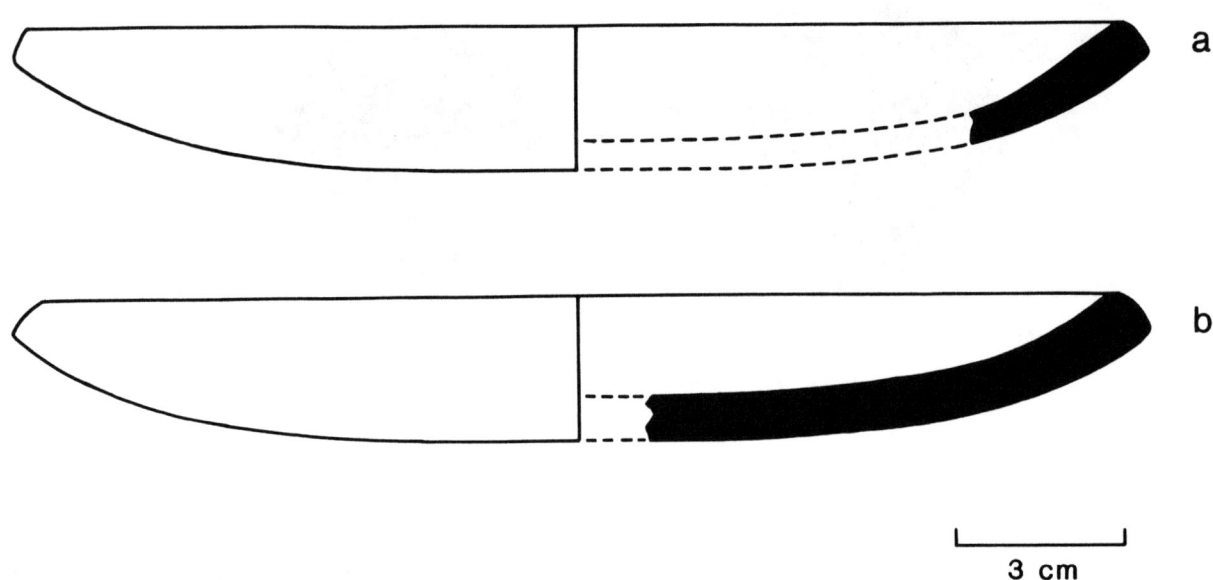

Figure 2.5. Probable potter's bats from the San José phase (Lupita Heavy Plain ware). *a,* found stored below the floor of House 6, Area C, San José Mogote. *b,* found in House 1 (Household Unit LSJ-1), Area A, Tierras Largas.

possibility that there were vessels for fermentation, dyeing, maize soaking, parching, decanting, slaking lime, evaporating salt, tanning, and leaching. Whether we will be able to recognize all these activities after the vessels have been in the ground for 3000 years is another question.

Raw Materials and Techniques—Payne

Figure 2.6. Fragment of lightly baked clay mold, apparently for making hemispherical bowls with pinched-in sides. Found in the debris just south of Structure 6, Area C, San José Mogote (late Tierras Largas phase).

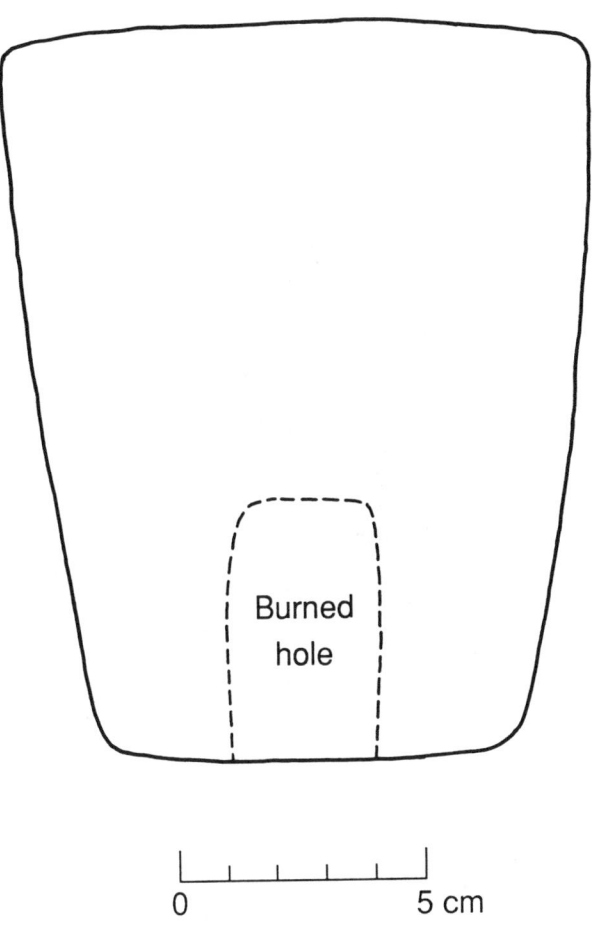

Figure 2.7. Lightly baked clay mold, probably for making flat-based bowls with vertical walls like those in Atoyac Yellow-white and Leandro Gray. The clay resembles that from the La Casahuatera locality near San Lorenzo Cacaotepec, and is similar to that used for *crema* wares during Monte Albán I. The burned hole may result from the burning of a wooden handle, used to speed up the drying of molded vessels by holding them near a fire. San José Mogote, Area B, Feature 62B of House 16 (San José phase).

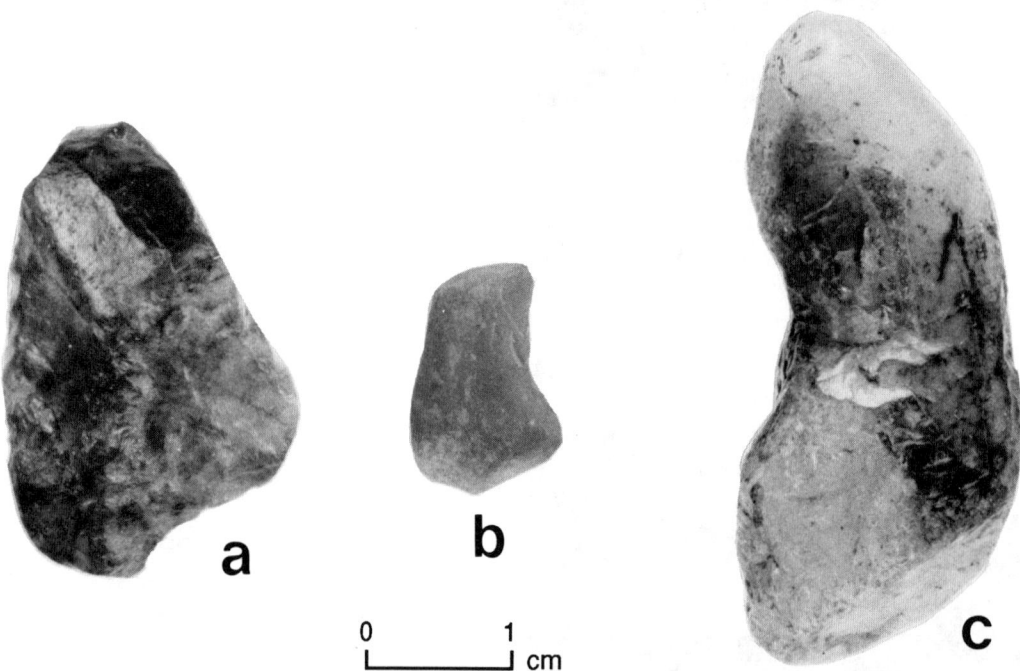

Figure 2.8. Quartz pebbles used for burnishing pottery in prehispanic Oaxaca. *a,* pebble found in the fill of Structure 1, Stages II-III, Area A, San José Mogote (San José phase). The rounded projection on the right is worn from burnishing. *b,* small pebble from Household Unit C1, Area A, San José Mogote, particularly worn on left side (San José phase). *c,* large pebble from Zone A, Cueva Blanca (Postclassic). This pebble, worn on both ends, was used to burnish G3M gray jars of the Monte Albán V period.

GLOSSARY OF CERAMIC TERMS

APPLIQUÉ—the attachment of decorative elements of clay body to a ware while both are in a similar state of dampness. Also known as "sprigging."

BAT, POTTER'S—a concave-convex disk of fired clay body used for turning ware during forming, and sometimes for decorating. Variously called a *tournette, plato,* or *platillo.*

BISQUE—a fired state of ware in which the product is made water-resistant. Firing temperature must reach at least 650° C (1200° F) to drive off the water of crystallization of the mineral ingredients.

BODY, CLAY—earth with a combination of nonmetallic minerals, having properties that enable it to be formed and fired into a useful product. Sometimes, inaccurately, called PASTE.

BURNISHING—making pottery shiny by rubbing to develop a reflecting surface. The nonplastic particles are forced into a parallel position by the use of a quartz burnisher on the almost dry ware. Most of the burnishers found in Oaxaca have been made of chert, chalcedony, and quartz crystal. (A hardness of 7 [Mohs] is desirable.)

CARBONIZING—a process in low-temperature pottery making that gives a surface coating of soot to the ware. Penetration is sufficient to give a permanent black to gray appearance to the ware. If the ware contains iron compounds, the body will be gray.

CARVING—(see EXCISING)

CLAY—a fine-grained plastic earth (chiefly aluminum silicate), the product of the disintegration of rocks by weather and other agents. *Residual* clays are those that have decomposed in place. They often contain coarse particles of other minerals. *Transported* clays are those that have decomposed elsewhere than where found, and have been carried to another place by water, ice, or wind. The latter clays are often very finely divided, but sometimes contain sufficient nonplastics to allow them to be used for thin wares.

Figure 2.9. Arroyo near San Marcos Tlapazola whose banks are a source of gray or yellowish-gray soil. Such soils fire red in an oxidizing atmosphere and black or gray in a reducing atmosphere.

CLAY, ALLUVIAL—the general term for clay bodies found in stream-transported deposits. This is one of the most common sources of Mesoamerican pottery bodies, found in valleys and closed depressions, and composed of the transported disintegration products of parent rocks.

CORES, SHERD—a layer within the interior of a sherd that differs in color from the surface. Gray to black cores are caused by rapid firing of wares, or by a change from a reduction atmosphere to an oxidizing atmosphere at the end of the firing schedule.

CONCENTRIC RING FORMATION—placing successive rings of clay body on a circular base to raise the walls of a vessel. The joints are then smeared together so that the wall becomes homogeneous. This, rather than coiling, was the common technique in Formative Oaxaca.

COILING—an alternative to CONCENTRIC RING FORMATION in which a continuous long rope of clay is used.

DECORATION—process used to embellish the surfaces of ceramic wares. See APPLIQUÉ, CARVING, EXCISING, INCISING, SGRAFFITO, PAINT.

DRY STRENGTH—a measure of the adhesive quality of dried clay bodies. Mixtures containing 50% or slightly more of finely divided clay minerals develop great strength when dry. Very large vessels with thin walls may be successfully made with the properly selected earths.

ENGOBE—a ceramic coating (or "slip") used to mask the clay body color. Engobes are always opaque and may be either white or colored; they are usually applied by dipping, but can be painted on.

EXCISING—decorating a ware by carving out a portion of the surface.

FELDSPAR—crystalline aluminum silicate, one of the most common ingredients in pottery clays.

FIRING—subjecting ceramic materials to the action of heat from various fuels. As ceramic art is a series of arrested reactions, firing temperatures and atmospheres must be carefully controlled to ensure a successful product.

FORMING—the process of manipulating plastic clay bodies. The result may be a useful or decorative object to be fired or used in the unfired stage.

Figure 2.10. Above-ground "kiln" in a dooryard at San Marcos Tlapazola. On the right one can see the load of new pottery vessels, which on this day consisted of large *comales* (pottery griddles) interspersed with smaller *platillos* (potter's bats). On the left one can see the wall of old jars and grinding stones against which the potters lean the load of new vessels. The fuel (which was dry maguey leaves and organ cactus stems) has been reduced to white ash beside and atop the load of new *comales*. On this day, no items broke during firing; the large sherds in the foreground were used to cover the mound of fuel.

GNEISS—a coarse-grained metamorphic rock rich in quartz, feldspar, mica, and/or hornblende.

GROG—a nonplastic ingredient of natural pottery bodies (or material added to compounded bodies) to control shrinkage during the drying and firing of ceramic wares. Grog may be sand, crushed rock, partly decomposed rock, or crushed, fired ceramic products.

HEMATITE—oxide of iron. Occurs naturally as a red powder or as a submetallic mineral known as specular hematite. These forms are also found in combination, and when finely ground, give a red pigment with fine bright granules.

IGNIMBRITE—a volcanic ash flow tuff, originally laid down as a series of glowing avalanches.

INCISING—(see SGRAFFITO)

IRON OXIDE—common constituent of most clays as the ferric oxide hematite (red to brown). Found in sedimentary clays as the ferrous oxide (gray-black). Gray colors in fired ware are due to the reduction to, or the retention of, the gray oxide form.

KAOLIN—a fine white clay with very low iron content. A major ingredient is kaolinite, a hydrous aluminum silicate, usually converted from feldspar.

LUTING—the joining of two preformed segments of a vessel during the plastic state.

MATURE—the condition of a given clay body when it is fired to a point near to vitrification or nonporosity.

MICA—a laminated hydrous disilicate of aluminum often observed in clay bodies originating from igneous or metamorphic rocks.

MOLD—a shaped form into which, or over which, clay body is placed in order to reproduce similar pieces of ware. Molds may be of wood, plaster, or bisque pottery. Shells, boulders, gourds, holes in sand or soil, and baskets have been used for molds.

Figure 2.11. Another view of the same above-ground "kiln" at San Marcos Tlapazola, with its load of new griddles and potter's bats. This photo shows how little would be left behind for an archaeologist looking for a firing site. Once the vessels have been removed, all that will remain is a deposit of ash and some refired sherds; even those may later be swept up, leaving no evidence of firing beyond a possible patch of burnt earth.

OXIDATION—a type of firing in which sufficient oxygen is admitted to the fire box to allow complete combustion of all hydrocarbons. A smoky fire indicates insufficient oxygen, and will result in gray or smudged surfaces on the ware.

PAINT—to apply ENGOBE or STAIN by dipping, pouring, brushing, or swabbing. See STAIN.

PASTE—a term for certain European compositions of porcelain bodies. It does not apply to Mesoamerican Formative ceramic mixtures. See BODY.

PEGMATITE—a very coarse igneous rock, usually granitic, often found in fissures and cracks of other rocks as a dike. It may contain large crystals of quartz, feldspar, and mica.

PLASTICITY—the property of a clay body which allows it to be deformed without rupturing.

REDUCTION—a type of firing in which the amount of oxygen in the firing chamber is limited so as to create a carbon monoxide atmosphere. This process consumes the oxygen in metallic oxides and reduces their chemical complexity.

SELF-SLIP—the addition of a thin coating of the same clay used for the clay body, sometimes to provide a smooth surface for burnishing.

SGRAFFITO—the process of scratching through an engobe, slip, or stain to reveal a contrasting colored body beneath; often called "incising."

SHRINKAGE—the loss of volume of a body after drying in air. Grog is included in both natural and compounded bodies to reduce shrinkage, control warpage, and increase thermal shock resistance.

SINTERING—a firing process that is arrested at the point where the mechanical water is driven off but not so high as to fuse the body to even partial vitrification. The usual range is between 350° and 650° F.

SLIP—(see ENGOBE)

STAIN—a coating of metallic oxides and water for the purpose of decoration, or for coloring engobes. A stain does not contain clay body, and can be applied post-firing.

WARPING—distortion of drying ware owing to irregular drying or low grog content. Occurs in firing at temperatures above those needed to mature the body.

WASH (see SLIP)—a very dilute mixture of pigment and water that is characterized by its thinness of application. While some scholars restrict this term to post-firing surface treatment, we distinguish it from an ENGOBE by thickness.

Chapter 3

Studies of Traditional Pottery Making in the Valley of Oaxaca, 1955–1973

Like many other archaeologists before us, we hoped to learn something about the ancient ceramics of the Valley of Oaxaca by observing the way pottery is made there today.

Four communities in the valley still make pottery in ways considered "traditional" by ethnographers. To be sure, "traditional" in this context does not mean "prehispanic," since more than 400 years have elapsed since the Spanish Conquest. Nevertheless, many of the techniques used in those villages are believed to go back to prehispanic times. In addition, some of the raw materials used by today's potters are virtually indistinguishable from those used in ancient times.

The four villages are Santa María Atzompa in the Etla arm of the valley; San Bartolo Coyotepec in the northern Valle Grande; San Andrés Ocotlán in the southern Valle Grande; and San Marcos Tlapazola in the Tlacolula arm. Perhaps the most frequently studied has been Atzompa (Hendry 1957, Young 1966, Stolmaker 1973), although Coyotepec has also had its share of attention (e.g., Foster 1955). Anna Shepard (1963) visited all four communities, as did William O. Payne (this volume). Our brief discussion is drawn from all these studies.

San Marcos

The simplest pottery making techniques are those of San Marcos Tlapazola, which Payne believes may provide numerous analogies for our Formative potters. San Marcos lies in the southern piedmont of the Tlacolula subvalley. Its potters need walk no further than the outskirts of their village to find suitable clay; it occurs in the banks of small arroyos in the piedmont (Fig. 2.9). The pot is begun by punching a depression into a cone of clay with the fist, roughing the vessel out by stroking with a corncob. Next the incipient pot is placed on a *platillo* which serves as a tournette or potter's bat. The *platillo* rotates slowly on an inverted jar while the potter scrapes the vessel smooth with a piece of gourd (Fig. 2.3). When greater height is needed, the potter adds concentric rings of clay which are pinched and smoothed into place. This is very much the way some Formative vessels appear to have been formed.

No formal kiln is used at San Marcos. Vessels are simply placed in a stack in the dooryard of the potter's house, rim down and base upward. The fuel, which can be as simple as dried maguey leaves or dried organ cactus, is then piled over the stack of pottery and ignited. When the firing is over, the pots are carefully removed; we observed a firing in San Marcos during which not one single vessel broke. What remains from such firing is nothing but a layer of fine ash; no archaeologist would ever be able to prove that pottery had been made in that dooryard (Fig. 2.11). This is roughly the situation we have in our Early Formative villages—plenty of ash, but no kilns and no proof of firing.

The pottery made at San Marcos today resembles Guadalupe Burnished Brown of our Guadalupe and Rosario phases, as well as the *café* ware of Monte Albán times. It is described by Shepard (1963:8) as a red-firing, "sand-tempered" ware. However, there are enough quartz grains already in the residual piedmont clays used at San Marcos so that actual sand does not have to be added to the clay.

Coyotepec

San Bartolo Coyotepec lies on the alluvial floor of the Valle Grande, and the clay used there is a transported alluvial clay of very fine texture. Once again, the vessel is punched into rough shape, then hand-modeled on a slowly rotating *platillo,* with concentric rings of clay added to raise the walls or add a neck to a jar.

Kilns at Coyotepec are subterranean and "smothered," providing a reducing atmosphere that turns the clay gray or black. The "untempered" clay fires to a "hard, dense body" (Shepard 1963:7) that is perfect for holding water but cannot be used for cooking over an open fire. Payne compares Coyotepec's clay with the alluvial clay body used for Delfina Fine Gray, a luxury ware of the San José phase. This fine gray type was also reduction fired, and so fine-grained that it lacked resistance to thermal shock (see Chapter 2). Later gray wares, such as Socorro Fine Gray of the Rosario phase and Types G3, G15, and G16 of the period Monte Albán I, were also made from an untempered,

21

transported alluvial clay with very fine aplastic particles, suitable for serving vessels but not for cooking pots.

Ocotlán

San Andrés Ocotlán is the village whose pottery making is perhaps least relevant to the Formative. Ocotlán was one of the last areas of the valley to have any substantial Formative population (Kowalewski et al. 1989), and it was particularly underpopulated during the Early Formative. Pots in San Andrés Ocotlán are formed by tamping and paddling the clay over a "mushroom" mold for which we have no Early Formative analogs. The clay used at Ocotlán is similar to that used in Coyotepec, but it fires orange because it is subjected to an oxidizing atmosphere. The kiln is subsurface, and firing is done slowly over many hours (Shepard 1963).

Atzompa

For a variety of reasons, Santa María Atzompa and its neighboring villages (San Lorenzo Cacaotepec and San Felipe Tejalapan) provide us with an important context for understanding the Early Formative pottery of the Valley of Oaxaca. Simply put, it is likely that the earliest ceramics made at sites like Tierras Largas, Hacienda Blanca, and San José Mogote were made with clays very much like those used at Atzompa. They were embedded in the same geological formations, and probably collected within five kilometers of Atzompa or Cacaotepec. To bring home this point, we have prepared Figure 3.1, which shows the relationship of geological resources to Tierras Largas phase villages of the Atzompa–Cacaotepec region.

Almost the entire western piedmont of the southern Etla subvalley is composed of Paleozoic metamorphic rocks, mainly Precambrian gneiss. While they are usually so altered that one cannot determine their original nature, many of these ancient formations appear to have metamorphosed from igneous rocks like granite or diorite. Scattered through them are pegmatite dikes, areas where coarse igneous rock has filled fissures. The metamorphic rocks contain a wealth of mineral such as magnetite, hematite, and mica, all of which were used by Early Formative peoples. In addition, both the metamorphics and the pegmatites are filled with quartz, feldspar, hornblende, and other minerals that show up in the pottery of the area.

The weathering of Precambrian gneiss produces clay. Abundant feldspar, a crystalline aluminum silicate, breaks down into a fine-grained plastic earth. Such clay may contain kaolinite, a hydrous form of aluminum silicate, present in much of our Formative pottery.

William Payne detected two primary sources for the clay in our ceramics. Most of the early wares were made from what he calls *residual clays,* those which formed *in situ* above weathering gneiss. A few wares were made from *transported clays,* clays that had been washed out onto the alluvial valley floor some distance from their parent rock formations. Residual clays are coarser and have minerals found exclusively in Paleozoic metamorphic rock. Transported clays are finer, and may contain particles washed onto the alluvium from other rock formations. In the case of the southern Etla subvalley, those other rock formations can include Cretaceous limestones (such as those underlying Cacaotepec, Atzompa, and Monte Albán), Tertiary sandstones and conglomerates, and Miocene volcanic tuffs (which poke up into the piedmont spur beneath San José Mogote).

Today's Atzompa potters use two kinds of *barro liso* ("smooth clay"). One is a black, transported clay from buried Pleistocene alluvium near the Atoyac River, east of Cacaotepec and Site 1–1–15 (Fig. 3.1). This *barro liso* fires buff and is preferred for fine wares. The other *barro liso* comes from Tejalapan in the piedmont southwest of Cacaotepec, and is derived from the Paleozoic metamorphics; it fires red and is preferred for large jars.

Depending on how fine or coarse they want their pottery to be, the Atzompa potters mix various amounts of *barro áspero* ("rough clay") with their *barro liso*. The coarser the aplastic content, the greater the resistance to thermal shock. *Barro áspero* thus serves as "grog" (see Glossary, Chapter 2). There are two sources for this grog, both located in the Precambrian gneiss in the piedmont west of Atzompa; in Figure 2.2*b* of Chapter 2 we saw an example of *barro áspero* from the southernmost of these two grog sources (near the hamlet of Santa Catarina Montaño). It is interesting that the Atzompa potters classify this material as *barro* ("clay"), since it appears to be weathered Precambrian gneiss on its way to decomposing into residual clay. *Barro áspero* is so hard that it must be beaten with a stick for up to an hour before it can be mixed with *barro liso;* once pulverized, however, it blends in well due to its high content of clay minerals.

It seems likely that *barro áspero* is what Shepard (1963) referred to as "altered diorite," considered by her to be the "temper" of Monte Albán's *crema* ware. However, since the Precambrian gneisses west of Atzompa may well have metamorphosed from something like granite, diorite, or granodiorite, the mineral content would be the same whether one calls the grog "gneiss" or "altered diorite." Moreover, Payne points out that many residual clays found in arroyo banks in the Precambrian gneiss could have been used just as they were found; they would already be

Figure 3.1 (facing page). Geological map of the area between San José Mogote and Oaxaca City (Etla district, northwest Valley of Oaxaca). The map shows the city of Oaxaca and three modern villages: San Felipe Tejalapan, San Lorenzo Cacaotepec, and Santa María Atzompa. It also shows five sites of the Tierras Largas phase: San José Mogote, Hacienda Blanca, Tierras Largas, and Sites 1–1–14 and 1–1–15.

Traditional potters from Atzompa use several types of clay: (1) black *barro liso* from the alluvium between Cacaotepec and Hacienda Blanca; (2) gray *barro liso* from the metamorphics north of Tejalapan; and (3) grog or *barro áspero* from the metamorphics southwest of Cacaotepec. They also collect hematite for red pigment from San Pablo Etla, 3 km northeast of Hacienda Blanca.

Other resources of the area include chert and chalcedony (from the limestones) and magnetite (from the gneisses of the Paleozoic metamorphic formations). The magnetite was made into mirrors at San José Mogote.

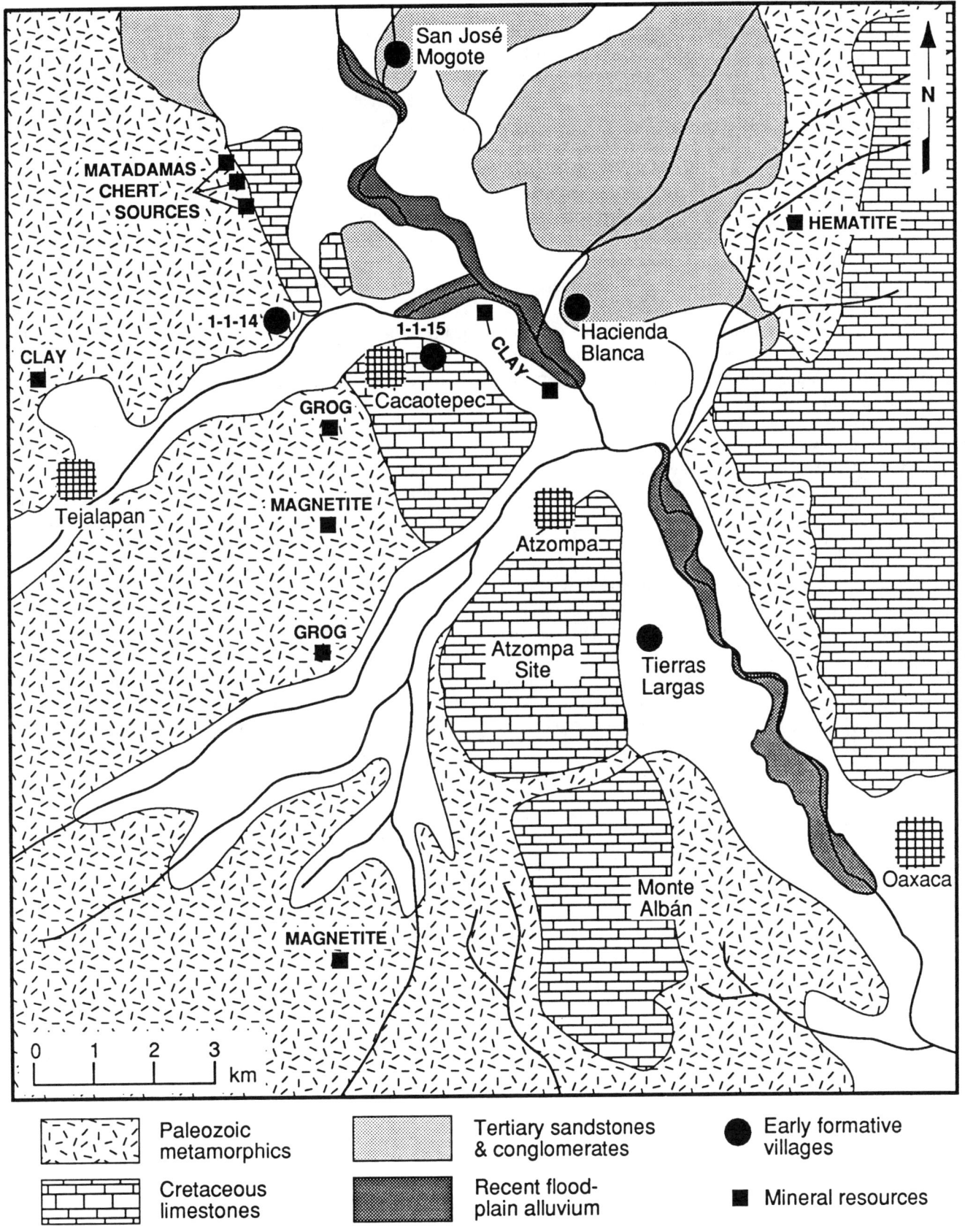

so rich in quartz, feldspar, mica, hornblende, and other nonplastics that no grog would need to be added. This seems to have been the case with the vast majority of our Early Formative pottery types, which were based on residual piedmont clays very like those from Cacaotepec, Atzompa, and Tejalapan.

One other clay, *barro crespo* (roughly meaning "gritty clay"), can be mined near the outskirts of Atzompa. It is used only when no better clay is available, since it is full of gravel and requires extensive sieving or screening.

Some pottery made at Atzompa is given a red wash or slip of *tierra colorada*. The red pigment in this special earth is hematite, which occurs at many localities in the Precambrian gneiss. Atzompa potters use hematite from San Pablo Etla, the source shown three kilometers northeast of Hacienda Blanca in Figure 3.1. However, Payne found several other sources which would be equally good, including one hematite deposit on Cerro del Fortín behind Oaxaca City's Hotel Victoria.

In sum, Figure 3.1 shows how easily the Early Formative villagers of San José Mogote, Hacienda Blanca, Tierras Largas, and Sites 1-1-14 and 1-1-15 could have obtained the mineral resources they needed. Residual clays and grog were available in the metamorphics of the western piedmont; transported clays were available in buried alluvial layers on the valley floor. Hematite for grinding into red pigment was available in the eastern piedmont; magnetite for polishing into small mirrors was available in the western piedmont. High-quality chert and chalcedony for chipped-stone tools were available in the limestones near Matadamas, southwest of San José Mogote. Metates and manos could be made from volcanic tuff or sandstone, or from igneous rocks in the pegmatite dikes. "Books" of mica for decorating costumes and masks were available in the Precambrian gneiss.

Pottery Making at Atzompa

The making of pots at Atzompa (Hendry 1957, Shepard 1963, Young 1966, Stolmaker 1973) resembles Payne's reconstruction of pottery making in our Early Formative sites (Chapter 2). *Barro liso* is spread out for three days on mats, then crumbled, with plant parts and large nonplastic particles removed. Then it is placed in water and kneaded to the right consistency. *Barro áspero* is pulverized with a club and sieved (formerly with twig sieves) to remove the larger nonplastics. It is then spread out on a mat while wet *barro liso* is rolled in it and kneaded; the amount of grog added depends on the size and amount of resistance to thermal shock the intended vessels will need.

The pot may be started by punching a fist into the clay, or by press-molding the clay over a previous vessel such as an inverted jar. This is interesting, because Payne believes that many of our Early Formative vessels were press-molded. The partially formed vessel is then placed on a *platillo* or potter's bat (infelicitously called a *molde* in Atzompa, though it has nothing to do with molding). The potter's bat is slowly turned on an inverted jar bottom while the potter adds concentric rings of clay, either to raise the height of the vessel, add a neck, or make some other modification. These rings are pinched and smoothed together with a piece of sheep or goat hide held between the potter's fingers; presumably, in ancient times deer hide was used. Ashes, or even dry potter's clay, are used to keep the vessel from sticking to the potter's bat.

Two artifacts whose use goes back to ancient times are the gourd scraper and the quartz pebble burnisher. A soft fragment of gourd is used by the Atzompa potters to scrape the vessel smooth as it rotates on the *platillo*; then it is burnished with a quartz pebble (easily found in the Tertiary conglomerates) to close the pores of the vessel and bring the finer clay particles to the surface. Identical quartz pebbles occur in all our Early Formative sites.

Finally, pots are fired for about an hour with fuel such as dried reeds or cornstalks to achieve a temperature of about 700° C. They are fired above ground, as we imagine most Early Formative firing to have been done, but today's kilns at Atzompa are too sophisticated to provide analogies for the Formative.

Ethnographic studies at Atzompa provide some perspective on work effort. Stolmaker (1973:57) calculates that a young woman with no children to care for can complete three dozen small jar bodies in a half day, with larger jars taking several hours to form. In cases where whole families collaborate on pottery making, it can take seven to twenty days to make enough vessels for a firing. The burnishing of jars with a quartz pebble may involve one and a half hours of work per dozen vessels, and some potters spend an hour a day pulverizing grog. These figures were collected, however, at a village that makes commercial quantities of pottery; the amount of time Early Formative villagers spent meeting their own needs may have been much less.

Finally, a persistent question is whether Early Formative potters were men, women, or whole families. We have no definitive answer for this. Whole families at Atzompa and San Marcos Tlapazola are involved in potting because it is a commercial enterprise. Men mine the clay, women form the pots, and the villagers often tell ethnologists that men were more involved in pot formation "in the past." We suspect that every Early Formative family was capable of meeting its needs for common, utilitarian, oxidized wares such as Tierras Largas Burnished Plain, Fidencio Coarse, Lupita Heavy Plain, and so on (see Chapters 8 and 12). However, when it came to luxury wares such as Delfina Fine Gray—reduction-fired and carved with motifs of pan-Mesoamerican significance—we suspect that only certain potters possessed the necessary skills. Whether those potters were men, women, or families is something we may never know.

Chapter 4

Site Formation Processes and the Quality of Sherd Collections

With a tip of the hat to our colleague Michael Schiffer (1976, 1987), let us now discuss the processes by which Oaxaca village sites formed, and the way in which those processes affect the quality of sherd collections. The reading of this chapter should be accompanied by examination of Figure 4.1, which is an idealized drawing of a Formative village.

In an earlier work, Flannery (1983:44–45) discussed seven analytical units of the early Oaxaca village. From smallest to largest these were the activity area, the feature, the man's or woman's work area, the house, the household unit, the residential ward, and the community. To these we would now like to add two more analytical units—the midden and the public building—and two types of natural deposits common in mountain valleys: arroyos and slopewash.

In the Early Formative villages of the Valley of Oaxaca, houses seem to have been spaced 20–40 m apart. The houses themselves were 3–4 m wide and 5–6 m long; their construction usually involved pine posts, wattle-and-daub walls, a thatched roof, and a stamped earth or clay floor with a light coating of sand. The door was usually on one of the long sides, and might have a threshold of stones. Other stones could appear in the bases of the wattle-and-daub walls, and there were sometimes silica "ghosts," or white exoskeletons, of reed mats on the floor. Better-preserved houses had activity areas, often marked by flint-chipping or shell-working debris. Interestingly enough, our houses rarely had hearths. For the San José phase, at least, this was because cooking was done in ceramic braziers.

Each house was part of a "household unit" of perhaps 300–400 m^2, consisting of the house itself and a "dooryard" or outdoor work area surrounding it. This outdoor area could have sheds, lean-tos, ramadas, storage pits, wells, ovens, activity areas, and household middens associated with it. It might, or might not, have burials.

Small villages, such as Tierras Largas or Fábrica San José, appear to have consisted of 5–10 household units. Large villages, such as San José Mogote, appear to have had residential wards composed of numerous household units, separated from each other by unoccupied areas. Frequently these unoccupied areas were characterized by rough terrain, with numerous arroyos and steep areas of slopewash where house construction would have been difficult.

At San José Mogote there were at least four such residential wards in the area we excavated, and an undetermined number on the piedmont spur to the east of our excavations. Each of the residential wards we excavated had large midden areas in it, too large to represent the debris from one household. We consider these to be multihousehold, or "barrio," middens.

Large communities were made up of several of these residential wards, and large communities frequently had public buildings. Those public buildings were usually on platforms, had specific astronomical orientations, and differed in construction from private residences. Sometimes they had features and activity areas associated with them, and occasionally even small middens, although most seem to have been swept clean while in use. Once an area of the village had been chosen as appropriate for public buildings, there might be a sequence of several such structures built virtually one above the other over time.

Every one of the analytical units mentioned above could produce potsherds, or even whole vessels. All these collections of ceramics were useful in the definition of ceramic types, forms, and decoration. However, not all were equally useful in defining phases, or in establishing the percentages of one type of pottery to another within a phase. We will now look at why that is so.

The Incorporation of Sherds into Households

A well-made wattle-and-daub house should last at least a decade, and there are wattle-and-daub houses in present-day Oaxaca villages that have lasted a quarter of a century. One of the variables affecting house life is the quality of the materials chosen. Pine posts have enough resin to discourage termites. Using high-quality clay (perhaps even pottery clay) for the daub, burnishing the surface, and whitewashing it (or even "slipping" it) with lime or kaolinite clay protects the wall from rain. It was

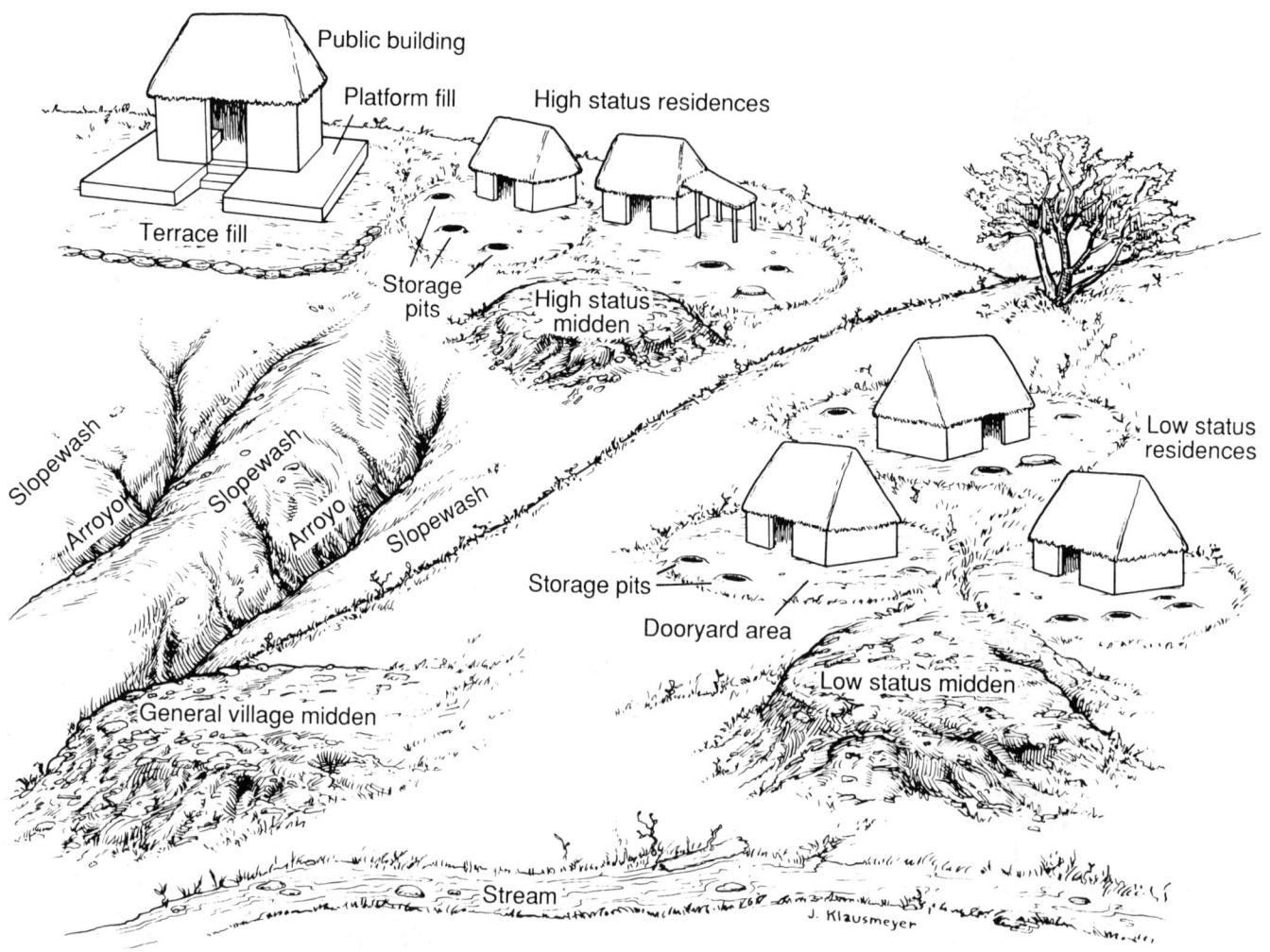

Figure 4.1. Idealized drawing of a large Formative village in the Valley of Oaxaca, showing the kinds of proveniences from which our sherd samples were drawn. The village consists of barrios or residential wards, some with residences of relatively high-status families, others with residences of relatively low-status families. Each family occupies a household unit, consisting of a residence and its surrounding dooryard and storage pits. Each barrio may have a midden, and there may be midden areas for the village as a whole. On a high point, the villagers have erected a public building on a platform, perhaps even on an artificial terrace. Leading down from high points are small arroyos and areas of slopewash.

As described in the text, sherd samples could come from house floors, storage pits, dooryards, middens for high- or low-status households, or general village middens. They could also come from platform fill, terrace fill, arroyo fill, or slopewash, all potentially problematic contexts.

clear from the chunks of prehistoric daub we found that great differences in quality (perhaps reflecting differences in human motivation, size of household, or status) characterized Early Formative houses.

Posts were also repaired frequently during the lifetime of a house, a fact that may have extended house life. Postmold patterns indicate that when posts became loose, stone wedges might be jammed into the ground to steady them (see Fig. 15.1, Chapter 15). In other cases posts were replaced, often leaving a pair of postmolds where only one might be expected; sometimes a smaller post was added as a "leaner" to prop up a larger post. Roofs were undoubtedly rethatched, although we have less information on that practice.

Floors were worn through constant traffic, becoming basin-shaped over time. Often they were resurfaced (up to four times in the case of one house), with a new layer of stamped clay laid over the old, and a new half-centimeter of river sand added (Fig. 4.2). Probably the sand, in addition to filling in the irregularities in the clay floor, provided a drier surface on rainy days. On such days, pure clay floors become muddy when people with wet feet enter the house. Two features indicated that rain runoff was a problem for house floors: (1) some doorways had sills or thresholds of stones to keep water out, and (2) some dooryards had drainage ditches to divert rain runoff away from the house or into a cistern (Fig. 15.4).

Ceramics, of course, were used in household units, and pots

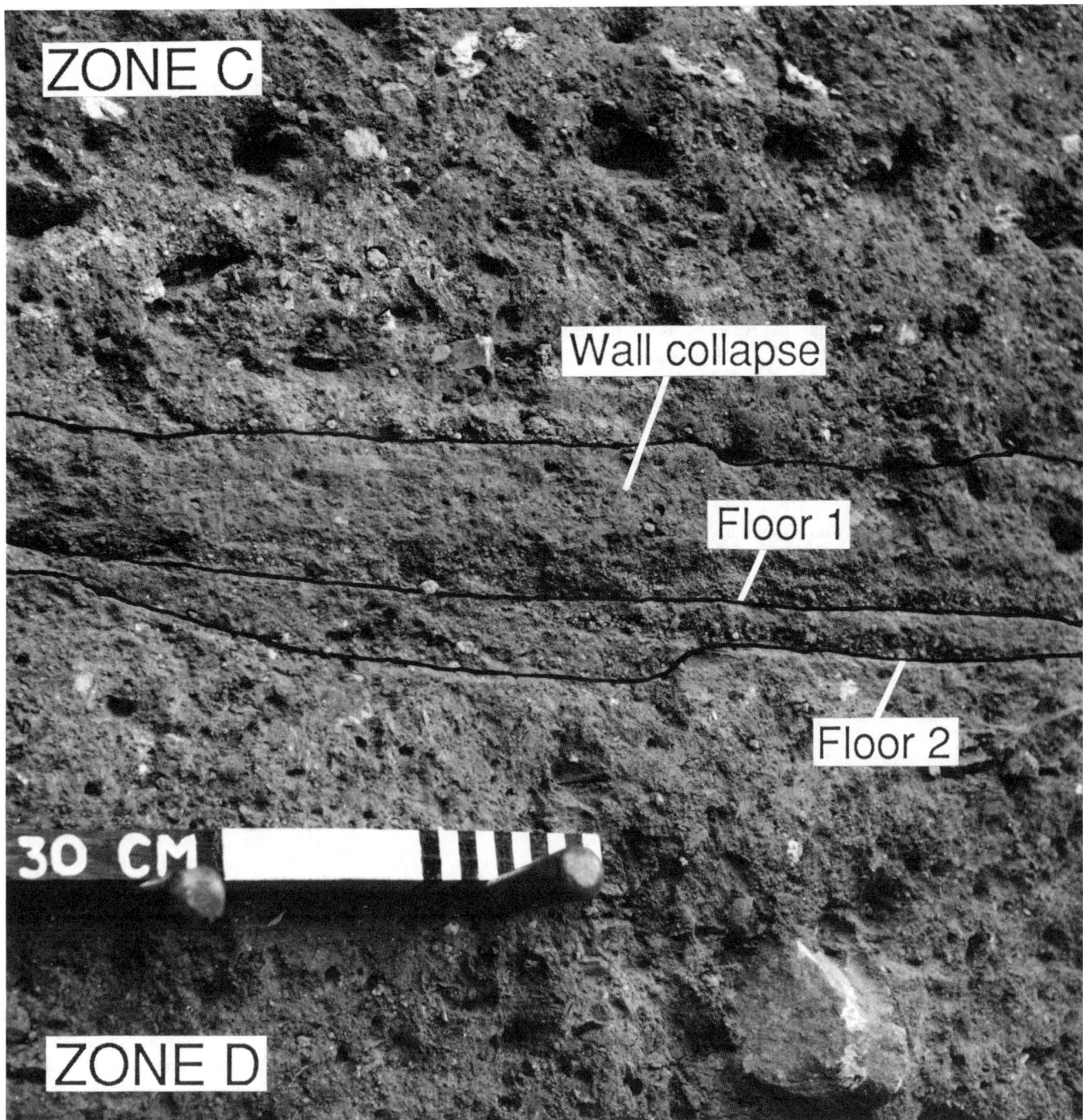

Figure 4.2. House 14, Area C, San José Mogote, seen in cross-section in the east profile of Square S18E. *Zone C* is a barrio midden overlying the house. *Wall collapse* is a layer of rain-melted clay from the collapse of House 14's wattle-and-daub walls. *Floor 1* is the uppermost of the house's two sand floors (in other words, a "floor resurfacing"). *Floor 2* is the lowermost of the house's two sand floors (in other words, the "original floor"). *Zone D* is a barrio midden underlying the house. Total length of the wooden scale is 30 cm. (For a plan view of this house and its dooryard midden, see Fig. 14.11.)

were broken inside and outside of the house. Small sherds were trodden into the sand of the floor and lost. In cases where floors had been resurfaced, there were tiny sherds trapped in earlier floors; however, they rarely amounted to a meaningful sample. Other sherds were swept into a corner, and sometimes even partial or restorable vessels were left resting against the wall. It seems likely, however, that the vast majority of sherds from broken vessels were swept up and removed from the house; no family was likely to let a thick carpet of sherds accumulate on the floor. Those sherds removed from the house probably went into one of two places: (1) nearby middens, or (2) open pits that had outlived their usefulness and needed to be filled in.

How is it, then, that some houses excavated by us had literally hundreds of sherds lying on the floor? We suspect that many of those sherds dated from shortly before the abandonment of the house. It seems unlikely to us that a family on the verge of abandoning an old house would bother to sweep it carefully. More than likely, they gathered up those items judged to be useful to them in their new residence, and left behind what they no longer needed.

The sherd sample from the floor of an Early Formative wattle-and-daub house, therefore, might consist of two kinds of sherds: (1) a modest number of sherds lost in the sand layer(s) during the lifetime of the house, and (2) a much larger number of sherds from vessels that had broken not long before abandonment. For example, if a house had been occupied for twenty years, we would not be surprised to learn that most of the sherds left behind on its floor dated to the last two years of its occupation. However, we could never claim that the entire collection from a house dated to so short a moment of time. Since the occupants of the house dug pits, postholes, graves, and other excavations in the soil around their house, they could even have incorporated occasional sherds of earlier periods into their household debris.

Some houses were evidently burned at the time of abandonment. This act produced massive quantities of burned daub, left behind when the walls collapsed. Still other houses were left abandoned until successive rainy seasons had melted the walls into a shapeless lens of clay. In either case, the collapsed or melted daub often formed a protective cap over the sherds on the house floor, sealing them off from lower strata. We tried to avoid including sherds from the collapsed daub layer in our samples from the house floor, because we knew that earlier sherds might have been included in the clay with which the walls were daubed. As might be expected, such separation was not always easy.

Small Middens Near Houses

A continuous task for Early Formative householders was the removal of ash, either from hearths or from charcoal braziers. We suspect that there were several stages to this. The first stage was evidently the temporary dumping of ash to one side of the house—most often to the south or east, which may have had something to do with prevailing northwesterly winds. Often, sherds were included in these small ashy middens, examples of which can be seen in the drawings of Houses 2 and 14 of San José Mogote (Chapter 14).

However, none of these middens seem large enough to represent the accumulated trash from the lifetime of a house; most are only a few meters square. We therefore suspect that at periodic intervals such debris was transported farther away, to more substantial middens that served an entire residential ward or even an entire hamlet. Sometimes this larger volume of trash was used to fill in arroyos or natural depressions on the site. In other cases, spread horizontally over areas more than 20 meters on a side, it became an actual stratigraphic layer at the site—the kind of layer an archaeologist might label "ashy brown midden" or "charcoal-flecked midden with abundant sherds."

Sherd collections from small middens near households, like the sherds from house floors, probably do not antedate the abandonment of the house by any substantial period of time. They presumably represent the last episodes of ash disposal from the house, and therefore never got transported to village or barrio middens. Of course, they could still contain some earlier sherds that had not previously been swept out of the house.

Sherds in the Dooryards of Household Units

Most Early Formative houses seem to have been surrounded by areas of outdoor work space, some of which could be 300–400 m². We have chosen to call such outdoor areas "dooryards," rather than "courtyards," because the latter term implies an enclosed space. While some households could include a house and a second building (cook shack, work shed, or ramada) flanking an open space, by and large Early Formative dooryards do not seem to have been walled off from the dooryards of their neighbors. (Of course, perishable cactus fences could have been present.)

Usually there were fewer sherds per square meter in dooryards than on house floors. Near the house itself, however, the density of sherds could be reasonably high. This suggests that broken vessels or even heaps of sherds might be tossed a short distance from the house, or even allowed to accumulate around the outer walls of the house. We did not find significant differences between the sherds found inside houses and the sherds found in those parts of the dooryard nearest the house. In some cases, particularly in Area A of San José Mogote, our sherd samples are described as coming from the "household unit" rather than the "house." This designation usually means that the sherds come predominantly from the dooryard adjacent to the house, or from an area including part of the house floor and part of the adjacent dooryard. Often we found that sherds in the house and the nearby dooryard had come from the same vessels, confirming their contemporaneity.

Bell-shaped Pits in Dooryards

One of the major sources of sherds in the dooryards of household units was the subterranean storage pit. These pits, usually "bottle-shaped" or "bell-shaped" in cross-section, had been excavated in the earth (or soft bedrock) of the dooryard. It seems likely that many were originally dug for the purpose of storing the household's annual crop of maize; it was not unusual for them to have the capacity for storing a metric ton of shelled maize. Some appeared to have been given an inner coating of clay or grass, perhaps to keep the grain clean.

The mouth and neck of these pits are much smaller than the large chamber at the bottom—hence, the "bottle shape" (Figs. 4.3–4.5). They may have been made this way to reduce the likelihood of inadvertently steppping into the pit; however, it is just as likely that the purpose was to provide a small mouth that could be sealed shut. Some bell-shaped pits still had collars of mud or clay around their mouths, and a number had large stone slabs—suitable as lids—associated with them. Sealing such a pit with a stone lid set in an airtight clay collar helps to preserve the stored grain, since it makes it likely that any insect pests that get into the pit will ultimately suffocate (Hall, Haswell, and Oxley 1956).

The sherds found in bell-shaped pits, of course, do not date to this early phase of their use. Ultimately each pit outlived its period of usefulness either because its walls began to collapse, or it became fouled or moldy, or some combination of the two (Fig. 4.3). At this point it became a convenient place into which to sweep household trash, and many of the sherds probably entered the pits in this way. However, the filling of bell-shaped pits was not necessarily a simple, one-step operation. It is clear from our excavations that the lower part of a pit might be filled, leaving the upper part as a depression in the dooryard (Fig. 4.4). After a lapse of time, this depression might then be filled with sherds of a later time period. Thus many bell-shaped pits had a stratigraphy of their own; such pits were anything but sealed deposits dating to a short period of time. Moreover, even those pits that were filled completely in one operation could have had sherds of several periods swept into them.

In spite of these problems, we did find some bell-shaped pits whose sherd samples appeared to be as good as those of most house floors or dooryards. To be sure, all that "good" means in such context is that the sample seems to be as restricted in time as the sample from a house floor—it could, in other words, contain sherds from the entire life span of the house. Another point to bear in mind is that the sherd sample dates not to the moment at which the pit was dug, but to the moment when someone decided to fill it in. Thus, a pit dug to store early Tierras Largas phase maize could have been filled in during late Tierras Largas phase times.

In some household units there were so many pits, and their contents were so different, that the following analogy occurred to us. Imagine all the wastebaskets in a large U.S. household. The wastebasket in the kitchen, the wastebasket in the master bedroom, the wastebasket in the children's bedroom, and the wastebasket in the bathroom would all have different contents. Not until the contents of all wastebaskets were combined in a single large trash barrel would we have anything like a representative sample of the household's trash. In our analogy, Formative bell-shaped pits would be like individual wastebaskets, while household middens would be like the large trash barrels you leave next to the curb, and barrio middens would be like local land fills.

Our conclusion is that while bell-shaped pits can provide large sherd samples (thousands of sherds, in some cases), they must be used with great caution (Fig. 4.5). In this volume we will look at the relationships of numerous pits to the houses with which they were associated. For pits in which we have confidence, we will give sherd-by-sherd counts; for others, we will simply give verbal assessments of the sherd contents as a supplement to the house floor counts. Used carefully, bell-shaped pits can enrich our understanding of the household units in which they occurred. Treated naively, as if they were "moments sealed in time," they can badly sabotage a sequence.

Community and Barrio Middens

At some point, the accumulating debris in household units had to be moved farther away. In the case of small hamlets on low piedmont spurs, such as Tierras Largas or Fábrica San José, this could probably have been accomplished just by carrying the debris to the edge of the piedmont spur and dumping it down the slope. Over time this would result in the building up of a substantial midden in which the debris of all households would be represented.

Under the right conditions, such a "community midden" could have great potential for an archaeologist interested in pottery chronology. Its strong points would include the fact that the whole range of ceramics used in the village should be represented. Suppose, for example, that the village included both high-status and low-status households (Chapter 15). In the community midden, both the fancier pottery used by high-status families and the drabber utilitarian pottery used by low-status families would be present. Any description of those deposits therefore would have the potential to cover the whole spectrum of pottery used (including rare types), rather than being restricted to the subset of ceramics used by one household.

Assuming that the community midden was set on relatively level ground, it might have the further advantage of preserving, in good stratigraphic order, a series of highly representative collections of the community's pottery that document its change over time. That is what every archaeologist hopes to find, but the hope is often greater than the reality. Community middens are not always set neatly on level ground and built up the way archaeologists would like them to be. In hilly areas like Oaxaca, debris is often dumped on slopes where the material continues to move downhill, or into arroyos that carry occasional rain runoff. The result can be a jumbled deposit whose excavation provides more confusion than clarity (see Arroyos and Slopewash, below).

In the case of large sites on piedmont spurs, like San José Mogote, there probably never were middens into which the debris of the entire community was dumped. Instead, each barrio

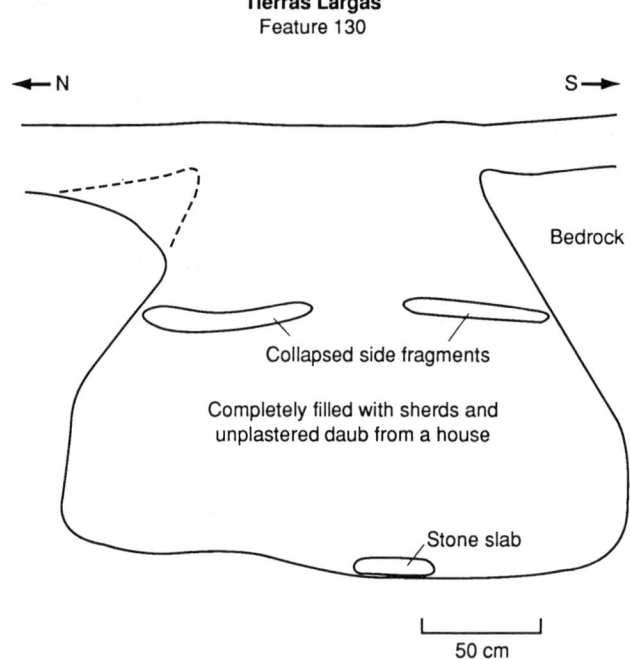

Figure 4.3. Feature 130 from Tierras Largas, an example of a large bell-shaped pit whose walls had begun to collapse over time, reducing its usefulness. (Redrawn from Flannery et al. 1970:65–66.)

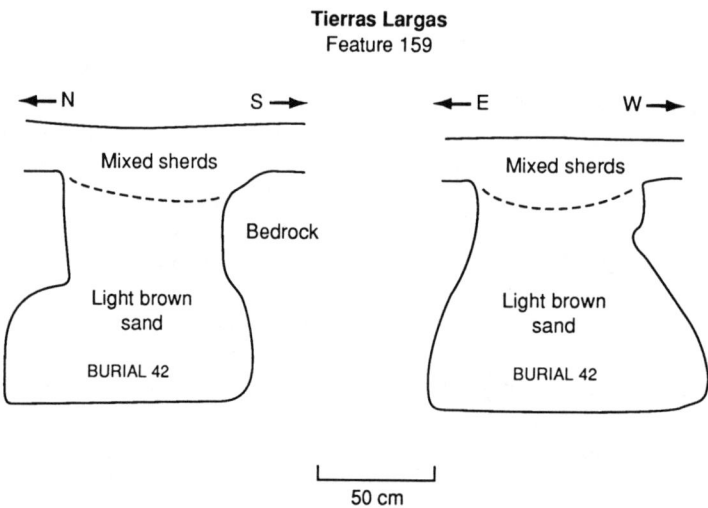

Figure 4.4. Feature 159 from Tierras Largas, an example of a small bell-shaped pit. The dashed line indicates that there were at least two periods in which this pit was filled—an earlier period, when light brown sand was used, and a later period when the pit's location was indicated only by a slight depression in the dooryard. (Redrawn from Flannery et al. 1970:65–66.)

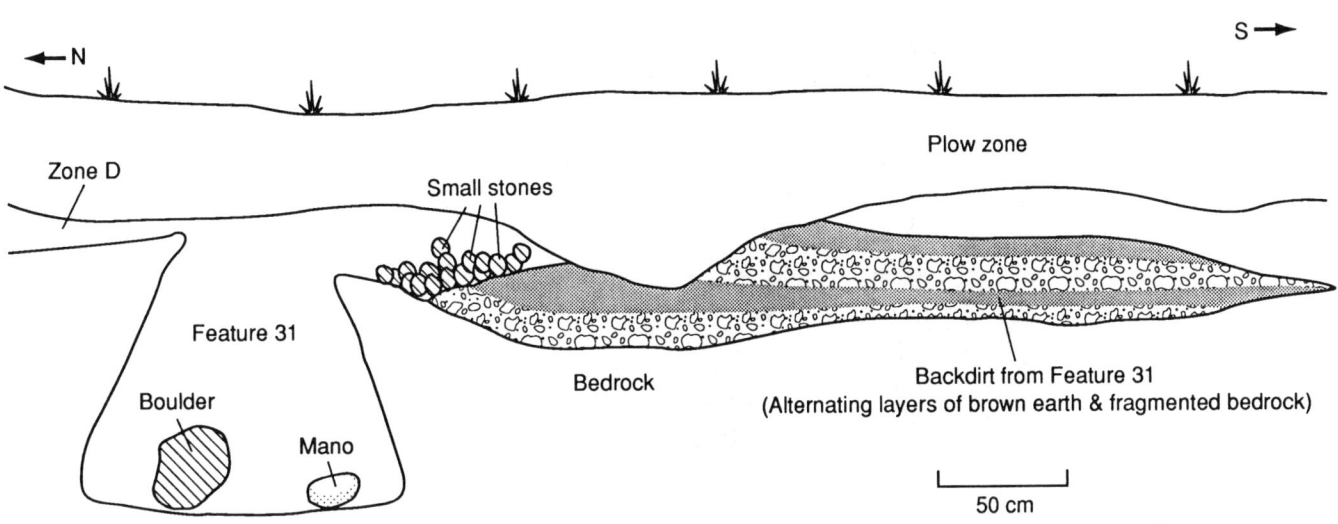

Figure 4.5. Feature 31 of San José Mogote, a bell-shaped pit and its associated backdirt, found while cutting the Area C profile at a point far south of the squares shown in Figure 9.2. This drawing illustrates why Formative sites have such complex stratigraphy, and bell-shaped pits are so problematic. The backdirt from digging a pit can be tossed on top of deposits that are actually younger than the pit, producing a kind of "reverse stratigraphy." In this case, because the pit was dug into bedrock, its backdirt was sterile and easily distinguished by its color. But what if it had been dug into earlier midden deposits, as was Feature 2 of Household Unit C3, Area A (see Fig. 14.3)?

or residential ward of the site appears to have found an appropriate place for the final disposal of its trash. Barrio middens were commonplace occurrences throughout San José Mogote. Sometimes they occurred on gentle slopes and gave the impression of having accumulated slowly over the years, providing a representative sample of sherds from many households. Other times they appeared as beds sloping at a 45° angle into natural depressions or old arroyos. In a later section of this report, we will see examples of several kinds of midden debris.

It should be noted that community middens, barrio middens, and household middens each provide different information. If the goal is establishing a chronology that will hold up over a wide area, the best midden to have is a community midden. In it, the differences between one household and another are homogenized into a comprehensive sherd assemblage for a segment of archaeological time.

Such a midden will not, however, show intracommunity differences, such as those between high-status and low-status households. To show those differences we need a series of barrio middens, at least one of which is from a high-status ward (or more if we can find them). Of course, even a good barrio midden will mask certain differences among households. For example, if one household has trade partners in Chiapas and another has trade partners in Puebla, that fact will only be clear if we dig individual houses or household middens.

In this volume we look at household and barrio debris to see if we can detect both synchronic and diachronic variation in ceramics. We are not sure that we have found any middens that are indisputably community-wide in content. But because we have excavated several different villages in different parts of the Valley of Oaxaca, we think we will have data on inter-community variation (Chapter 17).

Samples from Public Buildings

In addition to building houses, digging bell-shaped pits, and creating middens, Early Formative villagers erected public buildings. Such buildings were present from the beginning of the Tierras Largas phase onward, and increased in size and complexity during later periods.

While our earliest public buildings had wattle-and-daub walls, they differed from ordinary residences in several ways (Fig. 4.6). First, they were oriented roughly 8° west of true north (16°45′ W of magnetic north), an orientation shared by later public buildings of the San José, Guadalupe, and early Rosario phases. Second, they contained two or three times as many posts as the ordinary house, and those posts were set within the wattle-and-daub walls. Thus the walls themselves were weight-bearing, in contrast to some ordinary houses whose wattle-and-daub walls were set just outside the weight-bearing posts that supported the

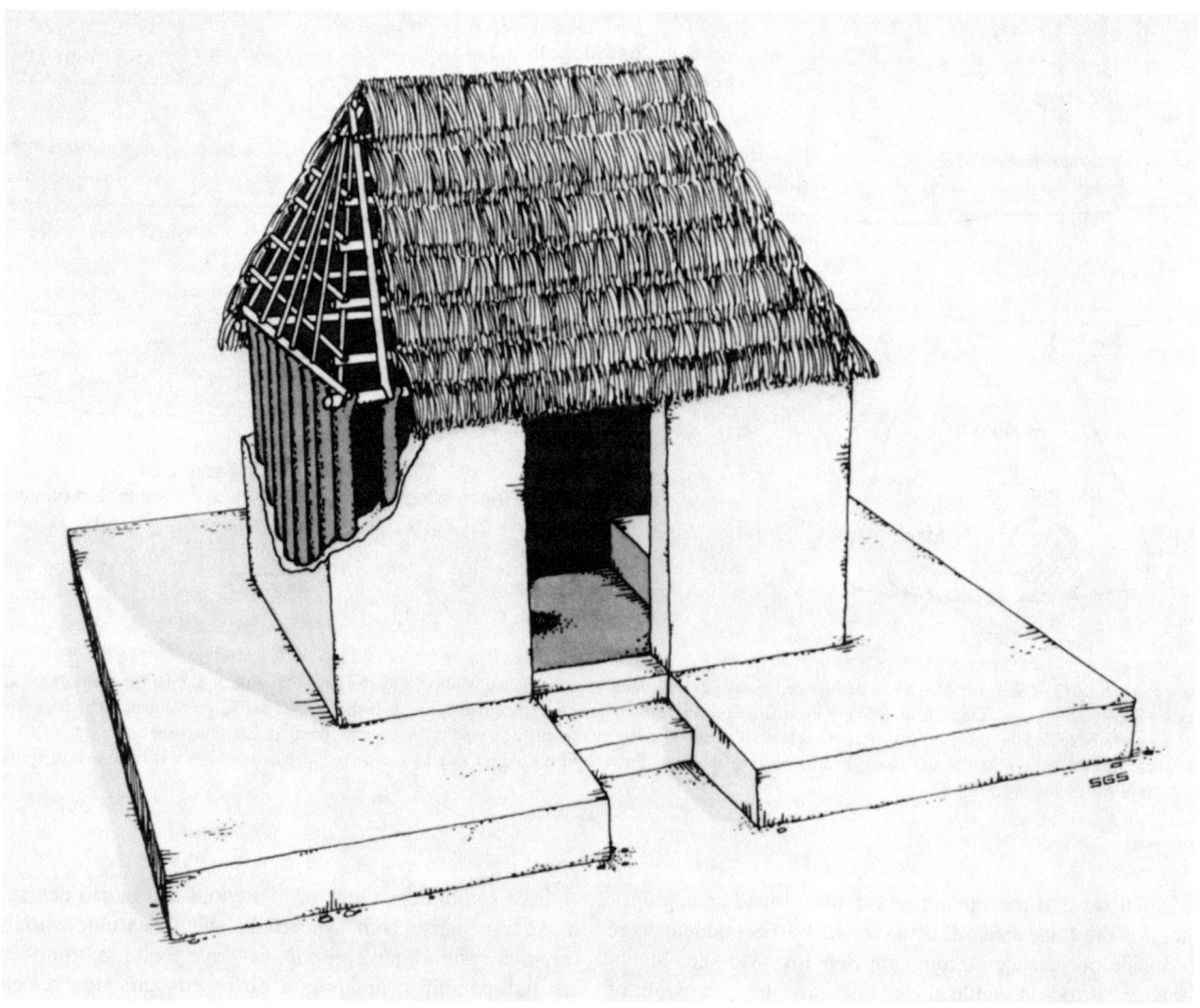

Figure 4.6. Artist's reconstruction of a typical public building of the Tierras Largas or early San José phase. The drawing is based on details of Structures 3, 5, and 6 of San José Mogote (see Chapter 11), but is not intended to represent any specific building.

The structure consists of a one-room wattle-and-daub building with a thatched roof, set on a low rectangular platform of crushed bedrock, clay, lime, and sand. The building and platform are coated with white lime plaster, and there may be an "apron" of white plaster surrounding the platform. The floor of the building is recessed 20–40 cm into the platform; there may be one step descending from the doorway into the room, and perhaps 1–2 steps (inset into the platform) descending from the door outside. The room may have a pit in the floor for powdered lime. It may also have a "sitting bench" along one or more walls. (Drawing by David Reynolds.)

roof (see, for example, House 2 of Area C, San José Mogote, shown in Figs. 14.7–14.8 of Chapter 14).

Third, the walls of public buildings were given a coating of white lime plaster (stucco) both inside and out. The floor was also surfaced with lime plaster, in contrast to the floors of ordinary houses, which were of stamped clay with a layer of sand. Fourth, several early public buildings had a lime-plastered storage pit built into the center of the floor, a feature no ordinary residence had. When discovered intact, these pits were filled with powdered lime, perhaps stored for use with some ritual plant such as tobacco or *Datura*.

Fifth, these early public buildings were set on rectangular platforms up to 40 cm high, also coated with lime plaster. The fill of the platforms contained stones, crushed volcanic tuff bedrock, sand, earth, and lime. Often, sherds were incorporated into the fill of the platform or the clay daub of the walls, which rose from the upper surface of the platform. We presume that these were sherds that happened to be lying nearby and accidentally got included in the construction material.

A sixth feature of these buildings—one that has caused some confusion in the secondary literature—is the fact that the floor of the building was not flush with the top of the platform. Rather, the floors were recessed between 20 and 40 cm into the platforms. (In the case of a floor recessed 40 cm into a 40 cm platform, the floor would actually be level with the base of the platform; thus it would be more accurate to say that the building was "surrounded" by a platform rather than "set on" a platform.)

The floors of such buildings had a low step just inside the door, allowing a person to enter by stepping down from the threshold. Virtually intact examples of such steps were recovered. There were evidently comparable steps just outside the door, allowing a person to reach the doorway by stepping up. These external steps occurred within small stairways inset in the platform, like most early Oaxaca stairways. While we have fragments of such outdoor stairways, no complete and intact examples were recovered. Once again, no ordinary houses had such stairways.

Some confusion in the secondary literature results from the way such public buildings collapsed. Once they were abandoned, it appears that in many cases the walls were deliberately knocked down and the area leveled so that a new public building could be built. However, the walls were knocked down only to the level of the top of the platform; the recessed floor area was simply filled with wall debris, often with a small sample of sherds trapped on the floor below the wall collapse. Once such a recessed floor area has been excavated and swept for photography, it looks *superficially* like a small inner court, and could give the erroneous impression that the buildings were composed of several rooms surrounding a recessed patio. That is not the case. The rectangular recessed area seen in photographs (for example, Fig. 11.8 of Chapter 11) is simply the lower 20–40 cm of a one-room building with a thatched roof, very like that of an ordinary house. Except for the area of the doorway, the recessed floor was surrounded by the post molds of the walls, sheared off at the level of the platform surface (Fig. 4.7).

While public buildings do not yield nice, representative samples of ceramics like those of households, it is necessary to date such buildings in order to understand their history and development. As will be seen in Chapters 11 and 18, we did this by (1) noting the building's position in the stratigraphic sequence; (2) collecting the sherds trapped under the plaster floor; (3) collecting the sherds incorporated into the construction fill of the platform; (4) collecting the sherds lying atop the floor, but trapped under the postabandonment wall collapse; and (5) collecting the sherds in the debris over the leveled building.

Finally, a warning: sherds from the fill of public buildings should not be used for the purpose of establishing chronological sequences (Fig. 4.8). Rather, chronological sequences should be established first and then used for the purpose of dating public buildings.

Arroyos and Slopewash

Because household units in Early Formative villages were spaced 20–40 m apart, at any given time there was considerable open space in the village. In the case of villages built on piedmont spurs, such as those in the Valley of Oaxaca, a great deal of that open space consisted of sloping ground. Rain striking that sloping ground often produced arroyos—gullies that were dry for part of the year, but carried rain runoff at various moments during the rainy season. Other areas might be subject to slopewash, the movement of soil downhill when the stabilizing vegetation had been removed. Early Formative villagers sometimes increased slopewash by leaving soft piles of midden that could easily wash downslope during rains. They also changed the contours of the terrain by placing buildings on high ground, or by constructing pyramidal mounds that were steeper than the angle of repose. Sometimes they attempted to counteract erosion by building artificial terraces on slopes. Inevitably, however, their activities disturbed the piedmont spur enough to promote more slopewash.

When the opportunity arises to cross-section such a village by means of extensive vertical profiles, it is revealing how much of the deposit is taken up with arroyo fill and slopewash. In an earlier publication (Flannery [ed.] 1976:71–73), we described a series of transect profiles, totaling 192.5 m in length, made at San José Mogote. These profiles revealed that residential wards occupied low natural rises on the site and were separated by slopes, natural depressions, and ancient erosion gullies into which the occupants threw their trash. The areas of arroyo fill and slopewash made up 80% of the deposits in those profiles, while undisturbed primary deposits constituted only 20%. This means that a pit made at random in such a site would have only about one chance in five of hitting primary deposits.

The irony is that the numbers of sherds in slopewash, arroyo fill, and artificial platform or terrace fill can be extraordinarily high. In the western portion of Area B at San José Mogote, an ancient arroyo had cut virtually to bedrock during the Early Formative, the result being that no one had lived there. During Middle Formative times, a massive program was initiated to fill the arroyo until it was level with the high points to either side. This was done so that the platform for a large public building could be placed over the former arroyo area. The process of filling in the arroyo involved spanning it with retaining walls of "bun-shaped" (circular planoconvex) adobes, then filling the areas between the retaining walls with basketload after basketload of earth. Occasional stones were added for stability. The variety of colors and textures of earth indicated many different sources for the fill, all of which contained sherds. Possibly, much of it represented dirt dug up from old midden areas.

Fig. 4.9 is a profile drawing of one section of this transect through Area B. While the profile is full of clear layers and color changes, it is useless for working out a stratigraphic sequence. From top to bottom—4.4 m in all—there is not one kilogram of primary deposit. The irony is that this area produced an estimated 60,000 potsherds, which many archaeologists would consider a good sample. From the standpoint of producing a quantitative chronology based on changing sherd types, however, the whole collection was useless, displaying both mixtures of time periods and inverted sequences. About all we got from the collection were some rim profiles that could be drawn.

The lessons we learned from our transect profiles were many. One lesson was that less than a quarter of a village may be

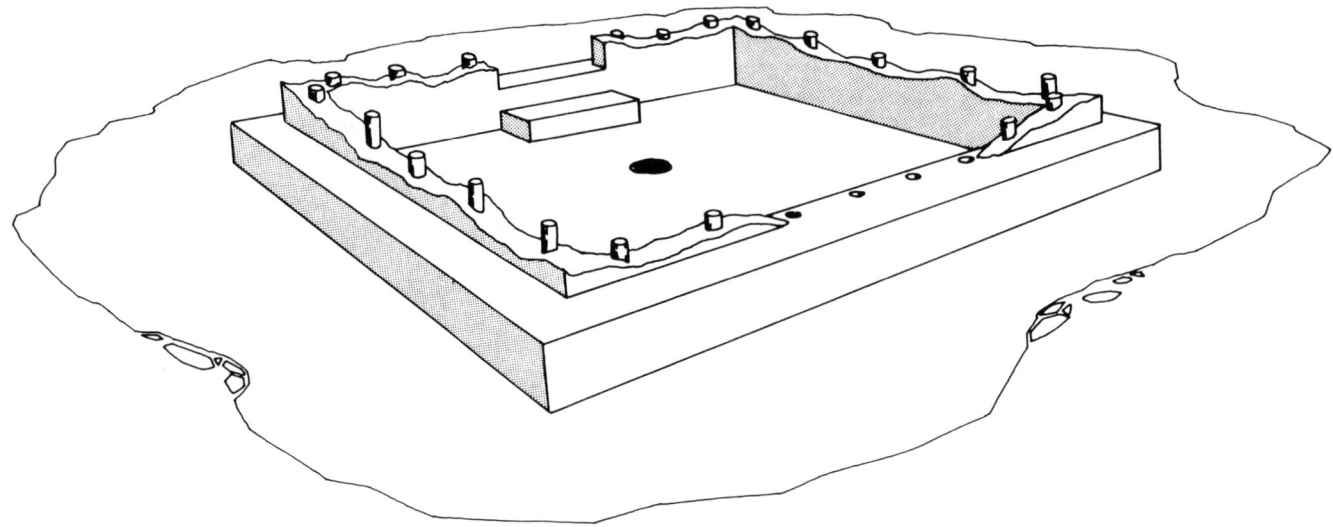

Figure 4.7. Artist's sketch of what a public building like the one shown in Figure 4.6 looks like after having been razed to make way for a new one. The edges of the plaster "apron" surrounding it are damaged; the walls of the building have been broken down to the level at which the pine posts enter the platform. The recessed floor (including the interior step and the centrally placed pit for lime) is still intact, but rapidly becomes covered by fallen plaster, and eventually by destroyed wall chunks and other fill. This fill may enclose and trap sherds that can be used in dating the building (see Chapter 11). This view of a destroyed public building is approximately what one is seeing in Figure 11.8.

primary deposit. Another was that deposits with the highest densities of sherds are not necessarily the most useful for chronology: 600 sherds from a household unit are probably worth more than 60,000 from arroyo fill. Still a third lesson was that the sherds lying on the surface are not necessarily a guide to what lies directly below. Finding lots of Early Formative sherds on the surface may only mean that you have a found a Middle Formative building with tons of earlier fill.

How Formative Villages Grew

Years ago, archaeologists working in the Near East used to think of *tells* as layer cakes of sherds and architectural features: Period 1 at the bottom, Period 2 above 1, Period 3 above 2, and so on. When a deep *sondage* on a given mound failed to produce evidence for Period 2, it was assumed to be missing, and a different mound was sought. Gradually, however, Near Eastern archaeologists began to discover that a second *sondage* on a different part of the same mound might uncover the missing period. *Tells*, in other words, did not grow "straight up."

One of the most eloquent descriptions of how *tells* actually grow has been provided by T. Cuyler Young, Jr., based on his work at Godin Tepe in western Iran (Young 1969; Young and Levine 1974). Godin Tepe, according to Young (pers. comm.), "grew upward in a spiral fashion, almost like the threads of a screw."

Picture a circular archaeological mound on which we can superimpose the dial of a giant imaginary clock. At six o'clock on the dial, the first house is built. The second house is built not directly above the first, but father away, perhaps near the *3* on the dial. The third house is built near the *12*, the fourth near the *9*. By now the first house has been abandoned and its ruins have become a slumped pile of mud brick. The fifth house is built near the *7*, and the occupants dump their midden debris over the

Figure 4.8 (facing page). Profile drawing of Area A, Barrio del Rosario Huitzo (lower levels only). This drawing illustrates how much of a Formative mound may consist of platform or public building fill. Zone F, at the bottom, represents the fill of Structure 4, an early Guadalupe phase platform for a public building. Thousands of basketloads of earth were used to fill in the spaces between adobe retaining walls in this platform; some of those basketloads of fill contained Guadalupe phase sherds, while others contained earth dug up in areas with San José phase sherds. The result is that sherd counts from Zone F cannot be used to establish a reliable chronology. Interesting sherds from the fill can be illustrated as examples of a particular pottery type, but cannot be precisely dated. In this volume we illustrate a number of sherds or restorable vessels from this zone, but specify that they are "from an early Guadalupe phase provenience that contains redeposited San José phase sherds." Zone F1, F2, and F3 are arbitrary excavation units, kept separate in order to see whether there was ceramic change from bottom to top within the fill of Structure 4; no change was detected.

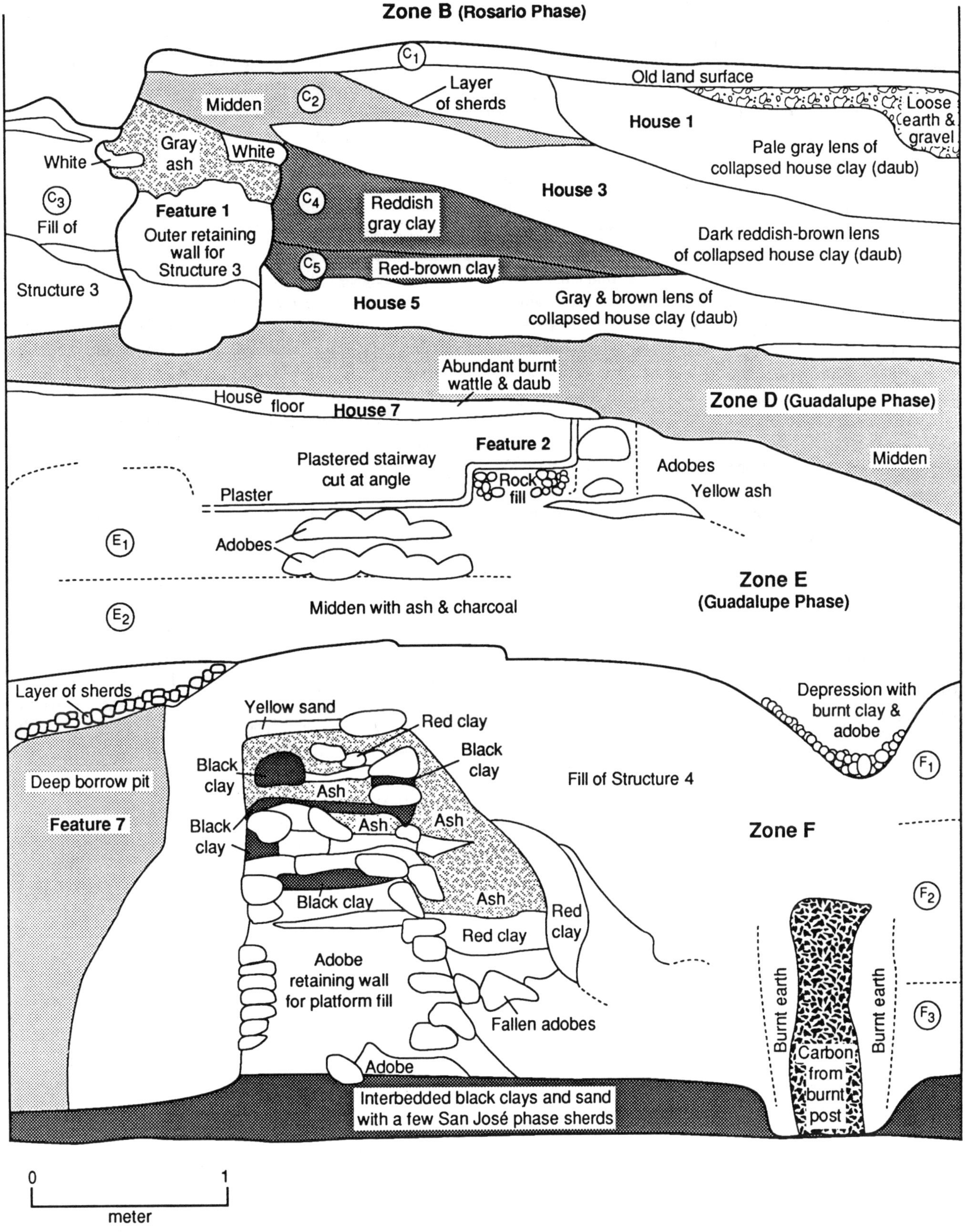

Site Formation Processes 35

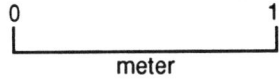

ruins of the first. Soon the dead are being buried in that midden by new householders who live near the *4*. And so it goes, with an early house buried beneath a midden, then beneath a cemetery, and still later beneath another house.

This, we believe, is also how Early Formative villages grew. Of course, they did not grow as neatly and regularly as the clock dial in the previous example, but neither did they grow "straight up." In Area A of San José Mogote, the first deposit on bedrock was a barrio midden. Above that came a series of four household units, one above the other. Then came the fill of a major public building; finally, deposition ended with the slopewash off some Protoclassic structures (Chapter 14). Other areas of the site showed the same alternating use as households, middens, cemeteries, and public buildings succeeded one another. Nowhere at San José Mogote was there a place where a single pit or trench would have recovered evidence of every period present at the site. The sequence had to be spliced together from excavations on several different parts of the site—at *3, 6,* and *9* on the dial, to continue our clock analogy.

To be truly useful on the regional level, of course, a sequence should be based on more than one site. The Pacific coastal plain of Chiapas and Guatemala provides a perfect example. Coe (1961), excavating at La Victoria, defined the Ocós and Conchas phases. Later, excavating at Salinas La Blanca (Coe and Flannery 1967), he defined the Cuadros and Jocotal phases, which fit between Ocós and Conchas. Later, Gareth Lowe (1975) defined the Barra phase which preceded Ocós. And more recently, Clark (1991) and Blake (1991)—working at Aquiles Serdán, Chilo, and Paso de la Amada—have inserted a Locona phase between Barra and Ocós, and a Cherla phase between Ocós and Cuadros. Only by working at several sites can a regionally useful chronology take shape. We have tried to do this for Oaxaca by excavating at Huitzo, San José Mogote, Tierras Largas, Fábrica San José, Abasolo, and Mitla.

Summary

Early Formative sites grew in complex and unpredictable ways and could consist of houses, pits, middens, public buildings, arroyos, and slopewash. As pointed out in this chapter, the sherd collections from such contexts differ greatly in quality. Community middens, because they contain a broad variety of ceramics from households of all kinds, probably provide the best collections for the purpose of defining ceramic phases. At the other end of the spectrum, small storage pits are likely to contain the least representative sherd collections. Some contexts, such as the fill of arroyos and public building platforms, do not provide good collections for defining periods at all; rather, they themselves need to be dated on the basis of more reliable collections.

Even when collections from a good community midden are available, this may not be enough to define a ceramic phase for an entire archaeological area. Every effort should be made to dig sites in several different parts of a region. We suspect that unnecessary new "phases" have been proposed in many parts of Mesoamerica simply because the collections from contemporaneous sites, located 15–30 km apart, look somewhat different.

A frequent complaint voiced by Mesoamerican archaeologists is that their colleagues "don't tell us where the sherds they illustrate come from." To this we can add our own complaint that they often don't tell us the contexts of the sherds counted in their tables. They give us the *proveniences*—"Pit 2, Level 3" or "Pit 4, Level 6"—but those are not the same as *contexts*. Examples of contexts would be "barrio midden," "dooryard of a household," "platform fill," or even "frankly, I'm not sure."

In this volume, we do several things not usually done in reports of this kind. First, we give the context of every sherd collection counted in our tables. Second, we keep those contexts separate; for example, midden layers are discussed in Chapters 9 and 13, household units in Chapters 10 and 14, public buildings in Chapters 11 and 18. Third, we tell you exactly where every sherd we illustrate came from. This attention to context has perhaps made every chapter (and certainly every figure caption) substantially longer. We sense, however, that real Mesoamerican archaeologists won't mind.

Figure 4.9 (facing page). A portion of the western Area B profile at San José Mogote, not far from its intersection with the Area C profile. This section of Area B is presented as an example of deposits that are worthless for establishing ceramic chronology. In this area, a former arroyo had been filled in during the Middle Formative by villagers who spanned its bed with retaining walls of bun-shaped adobes, stone, and clay. Between these retaining walls, thousands of basketloads of loose brown earth, yellow silt, brown clay, and other materials had been dumped until the arroyo was filled in. After the site was abandoned, a modern arroyo (top of drawing) cut through the same area, though not as deeply. Although this area produced an estimated 60,000 pottery sherds, not a single one was in primary context. Had we excavated this area by arbitrary levels (as so often happens on Formative Mesoamerican sites), the results would have misled our colleagues for years.

Site Formation Processes

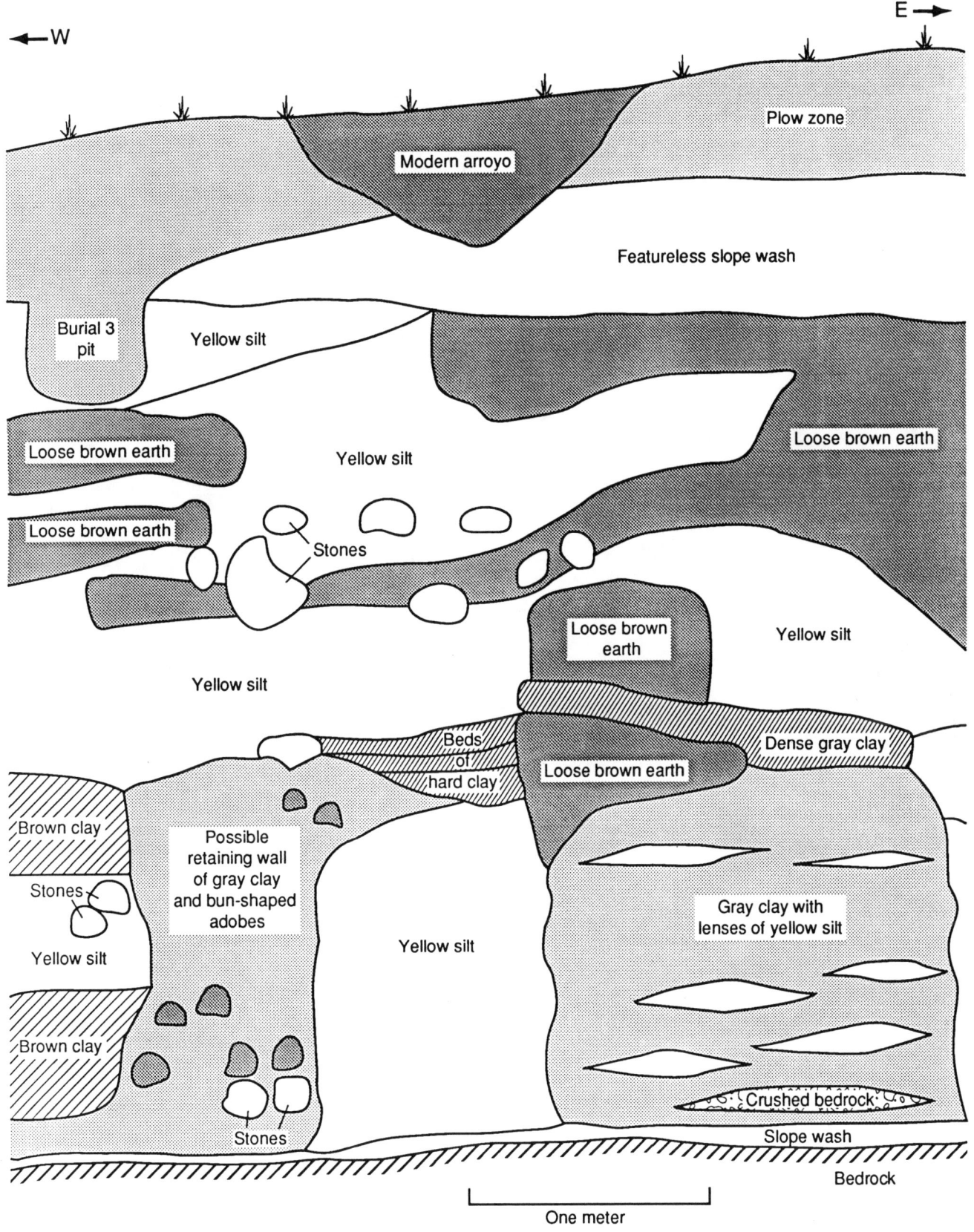

Chapter 5

Synchronic and Diachronic Variation in Ceramics

In many regions of the world, including Mesoamerica, pottery analysis is guided by an unstated and often unconscious assumption. That assumption is that variation between any two ceramic assemblages is a function of change over time. That is, when two adequate samples of sherds differ significantly, it is because one is earlier or later than the other.

In just as many regions of the world, including Mesoamerica, that assumption is demonstrably false. In Oaxaca, the sources of ceramic variation are so numerous that we do not as yet know how many factors are involved. To be sure, there was change over time, and much of it reflects synchronous changes in neighboring regions of Mesoamerica. As soon as hereditary differences in rank were present, however, there were differences in ceramic assemblage between higher status and lower status households. Some of those differences involved differential access to imported or local luxury wares, but some differences were even more basic than that.

For the Middle Formative Rosario phase, for example, Drennan (1976a:111–13) reports that bowls (especially decorated Socorro Fine Gray bowls) were more common around high-status households at Fábrica San José, while jars and other drab storage vessels were more common around low-status households. Here the pottery probably reflects different ranges of *activities* between such types of households, such as more frequent entertaining of elite guests by high-status households. And because there were apparently more high-status families at regional ceremonial centers, the status differences observed by Drennan often lead to differences in ceramic assemblage between large villages and small hamlets.

There were also regional differences which may have had little or nothing to do with status. Barrio del Rosario Huitzo, for example, had a different repertoire of motifs on Atoyac Yellow-white pottery when compared with San José Mogote (Plog 1976); both were ceremonial centers during the Guadalupe phase. San Sebastián Abasolo lacked some of the San José phase luxury wares seen in the Etla region, but used a fine white ware so far known only from the Tlacolula region (Chapter 17). Abasolo also had a Middle Formative vessel shape that may be associated with well irrigation; so far, no site outside the area where well irrigation is practiced has yielded such vessels. These differences in pottery assemblage could thus be *functional* as well as *status related*.

Finally, as early as 1970 we began to detect stylistic differences in San José phase pottery between barrios, or residential wards, at San José Mogote (Pyne 1976). Areas A and C of the site had significantly more depictions of the "fire-serpent" on gray pottery, while Area B had significantly more depictions of the "were-jaguar" on white pottery (Chapter 12). At first, like so many Mesoamericanists, we assumed that the differences might be chronological, with one motif succeeding the other over time. As work progressed, however, it became clear that that explanation would not work. All three areas of the site eventually produced the entire sequence from Tierras Largas phase to Guadalupe phase, and the differences in motif were present throughout the San José phase. Moreover, in Area C we had a sequence of ten San José phase houses, from early in the phase to late in the phase, all biased toward fire-serpent motifs. (Many of those houses are discussed in Chapter 16.)

For a variety of reasons, we do not believe that these differences in motif preference reflect differences in social rank; both higher status and lower status households are associated with each set of motifs. One possibility is that the two motifs may represent supernatural ancestors claimed by different descent lines within the community (Flannery and Marcus 1976b). More recently, Marcus (1989) has suggested that the two supernatural beings may reflect the widespread Mesoamerican dichotomy between Earth and Sky. We will have more to say about this in Chapter 12; for the purposes of this chapter, let us merely say that this example adds *differing social segments* to our list of causes for ceramic variation.

Summary

Separate chapters of this volume will be devoted to synchronic and diachronic variation. *Diachronic* variation is traditional chronological variation, a reflection of the changes in ceramics that take place as one moves vertically up the stratigraphic column for a region; it will be dealt with in Chapters 9, 13, and 14. Diachronic variation, however, is crosscut by *synchronic* variation, the set of differences seen as one moves horizontally away from the master stratigraphic column. Variation took place between high- and low-status households, between residential wards, between villages, and between subregions within the valley, all on the same time level. Those differences are discussed in Chapters 15, 16, and 17.

One of the most difficult tasks for us has been to determine which kinds of variation in our ceramic assemblages were diachronic and which were synchronic (functional, regional, rank-based, or social-segment–based). It is almost enough to make one long for the good old days, when all change was considered chronological.

Chapter 6

Types and Sherd Counts: Some Methodological Questions

There is no possible way we could present, in a volume of this size, every one of the hundreds of thousands of Early Formative sherds we washed and examined. What we will do is present a sample of sherds and whole vessels, selected on the basis of two criteria.

One criterion is whether or not the specimen is suitable for illustration. A whole vessel, a rim-to-base section, a decorated sherd, or a specimen that broadens our range of variation will be illustrated regardless of context. For example, if a Leandro Gray sherd shows an important vessel shape or decoration, it will be illustrated even if it comes from "cleaning the profile" or "platform fill."

The second criterion, relevant mainly to sherd count statistics, is quality of context (Chapter 4). For the purpose of establishing the percentage of one type to another within a phase, or one vessel form to another within a type, we will use only our best proveniences: house floors, dooryards, household middens, barrio middens, or sets of bell-shaped pits all of which are associated with the same house. We will not give statistical treatment to arroyo fill, slopewash, mixed construction fill, or any context whose nature and origin seem problematic. Thus the reader may see the drawing of an important sherd from mixed fill, but he or she will never see detailed sherd counts from mixed fill. We regard the latter as worse than no sherd counts at all.

The Order of Data Presentation

For each of the three Early Formative pottery assemblages of the Valley of Oaxaca—Espiridión, Tierras Largas, and San José—the order of data presentation will be as follows. First, we will give a brief narrative description of the assemblage. Second, we will describe and illustrate the pottery types on the basis of which that assemblage is defined.

Following those type descriptions, we will present three types of sherd counts. The first of these will be taken from superimposed layers of barrio midden. From within our sample of multilayered cross-sections of various Formative sites, we will select one or two with very clear natural or cultural stratigraphy: superimposed layers of barrio midden whose color and texture made them easy for our workers to separate. During the course of the Oaxaca project we came to refer to such areas as "Master Profiles" or "Control Sections." They were screened in their entirety through 6-mm mesh and every sherd saved.

The Control Sections we selected are usually the ones that document the change from one Formative phase to another, or the changes within a phase over time. We begin with such strata because we believe that barrio middens, precisely because they include the sherds from many households, are more representative of the phase as a whole. Thus, while they do not provide all the data we need to define a phase, they could be regarded as the backbone of any phase definition. All sherds within them were typed and counted.

The next set of sherd counts we provide will be taken from a sample of individual households within the same phase covered by the barrio middens. Depending on the circumstances of the household and its state of preservation, these sherd collections could come from the floor of the house; the surface of the dooryard adjacent to the house; or a set of bell-shaped pits in the dooryard, selected because their sherds seemed to be unmixed with those of other phases. In some cases, we supplemented the sherd count from a house with a narrative (nonquantitative) description of the sherds from an associated pit.

Like the midden samples from Master Profiles, our household samples were totally screened and all sherds counted. We believe their contribution is twofold. First, they provide a look at a thinner slice of time than the barrio middens give us. Second, they enable us to see those differences in ceramic assemblage which are synchronic rather than diachronic, such as the differences between high-status and low-status households.

Finally, we present the sherd counts from a sample of public buildings of the same phase. Those counts may include sherds trapped below the floor of the building, sherds lying on the floor after abandonment, or sherds higher up in the postabandonment debris. Our purpose is not to use those sherds to define a phase, but to show how a public building can be dated once the phase has been defined.

Honk If You Like Undecorated Body Sherds

Archaeologists digging Formative villages find thousands of sherds, and many of those are undecorated body sherds. For example, in Household Unit C3 of Area A at San José Mogote, there were 3,246 sherds of Fidencio Coarse (Table 14.1). Of those, 3,137 were undecorated body sherds. It is possible that all of the latter were from utilitarian jars, which tend to break into hundreds of fragments.

Mesoamerican archaeologists usually count every one of those plain body sherds, but they can't always explain why they do so. It can't be because they provide a lot of chronological information; in fact, when sherd counts are converted to percentages, such undecorated body sherds may be so numerous that they reduce everything else to insignificance. We have long felt that Mesoamerican archaeologists count plain body sherds primarily because they think it would be immoral not to. We didn't want to be immoral, so we counted ours also.

There are hints, however, that ignoring undecorated body sherds may not be as heinous a crime as we thought. Let us look at two examples.

In Iran's Deh Luran plain, Hole, Flannery, and Neely (1969:69–72) attempted to correlate levels at two early village sites by means of a Brainerd-Robinson Matrix of sherd frequencies (Robinson 1951; Brainerd 1951). Two different data sets were used. The first set involved the percentages of the nine major pottery types present at both sites; included were rims, decorated sherds, and undecorated body sherds, all dutifully counted. The second data set involved only Susiana Black-on-Buff (the decorated pottery type with the greatest number of design motifs) and did not include plain body sherds. This second data set produced by far the most satisfactory ordered matrix, one that kept all levels in their correct stratigraphic order (Hole, Flannery, and Neely 1969: Fig. 23). We conclude from this example that the elaborate decoration on Susiana Black-on-Buff pottery is more time-sensitive than gross pottery type counts. Furthermore, since there is apparently much less time-sensitive information in plain body sherds, the inclusion of large numbers of them in a data set may actually produce so much "noise" that the chronology is less refined.

A second example, drawn from the Valley of Oaxaca itself, is the multidimensional scaling program designed by Drennan (1976a, 1976b) for Fábrica San José. The variables used by Drennan consisted of highly specific vessel shapes and decorative modes within pottery types; undecorated body sherds were not used because they did not provide enough information. The resultant program enables anyone to place an unmixed sherd sample from good archaeological context (such as a house floor) along a continuum from the Guadalupe phase through the Rosario phase to Monte Albán I. Since this program relates to Middle Formative rather than Early Formative pottery, it will be discussed in a later volume.

These two examples suggest to us that once a basic pottery sequence has been established for a region, with all sherds dutifully classified and counted, it may be possible to streamline the chronology and stop spending so much time counting undecorated body sherds. We have continued to count such sherds in most tables in this volume because we have goals beyond chronology, such as establishing complete inventories of house contents. We suspect, however, that in the future we may stop counting plain body sherds without feeling the slightest bit immoral.

An Adequate Sample of What?

Midway through our first field season at San José Mogote, we were joined by a young man who was a veteran of Stuart Struever's excavations in the Lower Illinois Valley. A superb excavator and former supervisor at Apple Creek, he had never been to Mesomerica. Like all good North American archaeologists, he had a sense of how many sherds constituted "an adequate sample."

We parked the car in the village of San José Mogote and walked 100 m to the excavation. We could see the young man's eyes grow larger as he realized his feet never needed to touch the ground as he walked; he could stroll on a carpet of sherds. As we reached the excavation he looked around and said with disbelief: "There are more sherds on this one site than in the whole state of Illinois." An exaggeration, perhaps, but not an unusual reaction during one's first visit to Mesoamerica. At times, the enormous quantities of sherds that come out of Mesoamerican sites even overwhelm veteran Mesoamericanists.

Like his North American counterpart, the Real Mesoamerican Archaeologist also has a sense of how many sherds constitute "an adequate sample." When he visited us in the 1970s at San José Mogote, he asked us why we were still digging there; "You *must* have an adequate sample of sherds by now," was a frequent remark. Our reply was, and is, as follows: We did not dig Formative villages in Oaxaca to get an adequate sample of sherds. We dug to get an adequate sample of houses, features, burials, and public buildings. One midden, if it is the right midden, could give you a sample of sherds adequate to define a phase. It would not, however, give you an adequate sample of houses or public buildings. In Mesoamerica it is likely that in the course of recovering an adequate sample of houses and public buildings, you will recover 100 times an adequate sample of sherds.

Even today, we are not sure we have an adequate sample of houses, features, burials, and public buildings. But digging for fifteen years in search of such a sample affords us this luxury: instead of having to present all the sherds from all proveniences excavated, we can restrict ourselves to what we believe are the very best contexts. As for what constitutes an adequate sample of sherds, we believe not in an absolute number but in a rule of thumb—the "point of diminishing surprises." When each new house yields no type of sherd you have not seen many times before, you probably have an adequate sample.

Our Choice of Ceramic Typology

Any archaeologist who searches the literature on pottery typology in Mesoamerica is overwhelmed by the variety of definitions (e.g., Gifford 1960, 1976; Sabloff and Smith 1969, 1972; Smith, Willey, and Gifford 1960; Willey, Culbert, and Adams 1967). Types, wares, attributes, modes, and groups are defined differently by different authors. Our selection of one approach from dozens of good ones was guided by our number one goal: to make our pottery typology comparable to that used by our colleagues in neighboring areas.

Those neighboring areas include the Nochixtlán Valley (Spores 1972); the Tehuacán Valley (MacNeish, Peterson, and Flannery 1970); the Valley of Morelos (Grove 1987, Cyphers Guillén 1987); the Isthmus of Tehuantepec (Zeitlin 1979); the Grijalva Depression (Dixon 1959, Agrinier 1989); and the Gulf Coast (Coe and Diehl 1980). Slightly farther away we have the Basin of Mexico (Niederberger 1987) and the Pacific Coast of Chiapas and Guatemala (Coe 1961, Coe and Flannery 1967, Clark and Blake 1989, Clark 1991, Blake 1991).

These, then, were the areas to which we most wanted to relate our ceramics. To do so, however, we needed monograph-length publications to work from, publications with abundant illustrations and detailed pottery type descriptions such as those by Niederberger, Cyphers Guillén, Coe and Diehl, and MacNeish, Peterson, and Flannery. Short journal articles and book chapters could not serve our needs, nor could narrative descriptions of new phases or new ceramic complexes that have yet to be fully illustrated or defined. There are many such phases and complexes, and in the future when they are given full monographic treatment we will be able to expand our comparisons.

Our pottery types are binomial, like those of Coe and MacNeish. Each type encompasses a set of vessel forms, all featuring the same clay body and surface treatment, which occurred as a complex over all (or most) of the Valley of Oaxaca during a specified time period. Many of our types are designed to correlate with well-known coeval types described elsewhere. For example, our type Atoyac Yellow-white is the Oaxaca equivalent of Tehuacán's Canoas White, Tlapacoya's Cesto White, Chalcatzingo's Amatzinac White, Chiapa de Corzo's Period I-II "White Monochrome," and coastal Guatemala's Conchas White-to-Buff.

Below the level of the type, we regard individual vessel forms as important categories to be listed in our sherd counts. One level below this, we have singled out the kinds of decoration used on those vessel forms within a type. As might be expected, specific combinations of decoration and vessel form within a type are more time-sensitive than the type alone. Atoyac Yellow-white pottery lasts through several phases, but Atoyac Yellow-white cylindrical bowls with incised were-jaguars on them are virtually restricted to one phase. Indeed, were it not for the fact that it would cause massive problems correlating our ceramics with those of neighboring areas, one could probably justify creating types at the level of vessel shape/decoration rather than clay body/surface color/surface treatment.

As it is, our pottery typology—designed to facilitate correlations with colleagues who work on the Early and Middle Formative—will encounter problems enough when we try to unite it with the very differently designed Monte Albán sequence of Caso, Bernal, and Acosta (1967). Those problems will be dealt with in a later volume.

Chapter 7

The Espiridión Complex

Purrón Cave, in the southeast piedmont of the Tehuacán Valley, was excavated between 1961 and 1964 (MacNeish, Peterson, and Flannery 1970:3–6). Two stratigraphic levels in the cave, Zones K and K^1, yielded the oldest ceramics from the valley. The collection consisted of 127 sherds, all but 7 of them belonging to two pottery types: Purrón Coarse and Purrón Plain.

Both Purrón Coarse and Purrón Plain were undecorated buff wares, locally made, and occurring in simple shapes such as tecomates, jars, and hemispherical bowls (Fig. 7.1). Both the tecomates and hemispherical bowls could have been based on gourd prototypes. However, there were also stone bowls in the late preceramic Abejas phase that could have served as models for some of the Purrón vessels. Because of the small sample from Zones K and K^1 and the lack of comparable material from other sites, the Purrón ceramic complex remained unique and enigmatic for years.

In 1974, digging in Area C of San José Mogote, we uncovered an analogous, though not identical, collection of ceramics. In this case the collection came not from a cave living floor but from House 20, the remains of a small wattle-and-daub residence in Stratigraphic Zone H. This house may have been one of the first ever built on the site, its wall posts having been set in bedrock.

Area C, the westernmost area of San José Mogote excavated by us, is described more fully in Chapter 9. Reference to Fig. 9.3 of that chapter will indicate that the remains of House 20 rested on bedrock, and filled excavation squares S18K-S18N. They also extended partway into S19K-S19N and S17K-S17L, but had been truncated by later construction in Area C.

The sample of sherds, numbering 262, is somewhat larger than that from Zones K and K^1 of Purrón Cave. It includes 14 sherds, possibly all from one jar, which we have assigned to Purrón Plain; MacNeish examined these sherds in August of 1978 and agreed with our assessment. Also present were 14 sherds of a previously undescribed type, Espiridión Thin, which appears exclusively as hemispherical bowls with walls no thicker than 2.0–2.5 mm.

The bulk of the collection from House 20 consists of jars and hemispherical bowls of the type Tierras Largas Burnished Plain, a ware that goes on to reach its peak in the Tierras Largas phase. The range of vessel forms was much more limited than that seen in the Tierras Largas phase, however, and was entirely without plastic decoration. In the Tierras Largas phase, such decorative techniques as dentate stamping, rocker stamping, and rim ticking were often used, but we see none of that in House 20.

One other attribute should be mentioned. As the type description of Tierras Largas Burnished Plain will make clear (Chapter 8), there were chronologically significant variations in the ways in which Tierras Largas phase potters finished the inner surface of jars in this type. Jar interiors could be (1) pocked, (2) wiped, or (3) plain (smoothed). In the Espiridión material from House 20, however, there were 30 jar body sherds whose interior surface had simply been left rough and unfinished. By the time of the Tierras Largas phase, this "rough" variant had disappeared.

Purrón-Espiridión Comparisons

Originally we planned to call the House 20 collection "Purrón" rather than invent a new name for it. However, on closer inspection we noted some potentially significant differences. For one thing, the Espiridión collection lacks the tecomate shape that seems to have been so much a part of the Purrón material. The Purrón collection, for its part, lacks anything resembling Espiridión Thin. For the moment, therefore, we have decided to keep the two complexes separate, although they could be combined in the future if larger collections show that the differences are merely due to sampling error.

It should be noted that the combined collections total only 389 sherds. For this reason we have chosen to refer to Espiridión merely as a ceramic *complex* and not as a full-fledged chronological *phase*. MacNeish took much the same position with Purrón (MacNeish, Peterson, and Flannery 1970).

Both Purrón and Espiridión are characterized as much by what they lack as by what they include. They are totally without paint, wash, slip, or plastic decoration. Each looks like the area's first successful attempt to make simple pottery containers for storage (jars, tecomates) or individual servings (hemispherical bowls). We doubt that this early period of ceramic manufacture will ever show widespread and distinctive stylistic attributes. Indeed, it

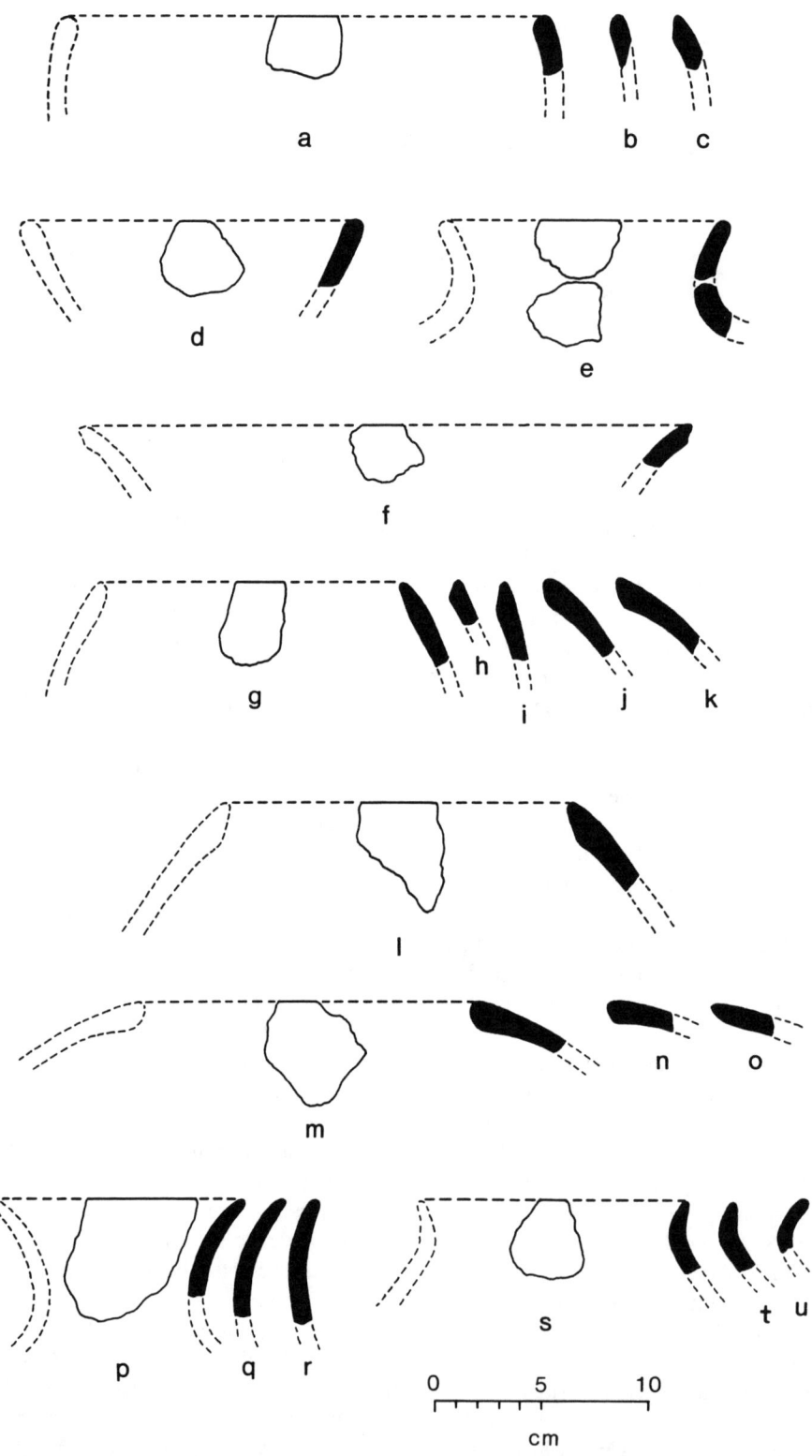

Figure 7.1. Pottery of the Purrón complex from the Tehuacán Valley. *a-f,* Purrón Coarse. *g-u,* Purrón Plain. *a-d,* hemispherical bowls. *e,* jar. *f,* bowl with outleaned wall. *g-l,* tecomates or incurved-rim bowls. *m-o,* tecomates. *p-r,* jars with tall necks. *s-u,* jars with short necks. (Redrawn from MacNeish, Peterson, and Flannery 1970: Figs. 8, 9.)

may be that at this time period, every collection of pottery from the Oaxaca-Puebla area will look a little different.

If Espiridión is ever promoted to the level of a phase, we suspect that House 20 will fall near the end of that phase. That suspicion is based on the fact that its frequency of Purrón Plain is low, and its frequency of Tierras Largas Burnished Plain is high, which suggests that the collection does not lie far from the beginning of the Tierras Largas phase. In addition, we wonder whether the prehistoric potters would really have made as many typological distinctions as we have. As Marcus (1983:42) put it earlier, "On one conceptual level Purrón Coarse, Ajalpan Coarse, Purrón Plain, Ajalpan Plain, and Tierras Largas Burnished Plain are just a collection of bowls and jars with minor variations, made from the same kinds of piedmont clays that formed *in situ* above the ancient metamorphic rocks of the Oaxaca-Puebla region."

The Origins of Pottery Making in Oaxaca

We do not believe that pottery making was invented in Oaxaca (or in Tehuacán) independently of the rest of Mesoamerica. In fact, we see the stone bowls of the late preceramic Abejas phase as possible imitations of pottery already being made elsewhere, while Tehuacán was still without that technology. We thus suspect that the inhabitants of the Valley of Oaxaca learned pottery making from their neighbors. We cannot as yet specify who those neighbors were, although we would guess that they lived to the south of Oaxaca rather than to the north. Sites such as Monagrillo in Panamá (Willey and McGimsey 1954) and Puerto Hormiga in Colombia (Reichel-Dolmatoff 1965) seem to have had ceramics before Mesoamerica did.

Thus the *technology* of pottery making may have been introduced into Oaxaca; however, it is not necessarily the case that the earliest *vessel forms* were introduced. We know that the preceramic occupants of the Valleys of Oaxaca and Tehuacán had used bottle gourds as containers for thousands of years (Cutler and Whitaker 1967, Whitaker and Cutler 1986), and many of the earliest pottery vessels in Oaxaca and Tehuacán resemble gourd prototypes. This is particularly true of the tecomates of the Purrón complex, the hemispherical bowls of Purrón and Espiridión, and the bottles of the Tierras Largas phase.

In fact, virtually every vessel shape known from the Purrón and Espiridión complexes could be duplicated by cross-sectioning a bottle gourd, one of the oldest containers known from Oaxaca and Tehuacán. The vessels themselves could have been produced by press-molding clay on the inside or outside of one of the gourd containers that had been used for thousands of years by hunter-gatherers of the preceding Archaic (Fig. 7.2).

If the top fifth of a spherical gourd was cut off, a tecomate was created (Fig. 7.2*a*). If a spherical gourd was cut in half, two hemispherical bowls were produced (Fig. 7.2*b*). And if one cut in half the typical wasp-waisted Mesoamerican water-carrying gourd, the result was two simple jars (Fig. 7.2*c*).

Since much of our Early Formative Oaxaca pottery was press-molded, it is reasonable to suggest that many Espiridión vessels were the result of press-molding a clay vessel inside or outside a gourd. For example, Espiridión Thin hemispherical bowls (see below) look very much like clay imitations of *jícaras* or hemispherical gourd bowls. Some hemispherical bowls from the subsequent Tierras Largas phase provide additional support for this possibility: they have dimples at the rim on opposite sides of the vessel, exactly where one would expect them if the clay vessel were press-molded inside a gourd that had been cross-sectioned through the stem scars (Figs. 7.2*f*, 7.3). Indeed, vessels that resemble gourd bowls are common throughout Oaxaca prehistory (Fig. 7.4).

Finally, a few other Tierras Largas phase vessels display fluting or gadrooning that initially could have been achieved by press-molding clay around the outside of a squash, pumpkin, or other cucurbit (Chapter 8).

Bottle Gourds as Prototypes in Other Regions

We are certainly not the first to suggest that gourds may have served as prototypes for early pottery. The same suggestion has been made in other parts of the world.

For example, Anthony Arkell has suggested that the prototype of early Egyptian pottery was the gourd. Arkell (1960:106) explains the origins of black-topped red pottery in predynastic Egypt as follows:

> Gourd bowls or cups in the Sudan always have a black rim, for when a gourd is cut in half to make two bowls, its rim is always fired, presumably in order to prevent it tasting or splintering. So that when potters came to copy these gourd bowls as drinking bowls, they naturally tried to reproduce the black rim, because a gourd would not look right without a black rim. The method of taking the bowl from the kiln red hot and placing it upside down in carbonizing material which they developed as being the easiest way of producing a black rim in pottery, led to the aesthetically more pleasing black-topped bowl.

For the southeast United States, Holmes (1903:124,127) stated that the gourd appeared "in some cases as a model for earthen vessels" such as one finds at Tarpon Springs, Florida. In the nineteenth century, Cushing (1886) also saw gourds as possible precursors of ceramic vessels in the southeast United States.

Farther afield, the general name for all bowls and dishes of the Hawaiians was *ipu*; this word was also the name for the gourd plant. Thus it has been suggested by some that the gourd, as a natural container, preceded the manufacture of vessels made of wood or other materials (Dodge 1943:17, 24). The bottle gourd has also been suggested as a prototype for some Chinese ceramics and bronzes (Wilson 1945:30–32).

V. Gordon Childe (1958:108–10) believed that the Danubian I globular vesels of around 3000 B.C. were "clearly derived from gourd models." Zeuner (1954:372) had earlier concluded that Danubian ceramic bottles were imitations of gourds.

The gourd also served as a prototype for early pottery in Peru (Tello 1960:320–21). In fact, even after pottery appeared, the

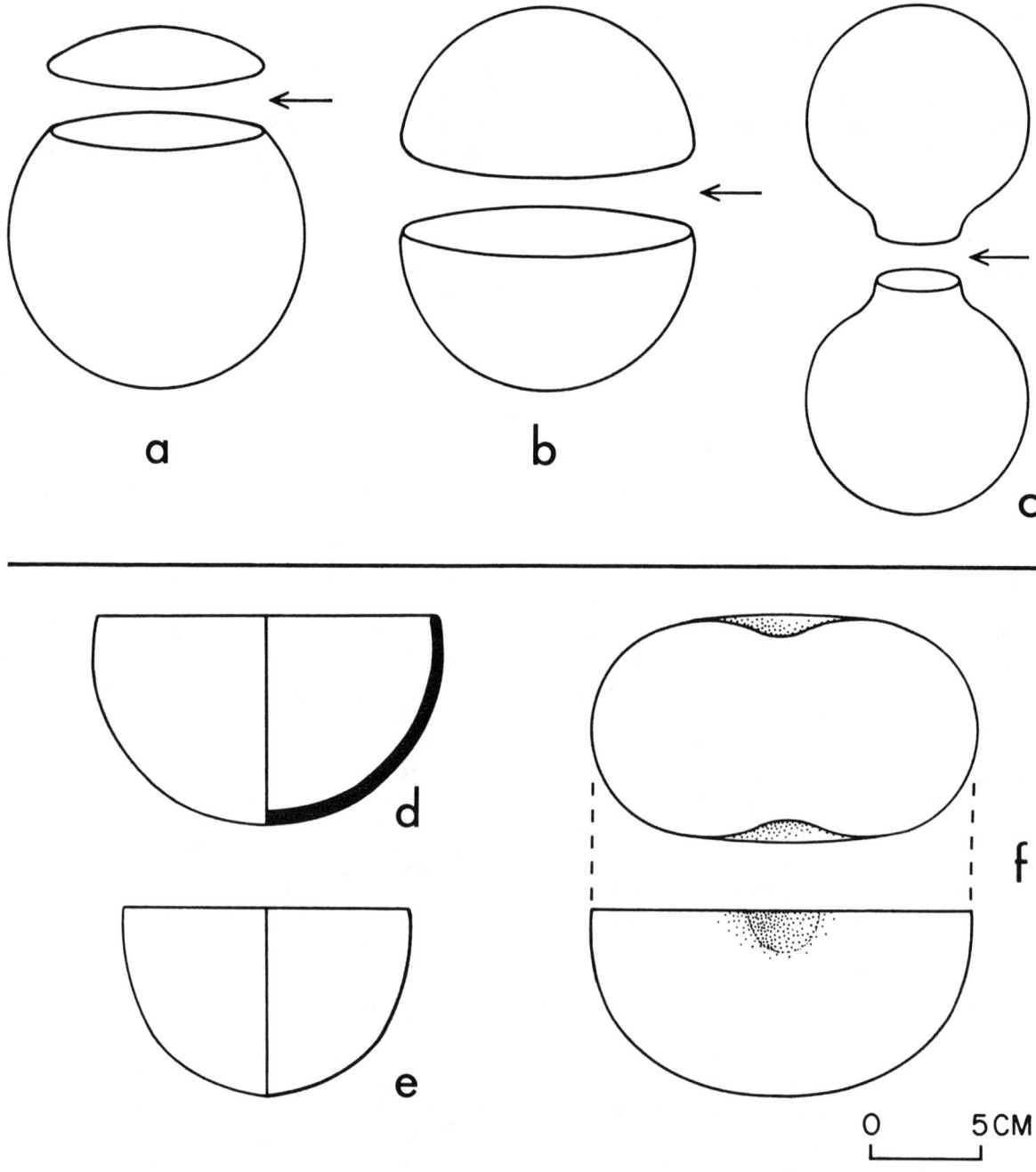

Figure 7.2. Vessel shapes of the Purrón and Espiridión complexes: possible prototypes for the (*a*) tecomate, (*b*) hemispherical bowl, and (*c*) jar, all achieved by cross-sectioning gourds. Reconstructions of (*d*) Purrón Plain bowl and (*e*) Espiridión Thin bowl. (*f*) Tierras Largas phase bowl with dimples suggesting gourd stem scars. (Redrawn from Marcus 1983a: Fig. 3.1.)

Espiridión Complex 49

Figure 7.3. Two vessels that may shed some light on the origins of pottery in Oaxaca. At the top is a gourd bowl from the Oaxaca market, produced by slicing a spherical gourd in half through the stem scars. At the bottom is a Tierras Largas Unburnished Plain bowl with pinched-in "dimples" on the sides, from Feature 142 at Tierras Largas. A pottery vessel such as the one at the bottom would result if it had been press-molded inside a gourd vessel like the one at the top, with its stem scars producing the dimples.

Figure 7.4. Are they gourd bowls or pottery vessels? These two Postclassic burial offerings from the Valley of Oaxaca show how similar some ceramics could be to gourd prototypes, even in later periods.

gourd continued to be used as a container in both the Andes and Mesoamerica.

Pottery Types of the Espiridión Complex

Let us now look at the Espiridión pottery from House 20 at San José Mogote, followed by our definitions of Espiridión complex pottery types. The collection of 262 sherds was as follows:

ESPIRIDION THIN
Hemispherical bowls: plain rims	3
Hemispherical bowls: plain body sherds	11
Total	14

PURRON PLAIN
Jar rims	1
Jar shoulders	1
Body sherds	12
Total	14

TIERRAS LARGAS BURNISHED PLAIN
Jar rims	2
Jar body sherds: rough interior	30
Jar body sherds: pocked interior	2
Jar body sherds: wiped interior	33
Jar body sherds: plain (smoothed) interior	102
Jar shoulders: unburnished interior	2
Hemispherical bowls: plain rims	3
Hemispherical bowls: basal curves	2
Hemispherical bowls: body sherds	58
Total	234

GRAND TOTAL	262

PURRON PLAIN

General Description

Purrón Plain is an unslipped, undecorated, unburnished ware, known so far from only one site in the Valley of Oaxaca. The only vessel form present in our small sample is a jar of the type called *olla with long flaring neck* in Tehuacán (MacNeish, Peterson, and Flannery 1970:22–24).

Chronological History

It is known principally from House 20 at San José Mogote, our only Espiridión phase provenience (Chapter 9). One additional sherd showed up in an early Tierras Largas phase provenience. We suspect that our excavations caught this pottery type very late in its history.

Clay Body: Tehuacán Valley

Specimens from Purrón Cave in the Tehuacán Valley had a clay body whose description sounds like the decomposition product of metamorphic rock. Nonplastic materials in the 0.5–1.5 mm range were quartz, quartzite, andesite, gneiss, shale, biotite (mica), limestone, calcite, marble, and diorite. Materials smaller than 0.5 mm were quartz, feldspar, magnetite, and biotite (MacNeish, Peterson, and Flannery 1970:22). The clay is described as light in color, "running to more yellowish tones," and having a porous and contorted appearance which suggests that it was not well mixed and levigated.

In general, this description fits the sample from San José Mogote, which also has a yellowish-white clay body with quartz, feldspar, magnetite, mica, and many of the same materials. However, we believe that our Purrón Plain is made from local Oaxaca clay, while MacNeish's is made from local Tehuacán clay. We therefore present Payne's description of our specimens.

Clay Body: Valley of Oaxaca

The clay body used for our Oaxaca variety of Purrón Plain is a residual clay, formed above Precambrian gneiss somewhere in the western piedmont of the valley. It may have been transported a short distance by water; the nonplastic materials seem to have been sorted and moved somewhat, but not enough for the particles to be rounded. Payne's best guess is that the clay may have come from an arroyo somewhere in the Cacaotepec area, where it had not been moved far from its parent material.

The clay is a kaolinite resulting from the decomposition of feldspar. Some samples are up to one-third clay, with the nonplastic materials including quartz, feldspar, hornblende, iron micas, and magnetite. The dominant color of the raw clay would have been white, like the Cacaotepec clay used today by the potters of Atzompa. The magnetite specks could also indicate a source somewhere in the Cacaotepec area, where Pires-Ferreira (1975, 1976) reports raw material suitable for magnetite mirrors eroding from Precambrian gneiss. An archaeological site called La Nopalera, discovered by Stephen Kowalewski (pers. comm.), lies on *crema* clay and magnetite deposits in the piedmont above Cacaotepec.

This clay was used as found, except for the removal of the largest nonplastic particles (all of those larger than 3.0 mm in diameter, and most of those larger than 1.5 mm).

Firing Temperature

It was fired at about 700° C in an oxidizing atmosphere, probably out in the open as the potters of San Marcos Tlapazola fire pottery today.

Color

Specimens from the Tehuacán Valley are described as follows: "The firing is very uneven, with the interior surface ranging from gray (2.5 YR 6/2) to red (10 R 7/8), and the lighter exterior varying from dark brown (10 R 4/4) to yellowish-white (7.5 YR 6/4)" (MacNeish, Peterson, and Flannery 1970:24). This description fits our Oaxaca specimens as well. The last thing the makers of this pottery were worried about was what color it would turn out to be.

Surface Treatment

Once again, the description of the Tehuacán specimens fits ours as well: "Exterior surfaces have been smoothed, probably while the clay was relatively wet, since there are few marks of any smoothing implement." No burnishing of any kind was carried out. "Interior surfaces are grainier; they have been rather crudely brushed, usually with a horizontal motion, during which process granules of temper were dragged along, scarring the surface" (MacNeish, Peterson, and Flannery 1970:24). However, jar interiors do *not* show the three distinctive varieties of surface finish seen in Tierras Largas Burnished Plain: pocked, wiped, and plain (smoothed).

Vessel Forms

Jars (Fig. 7.5). While the sample is very small, it appears that our Purrón Plain jars are like those called "ollas with long flaring necks" by MacNeish, Peterson, and Flannery (1970: Fig. 9, lower left). Such jars are described as having "globular to semiglobular bodies terminating in tall necks (over 5 cm) with flaring rims."

ESPIRIDION THIN

General Description

Espiridión Thin appears in only one vessel form: thin-walled, undecorated hemispherical bowls that look remarkably like gourd prototypes. This type provides us with our strongest suggestion that pottery in Oaxaca began as an effort to imitate gourd vessels.

Chronological History

This type is so far known only from the Espiridión complex. As in the case of Purrón Plain, our excavations may only have caught the very last stage in this type's history. In the Tierras Largas phase, it was fully replaced by better-made hemispherical bowls of Tierras Largas Burnished Plain.

Clay Body

Like Purrón Plain, Espiridión Thin is made from a yellowish-white kaolinite clay which probably comes from somewhere in the Cacaotepec piedmont; its parent material was undoubtedly Precambrian gneiss, and it contains the same range of nonplastic materials.

It differs from Purrón Plain mainly in the grain size of that aplastic material. In the case of Espiridión Thin, the clay had clearly been carefully winnowed to remove most particles larger than .05 mm in diameter. Payne suggests that this could have been done in one of two ways. The simplest of these is wind winnowing, a process similar to that practiced by some Native Americans of the Southwest U.S. An alternative would be the method used today in San Marcos Tlapazola, where clay is mixed with water and stirred until the larger nonplastic particles sink to the bottom. The finer fraction is then decanted into another container.

Firing Temperatures

It was fired at roughly 700° C in an oxidizing environment.

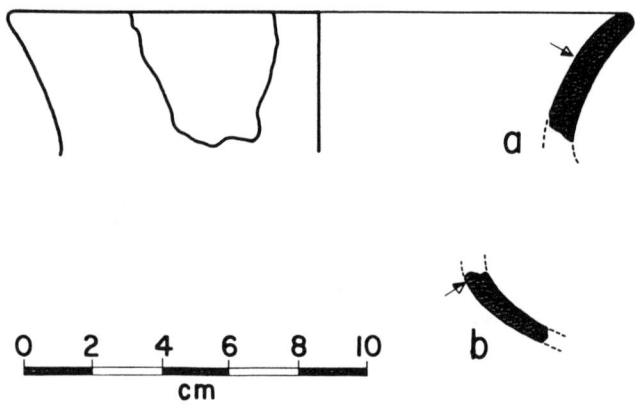

Figure 7.5. Purrón Plain pottery from House 20, Zone H, Area C, San José Mogote. *a,* jar rim, smoothed outside; smoothed inside only as far down as the arrow; left rough and sandy below. *b,* jar shoulder, barely smoothed at all outside; smoothed inside only as far down as the arrow; left rough and sandy below. (Espiridión complex.)

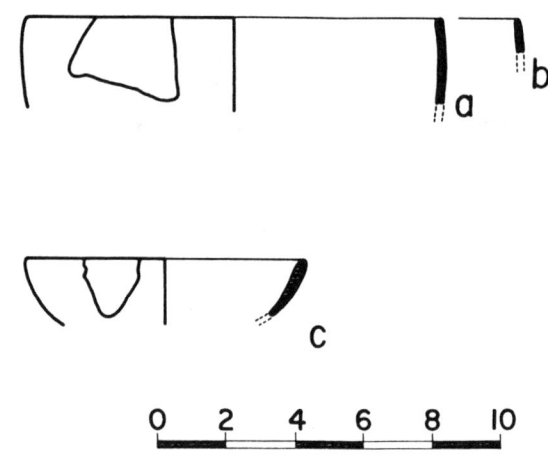

Figure 7.6. Espiridión Thin pottery from House 20, Zone H, Area C, San José Mogote. *a, b,* rims of small hemispherical bowls; *a* has glossy, uniform burnishing outside and streaky burnishing inside, while *b* has glossy, uniform burnishing on both surfaces. *c,* rim of small hemispherical bowl, smoothed inside and out, then lightly burnished on the outside only. (Espiridión complex.)

Color

Like Purrón Plain, Espiridión Thin shows very uneven firing, with surface colors ranging from dark brown to buff or even whitish buff. Because of its thinness, cores are usually the same color as the surface. The range of Munsell colors is the same given for Purrón Plain.

Surface Treatment

Smoothed while wet. When leather-hard, some bowls were burnished once with a quartz pebble, while others were not. The pattern of burnishing was variable (see below). Probably the burnishing was done to close the pores of the vessel so that it could hold liquids.

Vessel Forms

Hemispherical bowls (Fig. 7.6). The only vessel form in which this type occurs is a hemispherical bowl that appears to have been press-molded over a previous vessel, perhaps an inverted gourd bowl. Rims are blunt, either squared off or rounded off.
  Rim diameter: Estimated at 15–20 cm
  Height: Estimated at 10–15 cm
  Wall thickness: Usually 2.0–2.5 mm
  Surface treatment: Variable. Some bowls were unburnished; some were burnished only on the exterior, with the interior left smoothed but unburnished. A few were burnished in a streaky fashion on one surface, and given a more even (glossy) burnish on the other surface.
Decoration: None

TIERRAS LARGAS BURNISHED PLAIN

Because Tierras Largas Burnished Plain reached its peak in the Tierras Largas phase, its type description is given in Chapter 8. In our Espiridión sample, Tierras Largas Burnished Plain occurs in only two vessel shapes, jars and hemispherical bowls (Figs. 7.7–7.9). None of the usual Tierras Largas phase plastic decoration, such as rim ticking, dentate stamping, or rocker stamping, was present in House 20. As we have seen, the Espiridión jars also display one attribute not seen in the later Tierras Largas phase. Thirty of the jar body sherds were left completely rough and unfinished on the interior, rather than displaying one of the three common Tierras Largas phase attributes—that is, pocked, wiped, or plain (smoothed) interiors.

A Possible Figurine or Miniature Mask

It is our intention to devote a future volume of our Oaxaca reports to the Formative figurines recovered from San José Mogote, Huitzo, Abasolo, and other sites. The Espiridión deposits in House 20, however, produced one object worth mentioning here: our earliest possible candidate for a figurine.

The object is a small disk of lightly fired clay, modeled to depict the face of a puma or jaguar (Fig. 7.10). The clay body is

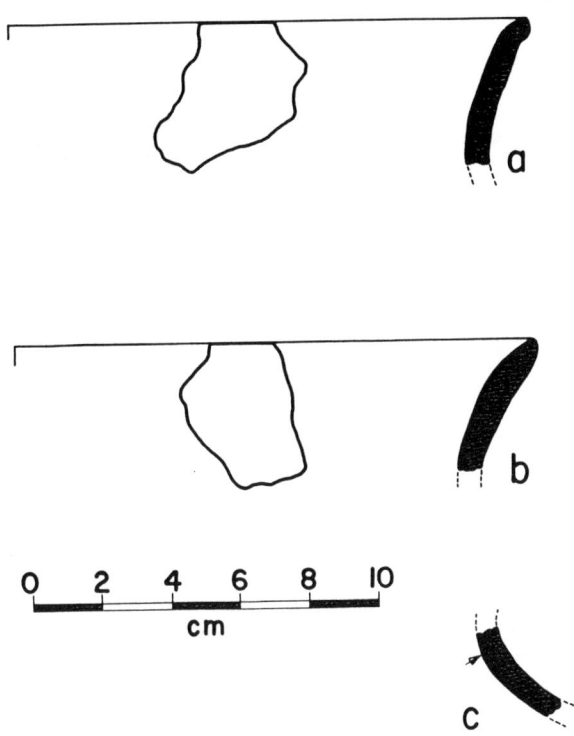

Figure 7.7. Tierras Largas Burnished Plain pottery from House 20, Zone H, Area C, San José Mogote. *a,* jar rim, smoothed inside, lightly burnished in streaks on the exterior and just inside the rim. *b,* jar rim, smoothed, then lightly and uniformly burnished on both surfaces. *c,* jar shoulder, well burnished outside; burnished inside only as far down as arrow, left rough below that. (Espiridión complex.)

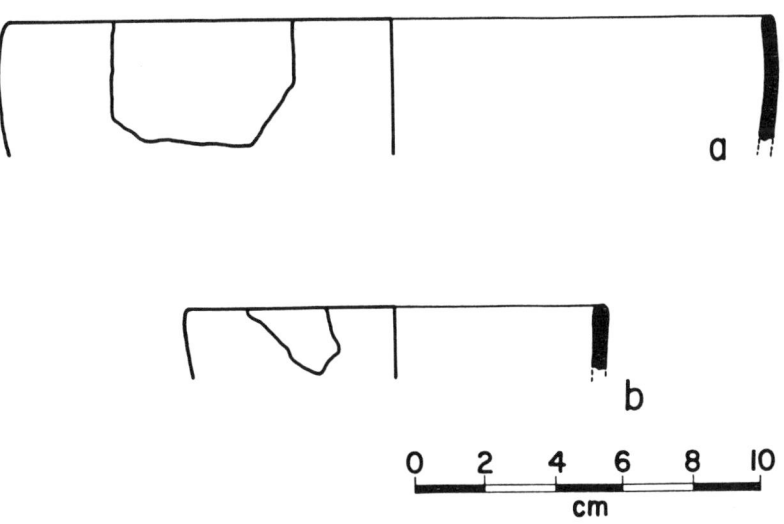

Figure 7.8. Tierras Largas Burnished Plain pottery from House 20, Zone H, Area C, San José Mogote. *a,* rim of hemispherical bowl, burnished in streaks both inside and out. *b,* rim of hemispherical bowl, lightly but uniformly burnished inside and out. (Espiridión complex.)

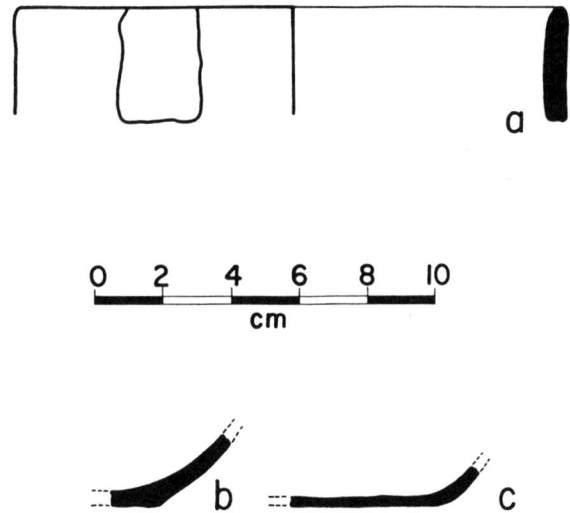

Figure 7.9. Tierras Largas Burnished Plain pottery from House 20, Zone H, Area C, San José Mogote. *a,* rim of hemispherical bowl, very lightly burnished inside and on top of rim; merely smoothed inside. *b,* base of hemispherical bowl, minimally burnished. *c,* base of hemispherical bowl. (Espiridión complex.)

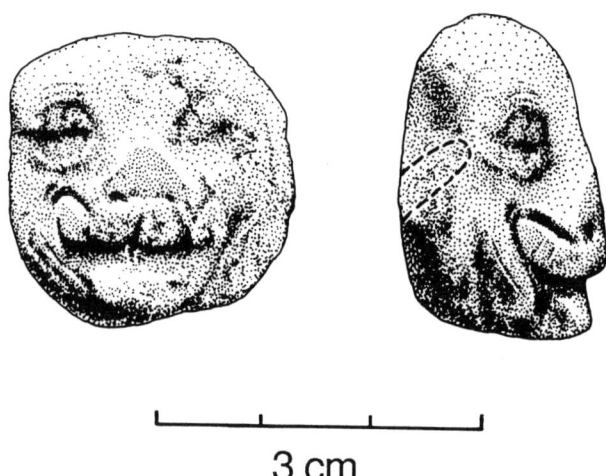

Figure 7.10. Puma or jaguar face modeled in lightly fired clay. The dashed line shows where this artifact has been perforated to receive an object like a slender stick. House 20, Zone H, Area C, San José Mogote (Espiridión complex).

similar to that used for Purrón Plain and Tierras Largas Burnished Plain, a residual piedmont clay formed by the breakdown of Precambrian gneiss. The feline head does not appear to have broken off from a torso; rather, it seems to be complete and self-contained, like an amulet, or perhaps a miniature mask. From the rear it has been perforated by an object like a small stick; the perforation was completed before firing, and its purpose is unknown. It could have been used to attach the feline head to some other object.

While crude and rather poorly preserved, this object is our oldest example of "art" in potter's clay from the Valley of Oaxaca. It is worth noting that the puma or jaguar was already considered a suitable subject for artistic depiction in the Espiridión complex, many centuries before were-jaguars were carved on San José phase pottery (Chapter 12).

Chapter 8

The Tierras Largas Phase

The Tierras Largas phase is the first period in our sequence that can actually be said to have a "style," one that is traceable from site to site over a wide area. The Valley of Oaxaca, the Valley of Nochixtlán in the Mixteca Alta, the Cuicatlán Cañada, and the Valley of Tehuacán in southern Puebla have all produced sites where that style is strongly represented. In the Basin of Mexico to the north and the Isthmus of Tehuantepec to the south, a few components of the style can be detected, albeit mixed with other elements.

The vessel forms of the Tierras Largas phase assemblage consist of jars with necks, hemispherical bowls of various kinds, and less frequently, bottles, tecomates, and flat-based bowls with outleaned walls. The jars were clearly for storage or cooking, and the hemispherical bowls were used mainly for individual portions of food.

The clay body of the assemblage could be described as burnished buff ware made from residual piedmont clays. Its dominant type, Tierras Largas Burnished Plain, is so drab that we were forced to turn to such details as the interior surface treatment of jars to provide enough attributes to measure chronological change.

Only when we look at the surface color and decoration of Tierras Largas pottery do we see its "style" emerge. Some jars were coated with red or orange iron oxide pigment. Many hemispherical bowls were given a red band at the rim, or a series of red stripes or chevrons. Other bowls might be painted completely red on one or both sides. Bottles could be all red, and tecomates could have a red band at the rim. In some cases, the red pigment was specular hematite.

Those red-on-buff hemispherical bowls, bottles, and tecomates link San José Mogote and Tierras Largas to other sites such as Yucuita in the Nochixtlán Valley, Rancho Dolores Ortiz in the Cuicatlán Cañada, Ajalpan in the Tehuacán Valley, Tlapacoya-Zohapilco in the Basin of Mexico, and Laguna Zope near Tehuantepec. Two of our Tierras Largas phase types, Avelina Red-on-Buff and Clementina Fine Red-on-Buff, provide most of the crossties with other regions. Two other types, Matadamas Red and Matadamas Orange, have ties with the Tehuacán Valley but not with a wider area.

Tierras Largas vessels occasionally show such attributes as gadrooning or fluting, dentate stamping, and plain rocker stamping. For the most part, these attributes suggest occasional contact with the Isthmus and the Chiapas-Guatemala coast rather than with Veracruz. One other pottery type of the Tierras Largas phase, although never common, reinforces our impression of occasional contact with Soconusco. This is a highly burnished black ware which reminds us so strongly of Ocós Black that we have called it by the same name.

Types of the Tierras Largas Phase

We now present descriptions of the pottery types used to define the Tierras Largas phase. While most of these types reached their peak in Tierras Largas times, none was absolutely restricted to that phase. As we have seen, Tierras Largas Burnished Plain began in the Espiridión complex; it lasted into the early San José phase. Avelina Red-on-Buff and Clementina Fine Red-on-Buff also lasted into the San José phase, although their decorative attributes were greatly reduced in number by then. Tierras Largas is therefore defined both by (1) the peak frequencies and decorative attributes of the types described in Chapter 8, and (2) the absence of the San José phase types described in Chapter 12. (Perhaps "near absence" would be a better phrase, since a few San José phase types make sporadic appearances late in the Tierras Largas phase.)

The Tierras Largas phase presents a problem for surface survey. One of its most commonly used horizon markers is the Avelina Red-on-Buff hemispherical bowl, whose maximum abundance and decorative variety admittedly occur in the Tierras Largas phase. Since this bowl lasted into the San José phase, however, it can also be expected to appear on the surface of early San José phase sites. To guarantee that a site belongs to the Tierras Largas phase, one should try to recover the more complex Avelina bowls (with multiple red stripes or chevrons) rather than those with only a simple band at the rim. One should also search for Matadamas Red and Matadamas Orange, and for Tierras Largas Burnished Plain jars with "pocked" interiors (see below).

TIERRAS LARGAS BURNISHED PLAIN

General Description

Tierras Largas Burnished Plain was the most common unslipped, unpainted utilitarian ware of the Espiridión and Tierras Largas phases. Its usual color is buff to brown (with darker firing clouds) and its rare decoration is limited to plastic techniques such as stamping, punctation, notching, or grooving. Vessel forms are jars, hemispherical bowls, flat-based bowls with outleaned walls, and occasional bottles or tecomates.

Chronological History

In our Espiridión complex collections, Tierras Largas Burnished Plain appeared only in two shapes: jars and hemispherical bowls. Neither had decoration. The jars displayed four attributes of internal surface finish that may have chronological significance; three of those continued into Tierras Largas times. The attribute restricted to the Espiridión complex was one in which the interior of the jar was simply left rough, rather than pocked, wiped, or plain (smoothed).

During early Tierras Largas times, jars and hemispherical bowls remained virtually the only vessel forms. Rough jar interiors disappeared; the most common attributes of internal surface finish were pocked interiors and wiped interiors (described below). By middle Tierras Largas times, wiped jar interiors were increasing in frequency, and they went on to reach their peak during the late Tierras Largas phase. Wiped interiors and plain (smoothed) interiors were running neck-and-neck in frequency by the beginning of the San José phase, while pocked interiors gradually disappeared.

At the start of the Tierras Largas phase there were perhaps seven jar rims to every three hemispherical bowl rims, but late in the phase the two vessel forms were equal in frequency, and during the early San José phase there were four hemispherical bowl rims to every jar rim. (That presumably happened because jars in Fidencio Coarse were so much harder, stronger, and more durable that they eventually replaced Tierras Largas Burnished Plain jars.) Flat-based bowls with outleaned walls also appeared during the middle and late Tierras Largas phase, but were always outnumbered by hemispherical bowls.

As for plastic decoration, various attributes characterized the Tierras Largas phase. Notches or slashes on the rims of hemispherical bowls were essentially Tierras Largas phase in date, disappearing early in the San José phase. Zoned dentate stamping, dentate rocker stamping, plain rocker stamping, and "micro" rocker stamping were essentially late Tierras Largas/early San José phase decorative modes. Flat-based bowls with outleaned walls, plus some rare bottles or tecomates, were the usual vessel forms showing such stamping. A few late Tierras Largas phase flat-based, outleaned-wall bowls had thickened grooved rims or gadrooned rims, like bowls of the Ocós phase from La Victoria, Guatemala. This was no surprise, since late Tierras Largas phase/early San José phase was the period to which virtually all Ocós-like traits were restricted.

Most, but not all, of our tecomates with zoned rocker stamping or zoned dentate stamping in Tierras Largas Burnished Plain appeared in early San José phase levels.

This pottery type began to disappear during the San José phase, as it was gradually replaced by harder, stronger wares fired at higher temperatures. By the late San José phase there were roughly seven hemispherical bowl rims to every three jar rims (the reverse of the situation during early Tierras Largas times). Flat-based, outleaned-wall bowls in Tierras Largas Burnished Plain had been virtually replaced by similar bowls in later wares by this time. A few dentate stamped or rocker stamped tecomates in Tierras Largas Burnished Plain survived into late San José phase, but not many. By the Guadalupe phase, this pottery type had disappeared.

In a few San José phase residences—such as Houses 1, 4, 5, and 9 in Area C of San José Mogote—we found fragments of burnished pottery ear spools in what appears to be Tierras Largas Burnished Plain.

Clay Body

The clay body is residual piedmont clay formed by the weathering and decomposition of Precambrian gneiss. This material is available just below the ground surface in many areas of the piedmont west of the Atoyac River; it contains quartz granules, feldspars in various stages of disintegration, iron micas, hornblende, and augite. This clay was used virtually as found, except for the removal of large nonplastic particles.

This clay body is similar to that used for many of the major San José phase wares, but it is coarser, suggesting that it was usually not winnowed. Nonplastic particles up to 4.0 mm in size occur frequently in the walls of Tierras Largas Burnished Plain jars. The only exceptions to this coarseness are provided by some hemispherical bowls made with an unusually fine clay body, one in which nonplastic particles greater than .05 mm in diameter are rare to absent. This relatively fine body was either painstakingly selected from deposits of older and more disintegrated gneiss, or was produced by winnowing the usual clay body to remove the coarser particles. Because these somewhat finer bowls were simply at one end of a continuum of particle size (with coarse jars at the other end of the continuum), it seemed pointless to single them out as a separate variety.

Firing Temperature

This ware was fired in an oxidizing atmosphere at about 700° C. The vessels were probably fired in the open, as they are at San Marcos Tlapazola today (see Chapter 2). The large number of dark firing clouds suggests that many pots were in contact with rocks, fuel, other vessels, or large sherds used to cover the ceramics being fired, resulting in areas that were incompletely oxidized.

Color

Surface colors are extremely variable, most commonly ranging from browns (7.5 YR 5/2; 10 YR 5/3) to light browns or buffs (7.5 YR 6/4; 10 YR 6/4); reds (2.5 YR 4/8; 5 YR 6/6) may also be present. Firing clouds are usually black to mahogany. It is not unusual for a single large jar to show almost the entire range of surface color for the ware.

Cores in brown sherds may be very close in color to the surface. However, many cores (especially those in vessels with great surface color variation) are dark gray (2.5 YR N3/ to 7.5 YR N4/), indicating that the vessels were fired rapidly (40–50 minutes).

Surface Treatment

As its name implies, this pottery type was characterized by burnishing. The burnishing was done only once, while the vessel was leather-hard, and was careless enough so that streaks of burnishing usually alternate with streaks of matte surface. This is the kind of streaky burnish which archaeologists sometimes erroneously refer to as "stick polish." However, it was clearly done with a quartz pebble, since (as Payne pointed out to us) pottery cannot be burnished with a stick.

Bowls were burnished, generally more carefully than jars, on both interior and exterior surfaces. One can still see the individual burnishing streaks on each bowl, but very little of the original matte surface of the vessel is noticeable.

Jars were less carefully burnished, with necks receiving the most thorough treatment, and lower parts of the body left predominantly matte. Even the interior of the jar neck might be burnished, often as far down inside as the juncture between neck and shoulder. We distinguished shoulder sherds that were internally burnished from those that were not, since the former seemed to increase over time.

Jars also showed the four attributes of interior surface treatment already mentioned above under Chronological History: rough, pocked, wiped, and plain (smoothed). Those attributes are described below under Jars. As we have seen, jar interiors left rough were restricted to the Espiridión complex; the other three attributes carried on into the Tierras Largas phase, with pocked interiors peaking early, and plain (smoothed) interiors peaking late.

Vessel Forms

Jars (Figs. 8.1–8.5). While a few Tierras Largas Burnished Plain jars could be considered to have globular bodies, most are too vertically elongated to fit that term. Necks are generally tall and their rims curve gently outward. The taller jars, with their more vertically elongated bodies (Figs. 8.1–8.2), are more likely to have rounded bases that would require a ring of braided grass, or a hollow in the ground, to keep them upright. The lower and more nearly spherical jars (Fig. 8.3) tend to have a circular, flattened facet on the base, like that seen on some hemispherical bowls.

Rim diameter: 12–30 cm, with most specimens in the 24 cm range.

Neck diameter: The narrowest part of the neck has a diameter roughly 70% of the rim.

Neck height: Usually 8–12 cm

Wall thickness (neck): 6–12 cm

Wall thickness (body): 6–10 cm except for bases, which may be 12 cm thick.

Volume: Those with a rim diameter of 12.5 cm and a height of 45 cm could have held ca. 19 liters; the largest Tierras Largas Burnished Plain jars might have held more than 40 liters, or about 10 gallons. These larger jars were probably for household water storage.

Decoration: None

Method of manufacture: According to Payne, Tierras Largas Burnished Plain jars were made in several stages. The lower half was made by press-molding clay over the inverted base of another jar. As is customary, the vessel serving as the mold would have been lightly dusted with dry clay or wood ash so the new vessel would not stick to it. Handfuls of clay were slapped on, then flattened, joined, and partially smoothed with the fingers, sometimes resulting in a rippled surface where the flattened handfuls were joined.

The upper half would have been press-molded in the same way, but with a circular hole left for the neck. Before adding the neck, the potter would have joined the upper and lower halves of the jar by the process Payne calls *luting*. A concentric ring of wet clay would be added to the rim of the lower half, the upper half would be pressed into that ring, and the two halves would be joined by smoothing.

Next, the neck could be added by stacking concentric rings of clay on the hole left in the upper half of the body. These rings could be smoothed and drawn up into the desired shape, and the rim given the desired flare. Finally, the interior could be finished by scraping, wiping, or smoothing, and the exterior could be burnished with a quartz pebble when the vessel was leather-hard.

Attributes of interior surface treatment: As already mentioned, there were four ways of treating the interiors of Tierras Largas Burnished Plain jars. The oldest—simply leaving the interior rough and unfinished—was restricted to the Espiridión complex and has already been described in Chapter 7. The other three attributes are as follows.

1. *Pocked interiors* (Fig 8.4). Some jars seem to have had their interiors scraped smooth while the vessel was in the leather-hard stage. The tool may have been a piece of gourd or a rounded-off sherd. The result of this scraping was that large quartz grains or other nonplastic particles were literally pulled out of the surface and briefly dragged along it, leaving a pocked, cratered, and striated surface.

58 | Early Formative Pottery of Oaxaca

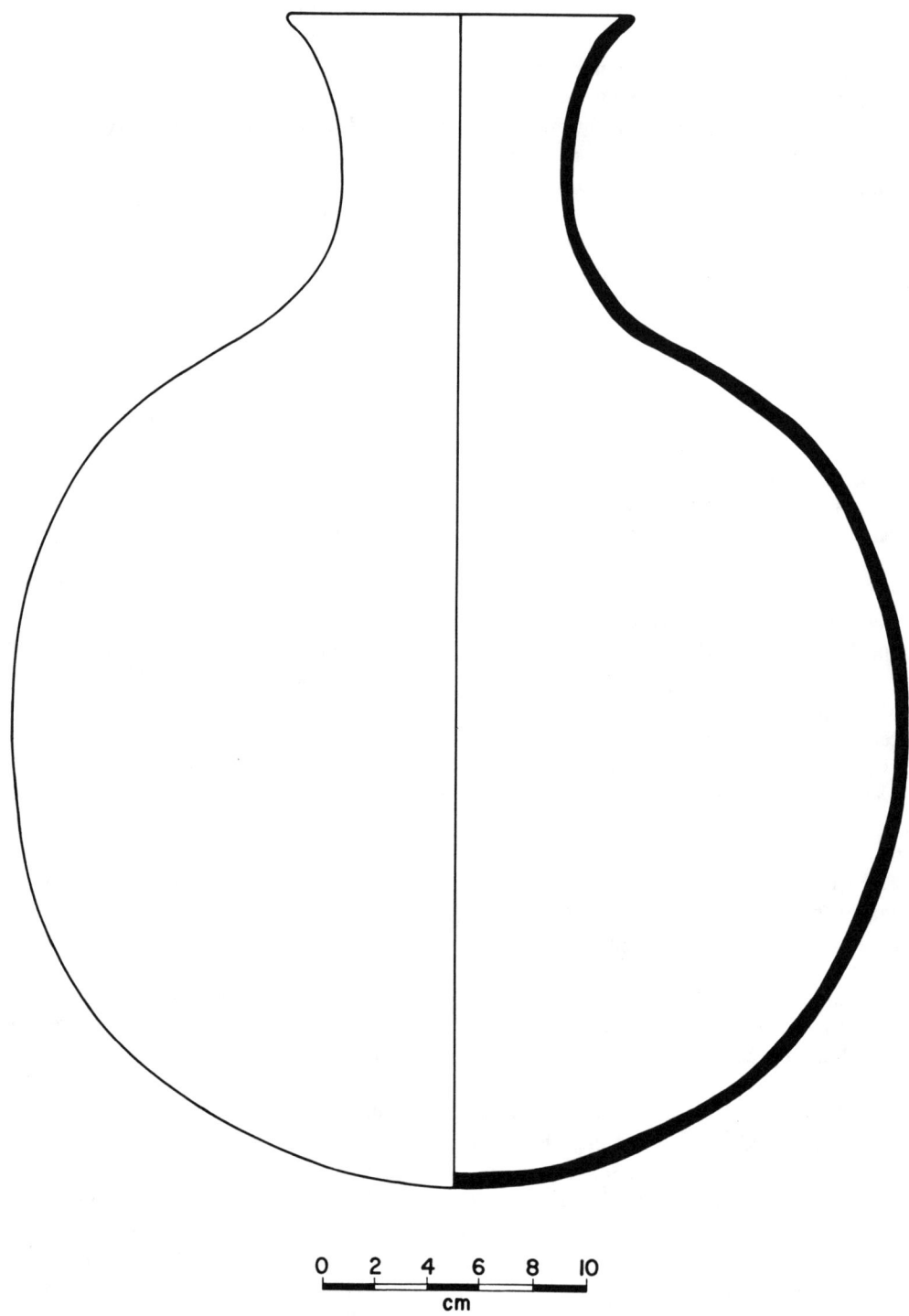

Figure 8.1. Tierras Largas Burnished Plain jar, Vessel 2 of Feature 57A, Tierras Largas (Tierras Largas phase). This is an example of a relatively tall jar with a vertically elongated body. The vessel is mahogany brown with gray firing clouds, and is burnished all over in the streaky style erroneously called "stick polish." (See also Fig. 8.2.)

Figure 8.2. Tierras Largas Burnished Plain jar, Vessel 2 of Feature 57A, Tierras Largas (Tierras Largas phase). This is the same vessel shown in Figure 8.1. (Height of vessel, 43 cm; maximum diameter, 34 cm.)

We were struck by the resemblance of these pocked surfaces to the so-called "Pox Pottery" described from shell mounds at Puerto Marquez, Guerrero by Charles Brush (1965). When Brush visited us in the early 1970s, we showed him our pocked sherds and were informed that they were, as we had suspected, just like his. In fact, he supplied us with some additional information that came as a surprise. For one thing, his term "Pox Pottery" referred to the interior surface treatment of plain buff-to-brown jars, and was not a separate pottery type. Second, he revealed that these pocked jars had been accompanied by other pottery types, including red-on-buffs like our Avelina and/or Clementina types (see below). By the end of our conversation with Brush, it was clear to us that his earliest pottery from Puerto Marquez was coeval with Tierras Largas or Early Ajalpan, not with Purrón or Espiridión as we had previously thought.

2. *Wiped interiors* (Fig. 8.5). Perhaps the most common mode of finishing off the interior of Tierras Largas Burnished Plain jars during the Tierras Largas phase was neither rough nor pocked, but wiped. As Figure 8.5 suggests, this was accomplished by wiping the interior of the jar with a wad of grass, coarse cloth, or some other fibrous substance which left countless rough, intersecting streaks. This wiping may have been done prior to the leather-hard stage, while the vessel was still damp. (We originally considered the term "brushed" for this mode of surface finish, but dropped it because we did not wish to imply the use of a brush.)

3. *Plain (smoothed) interior.* Some Tierras Largas Burnished Plain jar body sherds were simply smoothed with a wet hand or a piece of animal hide, leaving no interesting pocks, striations, or streaks. That was true of most Espiridión complex body sherds, and continued to be true of a third of the jar sherds during the Tierras Largas phase.

Hemispherical bowls (Figs. 8.6–8.9). These bowls, probably derived from gourd prototypes, were often given either a circular flat facet or a "dimple" on the base to enable them to sit upright on a flat surface in a way that gourd vessels cannot. While we refer to them generically as "hemispherical," not all are perfect hemispheres. A minority have rims that curve in or flare out slightly, and a few have rims that could be described as rolled or beaded (Fig. 8.7b). Most, however, have rims that are nearly vertical and seem to have been squared or rounded off as the rim of a gourd vessel might be. Even the dimple in the base may have been suggested by a cucurbit stem scar. Our sherd counts include rim sherds, body sherds, and sherds showing the distinctive curve between the wall and the dimpled base.

Rim diameter: 15–30 cm, with a few miniatures (e.g., 6 cm); most specimens are in the 16–24 cm range.

Height: Usually 10–16 cm

Wall thickness: Usually 4–8 mm

Volume: One complete specimen from Feature 40 at Tierras Largas (Fig. 8.8), with a rim diameter of 24 cm and a height of 11 cm, held 2.4 liters. Based on very similar vessels in other pottery types of the Tierras Largas phase, average volumes were probably in the 1.5-3.0 liter range.

Decoration: Rare to absent. The tops of some bowl rims are decorated with notches or slashes (sometimes referred to as "rim ticking") made with a maguey spine or a chipped-stone tool (Fig. 8.9). Even rarer are punctations atop the rim, also probably made with a maguey spine. A few specimens, late in the Tierras Largas phase, have rims which are thickened and have a shallow groove on top running around the entire circumference of the bowl. Such rims (which are wedge-shaped in cross-section) remind us of certain rims on Ocós phase vessels from La Victoria (Coe 1961:Fig. 19a-f, Fig. 21q, Fig. 23h, i).

Method of manufacture: Many of these bowls may have been made by press-molding clay over inverted gourd vessels or previous hemispherical bowls, in the manner already described for the lower halves of jars. Alternatively, some

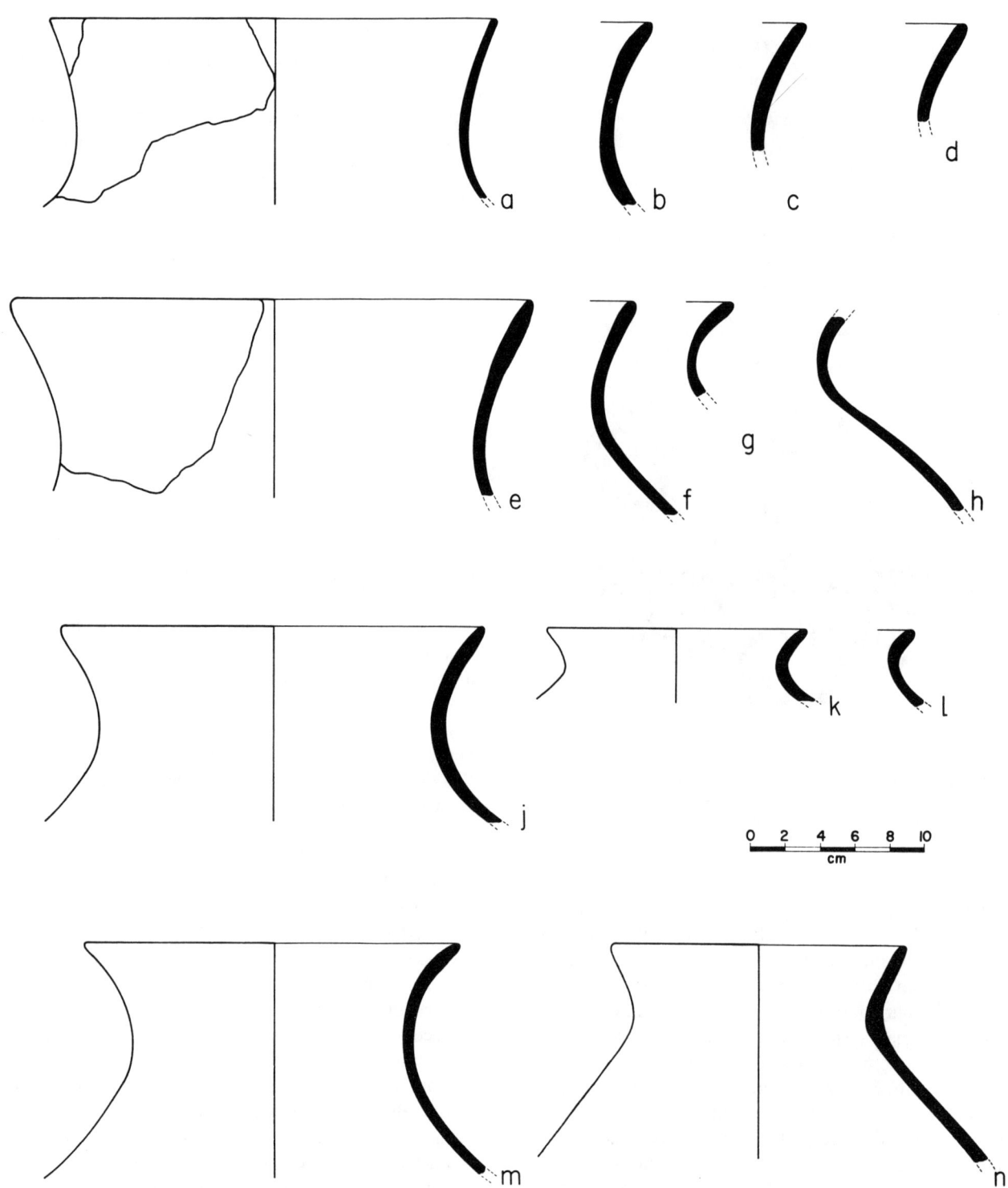

Figure 8.3. Tierras Largas Burnished Plain jar rims and shoulders from features at Tierras Largas (Tierras Largas phase). These are examples of lower and more nearly spherical jars. *a*, Feature 40. *b-d, f-h, k-m*, Feature 142. *e*, Feature 117-north. *j*, Feature 151-south. *n*, Vessel 1 of Feature 86. *h, j*, and *n* have pocked interiors.

Tierras Largas Phase

Figure 8.4. Interior of Tierras Largas Burnished Plain jar, showing "pocked" surface treatment. This way of scraping the inner surface, probably with a worn potsherd or similar tool, pulls the larger quartz grains and other nonplastic materials out, leaving a pitted surface similar to "Pox Pottery." Feature 117, Tierras Largas (Tierras Largas phase.)

Figure 8.5. Interior of Tierras Largas Burnished Plain jar, showing "wiped" surface treatment. A bundle of fiber or a piece of coarse cloth has been wiped across the interior of the vessel. Feature 42, Tierras Largas (Tierras Largas phase).

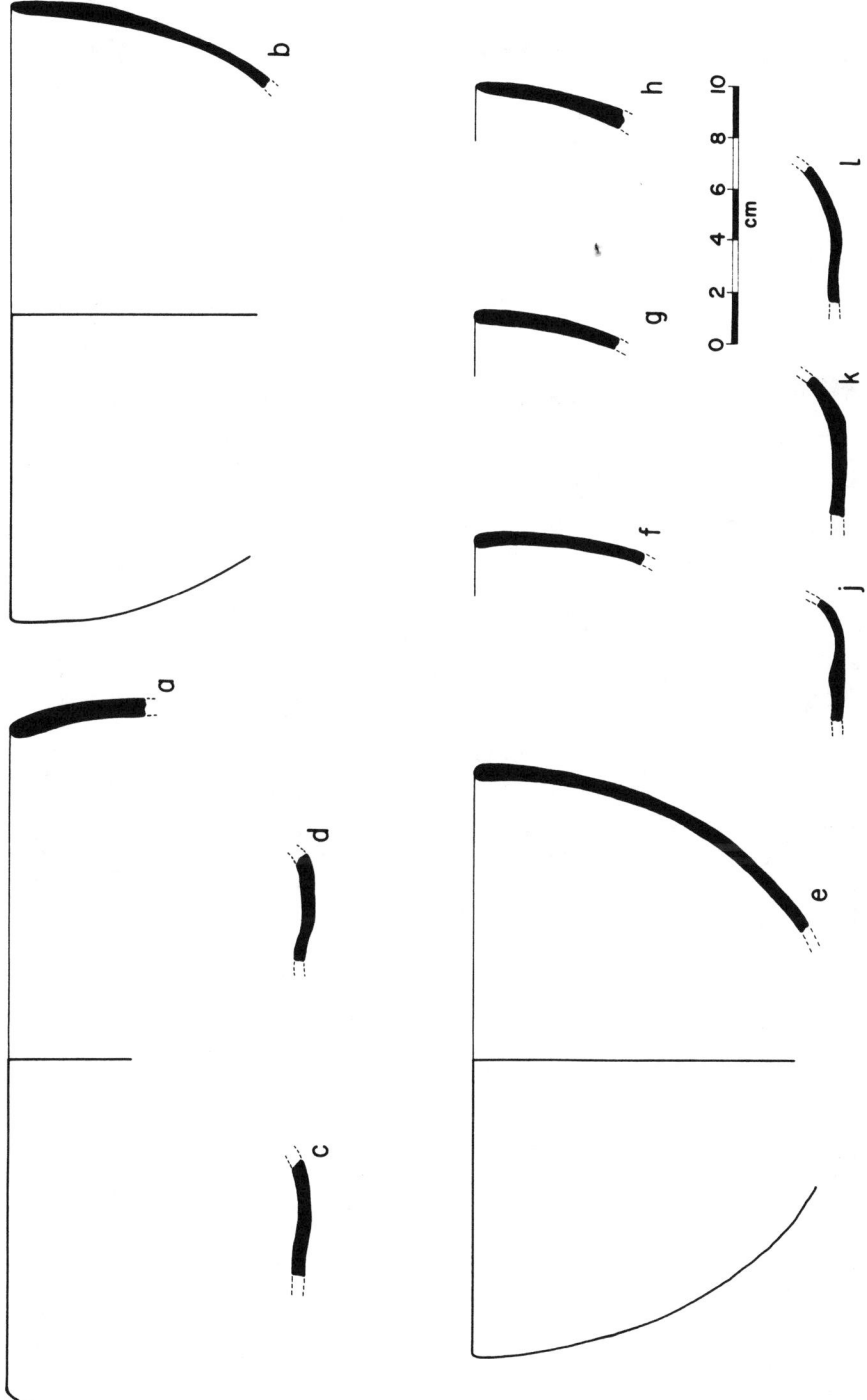

Figure 8.6. Tierras Largas Burnished Plain hemispherical bowls from Tierras Largas (TL) and San José Mogote (SJM). *a*, Zone G, Area C, SJM. *b*, Feature 142, Area B, TL. *c, d*, sherds from dimpled bowl bases, Feature 151, TL. *e*, Feature 17, TL. *f–h*, rim sherds from Feature 142, Area B, TL. *j*, sherd from dimpled base, Structure 5, Area C, SJM. *k*, sherd from flattened base, Structure 5, Area C, SJM. *l*, sherd from dimpled base, Feature 117, TL. (All specimens are Tierras Largas phase.)

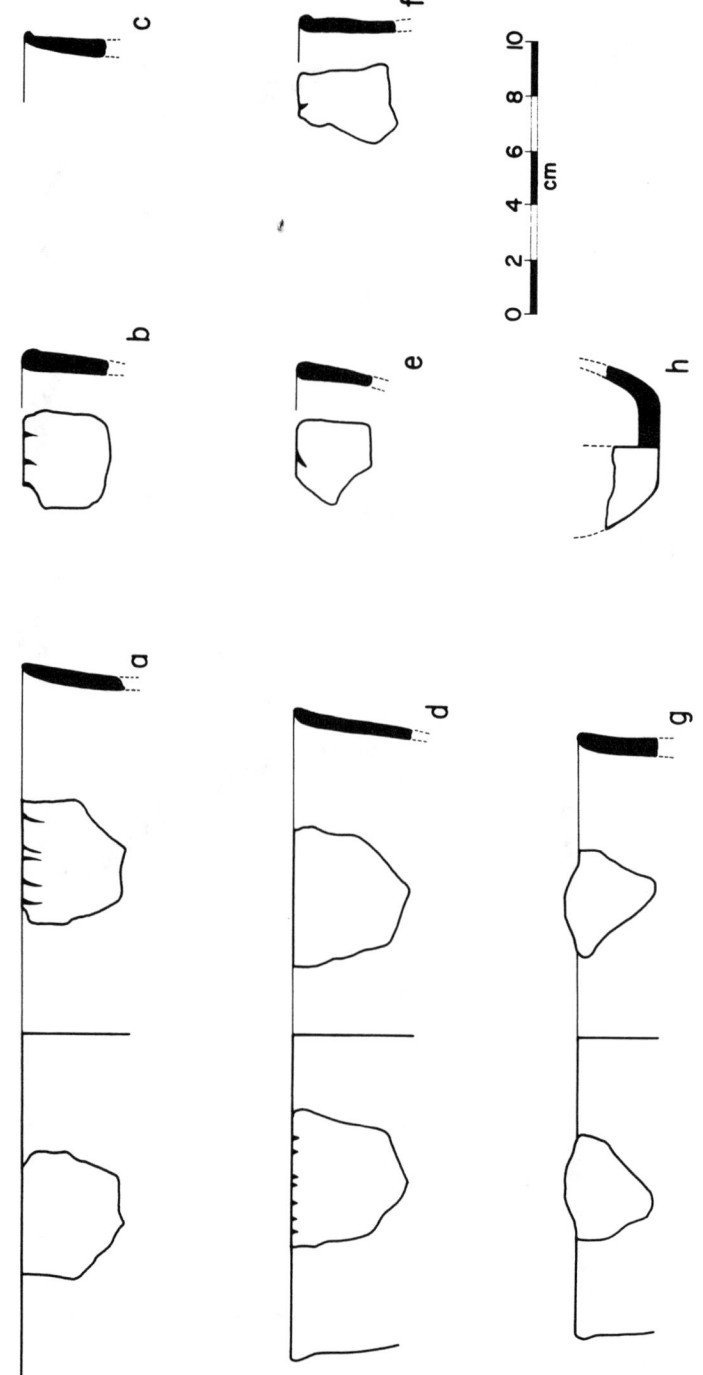

Figure 8.7. Tierras Largas Burnished Plain hemispherical bowls from Tierras Largas (TL) and San José Mogote (SJM). *a*, rim sherd with slashes on interior, Zone G, Area C, SJM. *b*, sherd from slightly beaded rim with interior slashes, Feature 142, Area B, TL. *c*, beaded rim, Structure 5, Area C, SJM. *d*, rim sherd with slashes on exterior, Feature 151, Area C, TL. *e*, *f*, rims with slashes on interior, Feature 142, Area B, TL (*f* is slightly beaded). *g*, sherd from eccentric rim, Feature 151, Area C, TL. *h*, base of small bowl, Feature 117-north, Area B, TL. (All specimens are Tierras Largas phase.)

may have been press-molded inside such vessels. They were then wiped smooth with a wet hand or animal hide, and burnished once with a quartz pebble when leather-hard.

If a deeper bowl was desired, concentric rings of clay could be added to the rim once the vessel had been removed from the bowl. For example, a partially reconstructed bowl from Feature 40 at Tierras Largas (Fig. 8.9) appears to have a rim which was built up 4 cm higher than its press-molded basal portion. Even the burnishing streaks on the bowl cannot completely hide the difference between the press-molded base and the added concentric rings.

Flat-based bowls with outleaned to slightly outcurved walls (Figs. 8.10–8.12a-c). These vessels (abbreviated in our charts as "outleaned-wall bowls") appeared in late Tierras Largas times, and are forerunners of one of the most common shapes of the San José phase. They remind us very much of similar bowls from the Lagunita phase of the Isthmus of Tehuantepec (Zeitlin 1979) and the Ocós phase of the Chiapas-Guatemala coast (Coe 1961). They differ from the typical "outleaned-wall bowl" of the San José phase in two ways. First, their method of manufacture is somewhat different. Second, they more frequently have walls that are slightly concave (i.e., curving slightly rather than simply leaning outward.) However, the outleaned/slightly outcurved walls form enough of a continuum so that we have treated them here as one vessel form, albeit with a range of variation. For one thing, it is often impossible to tell from a small rim sherd whether or not the wall had a slight curve to it.

Rim diameter: 14–30 cm, with an assumed average of about 24 cm.
Basal diameter: 8–24 cm, with an assumed average of about 18 cm (typically, 70% of the rim diameter).
Height: 3–10 cm (typically 30% of the rim diameter).
Wall thickness: Usually 4–10 mm
Basal thickness: Usually 4–12 mm
Volume: About 2 liters on average.
Decoration: Usually none. Some bowls, late in the Tierras Largas phase or early in the San José phase, have rims that are gadrooned, or thickened and grooved on top (Fig. 8.10c-f). Both decorative modes are reminiscent of the Ocós phase at La Victoria (Coe 1961: Fig. 19a-f, Fig. 21f-g). Occasionally, bowls with thickened and grooved rims may be rocker stamped (Fig. 8.11).
Method of manufacture: According to Payne, the flat bases of these bowls would have been made first, by rolling out a large disc of clay on a flat surface coated with dry clay or wood ash. Concentric rings of clay could then be added to produce a wall that varied from outleaned to slightly concave. This method differed from the San José phase technique (to be described later) in which the wall was made separately, from a long strip of clay. The difference in method of manufacture helps to account for the lack of uniformly outleaned walls in Tierras Largas Burnished Plain.

When leather-hard, the vessel was burnished once with a quartz pebble. Linear burnishing marks indicate that the base was burnished while the bowl was held stationary; the walls, on the other hand, were evidently burnished by rotating the vessel while the other hand gripped the pebble.

Other vessel forms (Figs. 8.12d-f, and 8.13–8.15). Tecomates and small bottles were also made in Tierras Largas Burnished Plain, but neither vessel form was particularly common. Some hemispherical or incurved-rim bowls may also have eccentric or unusual rims.

Other decorative modes (Figs. 8.16–8.19). Late in the Tierras Largas phase and early in the San José phase, rocker stamping, dentate stamping, dentate rocker stamping, and punctation were occasionally seen on Tierras Largas Burnished Plain vessels. In some cases it is clear that the vessel was a tecomate or a bottle. In other cases, we are dealing with decorated body sherds that cannot be assigned to a specific vessel form. There is even a form of "micro" rocker stamping, probably on bottles (Figs. 8.18, 8.19).

These plastic decorative attributes are so rare in Tierras Largas Burnished Plain that we suspect they were local imitations of vessels obtained in trade. The rocker stamped bottles make us think immediately of Tlatilco and Tlapacoya in the Basin of Mexico, although that was not the only region producing such vessels.

TIERRAS LARGAS UNBURNISHED PLAIN

General Description

In the course of analyzing some of our Tierras Largas and early San José phase proveniences, we came across a number of sherds that would have been classified as Tierras Largas Burnished Plain except for one fact: they were not burnished.

We kept these sherds separate from Tierras Largas Burnished Plain in case their distribution turned out to be temporally significant. We wondered if a "Tierras Largas Unburnished Plain" might have preceded the burnished version. If this were the case, we might expect to see unburnished bowls and jars give way to burnished bowls and jars over time.

As will be clear from the chronological history of these sherds (below), such was not the case. They were not present in our Espiridión sample (Chapter 7), and were no more frequent in early Tierras Largas than in late Tierras Largas (Tables 9.1–13.1). We therefore concluded that these were simply sherds from vessels originally intended to be Tierras Largas Burnished Plain, but which the potters had never gotten around to burnishing.

We have continued to keep these sherds separate from Tierras Largas Burnished Plain in this volume, not for chronological reasons but for what they tell us about *synchronic* variation. Tierras Largas Unburnished Plain sherds were more frequent at Tierras Largas, a small hamlet, than at San José Mogote, a large

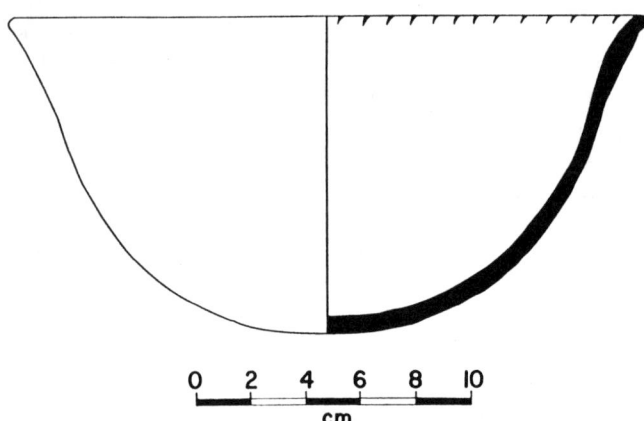

Figure 8.8. Tierras Largas Burnished Plain hemispherical bowl with slightly flaring rim; rim decorated with a series of nicks cut into the clay when it was leather-hard. Feature 40, Tierras Largas (Tierras Largas phase).

village with public buildings. Possibly, therefore, they tell us that ordinary potters in a hamlet were more likely to overlook the step of burnishing Tierras Largas Burnished Plain while it was leather-hard than were the more expert potters at the valley's largest village.

Chronological History

Tierras Largas Unburnished Plain was apparently restricted to the Tierras Largas phase, and occurs mostly in the context of ordinary households. A few sporadic sherds show up in San José phase deposits, but they may simply be redeposited sherds from Tierras Largas levels.

Clay Body, Firing Temperature, and Color

These are identical to Tierras Largas Burnished Plain.

Surface Finish

It was smoothed when wet, but never burnished.

Vessel Forms

Identical to Tierras Largas Burnished Plain, although most unburnished specimens are hemispherical bowls (Figs. 8.20–8.21).

One unburnished hemispherical bowl from the site of Tierras Largas has a crack part way down from the rim. According to Payne, the crack was present before firing. It probably occurred as the pot was drying, and the vessel was later fired without ever having been burnished. Perhaps the potter did not see any point in taking time to burnish a pot that already had a crack in it.

The clay body in this bowl was quite fine, almost fine enough to meet the standards of Clementina Fine Red-on-Buff (see below). This very fineness could also account for the crack, since vessels that lack sufficient nonplastic particles tend to shrink when drying. In general, this vessel reflects inexpert pottery making on several levels.

GENERAL CATEGORY: EARLY HIGHLAND RED-ON-BUFF PAINTED WARES

The transition from the Espiridión complex to the Tierras Largas phase was marked by the first appearance of jars, bottles, and hemispherical bowls in red-painted buff pottery, for which Payne (see Chapter 2 Glossary) prefers the term "red stained." Similar material occurs in the Tehuacán Valley, where the Ajalpan phase is characterized by Coatepec Red-on-Buff and Ajalpan Fine Red (MacNeish, Peterson, and Flannery 1970). Related red-on-buffs occur also at Moyotzingo in the Valley of Puebla (Jörg Aufdermauer, pers. comm.) and in looters' backdirt at Las Bocas, Puebla. In the Valley of Morelos, Cuautla Red-Slipped (Cyphers Guillén 1987:207) is an analogous type. Ronald Spores (1983:46 and pers. comm.) reports red-on-buffs identical to ours in his area K203 at Yucuita in the Nochixtlán-Yanhuitlán Valley. At Rancho Dolores Ortiz, near San Pedro Chicozapotes in the Cañada de Cuicatlán, Adriana Alaniz (1975) of the Centro Regional de Oaxaca (INAH) recovered similar ceramics. Farther away, the pottery type Pilli Red-on-Buff from Tlapacoya-Zohapilco (Niederberger 1987:562) resembles our material.

Thus, numerous highland valleys, from the Basin of Mexico south to Oaxaca, have red-on-buff hemispherical bowls, bottles, and jars similar enough to show widespread interaction at a time equivalent to our Tierras Largas phase. We do not see this complex, however, extending east into Veracruz or south past Tehuantepec (see Clark 1991: Fig. 8). In those tropical lowland areas, red-on-buff ceramics usually took the form of tecomates with plastic decoration. We now consider this "red-rimmed tecomate tradition" (Coe and Flannery 1967:25) to be a lowland phenomenon, more usefully contrasted with the red-rimmed hemispherical bowl tradition of the highlands than combined with it. That does not mean that red-rimmed tecomates did not reach the highlands; it simply means that the two areas look very different in terms of the relative proportions of vessel forms. The predominant utilitarian vessel of the lowlands was the neckless jar (tecomate); the predominant utilitarian vessel of the highlands was the necked jar (olla).

Local Oaxaca Types

After considerable contemplation, we have created two local Oaxaca red-on-buff pottery types: Avelina Red-on-Buff and Clementina Fine Red-on-Buff. The two types are not strikingly dissimilar, and we would not be upset in the future if they were treated simply as two varieties within the same type. For the present, however, we have decided to keep them separate until we know more about their synchronic and diachronic variation. Avelina Red-on-Buff, always the more common, was coarser and

Figure 8.9. Top and side views of Tierras Largas Burnished Plain hemispherical bowl with notches cut on rim. Feature 40, Tierras Largas (Tierras Largas phase).

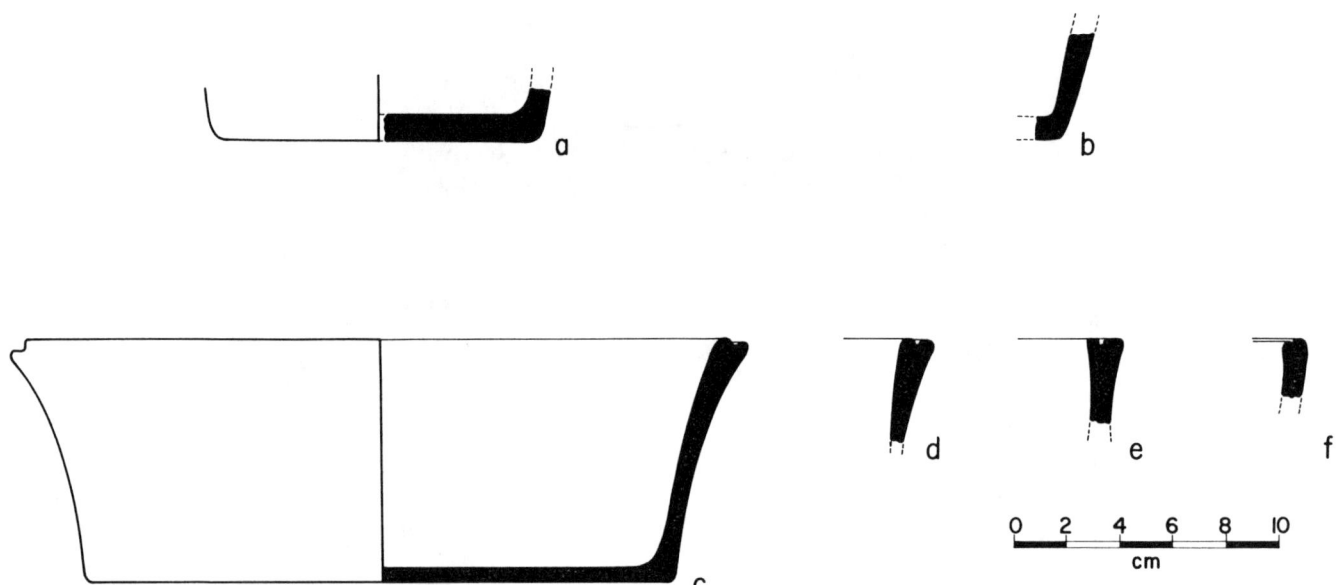

Figure 8.10. Tierras Largas Burnished Plain flat-based bowls from Tierras Largas (TL) and San José Mogote (SJM). *a*, basal sherd, Feature 148, Area C, TL. *b*, basal sherd, Zone G, Area C, SJM. *c*, flat-based bowl with "Ocós-like" grooved rim, Feature 142, Area B, TL. *d-f*, grooved rims from bowls similar to *c*, Area A, SJM (*d*, Household Unit C4; *e*, Household Unit C1; *f*, Household Unit C2). *a-c*, Tierras Largas phase; *d-f*, San José phase.

Figure 8.11. Two sherds from Tierras Largas Burnished Plain bowls with thickened rim; grooved on top of the rim, and decorated on the exterior with zoned rocker stamping. Area D, Tierras Largas (Tierras Largas phase).

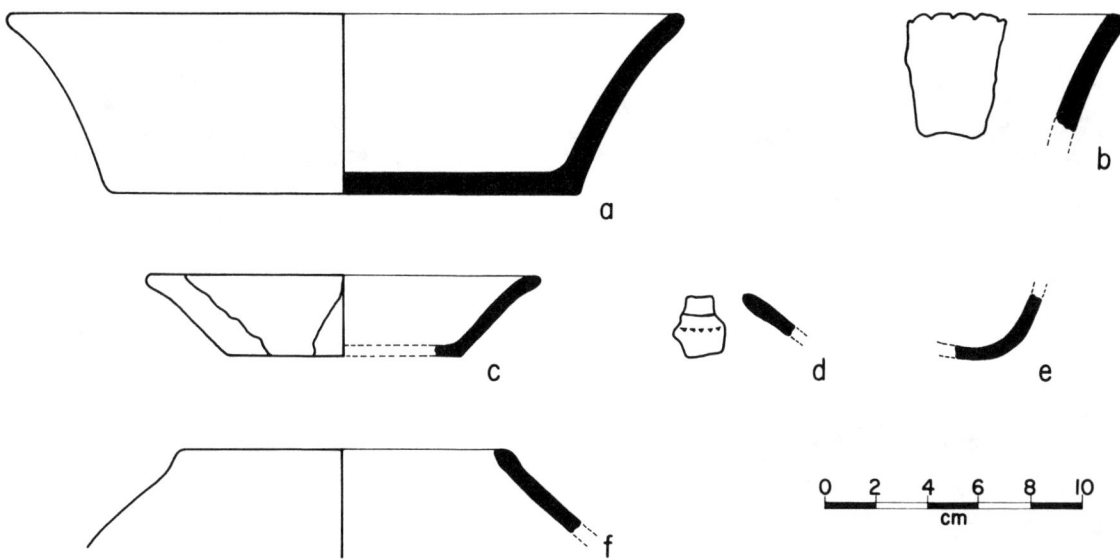

Figure 8.12. Tierras Largas Burnished Plain vessels from Tierras Largas (TL) and San José Mogote (SJM). *a,* flat-based bowl from Feature 86, TL. *b,* rim sherd with notches (probably from a bowl like *a*), Structure 5, Area C, SJM. *c,* small flat-based bowl, Feature 151, Area C, TL. *d,* rim of dentate-stamped tecomate (exterior view and profile), Household Unit C1, Area A, SJM (see also Fig. 8.13). *e,* basal angle sherd from bowl with dimpled base, Zone G, Area C, SJM. *f,* tecomate with turned-up rim, Feature 160-west, Area D, TL. (*a, b, c, e,* Tierras Largas phase; *d, f,* San José phase.)

Figure 8.13. Tierras Largas Burnished Plain tecomate rim with zoned dentate stamping, Household Unit C1, Area A, San José Mogote (San José phase). For a profile drawing of this sherd, see Figure 8.12*d*.

tended to be used more often for jars than for bottles. Clementina Fine Red-on-Buff, rarely used for jars, seems to be more common in affluent areas of larger villages.

AVELINA RED-ON-BUFF

General Description

Avelina Red-on-Buff is essentially Tierras Largas Burnished Plain to which a red iron-oxide paint has been added. Since the paint is often limited to a band encircling the rim of a hemispherical bowl, unpainted sherds from the lower parts of such bowls would have been classified by us as Tierras Largas Burnished Plain. Thus our sherd counts unavoidably inflate the numbers of Tierras Largas Burnished Plain sherds and deflate the numbers of Avelina Red-on-Buff sherds. Here is a case where one could get a more accurate impression of relative numbers by counting only rim sherds and ignoring body sherds.

Avelina Red-on-Buff differs from its sister type, Clementina Fine Red-on-Buff, in having a relatively coarser clay body, a darker core, a more crumbly texture, and a much higher proportion of jars. It also shows a wider range of painted designs, but this may only be because it is so much more common.

The red iron oxide pigment was sometimes simply painted on the surface of the vessel, a technique called "staining." In other cases (especially when one whole surface of the vessel was to

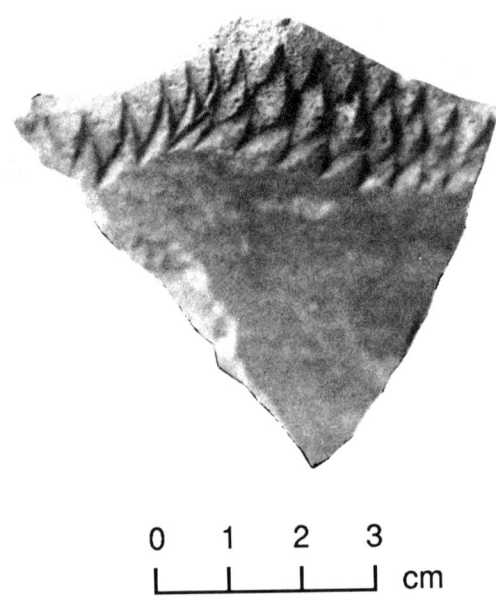

Figure 8.14. Sherds from Tierras Largas Burnished Plain bowls with thickened, incurved rims decorated with incised "rim ticking." Feature 116, Area B, Tierras Largas (Tierras Largas phase).

Figure 8.15. Sherd from Tierras Largas Burnished Plain bowl with eccentric rim, decorated on the exterior with rocker stamping. San José Mogote, Area C, fill in west end of Structure 6 (Tierras Largas phase).

be covered), it could be mixed with clay to form an actual red slip. It was not always possible to tell (especially on eroded sherds) which technique was used, so they have not been distinguished in our sherd counts.

Chronological History

Avelina Red-on-Buff appeared at the start of the Tierras Largas phase in the form of necked jars and hemispherical bowls. Both vessel shapes were like their counterparts in Tierras Largas Burnished Plain, and jars had interior surfaces that could be pocked, wiped, or plain. Hemispherical bowls had a red band at the rim (inside and out) at the very least, and sometimes had more extensive areas of red.

This type reached its peak of popularity and variety in late Tierras Largas times. In the case of jars, the most common traits were a wiped interior surface and curvilinear red bands painted on the exterior. In the case of hemispherical bowls, the most common forms of decoration were (1) a red rim band inside and out; (2) an all-red exterior with a rim band on the interior; (3) an all-red interior with a rim band on the exterior; (4) a design on one surface, with the opposite side left plain below the rim band; and (5) all red inside and out. Tecomates were rare and had no plastic decoration, just a simple red band at the rim.

Avelina Red-on-Buff survived into the early San José phase, though in lower frequency. Jars were rare by then, and pocked interiors had completely given way to wiped or plain interiors. Hemispherical bowls showed the same range of decorative modes, but declined in numbers as a later pottery type, San José Red-on-White, increased in popularity. By late San José times, Avelina had decreased to the point of rarity; there were almost no jars left in that type, and hemispherical bowls were almost always of the simplest type—the one with a simple red band at the rim. Of the other decorative modes, only the bowl with an all-red exterior and a rim band on the interior appeared with any frequency.

By the Guadalupe phase, Avelina Red-on-Buff was gone.

Clay Body

The clay body used for Avelina Red-on-Buff is a residual clay derived from decomposed Precambrian gneiss. It contains about 50% clay minerals and 50% nonplastic particles including quartz, feldspar, iron micas, hornblende, and augite. The clay was used as found except for removing the larger aplastic particles; it was neither refined, nor selected, as carefully as the clay body for Clementina Fine Red-on-Buff. As a result, Avelina Red-on-Buff contains numerous aplastic particles 1.0 mm in diameter, and occasional particles up to 4.0 mm.

Figure 8.16. Tierras Largas Burnished Plain body sherds with plastic decoration, all from Tierras Largas. *Top left,* plain rocker stamping, Feature 152-south, Area B. *Top right,* zoned rocker stamping, Feature 142, Area B. *Bottom,* interrupted rocker stamping with red pigment rubbed in, Feature 192, Area K. (All specimens Tierras Largas phase.)

The Avelina clay body substantially overlaps with that of Tierras Largas Burnished Plain, but jars in Tierras Largas Burnished Plain can contain even coarser particles than Avelina. According to Payne, jars in both wares were probably given a coarser clay body so that thicker and larger vessels could be produced. Such coarse vessels have greater resistance to thermal shock, which means that jars (in contrast to bowls) could be heated over a fire.

Firing Temperature

This ware was fired at roughly 700° C in an oxidizing atmosphere, perhaps in the open as is done today in San Marcos Tlapazola.

Color

Unpainted surfaces range from light brown (7.5 YR 6/4) to reddish brown (5 YR 4/4) with black firing clouds (10 YR 2/1). Cores are usually dark gray (10 YR 3/1), suggesting that firing was done at lower temperatures and under less controlled conditions than was the case with Clementina Fine Red-on-Buff. Painted (or slipped) surfaces vary fom brick red (10 R 4/4) when completely oxidized, to dusky red (10 R 3/3–3/4) on firing clouds.

Surface Treatment

Bowls were burnished with a quartz pebble on both surfaces after the red pigment had been applied. The burnishing streaks resemble those on Tierras Largas Burnished Plain. Jars were burnished on the exterior, and down inside the neck as far as the shoulder. Below that, they displayed the same wiped, plain, or (less frequently) pocked interior surfaces in Tierras Largas Burnished Plain. Tecomates were burnished on the outside, and a short distance down from the rim on the inside. Their interiors were generally wiped with the hand or a piece of hide while wet, leaving a plain interior like that seen on some jars.

Figure 8.17. Tierras Largas Burnished Plain body sherds with plastic decoration. *Left,* tecomate body sherd with zoned rocker stamping, San José Mogote, Zone G, Area C (Tierras Largas phase). *Right,* bowl body sherd with dentate stamping in columns; found on the surface of an Early Formative site at San Bartolo Coyotepec (Site 3–1–2 of the Valley of Oaxaca survey [Kowalewski et al. 1989: Fig. 3.1]).

Figure 8.19. Tierras Largas Burnished Plain body sherds with "micro" rocker stamping, shown twice natural size. Area D, Tierras Largas (Tierras Largas phase).

Figure 8.18 (left). Tierras Largas Burnished Plain sherd, possibly from a bottle. This sherd has very fine zoned "micro" rocker stamping in neat columns. Household Unit C3, Area A, San José Mogote (San José phase). Shown twice natural size.

Tierras Largas Phase

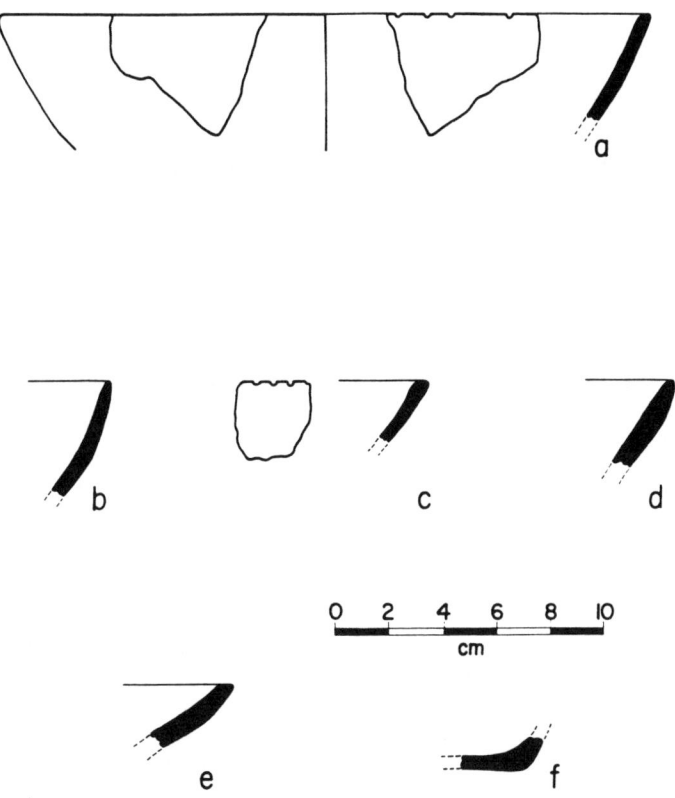

Figure 8.20. Tierras Largas Unburnished Plain bowls from Tierras Largas (TL) and San José Mogote (SJM). *a,* sherd from hemispherical bowl with punch marks on rim, Feature 75, TL. *b,* plain rim from hemispherical bowl, Feature 117, TL. *c,* notched rim from hemispherical bowl, Feature 75, TL. *d,* plain rim from hemispherical bowl, Feature 75, TL. *e,* plain bowl rim, Zone G, Area C, SJM. *f,* sherd from bowl base, Zone G, Area C, SJM. (All specimens Tierras Largas phase.)

Figure 8.21. Possible Tierras Largas Unburnished Plain body sherd, roughened by what appears to have been a comb or multi-toothed instrument of some kind. Area B, Tierras Largas (Tierras Largas phase).

Red Pigment

One of the diagnostic features of Avelina Red-on-Buff is the decoration of vessel surfaces with red iron oxide pigment, most often in the form of stripes or bands. Iron oxide in different stages of decomposition, and from different deposits, was used. It is not always possible to identify the type of pigment used, but at least two general varieties are evident.

Both magnetite and hematite occur in the Precambrian metamorphic formations of the Valley of Oaxaca. In their best preserved form, they could be made into iron-ore mirrors. In their most decomposed forms, they are broken down to the iron oxide which gives certain clay lenses their red color. One variety of red pigment—the one most commonly used for Avelina—was a completely disintegrated iron oxide. The other, used much less frequently, still contains recognizable fragments of sparkling hematite. Called "specular hematite," it was probably considered superior by Tierras Largas potters, because it was more often used on Clementina Fine Red-on-Buff. However, both varieties of iron oxide are locally available in the Precambrian gneiss of the Valley of Oaxaca, and traces of red pigment on metates and manos indicate that both were ground before being turned into a stain or slip.

Payne's experiments have shown that even clay with an iron content no greater than 2–3% can be mixed with water to form a slurry or simple red slip. When richer iron oxide pigment is added to this, the result is a slip that bonds well with the vessel surface and turns brick red. The makers of Avelina Red-on-Buff used a variety of pigments, some applied as a simple stain or paint, and some applied as a red slip. Because all the iron oxide deposits had some clay content, it is often impossible to know where to draw the line between the two.

Vessel Forms

Jars (Fig. 8.22). Like the Tierras Largas Burnished Plain jars already described, these vessels were made in two sections, each press-molded over an inverted jar. A hole was left in one section so that the neck could be built up by adding concentric rings. After the two molded halves had been joined by luting, the neck was finished and the jar allowed to dry until it was leather-hard. The red iron oxide stain was then applied, either with a brush or a swab of animal fur. Finally, the jar was burnished with a quartz pebble in the manner of Tierras Largas Burnished Plain vessels.

Rim diameter: 10–30 cm
  Height: Like that of comparable Tierras Largas Burnished Plain examples.
Wall thickness: 8–12 mm
Volume: Up to several gallons (few restorable examples were available for measurement).
Surface finish: On the outside, these jars show the same streaky burnishing seen on Tierras Largas Burnished Plain vessels. On the inside, they also show the same three modes of surface finish—pocked interiors, wiped interiors, or plain interiors.
Decoration: Red bands on the inside and outside of the rim. The exterior band may be accompanied by stripes or inverted chevrons extending down to the shoulder of the vessel. Designs can be rectilinear or curvilinear.

Hemispherical bowls (Figs. 8.23–8.28). These bowls resemble their Tierras Largas Burnished Plain counterparts, except for the fact that they are slightly less likely to have a flat, circular facet or a dimple on the base; many examples have completely rounded bases. While a great many Avelina Red-on-Buff hemispherical bowls were press-molded over gourds or previously made ceramic bowls, some show signs of having been built up differently. In the latter case, the potter seems to have begun with a flat disc of clay for the base, rotating it in one hand while he punched and squeezed it into a cuplike shape. Concentric rings of clay could then be added until the bowl had reached its desired depth, with each ring pinched to the next and finally smoothed to reduce the traces of manufacture.

A few Avelina Red-on-Buff bowls have "pinched-in sides"—that is, an area just below the rim where, on opposite sides, the wall has been pushed inward (Fig. 8.26b). Niederberger (1987) calls such vessels *bols pincés*.

Rim diameter: 14–28 cm, with a mode of about 20 cm and a mean in the 20–24 cm range.
Height: Usually 8–14 cm, with a mode of about 10 cm (50% of the modal rim diameter).
Wall thickness: 4–8 mm
Surface finish: Smoothed when wet, burnished once when leather-hard.
Volume: A complete example from Feature 24 at the site of Tierras Largas, with a rim diameter of 18 cm and a height of 11 cm, had a volume of 1.55 liters. Another from Feature 91 at the same site, with a rim diameter of 24 cm and a height of 13.5 cm, had a volume of 3.32 liters. Most probably had volumes in the 1.5–3.0 liter range.
Decoration: All examples have a red band at the rim, almost always on both sides (rare examples might have a rim band only on the exterior). While this was the most common form of decoration, our sherd counts reveal a great variety of additional decorative modes, peaking in late Tierras Largas. These included horizontal or diagonal stripes, chevrons, and other motifs. Plain interiors or exteriors could be contrasted with designs on the opposite surface. All-red interiors or exteriors could be combined with plain opposite surfaces, designs on the opposite surface, or all-red opposite surfaces. In short, virtually every combination could occur.

Tecomates (Figs. 8.22e, 8.29). These globular neckless jars were made in the same manner as the bodies of the jars already described: the two halves were made separately by press-molding pats of clay over the inverted lower portion of an old vessel. One

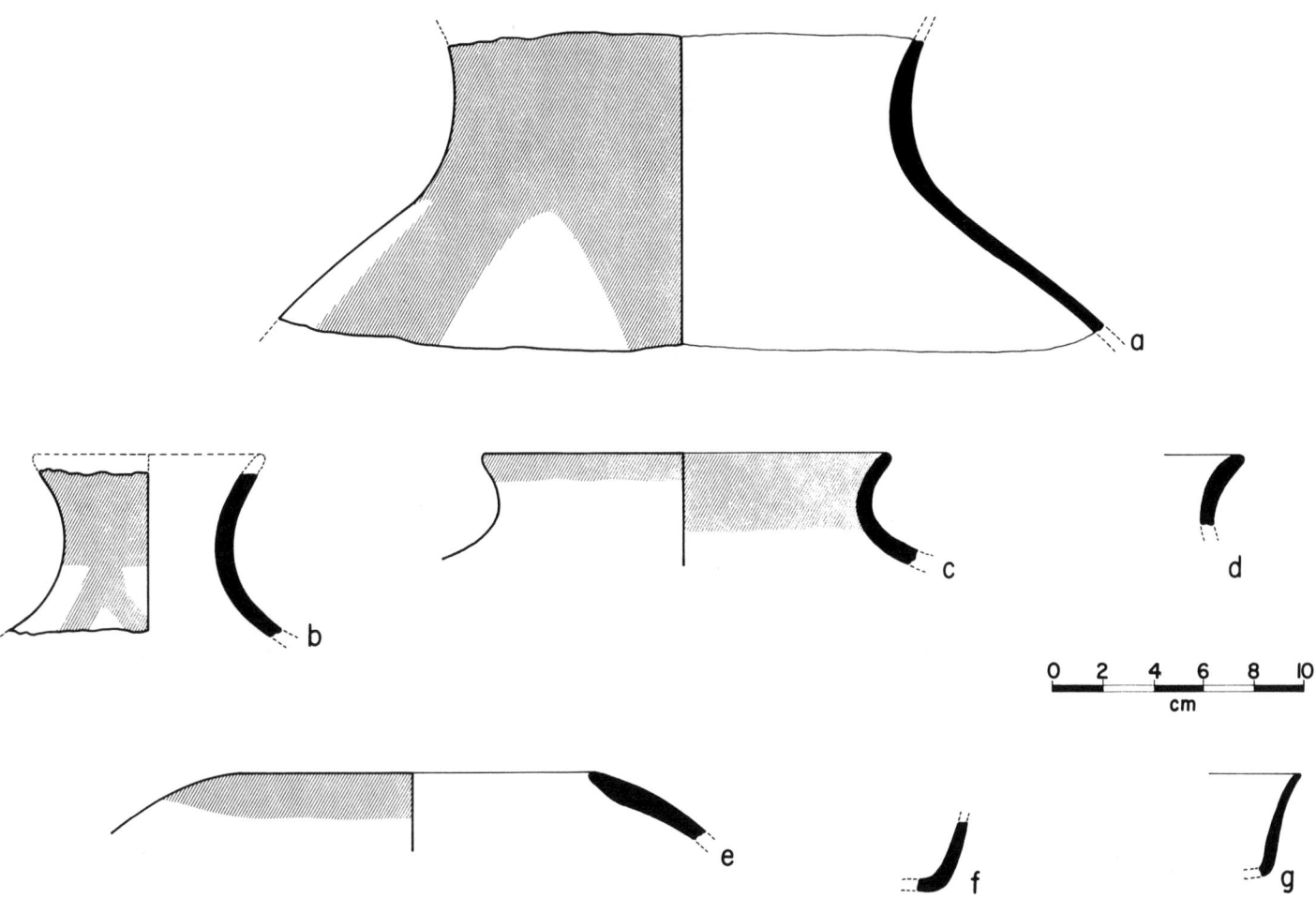

Figure 8.22. Avelina Red-on-Buff jars, tecomates, and minor vessel forms from Tierras Largas (TL) and San José Mogote (SJM). *a,* jar shoulder with nonspecular red stripes on outside, Zone G, Area C, SJM. *b,* jar shoulder with specular red stripes on outside, lightly burnished but plain buff inside, Feature 117, TL. *c,* jar rim with red bands inside and outside, Feature 142, TL. *d,* jar rim with traces of red band, Feature 142, TL. *e,* tecomate with nonspecular band at rim outside, no incised line delimiting rim band, Feature 75, TL. *f,* base of small vessel (probably a bowl or bottle) with specular red exterior, Household Unit C2, Area A, SJM. *g,* rim of small bowl with traces of red geometric design outside, Feature 117, TL. (*b, c, d, e,* and *g* are all from Household Unit LTL-1, Area B, TL, a Late Tierras Largas phase provenience.)

half was made with a hole for the mouth; after the two halves were luted, the neck was wiped with a damp piece of hide to smooth and shape the rim.

Rim diameter: 16–20 cm
Height: Unknown
Wall thickness: 4–10 mm
Volume: Unknown, but probably several gallons.
Decoration: A red band of paint at the rim.

Minor vessel forms (Fig. 8.22f, g). A few small bowls were also found, resembling the smallest of the flat-based bowls with outleaned walls in Tierras Largas Burnished Plain, but with the addition of red slip on the exterior. In some cases this took the form of geometric designs; in other cases, the whole exterior was slipped red.

CLEMENTINA FINE RED-ON-BUFF

General Description

Clementina Fine Red-on-Buff is a well-made, hard-fired, fine-grained ware used mainly for hemispherical bowls. The clay body is similiar to that used for Avelina Red-on-Buff, but is noticeably finer as the result of careful winnowing to remove large aplastic particles, and appears to have been *decanted* (see Chapter 2 Glossary). It also differs from Avelina in the fact that

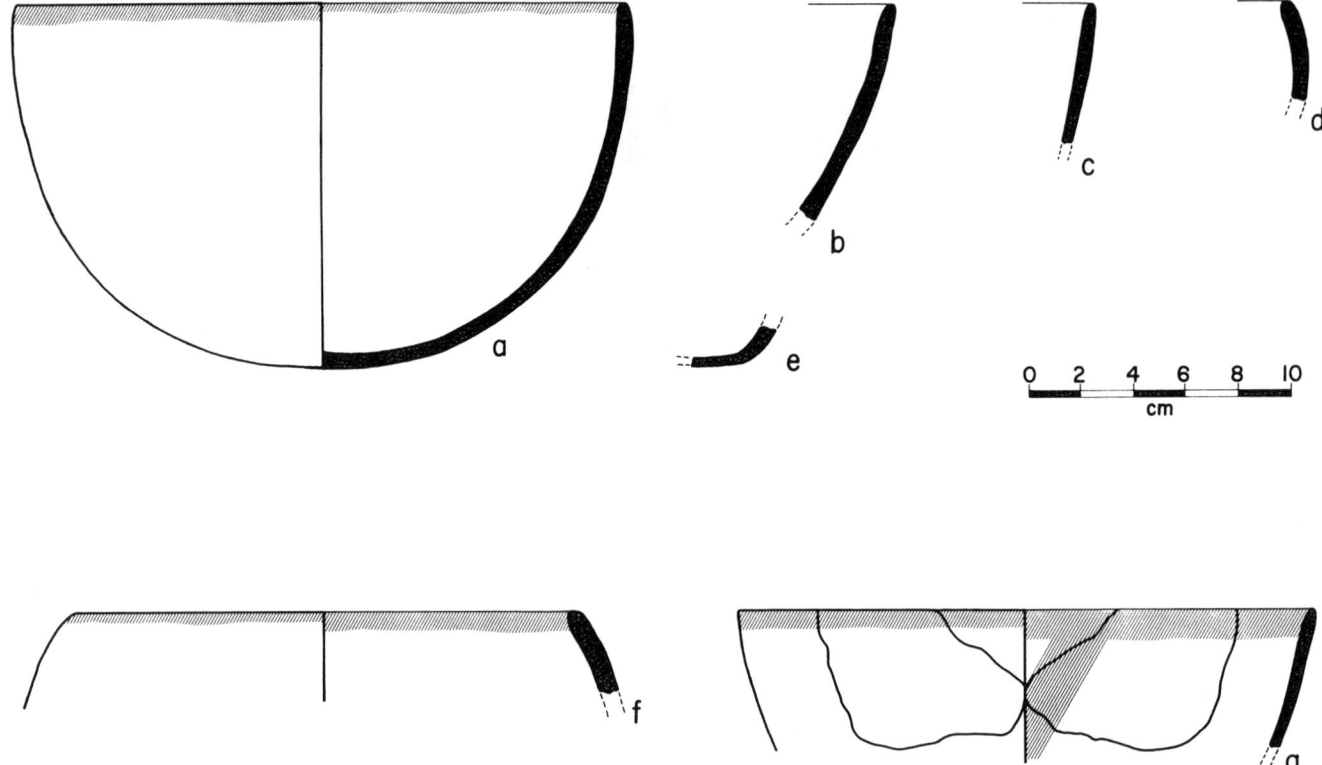

Figure 8.23. Avelina Red-on-Buff hemispherical bowls from Tierras Largas (TL) and San José Mogote (SJM). *a*, bowl with red band at rim inside and out, Feature 91, TL. (A red band at the rim inside and out was the most common attribute found on hemispherical bowls in this type.) *b*, bowl with red band at rim on inside only, Feature 142, TL. *c*, bowl similar to *b*, Feature 151, TL. *d*, bowl with red band at rim inside, totally red outside, Feature 117, TL. *e*, basal angle sherd, totally specular red outside, Feature 75, TL. *f*, bowl with unusually restricted mouth, red band at rim inside and out, Household Unit C4, Area A, SJM. *g*, bowl with specular red band at rim inside and out, diagonal bands inside, Feature 151, TL. (*a–e* and *g*, Tierras Largas phase; *f*, San José phase.)

its red stain or slip is much more likely to be specular hematite. While Clementina bowls show a variety of design modes (red rim bands, geometric motifs, all-red surfaces contrasted with plain surfaces), they lack the extreme variety seen in Avelina.

Clementina Fine Red-on-Buff is a rarer type than Avelina, and is more frequently seen at large villages like San José Mogote than at smaller hamlets like Tierras Largas. For example, only 29 Clementina sherds were found in Features 142 and 148, two large bell-shaped pits at Tierras Largas; indeed, only 58 Clementina sherds were recovered from the major features of Household Unit LTL-1 at that hamlet (see Table 10.1, Chapter 10). In contrast, 143 Clementina sherds were found in a relatively small section of Zone G, Area C, at San José Mogote, and 20 more were found in an even smaller sample of construction fill in Structure 5 of the same village (see Chapters 11 and 13). This distribution suggests that Clementina Fine Red-on-Buff was somewhat of a luxury ware.

Jars are virtually nonexistent in Clementina Fine Red-on-Buff, perhaps because the finer clay body would not have provided the resistance to thermal shock seen in coarser wares like Tierras Largas Burnished Plain or Avelina Red-on-Buff. However, precisely because of its fine clay body, Clementina was used for specular hematite–slipped bottles, miniature vessels, and an occasional exotic shape like the "double vessel" seen in Figure 8.36. For all these reasons we have treated it here as a separate pottery type rather than simply a fine variety of Avelina Red-on-Buff.

Chronological History

Clementina Fine Red-on-Buff had a temporal span not unlike that of Avelina Red-on-Buff. Present from the beginning of the Tierras Largas phase (but in low frequency), it reached its peak in late Tierras Largas times. Most bottles and exotic vessels occurred in the late Tierras Largas phase, with hemispherical bowls generally present throughout the history of the type. Clementina lasted into the San José phase, but by late San José times the hemispherical bowl with a simple red rim band (inside and out) was the only surviving vestige of the ware. It was gone by the Guadalupe phase.

As suggested above, Clementina Fine Red-on-Buff shows considerable synchronic variation, because it was present in greatest frequency and displays the greatest variety of decorative modes at the largest village in the valley.

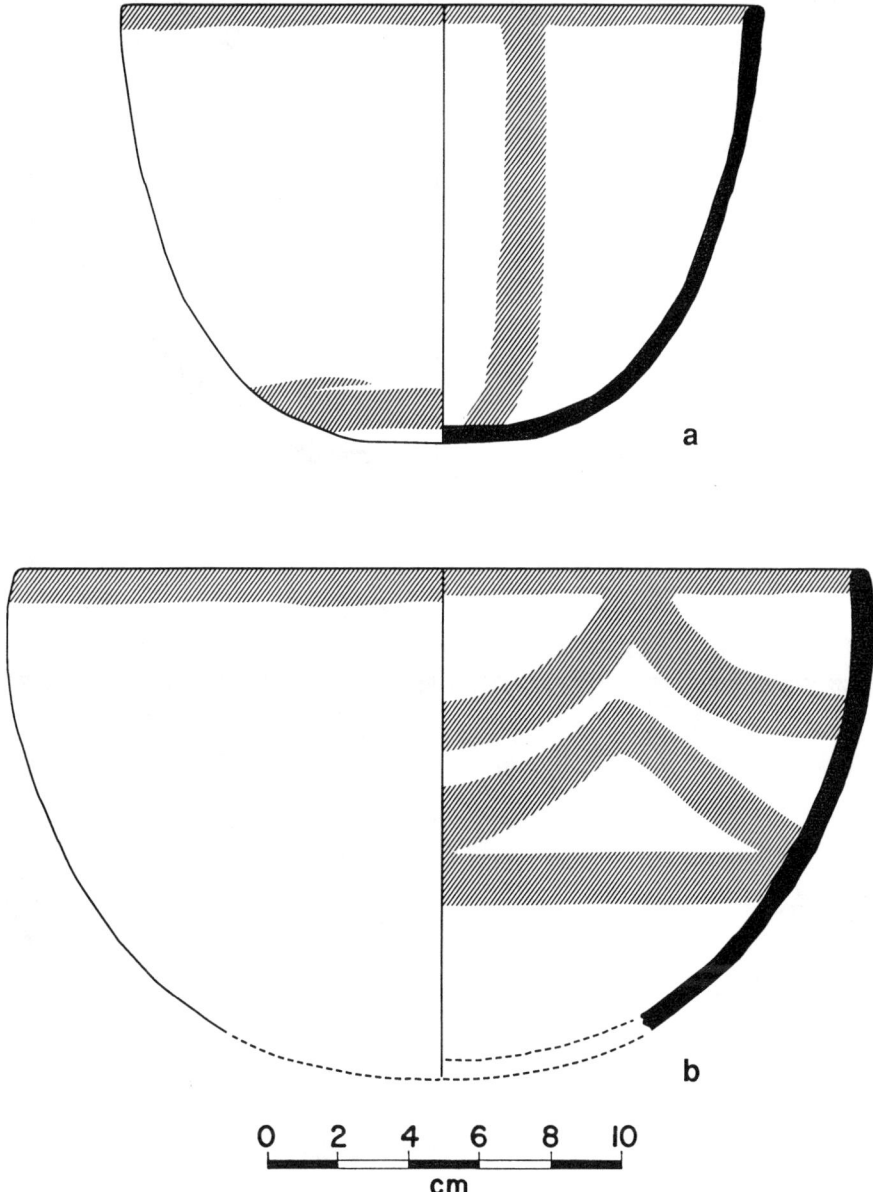

Figure 8.24. Reconstruction drawings of Avelina Red-on-Buff hemispherical bowls from Tierras Largas (Tierras Largas phase). *a,* bowl with red band at rim inside and out, vertical band inside, sloppy horizontal band at the base outside; the red is nonspecular (Feature 24). *b,* bowl with red band at rim inside and out, curvilinear design (nested chevrons or "sergeant's stripes") inside; the red is specular (Feature 58).

78   *Early Formative Pottery of Oaxaca*

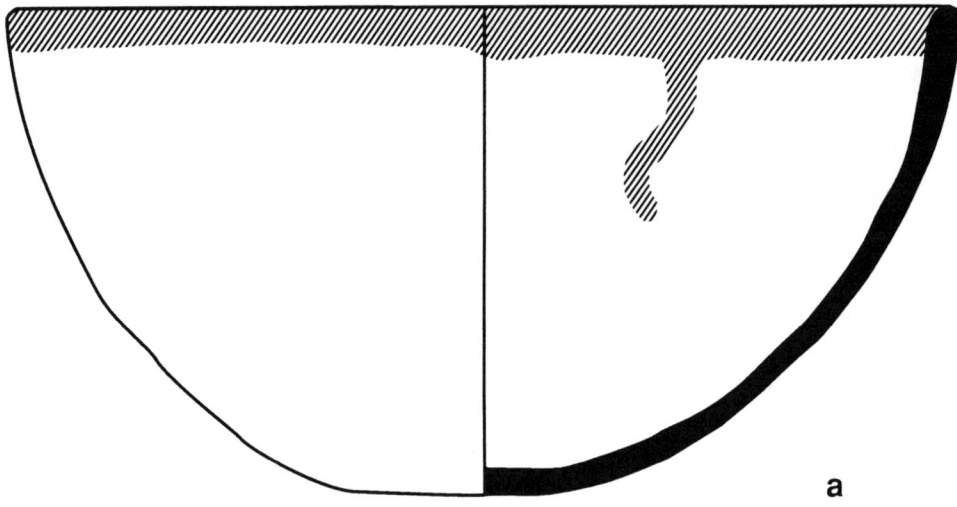

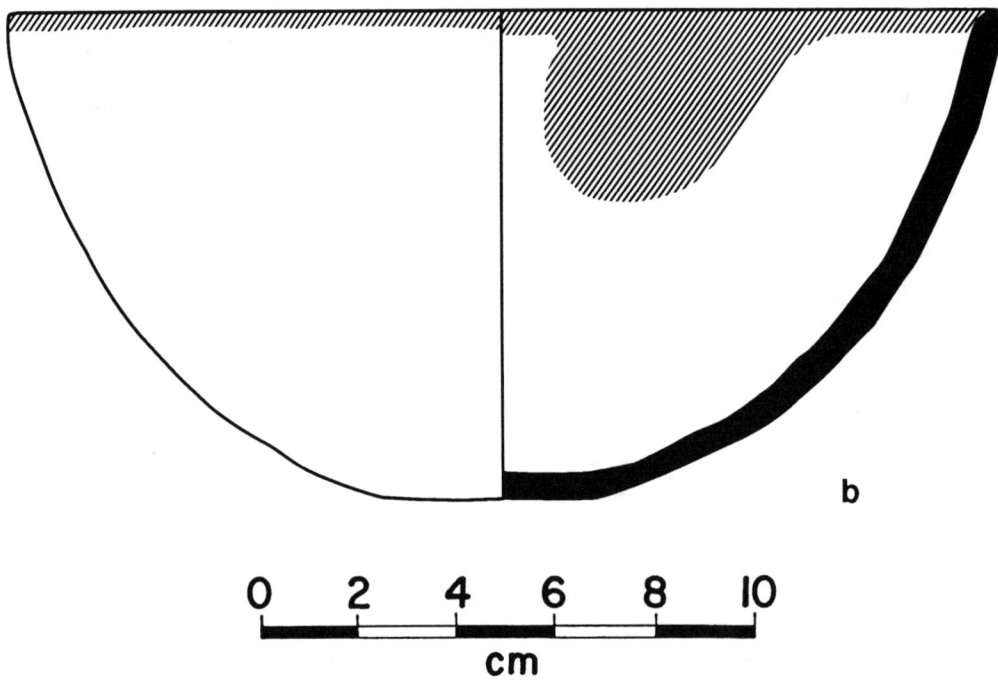

Figure 8.25. Reconstruction drawings of Avelina Red-on-Buff hemispherical bowls from Tierras Largas (Tierras Largas phase). *a,* bowl with red band at rim inside and out, and a wiggly vertical line descending from the rim inside; the red is nonspecular (Feature 73). *b,* bowl with red band at rim inside and out, and a sloppy circular bulge descending from the rim inside; the red is dull brick-red, and nonspecular (Feature 142).

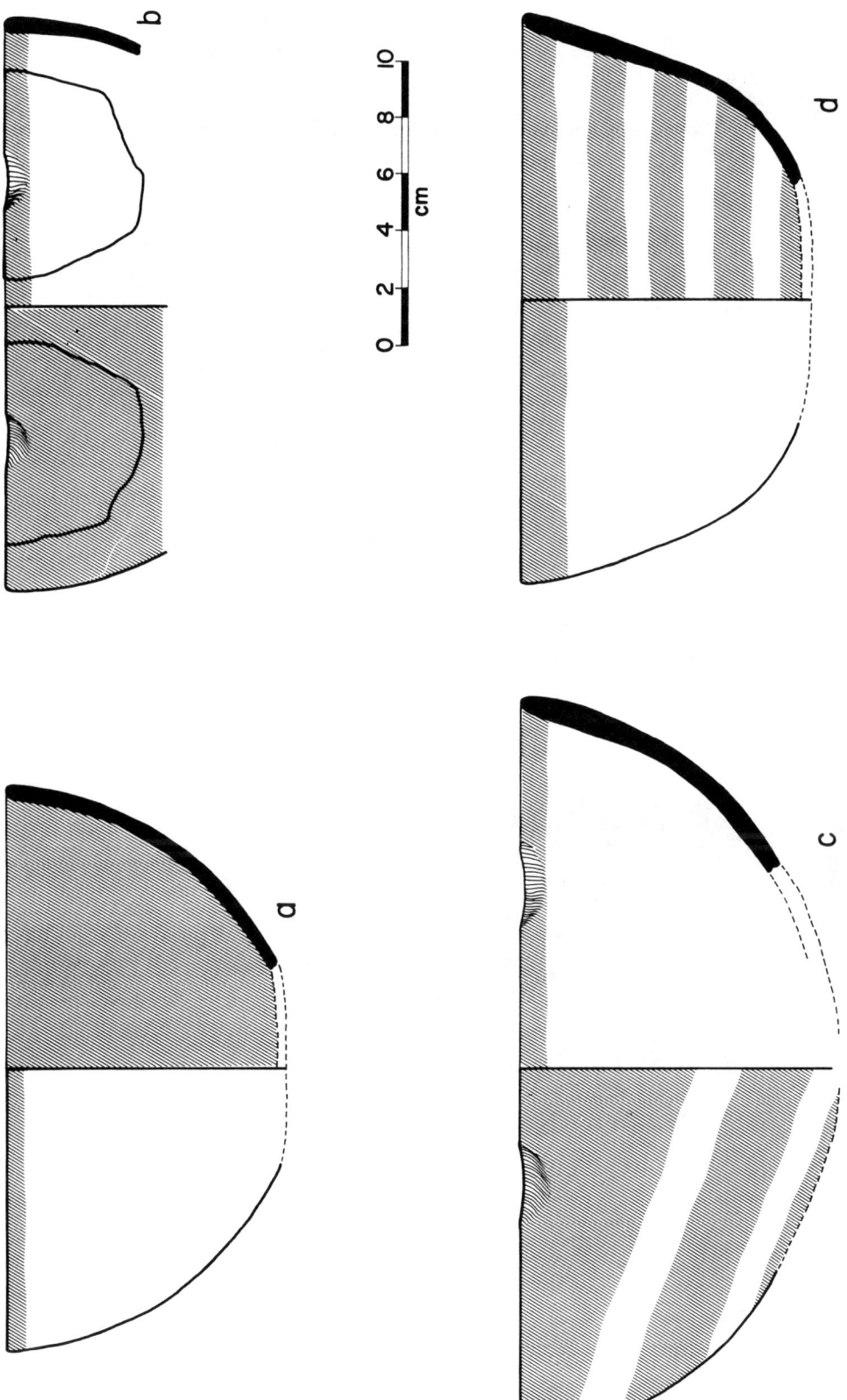

Figure 8.26. Reconstruction drawings of Avelina Red-on-Buff hemispherical bowls from Tierras Largas (Tierras Largas phase). *a*, bowl with red band at rim outside, all red inside (Feature 75). *b*, bowl with pinched-in sides, red band at rim inside, all red outside (Feature 148). *c*, bowl with pinched-in sides, red band at rim inside, geometric design (diagonal stripes) outside (Feature 57A). *d*, bowl with red band at rim outside, geometric design (horizontal stripes) inside; the red is specular (Feature 117). For a photo of *d*, see Fig. 8.27.

Figure 8.27. Avelina Red-on-Buff hemispherical bowl with red band at rim outside, geometric design (horizontal stripes) inside; the red is specular. Feature 117, Area B, Tierras Largas (Tierras Largas phase). For a reconstruction drawing of this vessel, see Fig. 8.26*d*.

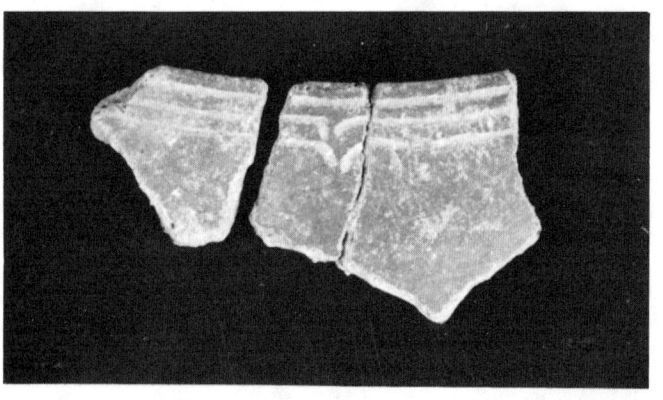

Figure 8.28. Three rim sherds from an unusual Avelina Red-on-Buff bowl with slightly restricted orifice. The bowl is slipped specular red outside and has a specular red band at the rim inside, below which is plain buff. It is incised on the outside with three parallel lines, two of which seem to form "music brackets" of the type associated with the were-jaguar. This bowl was found in San José phase levels at Operation A, San Sebastián Abasolo. Two of the sherds were found in Zone E2, while a third (which fitted together with one of those from E2) had been redeposited in Zone D2.

Tierras Largas Phase

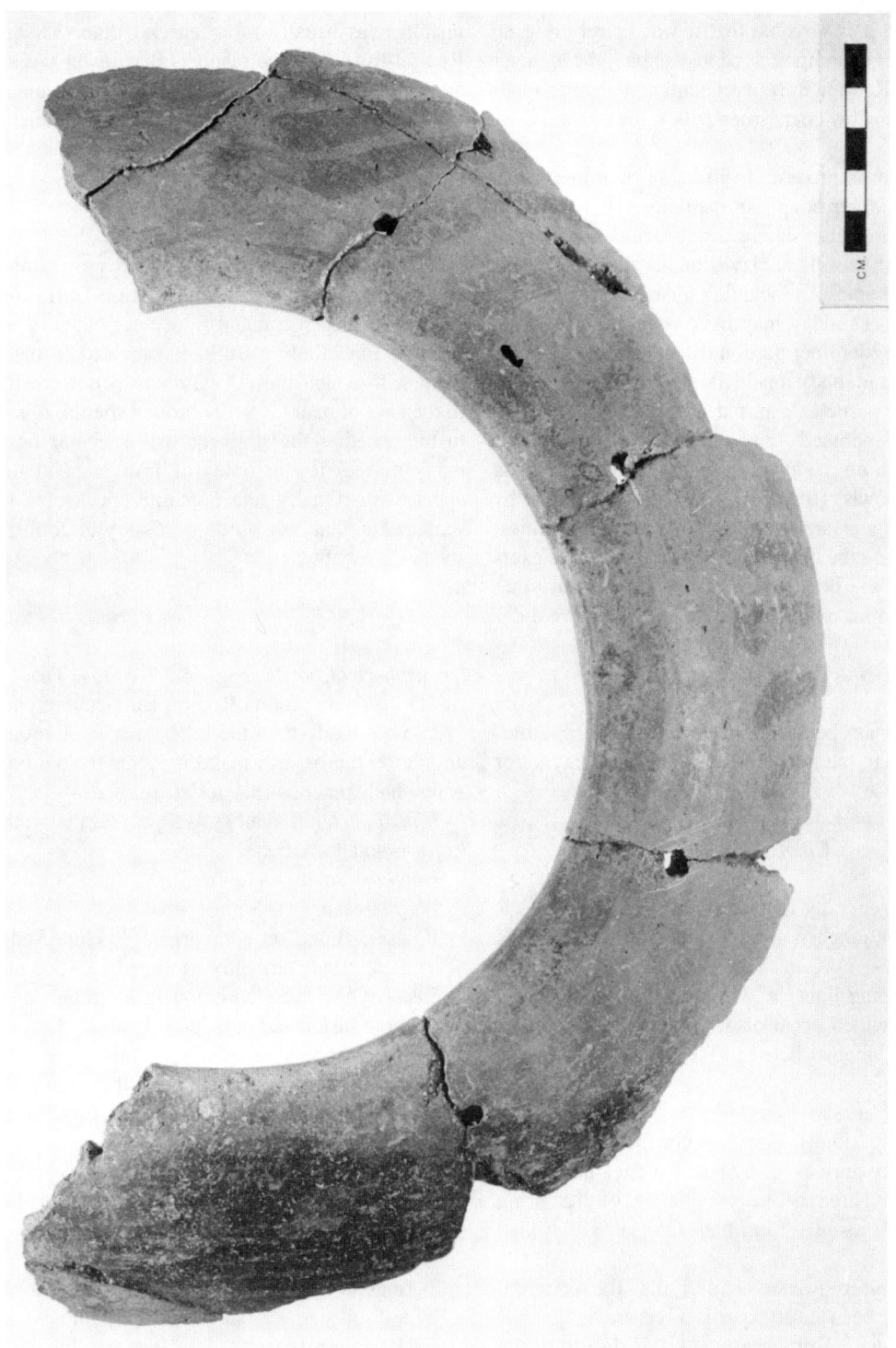

Figure 8.29. Overhead view of a badly weathered Avelina Red-on-Buff tecomate from Feature 116, Tierras Largas (Tierras Largas phase). This specimen has a red band at the rim, and what appear to be red finger streaks on the body below that. It has also been perforated for suspension.

Clay Body

The clay body used for Clementina Fine Red-on-Buff is a residual piedmont clay derived from the weathering of Precambrian gneiss. However, it is possible that it was merely dug up from deeper and more decomposed deposits than the coarser clays used in Avelina Red-on-Buff. Frequently, the same piedmont arroyo profile will show coarser deposits at the top and finer clays lower down.

This raw clay body was processed, probably by winnowing, in order to remove the larger nonplastic particles. This seems to have been done very carefully, since particle size does not usually exceed 0.05 mm. The resultant clay contains about 50% clay minerals and 50% small aplastics including quartz, feldspar, iron micas, and hornblende. The clay may have been allowed to sit for a while before having its finer portion decanted for use.

Use of a finely sorted body made it possible to construct vessels without aplastic particles exposed in the walls. Resultant surfaces are well smoothed and eventually burnished. Hemispherical bowls are on the average denser, harder, and less crumbly than Avelina bowls. However, we acknowledge that the coarsest Clementina bowls are close in texture to the finest Avelina bowls. Separating the two is a somewhat subjective exercise, and while we did the best we could, we are not sure that every investigator would make the separation exactly as we did.

Firing Temperature

This ware was fired at about 750° C in an oxidizing atmosphere. This is hotter than the temperature deduced by Payne for Avelina Red-on-Buff.

Color

Vessel surfaces are generally a uniform light brown (7.5 YR 6/4), although the color range is from reddish yellow (7.5 YR 7/6) to dark gray (5 YR 4/1). Cores tend to be slightly lighter in color, the modal hue being light yellowish brown (10 YR 6/4). The gray firing clouds which occur on some bowl surfaces may have been produced by contact between the fuel and the vessel wall.

Specimens produced at San José Mogote are less likely to show grayness and firing clouds. Some specimens from Tierras Largas are so extensively gray as to suggest that fires may occasionally have been smothered before completion of the firing schedule. This may have resulted from inexperience, rather than design.

As for the color of the iron oxide stain or slip, the examples which we judge to have been most expertly fired are red (7.5 R 4/6). The range, however, is from weak red (10 R 4/4) to dusky red (10 R 3/3–3/4). Often, the red pigment is specular.

Surface Treatment

Clementina vessels were carefully smoothed, and were burnished once with a quartz pebble when leather-hard. This burnishing was usually more careful than that applied to Avelina Red-on-Buff, and the result is that fewer vessels have a streaky appearance. Burnishing seems to have been especially careful on bowls that were stained or slipped completely red on one or more surfaces.

Red Pigment

The red iron oxide pigments used were similar to the varieties already described for Avelina Red-on-Buff. However, a significantly higher percentage of specular hematite was used for Clementina Fine Red-on-Buff, as opposed to the nonspecular pigment with which most Avelina vessels were stained or slipped. In the case of badly worn or eroded sherds, it is often not possible to tell whether the pigment was specular or not. In addition, many of the tiny particles of iron mica in the clay body can appear superficially like hematite specks, so very close microscopic examination may be necessary to confirm the presence of specular hematite.

Vessel Forms

Hemispherical bowls (Figs. 8.30–8.33). These bowls were very similar to their Avelina Red-on-Buff counterparts, but they were even more likely than the latter to have a circular flat facet or a dimple on the base to make it easier for the bowl to sit upright. A few had "pinched-in sides" (Fig. 8.33).

  Rim diameter: Usually 14–24 cm, although there are examples as small as 10 cm.
  Height: Usually 6–12 cm
  Wall thickness: 4–8 mm
  Volume: Based on comparable Avelina Red-on-Buff vessels, these bowls probably averaged 1.5–3.0 liters.
  Decoration: Most common is a simple red band at the rim (both inside and out), usually about 1.0 cm wide. There are also combinations such as those seen in Avelina (all red on one side vs. plain on the other; geometric design on one side vs. plain on the other; etc.), but our sample is much smaller than for Avelina.
  Manufacture: Like their Avelina Red-on-Buff counterparts, many of these bowls were press-molded outside or inside gourds, or over earlier bowls. Others, however (including some of the fanciest), were made by adding concentric rings of clay to a base that had been formed by punching and squeezing a flat disc of clay into a cup-like shape. The latter vessels were more likely to have a flat facet on the base, while those thought to be press-molded over gourds were more likely to have a rounded base.

Less common shapes. Bottles of fine-grained clay with tall, narrow necks (rim diameter, 3 cm) were present though rare during late Tierras Largas times (Figs. 8.34*b,* 8.35). The neck was completely slipped with specular red pigment, and the red extended a few centimeters over the rim and down into the interior. Some bottles may have been totally red-slipped.

Clementina tecomates were like their Avelina Red-on-Buff counterparts.

A rare "double vessel" was found in Feature 142 at Tierras Largas (Figs. 8.34*a,* 8.36). It consists of two miniature jars, modeled separately and then connected by a hollow tube so that any liquid in one could pass directly to the other. The rim diameter of each jar is about 5.0 cm, and its height about 9.5 cm. Each jar would have held about 0.25 liters. Red clay slip with hematite pigment was swabbed onto portions of the exterior, and both vessels were burnished once with a quartz pebble while leather-hard.

MATADAMAS RED

General Description

This is a red-slipped utilitarian ware used mainly for jars, and to a lesser extent for bottles and tecomates. Vessels are covered with a slip of naturally occurring red clay, with or without added iron oxide pigment. When such pigment is added, it may be specular hematite. Outer surfaces are burnished and range from dull red to maroon in color. This type is analogous to Ajalpan Coarse Red of the Tehuacán Valley (MacNeish, Peterson, and Flannery 1970:41). However, Matadamas Red is an earlier type and overlaps with Ajalpan Coarse Red only in the later part of its temporal span. It is readily distinguishable from its companion ware, Matadamas Orange, since the slip color ranges are mutually exclusive.

Chronological History

In the early Tierras Largas phase Matadamas Red was an extremely minor type, virtually restricted to jars with the same range of pocked, wiped, and plain interior surfaces seen in Tierras Largas Burnished Plain. It reached its peak in the late Tierras Largas phase, diversifying into jars, bottles, and tecomates, the latter sometimes rocker stamped. Pocked interiors declined during this period. Matadamas Red continued into the early San José phase mainly as jars with wiped or plain interiors; a few bottles and tecomates could still be found. By late San José times, this type had virtually run its course. It was absent in the Guadalupe phase.

Clay Body

The clay used for Matadamas Red was a residual piedmont deposit derived from decomposing Precambrian gneiss. It was probably used as found, except for the removal of large nonplastic particles. It contains roughly 50% clay minerals and 50% aplastic particles including quartz, feldspar, iron micas, hornblende, and augite. The most common aplastic particle size is about 1.0 mm in diameter, although particles up to 4.0 mm are present.

Firing Temperature and Color

Vessels were fired at roughly 700–720° C in an oxidizing atmosphere, resulting in unslipped surfaces that are brown (e.g., 10 YR 5/3). Cores range from yellowish red (5 YR 4/6) to very dark grayish brown (10 YR 3/2).

Slipped areas could be red (7.5 R 4/6, 10 R 4/6), but graded into weak red (10 R 4/4) or dusky red (10 R 3/6).

Black firing clouds are generally absent from jar rims and shoulders, suggesting that these vessels might have been fired in an upright position. There were, however, firing clouds on the lower parts of jars that had turned so black that it would not always be possible to classify isolated sherds from those areas correctly. (Under such reduced-atmosphere conditions, even the iron in the pigment turns black.) The presence of specular hematite particles on such blackened sherds would let us know the vessel had been slipped or stained red, but would not necessarily allow us to separate it from a type such as San José Specular Red.

Natural Red Clay Slip

Red clay (*barro colorado*) is locally available in piedmont deposits of decomposing gneiss, where it occurs as veins, lenses, or "pods" with relatively high iron content (perhaps 2–3%). This clay is reddish in color in its natural state. It was processed to remove nonplastic particles larger than 0.5 mm, either by winnowing or by mixing with water. In the latter technique, used today in San Marcos Tlapazola, the clay goes into solution in the water and the heavier particles sink to the bottom of the container. The finer fraction can then be decanted and some of the moisture allowed to evaporate.

In some cases it appears that the brilliance of the red color was enhanced by adding ground-up iron oxide pigment to the red clay slip. In cases where the added pigment was specular hematite, this color enhancement could be detected by us visually. In cases where the added pigment was nonspecular, the color of the original red clay was not sufficiently changed for us to detect it without more sophisticated mineralogical analysis.

Surface Treatment

Vessels were burnished very evenly and uniformly with a quartz pebble while leather-hard. Some of the best examples have a gloss which approaches that of double-burnished vessels from the San José phase.

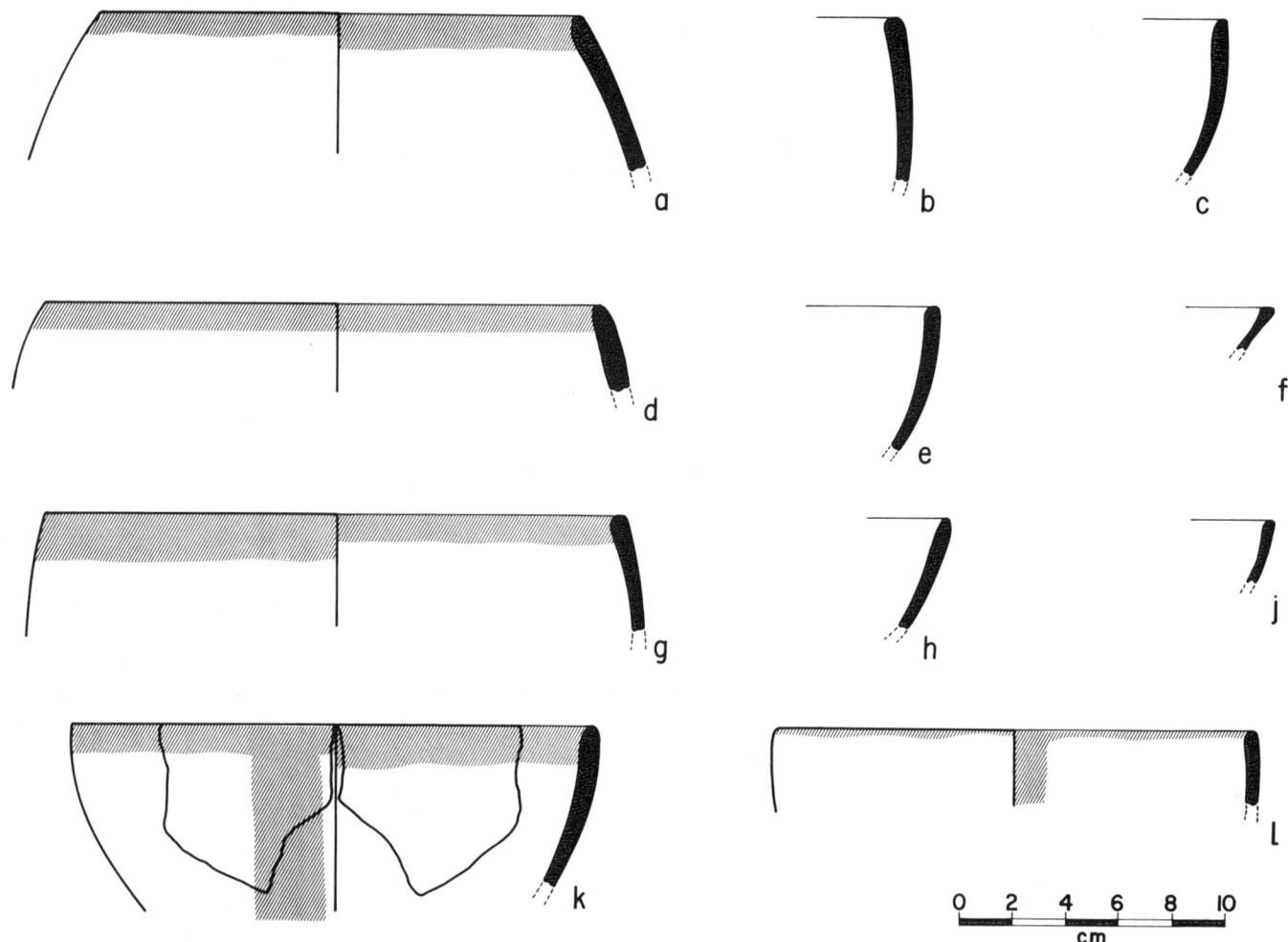

Figure 8.30. Clementina Fine Red-on-Buff hemispherical bowls present an uninterrupted sequence from those with a more restricted orifice (*a*) to those that were more open (*k*). No attempt to divide this continuum proved satisfactory; moreover, we doubt that the prehistoric potters saw any significant distinctions, since they gave all these bowls a red band at the rim inside and out. Here we see a series of such bowls from Tierras Largas (TL) and San José Mogote (SJM); all specimens are Tierras Largas phase. *a,* red band at rim inside and out, Feature 117, Area B, TL. *b, c,* bowls with red bands like *a,* Zone G, Area C, SJM. *d-h,* red band at rim inside and out, Zone G, Area C, SJM. *j,* red band at rim inside, all red outside, Zone G, Area C, SJM. *k,* red band at rim inside and out, geometric design (vertical red band) outside, Feature 100, Area B, TL. *l,* bowl with decoration similar to *k,* Feature 142, Area B, TL. (In the case of *a, b, e, f, h, j,* and *k,* the red is specular hematite.)

Vessel Forms

Jars (Figs. 8.37–8.38a-j). In general, the range of shapes in which these jars occur matches the range for jars in Tierras Largas Burnished Plain and Avelina Red-on-Buff. Bodies tend to be vertically elongated rather than globular, and rim forms range from funnel-like to outcurved. Matadamas Red jars differ from Avelina Red-on-Buff jars in that they are slipped red over their entire outer surface. Avelina jars were given only a red rim and some rectilinear or curvilinear stripes extending down to the shoulder; their lower halves were plain buff.

  Rim diameter: 10–30 cm

    Height: Apparently similar to Matadamas Orange jars (see below).

    Wall thickness: 8–12 mm

    Volume: Up to 10 gallons (?)

  Surface treatment: Burnished on the exterior and part way down inside the neck. Body interiors were left pocked, wiped, or plain like Tierras Largas Burnished Plain jar interiors.

  Decoration: A red slip covering the entire exterior, and extending down inside the neck as a red rim band (average width, 1.0 cm).

  Method of manufacture: Identical to that described for Tierras Largas Burnished Plain jars.

Bottles (Fig. 8.38k, l). Bottles with tall necks and rounded or carinated shoulders were made in this type. Since no complete

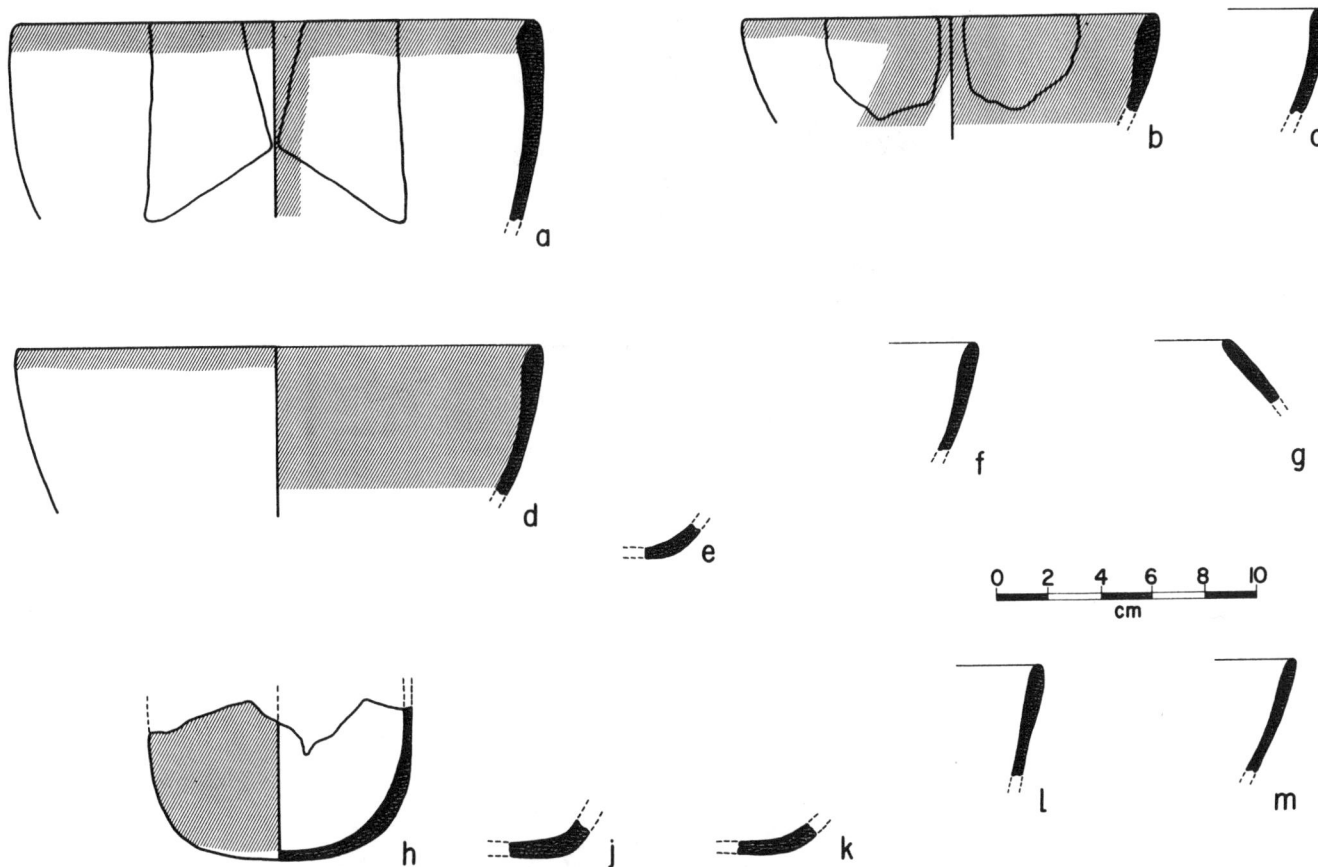

Figure 8.31. Clementina Fine Red-on-Buff hemispherical bowls from Tierras Largas (TL) and San José Mogote (SJM); all specimens Tierras Largas phase. *a*, red band at rim inside and out, geometric design (vertical red band) outside, Feature 100, Area B, TL. *b*, bowl with red rim and diagonal band outside, all red inside, Zone G, Area C, SJM. *c*, red band at rim inside, all red outside, Zone G, Area C, SJM. *d*, red band at rim outside, all red inside, Zone G, Area C, SJM. *e*, bowl base, red inside, Feature 75, TL. *f*, red band at rim outside, all red inside, Zone G, Area C, SJM. *g*, bowl that, in spite of its incurved rim profile, was treated like other hemispherical bowls: red band at rim outside, all red inside (Structure 5, Area C, SJM). *h*, bowl base, all red outside, Feature 117-north, Area B, TL. *j, k*, bowl bases similar to *h* (*j*, Zone G, Area C, SJM; *k*, Feature 142, Area B, TL). *l*, red band at rim inside, all red outside, Zone G, Area C, SJM. *m*, all red on both sides, Feature 86, TL. (In the case of *b, c, d, f, h, j, l,* and *m*, the red is specular hematite.)

examples were found, we can only assume that their overall dimensions were like those of bottles in Avelina Red-on-Buff and Clementina Fine Red-on-Buff. A slip of natural red to maroon clay covers the entire outer surface and is burnished to a gloss.

While reconstructing the manufacturing technique from our fragmentary examples is difficult, we believe these vessels were completely hand-modeled rather than press-molded. The base probably began as a disc of clay pounded and squeezed into a cup shape, then had concentric rings of clay added until the desired body was achieved. The neck was probably modeled separately (perhaps as a flat strip of clay rolled into a tube) and then luted to the body.

Tecomates (Figs. 8.38m–8.40). Globular neckless jars, sometimes with a turned-up rim, appeared in Matadamas Red. The body may have been made by joining two press-molded hemispheres, one with a circular hole left for the mouth. Alternatively, concentric rings of clay may have been added to a press-molded lower half. Rims could be simply rounded off, or drawn up with the fingers like the example in Fig. 8.39.

Rim diameter: 10–16 cm

Height: Unknown (no complete examples)

Wall thickness: 8–10 mm

Volume: Unknown

Decoration: A red slip covers the entire exterior and extends down inside the mouth as a red band (average width, 1.0 cm). During the San José phase (or occasionally in late Tierras Largas times), some tecomates had rocker stamping or zoned rocker stamping (Fig. 8.40).

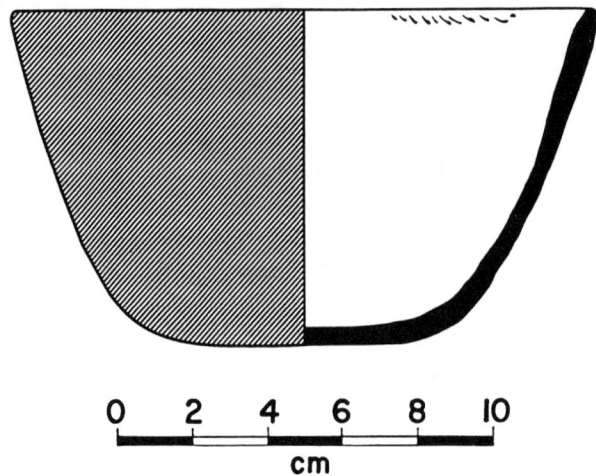

Figure 8.32. Clementina Fine Red-on-Buff hemispherical bowl, slipped specular red and completely burnished on the outside. The inside has been wiped, but not smoothed or burnished; cut marks shown on the rim may have resulted from the process of trimming the rim. Tierras Largas, Feature 117, Household Unit LTL-1, Area B (late Tierras Largas phase).

Figure 8.33. Clementina Fine Red-on-Buff hemispherical bowl with pinched-in sides, all red outside. Tierras Largas, Test Square 2851 (Tierras Largas phase).

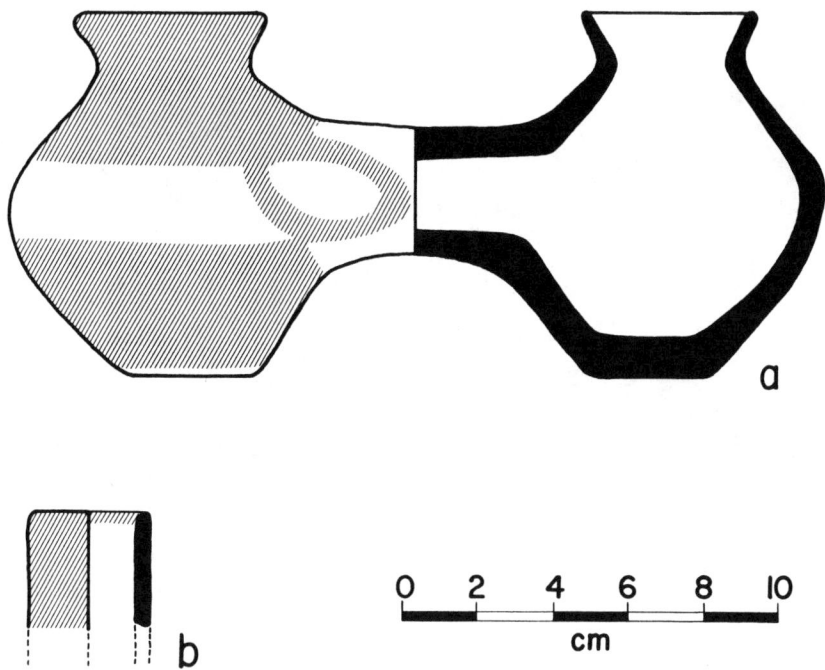

Figure 8.34. Clementina Fine Red-on-Buff vessels from Feature 142, Household Unit LTL-1, Area B, Tierras Largas (late Tierras Largas phase). *a,* unusual double vessel with specular red bands and loops on outside (see also Fig. 8.36). *b,* bottle neck sherd with red band at rim inside, all red outside (see also Fig. 8.35).

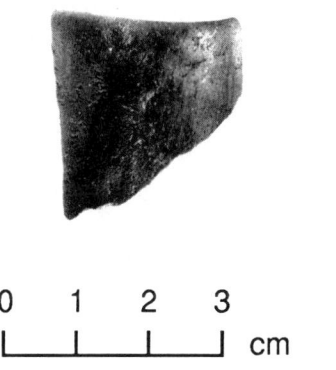

Figure 8.35. Rim sherd from neck of Clementina Fine Red-on-Buff bottle, red band at rim inside, all red outside. Feature 142, Household Unit LTL-1, Area B, Tierras Largas (late Tierras Largas phase). See also Figure 8.34*b.*

MATADAMAS ORANGE

General Description

Matadamas Orange is a distinctive pottery type of the late Tierras Largas and early San José phases. It consists of jars, hemispherical bowls, tecomates, and flat-based bowls with out-leaned walls, all coated with a distinctive orange slip. This slip occurs naturally in the Oaxaca piedmont as veins or "pods" of clay, stained orange or rust-colored by iron from Precambrian metamorphics. Of all Tierras Largas phase vessels, Matadamas Orange tecomates are the most likely to have plastic decoration such as rocker stamping, dentate stamping, and dentate rocker stamping. Frequencies of Matadamas Orange vary from site to site, possibly because certain villages had easier access to the source of orange slip.

Chronological History

Matadamas Orange was present, but not abundant, in early Tierras Largas times. At that point it was limited to jars, with wiped interiors predominating over pocked or plain interiors. By the late Tierras Largas phase, its variety had expanded to include hemispherical bowls (up to three bowls for every jar) and occasional tecomates (some dentate stamped, some rocker stamped).

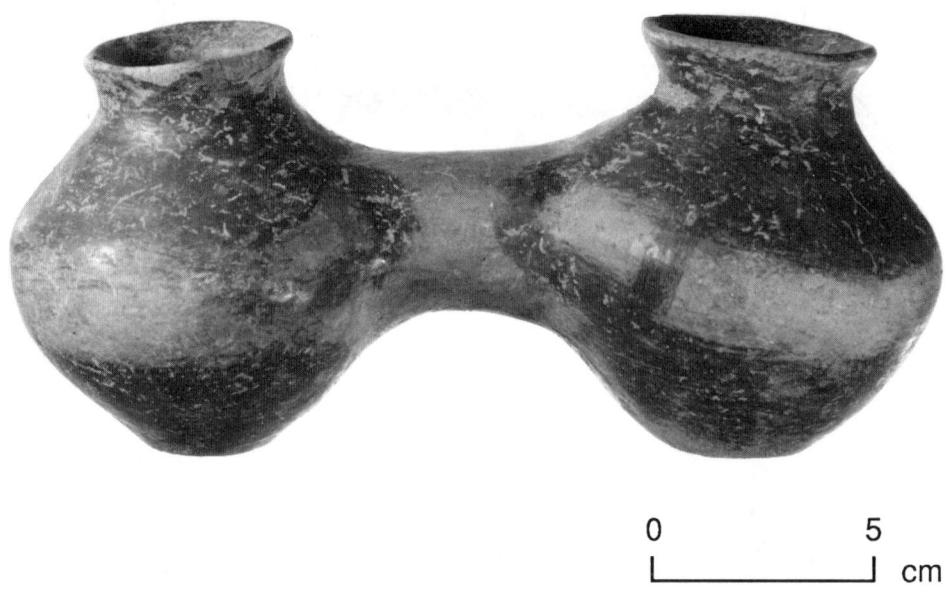

Figure 8.36. Unusual Clementina Fine Red-on-Buff double vessel, consisting of two small jars linked by a hollow bridge. Feature 142, Household Unit LTL-1, Area B, Tierras Largas (late Tierras Largas phase). See also Figure 8.34*a*.

Matadamas Orange probably hit its peak popularity about the time of the transition from Tierras Largas to San José. It also seems to have been more popular at the hamlet of Tierras Largas than at the large village of San José Mogote.

In the early San José phase, Matadamas Orange was a minor type occurring as jars, hemispherical bowls, tecomates, and a new vessel form—flat-based bowls with outleaned walls. Jars with pocked interior surfaces had died out, while wiped and plain interiors were about evenly represented. Tecomates could be rocker stamped or dentate rocker stamped, but outleaned-wall bowls were rarely decorated.

Matadamas Orange declined further in late San José times; it was virtually limited to jars and hemispherical bowls, since tecomates and outleaned-wall bowls in other wares were now more popular. By the Guadalupe phase, this pottery type had vanished.

Clay Body

The clay body used for Matadamas Orange, like that used for other Tierras Largas phase wares, is a residual piedmont clay derived from the weathering and decomposition of Precambrian gneiss. The clay was used as found except for removal of the larger nonplastic particles. Perhaps because it was often used for jars, it includes aplastics up to 4.0 mm in diameter. Composed of about 50% clay minerals and 50% nonplastic particles, the clay body includes such aplastics as quartz, feldspar, iron micas, hornblende, augite, and some olivine.

Firing Temperature

This type was fired at about 700° C in an oxidizing atmosphere.

Natural Orange Clay Wash/Slip

Like the red clay used for Matadamas Red, the orange slip used for Matadamas Orange is a clay that occurs naturally as veins, lenses, or pods in piedmont settings above metamorphic bedrock. The clay itself is a breakdown product of gneiss, and its orange color is the result of relatively high iron content (2–3%). Rather than a red to maroon color, however, this clay has an orange color not unlike that of rust on iron.

Since the ancient Zapotec did not have color terms that distinguished between red and orange (Córdova 1578), it could be legitimately asked whether it makes sense to distinguish between Matadamas Red and Matadamas Orange. We have done so because of the much greater tendency for Formative potters to use Matadamas Orange for dentate and rocker stamped tecomates. This suggests that, whether or not there was a term for "orange," ancient potters recognized the fact that plastic decoration would show up much more clearly against a pale orange background than against a dark red or maroon background.

Since the orange slip used for this type virtually lacked aplastic particles greater than 0.05 mm in diameter, it may have been carefully winnowed, and/or mixed with water as is done in San Marcos Tlapazola today. In the latter technique, clay mixed with

Figure 8.37. Matadamas Red jar neck from Feature 73, Tierras Largas (Tierras Largas phase). For a reconstruction drawing, see Figure 8.38*a*.

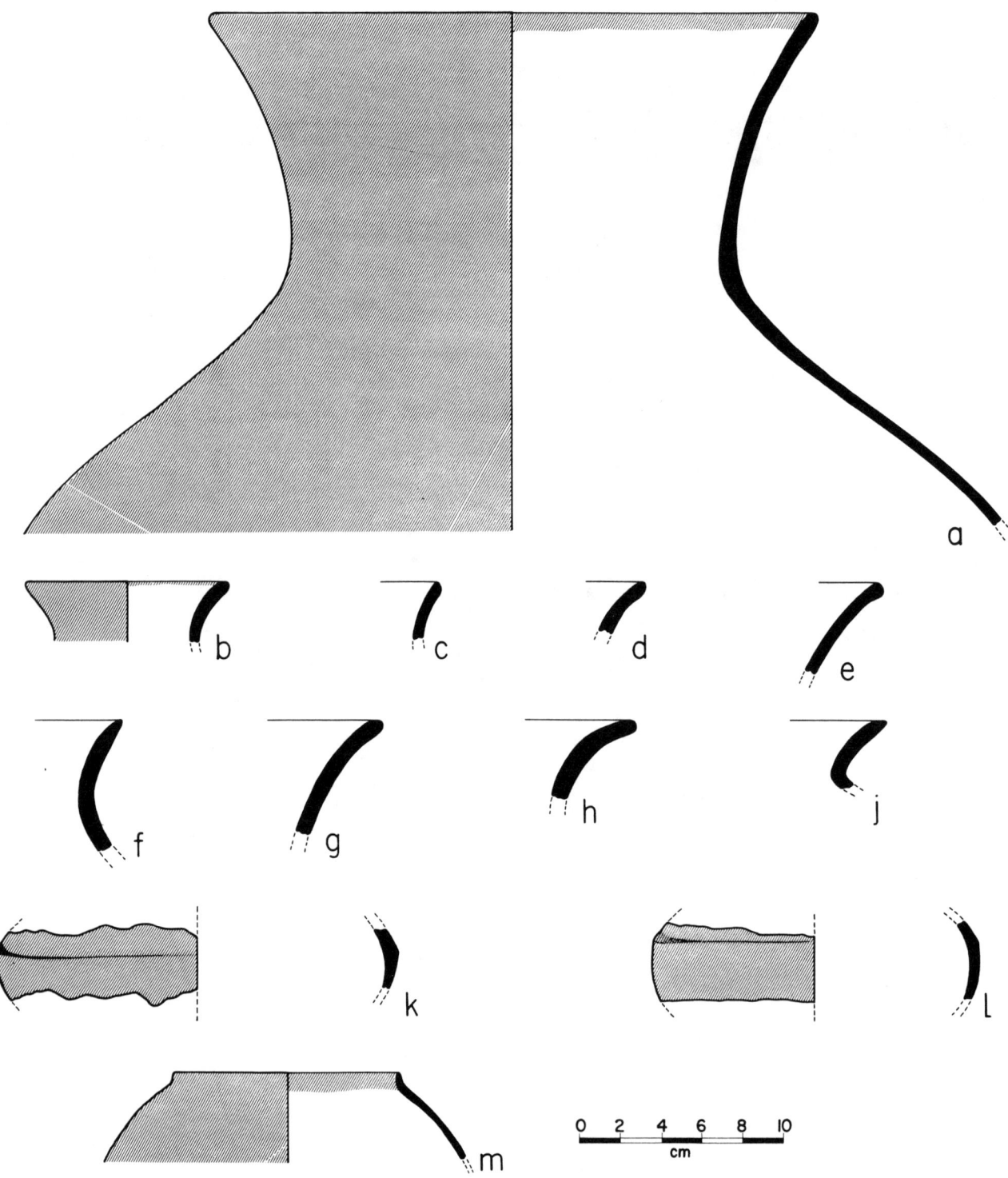

Figure 8.38. Matadamas Red vessels from Tierras Largas (TL) and San José Mogote (SJM). *a*, large jar with flaring neck, red band at rim inside, all red outside, Feature 73, TL (see also Fig. 8.37). *b*, small jar with flaring neck, red band at rim inside, all red outside, Feature 142, Area B, TL. *c-j*, rim sherds from jars with red band at rim inside, all red outside (*c, d, f*, Feature 117, Area B, TL; *e*, Feature 75, Area B, TL; *g, j*, Zone G, Area C, SJM; *h*, Zone D3 midden, Area A, SJM). *k, l*, sherds from the shoulders of bottles, all red outside (*k*, Zone G, Area C, SJM; *l*, Feature 117, Area B, TL). *m*, thin-walled tecomate with turned-up rim; red band at rim inside, all red outside; Household Unit C1, Area A, SJM (see also Fig. 8.39). In the case of *c, d, k,* and *l*, the red is specular hematite. (*h* and *m* are San José phase; all other specimens are Tierras Largas phase.)

Tierras Largas Phase

Figure 8.40. Matadamas Red body sherds with zoned interrupted rocker stamping (Tierras Largas phase). Area B, Tierras Largas.

Figure 8.39. Matadamas Red thin-walled tecomate with turned-up rim, all red outside, red band at rim inside. Household Unit C1, Area A, San José Mogote (San José phase). See also Figure 8.38*m*.

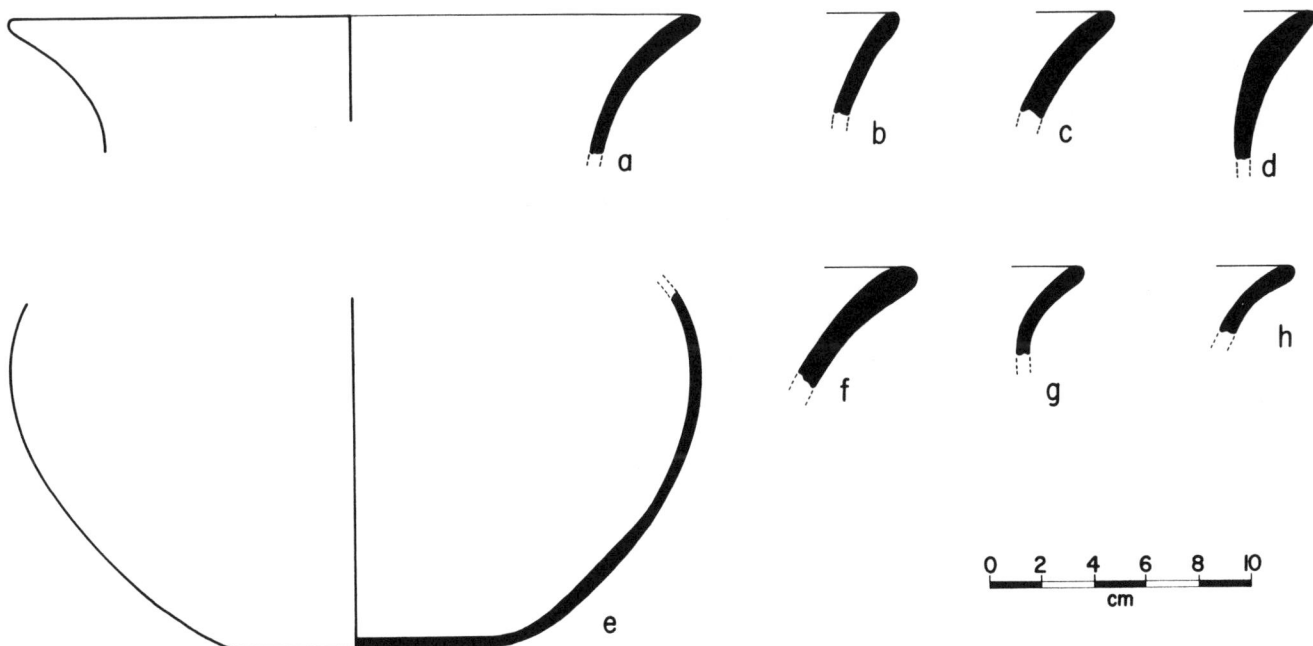

Figure 8.41. Matadamas Orange jar rims and bodies from Tierras Largas (TL) and San José Mogote (SJM). *a-d*, jar rims from Feature 148, TL. *e*, jar body with wiped interior, Feature 148, TL. *f*, jar rim, Structure 5, Area C, SJM. *g*, jar rim, Feature 148, TL. *h*, jar rim, Household Unit C4, Area A, SJM. (All specimens except for *h* are from Tierras Largas phase proveniences; *h* is San José phase.)

water is stirred so that clay minerals go into suspension while the heavier non-plastics sink to the bottom. Later, the much finer solution is poured off into another container.

The orange clay was swabbed onto vessels while wet, perhaps with a piece of animal fur. Because of its similar geological origin, this slip bonded well to the clay body of the vessel. Usually it was applied thickly enough to be considered a slip; however, we have many examples where the orange is thin enough to be described as a wash. In the case of some tecomates, the zoned orange band at the rim is thick enough to be a slip, while the areas of rocker stamping have only a thin wash. Of course, this is not a problem that would have bothered Formative potters; only archaeologists lose sleep over the terminological distinctions between "slip" and "wash."

Color

Unslipped surfaces of Matadamas Orange fall in the same color range as Tierras Largas Burnished Plain. For example, the unslipped interiors of jar necks were generally brown to buff (10 YR 5/3 to 5 YR 6/6). Cores varied from dark gray (10 YR 4/1, 5 YR 4/1) to light yellowish brown (10 YR 6/4).

On slipped surfaces, under what appear to be the best conditions, the orange clay fired 10 R 6/8; areas of firing clouds could be weak red (10 R 4/4–5/4). Other colors observed were 10 R 5/6–6/6, and occasionally 2.5 YR 4/6 or 5 YR 7/6. It should be noted that especially black or dark gray firing clouds could make the orange slip undetectable on some sherds.

Surface Treatment

The orange slip (or wash) was applied to both surfaces of bowls, and to the exterior surface of jars and tecomates. When leather-hard, vessels were burnished once with a quartz pebble. This burnishing was even and careful on both surfaces of bowls, and the upper halves of jars and tecomates. The lower halves of jars and tecomates were burnished less carefully, as were the exterior bases of some bowls.

Plastic Decoration

The most frequent attributes of plastic decoration were rocker stamping, dentate stamping, and dentate rocker stamping, usually on tecomates. Often this stamping was confined to zones, delimited by incised lines or shallow grooves. In most cases this plastic decoration was done before slipping or burnishing, and the decoration was somewhat softened by the burnishing. In a few cases, the plastic decoration was the last step before firing.

Payne speculates that the incising may have been done with a tool such as a maguey spine or an acacia thorn, while the dentate stamping may have been done with the serrated margin of a *Hechtia* leaf. We have no idea what instrument was used for rocker stamping.

Vessel Forms

Jars (Fig. 8.41). These vessels were similar in shape to, and manufactured the same way as, jars in Tierras Largas Burnished Plain. Both halves of the body were press-molded over an inverted jar, then luted, and concentric rings added to build up the neck. The orange slip was added with the hand or a swab of animal fur when the vessel was leather-hard. While the outer surface of the jar was then burnished once with a quartz pebble, jar interiors displayed the same range of finishes seen in Tierras Largas Burnished Plain: pocked, wiped, and plain.

One Matadamas Orange jar from Feature 148 at Tierras Largas (Fig. 8.41e) stands out as being more globular and thin-walled than was the norm. This jar appears to have been built up entirely by adding concentric rings to a basal disk of clay, rather than having been press-molded.

Rim diameter: 12–30 cm (most are 20–24 cm).
Height: One complete specimen from Feature 57A at Tierras Largas has a rim diameter of 12.5 cm and a height of 45 cm. This suggests that the height may be roughly four times the rim diameter.
Wall thickness: 4–12 mm
Volume: The specimen from Feature 57A at Tierras Largas (see above) had a volume of 19 liters. Some of the larger jars may therefore have had volumes of over 40 liters, or about 10 gallons. We presume that such jars would have been used for storage.
Plastic decoration: None

Hemispherical bowls (Figs. 8.42, 8.43a, b). These bowls were made in the same manner as their Tierras Largas Burnished Plain counterparts. Some were press-molded over an inverted gourd vessel or previous bowl. In other cases, a basal disc of clay was punched and squeezed into a cuplike shape; then concentric rings of clay were added until the wall was the desired height. When the bowl was leather-hard, the orange slip was swabbed over both surfaces and the vessel burnished once with a quartz pebble.

Rim diameter: 15–32 cm, with most 20–24 cm.
Height: Usually about 50% of the rim diameter.
Wall thickness: 4–10 mm
Volume: Roughly 1.5–3.0 liters.
Plastic decoration: Almost nonexistent. A few rare examples are incised, slashed, or notched on or near the rim.

Tecomates (Figs. 8.43h-k, 8.44–8.49). These globular jars are like their counterparts in Matadamas Red, except that a few have plastic decoration in the form of zoned incising, plain or false rocker stamping, and dentate stamping. Such attributes appear late in the Tierras Largas phase.
Rim diameter: 12–24 cm
Height: One nearly complete example with a rim diameter of 14 cm has a height of 13 cm.
Wall thickness: 4–12 mm

Volume: Unknown, but estimated at over 2 liters for most specimens.

Decoration: On specimens without plastic decoration, an orange slip covers the whole exterior (interiors left plain). On plastic-decorated specimens, the orange slip may be restricted to plain bands (isolated by incised lines) that separate unslipped zones with plain or false rocker stamping, dentate stamping, or shell edge rocker stamping (Figs. 8.44–8.48). One tecomate body sherd, unfortunately redeposited in fill, shows very "Ocós-like" zoned punctation between shallow grooves (Fig. 8.49).

Minor vessel forms. Occasional flat-based bowls with outleaned walls occurred in the late Tierras Largas phase (Fig. 8.43d, e). In shape and dimensions they resemble their Tierras Largas Burnished Plain counterparts, except for the addition of Matadamas Orange slip on the exterior. These vessels continue in low frequency into the early San José phase.

In early San José phase times, Matadamas Orange slip was used on an occasional flat-based cylinder (Fig. 8.43c, f, g). Some of these vessels even show the kind of incising or punctation typical of the San José phase (Fig. 8.43g).

OCOS BLACK

General Description

This is a double-burnished, glossy black ware appearing mainly in the form of bottles, tecomates, and flat-based bowls (cylindrical or outleaned-wall). It is so rare in our collections, and so similar in appearance to Ocós Black from La Victoria (Coe 1961:54), that we have provisionally borrowed Coe's name. For example, we recovered thin-walled tecomates with zones of dentate stamping set off by shallow grooves, which are very reminiscent of Ocós sherds (Coe 1961: Figs. 48–49). At the same time, some of our vessels do not match Coe's, and appear to be made of local clay. We therefore suspect that our sample includes both an "Ocós Black, Ocós Variety" (imported) and an "Ocós Black, Oaxaca Variety" (local), difficult to separate without a microscope.

Chronological History

This rare type occurs mainly in the late Tierras Largas and early San José phases, which has implications for the dating of the Guatemalan coastal sequence. Ocós Black appears in the Tierras Largas phase as bottles and tecomates, often dentate or rocker stamped. At this time period, almost our entire sample comes from San José Mogote, especially around public buildings. The type peaks in the early San José phase as cylinders, bottles, and outleaned-wall bowls. While there were noticeable amounts found in the houses of Area A at San José Mogote, very little appeared in the houses of Area C at the same site. Thus, there was strong synchronic variation in the distribution of this type, suggesting that it may have been a luxury ware that reached only those households that had the right trade partners.

Clay Body

Complicating our definition of Ocós Black is the fact that while most sherds appear to contain local raw material, others seem to be from imported pieces. We therefore suspect that Oaxaca potters obtained some Ocós Black from other regions and successfully imitated it. The Oaxaca Variety vessels are made of residual piedmont clays that formed above Precambrian gneiss, such as those used for Leandro Gray, or transported valley floor alluvial clays such as those used for Delfina Fine Gray (see Chapter 12). Tentatively, it appears that the coarser piedmont clays were used for tecomates, while the finer alluvial clays were used for bottles or bowls. It is worth noting that the latter vessels constitute the first use in our ceramic sequence of the alluvial clays that are so important at San Bartolo Coyotepec today.

Firing Temperature

Probably 720–730° C in a strongly reducing atmosphere. The fuel may have been some resinous material, probably pine, which produced the characteristic black surface.

Color

The Oaxaca Variety clay body fires an even dark gray (7.5 YR N4/) throughout. The color of the strongly reduced exterior surface is usually black (7.5 YR N2/), although occasional examples may be classed as "very dark gray" (7.5 YR N3/) in the Munsell system.

Surface Treatment

The surface of Ocós Black, Oaxaca Variety, was smoothed, then burnished twice (once when leather-hard, again when completely dry) with a quartz pebble. This variety was never slipped; it merely gives that impression because the double burnishing brings so many fine particles to the surface. It is worth noting that this is the first double-burnished pottery type to appear in our sequence.

Simulation of the Variety

It was not necessary for Payne to simulate the local variety of this pottery type, since it is simulated every week by the potters of San Bartolo Coyotepec. Using a fine-grained valley floor alluvial clay that has been transported far from its parent material, the Coyotepec potters fire their vessels in a neutral or weakly oxidizing atmosphere almost until the end of the process. As a final stage the fuel is increased and the fire smothered, so that firing ends in a strongly reducing atmosphere to turn the surface of the pottery black. The use of pine as a fuel increases the reducing atmosphere because of the resinous fumes. Coyotepec

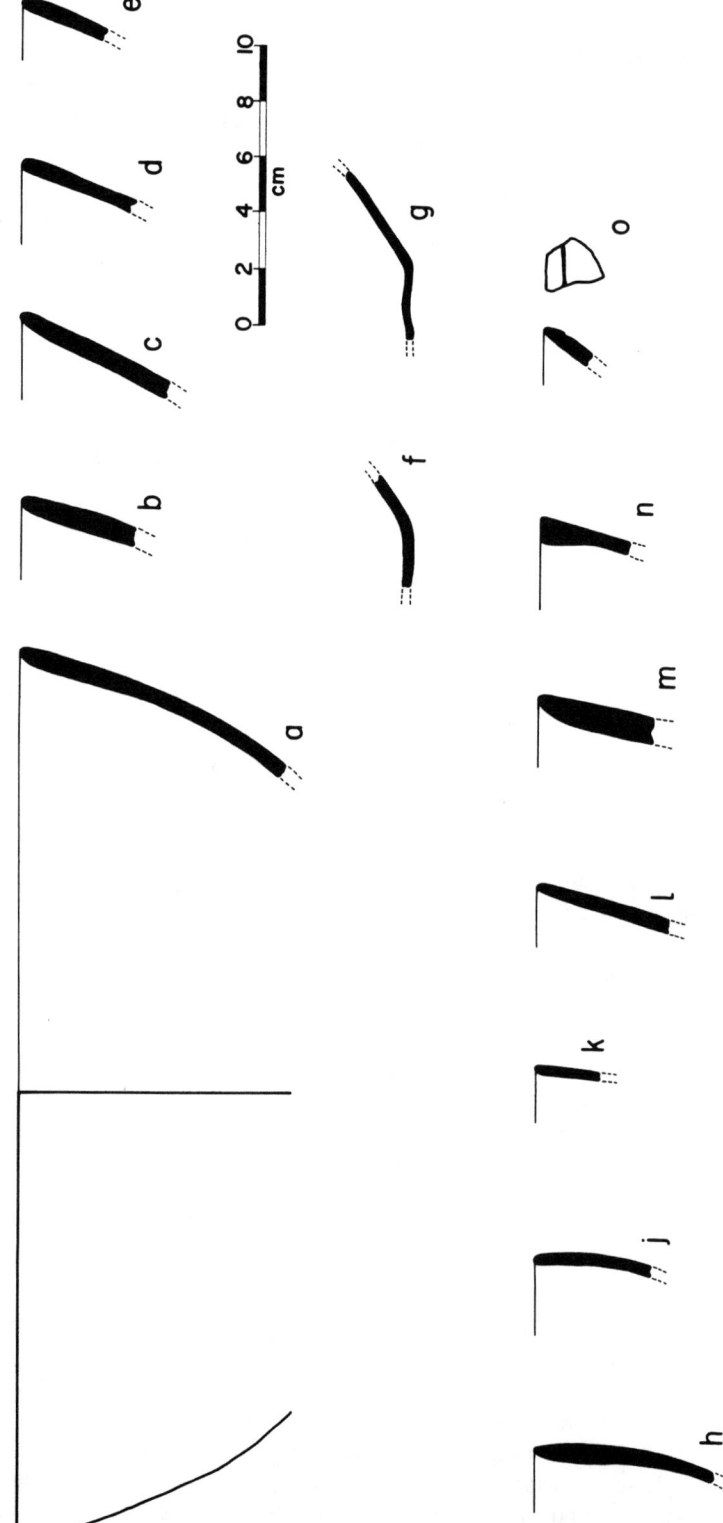

Figure 8.42. Matadamas Orange hemispherical bowls from Tierras Largas (TL) and San José Mogote (SJM). *a-e*, bowl rims from Feature 148, TL. *f, g*, bowl bases, Feature 148, TL (*f* is an example of a rounded base; *g* is an example of a dimpled base). *h-l*, bowl rims from Feature 148, TL. *m*, bowl rim from Zone D2 midden, Area A, SJM. *n*, hemispherical bowl with thickened, flat-topped rim, Zone D2 midden, Area A, SJM. *o*, bowl rim with single groove on exterior, Household Unit C2, Area A, SJM. (*a-l*, Tierras Largas phase; *m-o*, San José phase.)

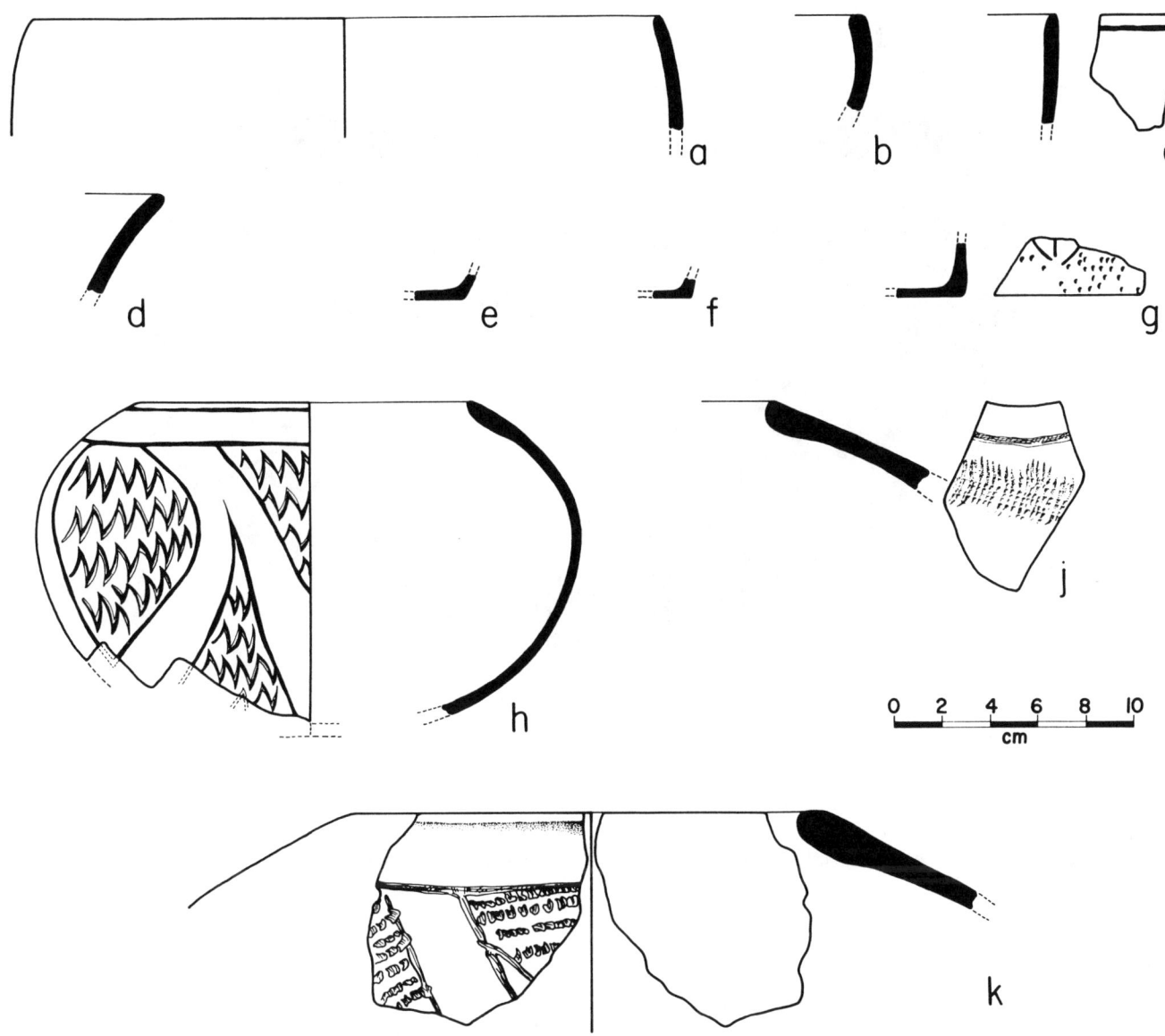

Figure 8.43. Matadamas Orange vessels from Tierras Largas (TL) and San José Mogote (SJM). *a, b,* hemispherical bowls, Feature 148, TL. *c,* cylinder rim with single groove on exterior, Household Unit C4, Area A, SJM. *d,* rim of outleaned-wall bowl, Household Unit C4, Area A, SJM. *e,* base of outleaned-wall bowl, Household Unit C3, Area A, SJM. *f,* cylinder base, plain, Household Unit C3, Area A, SJM. *g,* cylinder base with zoned punctation on exterior, Zone D1 midden, Area A, SJM. *h,* tecomate with false rocker stamping in zones, Feature 116-west, Area B, TL (see also Fig. 8.44). *j,* tecomate rim with possible shell-edge stamping, Household Unit C3, Area A, SJM (see also Fig. 8.45). *k,* tecomate rim with zoned dentate stamping, Zone D3 midden, Area A, SJM (see also Fig. 8.45). (*a, b,* and *h* are Tierras Largas phase; all other specimens are San José phase.)

Figure 8.44. Matadamas Orange tecomate with false rocker stamping in zones. Feature 116-west, Area B, Tierras Largas (Tierras Largas phase). See also Figure 8.43*h*.

black ware does not have exactly the same gloss as Ocós Black, Oaxaca Variety, but that probably reflects different styles of burnishing.

Plastic Decoration

Plastic decoration includes fine-line incising (*sgraffito*); shallow grooving; zoned dentate stamping; and zoned, very fine rocker stamping. The fine line incising was done after the second burnishing, and dry red pigment was rubbed into the lines after firing. The shallow grooving was done just before the second burnishing, with the burnishing giving the grooves their soft, "Ocós-like" appearance. Dentate stamping was done after the second burnishing, with dry red pigment rubbed into the "tooth marks" after firing.

Post-Firing Addition of Red Pigment

As indicated above, dry red pigment might be rubbed into the fine-line incising, fine rocker stamping, or dentate stamping on this variety. In some cases, even plain areas of the vessel have such pigment. The material appears to be finely ground, dry red hematite powder (7.5 R 4/8), and is usually fugitive.

Vessel Forms

Bottles (Figs. 8.50–8.51). Most bottles have a squat, globular lower body, but they can also have a prominent, almost carinated shoulder which gives them a composite silhouette. Bottle necks (based on a very small sample) must have been tall and narrow. All bottles are double-burnished to the point where they look like black glass.

Such bottles do not characterize the Ocós Variety of this pottery type, and are therefore one of the distinguishing characteristics of the Oaxaca Variety. Almost certainly the affinities of this vessel shape lie to the north, in Morelos and the Basin of Mexico.

Diameter of body: 10–14 cm
Wall thickness: 2–5 mm
Other dimensions: Unknown
Plastic decoration: A few have incising that is more reminis-

Figure 8.45. Matadamas Orange tecomate rims with plastic decoration (San José phase). *Left,* tecomate with band at rim and possible shell-edge stamping, Household Unit C3, Area A, San José Mogote (see also Fig. 8.43*j*). *Right,* tecomate with band at rim and zoned dentate stamping, Zone D3 midden, Area A, San José Mogote (see also Fig. 8.43*k*).

Figure 8.46. Matadamas Orange tecomate with plain band at rim followed by a band of interrupted rocker stamping. Fragments of this vessel were found in Features 134 and 135, Area B, Tierras Largas (late Tierras Largas phase).

Figure 8.47. Matadamas Orange tecomate rims with plastic decoration, all from Tierras Largas. *a,* tecomate with plain band at rim and zoned dentate stamping done with a very fine tool, Feature 148. *b,* tecomate with plain band at rim and zoned rocker stamping done with a very fine tool, Feature 151. *c,* tecomate with burnished band at rim and vertical incised lines, Feature 157. (Features 148 and 151 had late Tierras Largas phase material; Feature 157 was a Guadalupe phase provenience, but contained some redeposited Tierras Largas phase sherds.)

Figure 8.48. Matadamas Orange tecomate body sherds with plastic decoration, all from Area D of Tierras Largas. *a,* true rocker stamping. *b,* zoned interrupted rocker stamping. *c, d,* zoned dentate stamping. (All specimens are late Tierras Largas phase or early San José phase.)

Figure 8.49. Matadamas Orange tecomate body sherd with shallow grooves outlining zones of punctation. The decorative style recalls some zoned stamped vessels of the Ocós phase from La Victoria, Guatemala (Coe 1961: Fig. 47 *a, b*). This sherd, which probably dates to the late Tierras Largas phase, was found redeposited in the rubble between Floors 2 and 3 of Structure 13, a Monte Albán II temple on Mound 1, San José Mogote.

Figure 8.51. Ocós Black, Ocós Variety: sherds from a thin-walled tecomate or bottle with zoned dentate stamping on a highly burnished black surface. San José Mogote, Area C, Zone G (Tierras Largas phase).

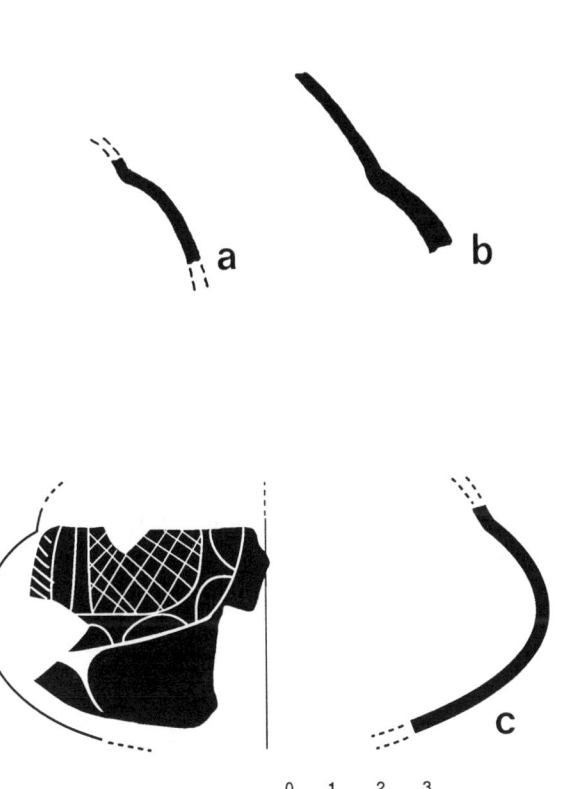

Figure 8.50. Ocós Black, Oaxaca Variety: bottles from Area A, San José Mogote (San José phase). *a, b,* sherds from bottle shoulders, undecorated, found in Household Unit C4 and the Zone D1 midden. *c,* bottle body sherd with pan-Mesoamerican motif, done on the outside with fine-line engraving; dry red pigment has been rubbed into the design (Zone D1 midden).

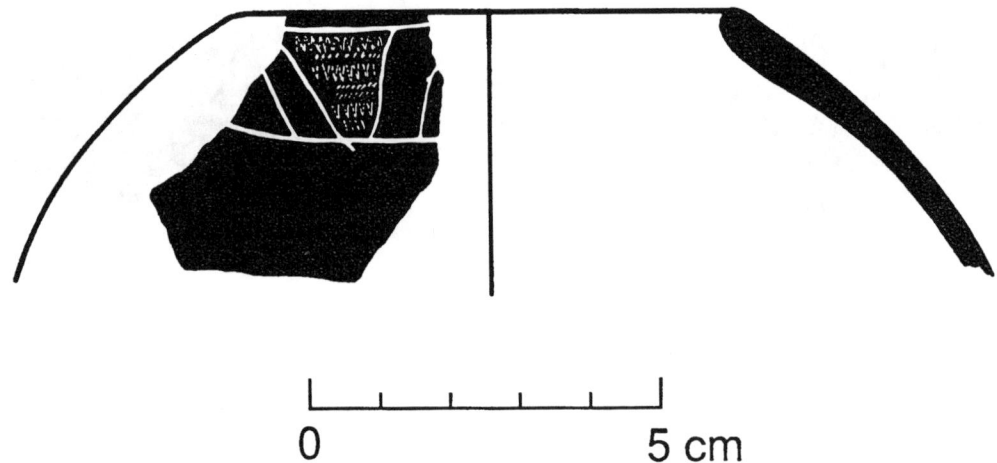

Figure 8.52. Ocós Black, Ocós Variety: tecomate rim with zoned interrupted dentate "micro" rocker stamping. Found amid the fallen plaster covering the floor of Structure 6, Area C, San José Mogote (late Tierras Largas phase). For an enlargement of this unusual sherd, see Figure 8.53.

Figure 8.53. Ocós Black, Ocós Variety: tecomate rim with zoned interrupted dentate "micro" rocker stamping. Both the double-burnished high gloss and the rocker stamping are reminiscent of Ocós Black specimens from La Victoria, Guatemala (Coe 1961: Figs. 22a, 47e). Found amid the fallen plaster covering the floor of Structure 6, Area C, San José Mogote (late Tierras Largas phase). For a reconstruction of the vessel, see Figure 8.52.

cent of Basin of Mexico designs than anything from the south (Fig. 8.50c). Others have zoned dentate stamping more reminiscent of Ocós than anything from the north (Fig. 8.51).

Tecomates (Figs. 8.52, 8.53). These are small, thin-walled vessels whose rims are blunt or gently rounded to very slightly tapered in profile. Such tecomates do characterize the Pacific Coast of Guatemala where Ocós Black was originally described (Coe 1961: Fig.22).

Rim diameter: 6–10 cm
Wall thickness: 2–5 mm
Other dimensions: Unknown
Plastic decoration: A few tecomates have fine-line incising at the rim, usually in the form of a rim band set off from the rest of the vessel. Sometimes there are zones of dentate stamping or very fine rocker stamping, delimited by shallow grooves or very fine lines. Dry red pigment may be rubbed into the plastic decoration.

Flat-based bowls with vertical (or nearly vertical) walls (Fig. 8.54a-j). These "cylinders" may represent the "ideal" after which many of our Leandro Gray cylinders were modeled (Chapter 12). The juncture between base and lower wall is a virtual right angle, and the rims tend to be slightly tapered and rounded off in profile.

Tierras Largas Phase

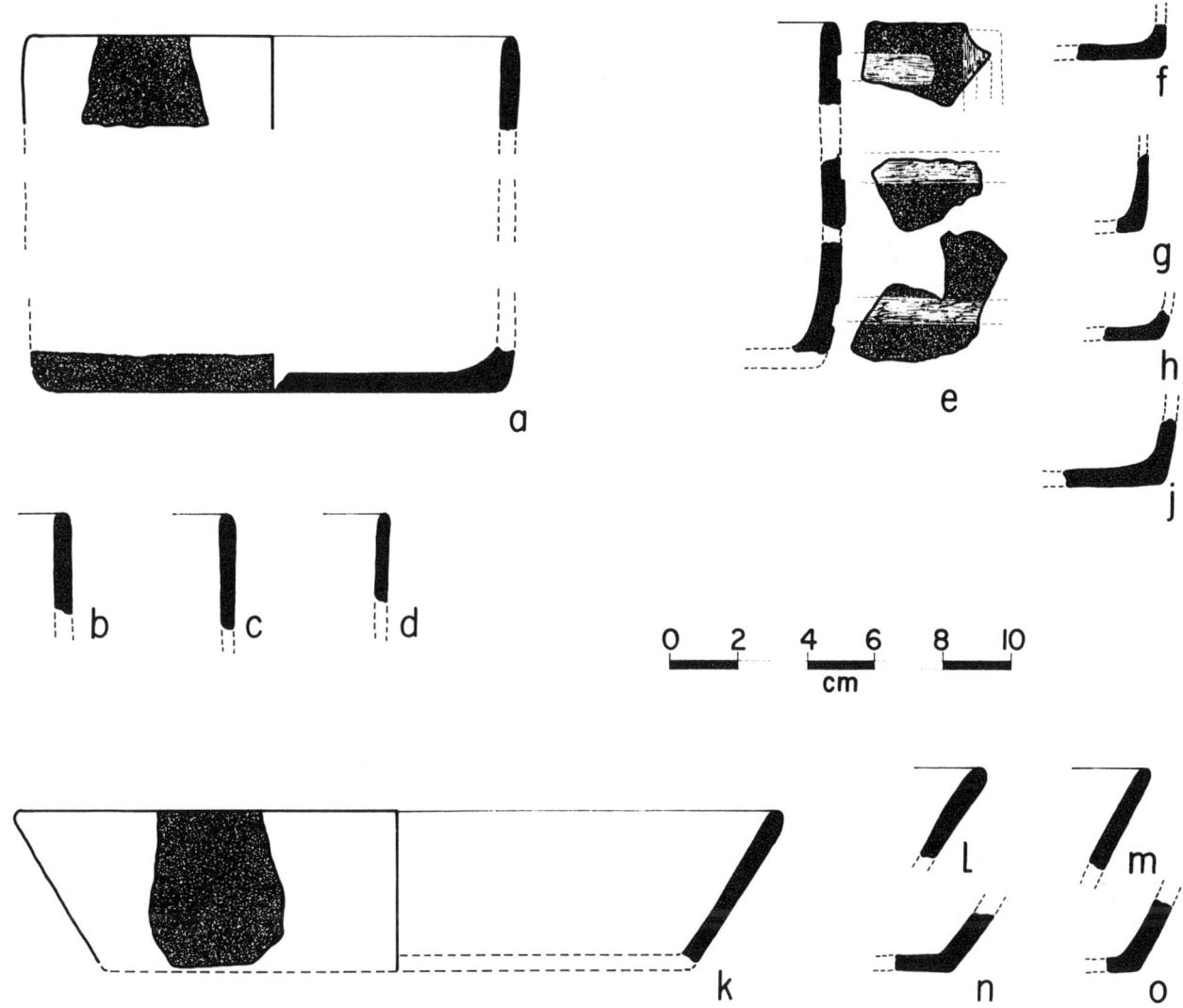

Figure 8.54. Ocós Black, Oaxaca Variety: cylinders and outleaned-wall bowls from Area A of San José Mogote (San José phase). *a*, fragments arranged to show what a typical cylinder may have looked like (rim sherds from Household Unit C4; basal sherds from the Zone D2 midden). *b-d*, cylinder rims, undecorated (*b*, Household Unit C3; *c*, Household Unit C4; *d*, Zone D1 midden). *e*, cylinder with excised design on outside, Zone D1 midden. *f-j*, basal angle sherds of cylinders (*f, h*, Household Unit C4; *g*, Household Unit C1; *j*, Zone D1 midden). *k*, outleaned-wall bowl, covered with dry red pigment, Household Unit C1. *l, m*, rims of bowls similar to *k* (*l*, Household Unit C1; *m*, Zone D1 midden). *n-o*, basal sherds from bowls similar to *k* (both from Household Unit C1).

Rim diameter: 12–18 cm
Basal diameter: Virtually the same as the rim diameter.
Height: Normally about two-thirds the rim diameter.
Wall thickness: 4–8 mm
Plastic decoration: Rare. A few San José phase cylinders have excised designs on the outside. No single design could be reconstructed from our fragmentary specimens, but the few traces recovered suggest motifs like those on Leandro Gray cylinders. Dry red pigment had been rubbed into some excisions.

Flat-based bowls with outleaned walls (Fig. 8.54k-o). These outleaned-wall bowls are like the best Leandro Gray specimens of the San José phase (Chapter 12). Their rims are usually plain, direct, and gently rounded, but can be either slightly tapered or slightly expanding. Coe (1961: Fig. 22*o, p*) illustrates similar bowls in Ocós Black, Ocós Variety.

Rim variety: 18–24 cm
Height: Normally one-fourth to one-third the rim diameter.
Wall thickness: 4–8 mm
Plastic decoration: None

Chapter 9

The Transition From Espiridión Complex to Tierras Largas Phase: Midden Stratigraphy

We have already mentioned Area C of San José Mogote in Chapter 7. This area, covering the extreme western tip of the piedmont spur on which the site is located, may well have been the earliest locus of settlement (Fig. 9.1). It is the only area of the site to produce deposits of the Espiridión complex; it is also the only area to produce early Tierras Largas phase remains.

The three major landmarks of Area C are (1) a long, vertical cut bank, left by adobe makers prior to our arrival; (2) a large fig tree whose roots have disturbed an area roughly 6 × 7 m in extent; and (3) a brick threshing floor dating from the era of large haciendas in the Valley of Oaxaca.

We shaved the vertical cut bank in order to turn it into the Master Profile for Area C; it will be described in more detail in Chapter 13. We left the large fig tree on a pedestal as we dug around it. The area near the brick threshing floor, known as the Threshing Floor Sector of Area C, produced our oldest Formative deposits: House 20 of the Espiridión complex (Chapter 7), overlain by several midden levels of the Tierras Largas phase. It is that midden and house floor stratigraphy that will be covered in this chapter.

The Threshing Floor Sector

As can be seen in Figure 9.2, we established a grid of 1 × 1 m squares that covered all of Area C. Zero datum for this grid was a *mojonera,* or permanent stone boundary marker, sunk in the ground at one corner of Sr. Espiridión Hernández's property. From this *mojonera,* squares ran magnetic north–south along the Master Profile we had carved from the vertical cut bank left by adobe makers. Numbers were used along this axis of the grid; letters were used to mark the east–west axis. Thus, the southeast corner of Square S16C was located 16 m south of the *mojonera* and 3 m east of the Master Profile.

In 1969, Kathryn Blair Vaughn made a deep sounding, designated Test 1, in Squares S17M and S17N of the Threshing Floor Sector. This test was made late in the field season, and when the sherds were washed and analyzed, they appeared to include the earliest Formative material we had found so far. In 1974, when we resumed excavation in Area C, Marcus expanded Vaughn's excavation to include Squares S17H–S17N and S18H–S18N. Eventually, other squares were excavated on all sides of Marcus's excavation.

Overlying bedrock in Squares S18K–S18N, Marcus found the surviving remnant of House 20, described in Chapter 7; its remains extended into S17K and S17L, and may have been grazed by Vaughn in S17M. Farther to the west, in Squares S18J and S18I, Marcus found only sterile clay overlying bedrock. This lowermost stratigraphic layer was called Zone H.

Our account of the various levels in the Threshing Floor Sector will follow Figure 9.3, the stratigraphic profile that results from drawing the south wall of Squares S18H–S18N. The sherd counts from that sector are given in Table 9.1.

Bedrock

Bedrock in the Threshing Floor Sector of Area C was soft, greenish-white volcanic tuff, penetrated in places by postmolds from houses. The three deepest postmolds apeared to be from House 20, our only Espiridión complex house.

Zone H

As Figure 9.3 shows, Zone H had two facies. In Squares S18J and S18I we have described its downhill facies as sterile greenish-black clay, and that appears to have been the zone's original composition. At San José Mogote such clay naturally forms above volcanic tuff through weathering and humic acids.

In the area of Squares S18N-S18K, however, we have labeled Zone H "House 20." That is because the floor of House 20 was dug down through the greenish-black clay already mentioned. This exposed a gently sloping area of bedrock that could serve as a house floor, once it had been given a light coating of sand to fill in all the natural hollows and irregularities. Thus, the uphill facies of Zone H consisted of ashy, chocolate-brown house fill and burned daub fragments from House 20.

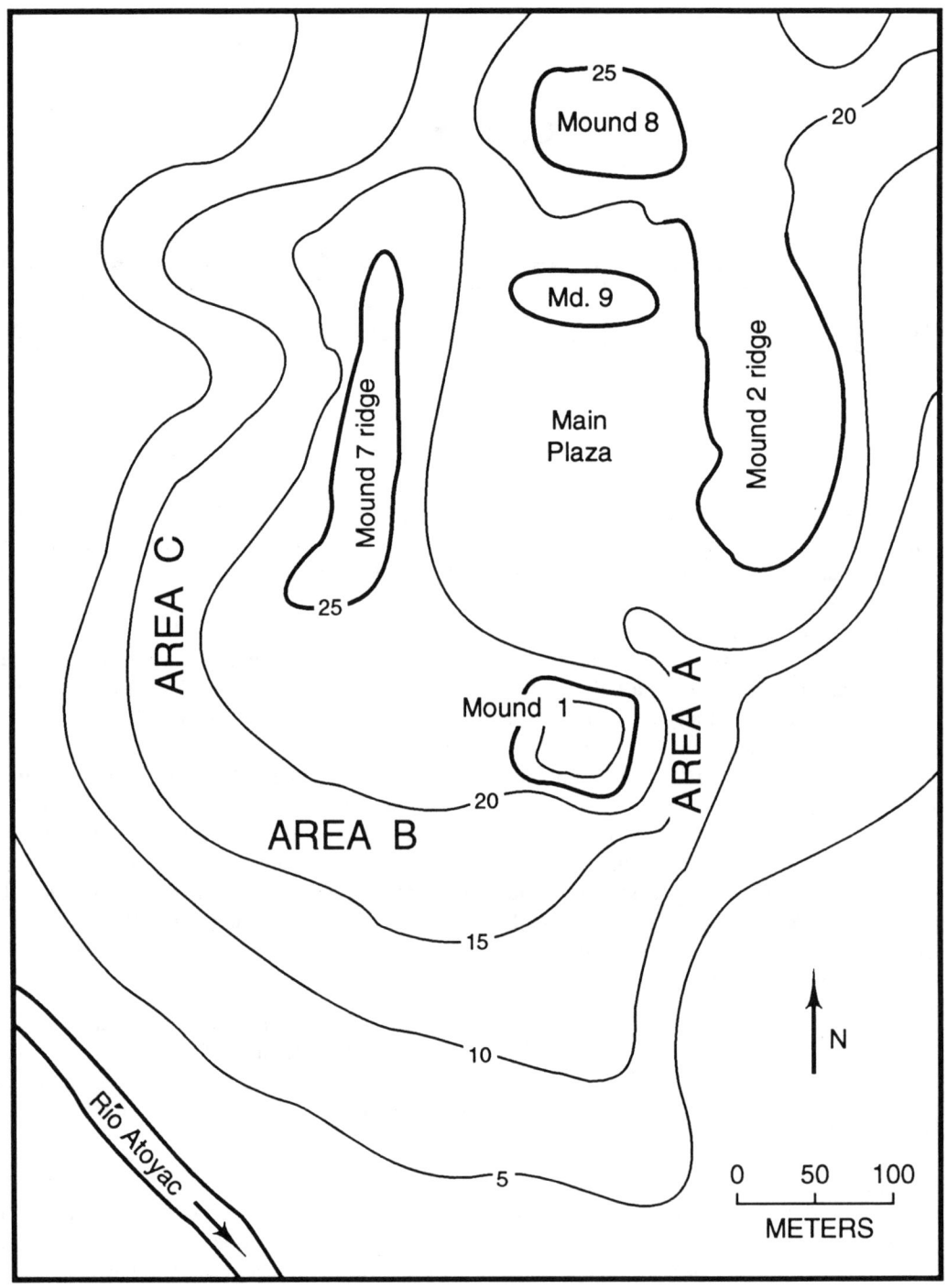

Figure 9.1. Simplified map of San José Mogote, showing Areas A, B, and C as well as other landmarks. Contour interval is 5 m (above an arbitrary datum; the absolute altitude of the Main Plaza is 1610 m).

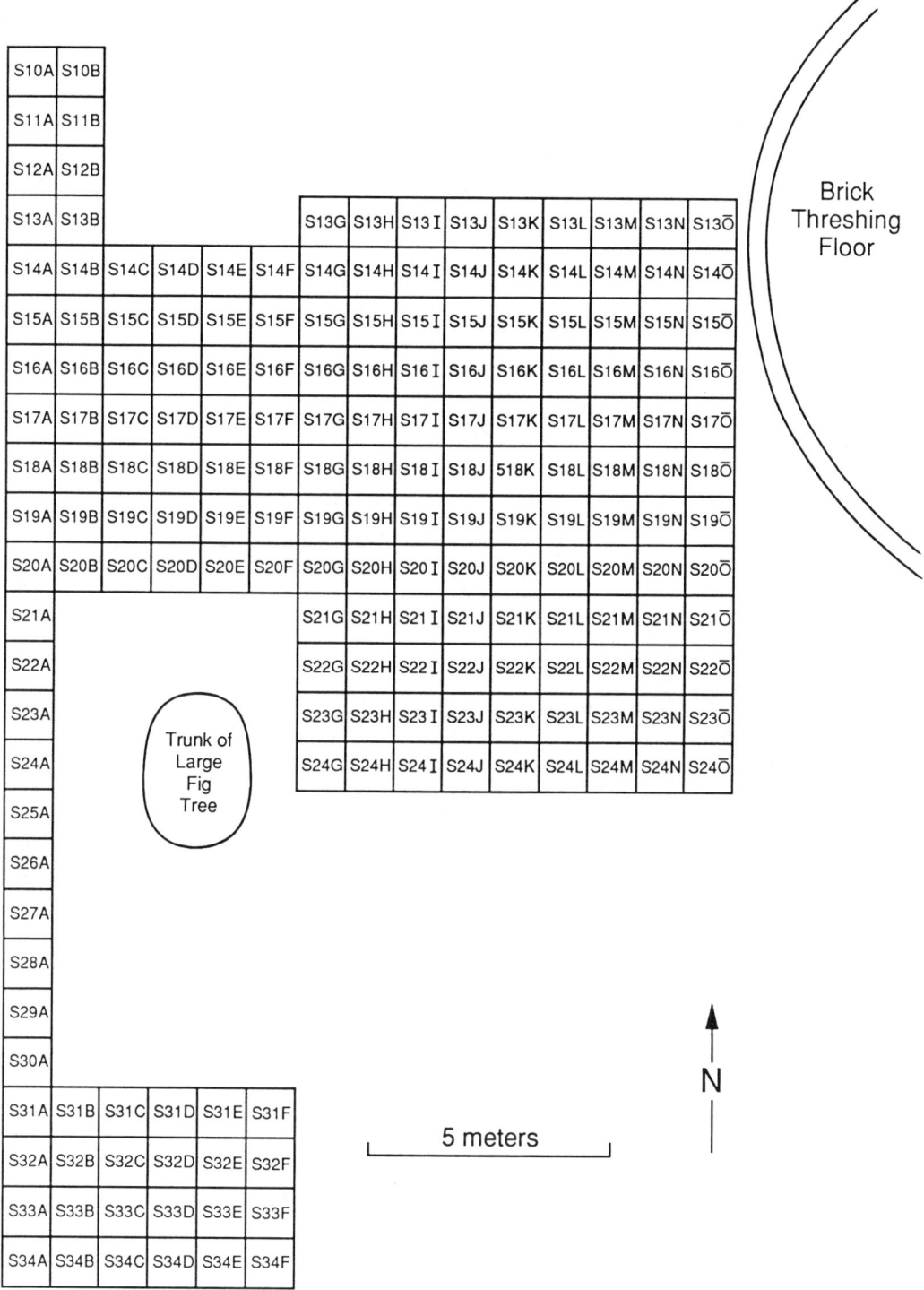

Figure 9.2. The Master Grid of 1 × 1 m squares established for Area C, San José Mogote (on this version, only the squares that were actually excavated are shown). As explained in the text, the north-south axis of the grid employs numbers (10–34) that run south from the boundary monument used as the datum point. The east-west axis uses letters (A through O) that run east from the original Master Profile cut in 1969 (the letter O was given an overbar to distinguish it from zero). In this drawing, the Control Section of the Master Profile runs along the western border of the N-S column of Squares S10A-S34A. Figure 9.3 shows the south profile of Squares S18H-S18N after they had been excavated. House 20, our best provenience of the Espiridión complex, lay mainly in Squares S18K-S18N, S19K-S19N, and S17K-S17L (see Chapter 7).

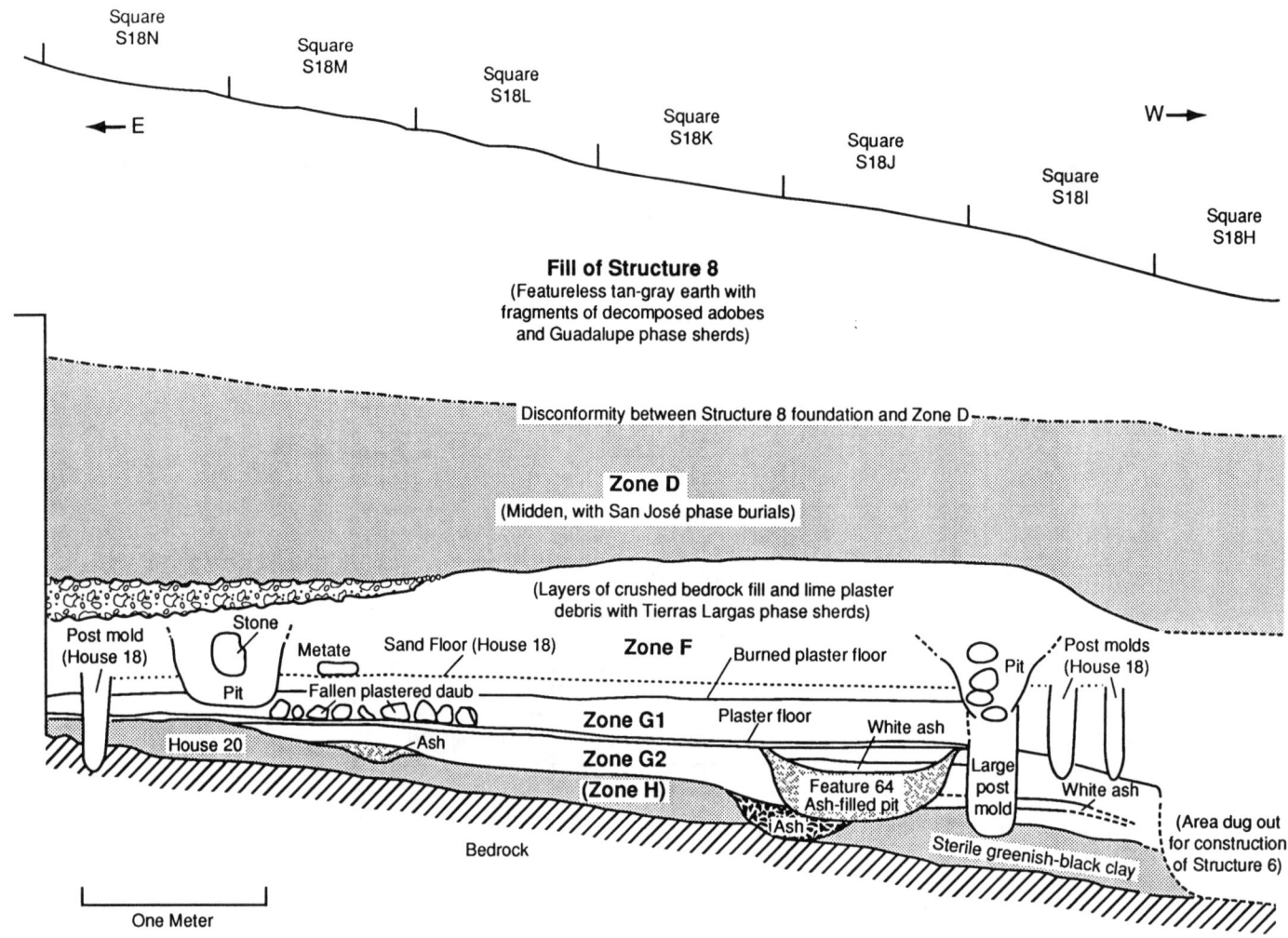

Figure 9.3. The south profile of Squares S18H–S18N of the Threshing Floor Sector, Area C, San José Mogote. For a closeup photograph of Square S18L, see Figure 9.4.

On the border between Squares S18K and S18J, the profile shows an area of ash separating the two facies of Zone H. This was not a pit or a hearth, but a shallow trench to the west of House 20, possibly dug to divert rain runoff. Its filling with ash postdated the house.

Obviously, since the downhill facies of Zone H was sterile, all sherds listed in Table 9.1 as coming from Zone H are from House 20.

Zone G2

Zone G2 was an ashy midden layer that we assigned to the middle of the Tierras Largas phase (Fig. 9.4). It had none of the Tierras Largas Burnished Plain jars with their interior surfaces left rough, which had been such an interesting part of the Espiridión sherd sample. Instead, Zone G2 showed the usual Tierras Largas phase range of pocked, wiped, and plain jar interiors, with the wiped version predominating. This zone was extensive enough to represent a barrio midden.

Zone G2 did not have even one sherd from those pottery types that became important in the San José phase. It also did not have sherds of Matadamas Orange, a common type in later Tierras Largas times. It did, however, produce one Ocós Black body sherd, and the rim of a fine buff bottle of foreign manufacture. Zone G2 also had one sherd of Purrón Plain, which might have been redeposited from House 20.

This zone was interrupted in places by postmolds and an ash-filled pit (Feature 64) intrusive from later levels.

The G2–G1 Boundary

Zones G2 and G1 were separated by a floor made of white lime plaster. This floor appeared to be the kind that served as an "apron" surrounding some of our Tierras Largas phase public buildings (see Fig. 4.7, Chapter 4). The presence of numerous fragments of lime-plastered daub on the floor in Square S18M indicated that we probably were dealing with such an "apron."

Zone G1

Zone G1 was a layer of midden and construction debris, presumably including fragments of a destroyed Tierras Largas phase public building like those described in Chapter 4. We would assign G1 to the late Tierras Largas phase, and have stratigraphic evidence that it is ultimately related to Zone G of the Master Profile for Area C (see Figs. 13.1–13.4).

Out of a sample of 173 sherds, Zone G1 had only three sherds of a pottery type that became important in the San José phase. That type was Atoyac Yellow-white, and all three sherds were from early vessel forms, such as bottles and hemispherical bowls. Since Zone G1 was sealed beneath a plaster floor and a house of the Tierras Largas phase (see Fig. 9.3), these Atoyac Yellow-white sherds cannot be intrusive. They confirm our evidence (from other proveniences) that some common San José phase types made their first appearance in the late Tierras Largas phase, though in low frequency.

The G1-F Boundary

Separating Zones G1 and F was a second lime-plastered floor resembling the "aprons" that usually surrounded Tierras Largas phase public buildings. However, as can be seen in Figure 9.4, this floor was burned almost black. Lying immediately above it was a 10-cm-thick layer of dark debris, apparently from the burning and razing of a lime-plastered building.

Zone F

Zone F was a relatively amorphous layer of crushed bedrock fill and lime plaster debris with late Tierras Largas phase sherds. It appeared to correlate with Zone F of the Master Profile for Area C, a stratum containing several small Tierras Largas phase public buildings. We believe that Zone F accumulated over a period of time greater than the lifetime of any one building, but it had no natural breaks in it except for House 18 (see below).

Out of a sample of 379 sherds, Zone F had only four sherds of Atoyac Yellow-white, and two vessels combining Atoyac Yellow-white engobe with either Avelina Red-on-Buff or Matadamas Red pigments. Such "hybrid" vessels are typical of the late Tierras Largas phase. Zone F was also the first stratum of the Threshing Floor Sector to have Matadamas Orange sherds.

House 18

House 18 consisted of a sand-covered house floor and three postmolds, all belonging to an ordinary wattle-and-daub house of the late Tierras Largas phase. A metate fragment and 54 sherds lay on the area of floor we recovered.

House 18 was contained within Zone F. It overlay the 10-cm-thick area of burned debris in basal Zone F, separating it from the crushed bedrock fill and lime plaster debris of upper Zone F. However, to the north—in squares that are not shown in Figure 9.3—there were no remains of House 18, and basal Zone F graded into upper Zone F without any observable stratigraphic break. Our sherd sample for Zone F comes from the latter squares.

Conclusion

Zone H of the Threshing Floor Sector, already discussed in Chapter 7, belongs to the Espiridión complex. It lacks paint or decoration of any kind, and features Tierras Largas Burnished Plain jar sherds with a rough interior not seen in any Tierras Largas phase sherd samples.

The transition to the Tierras Largas phase is marked by the appearance by Avelina Fine Red-on-Buff and an increase of pocked and wiped jar interiors in Tierras Largas Burnished Plain. As late as Zone G2, which we assign to the middle Tierras Largas phase, Matadamas Orange was rare to absent. No sherds from pottery types of the San José phase were present in middle Tierras Largas.

By the time of Zones G1 and F, which we assign to the late Tierras Largas phase, the full complement of pottery types for the phase was present, including Matadamas Orange. A few sherds of San José phase types occur in these late Tierras Largas phase levels, most notably Atoyac Yellow-white. However, the vessel forms in which Atoyac Yellow-white first appears are ones typical of the Tierras Largas phase: bottles, hemispherical bowls, and bowls with pinched-in sides resembling gourds with stem scars.

Ocós Black makes its first appearance in middle Tierras Largas times. Regardless of the region from which it may originally have come, by late Tierras Largas times it was being imitated on local Oaxaca clay.

Figure 9.4. The south profile of Square S18L of the Threshing Floor Sector, Area C, San José Mogote. This sector, begun as "Test 1" by Kathryn Blair Vaughn in 1969, was completed by Marcus in 1974. It yielded the oldest Formative remains so far found in the Valley of Oaxaca.

At the bottom we see stratigraphic Zone H, the ashy, chocolate-brown fill of House 20 (Espiridión complex). Above that is Zone G2, a layer of ashy midden from near the midpoint of the Tierras Largas phase.

Dividing Zones G2 and G1 is a plaster floor of the type usually found as an "apron" surrounding the low platforms of Tierras Largas phase public buildings. Zone G1 contains the debris from the destruction of such a building, including the triangular chunk of lime-plastered daub at far left.

Dividing Zones G1 and F is another plaster floor, this one burned almost black. Above it is 10 cm of dark debris from the burning and razing of a lime-plastered building. Only a centimeter or two above the card marked "F," however, we see a disconformity between this dark debris and a whiter, overlying layer. That disconformity is the sand floor of House 18, a late Tierras Largas phase residence (see Fig. 9.3).

TABLE 9.1
Sherds from the Threshing Floor Sector of Area C, San José Mogote

	Stratigraphic Zones				
	H	G2	G1	F	H. 18
ESPIRIDION THIN					
Hemispherical bowls: plain rims	3	-	-	-	-
Hemispherical bowls: plain body sherds	11	-	-	-	-
Total	14	-	-	-	-
PURRON PLAIN					
Jar rims	1	-	-	-	-
Jar shoulders	1	-	-	-	-
Body sherds	12	1	-	-	-
Total	14	1	-	-	-
TIERRAS LARGAS BURNISHED PLAIN					
Jar rims	2	5	5	11	1
Jar body sherds: rough interior	30	-	-	-	-
Jar body sherds: pocked interior	2	58	12	29	5
Jar body sherds: wiped interior	33	111	29	68	13
Jar body sherds: plain (smoothed) interior	102	62	25	56	10
Jar shoulders: unburnished interior	2	-	-	-	-
Jar shoulders: burnished interior	-	7	6	3	-
Hemispherical bowls: plain rims	3	25	11	38	1
Hemispherical bowls: notched/slashed rims	-	1	1	1	-
Hemispherical bowls: thickened, grooved rim	-	-	1	-	-
Hemispherical bowls: basal curves	2	5	6	4	3
Hemispherical bowls: body sherds	58	68	44	83	7
Outleaned-wall bowls: plain rims	-	1	-	2	-
Misc. body sherds: dentate rocker stamping	-	1	-	-	-
Total	234	344	140	295	40
TIERRAS LARGAS UNBURNISHED PLAIN					
Rims too small to show shape	-	-	1	-	-
Miscellaneous body sherds	-	-	1	-	-
Total	-	-	2	-	-
AVELINA RED-ON-BUFF					
Jar rims	-	11	-	2	1
Jar shoulders: burnished, rect. design exterior	-	3	2	1	-
Jar body sherds: pocked interior, design exterior	-	7	-	3	-
Jar body sherds: wiped interior, design exterior	-	11	1	9	2
Jar body sherds: plain interior, design exterior	-	10	1	7	3
Hemispherical bowl rims: red rim band only	-	18	4	23	2
Hemisph. bowl rims: red band int., all red ext.	-	5	1	5	1
Hemisph. bowl rims: red band ext., all red int.	-	4	1	2	-
Hemispherical bowl body sherds: all red ext., plain int.	-	7	1	5	1
Hemispherical bowl body sherds: plain ext., all red int.	-	5	1	3	-
Hemispherical bowl body sherds: miscellaneous	-	10	2	3	1
Total	-	91	14	63	11
CLEMENTINA FINE RED-ON-BUFF					
Hemispherical bowl rims: red rim band only	-	1	1	-	-
Hemispherical bowl rims: all red, both sides	-	2	1	1	-
Hemispherical bowl body sherds: all red ext., plain int.	-	2	1	-	-
Hemispherical bowl body sherds: plain ext., all red int.	-	3	-	-	-
Hemispherical bowl body sherds: all red, both sides	-	4	1	1	-
Hemispherical bowl body sherds: miscellaneous	-	-	-	-	1
Bottle neck (all red exterior)	-	1	-	-	-
Bottle body sherd (all red exterior)	-	-	1	-	-
Total	-	13	5	2	1
MATADAMAS RED					
Jar rims	-	-	-	3	-
Jar body sherds	-	2	-	-	1
Total	-	2	-	3	1
MATADAMAS ORANGE					
Jar shoulders: burnished interior	-	-	-	2	-
Hemispherical bowls: plain rims	-	-	-	2	-

TABLE 9.1 (continued)

	Stratigraphic Zones				
	H	G2	G1	F	H. 18
Miscellaneous unclassified body sherds	-	-	-	-	1
Total	-	-	-	4	1
OCOS BLACK					
Body sherd	-	1	1	-	-
Total	-	1	1	-	-
ATOYAC YELLOW-WHITE					
Bottles: body sherds	-	-	1	-	-
Outleaned-wall bowls: plain rims	-	-	1	-	-
Hemispherical bowls: plain rims	-	-	-	3	-
Hemispherical bowls: thickened, eccentric rims	-	-	1	-	-
Oval bowls with pinched-in sides: rims	-	-	-	1	-
Total	-	-	3	4	-
"HYBRID" VESSELS					
Hemispherical bowl rims:					
Atoyac Yellow-white ext., Avelina Red-on-Buff int.	-	-	-	1	-
Atoyac Yellow-white ext., Matadamas Red int.	-	-	-	1	-
Total	-	-	-	2	-
POSSIBLE FOREIGN WARES					
Non-local fine buff bottle rim	-	1	-	-	-
Total	-	1	-	-	-
UNCLASSIFIED SHERDS					
Plain body sherds	-	5	8	6	-
Total	-	5	8	6	-
GRAND TOTAL	262	458	173	379	54

Chapter 10

A Sample of Tierras Largas Phase Households

We now look at the sherds from a small sample of Tierras Largas phase households. All are households where we have had to rely on sherds from associated features because the house floors themselves did not yield good samples.

1. Household Unit LTL-1, Area B, Tierras Largas (Figs. 10.1, 10.2)

Household Unit LTL-1 dated to the late Tierras Largas phase. Archaeological remains consisted of (1) a rectangular postmold pattern indicating a house, and (2) a set of bell-shaped pits in the adjacent dooryard (Winter 1972: Table 7; Flannery et al. 1970:63–65; Flannery 1972: Fig. 7). Four of the bell-shaped pits were judged to have good samples of sherds; these were Features 75, 86 (Fig. 10.3), 117, and 142 (Fig. 10.4). The collections from those four pits, totaling 3,877 sherds, were subjected to a Brainerd-Robinson seriation (Robinson 1951; Brainerd 1951) by Yda Schreuder, a University of Michigan graduate student, using the 28 ceramic attributes given in the Appendix to this chapter. Her seriation arranged the four features in the following order:

Feature 142 (youngest)
Feature 75
Feature 117
Feature 86 (oldest)

The contents of these four features are given in Table 10.1. Several points are worth mentioning. We note an overall decrease in pocked interiors of Tierras Largas Burnished Plain jars between Feature 86 and Feature 142, accompanied by an overall increase in wiped and plain (smoothed) interiors. We also note that the two earliest pits, Features 86 and 117, are without any pottery types characteristic of the San José phase. San José phase types Fidencio Coarse, Leandro Gray, Atoyac Yellow-white, and San José Red-on-White do appear in the two latest pits, Features 75 and 142. However, they amount to only 52 sherds out of the 2,910 in those two pits. This is about what one might expect if the pits had originally been dug in the Tierras Largas phase, but were filled in very late in the phase, when a few San José phase types had already made an appearance.

2. Household Unit LTL-3, Area C, Tierras Largas (Fig. 10.5)

Household Unit LTL-3 also dated to the late Tierras Largas phase. Archaeological evidence included (1) an alignment of postmolds indicating a house, (2) four bell-shaped pits in the adjacent dooryard, and (3) a storage area with two manos, two metates, and a large Tierras Largas Burnished Plain jar (Winter 1972: Table 7; Flannery et al. 1970:63–65; Flannery 1972: Fig. 7). Two of the pits were judged to have fairly good samples of sherds; those were Features 148 and 151. When Yda Schreuder added these features to her Brainerd-Robinson matrix, they came out close together between Features 117 and 75 of Household Unit LTL-1, as follows:

Feature 75 (youngest)
Feature 148
Feature 151
Feature 117 (oldest)

The contents of these two pits, totaling 1,499 sherds, are given in Table 10.2. Tierras Largas Burnished Plain jars show a decrease in pocked interiors and an increase in wiped interiors over time like the trends seen in Household Unit LTL-1. We also find some sherds characteristic of the San José phase, such as Fidencio Coarse, Leandro Gray, and Atoyac Yellow-white, especially in Feature 148. Once again, this is about what we would expect if the pits had originally been dug in Tierras Largas times, but were filled in very late in the phase, after a few San José phase types had begun to appear.

3. Feature 100 at Tierras Largas

This bell-shaped pit was probably set in the dooryard of a late Tierras Largas phase house (Winter 1972: Table 10). When added to Yda Schreuder's Brainerd-Robinson seriation, this pit

TABLE 10.1
Sherds from Household Unit LTL-1, Area B, Tierras Largas

	F. 86	F. 117	F. 75	F. 142
TIERRAS LARGAS BURNISHED PLAIN				
Jar rims	5	17	38	84
Jar body sherds: pocked interior	225	200	150	187
Jar body sherds: wiped interior	11	89	360	613
Jar body sherds: plain (smoothed) interior	85	116	343	445
Jar shoulders: burnished interior	2	3	29	66
Hemispherical bowls: plain rims	1	8	25	30
Hemispherical bowls: notched/slashed rims	-	-	1	3
Hemispherical bowls: basal curves	-	1	3	7
Hemispherical bowls: body sherds	24	21	83	101
Outleaned-wall bowls: plain rims	1	-	-	-
Outleaned-wall bowls: thickened, grooved rim	-	-	-	4
Outleaned-wall bowls: plain flat bases	-	-	-	7
Outleaned-wall bowls: plain body sherds	-	-	-	20
Tecomate body sherds: plain rocker stamping	-	-	-	1
Misc. unclassified rims (incl. miniatures)	2	-	3	-
Misc. unclassified bases (incl. miniatures)	-	1	-	-
Total	356	456	1035	1568
TIERRAS LARGAS UNBURNISHED PLAIN				
Jar rims	-	-	-	1
Hemispherical bowls: plain rims	-	1	1	-
Hemispherical bowls: notched/slashed rims	-	-	1	-
Hemispherical bowls: pinched rims	-	-	3	-
Hemi. bowls w/pinched-in sides (whole vessel)	-	-	-	1
Total	0	1	5	2
AVELINA RED-ON-BUFF				
Jar rims	-	-	1	2
Jar shoulders: burnished, rect. design exterior	-	2	3	1
Jar body sherds: pocked interior, rect. design exterior	1	4	-	1
Jar body sherds: pocked interior, curv. design exterior	-	1	-	-
Jar body sherds: wiped interior, rect. design ext.	-	2	6	15
Jar body sherds: wiped interior, curv. design ext.	-	5	-	2
Jar body sherds: plain int., rect. design ext.	-	1	6	8
Jar body sherds: plain int., curv. design ext.	-	4	2	-
Hemispherical bowl rims:				
red rim band only	2	8	15	13
red rim band int., all red ext.	1	2	6	2
red rim band int., design ext.	1	1	-	-
red rim band ext., all red int.	1	2	9	2
red rim band ext., design int.	-	4	-	5
all red on both sides	-	-	-	1
Hemispherical bowl body sherds:				
all red ext., plain int.	2	5	6	8
design on ext., plain int.	2	3	-	1
plain ext., all red int.	-	3	4	4
plain ext., design int.	1	6	1	1
all red ext., design int.	-	1	-	-
design on both sides	-	-	-	1
misc. body sherds	4	2	1	2
Hemisph. bowls: basal curve sherds	1	1	1	2
Tecomate rims: red band at rim	-	-	8	-
Misc. unclassified rims (incl. miniatures)	-	1	-	-
Total	16	58	69	71
CLEMENTINA FINE RED-ON-BUFF				
Hemispherical bowl rims: red rim band only	1	-	3	5
Hemisph. bowl rims: red rim band int., all red ext.	1	3	3	1
Hemisph. bowl rims: red rim band int., design ext.	1	-	-	1
Hemisph. bowl rims: red rim band ext., all red int.	-	-	1	3
Hemisph. bowl rims: all red on both sides	1	-	-	1
Hemisph. bowl body sherds: all red ext., plain int.	2	9	3	1
Hemisph. bowl body sherds: design ext., plain int.	-	1	-	-
Hemisph. bowl body sherds: design ext., all red int.	-	-	1	-
Hemisph. bowl body sherds: plain ext., all red int.	-	1	1	1

TABLE 10.1 (continued)

	F. 86	F. 117	F. 75	F. 142
Hemisph. bowl body sherds: plain ext., design int.	-	1	-	-
Hemisph. bowl body sherds: all red ext., design int.	1	-	-	-
Hemisph. bowl body sherds: all red on both sides	-	2	-	-
Hemisph. bowls: basal curve sherds	-	2	1	3
Double vessel (whole vessel)	-	-	-	1
Bottle rims	-	-	-	1
Miscellaneous unclassified rims (incl. miniatures)	-	-	-	1
Total	7	19	13	19
MATADAMAS RED				
Jar rims	-	3	1	6
Jar body sherds: pocked interior	2	3	-	-
Jar body sherds: wiped interior	-	10	7	11
Jar body sherds: plain interior	2	4	7	4
Jar shoulders: burnished interior	-	2	-	3
Bottle shoulders	-	1	-	1
Tecomate body sherds: zoned rocker stamping	-	-	-	2
Total	4	23	15	27
MATADAMAS ORANGE				
Jar rims	-	2	1	-
Jar body sherds: pocked interior	-	1	-	-
Jar body sherds: wiped interior	-	2	8	-
Jar body sherds: plain interior	-	1	4	-
Hemispherical bowls: body sherds	-	-	1	-
Tecomate body sherds: dentate rocker stamping	-	1	-	-
Total	0	7	14	0
FIDENCIO COARSE				
Tecomate rims	-	-	2	2
Jar rims, unburnished	-	-	-	1
Plain body sherds	-	-	7	27
Total	0	0	9	30
LEANDRO GRAY				
Bottle rim or neck sherds	-	-	2	-
Outleaned-wall bowls: plain flat bases	-	-	-	1
Plain body sherds	-	-	3	-
Total	0	0	5	1
ATOYAC YELLOW-WHITE				
Cylinder rims: plain	-	-	-	1
Plain body sherds	-	-	3	1
Total	0	0	3	2
SAN JOSE RED-ON-WHITE				
Incurved-rim bowls: rims	-	-	1	-
Plain body sherds	-	-	1	-
Total	0	0	2	0
UNCLASSIFIED SHERDS				
Rims	-	3	-	1
Body sherds	4	13	-	19
Total	4	16	0	20
GRAND TOTAL	387	580	1170	1740

TABLE 10.2
Sherds from Household Unit LTL-3, Area C, Tierras Largas

	F. 151	F. 148
TIERRAS LARGAS BURNISHED PLAIN		
Jar rims	15	13
Jar body sherds: pocked interior	152	44
Jar body sherds: wiped interior	56	216
Jar body sherds: plain (smoothed) interior	140	129
Jar shoulders: burnished interior	10	1
Hemispherical bowls: plain rims	5	9
Hemispherical bowls: notched/slashed rims	1	4
Hemispherical bowls: basal curves	3	6
Hemispherical bowls: body sherds	21	55
Outleaned-wall bowls: plain rims	2	-
Outleaned-wall bowls: plain flat bases	-	1
Total	405	478
TIERRAS LARGAS UNBURNISHED PLAIN		
Jar rims	1	-
Hemispherical bowls: body sherds	1	-
Miniature vessels: rims	2	-
Total	4	-
AVELINA RED-ON-BUFF		
Jar body sherds:		
pocked interior, curvilinear design ext.	-	1
wiped interior, rectilinear design ext.	-	1
wiped interior, curvilinear design ext.	-	1
plain interior, rectilinear design ext.	2	1
plain interior, curvilinear design ext.	1	-
Hemispherical bowl rims:		
red rim band only	1	1
red rim band int., all red ext.	-	1
red rim band int., design ext.	1	-
red rim band exterior, all red int.	-	1
red rim band exterior, design int.	2	-
all red on both sides	1	-
Hemispherical bowl body sherds:		
all red exterior, plain interior	1	1
design exterior, plain interior	1	-
design exterior, all red interior	-	1
plain exterior, all red interior	-	1
plain exterior, design interior	3	-
design on both sides	-	1
miscellaneous	1	-
Hemisph. bowl rims: basal curves	-	1
Misc. unclassified rims (incl. miniatures)	-	1
Total	14	13
CLEMENTINA FINE RED-ON-BUFF		
Hemispherical bowl rims:		
red rim band only	1	7
red rim band interior, all red exterior	1	1
red rim band exterior, all red interior	1	2
Hemispherical bowl body sherds:		
all red exterior, plain interior	2	-
Total	5	10
MATADAMAS RED		
Jar body sherds: pocked interior	1	-
Jar body sherds: wiped interior	-	4
Jar shoulder: burnished interior	-	1
Total	1	5
MATADAMAS ORANGE		
Jar rims	-	11
Jar body sherds: pocked interior	-	5
Jar body sherds: wiped interior	1	207
Jar body sherds: plain interior	1	39

TABLE 10.2 (continued)

	F. 151	F. 148
Hemispherical bowls: plain rims	-	34
Hemispherical bowls: basal curves	-	4
Hemispherical bowls: body sherds	-	85
Tecomate rims: dentate stamping	-	1
Tecomate rims: fluted	-	1
Tecomate body sherds: rocker stamping	-	1
Miscellaneous unclassified body sherds	-	1
Total	2	389
FIDENCIO COARSE		
Plain body sherds (mostly from jars)	8	83
Total	8	83
LEANDRO GRAY		
Bottle body sherds, fluted	-	1
Outleaned-wall bowls: plain flat bases	1	1
Tecomate rims	-	2
Plain body sherds	3	25
Total	4	29
ATOYAC YELLOW-WHITE		
Bottle body sherds, fluted	-	2
Outleaned-wall bowls: plain rims	-	4
Cylinders: plain rims	1	1
Cylinders: incised rims	-	1
Plain body sherds	2	10
Total	3	18
SAN JOSE RED-ON-WHITE		
Hemispherical bowls: rims	1	-
Total	1	-
LUPITA HEAVY PLAIN		
Tecomate body sherds:		
interrupted rocker stamping	1	-
Spouted trays: spout sherds (?)	1	-
Total	2	-
"HYBRID" VESSELS		
Outleaned-wall bowls, Atoyac Yellow-white outside, Matadamas Orange inside: plain flat bases	-	1
Total	-	1
SAN JOSE BLACK-AND-WHITE		
Cylinders: plain rims	-	1
Total	-	1
UNCLASSIFIED SHERDS		
Rims	-	1
Body sherds	8	14
Total	8	15
GRAND TOTAL	457	1042

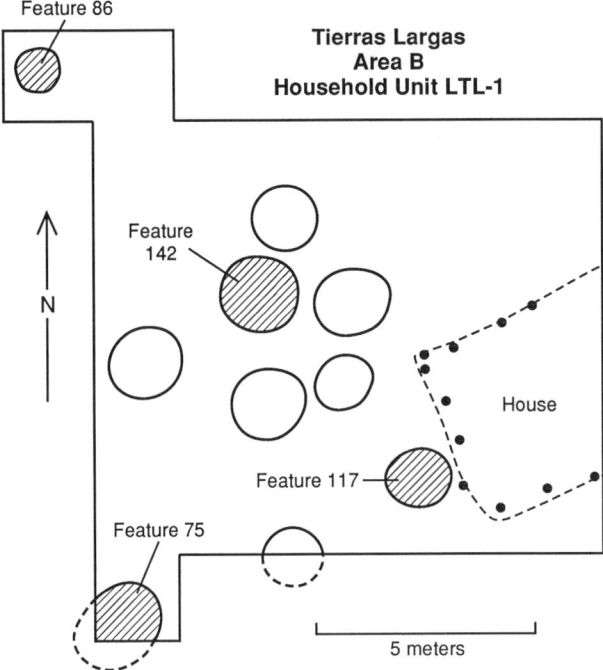

Figure 10.1. Plan view of Household Unit LTL-1 from Tierras Largas (late Tierras Largas phase). The black dots represent postholes, with the dashed line indicating the approximate area of the house floor. The large circles are bell-shaped pits; those shown with hachure were judged to have an adequate sherd sample for analysis. (Redrawn from Flannery 1972: Fig. 7; excavation by M. Winter.)

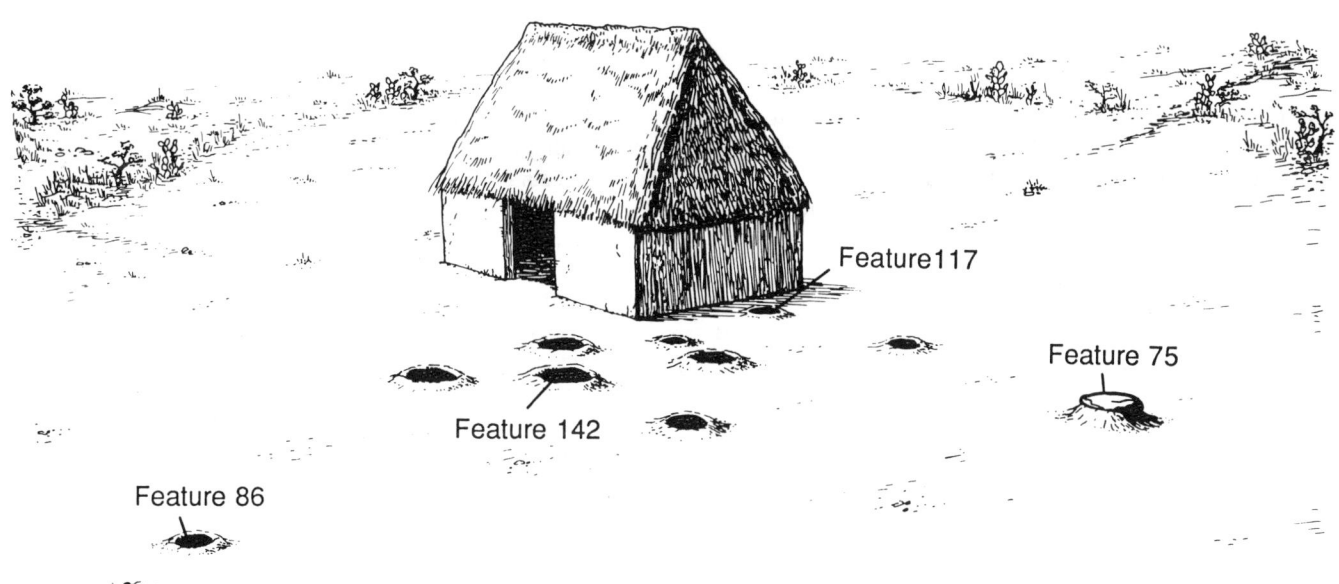

Figure 10.2. Artist's reconstruction of Household Unit LTL-1, Tierras Largas, as it might have looked late in the Tierras Largas phase. The view is from the northwest, and shows the numerous bell-shaped pits in the dooryard. (Drawing by David Reynolds.)

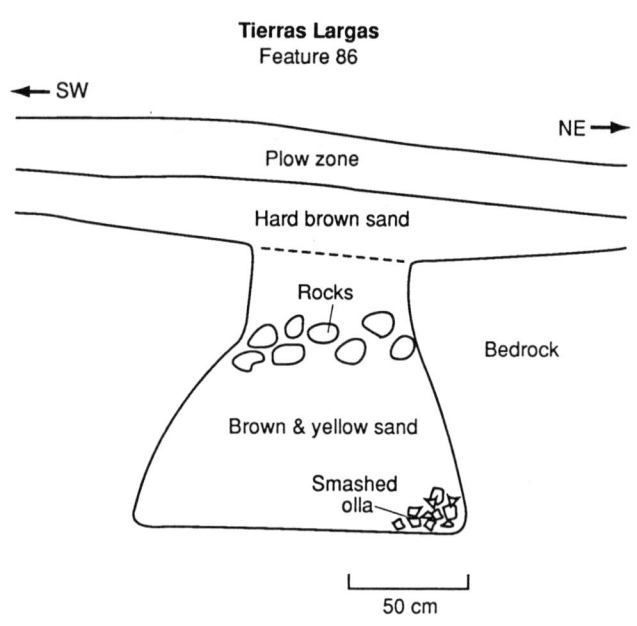

Figure 10.3. Feature 86, a bell-shaped pit associated with Household Unit LTL-1 at Tierras Largas. This feature came out on the early end of Y. Schreuder's seriation of features.

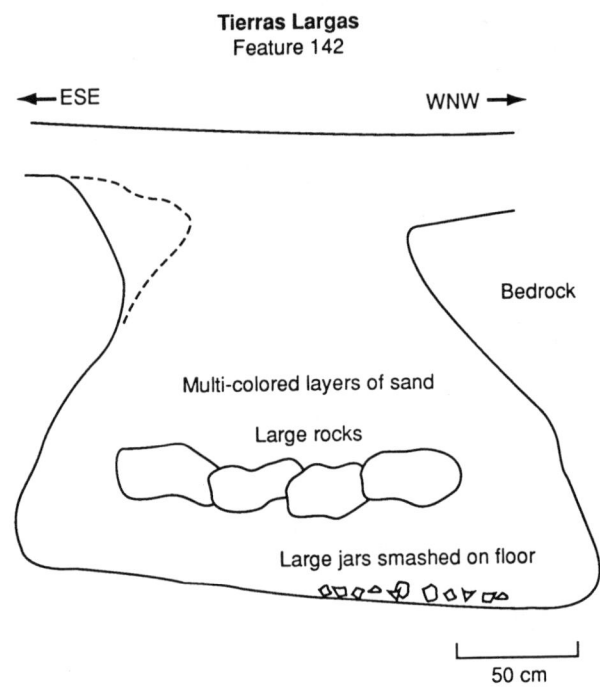

Figure 10.4. Feature 142, a bell-shaped pit associated with Household Unit LTL-1 at Tierras Largas. This feature came out on the late end of Y. Schreuder's seriation of features.

fits best between Features 86 and 117 of Household Unit LTL-1. Like those two pits, Feature 100 contained no San José phase sherd types at all, suggesting that it was filled in well before the end of the Tierras Largas phase. The 323 sherds from Feature 100 were as follows:

TIERRAS LARGAS BURNISHED PLAIN
Jar rims	4
Jar body sherds: pocked interior	176
Jar body sherds: wiped interior	33
Jar body sherds: plain interior	60
Jar shoulders: burnished interior	3
Hemispherical bowls: notched/slashed rims	3
Hemispherical bowls: body sherds	13
Misc. unclassified body sherds	1
Total	293

AVELINA RED-ON-BUFF
Jar rims	1
Jar body sherds:	
pocked interior, curvilinear design exterior	1
Hemispherical bowl rims: red rim band only	1
Hemispherical bowl rims:	
rim band interior, all red exterior	1
rim band interior, design exterior	2

Hemispherical bowl body sherds:	
all red exterior, plain interior	4
plain exterior, design interior	1
miscellaneous body sherds	1
Total	12

CLEMENTINA FINE RED-ON-BUFF
Hemispherical bowl rims: red rim band only	3
Hemispherical bowl body sherds:	
plain exterior, all red interior	2
Misc. hemispherical bowl body sherds	2
Total	7

MATADAMAS RED
Jar body sherds: pocked interior	7
Jar body sherds: wiped interior	2
Total	9

UNCLASSIFIED SHERDS
Body sherds, fluted	2
Total	2

GRAND TOTAL	323

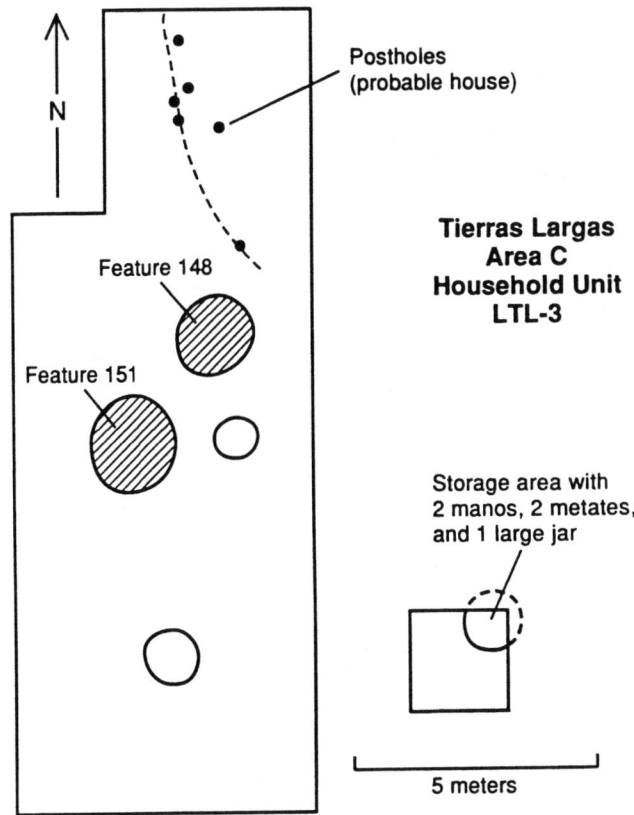

Figure 10.5. Plan view of Household Unit LTL-3 from Tierras Largas (late Tierras Largas phase). The black dots represent postholes, with the dashed line indicating the approximate limits of the house floor. The large circles are bell-shaped pits; those shown with hachure were judged to have an adequate sherd sample for analysis. (Redrawn from Flannery 1972: Fig. 7; excavation by M. Winter.)

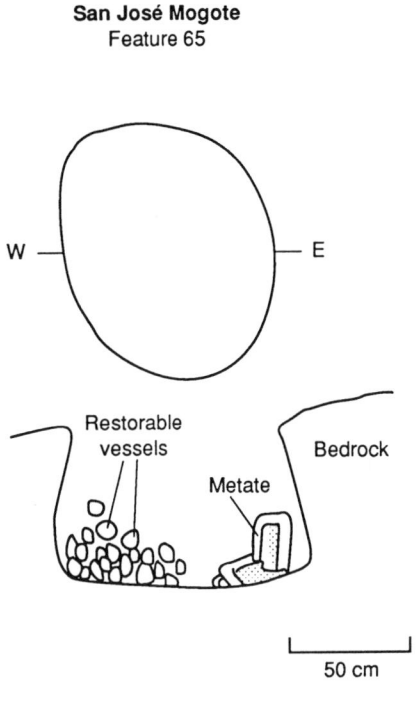

Figure 10.6. Feature 65 of San José Mogote, the lower part of a bell-shaped pit excavated into bedrock near the Area B Master Profile. Tierras Largas phase (excavation by John W. Rick).

4. Feature 65, Area B, San José Mogote (Fig. 10.6)

Feature 65 was a bell-shaped pit dug into bedrock in Square N2E8 of Area B at San José Mogote, not far from the Area B Master Profile shown in Figure 15.3, Chapter 15. It is likely that this feature was part of a late Tierras Largas phase household unit which is now partially buried under a modern house. The contents of the pit included a well-made metate, three partially restorable vessels, and a sample of 84 sherds, which were as follows:

TIERRAS LARGAS BURNISHED PLAIN
Jar rims	7
Jar body sherds: pocked interior	3
Jar body sherds: wiped interior	9
Jar body sherds: plain interior	11
Hemispherical bowls: plain rims	14
Outleaned-wall bowls: plain rims	4
Tecomate body sherds: zoned, fine dentate stamping	1
Total	49

AVELINA RED-ON-BUFF
Hemispherical bowl rims: red rim band only	3
rim band exterior, design interior	1
rims too small to show attributes	1
Hemispherical bowl body sherds	8
Total	13

CLEMENTINA FINE RED-ON-BUFF
Hemispherical bowl body sherds plain interior, design exterior	1
Total	1

MATADAMAS RED
Jar rims	1

Hemispherical bowls: plain rims	1
Miscellaneous bowl base	1
Total	3
MATADAMAS ORANGE	
Jar rims	3
Jar shoulders: burnished interior	1
Hemispherical bowls: plain rims	5
Outleaned-wall bowls: plain rims	2
Outleaned-wall bowls: plain flat bases	1
Total	12
ATOYAC YELLOW-WHITE	
Bottle: body sherd, fluted	1
Outleaned-wall bowls: plain rims	3
Outleaned-wall bowls: plain flat bases	2
Total	6
GRAND TOTAL	84

Note that all but six of the sherds from Feature 65 were from Tierras Largas phase types. The remaining six sherds are of Atoyac Yellow-white, but they all come from vessel forms typical of the late Tierras Largas phase, such as fluted bottles and undecorated outleaned-wall bowls.

The three restorable vessels also suggest a date toward the end of the Tierras Largas phase. They are (1) a Tierras Largas Burnished Plain hemispherical bowl, (2) a Matadamas Orange jar, and (3) an Atoyac Yellow-white cylinder.

Summary

Sherd counts from Households LTL-1 and LTL-3 at Tierras Largas do not vary dramatically from those of late Tierras Largas phase midden levels. However, that is probably because the features we used in our counts were chosen with great care. Not all features provide such a representative sample. Using a group of features from the same household, such as was done with LTL-1, helps to smooth out the differences among individual pits. Indeed, some of the largest bell-shaped pits may have acted as miniature middens into which sherds were swept for a considerable period of time. Others, however, had special-purpose contents and do not provide a good view of the whole ceramic assemblage. We continue to have reservations about the use of sherd samples from pits, and urge that they be evaluated carefully against good midden deposits.

APPENDIX TO CHAPTER 10

The 28 Variables Used in Yda Schreuder's Brainerd-Robinson Seriation of Tierras Largas Phase Features (1974)

TIERRAS LARGAS BURNISHED PLAIN
- Jar rims
- Jar body sherds, pocked interior
- Jar body sherds, wiped interior
- Jar body sherds, plain interior
- Jar shoulders, burnished interior
- Hemispherical bowl rims, plain
- Hemispherical bowls, basal curves
- Hemispherical bowls, plain body sherds

AVELINA RED-ON-BUFF
- Jar body sherds, wiped interior, rectilinear design exterior
- Jar body sherds, wiped interior, curvilinear or indeterminate design exterior
- Jar body sherds, plain interior, rectilinear design exterior
- Hemispherical bowl rims, red rim band only
- Hemispherical bowl rims, red rim band interior, all red exterior
- Hemispherical bowl rims, red rim band interior, design exterior
- Hemispherical bowl rims, red rim band exterior, all red interior
- Hemispherical bowl rims, red rim band exterior, design interior
- Hemispherical bowl body sherds, all red exterior, plain interior
- Hemispherical bowl body sherds, design exterior, plain interior
- Hemispherical bowl body sherds, plain exterior, all red interior
- Hemispherical bowl body sherds, plain exterior, design interior

MATADAMAS RED
- Jar rims
- Jar body sherds, pocked interior
- Jar body sherds, wiped interior
- Jar body sherds, plain interior

MATADAMAS ORANGE
- Jar body sherds, wiped interior
- Jar body sherds, plain interior
- Hemispherical bowl rims, plain
- Hemispherical bowls, basal curves

Chapter 11

Dating Tierras Largas Phase Public Buildings

In Chapter 4, we described the lime-plastered public buildings of the Tierras Largas and early San José phases, most of which were found in Area C of San José Mogote. While we don't know the exact function of those structures, we think they might be analogous to the "men's houses" of ethnographically documented autonomous village societies and minimal chiefdoms. In this chapter we describe the way in which three of those buildings—Structures 3, 5, and 6—were dated with sherd collections.

Our format for dating each structure consists of a series of questions and answers. We will first ask which stratigraphic units preceded the building of the structure, and what date the pottery samples of those units showed. We will next ask about sherds that might have been included in the fill of the building, or trapped between earlier and later floors. We will then ask about sherds left behind on the floor of the building when it was abandoned. Finally, we will ask what kinds of sherds occurred in the overlying layer of debris that followed abandonment and collapse of the building.

Structure 3

Structure 3 was found in Zone F of the Area C Master Profile at San José Mogote (Figs. 13.1–13.4). The room seems to have been about 4 m on each side and was built on a platform that, although badly destroyed, evidently extended well beyond the room in every direction. The floor of the room was inset 44 cm into the platform.

A plan view of the remains of Structure 3 can be seen in Figure 11.1. A cross-section of those remains, as they appeared in the Master Profile for Area C, can be found in Figure 11.2. For a photograph of Structure 3 in the process of being excavated, see Figure 11.3.

1. What stratigraphic zone preceded the building of Structure 3?

Answer: Zone G in the Control Section of the Area C Master Profile, whose contents are described in Table 13.1 of Chapter 13.

2. What other units might have preceded its construction?

Answer: To the south of Structure 3 was a surviving patch of the apron of lime-plastered floor that had surrounded it. Sealed beneath this lime plaster was some artificial fill, placed there to level the apron. The sherds carefully troweled out of this fill were as follows:

TIERRAS LARGAS BURNISHED PLAIN
    Jar rims   3
    Jar body sherds: pocked interior   6
    Jar body sherds: wiped interior   15
    Jar body sherds: plain interior   9
    Jar shoulders: burnished interior   2

AVELINA RED-ON-BUFF
    Hemispherical bowl rims:
        red rim band only   2
        red rim band interior, all red exterior   3
    Hemispherical bowls: basal curves   1

MATADAMAS RED
    Jar rims   1

3. Were there sherds trapped in the construction fill of the structure itself?

Answer: Yes, there were 215 sherds trapped between Floor I and Floor II of Structure 3. These sherds are probably representative of the ceramics that were lying nearby when the second of the building's plaster floors was laid down. Removed with the point of a trowel, these sherds were:

TIERRAS LARGAS BURNISHED PLAIN
    Jar rims   5
    Jar body sherds: pocked interior   36
    Jar body sherds: wiped interior   45
    Jar body sherds: plain interior   49

Jar shoulders: burnished interior	4
Hemispherical bowls: plain rims	3
Hemispherical bowls: body sherds	42
Total	184

AVELINA RED-ON-BUFF
Jar body sherds: wiped interior, curvilinear design exterior	2
Hemispherical bowls:	
red rim band only	3
rim band interior, all red exterior	1
Hemispherical bowl body sherds:	
all red exterior, plain interior	1
plain exterior, all red interior	1
plain exterior, design interior	1
Total	9

CLEMENTINA FINE RED-ON-BUFF
Hemispherical bowl rims:	
red rim band only	4
rim band exterior, all red interior	2
Hemispherical bowl body sherds:	
all red exterior, plain interior	1
plain exterior, all red interior	1
Total	8

MATADAMAS RED
Jar body sherds: wiped interior	5
Jar body sherds: plain interior	7
Total	12

UNCLASSIFIED SHERDS
Body sherds	2
Total	2

4. What did the postabandonment sherds overlying the building look like?

Answer: There were 73 sherds lying among the bits of fallen white plaster on the floor of Structure 3 after its abandonment. They were as follows:

TIERRAS LARGAS BURNISHED PLAIN
Jar body sherds: pocked interior	4
Jar body sherds: wiped interior	5
Jar body sherds: plain interior	11

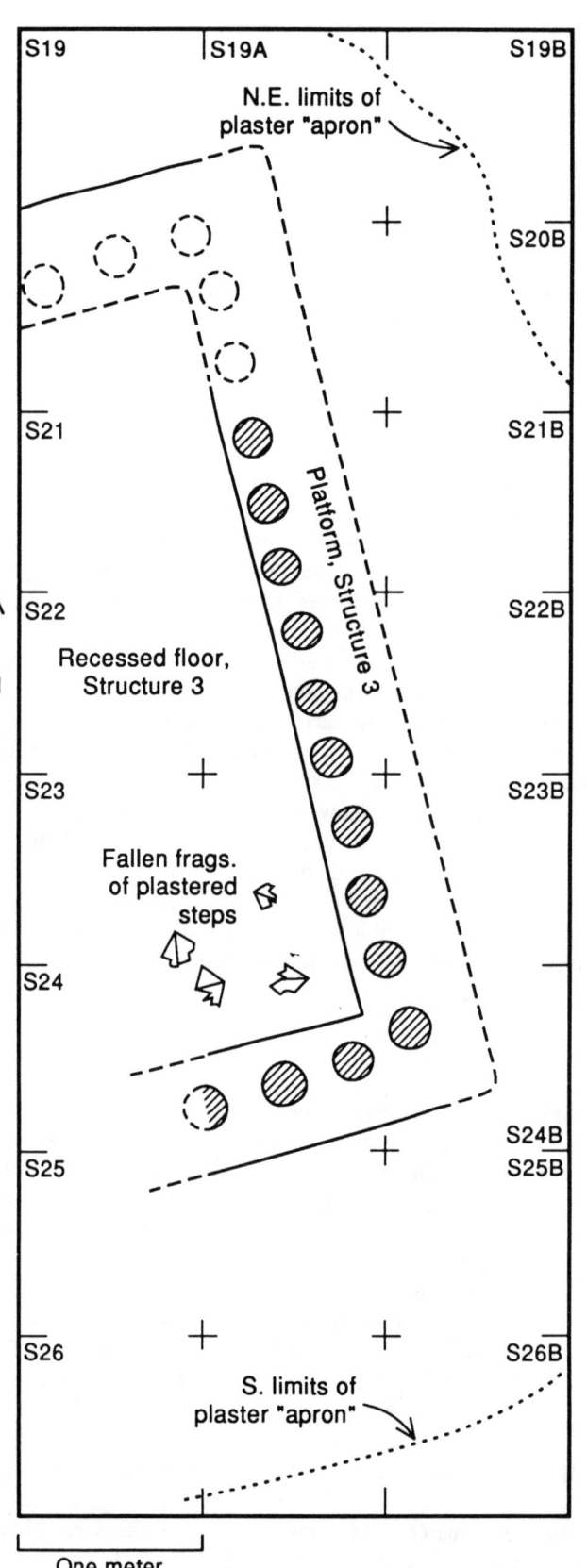

Figure 11.1 (right). Plan view of Structure 3 at San José Mogote, a Tierras Largas phase public building. This structure was a one-room building on a low platform surrounded by a plaster "apron," much like the building shown in Figure 4.6 (Chapter 4); it had broken down in much the way shown in Figure 4.7. The hachured circles represent postmolds. This structure can be located within Area C of San José Mogote by comparing the square designations with those shown in Figure 9.2.

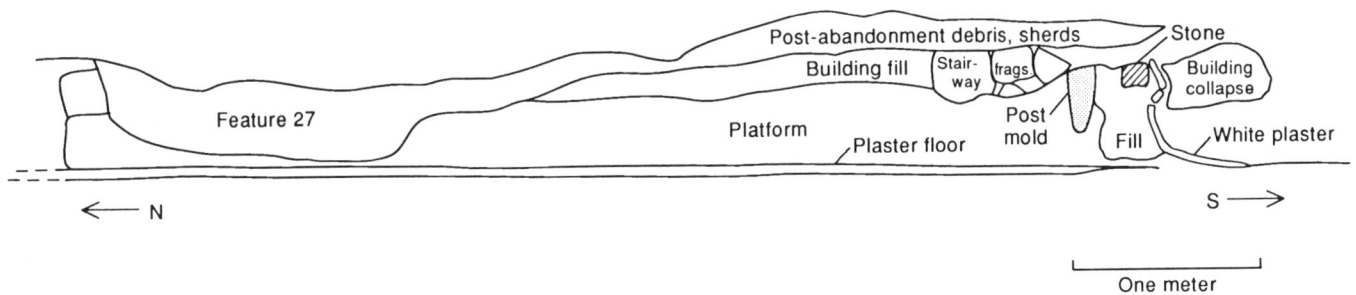

Figure 11.2. Simplified cross-section of the collapsed remains of Structure 3, San José Mogote, as it appeared between Squares S21 and S25 of the Master Profile of Area C (see Fig. 13.2).

Figure 11.3. Working in Square S25A of the Area C Master Profile, Joseph W. Hopkins uses a paintbrush to expose the point where the lime-plastered "apron" around Structure 3 curves up to form the 40-cm vertical south face of the structure's platform. (The postmold shown in Fig 11.2 lies just behind the bowl of Hopkins' pipe.) A large section of white-plastered building collapse (also shown in Fig. 11.2) can be seen in the profile about 30–50 cm above the paintbrush. The dark stains on the lower part of the profile represent moisture from the severed roots of a modern tree.

Jar shoulders: burnished interior	4
Hemispherical bowls: plain rims	6
Hemispherical bowls: basal curves	2
Hemispherical bowls: body sherds	21
Total	53

AVELINA RED-ON-BUFF

Jar rims	1
Jar shoulders:	
plain interior, all red exterior	1
Hemispherical bowls:	
red rim band only	7
rim band interior, all red exterior	3
rim band exterior, all red interior	1
rim band exterior, design interior	1
Hemispherical bowl body sherds:	
plain interior, all red exterior	5
Total	19

"HYBRID" VESSEL: ATOYAC YELLOW-WHITE OUTSIDE, AVELINA RED-ON-BUFF INSIDE

Oval bowls with pinched-in sides: rims	1
Total	1

5. What stratigraphic zone followed the abandonment of Structure 3?

Answer: Zone E in the Control Section of the Area C Master Profile, whose contents are described in Table 13.1 of Chapter 13.

Conclusion

Structure 3 clearly dates to the Tierras Largas phase. The 215 sherds trapped in its construction fill do not include a single fragment that is not typical of the phase. Even the postabandonment debris contains only one sherd that is slightly unusual. That sherd combines Avelina Red-on-Buff treatment (a Tierras Largas attribute) with an Atoyac Yellow-white slip (a San José phase attribute). Such "hybrid" vessels are known from the late Tierras Largas phase and early San José phase.

Structure 5

Structure 5 appeared in the Master Profile of Area C, San José Mogote (see Figs. 13.1–13.4). The room itself is estimated to have been a little over 4 m on a side; the platform on which it stood extended well beyond the room in every direction. The floor of the room was inset nearly 40 cm into the platform. A cross-section of the remains of Structure 5 can be seen in Figure 11.4.

1. What stratigraphic zone preceded the building of Structure 5?

Answer: Zone G in the Control Section of the Area C Master Profile, whose contents are described in Table 13.1 of Chapter 13.

2. What other units might have preceded its construction?

Answer: No other pre-construction units were found.

3. Were there sherds trapped in the construction fill of the structure itself?

Answer: Yes, there were 829 sherds trapped in the earth-and-crushed-bedrock fill of the platform and wall foundations of Structure 5. They were as follows:

TIERRAS LARGAS BURNISHED PLAIN

Jar rims	16
Jar body sherds: pocked interior	89
Jar body sherds: wiped interior	212
Jar body sherds: plain interior	133
Jar shoulders: burnished interior	5
Hemispherical bowls:	
plain rims	51
notched/slashed rims	1
basal curves	9
body sherds	209
Outleaned-wall bowls:	
notched rims	1
plain body sherds	1
Total	727

AVELINA RED-ON-BUFF

Jar body sherds:	
wiped interior, rect. design exterior	11
wiped interior, curv. design exterior	2
plain interior, curv. design exterior	1
Hemispherical bowl rims:	
red rim band only	12
rim band interior, all red exterior	1
rim band interior, design exterior	3
rim band exterior, all red interior	1
rim band exterior, design interior	1
Hemispherical bowl body sherds:	
all red exterior, plain interior	1
plain exterior, all red interior	1
plain exterior, design interior	2
miscellaneous body sherds	4
Miscellaneous unclassified body sherds	1
Total	41

CLEMENTINA FINE RED-ON-BUFF

Hemispherical bowl rims:	
red rim band only	7
red rim band exterior, red interior	1

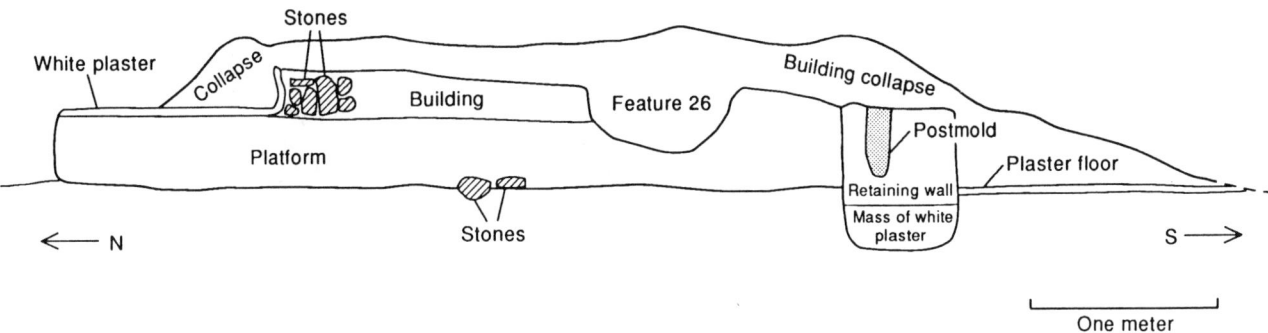

Figure 11.4. Simplified cross-section of the collapsed remains of Structure 5, San José Mogote, as it appeared between Squares S28 and S32 of the Master Profile of Area C (see Fig. 13.4).

Hemispherical bowl body sherds: misc.	5
Hemispherical bowls: basal curves	7
Total	20
MATADAMAS RED	
Jar body sherds: pocked interior	2
Jar body sherds: wiped interior	2
Jar body sherds: plain interior	5
Total	9
MATADAMAS ORANGE	
Jar rim	2
Jar body sherds: wiped interior	1
Hemispherical bowls: plain rims	1
Total	4
OCOS BLACK	
Thin-walled tecomates with zoned rocker stamping: body sherds	1
Total	1
FIDENCIO COARSE	
Jar shoulders: sloppy jabs	1
Plain body sherds	2
Total	3
LEANDRO GRAY	
Bolstered-rim bowls: burnished exterior	1
Plain body sherds	4
Total	5
ATOYAC YELLOW-WHITE	
Bottle rim/neck sherds	2
Outleaned-wall bowls: plain rims	1
Cylinders: plain rims	1
Cylinders: plain flat bases	1
Tecomate rims	1
Miscellaneous decorated body sherds	2
Total	8
LUPITA HEAVY PLAIN	
Tecomate body sherds: rocker stamping	1
Outleaned-wall bowls: plain flat bases	1
Miscellaneous decorated body sherds	1
Plain body sherds	2
Total	5
UNCLASSIFIED SHERDS	
Rim sherds	1
Body sherds	5
Total	6

4. What were the postabandonment sherds overlying the building like?

Answer: There were 91 sherds lying among the bits of fallen white plaster on the floor of Structure 5 after its abandonment. They were as follows:

TIERRAS LARGAS BURNISHED PLAIN	
Jar body sherds: pocked interior	1
Jar body sherds: wiped interior	3
Jar body sherds: plain interior	6
Hemispherical bowls: plain rims	5
Hemispherical bowls: body sherds	11
Total	26
AVELINA RED-ON-BUFF	
Jar body sherds:	
wiped interior, rect. design exterior	2
plain interior, curv. design exterior	3
Hemispherical bowl rims:	
red rim band only	4
rim band interior, all red exterior	2
rim band exterior, all red interior	1

Hemispherical bowl body sherds:
  all red exterior, plain interior   3
  plain exterior, all red interior   5
  miscellaneous body sherds   8
Total   28

CLEMENTINA FINE RED-ON-BUFF
Hemispherical bowl rims:
  red rim band only   2
Hemispherical bowls: misc. body sherd   1
Total   3

MATADAMAS ORANGE
Jar rims   2
Hemispherical bowls: rims   3
Hemispherical bowls: body sherds   5
Tecomate body sherds: rocker stamp   3
Total   13

LEANDRO GRAY
Outleaned-wall bowls: plain rims   3
Cylinders: excised rims   3
Miscellaneous excised body sherds   4
Total   10

ATOYAC YELLOW-WHITE
Cylinders: plain rims   3
Tecomate body sherds: rocker stamp   4
Plain body sherds   2
Total   9

XOCHILTEPEC WHITE
Body sherds   1
Total   1

LA MINA WHITE
Body sherds   1
Total   1

5. What stratigraphic zone followed the abandonment of Structure 5?

Answer: Zone E in the Control Section of the Area C Master Profile, whose contents are described in Table 13.1 of Chapter 13.

Conclusion

Structure 5 probably was built very late in the Tierras Largas phase. Of the 829 sherds trapped in the fill of the platform and wall foundation, at least 808 are typical Tierras Largas phase sherds. The remaining 21 sherds are from types that make their first appearance toward the end of the Tierras Largas phase and go on to reach maximum popularity in the San José phase. Even the latter sherds, however, are from vessel forms that occur early in the chronological history of the type: bottles, tecomates, and flat-based bowls, for example, all of which are known from the Tierras Largas phase. In the postabandonment debris overlying Structure 5, 70 of 91 sherds are from common Tierras Largas phase types; the remaining 21 are all from types that were present during the Tierras Largas–San José phase transition. No sherds from vessels restricted to the San José phase were present in any of the collections used to date Structure 5.

Structure 6

Structure 6 (Figs. 11.5–11.8) was one of the best preserved of all the Tierras Largas phase public buildings found in Area C. Like Structures 3 and 5, it was built on a rectangular platform of crushed bedrock, lime, clay, and sand, oriented roughly 8° west of true north. Its floor was sunk roughly 40 cm below the upper level of this platform. If we allow for all the warping and distortion caused by the destruction of the building and the weight of the overburden, its floor area measured roughly 5.33 m east–west and 4.30 m north–south.

The vertical walls of the room were of wattle-and-daub 50–60 cm thick, and rose directly from the surface of the platform; in places, their foundations included stones 2 courses high. These wattle-and-daub walls were built around a series of vertically set posts about 16 cm in diameter, driven all the way through the platform and into bedrock. The posts were set approximately 40–80 cm apart, which meant that there might be anywhere from 7 to 12 posts per wall. The doorway was on the south side and seems to have been 1.0–1.5 m wide. One entered by means of a step which was about half the distance down from the threshold to the floor.

The platform, the step, the inside and outside of the building, and the floor were all coated with several layers of lime plaster or stucco. In some places, it appeared that the building had been plastered at least three separate times. Also plastered several times was a cylindrical pit 36 cm in diameter and 38 cm deep, which had been built into the center of the floor as part of the original construction of the building (Fig. 11.6, right). This pit, designated Feature 56, was filled to the brim with powdered lime when found.

Elsewhere (Drennan 1983a:48; Marcus and Flannery n.d.), we have expressed agreement with Michael D. Coe's suggestion that this powdered lime was probably stored to use with some narcotic, such as tobacco. Powdered tobacco was widely used in offerings by other Oaxacan peoples (Furst 1978), and several sixteenth-century *relaciones* from Zapotec towns list tobacco as an important plant.

Because of later destruction, it was not possible to measure the platform that surrounded and supported Structure 6, but it was evidently larger than 8 × 8 m. Some clues to the construction of the building were provided by collapsed roof material found among the pieces of fallen plaster on the floor. One fragment of fallen daub bore the impression of what seems to have

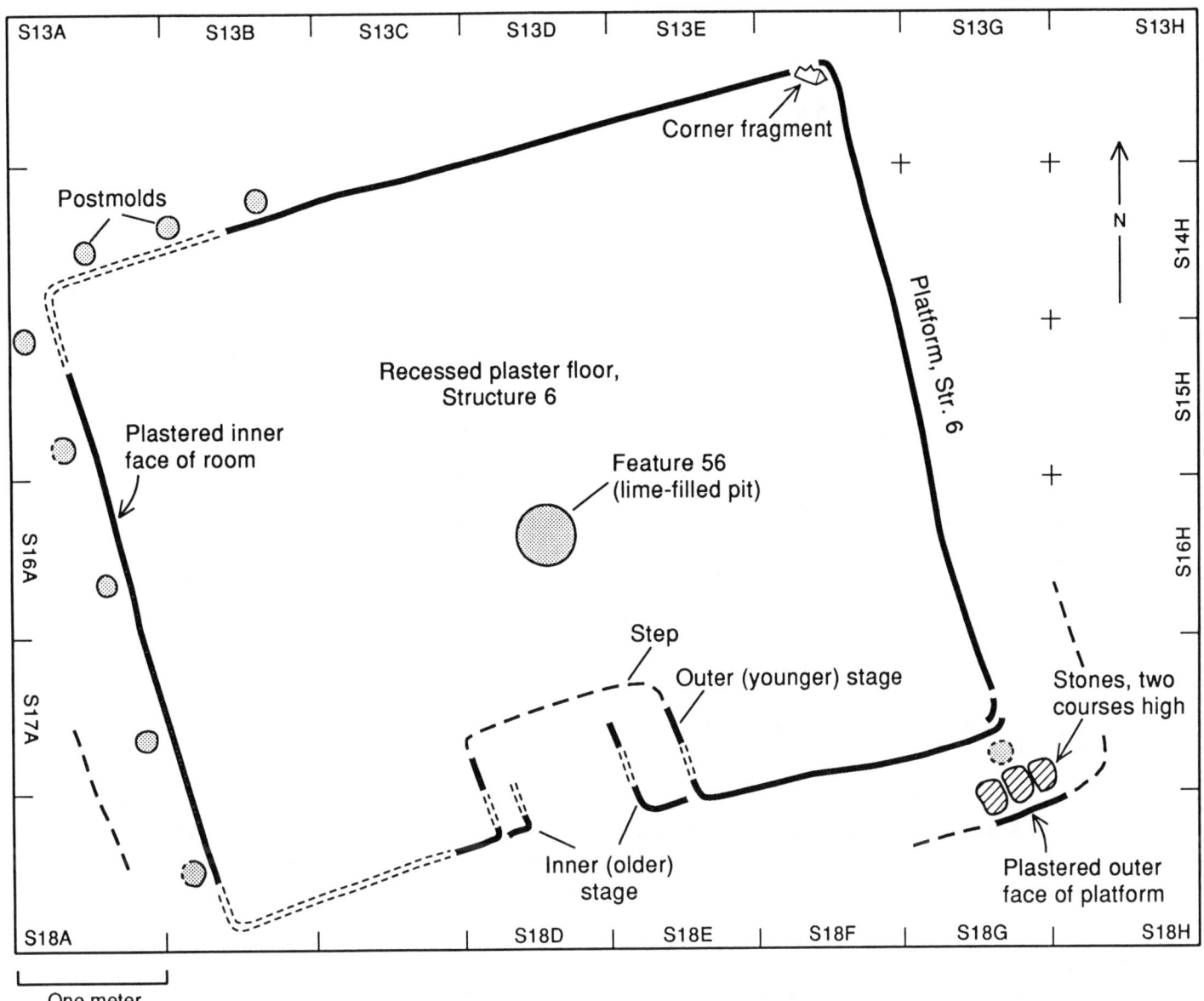

Figure 11.5. Plan view of Structure 6 at San José Mogote, a Tierras Largas phase public building. This structure was a one-room building on a low platform surrounded by a plaster "apron," much like the building shown in Figure 4.6 (Chapter 4); it had broken down in much the way shown in Figure 4.7. The stippled circles represent postmolds; Feature 56 was a lime-filled pit (see Fig. 11.6, right). This structure can be located within Area C of San José Mogote by comparing the square designations with those shown in Figure 9.2.

been a roof beam 11 cm in diameter. Some 7 cm of clay daub had been applied to this beam and given a half-centimeter coat of pure white lime plaster.

Traces of reeds and reed matting were also found. This substantiated our evidence from Structure 15, a similar building whose roof evidently burned. In the case of Structure 15, carbonized remains of reed mats (*petates*), reeds (*Phragmites* sp.), and reed canary grass (*Phalaris* sp.) suggested that roofs were constructed by lashing reed mats over the roof beams and thatching them with reed canary grass or *Phragmites*.

1. What stratigraphic zone preceded the building of Structure 6?

Answer: Zone G in the Control Section of the Area C Master Profile, whose contents are described in Table 13.1 of Chapter 13.

2. What other units might have preceded its construction?

Answer: Since Structure 6 was consolidated for posterity (Fig. 11.8), rather than being taken apart bit by bit, we do not know whether there were any other sherds trapped beneath its floor.

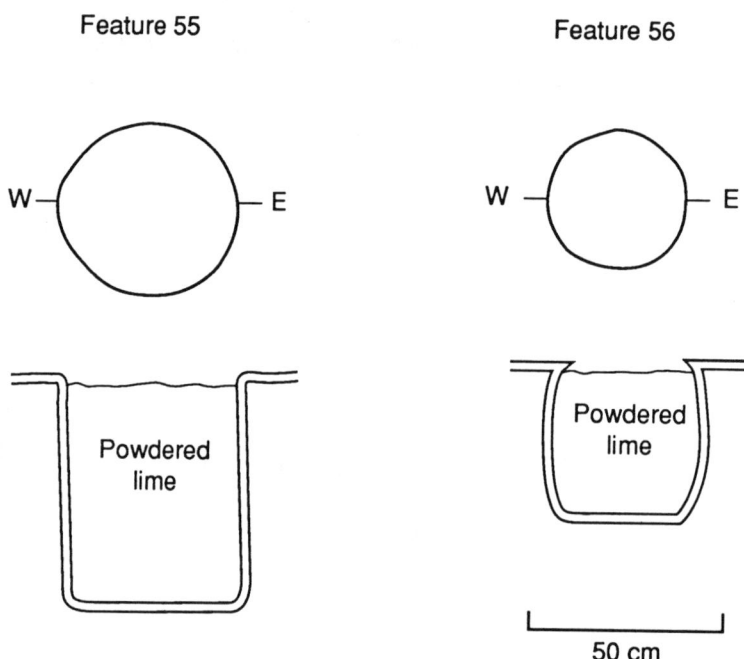

Figure 11.6. Plastered pits containing powdered lime, found in Tierras Largas phase public buildings in Area C, San José Mogote. Feature 56 was found in Structure 6 (Fig. 11.5), while Feature 55 was found in Structure 15 (see text).

3. Were there sherds trapped in the construction fill of the structure itself?

Answer: There were occasional sherds trapped between the first, second, and third plaster floors. However, since the third floor was consolidated for posterity, such sherds were only visible in the profiles of later pits that intruded through the floor of Structure 6.

For example, in the northwest corner of the floor there was a later intrusion that revealed sherds trapped between Floors II and III. Those sherds were as follows:

TIERRAS LARGAS BURNISHED PLAIN
   Hemispherical bowls: notched/slashed rims   1

AVELINA RED-ON-BUFF
   Jar rims   1
   Jar body sherds   1
   Hemispherical bowl rims: red rim band only   1
   Hemispherical bowl body sherds:
      all red exterior, plain interior   1

In the northeast corner of the floor was another disturbance that allowed us to see a few sherds trapped between Floor I and Floor II. Included were 3 rims and 19 body sherds from a Tierras Largas Burnished Plain hemispherical bowl. In this case, it looked as if the sherds had been deliberately laid flat on Floor I (within a thin layer of sand and clay) to provide partial support for the new layer of plaster—Floor II.

4. Did any sherds, dating to the period of use of Structure 6, appear to have been left lying on Floor III?

Answer: No. The floor appeared to have been swept clean. This was typical of most of our public buildings.

5. What were the postabandonment sherds overlying the building like?

Answer: There were 399 sherds lying among the bits of fallen plaster on the floor of Structure 6 after its abandonment. Because so much of Structure 6 was preserved, we were able to divide its floor into quadrants (NW, SW, NE, SE) and excavate the postabandonment debris of each quadrant separately. This was done so that, should one quadrant turn out to have intrusive later material, that material would not contaminate the whole collection of sherds. As it turned out, all intrusive features were so easy to work around that contamination by later sherds was not a problem. Table 11.1 lists our collection of postabandonment sherds by quadrant.

Figure 11.7. Standing in Square S17A of Area C, San José Mogote, Henry T. Wright works to expose the western side of Structure 6's recessed floor. In this view, looking south along the Area C Master Profile, the juncture between the horizontal plaster floor and the base of the west wall appears as a line running across the photograph from upper left to lower right. Wright is systematically following the vertical face of the west wall, coring out postmolds (like the one near his left elbow) and leaving fallen chunks of lime plaster on pedestals.

Figure 11.8. Workers build a protective stone wall around the surviving floor of Structure 6, Area C, San José Mogote (view from the east). This photo shows many of the details seen in Figure 4.7. For example, one can see the way the floor of the room was recessed into the underlying platform. At this stage of excavation, the floor has been swept clean of sherds and fallen plaster fragments; the interior step has been repaired with cement; and the centrally placed pit (Feature 56) has been emptied of its powdered lime.

TABLE 11.1
Sherds from the Debris Lying on the Floor of Structure 6 after Its Abandonment (Given by Quadrants)

	Quadrants			
	NW	SW	NE	SE
TIERRAS LARGAS BURNISHED PLAIN				
Jar rims	10	14	1	4
Jar body sherds: pocked interior	2	3	-	-
Jar body sherds: wiped interior	18	30	2	24
Jar body sherds: plain interior	15	18	1	10
Jar shoulders: burnished interior	6	2	-	5
Hemispherical bowls: plain rims	12	17	14	4
Hemispherical bowls: notched/slashed rims	-	2	-	-
Hemispherical bowls: thickened, wedge-shaped rim	-	3	-	-
Hemispherical bowls: eccen. rim tab, rocker stamping	1	-	-	-
Hemispherical bowls: basal curves	-	2	-	1
Hemispherical bowls: body sherds	10	13	30	15
Outleaned-wall bowls: plain rims	-	1	-	-
Outleaned-wall bowls: plain bases	-	-	-	1
Possible cylinder base	1	-	-	-
Miscellaneous unclassified rims	3	2	1	2
Miscellaneous unclassified bases	2	3	2	1
Total	80	110	51	67
TIERRAS LARGAS UNBURNISHED PLAIN				
Hemispherical bowls: plain rims	-	1	-	-
Total	-	1	-	-
AVELINA RED-ON-BUFF				
Jar rims	-	4	-	1
Jar body sherds:				
pocked interior, rectilinear design ext.	1	-	-	-
pocked interior, curvilinear design ext.	-	-	-	1
wiped interior, rectilinear design ext.	3	8	-	-
plain interior, rectilinear design ext.	1	-	-	-
Hemispherical bowl rims:				
red rim band only	6	6	1	7
rim band int., all red ext.	3	4	-	4
rim band int., ext. design	1	-	1	-
rim band ext., all red int.	-	-	-	2
rim band ext., int. design	1	-	-	-
all red, both sides	1	-	-	1
Hemispherical bowl body sherds:				
exterior all red, interior plain	-	1	-	5
all red, both sides	-	1	-	-
Bottle neck: rim band int., all red ext.	-	1	-	-
Tecomates: specular red rim band	-	2	-	-
Tecomates: all specular red outside	-	1	-	-
Total	17	28	2	21
CLEMENTINA FINE RED-ON-BUFF				
Hemispherical bowl rims:				
red rim band only	-	2	1	-
rim band interior, all red exterior	-	3	-	-
all red, both sides	1	-	-	-
Hemispherical bowl body sherds:				
plain interior, all red exterior	3	-	-	2
all red, both sides	2	-	-	-
Total	6	5	1	2
MATADAMAS RED				
Jar rims	1	1	1	-
Hemispherical bowls: plain rims	2	1	-	-
Total	3	2	1	-
MATADAMAS ORANGE				
Hemispherical bowls: plain rims	-	1	-	-
Total	-	1	-	-

TABLE 11.1 (continued)

	Quadrants			
	NW	SW	NE	SE
POSSIBLE FOREIGN WARES				
Unknown red-on-white hemispherical bowl, white outside, red inside	-	1	-	-
Total	-	1	-	-
GRAND TOTAL	106	148	55	90

6. What other excavation units were found above Structure 6?

Answer: Structure 15—another Tierras Largas phase public building—was found directly above Structure 6. Its ground plan was so similar to Structure 6's that its centrally placed pit full of powdered lime (Feature 55) intruded through the floor of Structure 6 less than half a meter northeast of Feature 56 (Fig. 11.6, left).

7. What major stratigraphic zone followed Structure 6?

Answer: Zone E in the Control Section of the Area C Master Profile, whose ceramics are given in Table 13.1 of Chapter 13, overlay Structure 15.

Conclusion

Since Structure 6 overlies Zone G, it presumably falls somewhere in the second half of the Tierras Largas phase. However, as Table 11.1 reveals, the building had no San José phase pottery types whatsoever, even in its postabandonment debris. That fact, coupled with our discovery that it was overlain by yet another Tierras Largas phase building (Structure 15), suggests that Structure 6 was earlier than Structure 5.

Chapter 12

The San José Phase

Near the end of the second millennium BC and in the initial centuries of the first, conditions over much of Mesoamerica evidently favored demographic growth, craft specialization, increased interregional exchange, greater disparities in social rank, and more elaborate ceremonialism. These changes, moreover, seem to have affected certain communities earlier to a greater degree than others. San Lorenzo in Veracruz, San José Mogote in Oaxaca, Chalcatzingo in Morelos, Coapexco, Tlapacoya, Tlatilco and possibly Cuicuilco in the Basin of Mexico are among the sites which illustrate these tendencies to varying degrees.

[Tolstoy 1989b:275]

In simplest terms, one could describe the San José phase pottery assemblage as one in which flat-based bowls had largely replaced hemispherical bowls. Those flat-based bowls varied from cylinders with vertical walls to open bowls with outleaned walls. The designs carved on such vessels were so distinctive of the period that one could potentially define the San José phase on the basis of vessel form and decoration, without even referring to surface color.

There was, however, also an explosion of surface color when compared with the Tierras Largas phase. No longer limited to buff, red, or red-on-buff, San José phase pottery could also be gray, black, white, black-and-white, or red-on-white. Vessel forms showed an equivalent diversity. Bottles gave way to jars with tall vertical necks. Jars with flaring necks increased in size, and many had plastic decoration such as jabs, slashes, or punctations. Tecomates grew heavier and had many varieties of rocker stamping and punctation. There were also charcoal braziers/potstands, multicompartment vessels, spouted trays, pigment dishes, huge bowls like washtubs with bolstered rims, and effigy vessels of various kinds.

From a purely aesthetic standpoint, one could describe the San José phase assemblage as one of the most colorful, attractive, and varied in the history of the Valley of Oaxaca. Not until Monte Albán II—with its blacks, grays, reds, red-on-oranges, white-rimmed blacks, and red-on-creams—would anything like it be seen again (Caso, Bernal, and Acosta 1967).

While the pottery of the Tierras Largas phase was the first to contain enough stylistic information to identify the valleys of Oaxaca, Nochixtlán, Tehuacán, and the Cuicatlán Cañada as nodes in a network of interaction, the pottery of the San José phase outdid it. San José phase pottery reflected a stylistic horizon that was virtually pan-Mesoamerican. That horizon stretched from Tlatilco in the Basin of Mexico to Copán in Honduras, including not only the sites in the quotation from Tolstoy, above, but also from Mirador-Plumajillo and Chiapa de Corzo in Chiapas, Salinas La Blanca in Guatemala, and many other villages.

Tolstoy quite rightly points out that this was a period of emerging differences in social rank, with increases in interregional interaction at least partly stimulated by a relentless desire for status paraphernalia from distant regions. Along the exchange networks that sprang up, new ideas about the decoration of pottery traveled rapidly. Black ware, white ware, differentially fired white-and-black ware, and red-on-white bichromes became commonplace. Also widespread were a whole series of excised and incised designs that became pan-Mesoamerican. Those designs include depictions of what may be supernatural beings, great natural forces, or cosmological symbols. The San José phase may not be the period in which those symbols first arose, but it was the first period in which they appeared on ceramics.

"Earth" and "Sky" in the Symbolism of the San José Phase

For a variety of reasons, summarized in *The Cloud People* (Flannery and Marcus 1983), we suspect that the villagers of the San José phase were speakers of an Otomanguean language, probably an early form of Zapotec. Ethnohistoric data tell us that the Otomangueans—the Zapotec, Mixtec, and their linguistic relatives—saw Earth and Sky as two major cosmological divisions of their world. Indeed, the Earth/Sky dichotomy was widespread in ancient Mesoamerica, even beyond the territory occupied by Otomanguean speakers.

Ethnohistoric sources and sixteenth-century dictionaries suggest that Earth and Sky were not merely cosmological provinces, but supernatural influences on humans. The power of Earth was symbolized for the Zapotec in *xòo*, "earthquake," a fearsome reminder that Earth was alive and could become angry. The power of Sky was symbolized by *cociyo*, "lightning," a serpentine bolt of fire which demonstrated to humans that Sky was also alive and could become angry.

It was not easy to depict Earth and Sky symbolically, but we believe that San José phase villagers created the appropriate motifs by showing those forces in their "angry state,"—that is, by depicting Earth as "earthquake" and Sky as "lightning." We further believe that these forces can be detected in the two supernatural beings Covarrubias (1957) and Coe (1965) defined as the "were-jaguar," and the "fire-serpent" or "sky-dragon." Our suspicion is that the fire-serpent represents lightning quite literally, as a serpent of fire in the darkened sky. The were-jaguar, on the other hand, represents earthquake as a human with a feline mouth and a fissure in his skull left by the temblor. Vegetation is often shown growing in the fissure.

In some parts of Mesoamerica, such as the Basin of Mexico, the fire-serpent may be realistically depicted as a snake with flames rising from his eyebrows (Fig. 12.1*a*). He can, however, be shown simply as a series of excised bars, a set of upside-down U-motifs depicting his gums, and a set of sine curves representing his eyebrow flames (Fig. 12.1*d, f, h*). This is the way he is usually depicted in Oaxaca (Fig. 12.2*b, c*).

The were-jaguar can be depicted realistically as a grotesque human with a snarling feline mouth and a cleft skull (Fig. 12.2*d*). In Oaxaca, however, he is usually reduced to a stylized cleft-skull mask on a background of fine-line hachure, framed by giant "music brackets" (Fig. 12.2*e, f*). To be sure, the San José phase occasionally produced more realistic were-jaguars (Fig. 12.3), but the vast majority of all were-jaguars and fire-serpents in Oaxaca were highly stylized. Often those stylized supernatural forces were accompanied by other pan-Mesoamerican motifs such as the St. Andrew's cross (Fig. 12.4).

Pyne (1976) has presented statistical evidence that in Oaxaca these two supernatural beings—expressed by a variety of free-standing motifs—were more strongly associated with residential groupings than with public buildings. Their distribution was almost mutually exclusive; households with high frequencies of fire-serpents showed a negative statistical association with the were-jaguar, and vice versa.

Small hamlets like Tierras Largas and Abasolo tend to have motifs related to only one of these supernaturals, but the large village of San José Mogote had separate residential wards associated with each. Specifically, Areas A and C of San José Mogote were associated with the fire-serpent, as were the smaller sites of Tomaltepec and Abasolo. Area B of San José Mogote, on the other hand, was associated with the were-jaguar, as were the smaller sites of Tierras Largas and Abasolo. Moreover, fire-serpents tend to occur on Leandro Gray and Delfina Fine Gray vessels, while were-jaguars tend to occur on Atoyac Yellow-white.

Burial vessels with these pan-Mesoamerican motifs also had an interesting distribution. When the burials were those of persons old enough to be sexed by a biological anthropologist, pots bearing such motifs occurred only with males. This distribution is the opposite of the situation at Tlatilco in the Basin of Mexico, where such motifs tend to occur with females (Tolstoy 1989b:290). This difference is fascinating because Tolstoy (1989a:117) believes, on the basis of burial position, that there were two intermarrying groups at Tlatilco and that "the in-marrying spouse was most often a male." At San José Mogote, on the other hand, we believe that there were at least two intermarrying groups and that the in-marrying spouse was most often a female. Such differences may be pertinent to social relations between the two regions.

For Oaxaca, as we have mentioned, Marcus (1989:170) has suggested that the were-jaguar and fire-serpent motifs represent not actual deities, but stylized depictions of Earth and Sky:

> While the Otomangueans revered sky and earth as two normally benevolent supernatural forces, both ethnohistory and ethnography suggest that they were more fascinated by the way those two supernaturals manifested their anger. Therefore, we might expect Otomanguean depictions of sky and earth to capture these supernatural forces in their "angry" state rather than their benevolent one. The sky revealed its anger by producing lightning, a powerful visual image. I suggest that the Formative Zapotec captured this impressive supernatural by excising with bold, strong strokes the "fire-serpent" motif. This motif was often placed on gray or black vessels at a 45° angle, perhaps an attempt to capture both the movement of lightning and the color of the overcast sky. The motif usually includes three elements: (1) *raspada* bars that are broad and deep, (2) finer-lined flames or flame-scrolls, and (3) inverted U-shaped elements. Coe (1965b, 1973) has interpreted these elements as the "paw-wing" motifs, "flame-eyebrows," and the "gums" of the "fire-serpent" or "sky-dragon."
>
> The earth showed its anger by opening its surface, emitting loud noises, and moving itself from side to side. These fissures, tremors, and quakes also provided powerful impressions. I suggest that Formative Otomangueans represented this by means of the "were-jaguar" motif which usually

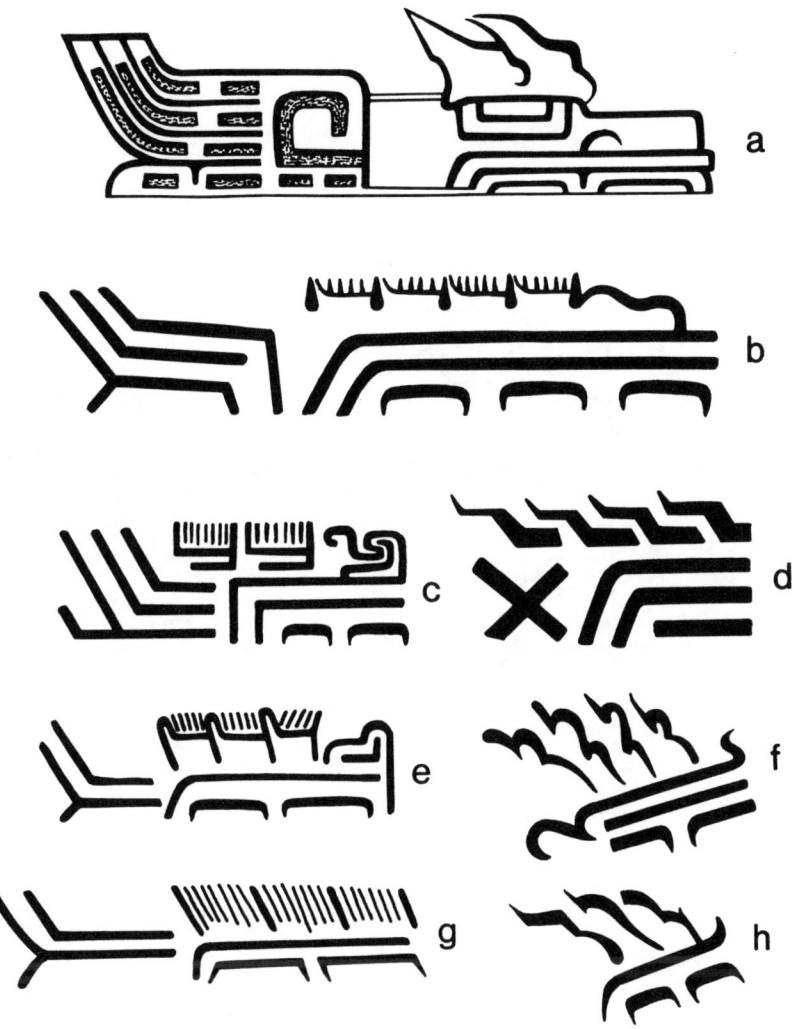

Figure 12.1. Representations of the fire-serpent (Sky) on the pottery of Tlatilco, Basin of Mexico. Beginning with the most realistic representation at *a*, the series proceeds to more abstract representations at *g* and *h*. (Redrawn from Covarrubias 1957: Fig 9.)

includes at least two of the following elements: (1) a cleft, (2) oversized "music brackets," (3) small dots or circles in the "tabs" to either side of the cleft, and (4) fine-line hachure. While the cleft has been proposed as representing the sagittal furrow of the jaguar's head (Coe 1972:2), a case can be made that the cleft represents a fissure in the surface of the earth. This view is reinforced by the fact that sometimes emanating from these fissures are plants, occasionally maize (Coe 1973, Joralemon 1971) or, in much later times, human figures. Similar clefts are shown in the later codices, representing the places from which the "original Mixtecs" emerged from the earth (Smith 1973: Fig. 5). (Earlier we discussed the Mixtec term *ñuhu* which can mean sacred, earth, fire, or spirit; the earliest Mixtec were *ñuhu*, both sacred and earthly, emerging from a cleft or fissure in the earth.)

To return to Formative Oaxacan depictions of the "were-jaguar," we sometimes see four circles surrounding a central bar or "trough" in addition to the cleft; this may be a convention for the four Mesoamerican world quarters or the four "corners" of the earth (Parsons 1936:313). The central bar, in contrast, may refer to the center or interior of the earth.

Thus, the "were-jaguar" motif in its most complete form may be the Otomanguean manifestation of the earth, earthquake's fissure, the four world quarters, and the earth's interior. It will be remembered that Otomanguean ritual honoring the earth, as revealed ethnographically, involved the burial of offerings in the earth and in agricultural fields (e.g. Beals 1973:98; DeCicco 1969:364). Interestingly enough, while it does not lie in the Otomanguean-speaking region, the site of La Venta seems to have at least three permanent buried were-jaguar offerings which may have been dedicated to the earth. Jaguar mosaic pavements 1, 2, 3 in Complex A (Coe 1965: Fig. 45) display many of the elements we have just described, including the cleft and the four elements flanking a central bar or "trough." Thus, these labor-intensive buried offerings may both represent the earth as well as honor it. [Marcus 1989:170–73]

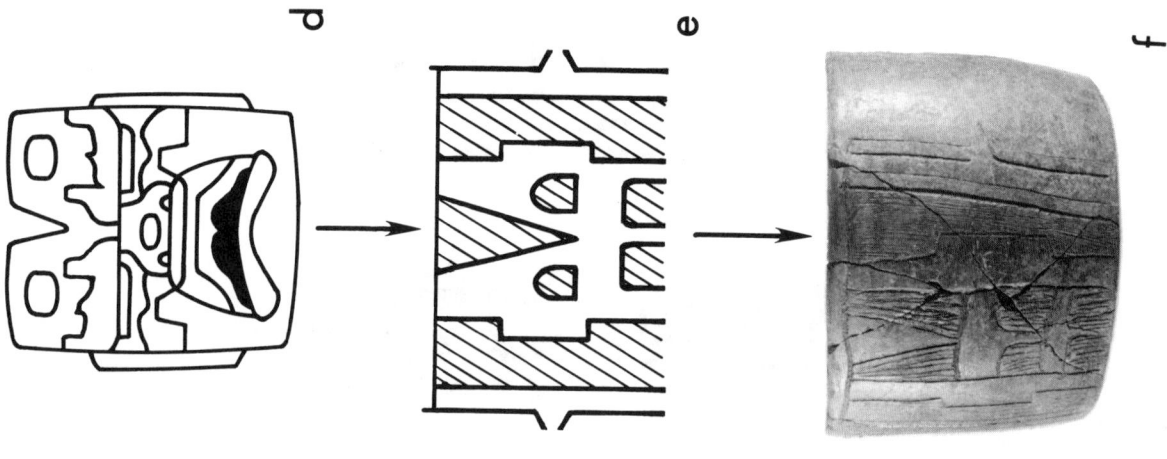

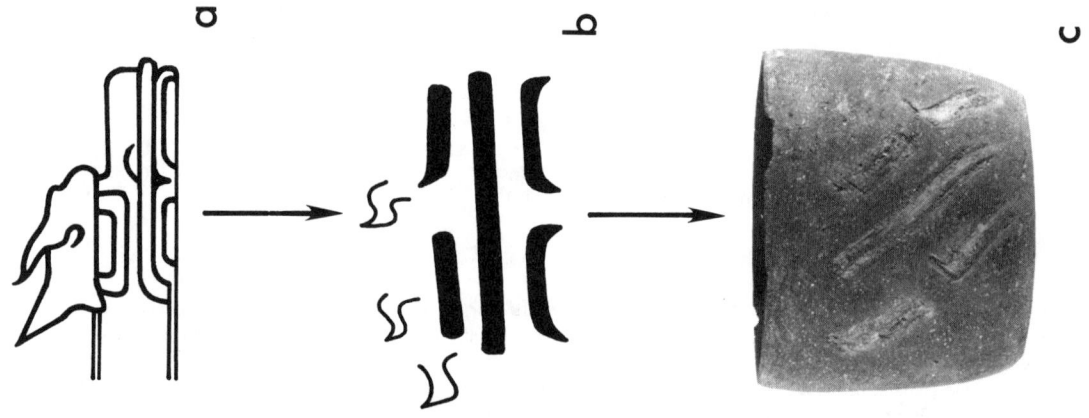

Figure 12.2. The derivation of the most common fire-serpent (Sky or Lightning) and were-jaguar (Earth or Earthquake) motifs used in the San José phase (redrawn from Flannery and Marcus 1976b: Fig. 6).

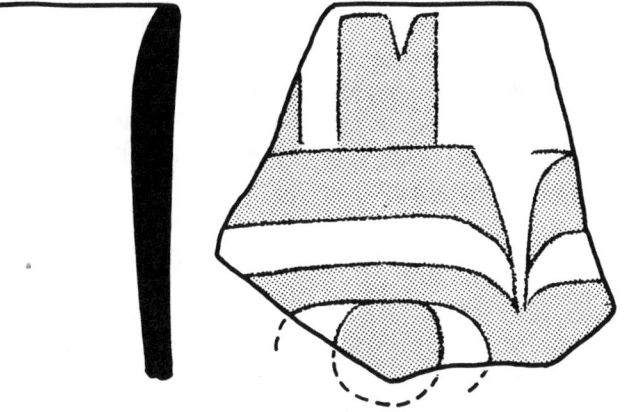
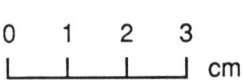

Figure 12.3. A rim sherd from an Atoyac Yellow-white cylindrical bowl with a relatively realistic incised were-jaguar motif on the exterior. The design is highlighted by differential burnishing: the area shown as shaded is left matte, while the remainder is double-burnished. The design seems to be the face of a were-jaguar with cleft-head elements rising from his eyebrows. San José Mogote, Area C, cleaning profile at the level of the San José phase deposits.

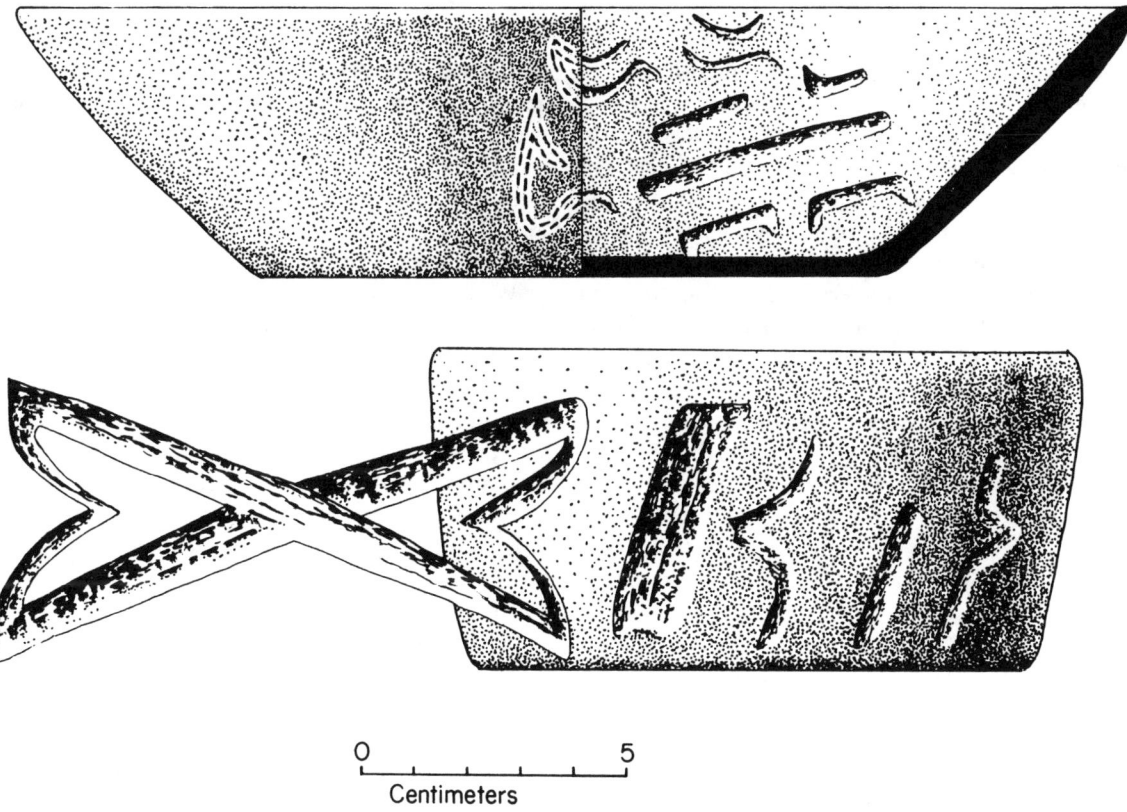

Figure 12.4. Reconstruction drawings of vessels from the fill of Structure 1, San José Mogote, a San José phase public building. The Leandro Gray outleaned-wall bowl at the top has Pyne's Motif 1 excised on the interior. The San José Black-and-White cylinder at the bottom has Pyne's Motif 11 excised on the outside, next to a St. Andrew's Cross.

An Inventory of Free-Standing Motifs

In her original study of 595 decorated sherds from the San José phase, Pyne (1976) distinguished eighteen free-standing motifs. Seven of these were considered to be variants of the fire-serpent (Sky); seven were considered to be variants of the were-jaguar (Earth); and four did not fit either of those two categories. The four latter motifs seem to be specific to Oaxaca, rather than pan-Mesoamerican. Since they frequently occur on the same pottery types as the first 14 motifs, and are treated in many of the same ways, they may have some local cultural or cosmological significance (Pyne 1976:274).

Space did not permit the illustration of all eighteen of Pyne's motifs in her original 1976 paper. In this chapter, therefore, we present several variants of each of her motifs (Figs. 12.5–12.16).

The Origins of the "Double-Line-Break" Motif

Another of the decorative techniques making its first appearance in the San José phase was the "double-line-break." This is the term coined by Michael Coe (1961) for a form of incised decoration usually occurring on white-ware bowls; in the case of the Valley of Oaxaca, it usually appears on flat-based bowls (vertical-walled to outleaned-wall) in Atoyac Yellow-white.

Such bowls typically have a series of two, three, or four parallel incised lines running around the bowl just below the rim. (In the case of outleaned-wall bowls, the lines are on the inside; in vertical-wall bowls, they are on the outside.) At intervals, one line may turn up or down to meet the others, or the lines may be separated by a free-standing motif. It is these points, where the flow of the parallel lines has been interrupted, that are referred to as double-line-breaks. Beginning in low frequency early in the San José phase, this form of incised decoration increases through time, reaching its greatest popularity during the Middle Formative. (Indeed, in a few other regions of Mesoamerica, "double-line-breaks" do not appear at all until Middle Formative times.)

In general, double-line-break motifs have been treated as mere decorations without iconographic significance. We believe, however, that we have recovered evidence for the evolution of the double-line-break out of the Earth or were-jaguar motif already discussed above.

Figure 12.17 shows part of an Atoyac Yellow-white bowl, from Area C of San José Mogote. Four parallel incised lines encircle the vessel just below the rim. The third line from the top forms the cleft head symbol of the were-jaguar (Pyne's Motif 13); the second line from the top forms a pair of "music brackets" like those often accompanying were-jaguar motifs (for example, in Pyne's Motif 8).

Figure 12.18 shows the rim sherd of an Atoyac Yellow-white vertical-wall bowl or "cylinder," also from Area C of San José Mogote. Three parallel incised lines encircle the vessel just below the rim; they appear to form an inverted version of the cleft head of the were-jaguar (see Pyne's Motifs 12–13). This white cylinder was heavily smudged with carbon.

These two sherds, and others like them, suggest that double- and triple-line-breaks may not be "iconographically neutral" forms of decoration after all. In the Early Formative, at least, they may have originated as simplified versions of Earth motifs. Later on—for example, during the Middle Formative—they may have diversified into a whole range of variants that had less iconographic significance.

An Inventory of Double-Line Breaks

During the 1970s, Stephen Plog undertook an analysis of double-line-break motifs from San José Mogote, Tierras Largas, Abasolo, Huitzo, and Fábrica San José (Plog 1976). He divided the motifs into 139 categories, or "design elements," to which numbers were assigned. All 139 of Plog's design elements are given in Figures 12.19–12.21, and the total counts of each design at every site are given in Table 12.1.

Since Plog's analysis is already published in detail, we only briefly summarize it here. Using a Gravity Model and a series of similarity coefficients (Pearson's r, Spearman's r, and Brainerd-Robinson), Plog compared all five Oaxaca villages with regard to shared double-line-break design elements. He found that Huitzo and San José Mogote—which were probably competing ceremonial centers during the Guadalupe phase—shared fewer designs than would have been predicted from the distance between them. He also found that Fábrica San José, Tierras Largas, and Abasolo shared more designs with San José Mogote than would have been predicted, probably because those smaller sites treated San José Mogote as a local ceremonial center with which they interacted frequently.

While there was some chronological change in design elements over time, it does not seem to have altered the relationships just mentioned (see discussion in Plog 1976:270). For example, even though most of the San José Mogote data set was drawn from the San José phase, and most of Fábrica San José data set was drawn from the Guadalupe phase, those two sites appear quite similar with regard to design elements.

Plog was using double-line-break motifs to measure the similarities and differences among pottery collections at different villages within the same valley. His success makes us wonder whether his methods could be applied on a wider scale in the future, comparing one valley to another. Such a possibility seems likely, since Agrinier (1989) has recently compared the pottery assemblages of Mirador-Plumajillo (Chiapas), San Lorenzo (Veracruz), and Salinas La Blanca (Guatemala) with considerable success by the use of Brainerd-Robinson matrices.

In preparation for a wider extension of Plog's approach, we present the 41 most common double-line-break elements on Canoas White pottery of the Tehuacán Valley, Puebla (Fig. 12.22). One can immediately see that Tehuacán shares many design elements with Oaxaca, but we cannot proceed beyond that observation without having the total counts for each design element from Tehuacán. In Chapter 19 we attempt to show that the double-line-breaks of Tlapacoya-Zohapilco are very similar

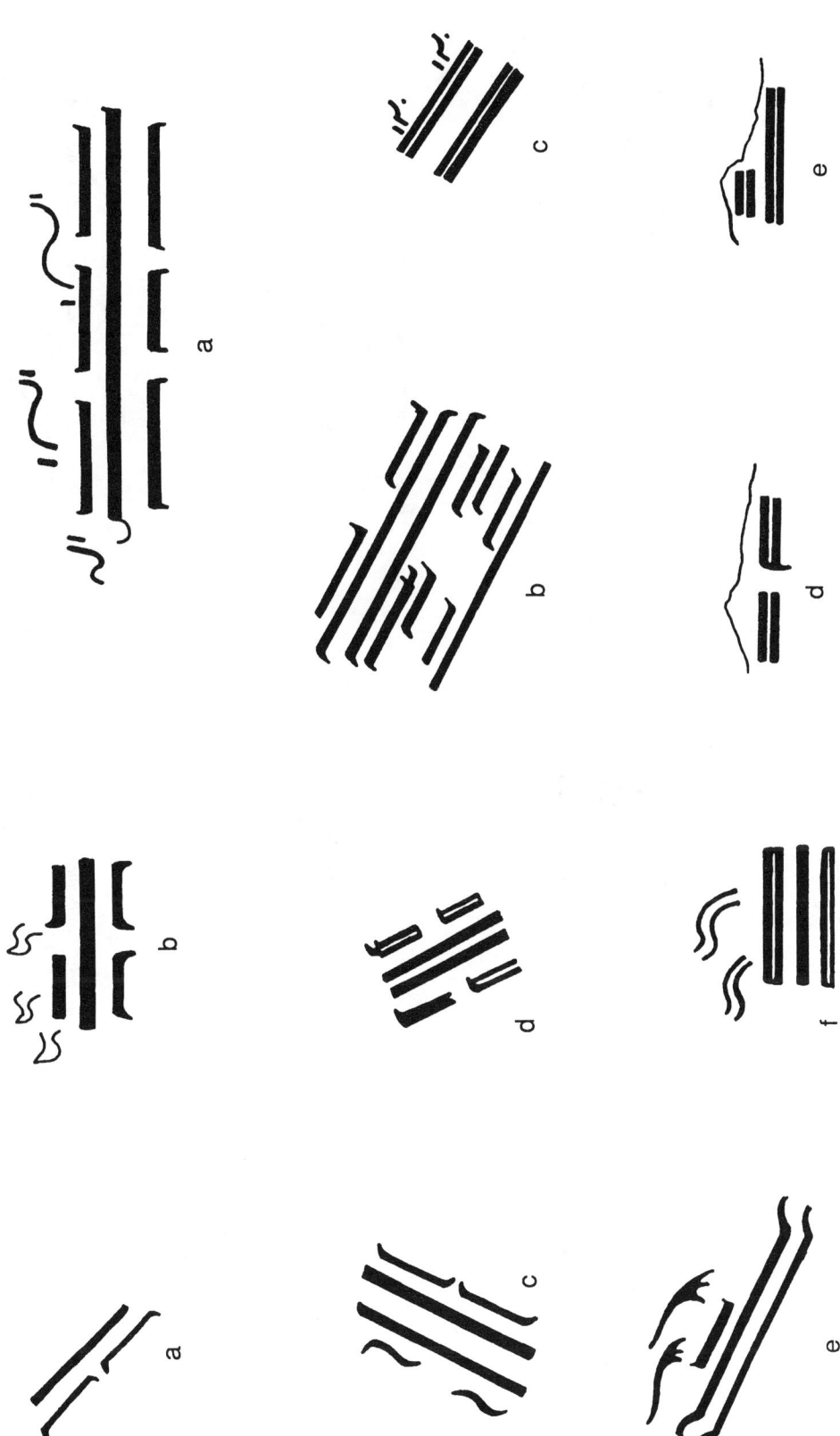

Figure 12.5. Variants of Pyne's Motif 1 (fire-serpent), Valley of Oaxaca. *a*, Leandro Gray cylinder, Zone D2 midden, Area A, San José Mogote (SJM). *b*, Leandro Gray outleaned-wall bowl, Zone D1 midden, Area A, SJM. *c*, Leandro Gray cylinder, Burial 4, Abasolo. *d*, Leandro Gray cylinder, Burial 4, Abasolo. *e*, Leandro Gray cylinder, Zone D1 midden, Area A, SJM. *f*, Leandro Gray cylinder, Household Unit C3, Area A, SJM. (All examples San José phase.)

Figure 12.6. Variants of Pyne's Motifs 1 (*a–c*) and 2 (*d, e*) (fire-serpent) from Tierras Largas, Valley of Oaxaca. *a*, Leandro Gray outleaned-wall bowl, Burial 20. *b*, Leandro Gray outleaned-wall bowl, Area K. *c*, Leandro Gray cylinder, Area E. *d, e*, Leandro Gray cylinders, Area E. (All examples San José phase.)

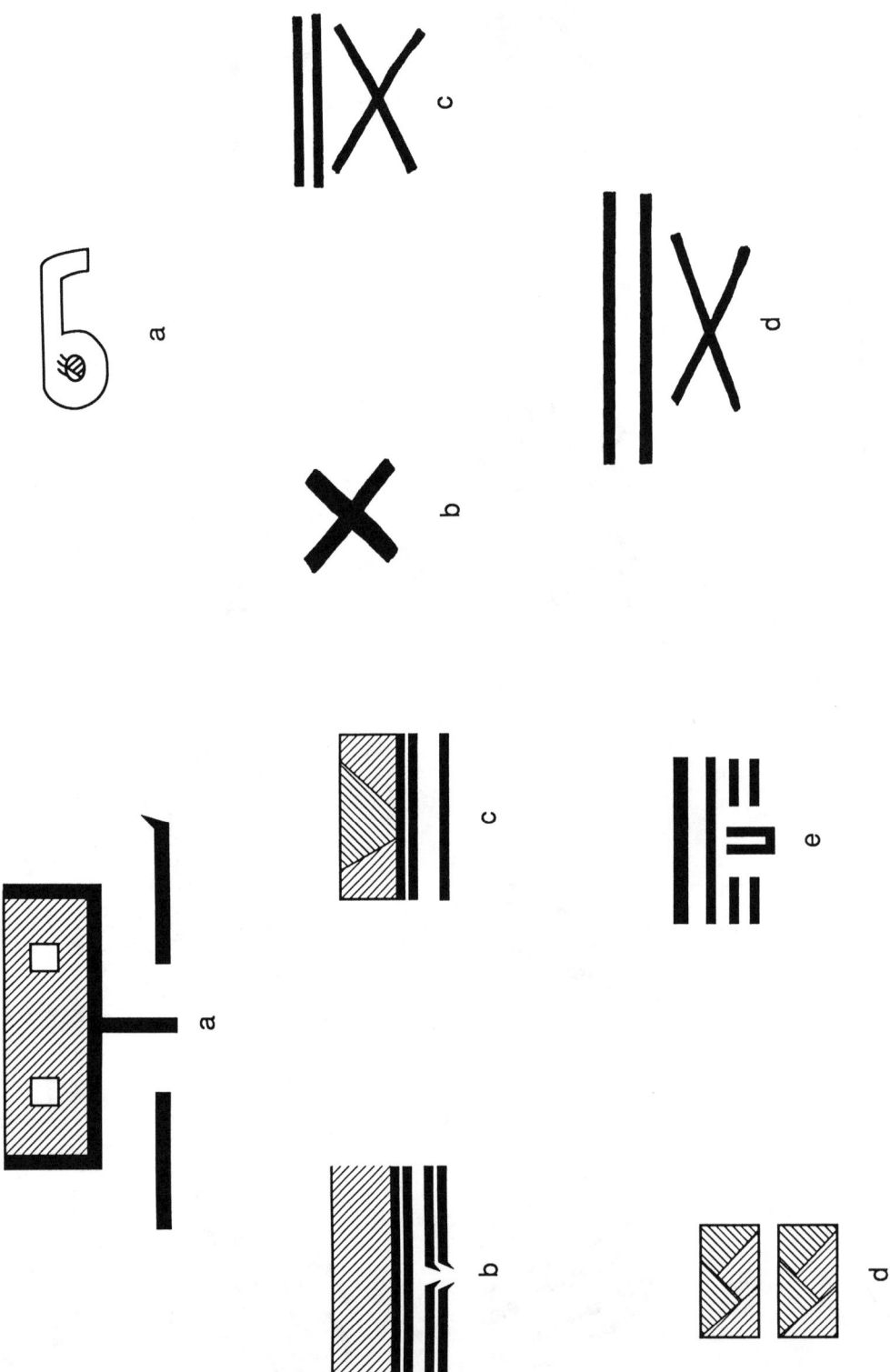

Figure 12.7. Variants of Pyne's Motifs 3 (*a, b*), 4 (*c, d*), and 5 (*e*), Valley of Oaxaca. *a*, Leandro Gray cylinder, Area C, San José Mogote (SJM). *b*, Delfina Fine Gray cylinder, Household Unit C2, Area A, SJM. *c*, Leandro Gray cylinder, Area A, Tierras Largas. *d*, Leandro Gray cylinder, House 6, Area C, SJM. *e*, Leandro Gray cylinder, Household Unit C3, Area A, SJM. (All examples San José phase.)

Figure 12.8. Variants of Pyne's Motifs 6 (*a*) and 7 (*b-d*) from San José Mogote, Valley of Oaxaca. *a*, Leandro Gray cylinder, Area C. *b*, Leandro Gray outleaned-wall bowl, Household Unit C3, Area A. *c*, Leandro Gray cylinder, House 7, Area C. *d*, Leandro Gray outleaned-wall bowl, Household Unit C3, Area A. (All examples San José phase.)

San José Phase

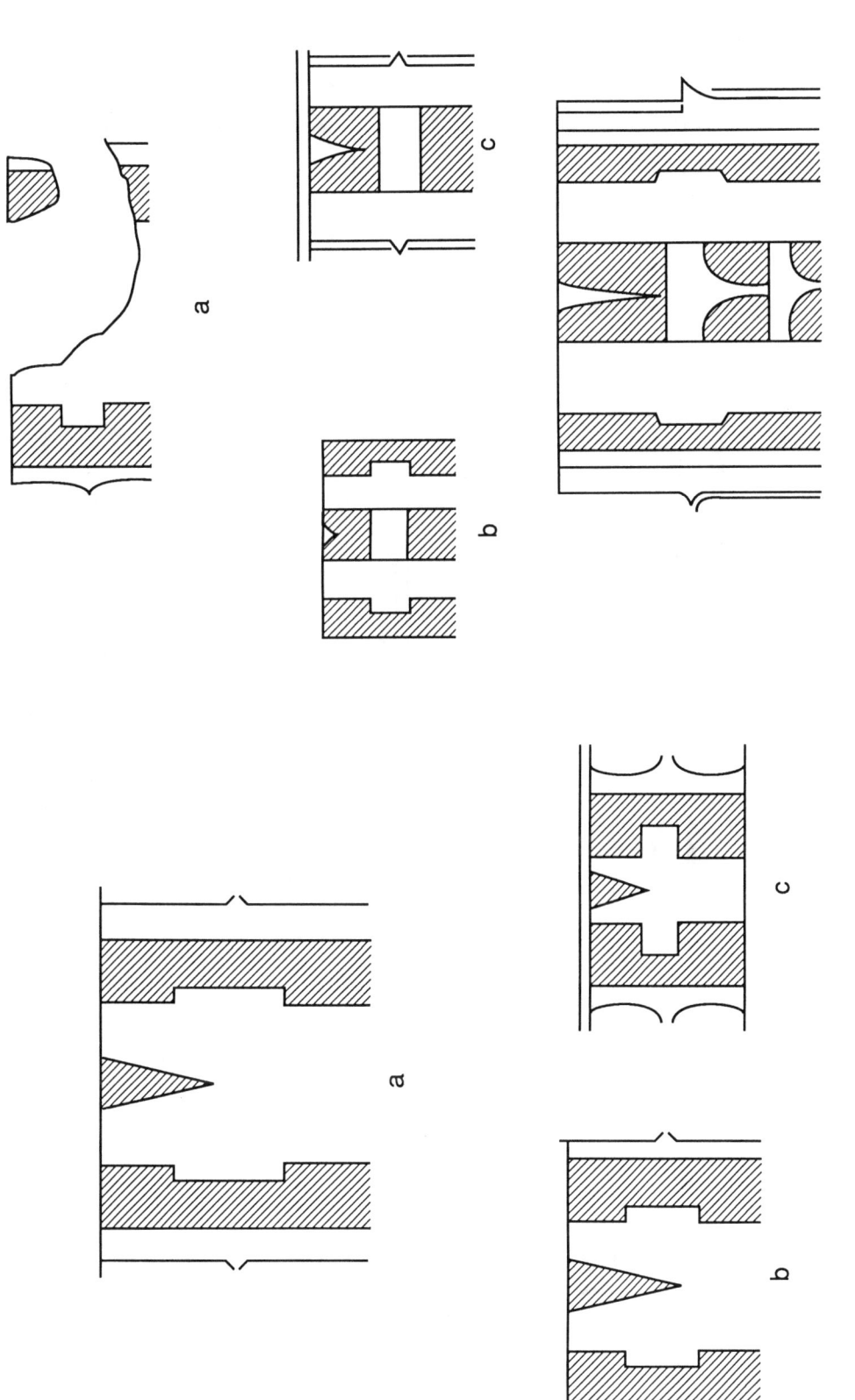

Figure 12.9. Variants of Pyne's Motif 8 (were-jaguar) from Tierras Largas, Valley of Oaxaca. *a*, Leandro Gray cylinder, House 1, Area A. *b*, Leandro Gray cylinder, Feature 4, Area A. *c*, Leandro Gray cylinder, Area D. (All examples San José phase.)

Figure 12.10. Variants of Pyne's Motifs 9 (*a*) and 10 (*b-d*) (were-jaguar), Valley of Oaxaca. *a*, Leandro Gray cylinder, Feature 160, Tierras Largas (TL). *b*, Leandro Gray cylinder, Area D, TL. *c*, Leandro Gray cylinder, Household Unit C4, Area A, San José Mogote. *d*, Leandro Gray cylinder, Feature 4, Area A, TL. (All examples San José phase.)

144 *Early Formative Pottery of Oaxaca*

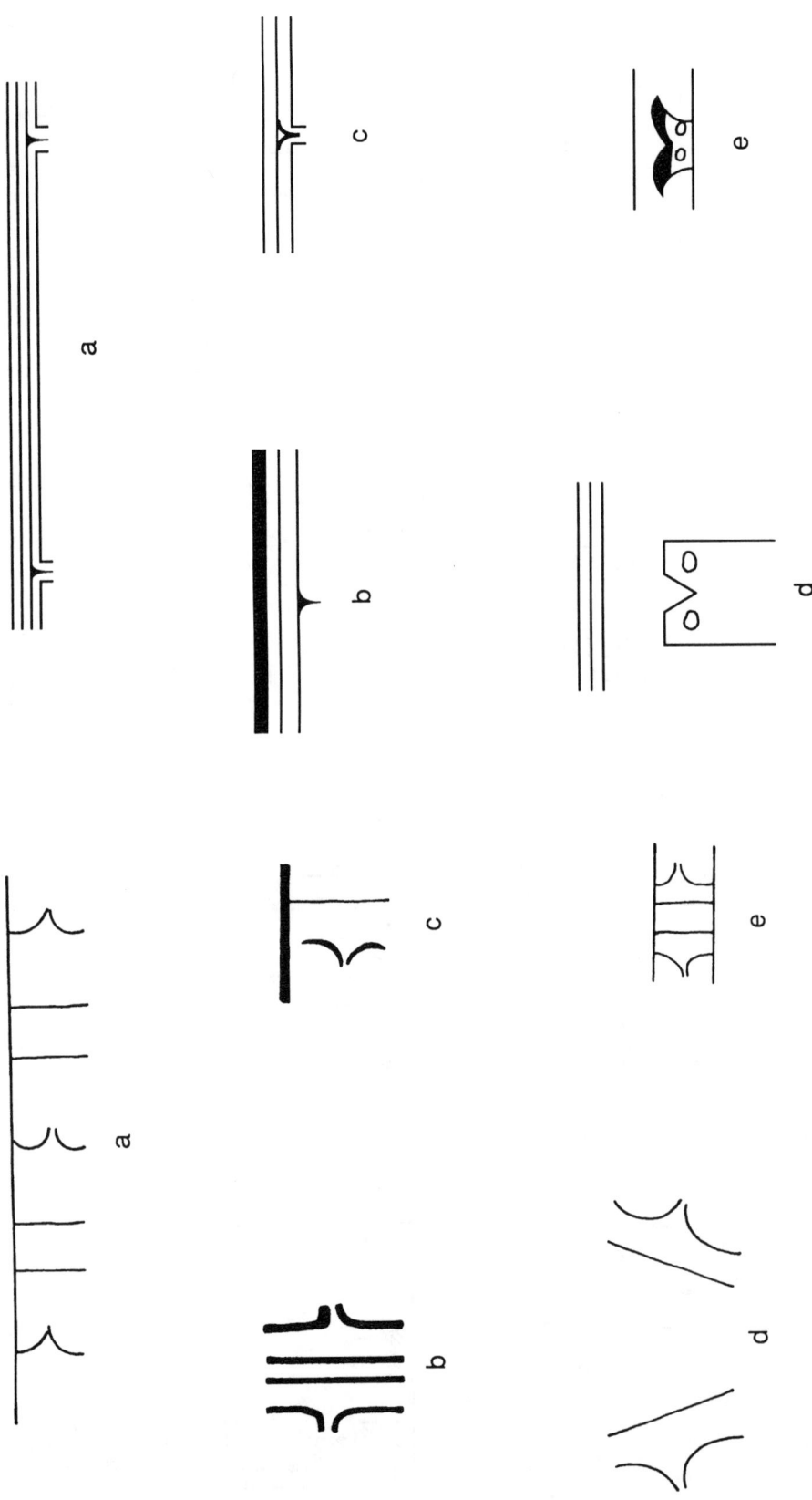

Figure 12.11. Variants of Pyne's Motif 11, Valley of Oaxaca. *a*, Leandro Gray outleaned-wall bowl, Household Unit C3, Area A, San José Mogote (SJM). *b*, Leandro Gray cylinder, Zone D1 midden, Area A, SJM. *c*, Leandro Gray cylinder, House 1, Area A, Tierras Largas (TL). *d*, Leandro Gray outleaned-wall bowl, House 1, Area A, TL. *e*, Leandro Gray cylinder, House 1, Area A, TL. (All examples San José phase.)

Figure 12.12. Variants of Pyne's Motif 12, Valley of Oaxaca. *a*, Atoyac Yellow-white cylinder, House 7, Area C, San José Mogote (SJM). *b, c, d*, Atoyac Yellow-white cylinders, Area C, SJM. *e*, Xochiltepec White cylinder, Zone E2, Area A, Huitzo. (*a–d* are from San José phase proveniences; *e* is from a Guadalupe phase provenience.)

San José Phase

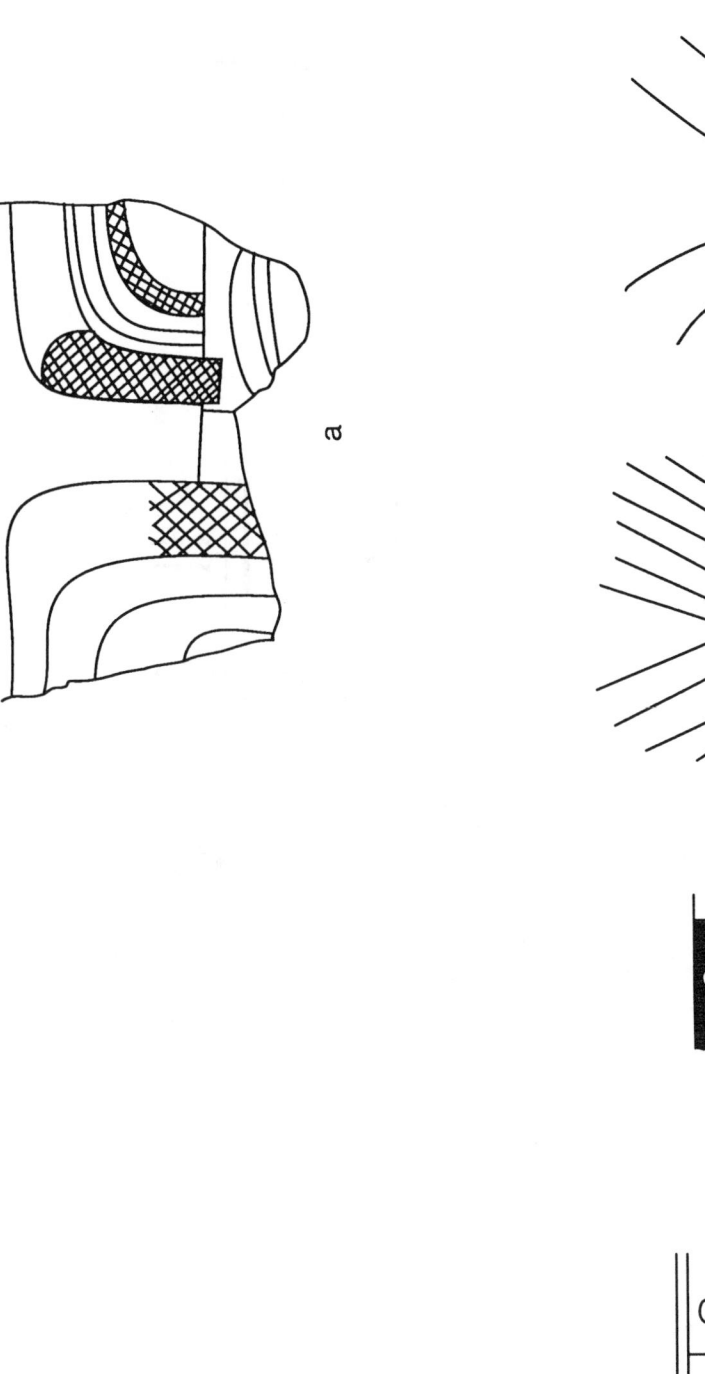

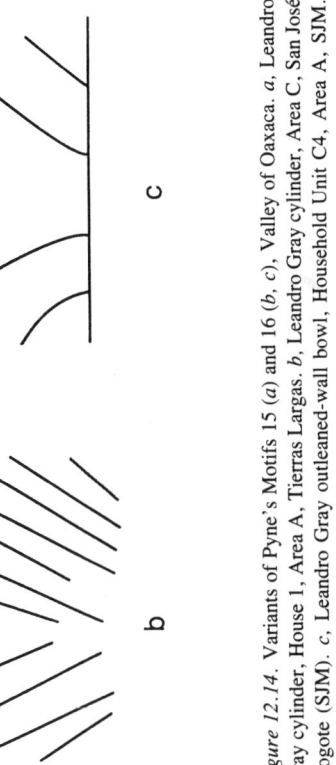

Figure 12.14. Variants of Pyne's Motifs 15 (*a*) and 16 (*b, c*), Valley of Oaxaca. *a*, Leandro Gray cylinder, House 1, Area A, Tierras Largas. *b*, Leandro Gray cylinder, Area C, San José Mogote (SJM). *c*, Leandro Gray outleaned-wall bowl, Household Unit C4, Area A, SJM. (All examples San José phase.)

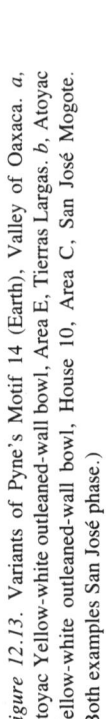

Figure 12.13. Variants of Pyne's Motif 14 (Earth), Valley of Oaxaca. *a*, Atoyac Yellow-white outleaned-wall bowl, Area E, Tierras Largas. *b*, Atoyac Yellow-white outleaned-wall bowl, House 10, Area C, San José Mogote. (Both examples San José phase.)

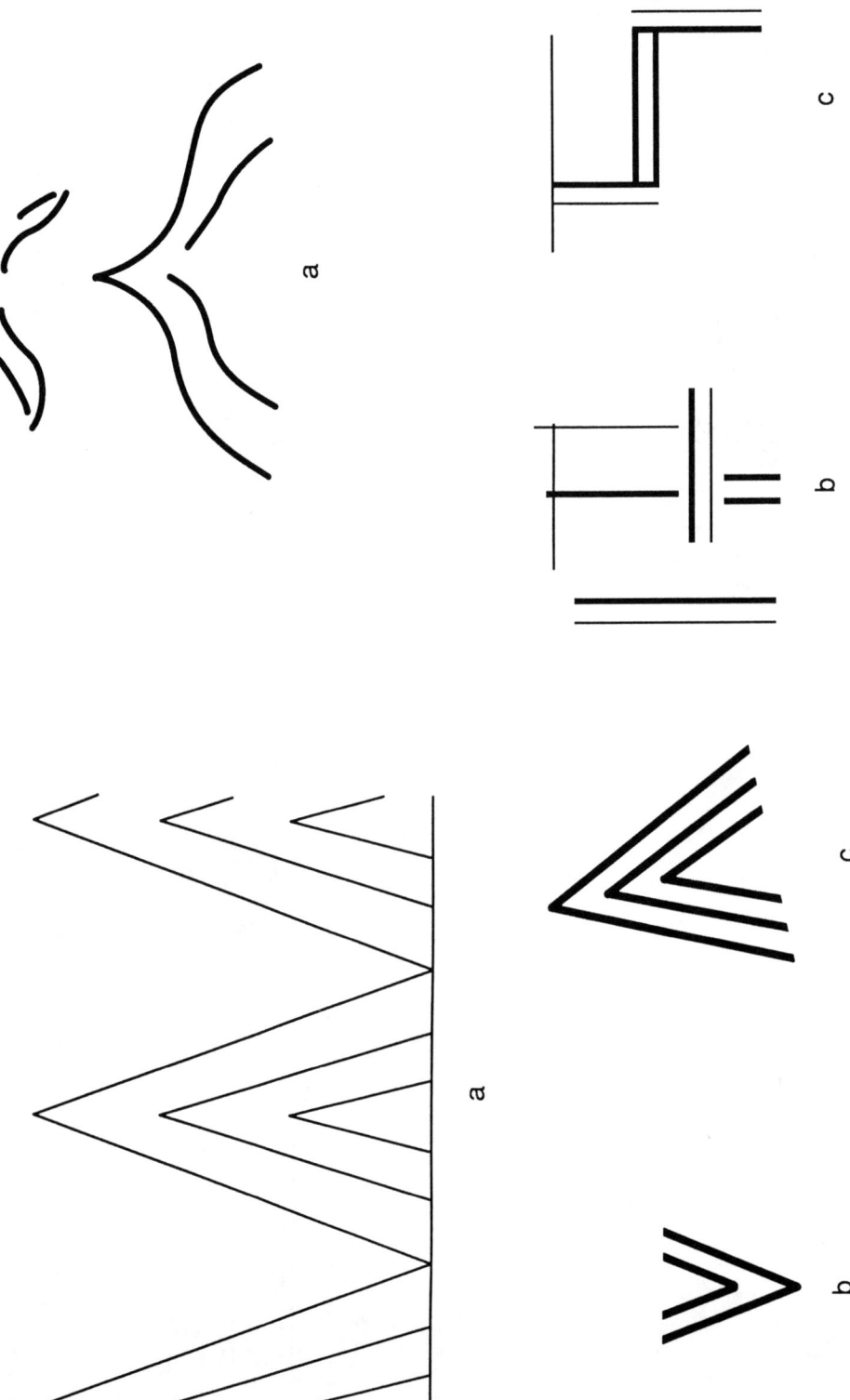

Figure 12.15. Variants of Pyne's Motif 17 from San José Mogote, Valley of Oaxaca. *a*, Leandro Gray cylinder, Household Unit C4, Area A. *b*, Leandro Gray cylinder, Zone D2 midden, Area A. *c*, Leandro Gray cylinder, Zone D1 midden, Area A. (All examples San José phase.)

Figure 12.16. Variants of Pyne's Motifs 17 (*a*) and 18 (*b*, *c*), Valley of Oaxaca. *a*, Leandro Gray cylinder, Household Unit C4, Area A, San José Mogote (SJM). *b*, Leandro Gray cylinder, Area K, Tierras Largas. *c*, Leandro Gray cylinder, Household Unit C4, Area A, SJM. (All examples San José phase.)

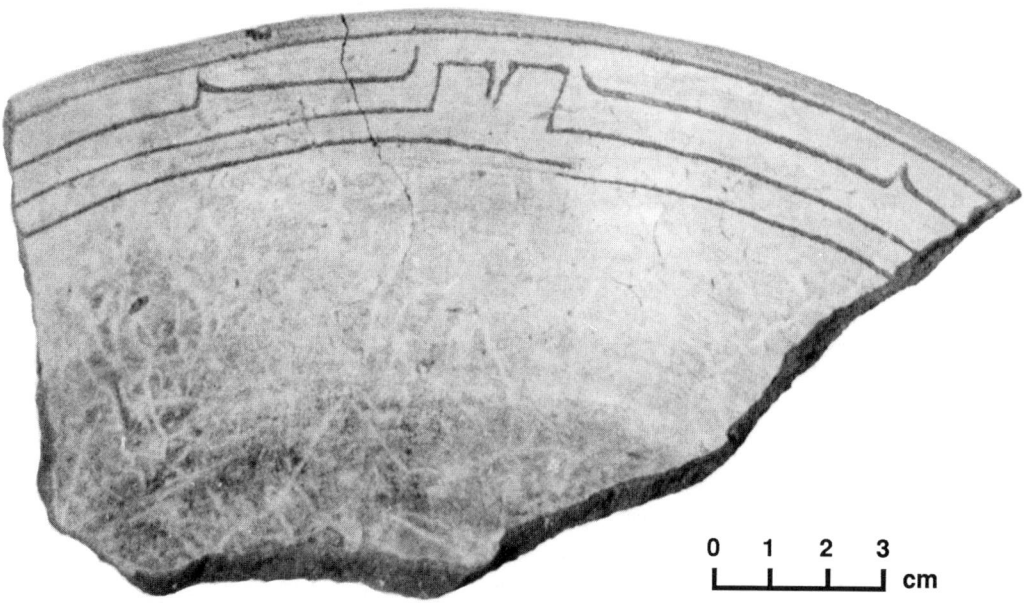

Figure 12.17. Atoyac Yellow-white outleaned-wall bowl sherd from San José Mogote, Area C, Zone C (San José phase). A variety of elements can be seen in the four parallel incised lines that run around the inside of the rim. In the center—formed by the third line from the top—is the cleft head of the were-jaguar (Pyne's Motif 13). To either side, formed by the second line from the top, are two "music brackets" of the type often associated with the were-jaguar. This bowl and others like it suggest that many common double-line-breaks seen on Atoyac Yellow-white vessels are simplified versions of Earth (were-jaguar) motifs.

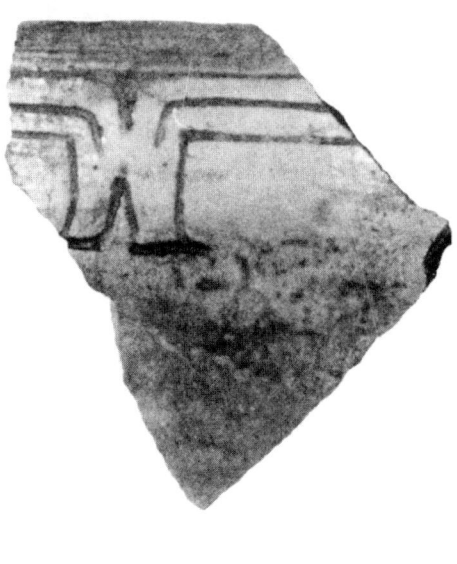

Figure 12.18. Rim sherd from an Atoyac Yellow-white cylinder found in Zone D, Area C, San José Mogote (San José phase). An interesting motif is formed by the three parallel incised lines that run around the outside of the rim. The motif appears to be an inverted form of the cleft head of the were-jaguar (Pyne's Motifs 12–13). As can be seen in the photograph, this white cylinder was heavily smudged with carbon. This vessel and others like it suggest that many common double-line-breaks seen on Atoyac Yellow-white vessels are simplified versions of Earth (were-jaguar) motifs.

TABLE 12.1
"Double-Line-Break" Motifs on Atoyac Yellow-white Vessels: Number of Occurrences of the 143 Most Common Motifs at San José Mogote, Huitzo, Tierras Largas, and Abasolo

Motif No.	S. José Mogote	Huitzo	Tierras Largas	Abasolo	Motif No.	S. José Mogote	Huitzo	Tierras Largas	Abasolo
1	4	16	8	1	65	—	—	1	—
2	1	—	—	—	66	—	—	1	—
3	—	11	—	—	67	—	—	4	—
4	4	4	1	—	68	—	—	1	—
5	1	1	—	—	69	—	—	1	—
6	3	—	1	—	70	—	—	1	—
7	—	—	1	—	71	1	—	—	—
8	1	4	—	—	72	1	—	—	—
9	5	7	—	—	73	1	—	—	—
10	1	4	3	—	74	—	1	—	—
11	2	—	—	—	75	—	—	1	—
12	—	1	—	—	76	—	—	2	—
13	—	1	—	—	77	1	—	—	—
14	1	—	—	—	78	1	—	—	—
15	—	1	1	—	79	1	1	—	—
16	—	1	—	—	80	—	1	—	—
17	1	—	—	—	81	1	—	—	—
18	—	1	—	—	82	—	1	—	—
19	2	3	—	—	83	—	1	—	—
20	—	2	—	—	84	—	1	—	—
21	—	1	—	—	85	—	1	—	—
22	—	1	—	—	86	1	—	—	—
23	—	—	—	1	87	1	—	—	—
24	—	—	—	1	88	1	—	—	—
25	—	2	—	—	89	—	—	1	—
26	—	3	—	—	90	—	—	—	1
27	—	1	—	—	91	1	—	—	—
28	—	1	—	—	92	1	—	—	—
29	—	1	—	—	93	1	—	—	—
30	—	1	—	—	94	1	—	—	—
31	3	13	—	—	95	1	—	—	—
32	1	—	—	—	96	1	—	—	—
33	—	—	1	—	97	—	—	1	—
34	—	1	—	—	98	—	—	1	—
35	2	107	—	—	99	1	—	—	—
36	—	2	—	—	101	—	1	—	—
37	—	2	—	—	102	1	—	—	—
38	—	1	—	—	103	—	1	—	—
39	—	1	—	—	104	—	1	—	—
40	1	52	—	—	105	—	1	—	—
41	1	—	—	—	106	2	—	1	—
42	—	2	—	—	107	1	—	—	—
43	—	1	—	—	108	1	—	—	—
44	—	1	—	—	109	1	—	—	—
45	—	1	—	—	110	1	—	—	—
46	—	1	—	—	111	—	—	1	—
47	—	—	1	1	112	—	—	1	—
48	1	1	7	—	113	—	—	—	1
49	5	—	15	—	114	—	—	—	1
50	2	1	17	—	115	—	1	—	—
51	2	—	8	—	116	—	1	—	—
52	3	—	9	—	118	—	1	—	—
53	4	—	8	1	119	—	1	1	—
54	12	1	11	5	121	1	—	—	—
55	—	—	2	—	122	1	—	—	—
56	—	—	1	—	123	—	—	1	—
57	—	—	1	—	124	—	—	1	—
58	—	—	3	—	125	—	—	1	—
59	—	—	3	—	127	—	—	1	—
60	—	—	1	—	128	—	—	1	—
61	1	—	—	—	129	—	—	1	—
62	1	—	—	—	130	—	—	1	—
63	1	—	—	—	131	—	—	1	—
64	—	—	4	—	132	—	—	1	—

TABLE 12.1 (continued)

Motif No.	S. José Mogote	Huitzo	Tierras Largas	Abasolo
133	—	—	1	—
134	—	—	1	—
135	—	1	—	—
136	—	1	1	—
137	1	—	—	—
138	1	—	—	—
139	—	—	1	—
140	—	—	1	—
141	—	—	2	—
142	—	—	1	—
143	—	1	—	—
TOTAL	94	274	143	13

SOURCE: Plog n.d.
Note that numbers 100, 117, 120, and 126 were not assigned.

to those of Oaxaca, while the double-line-breaks of Chalcatzingo are very different.

Pottery Types of the San José Phase

We now present our descriptions of the pottery types characteristic of the San José phase. Some of those types first appeared late in the Tierras Largas phase, and others lasted well into the Guadalupe phase, but they combined for a time to give the San José phase its distinctive character.

Perhaps the most useful horizon marker of the San José phase was Leandro Gray, a double-burnished, reduced-fired ware used mainly for flat-based bowls with a variety of wall angles. The cubic contents of those bowls suggest that they were for individual portions of food. They were also a major medium for excised pan-Mesoamerican motifs. Any surface survey that does not include Leandro Gray cannot be said to have done justice to the settlement pattern of the San José phase. It was the first gray ware manufactured in a region that was to become famous for its gray wares.

Also important in the San José phase were Atoyac Yellow-white, a white-slipped ware used as the major medium for incised double-line-breaks; San José Red-on-White, a bichrome ware; San José Black-and-White, a "white-rimmed black" ware; and Delfina Fine Gray, an export ware with pan-Mesoamerican excised motifs. The common utility wares of the San José phase were Fidencio Coarse, used mainly for cooking and storage jars; and Lupita Heavy Plain, used mainly for tecomates and charcoal braziers/potstands. Many of the tecomates of the San José phase had plain, false, or interrupted rocker stamping.

FIDENCIO COARSE

General Description

Fidencio Coarse is a drab reddish brown utilitarian ware, used primarily for cooking vessels and storage vessels. Chief among those were necked jars (*ollas*), followed by tecomates or neckless jars. One of the type's distinguishing characteristics is a carelessly applied dull red wash of *barro colorado*, whose surface color range can grade into purplish brown or reddish gray. Poor firing and later burning over hearths contribute to this type's often drab, dark appearance. Fidencio Coarse jar body sherds were probably the most common single item recovered from San José and Guadalupe phase deposits; the ware's resistance to thermal shock enabled it gradually to replace Tierras Largas Burnished Plain over time.

Chronological History

The clay body used for Fidencio Coarse first showed up toward the end of the Tierras Largas phase, in the form of molds for making other kinds of pottery. Possibly, even at that early time period, its heat-resistant mix of coarse aplastic materials was appreciated. A few tecomates and jars of this type show up in late Tierras Largas deposits, but it was really in the San José phase that Fidencio Coarse emerged as a major type.

From the beginning of the San José phase onward, Fidencio Coarse displayed variations in surface treatment and plastic decoration that are useful for establishing a chronology. For example, our San José phase sample of jars, while largely unburnished, nevertheless shows that about 40% of the rims had been burnished once with a quartz pebble—perhaps a legacy from Tierras Largas Burnished Plain. By the Guadalupe phase, burnished rims had dropped to 20% of the total.

Jar shoulders could be decorated with neat punctation, sloppy jabs, paired jabs, crosshatching, brushing, herringbone slashes, or appliqué lugs of the type Drennan (1976) calls "gopher grips." However, there was temporal variation in this repertoire. Paired jabs on jar shoulders are so far known only from the San José phase, and may turn out to be a good horizon marker. The San José phase seems to lack crosshatching, brushing, herringbone slashes, and "gopher grips"; all four of those attributes peak in the Guadalupe phase, with the gopher grips being a potentially good horizon marker.

By the Rosario phase, burnished jar rims had virtually disappeared, as had virtually all forms of plastic decoration on jar shoulders. By this time, the makers of Fidencio Coarse were gradually changing its clay body and the color of its *barro colorado* wash; the most likely explanation is that new raw material sources and more fully oxidizing kilns were being used. Fidencio Coarse eventually evolved into Monte Albán Type C2, a red-on-*crema* type of Monte Albán I (Caso, Bernal, and Acosta 1967).

In addition to the stylistic changes described above, Fidencio Coarse storage jars seem to show a steady increase in size and cubic capacity over time. While this could reflect technological change (i.e., the ability to make and fire bigger jars), we suspect it may have to do with increases in household size and storage needs.

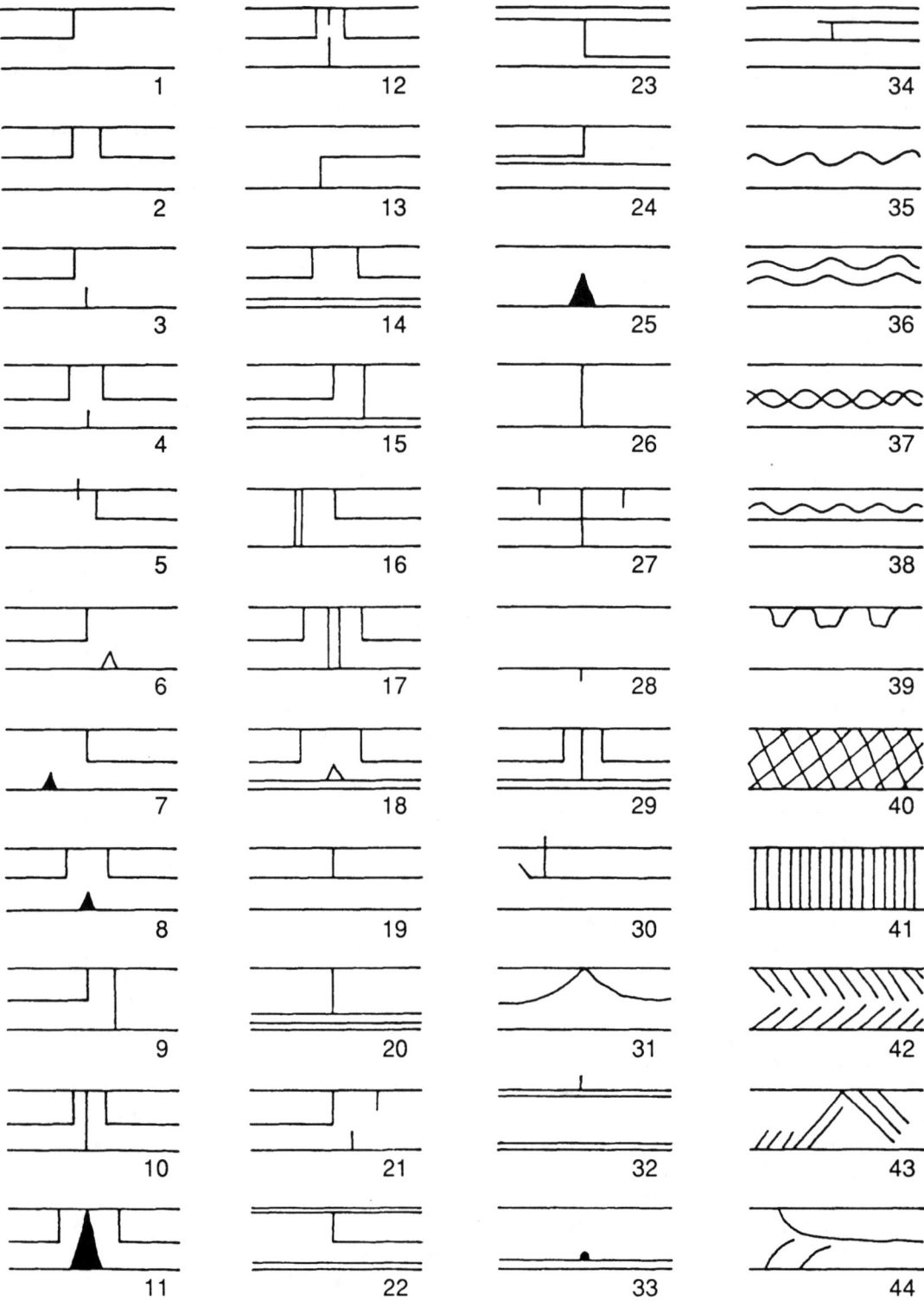

Figure 12.19. Plog's design elements 1 to 44, Atoyac Yellow-white pottery.

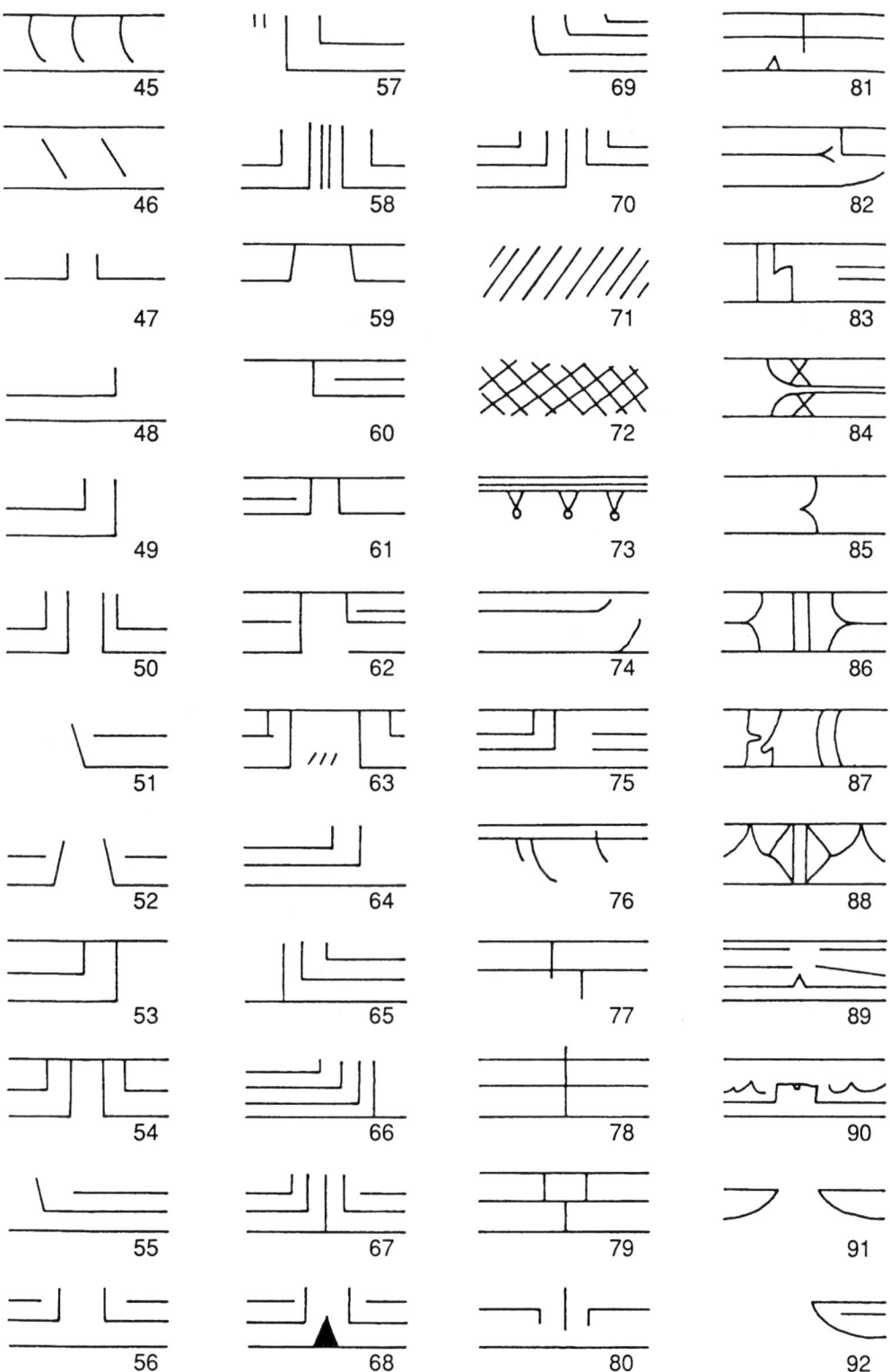

Figure 12.20. Plog's design elements 45 to 92, Atoyac Yellow-white pottery.

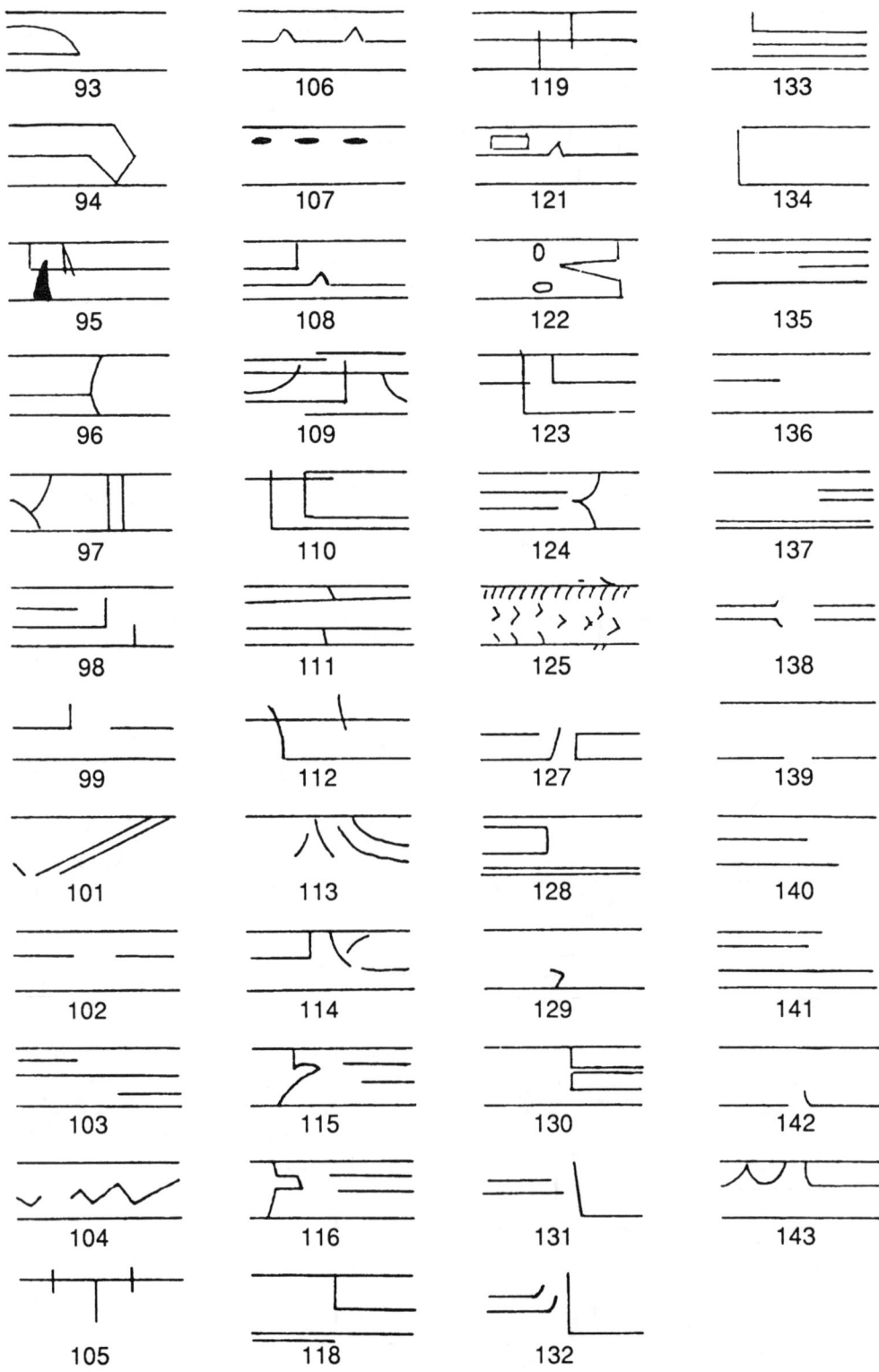

Figure 12.21. Plog's design elements 93 to 143, Atoyac Yellow-white pottery. (Note that numbers 100, 117, 120, and 126 were not assigned.)

Figure 12.22. The 41 most common double-line-break design elements on Canoas White pottery of the Tehuacán Valley (redrawn from MacNeish, Peterson, and Flannery 1970: Fig. 32).

Clay Body

The clay body is a residual piedmont clay resulting from the decomposition of Precambrian gneiss. It was used essentially as found, except perhaps for the picking out of the larger nonplastic materials. By inspection, roughly 30–35% of the volume of the body is aplastic materials, including angular fragments of quartz, biotite mica, partially decomposed particles of feldspar and hornblende, and occasional fragments of garnet, all in a base of kaolinite clay. The clay may have been winnowed before use, but all the nonplastic particles would have occurred naturally in the clay beds; none were added. Particles run from 0.25 to 5.0 mm in diameter, with most in the 1.0 mm range.

Firing Temperature

It was probably fired at around 700–720° C in an oxidizing temperature. The purpose of firing at such a low temperature is to produce a ware that will resist thermal shock; this would be especially necessary in the case of cooking jars.

Color

The color of the fired surface varies from reddish brown (5 YR 5/4) to dark reddish brown (5 YR 3/2) to light yellowish brown (10 YR 6/4), except where later burned or smoked during cooking. In the latter case, the surface may be dark gray or even carbonized black.

In sherd cross-sections, one can see a dark grayish brown core (2.5 Y 4/2), sandwiched between outer layers that run from light gray (2.5 Y 7/2) to light reddish brown (5 YR 6/4). The dark core probably reflects the relatively low firing temperature mentioned above.

Surface Treatment

The interior surfaces of vessels were scraped with a piece of gourd or the edge of a sherd. The interior, from the mouth to the inside of the shoulder, was then smoothed with something like a piece of animal hide. The exterior surface was smoothed in the same way. In less than half the cases (and with decreasing frequency over time), jar necks and shoulders might be lightly burnished once with a quartz pebble.

The Application of Red Wash

As Figure 2.1 of Chapter 2 shows, pods of *barro colorado* occur in the weathered Precambrian metamorphics of the Valley of Oaxaca, often in the upper piedmont. Fidencio Coarse was characterized by the application of a sloppy red wash of this iron-rich clay over certain parts of the vessel. In the case of jars, the neck is frequently red while the lower part of the vessel is not; in other examples, the shoulder may be red but not the neck. Where plastic decoration was present in zones, the red wash was often daubed carelessly over the areas between zones. At times it seems to have been applied while so wet that it ran down the vessel in long trickles. Of course, some sherds of cooking pots are so badly burned that the wash can barely be detected. In the late Guadalupe and Rosario phases, when Fidencio Coarse was evolving toward Monte Albán C2, it was not unusual for the *barro colorado* to be daubed on in broad stripes around the shoulder or upper body.

Where the vessel is unburnished, the stain varies from weak red (7.5 R 5/4) to light red (2.5 YR 6/6); where burned in cooking, it may be reddish brown (2.5 YR 4/4) or even darker. Where burnishing has been carried out over the wash, it may be reddish brown (2.5 YR 4/4) to weak red (7.5 R 5/4), except where burned.

Vessel Forms

Jars (Figs. 12.23–12.29). Where complete specimens are available, they appear to have been made in two stages. The lower half of the pot was molded over another *olla;* the upper half and the neck were added by means of concentric rings of clay, which were then smoothed. On the inside, the jar was finished with a piece of cloth or hide. Outside surfaces were scraped (possibly with a piece of gourd), then finished with a piece of cloth or hide. Rims are flaring or rolled outward.

Rim diameter: Most examples are in the 18–24 cm range, with some rims as small as 14 cm or as large as 30 cm. During the San José phase, rims in the 14–18 cm range reach their peak; by the end of the Guadalupe phase and the beginning of Rosario, rims in the 24–30 cm range reach their peak. A single specimen from the Guadalupe phase had a rim diameter of 40 cm.

Diameter of body: Usually about 1.5 times the rim diameter.

Estimated volume: Hard to estimate due to a lack of restorable specimens, but judging by *ollas* in other wares, average volumes would have exceeded 32 liters (8 gallons) in the San José phase and 48 liters (12 gallons) in the Guadalupe phase.

Height: Difficult to estimate, because so few restorable examples could be found.

Wall thickness: Variable. Near the contact between neck and shoulder, walls are usually 8–10 mm thick, but a few examples were as thin as 6 mm or as thick as 14 mm.

Surface finish: Burnishing of Fidencio Coarse jar necks was an attribute that varied through time. In the early San José phase, fully 40% of the jar neck sherds showed burnishing, but through time the percentage of unburnished necks increased. In Guadalupe times, unburnished jar neck sherds outnumbered burnished ones by 4 or 5 to 1. By the Rosario phase, Fidencio Coarse jar necks were virtually never burnished.

Plastic decoration: Neat punctation, paired jabs, sloppy jabs, herringbone slashes, and so on, are included in the series of attributes that varied through time. Plastic decoration was often set off from the rest of the vessel by incised zoning lines. In general, the usual red wash was applied to the areas in between the decorated zones, with the plastic-decorated areas left unstained.

Such zoned plastic decoration was rare in the early San José phase; for example, for every 50 jar neck sherds there might be only 5 or 6 sherds from decorated jar shoulders. By Guadalupe times, zoned plastic decoration had increased to the point where there was often one decorated jar shoulder sherd for every jar neck sherd. This form of decoration then declined rapidly, becoming virtually nonexistent in the Rosario phase.

Tecomates (Figs. 12.30–12.32). These globular neckless jars were built up through concentric rings of clay; the bodies were scraped and then smoothed with a piece of cloth or animal hide. Rim profiles usually have the thickened "comma shape" typical of the period, although a few are tapered. Holes for suspension are a common feature.

Rim diameter: 10–24 cm, with an average somewhere in the 15–20 cm range.

Diameter of body: Anywhere from 1.5 to 2 times the rim diameter.

Height: Difficult to estimate; probably about the same as the rim diameter.

Wall thickness: 6–10 mm except for the thickened rims, which may reach 12 mm.

Volume: Difficult to estimate due to a lack of restorable vessels, but most would have held at least 2 gallons.

Decoration: Tecomates were smoothed but never burnished; most are plain, except for the usual red wash. During the San José phase, a few tecomate bodies were decorated with rocker stamping or false rocker stamping, sometimes enclosed between incised zoning lines. During the Guadalupe phase, a few vessels had the same kind of plastic decoration

San José Phase

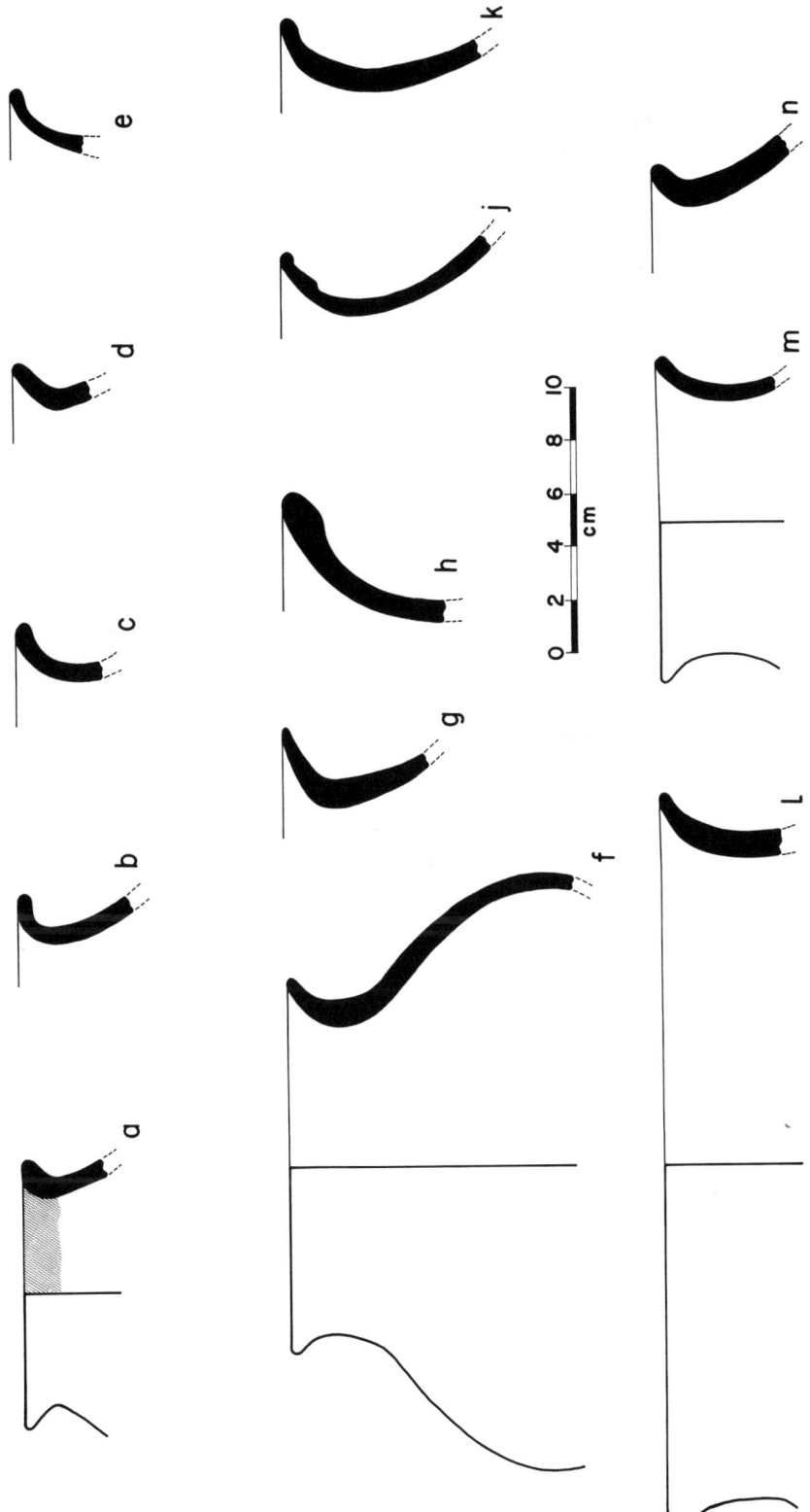

Figure 12.23. Fidencio Coarse jar necks from San José Mogote (SJM) and Barrio del Rosario Huitzo. All specimens have a drab red wash outside; *a* has a band of drab red wash inside the rim. *a–e* are lightly burnished outside; *f–n* are unburnished. *a*, House 3, Area A, Huitzo. *b*, Household Unit C2, Area A, SJM. *g, h, l, m*, Household Unit C3, Area A, SJM. *c, k*, Structure 1, Stages II-III, Area A, SJM. *e, f, j, n*, Zone D1 midden, Area A, SJM. The two Huitzo specimens are Guadalupe phase; all others are San José phase.

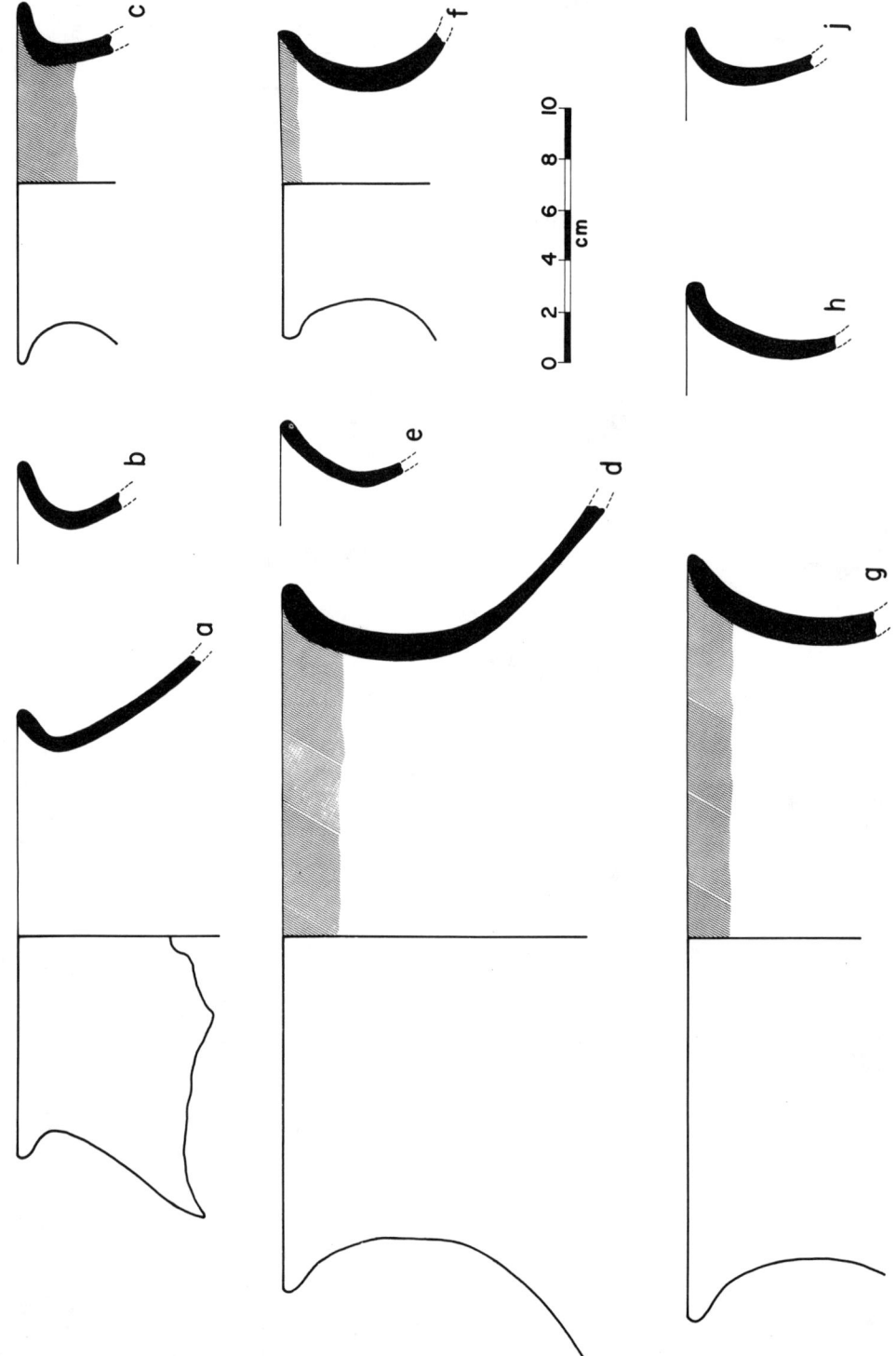

Figure 12.24. Fidencio Coarse jar necks from San José Mogote (SJM), Tierras Largas (TL), and Barrio del Rosario Huitzo. All specimens have a drab red wash outside, and are lightly burnished; c, d, f, and g also have a band of drab red wash inside the rim. a, Feature 112, TL. b, d, e, h, Zone D1 midden, Area A, SJM. c, j, Zone D, Area A, Huitzo. f, Household Unit C4, Area A, SJM. g, Zone D2 midden, Area A, SJM. All specimens from SJM are San José phase; all others are Guadalupe phase.

San José Phase

Figure 12.25. Fidencio Coarse jar shoulders with zoned, neat, punctationlike jabs, all from Area A of San José Mogote (San José phase). *a, c,* Household Unit C4. *b, e,* Zone D1 midden. *d,* Household Unit C2. *f,* Zone D2 midden.

as Fidencio Coarse jar shoulders: herringbone incising, neat punctation or sloppy jabs, etc. In those cases, the rim of the tecomate (as well as the zoning stripes) had a band of *barro colorado* while the plastic decoration was confined to plain areas (see Fig. 12.32*h*).

Hemispherical bowls (Fig. 12.33). These resemble hemispherical bowls in Tierras Largas Burnished Plain and Lupita Heavy Plain, but are characterized by the typical red wash of *barro colorado* seen on other Fidencio Coarse vessels. Rim profiles are blunt to tapered.

Rim diameter: 10–20 cm
Height: 3–12 cm
Wall thickness: 6–10 mm
Volume: Based on similar vessels in Avelina Red-on-Buff (see Chapter 8), these bowls probably held 1.0–1.5 liters.
Decoration: A thin wash of *barro colorado* sometimes daubed on in stripes; no plastic decoration.

LEANDRO GRAY

General Description

Leandro Gray was a reduction-fired, highly burnished, often streaky or cloudy gray ware, used primarily for bowls and less frequently for tecomates, jars, and a variety of exotic forms including effigies and miniatures. A hallmark of the San José phase, it was the first major gray ware produced in the Valley of Oaxaca, and therefore initiates the tradition of gray ware seen later at Monte Albán. It was also the preferred medium for carved designs of pan-Mesoamerican iconographic significance, such as the fire-serpent and the St. Andrew's cross. Clearly linking the Valley of Oaxaca into a network of shared stylistic conventions extending from Tlapacoya in the north to Copán in the south, Leandro Gray was widely traded and has been petrographically detected in foreign areas. Its counterparts in other areas include Calzadas Carved from the Gulf Coast (Coe and Diehl 1980) and

Figure 12.26. Fidencio Coarse jar shoulders with paired jabs, all from Area A, San José Mogote (San José phase). *a-c,* Zone D1 midden. *d, e,* Household Unit C1. *a* and *b* have necks that are smoothed, but not burnished.

Figure 12.27. Fidencio Coarse jar shoulders with paired, stepped jabs, Household Unit C3, Area A, San José Mogote (San José phase). The upper specimen has a neck that is smoothed but not burnished; the lower specimen has a neck with streaky burnishing.

Volcán Burnished from Tlapacoya-Zohapilco (Niederberger 1987).

Most Leandro Gray vessels appear to have functioned in the serving of prepared food (in all sizes from individual to family-sized portions). Some vessels may have served for light storage; none appear to have been used for cooking. Perhaps because of the high level of iconographic information they carried, Leandro Gray bowls seem often to have been included in burials, and certain of their carved designs show strong synchronic variation among residential wards (Chapter 16).

Chronological History

Leandro Gray is one of those wares that serves to establish the boundary between the Tierras Largas and San José phases. One or two stray sherds occur in contexts that could be terminal Tierras Largas, or transitional Tierras Largas/San José. Those earliest Leandro Gray sherds are from bottles, tecomates, and flat-based bowls with outleaned walls—all vessel shapes typical of late Tierras Largas times.

Early in the San José phase, Leandro Gray exploded in frequency and diversity. The most common shapes were bowls, with the flat-based, outleaned-wall kind still slightly more common (52%) but the deep cylindrical kind gaining in numbers (48%). Excising (carving) was at its peak during this subphase, while incising (*sgraffito*) was rare; for example, only 22 out of every 1,000 rims of outleaned-wall bowls show incising. Cylinders and bolstered-rim bowls were abundantly excised, often with dry red pigment rubbed into the carved or roughened areas. Other vessel forms peaking in the early San José phase were pigment dishes and spouted trays. Interrupted rocker stamping, a distinctive decorative attribute, also reached its peak at this time.

Late in the San José phase, cylindrical bowls had increased to the point where there were 60 of them to every 40 outleaned-wall bowls. Incising on cylinders was increasing relative to excising. Outleaned-wall bowls were still largely undecorated in comparison with cylinders, but excision continued to be their main form of decoration. It is possible that such bowls were rarely incised because *sgraffito* does not show up well against Leandro Gray's dark, streaky background. Bolstered-rim bowls, spouted trays, jars with vertical necks, and other minor vessel forms

Figure 12.28. Fidencio Coarse jar shoulders with zoned areas of sloppy jabs, all from Area A of San José Mogote (San José phase). *a,* Household Unit C3. *b,* Household Unit C2. *c,* Zone D2 midden. *d,* Zone D1 midden. *b* has a neck that is lightly burnished.

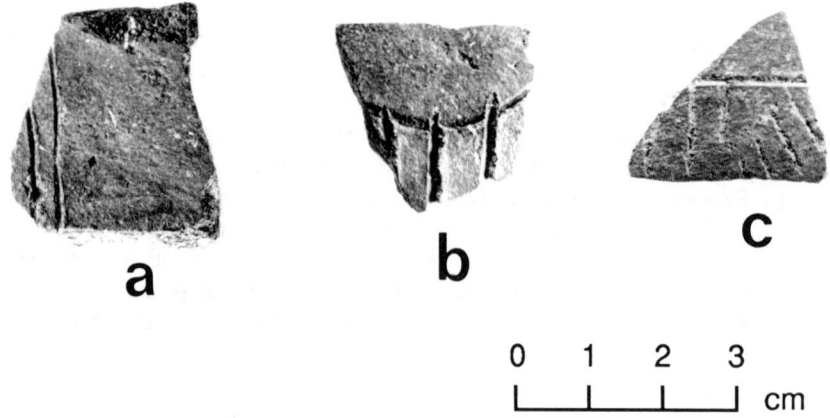

Figure 12.29. Fidencio Coarse body sherds from jars or tecomates with plastic decoration, all from Area A of San José Mogote (San José phase). *a,* jar with long parallel incised lines, Household Unit C3. *b,* sherd with long parallel lines in zone, Zone D2 midden. *c,* sherd with rows of slashes in zone, Household Unit C1.

Figure 12.30. Fidencio Coarse tecomate with punctation and incising in zones, drab red wash outside zones. Tierras Largas, Area C, above Feature 151 (San José phase).

continued, and some vessels had "grater bowl" interiors that were more decorative than functional.

In the Guadalupe phase, Leandro Gray declined in popularity and underwent a series of changes that reflect Middle Formative preferences. Excising in the form of pan-Mesoamerican motifs, such as fire-serpents and St. Andrew's crosses, virtually disappeared. Cylindrical bowls declined to the point where there was only one of them for every four outleaned-wall bowls. Bowls with walls that were outcurved (rather than outleaned) became more common, as did eccentric rims. Both outleaned- and outcurved-wall bowls were largely undecorated, and when they did have decoration it was usually an incised motif shared with Socorro Fine Gray, a Middle Formative pottery type.

In the Rosario phase, Leandro Gray survived only as a very minor type, occurring in typical Middle Formative shapes. It disappeared sometime before Monte Albán I.

Clay Body

The clay body is a residual piedmont clay resulting from decomposed Precambrian gneiss. It was used as found, except perhaps for winnowing or sieving out the larger nonplastic inclusions before use. All the remaining aplastic particles would have occurred naturally in the clay beds; none appear to have been added. By inspection, roughly 30–35% of the volume of the clay body is made up by this nonplastic material; the bulk of the visible particles run from 0.1 to 1.0 mm in diameter, with most in the 0.5 mm class. Included are angular fragments of quartz,

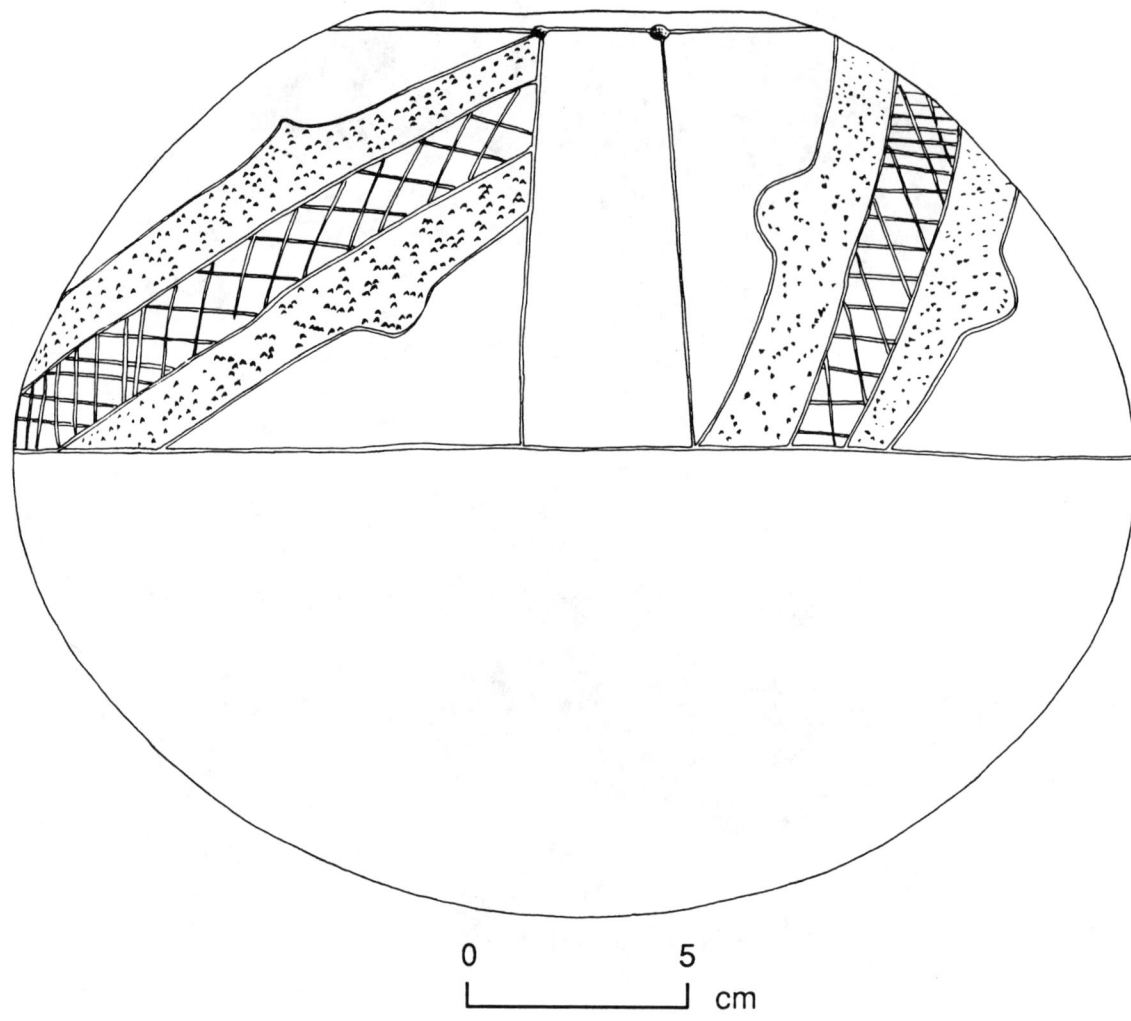

Figure 12.31. Reconstruction drawing of same Fidencio Coarse tecomate seen in Figure 12.30. The drawing shows more clearly than the photograph that this vessel was perforated for suspension.

biotite mica, partially decomposed particles of feldspar and hornblende, and occasional fragments of garnet, all in a base of kaolinite clay. Occasionally, small particles of volcanic tuff (ignimbrite) occur, and could constitute an exception to our general rule that nothing was added to the naturally occurring aplastics. Even this is not certain, however, because it could merely reflect a different clay body source from another part of the valley. The slightly finer appearance of Leandro Gray (when compared with types like Fidencio Coarse and Lupita Heavy Plain) is due to the fact that the clay body was selected more carefully, and has fewer particles over 1.0 mm.

The above description fits 95% of all Leandro Gray vessels. However, several burial offerings from San José Mogote and San Sebastián Abasolo provide exceptions to this description. These vessels—apparently made especially for burials, rather than having been used around the house—are made from black sedimentary clay from the valley floor, partly derived from Miocene volcanic tuff (ignimbrite). Although similar in shape and design to other Leandro Gray vessels, they are considerably finer-grained (see, for example, Figs. 12.49 and 12.60). It is possible that this finer clay body was used to make Leandro Gray vessels only when especially high-quality examples were desired, either for burials or for export outside the valley. Whatever the case, these atypical vessels show that San José phase potters were already familiar with the black alluvial clays used later for Monte Albán gray wares. The fact that either residual piedmont clays or sedimentary valley clays could be used for Leandro Gray may help explain some of the variation in exported vessels of this type (see below).

San José Phase

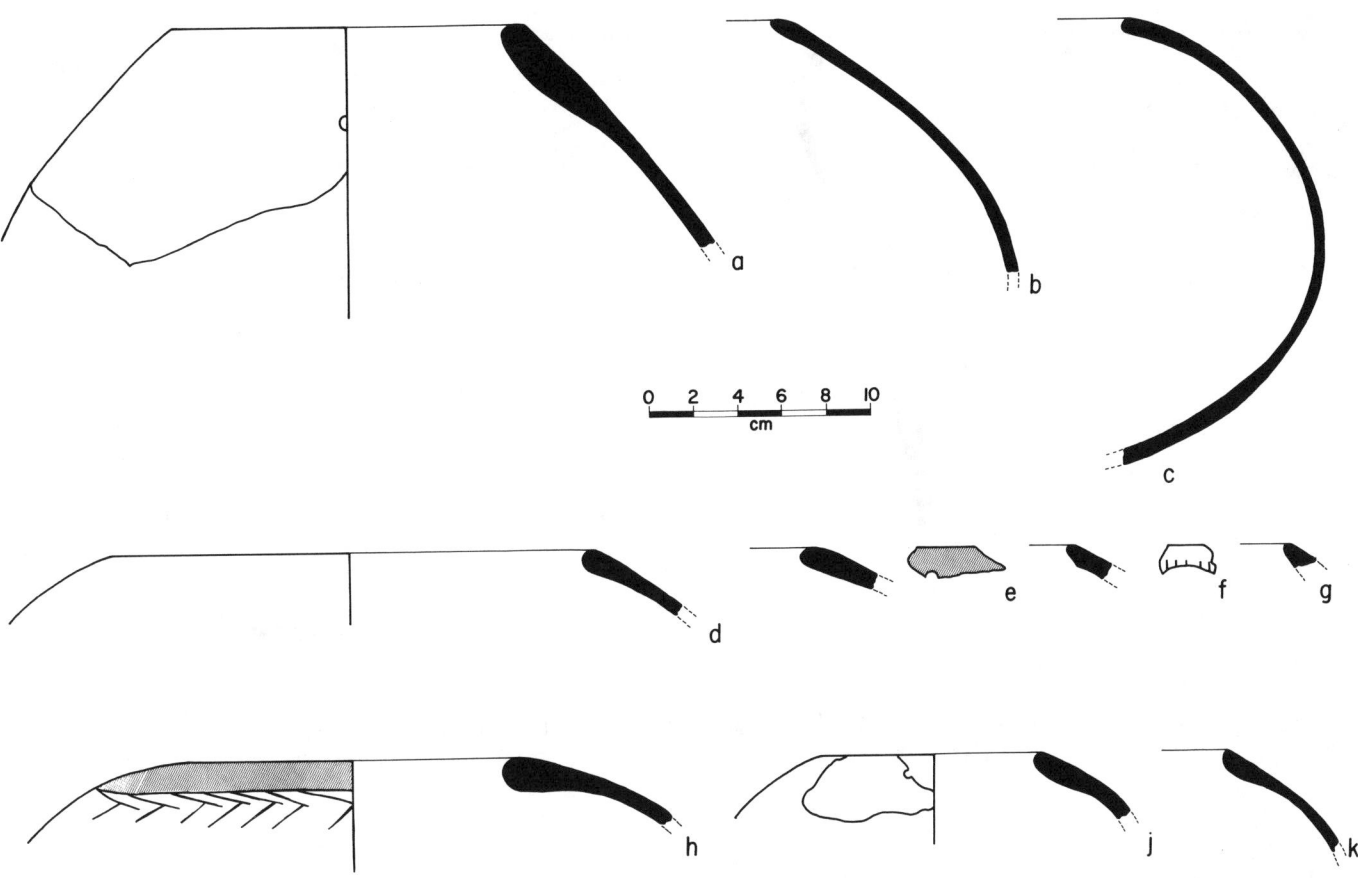

Figure 12.32. Fidencio Coarse tecomates from Tierras Largas (TL), San José Mogote (SJM), and Barrio del Rosario Huitzo. *a, b,* Guadalupe phase examples from Feature 112, TL. *c,* San José phase example from above Feature 151, TL. *k,* San José phase example from above Feature 142, TL (this specimen has a band of burnishing at the rim). *d, f,* San José phase examples from Household Unit C3, Area A, SJM (*f* has incised decoration on the exterior, some 1.5 cm below the rim). *g,* San José phase example from Zone D2 midden, Area A, SJM. *h, j,* Guadalupe phase examples from cleaning the profile, Area A, Huitzo. *h* has herringbone slashes on the exterior, and the red wash is confined to a band at the rim (shaded). *e* has been shaded to indicate that its wash may have been confined to the rim, as in the case of *h*. Both *e* and *j* show signs of having been perforated for suspension, with the perforation appearing as a crescent-shaped notch in the edge of the sherd.

Firing Temperature

It was probably fired at 700–720° C, in a reducing atmosphere. To fire Leandro Gray at a higher temperature might have destroyed the characteristic double burnish. Such reduction firing need not require an elaborate kiln; Atzompa potters today achieve reduction merely by piling dirt over the usual cover of sherds on the rack of pots being fired (Stolmaker 1973:74).

Color

Cross-sections of sherds show that the clay body most frequently turns out very dark gray (10 YR 3/1), but it may grade into mousey brown (7.5 YR 5/4), dark red (2.5 YR 3/6), or dark reddish brown (2.5 YR 3/5). The burnished surface is usually dark gray (10 YR 4/1), but may grade into dark grayish brown (10 YR 3/2); light spots or streaks on the surface may even be pale brown (10 YR 6/3).

Surface Treatment

One of the attributes of Leandro Gray is a streaky or cloudy appearance, dark gray alternating with pale brown. This attribute seems to have resulted from one of two alternative surface treatments.

1. In the majority of cases, the vessel was not given a wash, but was burnished twice with a quartz pebble (once when leather-hard, once when completely dry) to bring the clay component to the surface and achieve a hard, high gloss. In this case, the streaky effect is caused by irregular burnishing, with the dark gray streaks being glossy high points and the pale brown streaks being matte low points.

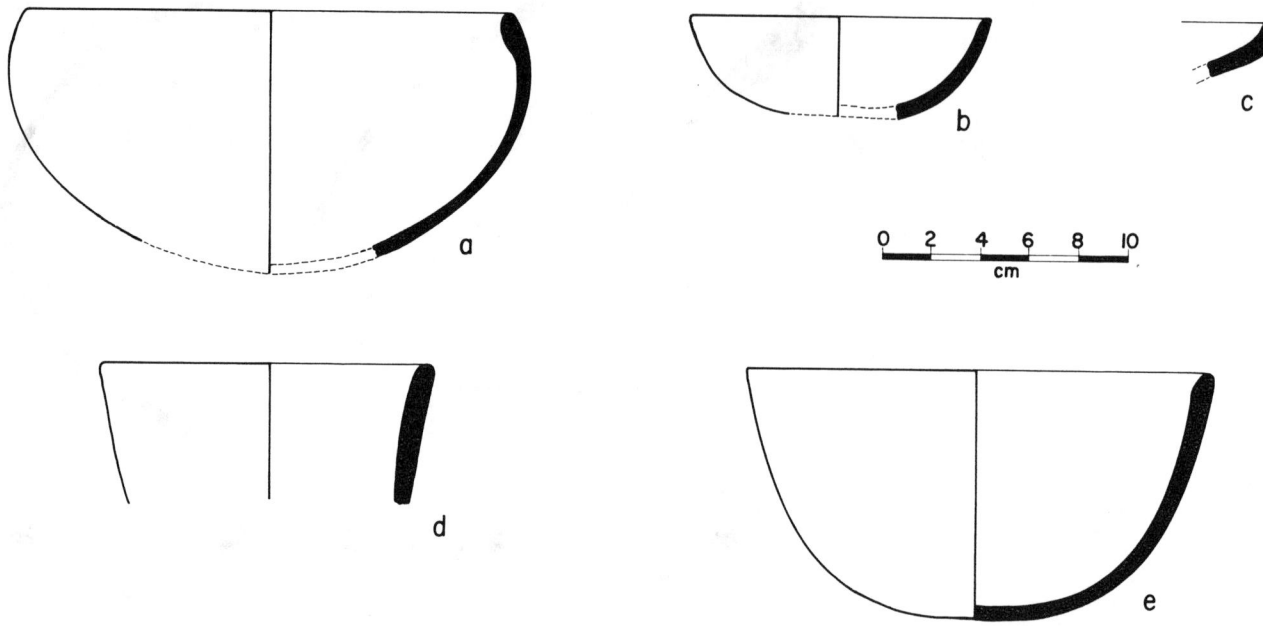

Figure 12.33. Examples of Fidencio Coarse hemispherical bowls from the site of Tierras Largas. All have a drab red wash on the outside. *a,* San José phase example from Feature 1, House 1, Area A. *e,* San José phase example from Test Square 3091, Area B. *b, c,* and *d,* Guadalupe phase examples from Feature 112.

2. In a minority of cases, the usual streaky effect was simulated not by burnishing, but by the application of a thin kaolinite wash. This wash was brushed on unevenly while the vessel was wet, then burnished (once) evenly with a quartz pebble. The alternate streaky bands of dark gray and pale brown give the same superficial appearance as the double-burnished surface described above. Such vessels lack the high gloss of double-burnished Leandro Gray.

Plastic Decoration

The most frequent type of decoration on Leandro Gray was excising or carving, called *raspada* by Mexican archaeologists. Such excising occurred very frequently on cylindrical bowls and bolstered-rim bowls, less frequently on other vessel forms; it was carried out after burnishing. Sometimes the excising was combined with incising (*sgraffito*) to form the Oaxaca versions of pan-Mesoamerican iconographic motifs. In the case of the so-called fire-serpent, for example, his stylized jaws and gums were done by excising, and the flames rising from his eyebrows by incising. Rarely was Leandro Gray decorated by incising alone, although fine-line hachure was a frequent component of some motifs.

As with other San José phase types, the excising appears to have been done with something resembling a slat of cane (*carrizo*), while the incising was done with something like the spine from the tip of a maguey leaf (*espina de maguey*). However, we cannot help but suspect that carved wooden bowls and/or pyroengraved gourd vessels served as the original prototypes for this type of excised pottery.

Post-Firing Addition of Red Pigment

In many cases, areas carved or roughened on Leandro Gray vessels were filled with dry red pigment. The pigment appears to be ground hematite powder, occasionally specular but usually nonspecular. Its color is roughly 7.5 R 4/8 in the Munsell system. The red pigment was applied after firing and can be very fugitive; it served to accent the excised designs.

Leandro Gray as an Export Ware

In 1972, Michael Coe allowed one of our Oaxaca project members, Nanette Pyne, to take small pieces off some excised gray sherds ("Calzadas Carved") from his excavations at San Lorenzo, Veracruz. Those particular gray sherds had struck Pyne as having motifs that looked more typical of the San José phase in Oaxaca than the San Lorenzo phase in Veracruz. William O. Payne's microscopic comparison of these samples with our Leandro Gray and Delfina Fine Gray sherds showed that several "Calzadas Carved" bowls were, in fact, made of the same clay as vessels found frequently at San José Mogote. Of the two wares, Delfina Fine Gray was perhaps the most widely exported because of its high quality, but Leandro Gray was occasionally exported as well (see discussion in our type description for Delfina Fine Gray).

Muriel Porter Weaver (1967:29–30) reported on an excised vessel from Tlapacoya in the southern Basin of Mexico whose clay body included Oaxaca-style volcanic tuffs. While the dark gray cylinder on the left in Weaver's photograph looks remarkably like a Leandro Gray vessel, its aplastic inclusions sound more like those found in Delfina Fine Gray. However, as mentioned above, a small percentage of Leandro Gray vessels were made with black sedimentary clays from the valley floor. Since those clays contain ignimbrite, it is possible that the vessel on the left in Weaver's illustration is a fine-grained Leandro Gray cylinder made for export.

More recently, Christine Niederberger has defined a pottery type from Tlapacoya which she calls "Atoyac Fine Gray" (Niederberger 1987:564–65). From her description, Atoyac Fine Gray sounds very much like Delfina Fine Gray (see discussion below). However, the fire-serpent motif on the cylinder she illustrates in her Fig. 4.71 is remarkably similar to some we found on Leandro Gray.

Niederberger (1987:564) considers Atoyac Fine Gray a trade ware from outside the Basin of Mexico ("un type d'origine exogene"). However, thin sections of her Atoyac Fine Gray did not precisely match thin sections of the Delfina Fine Gray sherds we had loaned her; the latter contained "a greater proportion of metamorphic material" than was found in those Delfina Fine Gray sherds. We do not see this as a problem, because sedimentary valley floor clays from the Valley of Oaxaca can contain varying proportions of volcanic tuff or Precambrian metamorphics, depending on which areas of the piedmont they are washed down from. Examples of Delfina Fine Gray made near Mitla might contain more ignimbrite, while examples made near Atzompa might contain more metamorphics.

We strongly suspect that both Delfina Fine Gray and Leandro Gray were exported from Oaxaca to the Basin of Mexico. We agree with Niederberger that her Atoyac Fine Gray is a trade ware, most probably from Oaxaca. We further suspect that while most of her examples are what we would call Delfina Fine Gray, some may be fine-grained versions of Leandro Gray.

Vessel Forms

Bottles (Fig. 12.34–12.35). This was one of the earliest shapes in which Leandro Gray occurred, appearing just at the end of the Tierras Largas phase or during the transition from Tierras Largas to early San José. Like their Xochiltepec White and Atoyac Yellow-white counterparts, Leandro Gray bottles had tall narrow necks. Their bodies—usually globular—were sometimes fluted, perhaps in imitation of a cucurbit.

Rim diameter: 3.5–7.0 cm
Height of neck: 8–12 cm
Diameter of body: Estimated to be 12–30 cm
Wall thickness: 4–10 mm
Decoration: Most are plain. Some have grooving or fluting on the body which makes it resemble a squash. This was a widespread Early Formative attribute.

Flat-based bowls with outleaned walls (Figs. 12.36–12.41). These "outleaned-wall bowls," as they are called in our sherd tables and figure captions, were a legacy from late Tierras Largas times. Typically their walls lean outward at an angle of 20–60° relative to the flat base.

Rim diameter: Usually 24–36 cm, with a mode of about 32 cm. Occasional bowls were as small as 20 cm or as large as 40 cm.
Height: Normally one-fourth to one-third the rim diameter.
Basal diameter: Normally about two-thirds the rim diameter.
Wall thickness: Usually 5–10 mm
Volume: One specimen with a rim diameter of 21 cm held 840 milliliters, or one adult serving. Another with a rim diameter of 31 cm held 2.3 liters; the latter might have provided servings for 3–4 persons. More than half of these bowls would have held a meal for a nuclear family.
Decoration: Excised designs (or a combination of excising and *sgraffito*) occur on the interior surfaces of some outleaned-wall bowls. The design tends to be a free-standing motif that occurs only twice (on opposite sides of the bowl); thus many wall sherds from a badly broken bowl will appear to be plain. Most of the excised designs are local versions of pan-Mesoamerican motifs.

An occasional San José phase rim sherd shows incised parallel lines, sometimes with a "double-line break" motif like those seen in Atoyac Yellow-white. The frequency of such rims, however, is very low until the end of the San José phase and the start of Guadalupe. During the Guadalupe phase, double-, triple-, and even quadruple-line breaks were not uncommon (Fig. 12.78), but by this time Leandro Gray was a relatively minor ware. Such incised gray bowls resemble Río Salado Gray vessels from the early Santa María phase in the Tehuacán Valley (MacNeish, Peterson, and Flannery 1970: Fig. 42).

Also present in both San José and Guadalupe times, but in very low frequency, were bowls with pseudo "grater bowl" or *molcajete* designs incised on the interior surface of the flat base (Fig. 12.74*a-j*; Fig. 12.75*c*). Their rarity in Oaxaca is striking in view of their great popularity in Formative Tehuacán.

Method of manufacture: Our earliest examples of these bowls appear to have been made from a circular slab of clay (the base), with walls built up by adding concentric rings of clay. A groove running along the contact between wall and base clearly indicates where the two parts of the vessel were joined and the concentric rings smoothed out. Many of the later examples of this vessel form, however, appear to have been press-molded inside or outside of previous bowls. Both surfaces of the bowl were burnished with a quartz pebble while leather-hard; the interior surface was later given a second burnishing when completely dry.

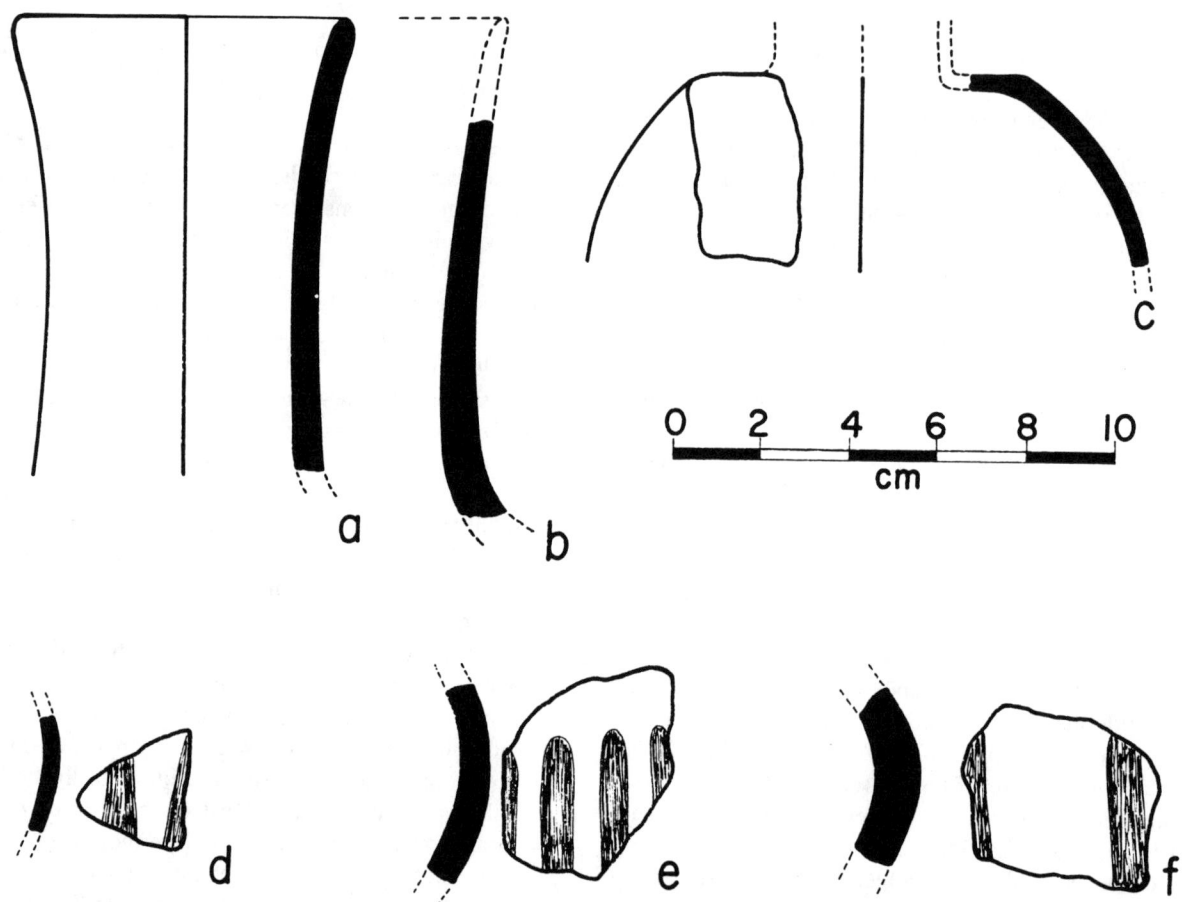

Figure 12.34. Leandro Gray bottle sherds from San José Mogote (SJM) and Tierras Largas (TL). *a,* bottle neck from cleaning profile of Zone D, Area C, SJM (associated with the feet of an adult burial removed by adobe makers). *b,* bottle neck from debris atop Structure 5, Area C, SJM. *c,* carinated bottle shoulder from Feature 75, TL. *d-f,* body sherds from fluted bottles, Area A, SJM (*d, f,* Zone D2 midden; *e,* Zone D1 midden). *b* and *c* date to the late Tierras Largas phase or the transition from Tierras Largas phase to San José phase. (All other specimens San José phase.)

Flat-based bowls with vertical, or nearly vertical, walls (Figs. 12.42–12.58). These "cylinders," as they are called in our sherd tables and figure captions, have walls that are vertical or lean outward only slightly (no more than 10° from vertical). Obviously, these bowls are one end of a continuum in which outleaned-wall bowls are the opposite end. However, it is also clear that the prehistoric potters saw a difference between the two: they put their carved designs on the *interiors* of outleaned-wall bowls and on the *exteriors* of cylinders, where they would be most easily seen. We tried to make our division between the two vessel forms roughly where that interior/exterior design dichotomy occurred: that is, somewhere between a wall angle of 10° and a wall angle of 20°.

Rim diameter: Most examples fall between 10 cm and 24 cm, with a peak between 16 cm and 18 cm. Rare specimens were as small as 7 cm or larger than 26 cm.

Height: Normally about two-thirds the rim diameter.

Basal diameter: Normally about four-fifths the rim diameter.

Wall thickness: Usually 5–8 mm, with the full range being 3–11 mm.

Volume: Two cylinders with rim diameters of 10–11 cm held 450 milliliters each, and may have been for individual servings of food (both these cylinders were offerings for burials). A specimen with a rim diameter of 16 cm held 1.55 liters and thus may have provided 3–4 individual servings. In general, about two-thirds of the Leandro Gray cylinders would have held one meal for a nuclear family.

Decoration: Excised designs (or a combination of excising and *sgraffito*) were very common. Since the designs tended to occur only once or twice on a cylinder, even a ratio of three plain rim sherds to every excised sherd would suggest that most cylinders were decorated. Motifs were generally the pan-Mesoamerican kind, such as the fire-serpent or were-jaguar, often with dry red pigment rubbed into the excising.

Method of manufacture: Most cylinders appear to have been press-molded, perhaps over a lightly baked mold like the one shown in Figure 2.7. Some appear to have been press-molded against a previous vessel; whether the potter molded the new vessel inside or outside the old one may

from plain and direct to slightly tapered in cross-section. While many tecomates are incised (usually just a line encircling the rim), still others are plain. None have rocker or dentate stamping; a high-gloss burnish, rather than plastic decoration, seems to have been the desired effect.

Rim diameter: Most are 12–22 cm, although one small tecomate found with a burial has a diameter of only 9 cm.

Height: Usually about two-thirds the rim diameter.

Wall thickness: Usually 6–8 mm, with a few up to 12 mm.

Decoration: When present, decoration may be limited to one or two incised lines forming a band around the rim. Occasional tecomates have wide, shallow grooves forming a rim band. In other cases, such grooves appear as vertical fluting, perhaps in imitation of a cucurbit. Dry red pigment may be rubbed into the incisions.

Method of manufactre: Built up by concentric rings from a base that had been pounded into the shape of a cup.

Bowls with incurved rim (Figs. 12.65–12.66). Sometimes called "bowls with a restricted orifice," these vessels can be difficult to separate from thin-walled tecomates. Figure 12.65 will perhaps aid in demonstrating where we drew the line between the two forms, as they tend to grade into one another. Incurved-rim bowls tend to be deeper and narrower than the specimens we have called "hemispherical bowls"; they may even be pear-shaped, with a globular body gradually contracting into something like an incurved-rim collar or neck (e.g., Fig. 12.65e). A few specimens, however, fall on the border between "hemispherical bowl" and "incurved-rim bowl" (see, for example, Fig. 12.65g, h).

Rim diameter: 14–24 cm

Height: About three-fourths the rim diameter.

Wall thickness: 4–8 mm

Decoration: Rare. Some bowls have incised lines around the outside of the rim, and a few have more complicated *sgraffito* patterns (e.g., Fig. 12.65j).

Hemispherical bowls (Fig. 12.65k, m; Fig. 12.70a). Hemispherical bowls with wide open mouths and a slightly flattened circular area on the base, such as we found in Tierras Largas Burnished Plain, are rare in Leandro Gray. The Leandro version includes vessels shallower than any recovered in the Tierras Largas phase (see, for example, Fig. 12.70a). Our sample is so small that we hesitate to give a range of measurements; all we can say is that these bowls are in the *general* size range of hemispherical bowls in Tierras Largas Burnished Plain.

Bowls with bolstered rim (Figs. 12.67–12.68). This type of bowl was an extremely important vehicle for excised pan-Mesoamerican motifs. Our specimens show very strong resemblances to bolstered-rim bowls in Calzadas Carved and Limón Carved-Incised from San Lorenzo, Veracruz (Coe and Diehl 1980: Figs. 138–45) and Mirador-Plumajillo, Chiapas (Agrinier 1989: Fotos 1, 2); they also show ties to Carved Gray of the late Amate subphase at Chalcatzingo (Cyphers Guillén 1987: Fig. 13.8) and

Figure 12.35. Leandro Gray bottle neck found while cutting the profile, Area C, San José Mogote. Early San José phase deposits.

have depended on whether he or she wanted the new vessel to be larger or smaller. Wood ash was probably spread over the previous vessel so that the new one would not stick to it.

Cylinders were burnished once on both surfaces with a quartz pebble while leather-hard; the exterior surface was burnished again when completely dry. Excising and incising were done after the final burnishing.

Tecomates (Figs. 12.59–12.64). Tecomates, incurved-rim bowls, and hemispherical bowls in Leandro Gray formed a continuum, all based on a sphere but differing in the horizontal plane through which the sphere had been cut. Leandro Gray tecomates tend to be thinner, smaller, and better made than their counterparts in Atoyac Yellow-white or Lupita Heavy Plain. Rims vary

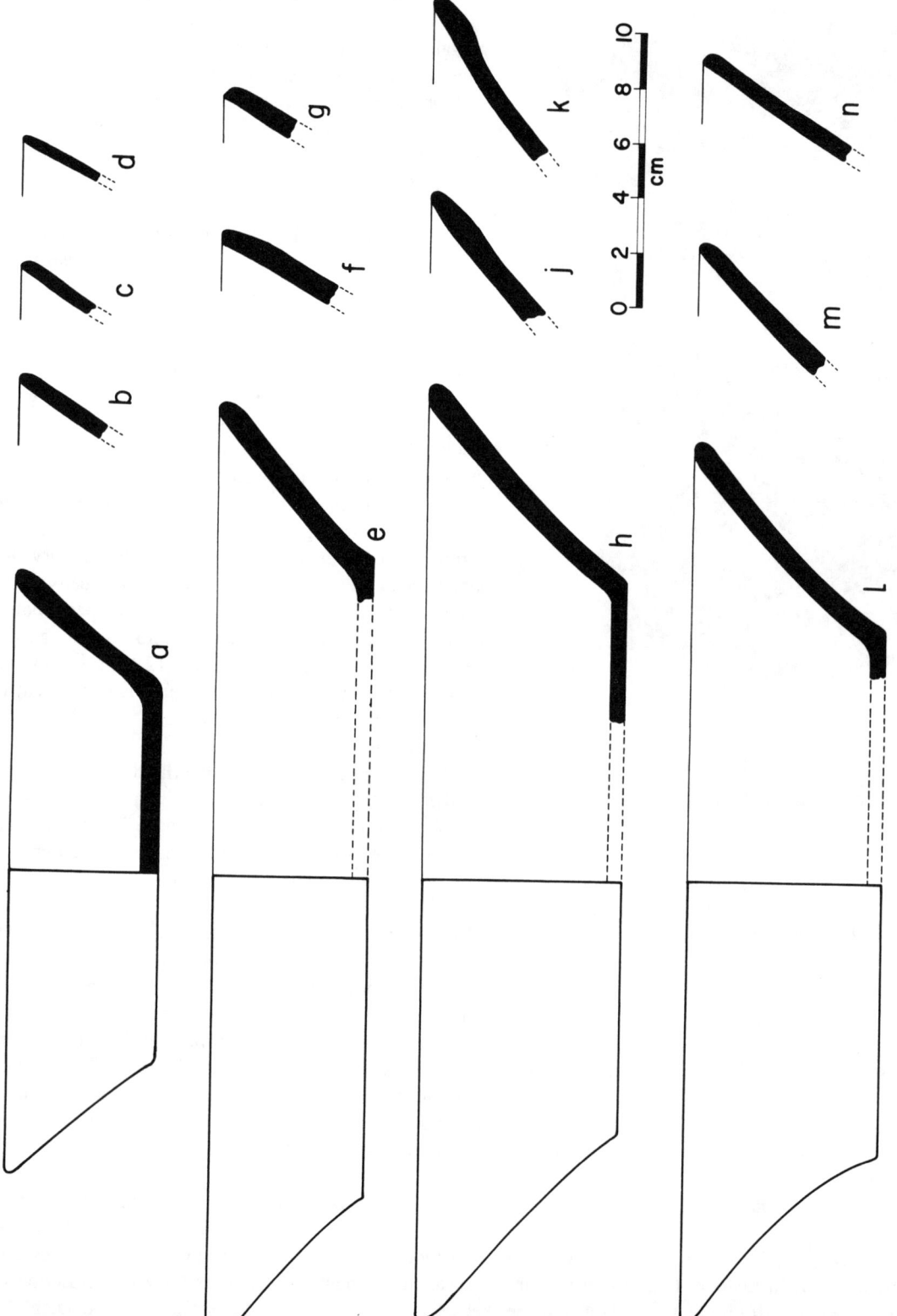

Figure 12.36. Leandro Gray bowls with flat base and outleaned walls, undecorated, from San José Mogote (SJM) and Huitzo. *a,* Vessel 3, House 2, Area C, SJM. All other SJM examples are from Area A, as follows: *m,* Household Unit C2; *c, e, h-k,* Household Unit C4; *l, n,* Zone D1 midden; *b, f,* Zone D2 midden. *g* is from Zone E2, Area A, Huitzo, a Guadalupe phase provenience. (All other proveniences San José phase.)

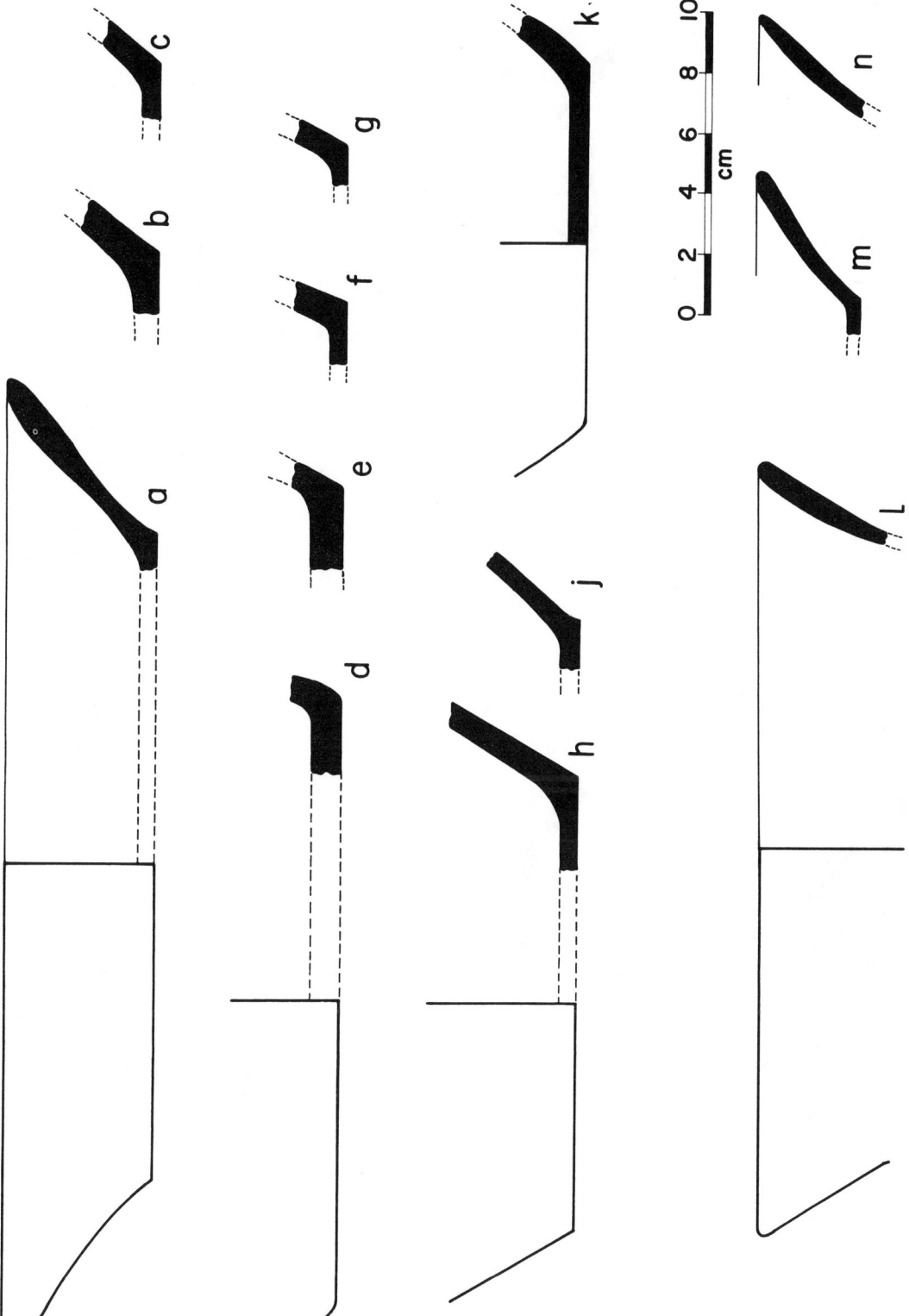

Figure 12.37. Leandro Gray bowls with flat base and outleaned walls, undecorated, from San José Mogote (SJM) and Huitzo. All SJM specimens are from Area A, as follows: *a-e, j-k*, Household Unit C3; *f*, Household Unit C4; *h*, Zone D1 midden; *g*, Zone D3 midden. All Huitzo specimens are from Area A, as follows: *n*, Zone C4; *l, m*, Zone F3. *a-k* are all San José phase; *n* is Guadalupe phase; *l, m* are from a Guadalupe phase provenience that could contain redeposited San José phase sherds.

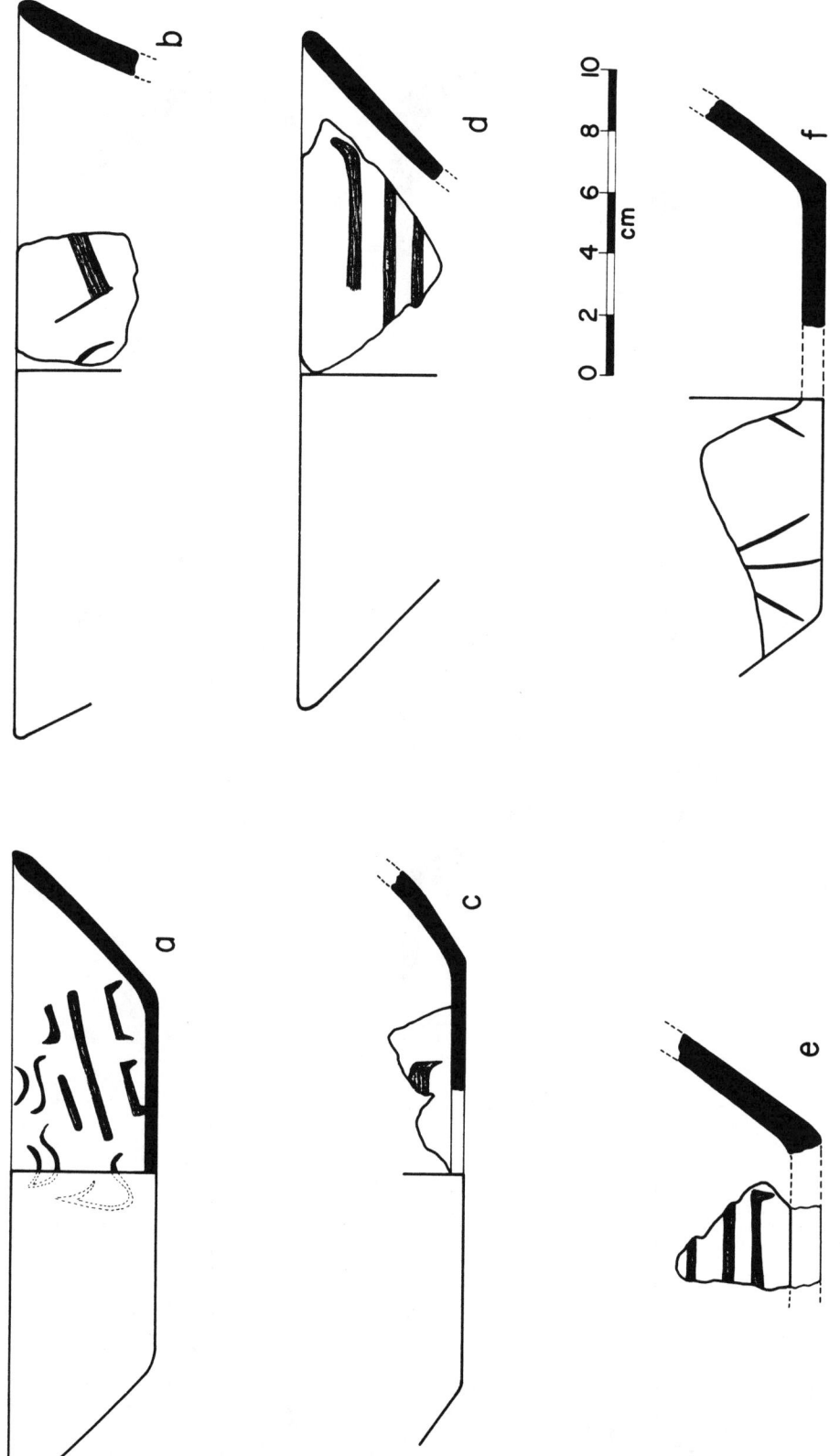

Figure 12.38. Leandro Gray bowls with flat base and outleaned walls, excised. All specimens come from the Zone D midden, Area A, San José Mogote, and probably all date to a relatively short period within the San José phase. All but *f* show some variant of the fire-serpent motif (Sky) carved on the interior of the bowl. *f* is unusual in that it is excised on the outside. *a-d, f,* Zone D1; *e,* Zone D3.

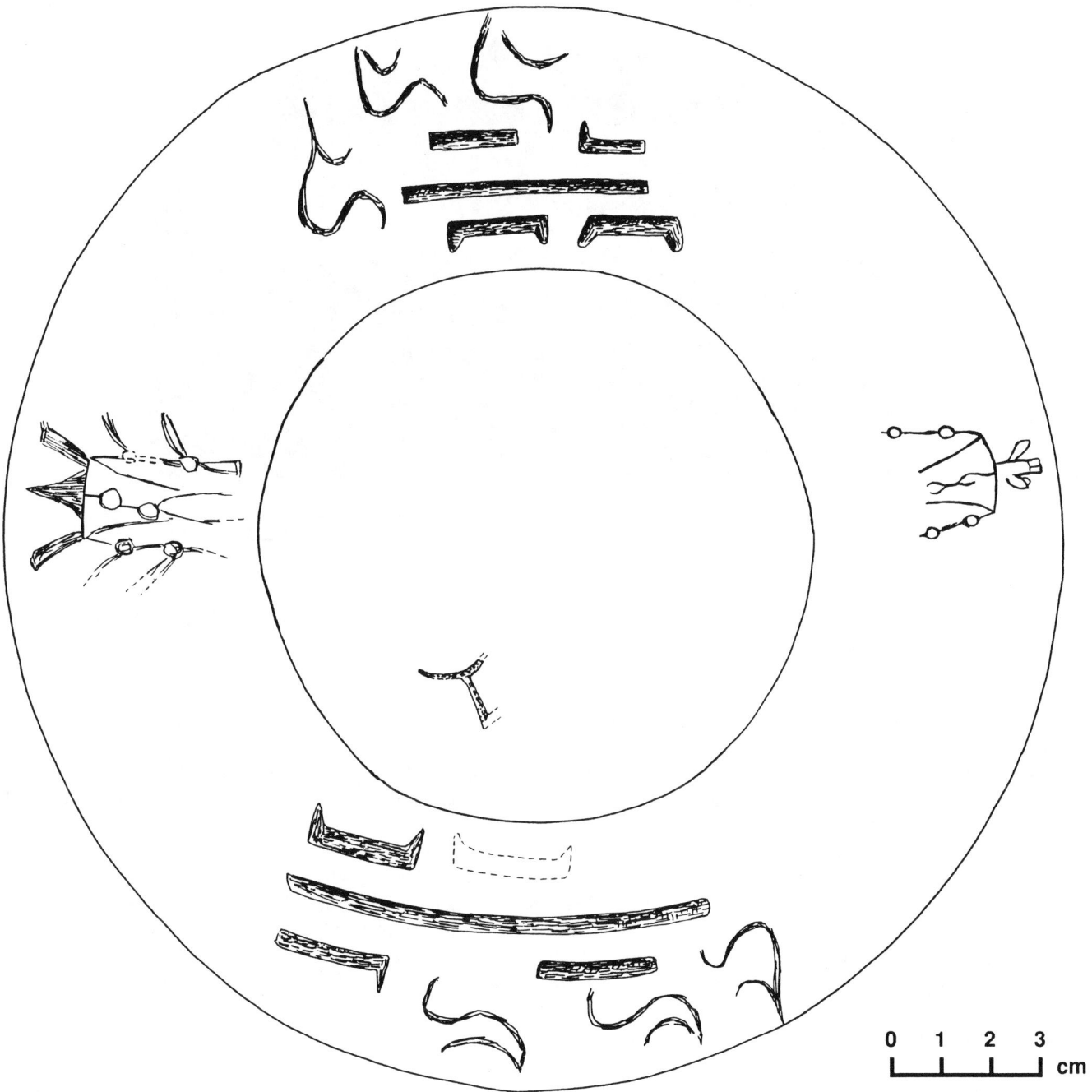

Figure 12.39. Top view of reconstructed Leandro Gray bowl with flat base and outleaned walls, showing interior decoration. The fire-serpent motifs (Pyne's Motif 1) were heavily excised when the clay was leather-hard, *before* firing. The stick figures of costumed humans were engraved onto the bowl with a sharp instrument *after* firing. Zone D1 midden, Area A, San José Mogote (San José phase).

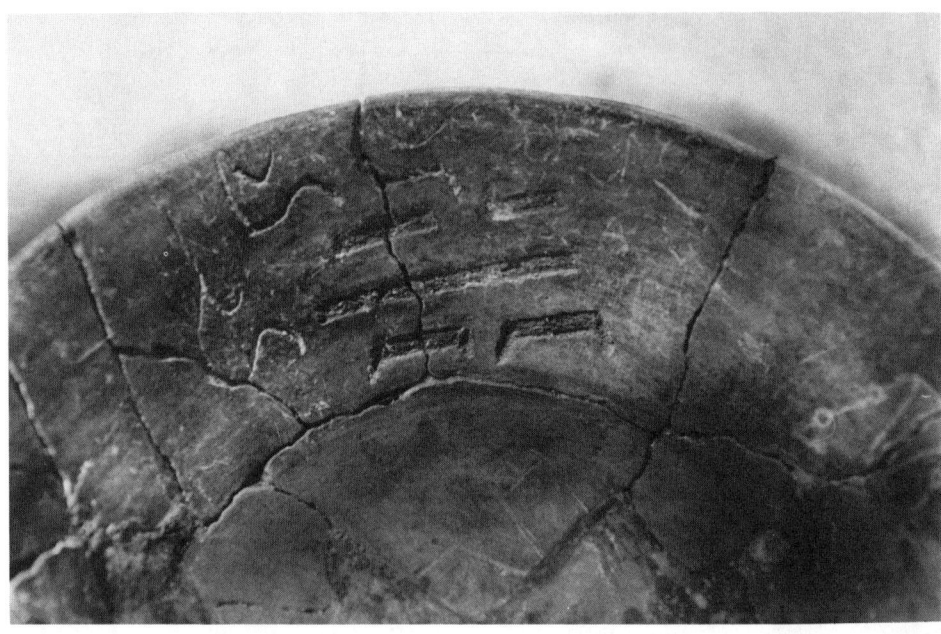

Figure 12.40. Close-up of Leandro Gray bowl shown reconstructed in Figure 12.39. Pyne's Motif 1 was produced by combining incised eyebrow flames with excised U-motifs.

Volcán Burnished from Tlapacoya-Zohapilco in the Basin of Mexico (Niederberger 1987: Fig. 391).

These bowls have their rims externally bolstered through the addition of an extra concentric ring of clay. An interesting feature of these vessels is that although they are "open" (i.e., with outleaned walls), the excised designs are almost always on the *exterior*. Indeed, the outer surface of the bowl below the rim is often left unburnished; it may even be roughened so that dry red pigment can be rubbed onto it. Over this rough surface such elements as crossed bands, "music brackets," flame eyebrows, U-motifs, and other components of the fire-serpent were excised. The rest of the bowl was double-burnished.

Rim diameter: Three-fourths of the bowls are in the 18–26 cm range, with a mode of 20–22 cm and occasional examples as small as 14 cm or as large as 40–60 cm.

Height: Usually one-third the rim diameter.

Wall thickness: 4–12 mm, with a mode of 7 mm.

Decoration: Frequent, including excising (*raspada*), incising (*sgraffito*), or some combination of the two. While the rim and interior of the vessel were burnished, the exterior could be deliberately roughened or left unsmoothed and unburnished. Apparently this was considered an appropriate background for carved designs.

Jars with vertical necks (Fig. 12.69). These are jars with a globular body and a relatively tall, vertical-sided neck that is built up by concentric rings of clay. Rims are either of the plain direct type, or slightly tapered-rounded in profile. The necks—usually as simple and straight as a pipe—probably evolved out of earlier bottle necks. Very similar jars were described by Dixon (1959: Fig. 1*f*) from Chiapa de Corzo I.

Rim diameter: 10–18 cm

Height of neck: 6–10 cm

Diameter of body: Usually unknown. One specimen with a rim diameter of 10 cm has a body diameter of at least 28 cm.

Wall thickness: Usually 5–9 mm

Decoration: Usually none. A few San José phase examples have a raised bulb on the outside of the neck (Fig. 12.69*f, g, h, j*), sometimes outlined or accompanied by incised lines. The bulb appears to have been pushed through from the inside of the neck with the potter's thumb. Dixon (1959: Fig. 2*e*) illustrates a similar bulb on a "vertical-wall bowl" (possibly a vertical-wall jar neck?) from Chiapa de Corzo I.

Oval bowls with pinched-in sides. These vessels, rare in Leandro Gray but not in other wares, look as if they had been press-molded inside gourd bowls that had been sectioned through the stem scars. Of course, they could also be produced by pinching in the opposite rims of a typical hemispherical bowl. Niederberger (1987: Figs. 511, 512) illustrates similarly shaped vessels (called *bols pincés*) in several wares at Tlapacoya-Zohapilco.

San José Phase

Figure 12.41. Leandro Gray bowl with flat base and outleaned walls, excised on the interior with an elaborate version of Pyne's Motif 1. Burial 20, Tierras Largas (San José phase).

174 — Early Formative Pottery of Oaxaca

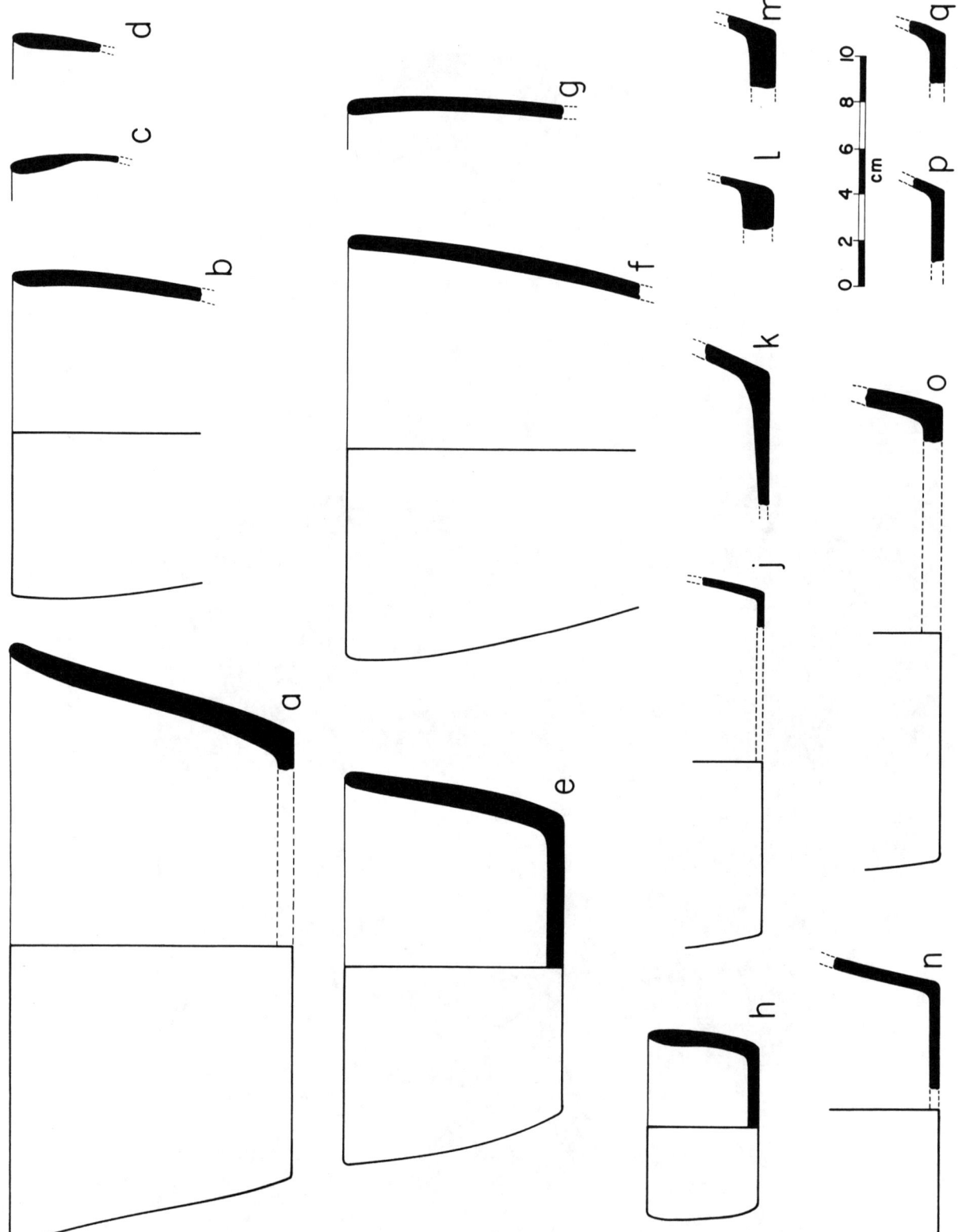

Figure 12.42. Leandro Gray cylinders or bowls with nearly vertical walls, undecorated, from San José Mogote (SJM) and Huitzo. All SJM specimens are from Area A, as follows: *d, e, h,* Household Unit C2; *b, f, k, n,* Household Unit C3; *c, g, l, m, o,* Household Unit C4; *a, j,* Zone D1 midden. All Huitzo specimens are from Area A, as follows: *p,* fill of Structure 4; *q,* Zone F2. *a–o* are all San José phase; *p–q* are from Guadalupe phase proveniences that could contain redeposited San José phase sherds.

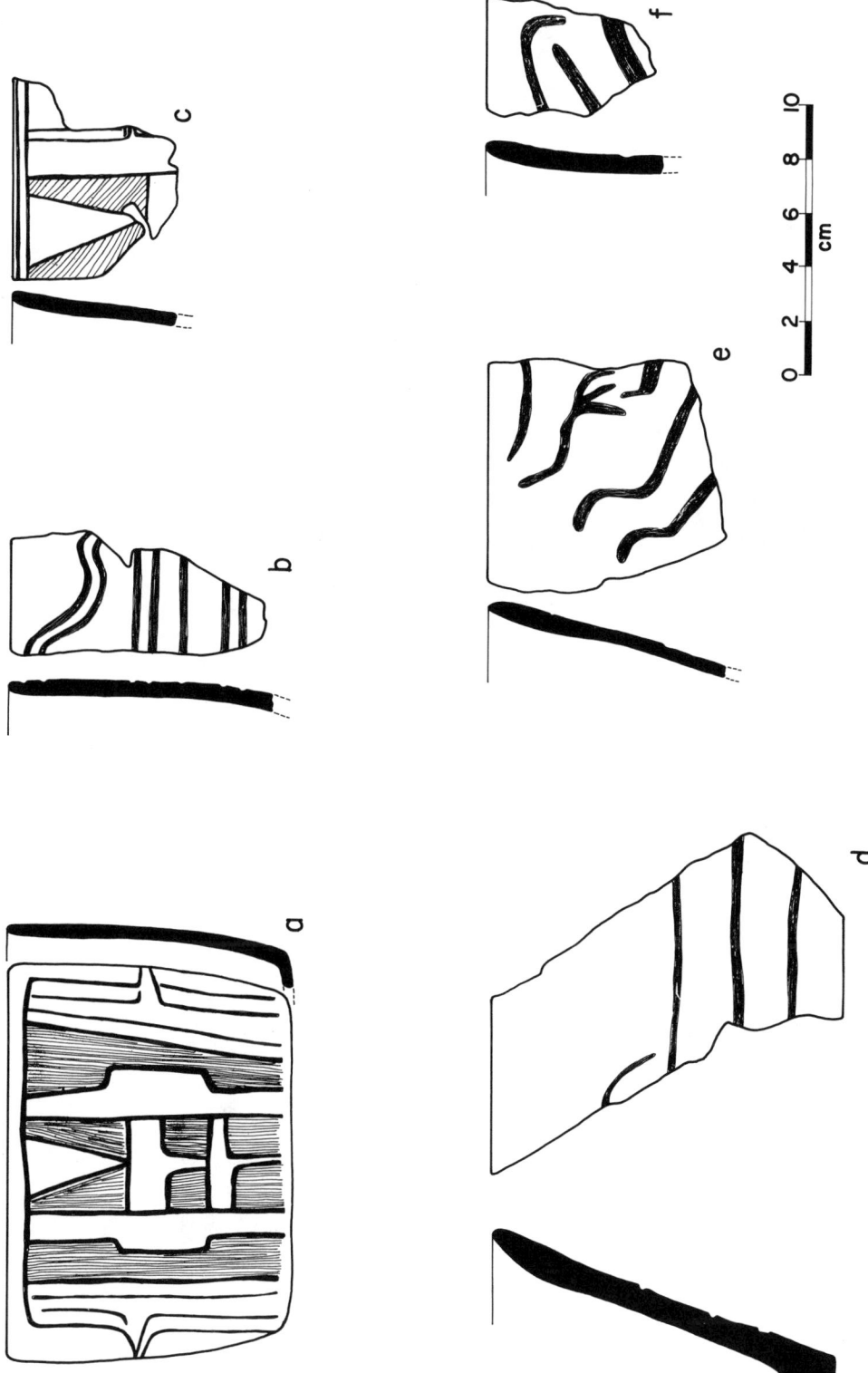

Figure 12.43. Leandro Gray cylinders or bowls with nearly vertical walls, excised, from San José Mogote (SJM) and Tierras Largas (TL). *a,* Vessel 2, Feature 4, House 1, Area A, TL, with a were-jaguar (Pyne's Motif 8) depicted by a combination of excising and fine-line hachure. *b,* cylinder rim with dry red pigment in excising, Household Unit C3, Area A, SJM. *c,* cylinder with excised and fine-line hachured design similar to that on *a,* Household Unit C4, Area A, SJM; dry red pigment rubbed into the design. *d-f,* bowl rims with excising on the outside, all from Zone D1 midden, Area A, SJM (*e* has dry red pigment rubbed into the excising). All specimens are San José phase.

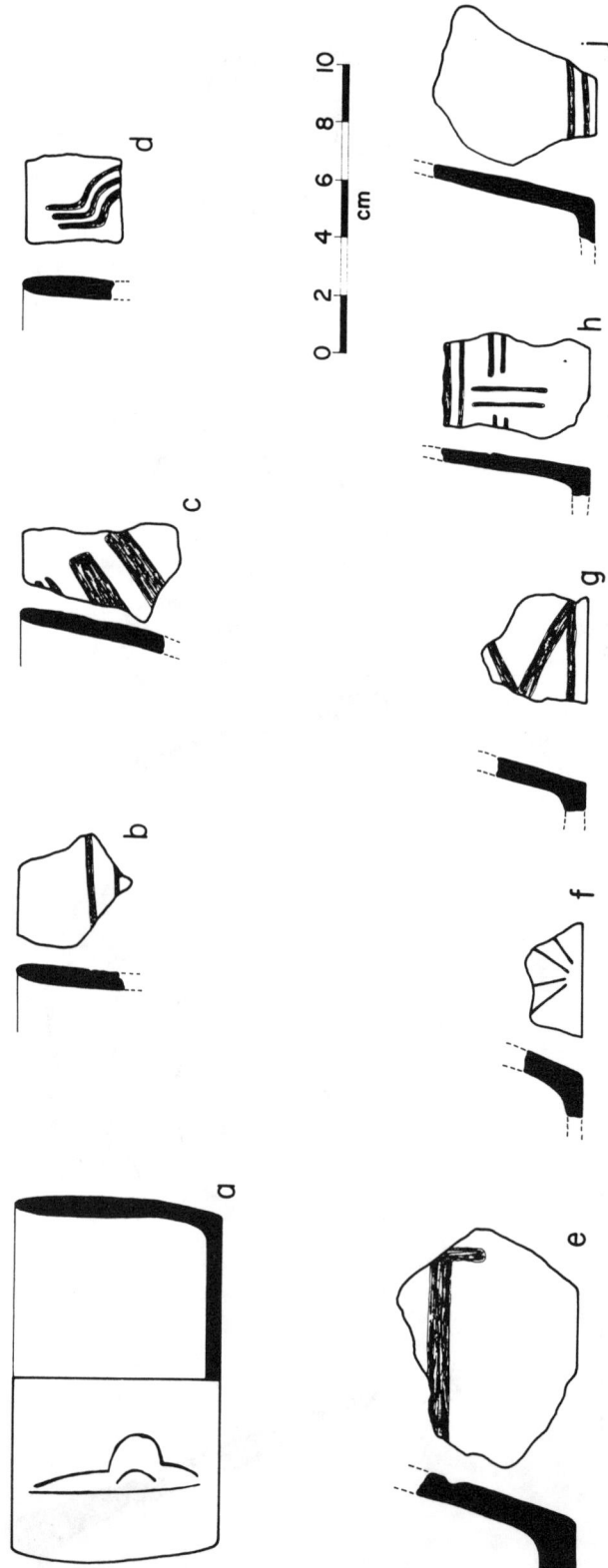

Figure 12.44. Leandro Gray cylinders or bowls with nearly vertical walls, excised, all from Area A of San José Mogote (San José phase). *a,* cylinder from Zone D1 midden. *b, d,* Household Unit C3. *c,* Household Unit C4. *e-j,* cylinder bases with incising (*f*) or excising (*e, g-j*) on the outside. *j,* Household Unit C2. *e, h,* Household Unit C3. *f,* Household Unit C4. *g,* Zone D2 midden.

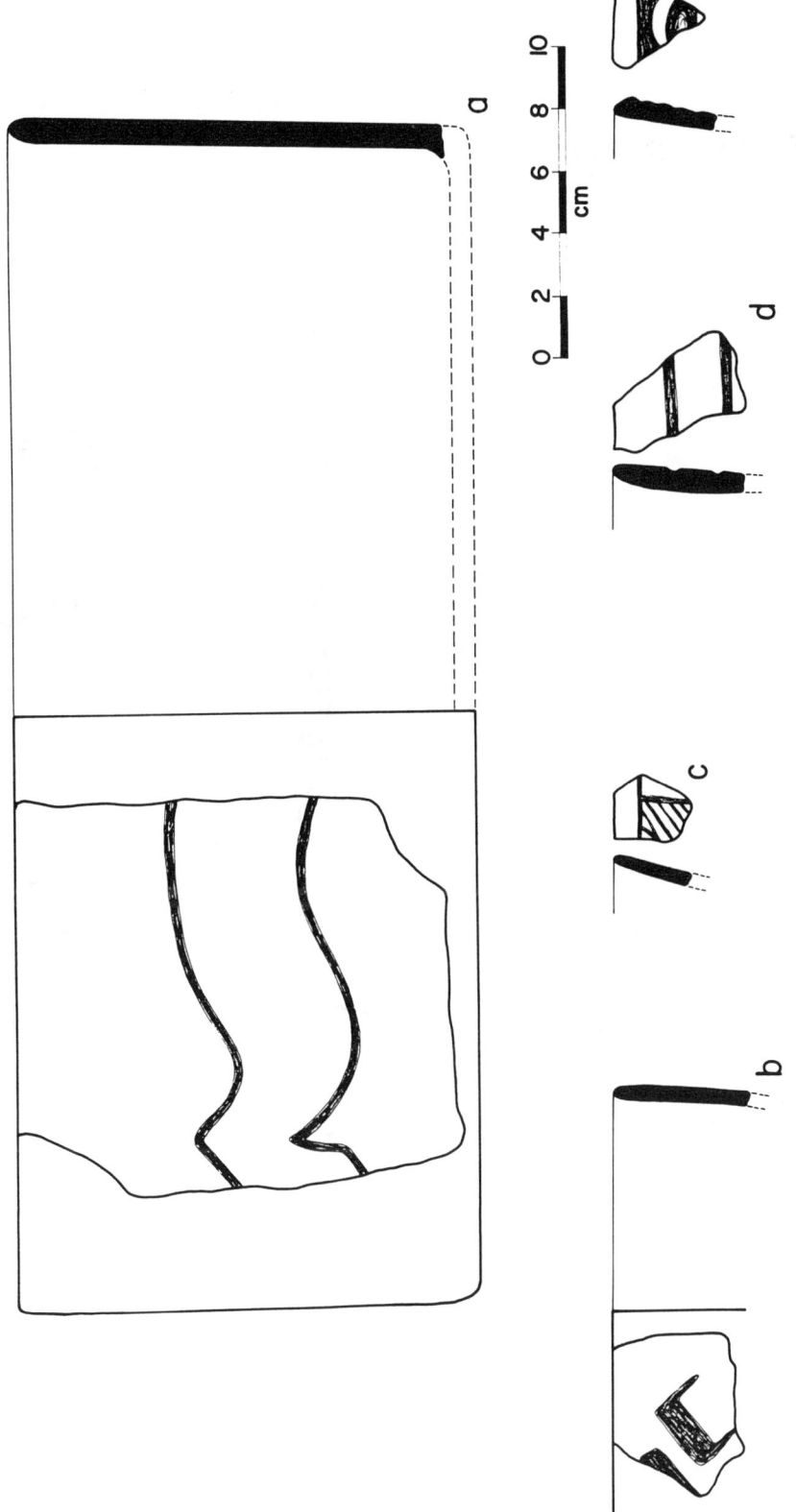

Figure 12.45. Leandro Gray cylinders, excised. *a*, rim sherd found while cleaning profile, Zone D, Area C, San José Mogote (SJM). *b*, Zone F1, Area A, Huitzo. *c–e*, cylinder rims from Area A, SJM, with traces of dry red pigment rubbed into the excised areas (*d*, Household Unit C2; *c*, Household Unit C3; *e*, Household Unit C4). All specimens are from San José phase proveniences except for *b*, which comes from a Guadalupe phase level that could contain redeposited San José phase sherds.

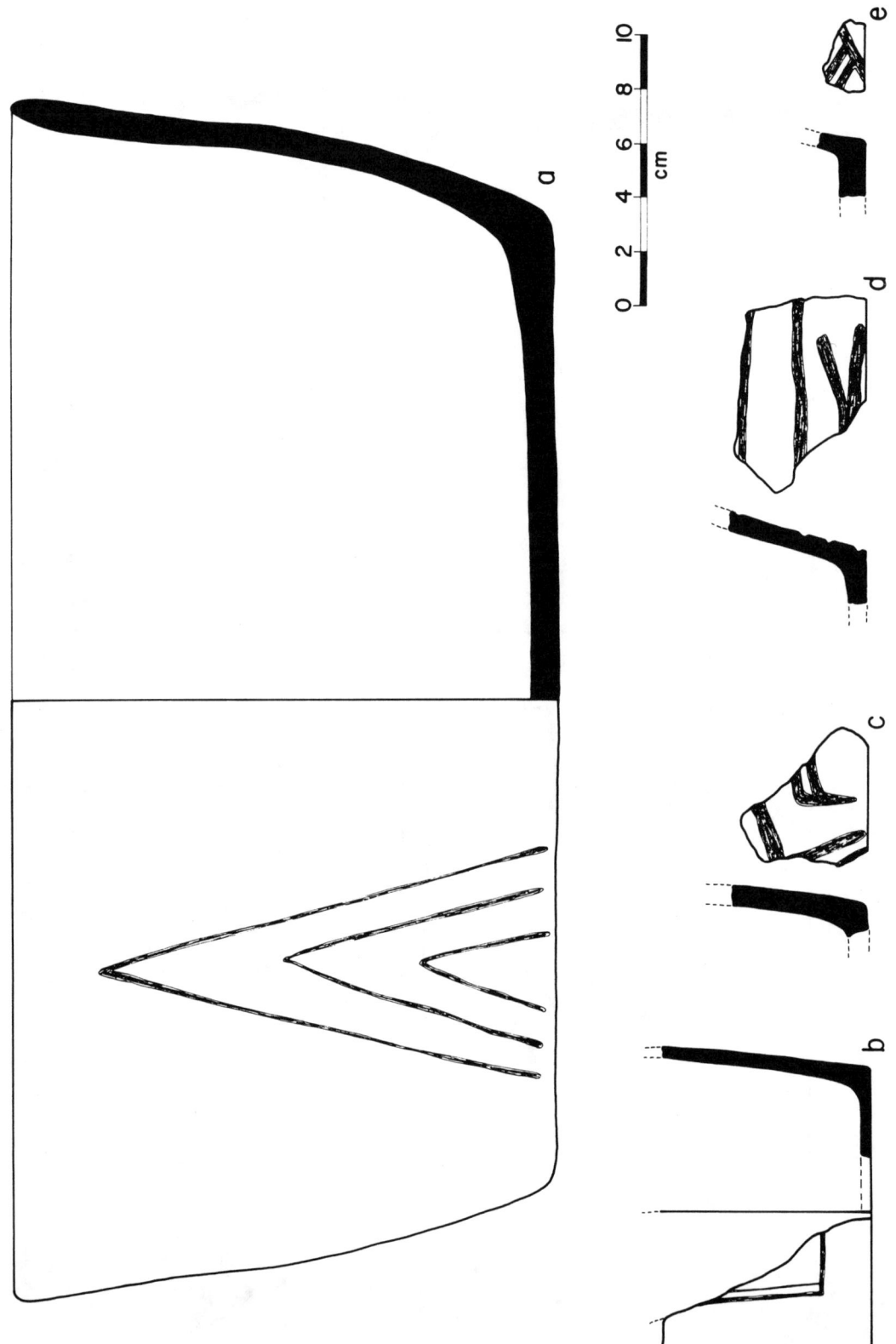

Figure 12.46. Leandro Gray cylinders or bowls with nearly vertical walls, excised, all from Area A, San José Mogote. *a*, Household Unit C4. *b-d*, Household Unit C3. *e*, cylinder base with dry red pigment rubbed into excising, Zone D2 midden.

Figure 12.47 (above). Leandro Gray cylinder with stylized were-jaguar (Earth) motif that combines excising and fine-line hachure. Vessel 2 of Feature 4, House 1, Area A, Tierras Largas (San José phase).

Bowls with gadrooned rim (Fig. 12.70b-d). These unusual vessels, found mainly in the early part of the San José phase, are reminiscent of gadrooned bowls in Ocós Buff from La Victoria, Guatemala (Coe 1961: Fig. 21*f, g*).

Spouted trays (Figs. 12.71–12.73). These shallow vessels, clearly designed to allow a liquid of some kind to be mixed and poured, were first described at Tlatilco by Muriel Porter (1953: Plate 10G). They are also common at Tlapacoya-Zohapilco, where they have been called *plats a bec verseur* (Niederberger 1987: Fig. 560). In Oaxaca, this vessel form is more common in Leandro Gray than in any other type, and appears to be restricted to the San José phase. While the spout is distinctive, the tray itself resembles the vessel we call a "pigment dish" (see below).
Dimensions: Our most complete example had a tray diameter of 16 cm, and a spout roughly 3.5 cm long which tapers to 2 cm wide at the tip.
Decoration: Parallel zigzag lines or crosshatching may be incised on both sides of the spout.

Pigment dishes (Fig. 12.74k-q). These vessels, shaped like small ashtrays, were clearly used for liquid pigment; traces of red or yellow mineral paint can be detected clinging to the interior surface. There is, however, one problem with the identification of this vessel form: the sherds from a broken pigment dish are difficult to tell from spouted tray sherds that do not include part of the actual spout. Thus, our sherd tables include the category "pigment dishes/spouted trays."
Rim diameter: 8–14 cm
Height: One-sixth to one-fourth the rim diameter.

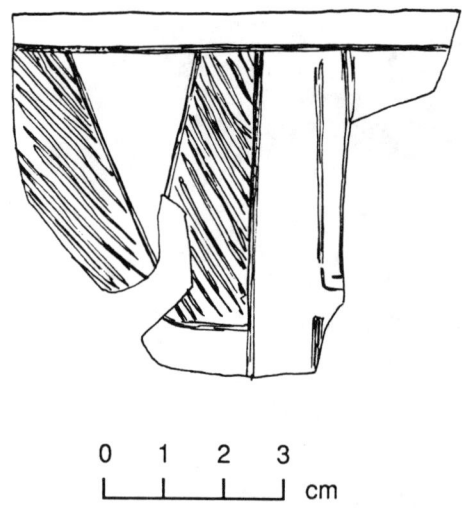

Figure 12.48. Rim sherd from Leandro Gray cylinder with incising and fine-line hachure on the outside. The design seems to be Pyne's Motif 10 (were-jaguar). Household Unit C4, Area A, San José Mogote (San José phase).

Wall thickness: 4–8 mm
Decoration: None
Volume: Those with a rim diameter of 12 cm might have held 300 ml of liquid; most pigment dishes were smaller than this, in the 200 ml range.

Multicompartment vessels (Fig. 12.75b). These rare vessels are similar in shape and dimensions to more complete examples in Lupita Heavy Plain. They resemble the multicompartment condiment trays used in some restaurants, and may have had a similar use. Dixon (1959: Fig. 11a) illustrates a multicompartment vessel similar to ours from Chiapa de Corzo I. It is described as having "a well-polished medium gray slip on the exterior surfaces" (Dixon 1959:12). Drucker (1952:122) also reports a vessel of this type from La Venta.

Bird effigy vessels (Figs. 12.75a, 12.76). Occasional fragments of bird effigy vessels occur in San José phase deposits; they are more common in later periods. One sherd from the Zone D midden in Area A at San José Mogote may have been part of a bird effigy ocarina. The wings were depicted by incised tabs, with red pigment rubbed in the incising.

Bowls with "grater bowl" design incised on base (Figs. 12.74a-j, 12.75c). "Grater bowl" or "pseudo-*molcajete*" bases are relatively rare in the San José phase, especially when one compares Oaxaca to the Basin of Mexico. What is interesting is that such bases occur relatively early in Oaxaca, even though they never become common. In some parts of Mesoamerica, "grater bowl" bases do not appear until the Middle Formative.

Miscellaneous vessels with rare decorative techniques (Fig. 12.77). Occasional Leandro Gray vessels show attributes such as three-dimensional sculpturing, or the division of a tecomate into lobes resembling those of a cucurbit.

Later vessel forms. During the San José phase, one sees hints of vessel forms that were to become more common in the Middle Formative Guadalupe and Rosario phases. While we include a few illustrations of such vessels here for completeness, their full description will be deferred to the Middle Formative pottery volume. Such relatively late forms include composite silhouette bowls (Fig. 12.75d, e); bowls with scalloped rims (Fig. 12.70e-g); and vessels with loop or strap handles (Fig. 12.70h-k).

Another late form is a bowl whose walls *curve* outward rather than simply *leaning* outward. While such bowls were occasionally made during the San José phase (Fig. 12.78a), it was not until the Guadalupe phase that they became common (Fig. 12.78l-u). Often these bowls have parallel incised lines encircling the inside of the rim; they may even have double-line-break motifs (Fig. 12.78m).

ATOYAC YELLOW-WHITE

General Description

A hallmark of the San José and Guadalupe phases, Atoyac Yellow-white was produced by covering our typical reddish brown, residual weathered gneiss clay body with a relatively iron-free kaolinite slip. This slip (or *engobe* in Payne's terminology) was usually yellow-white, but could be cream or white-to-buff. The color difference could reflect either different kaolinite sources, or different skills at purifying the dry clay material. Atoyac Yellow-white was used mainly for bowls of various sizes and shapes, some jars and tecomates, and a whole series of less abundant forms such as bolstered rim bowls, spouted trays, and so on. Most vessels appear to have been either for serving food (from individual portions to family-sized portions) or for light storage; none appear to have been used for cooking.

Atoyac Yellow-white was also the preferred vehicle for a set of pan-Mesoamerican motifs, such as the double-line-break and the were-jaguar. As such, it takes its place as one more "species" within a large "genus" of white-slipped Formative types, including Canoas White in the Tehuacán Valley; Reyes White in the Nochixtlán Valley; Altica White in the Teotihuacán Valley; Pilli White and Cesto White from Tlapacoya-Zohapilco; Moyotzingo White Monochrome from the Valley of Puebla; Amatzinac White from Chalcatzingo, Morelos; Vergel White-to-Buff at Chiapa de Corzo and Padre Piedra, Chiapas; Burrero Cream from Santa Cruz, Chiapas; and Conchas White-to-Buff from the Guatemalan Pacific coast. Here is a situation where we badly need an overarching generic term for all these white wares—either one that recognizes the priority of the first type awarded a binomial title (Conchas White-to-Buff), or a more region-neutral term such as "white-slipped reddish-brown wares."

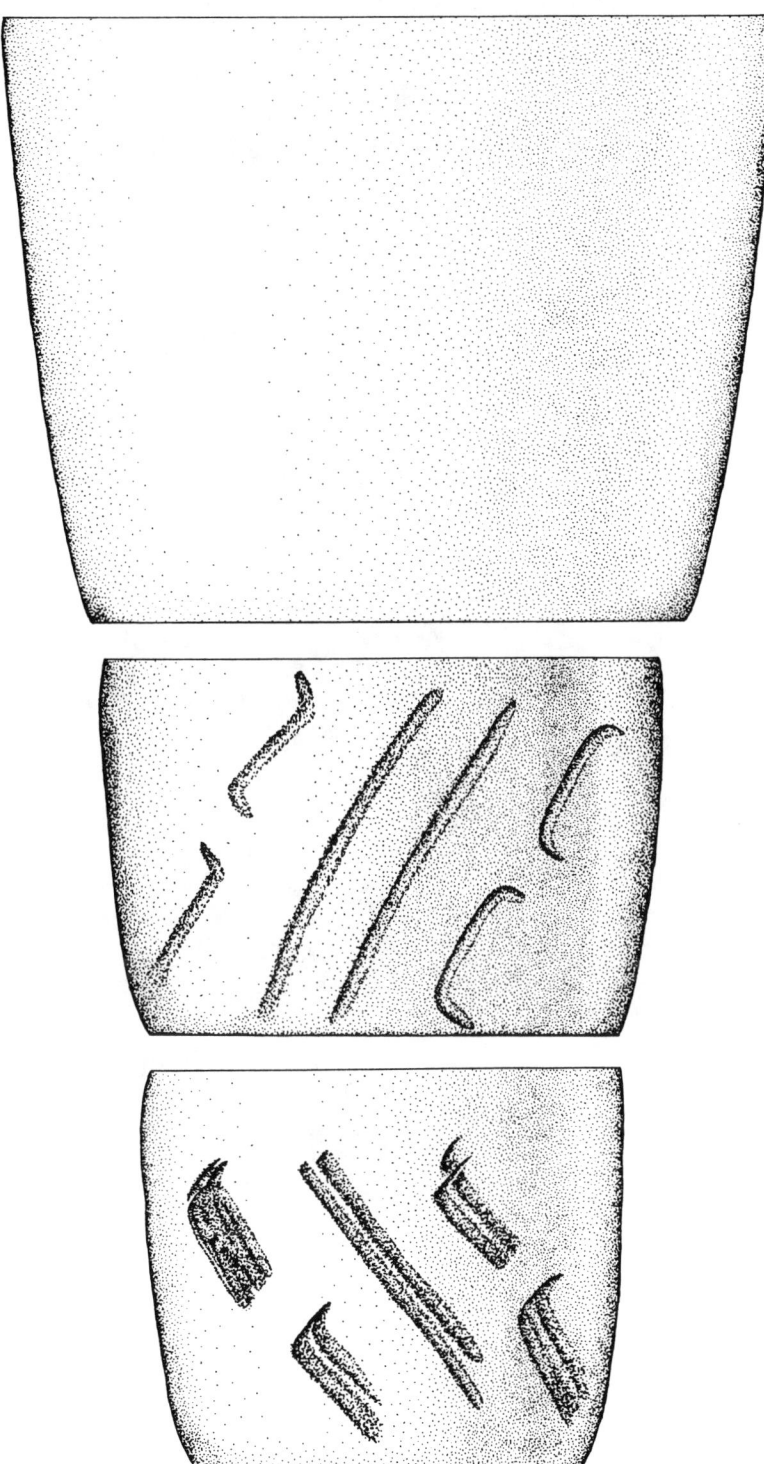

Figure 12.49. Leandro Gray cylinders from Burial 4, Area A, San Sebastián Abasolo (San José phase). *Top,* Vessel 1, an undecorated cylinder. *Middle,* Vessel 2, with stylized fire-serpent (Sky or Lightning) in deep grooves. *Bottom,* Vessel 3, with excised fire-serpent (Sky or Lightning). Rim diameter of Vessel 1: 16.2 cm.

Figure 12.50. Leandro Gray cylinders with variants of the fire-serpent motif found with Burial 4 at San Sebastián Abasolo (San José phase). *Top*, Vessel 3. *Bottom*, Vessel 2 (see also Fig. 12.49).

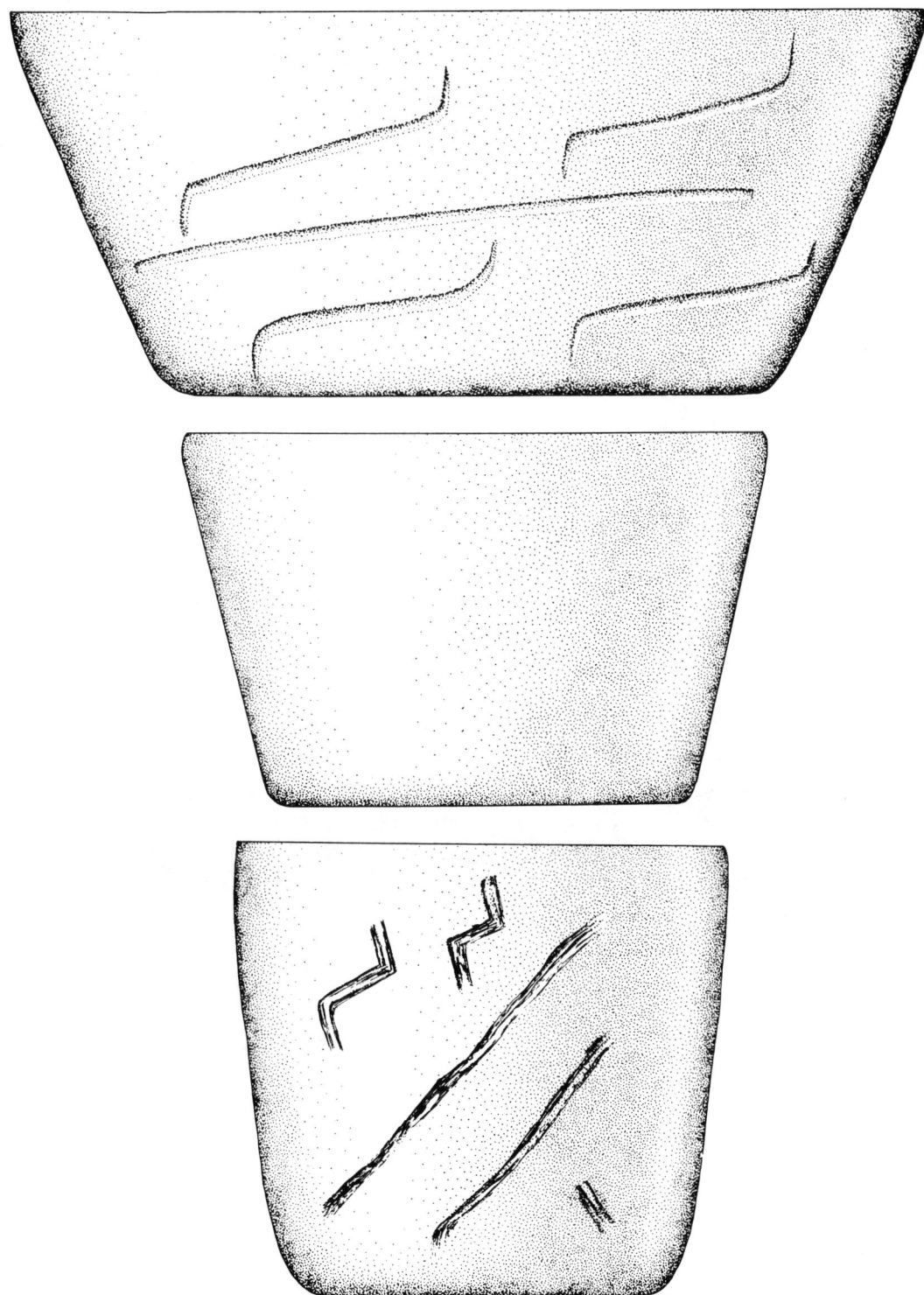

Figure 12.51. Leandro Gray bowls from Burial 1, Area A, San Sebastián Abasolo (San José phase). *Top,* Vessel 1, with stylized fire-serpent motif in deep grooves; in spite of the fact that this vessel has relatively outleaned walls, it was decorated on the outside. *Middle,* Vessel 2, an undecorated bowl with nearly vertical walls. *Bottom,* Vessel 3, a cylinder with excised fire-serpent motif. Rim diameter of Vessel 1: 30 cm.

Figure 12.52. Leandro Gray bowl with fire-serpent (Sky or Lightning) motif, shown reconstructed in Figure 12.51. Vessel 1, Burial 1, San Sebastián Abasolo (San José phase).

Figure 12.53. Leandro Gray bowl with nearly vertical walls, excised with Pyne's Motif 1 (fire-serpent). Vessel 1, Burial 5, Area C, San José Mogote (San José phase). Chalk has been rubbed into the excising so that the design will show up in the photograph.

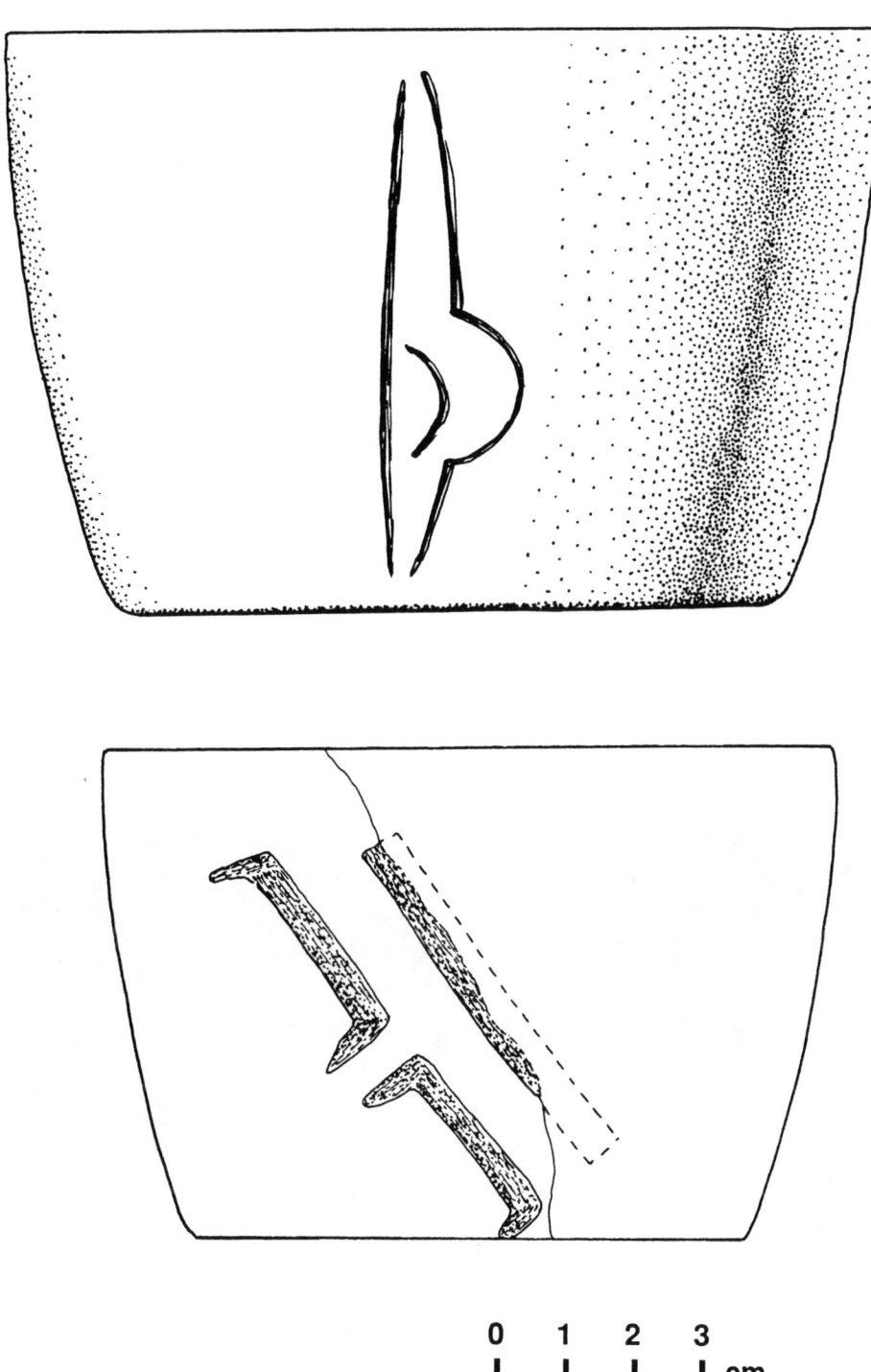

Figure 12.54. Leandro Gray cylinders with excised designs, both from Area A of San José Mogote (San José phase). *Top,* specimen with unusual design, Household Unit C2. *Bottom,* specimen with Pyne's Motif 1, Zone D2 midden; dry red pigment has been rubbed into the excising.

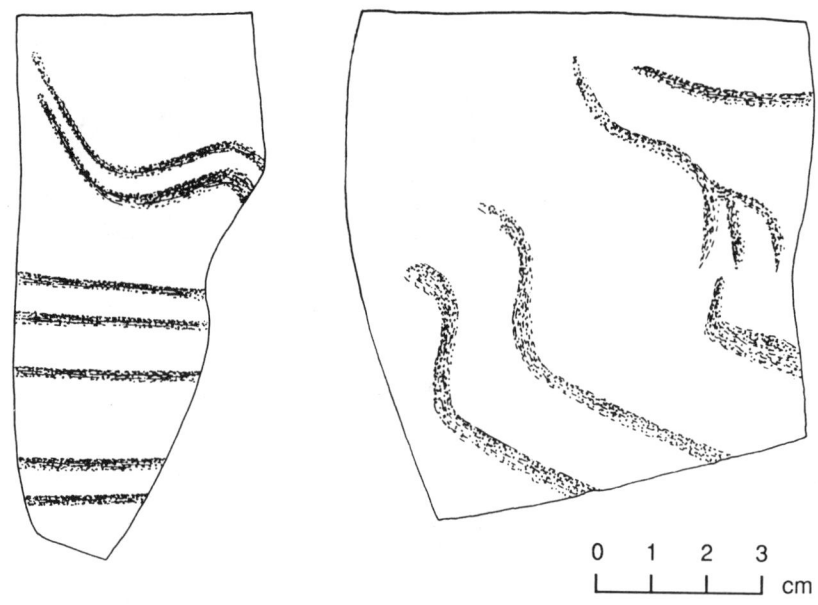

Figure 12.55. Rim sherds from Leandro Gray cylinders with variants of Pyne's Motif 1 excised on the outside, both from Area A of San José Mogote (San José phase). *Left,* Household Unit C3. *Right,* Zone D1 midden.

Figure 12.56. Rim sherds from Leandro Gray cylinders with Pyne's Motif 1 excised on the outside. San José Mogote, Area C, cutting profile at level of San José phase deposits.

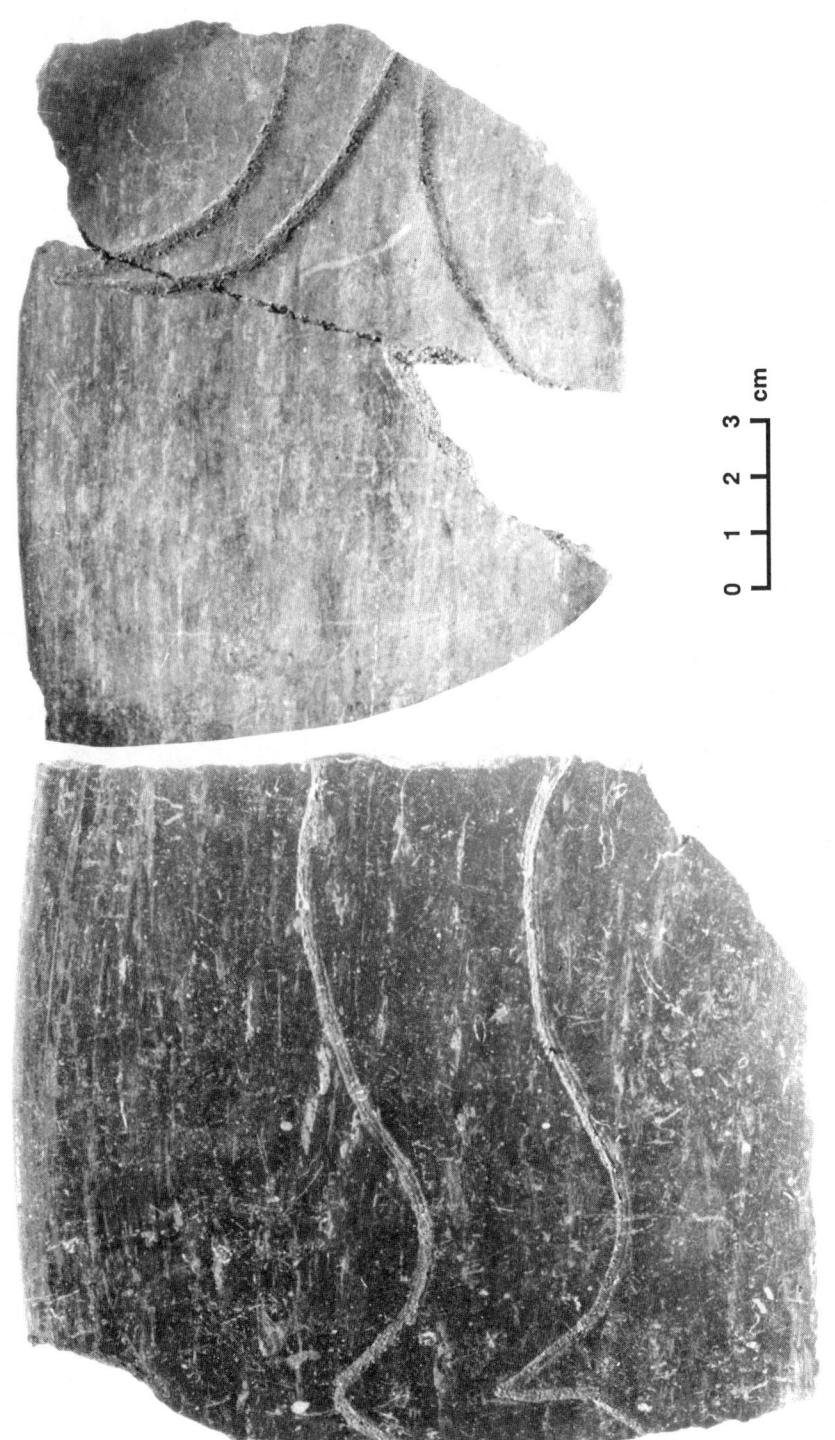

Figure 12.57. Rim sherds from Leandro Gray cylinders with designs of only local distribution, excised on the outside. The sherd on the right shows the horizontal streaks often produced by double burnishing. San José Mogote, Area C, Zone D (San José phase).

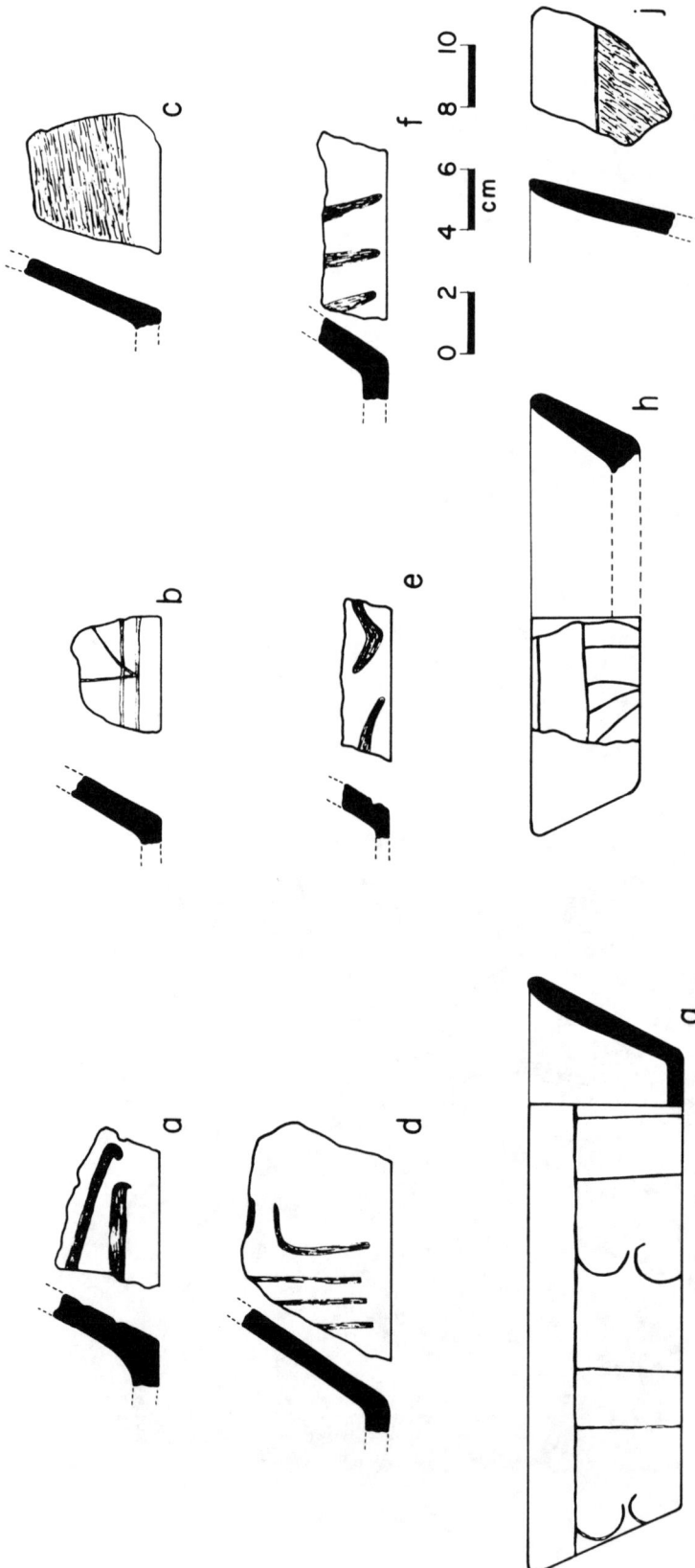

Figure 12.58. Occasionally, San José potters decorated the exterior of Leandro Gray bowls whose walls leaned outward at an angle greater than 10%, treating them as if they were cylinders. In this illustration, *a–f* are basal angle sherds from flat-based bowls; *g–h* are shallow, outleaned-wall bowls. All specimens are from Area A, San José Mogote (San José phase). *a* and *b* are self-slipped but not burnished on the outside, and are excised, with dry red pigment rubbed into the excisions. *c*, also self-slipped but not burnished on the outside, has its wall roughened by coarse brushing with dry pigment rubbed into it. *d* and *e*, also self-slipped but unburnished outside, have excising with dry red pigment rubbed in. *f*, totally self-slipped and burnished, has no trace of red pigment. *g* and *h* are self-slipped and burnished on the outside only as far down as the first horizontal incised line below the rim; below that they are left rough, and decorated with incised lines. *j* is also self-slipped on the inside, and on the outside as far down as the first horizontal incised line; below that it is roughened by coarse brushing, with dry red pigment rubbed in. *a*, *e*, and *f* have variants of Pyne's Motif 1, while *d* and *g* have variants of her Motif 11. *b*, Household Unit C1; *f*, *g*, Household Unit C3; *a*, Household Unit C4; *d*, *h*, Zone D1 midden; *c*, *e*, Zone D2 midden; *j*, Zone D3 midden.

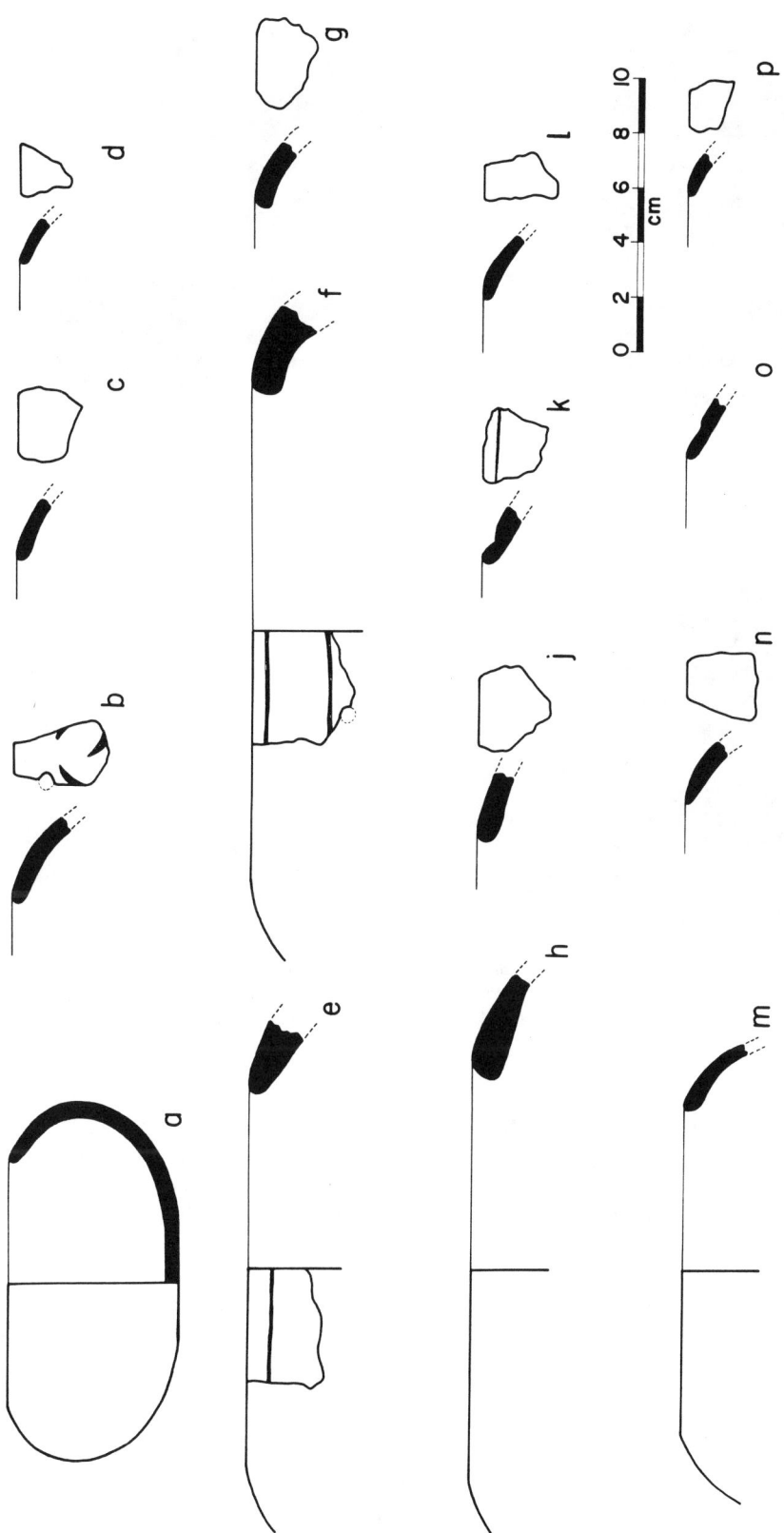

Figure 12.59. Leandro Gray tecomates from San José Mogote (all San José phase). *a*, complete tecomate from Burial 7, Zone D, Area C. *b*, tecomate rim with excising and hole drilled for suspension, Area A, Zone D1 midden. *e, f,* and *k*, tecomate rims with incised lines delimiting a plain band at the rim; *f* has red pigment in the incising, and has been perforated for suspension. *c, d, g, h, j, l* and *m-p* are plain tecomate rims. *b-p* are all from Area A, as follows: *c, h,* Household Unit C1; *d, e, j, l, m, o,* Household Unit C3; *g,* Household Unit C4; *b, k, n, p,* Zone D1 midden; *f,* Zone D2 midden.

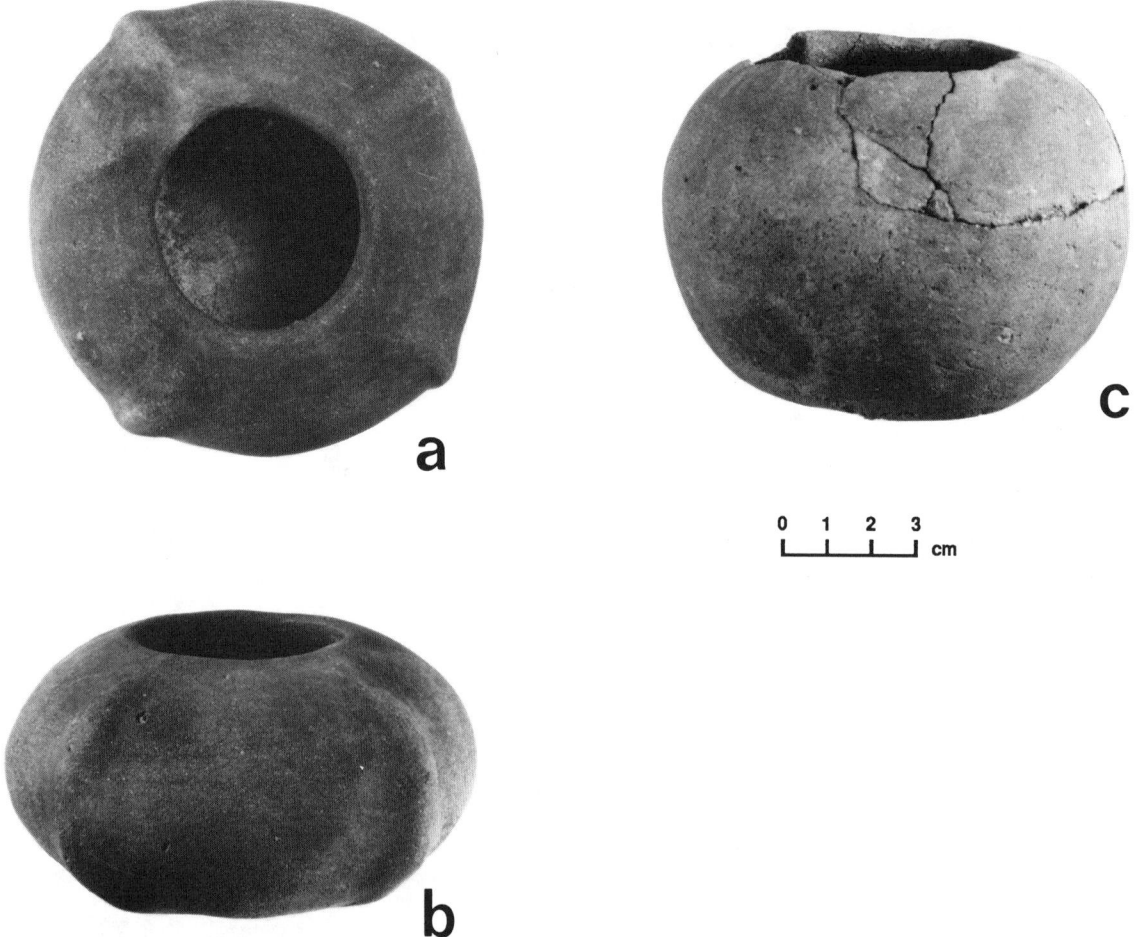

Figure 12.60. Vessels 1 and 2 from Burial 2, San Sebastián Abasolo (San José phase). The vessels are Leandro Gray in color, shape, and clay body, but appear to have been made specifically as burial offerings. Probably because of the haste with which they were made, they lack the double burnishing seen on typical Leandro Gray tecomates. *a, b,* top and side views of Vessel 1, a squash effigy tecomate. *c,* Vessel 2, a simple tecomate.

Of course, there are some chronological differences among these white wares. Some, like Atoyac Yellow-white and Pilli White, begin far back in the Early Formative and carry carved/incised were-jaguar designs. Others, like Conchas White-to-Buff and Canoas White, are known mostly as wares with double-line-breaks from early in the Middle Formative. Those differences, however, are minor compared to the amazing similarity the various types display over tens of thousands of square kilometers. And since we have already argued that the double-line-break developed iconographically out of a stylized were-jaguar (Figs. 12.17–12.18), it would be a mistake to overemphasize the Early Formative/Middle Formative boundary.

When a group of pottery types has such widespread significance, it is worth speculating about their ultimate origin. In our opinion, one clue lies in their relationship to a luxury export ware of the same time period: Xochiltepec White (described later in this chapter). Xochiltepec White, whose place of origin is not known with absolute certainty, was made from a kaolinite so iron-free that it fired pure white—literally "white clear through"—and consequently needed no slip. It was widely traded, appearing in areas as diverse as the Basin of Mexico, the Tehuacán Valley, the Valley of Oaxaca, and the southern Gulf Coast. Coe and Diehl (1980) could plausibly argue that it originated in Veracruz or Tabasco, but equally iron-free kaolinites occur in the Mesoamerican highlands.

We propose two alternative scenarios for the relationship between Xochiltepec White and the more abundant "white-slipped reddish-brown wares." In our first scenario, the latter wares appeared first; in response, someone living near an iron-free kaolinite source decided to produce a luxury version of them for export. In our second scenario, Xochiltepec White appeared first; in response, potters with limited access to iron-free kaolinite

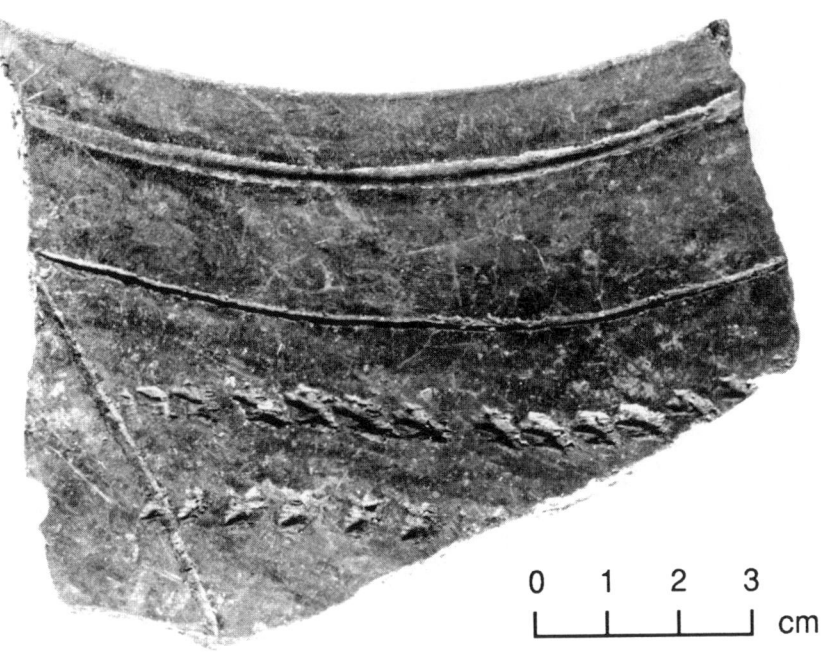

Figure 12.61. Leandro Gray tecomate rim with a plain rim band outlined by incising, a perforation for suspension, and a body divided into zones decorated with what appears to be interrupted dentate stamping of some kind. San José Mogote, Area C, straightening profile at level of San José phase deposits.

Figure 12.62. Leandro Gray tecomate rims from Area B of Tierras Largas (San José phase). *Left,* tecomate with a plain band at the rim, and zoned rocker stamping. *Right,* small tecomate with zoned plastic decoration of some kind.

Figure 12.63. Leandro Gray body sherd with "micro" rocker stamping, shown twice natural size. San José Mogote, Area A, Household Unit C4 (San José phase).

Figure 12.64. Leandro Gray body sherd with dentate stamping, San José Mogote, Area A, Zone D2 midden (San José phase).

began making local imitations of Xochiltepec White by covering reddish-brown vessels with off-white slips. While neither scenario can be confirmed at the moment, we tend to prefer the second.

Chronological History

Atoyac Yellow-white made its first appearance toward the end of the Tierras Largas phase. In stratigraphic Zones G and F of Area C at San José Mogote, and in Area B of Tierras Largas, a few sherds show up during the transition from Tierras Largas phase to San José phase. The earliest shapes seem to be mainly bottles and flat-based, outleaned-wall bowls, both typical late Tierras Largas phase vessel forms.

Not until early San José times, however, did Atoyac Yellow-white occur in significant quantities. Early San José was perhaps the peak moment for tecomates in Atoyac Yellow-white, as well as for interrupted rocker stamping, which was one of the decorative attributes of those vessels.

In the early San José phase there were approximately three outleaned-wall bowls to every two cylindrical bowls. Most outleaned-wall bowls were plain; for example, no rims with incised parallel lines appear in the basal levels of Area A at San José Mogote, a relatively early set of San José phase proveniences. As middle San José times approached, incised parallel lines with double-line-breaks seem to have evolved as a simplified and more abstract reference to the were-jaguar; they increased over time. Bowls with giant "macrorims," some the size of washtubs, also characterized the middle San José phase.

Late in the San José phase, cylindrical bowls had increased to the point where there were about 45 of them to every 55 outleaned-wall bowls. Parallel incised lines on outleaned-wall bowls were increasing, and double-line-break motifs were diversifying. The white cylinder was the favored medium for the stylized were-jaguar, but this set of motifs showed great synchronic variation, occurring in some residential wards but not in others (Chapter 16). Among other decorative attributes of the late San José phase, interrupted rocker stamping seems to have declined while false rocker stamping increased. As the San José phase drew to a close, jars with outcurved or flaring rims began to outnumber jars with vertical necks.

Atoyac Yellow-white went on to be the dominant pottery type of the Guadalupe phase, but its vessel shapes changed to reflect early Middle Formative preferences. Cylindrical bowls declined in frequency to the point where there was only about one cylinder to every six or seven outleaned-wall bowls. Incising had virtually replaced excising; no outleaned-wall bowls, and only a few rare cylinders, were excised. On the other hand, there were as many outleaned-wall bowl rims with parallel incised lines as without them—a sign of the Middle Formative. By this time, virtually all jars showed outcurved or flaring rims; the vertical, tubelike jar neck of earlier times had disappeared.

In the Rosario phase, Atoyac Yellow-white was an extremely minor component, rare to absent in most proveniences.

Clay Body

The clay body is a residual piedmont clay resulting from the decomposition of Precambrian gneiss. It was used virtually as found, except for winnowing or sieving to remove the larger nonplastic particles. The slightly finer appearance of Atoyac Yellow-white (when compared with Fidencio Coarse or Lupita Heavy Plain) is due to the fact that the clay body was selected more carefully, and winnowed so that it had very few particles

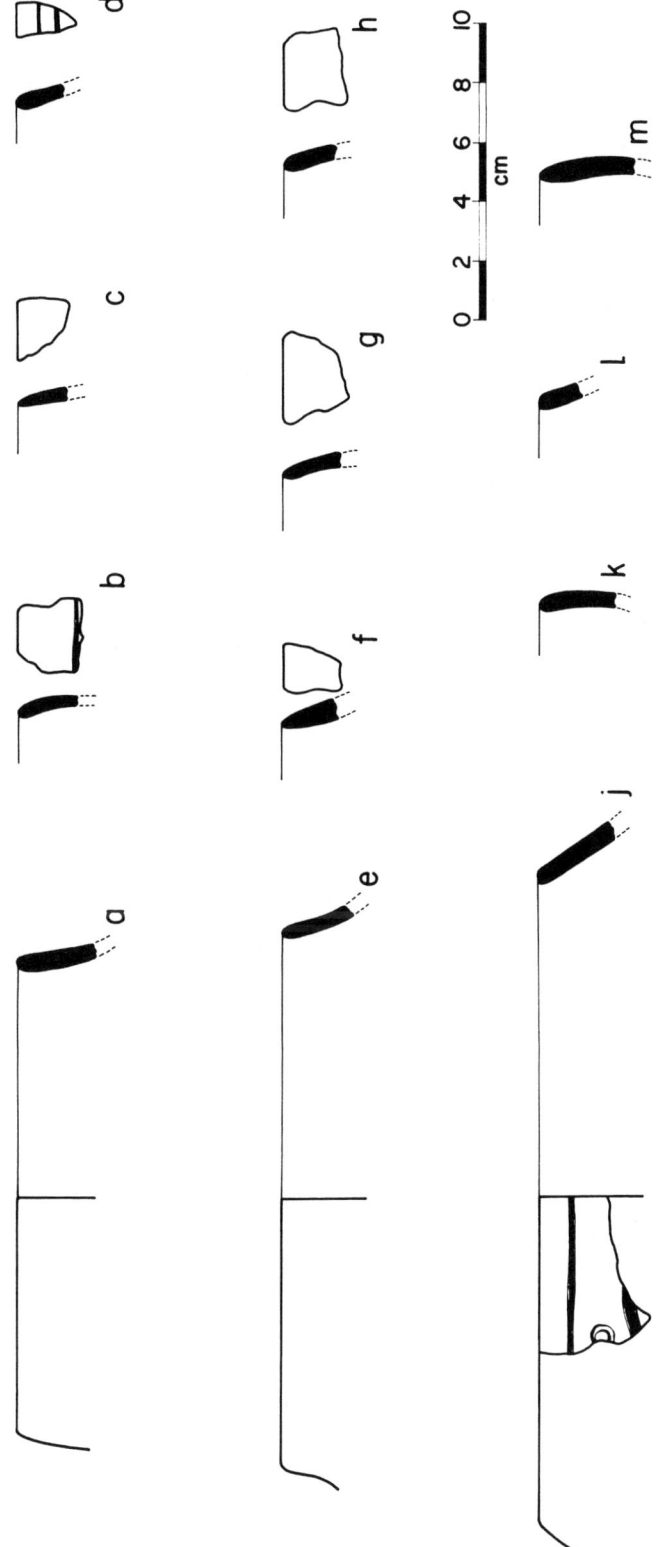

Figure 12.65. Leandro Gray bowls from San José Mogote (SJM) and Huitzo, ranging from hemispherical to incurved-rim in shape. All are plain except for *b* and *d*, which have shallow grooves on the outside, and *j*, which has shallow grooves and a circular ("cane-end") impression. *a–j* are San José phase specimens from Area A, SJM, as follows: *b*, *g*, Household Unit C1; *f*, Household Unit C3; *e*, Household Unit C4; *a*, *d*, *h*, *j*, Zone D1 midden; *c*, Zone D2 midden. *k–m* are Guadalupe phase specimens from Area A of Huitzo, as follows: *k*, *l*, House 1; *m*, Zone D.

194 Early Formative Pottery of Oaxaca

Figure 12.66. Sherd from Leandro Gray bowl with incurved rim, decorated on the outside by excising and the three-dimensional modeling of what may be the ear from an effigy face. San José Mogote, Area C, cutting profile at level of San José phase deposits.

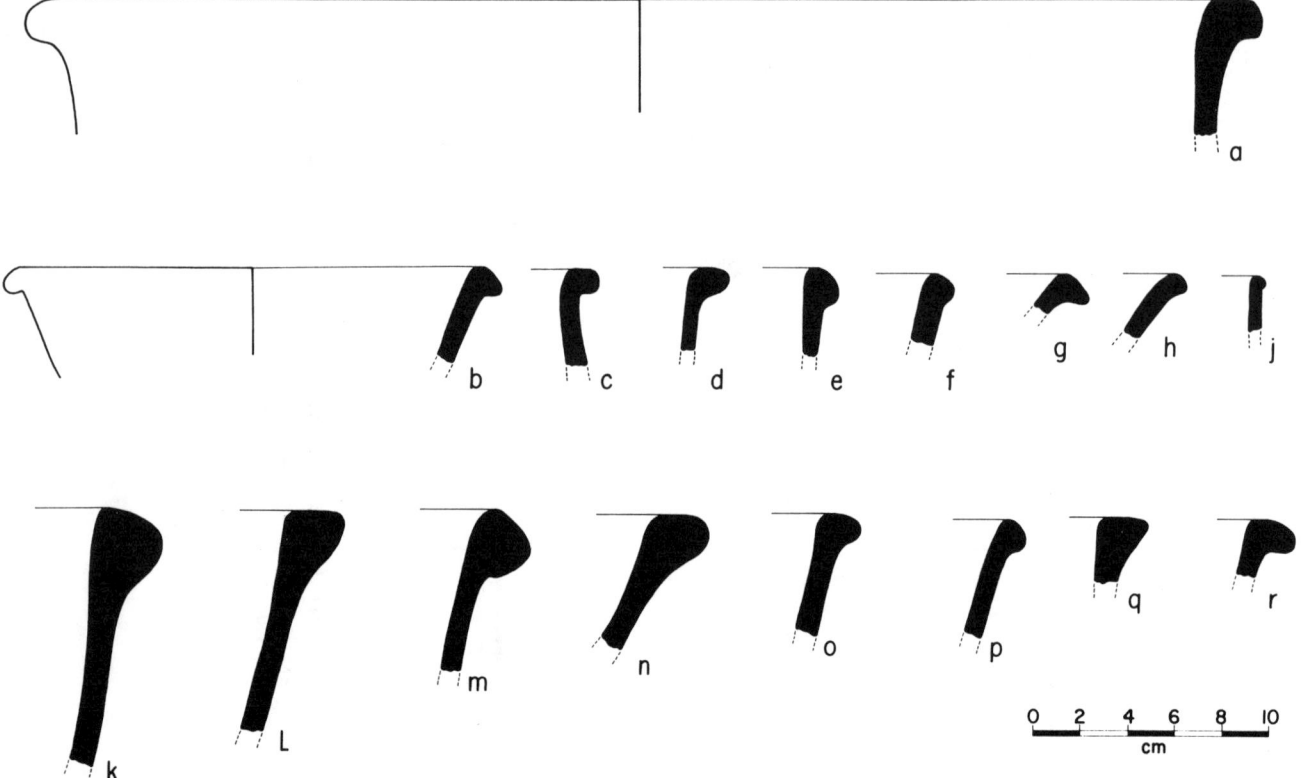

Figure 12.67. Leandro Gray bowls with bolstered rim, undecorated, all from Area A of San José Mogote. *a, d, m, n, p,* Household Unit C3; *k,* Household Unit C4; *c, h, j, l, o, q,* Zone D1 midden; *b, f, g, r,* Zone D2 midden; *e,* Zone D3 midden.

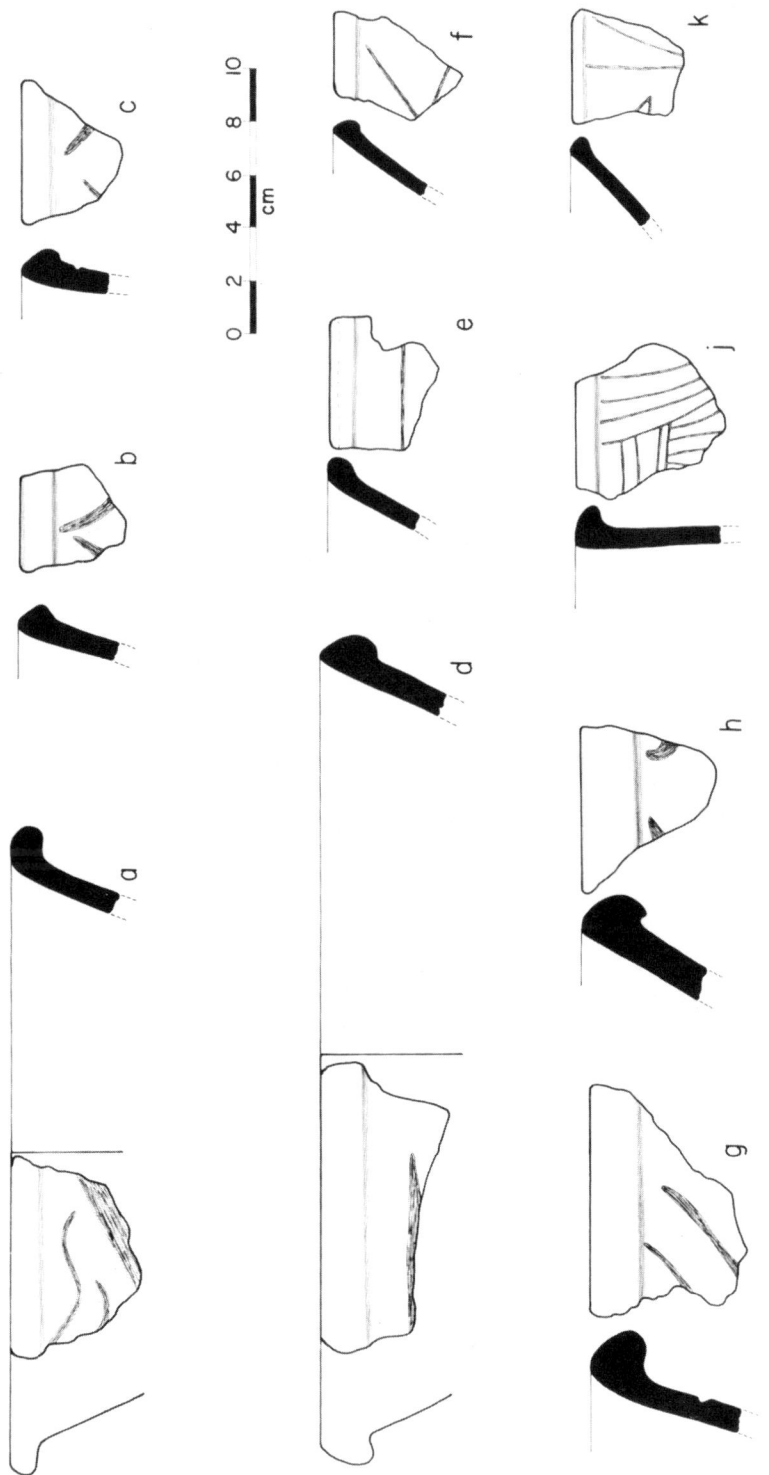

Figure 12.68. Leandro Gray bowls with bolstered rim, decorated on the outside, all from Area A of San José Mogote (San José phase). *a-c*, all from Household Unit C3, are fully burnished and have excised designs (probably Pyne's Motif 1) on the outside. *d-k* are burnished on the inside and on the top and outer edge of the bolstered rim, but are left unburnished on the outside below the rim. *d-h* are excised on the unburnished outer surface, with dry red pigment rubbed into the excising. *j* and *k* are incised on the unburnished outer surface and show no pigment. *j*, Household Unit C3; *e, g, h, k*, Zone D1 midden; *d, f*, Zone D2 midden.

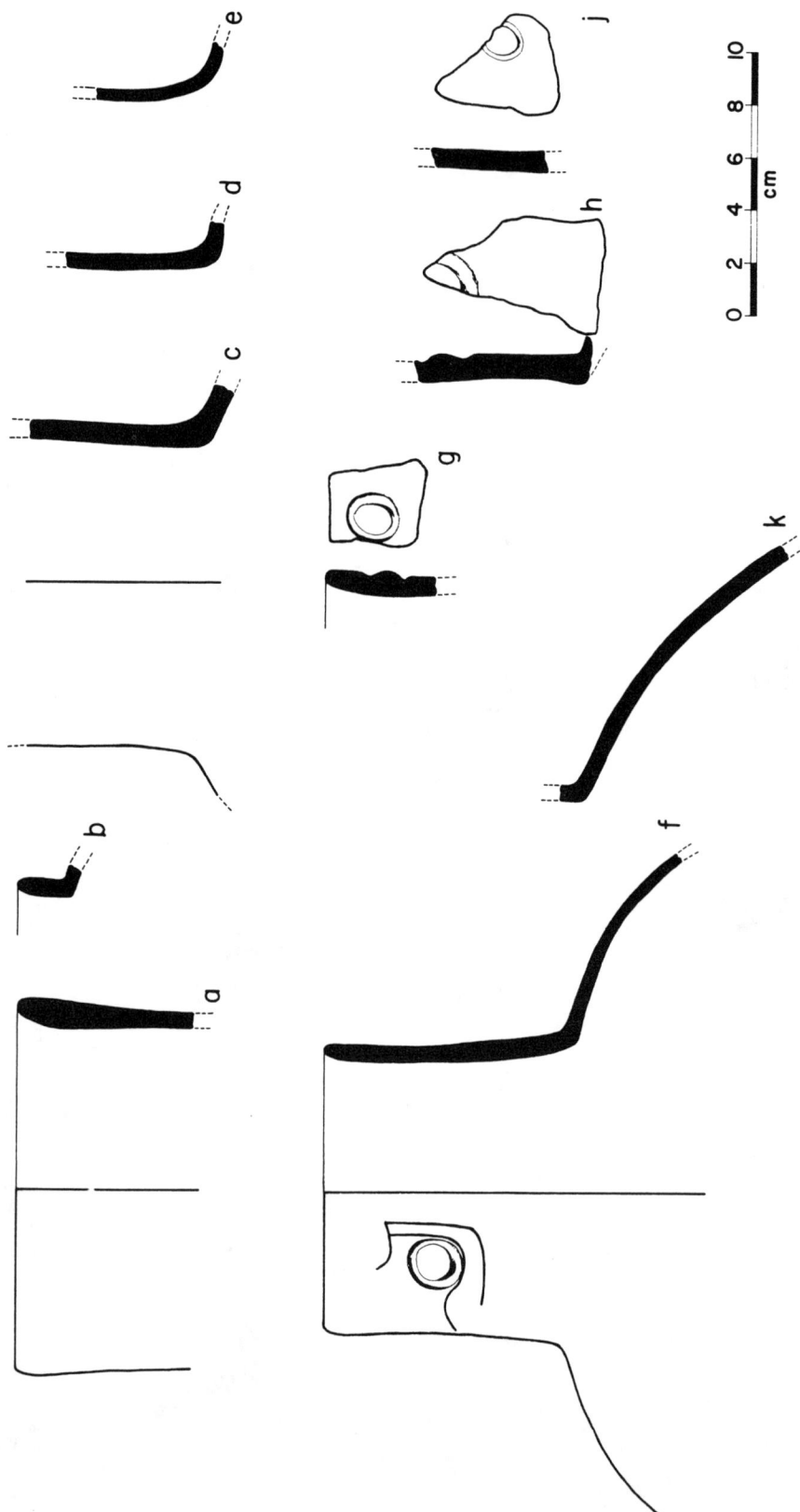

Figure 12.69. Leandro Gray jar necks and shoulders from Area A, San José Mogote (San José phase). *a–e*, jars with vertical necks, plain (*b*, Household Unit C3; *a, c, d*, Zone D1 midden; *e*, Zone D2 midden). *f*, jar with vertical neck, showing a raised bulb outlined by incising or cane-end impression on the exterior, Household Unit C3. *g–j*, jar neck sherds with raised bulbs on the exterior (*g*, Household Unit C4; *h, j*, Zone D2 midden). *k*, jar shoulder, Household Unit C3.

San José Phase

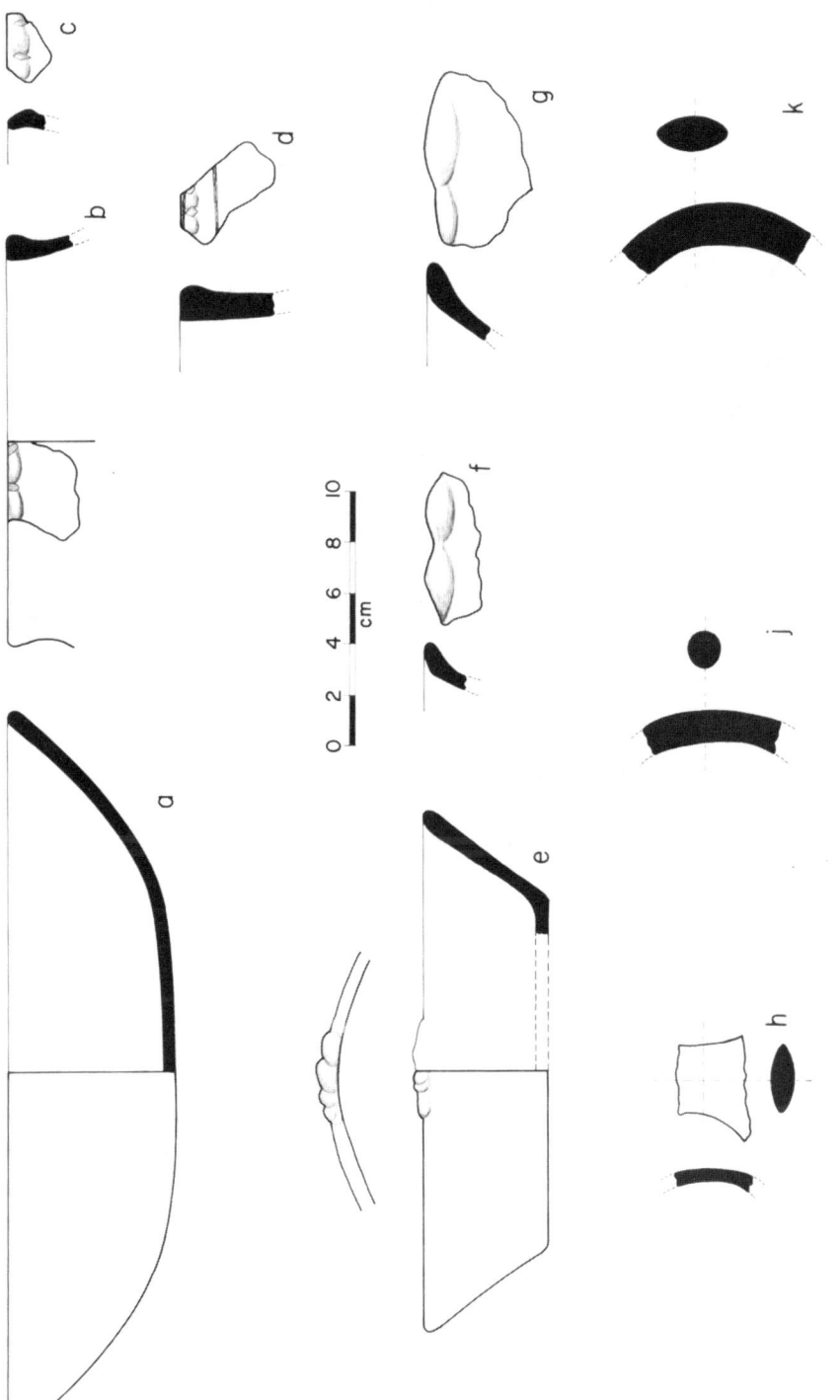

Figure 12.70. Leandro Gray vessels from San José Mogote (SJM) and Barrio del Rosario Huitzo. *a,* hemispherical bowl, traces of red paint inside and outside, Household Unit C3, Area A, SJM. *b-d,* bowls with gadrooned rims (*b,* Household Unit C4, Area A, SJM; *c-d,* Household Unit C3, Area A, SJM). *e-g,* bowls with scalloped rims (*e,* ashy midden south of House 2, Area C, SJM; *f, g,* Zone E2, Area A, Huitzo). *h-k,* fragments of handles (*h,* Zone F3, Area A, Huitzo; *j,* Structure 4, Area A, Huitzo; *k,* Zone D, Area A, Huitzo). All specimens from SJM are San José phase; all specimens from Barrio del Rosario Huitzo are Guadalupe phase.

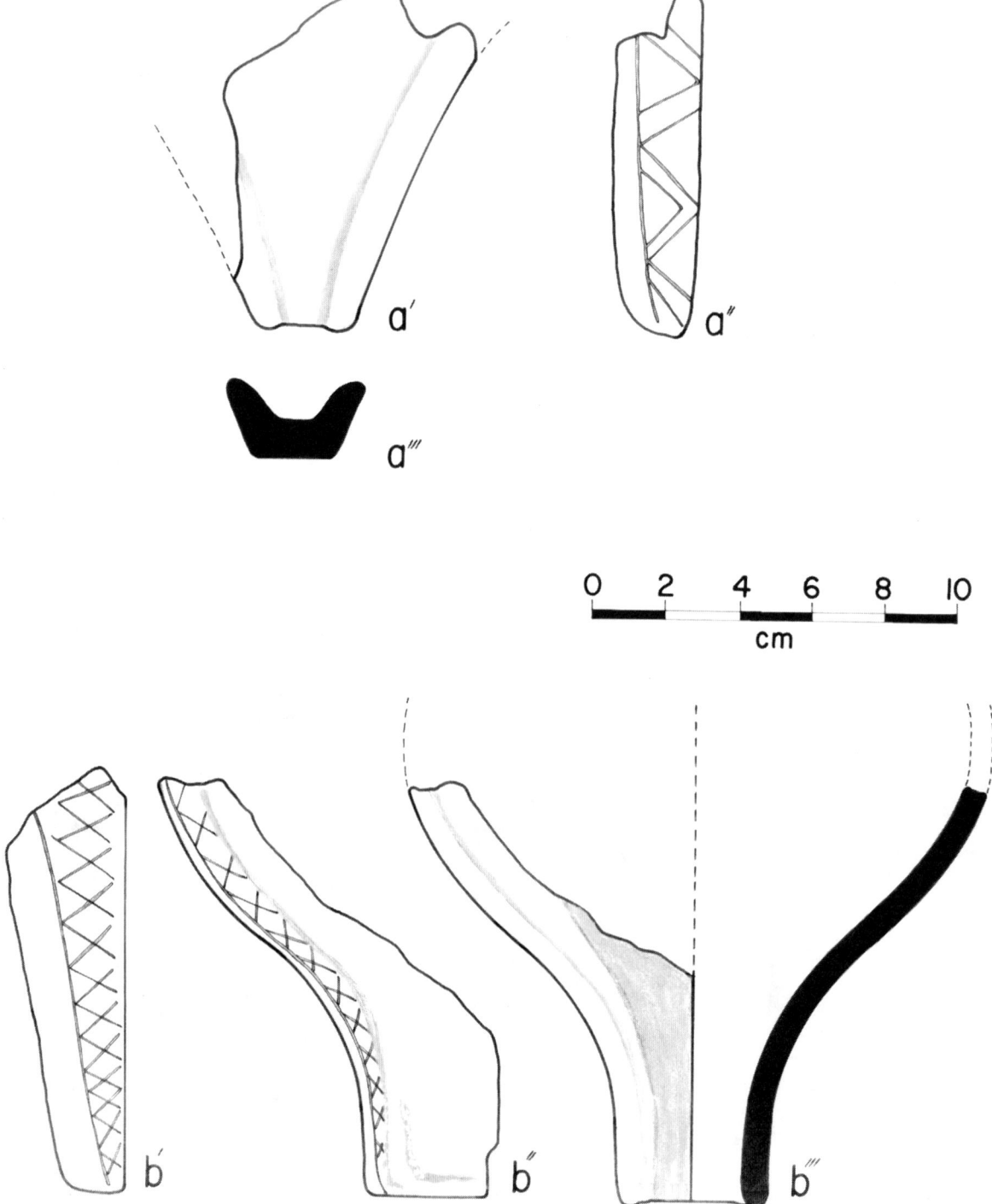

Figure 12.71. Leandro Gray spouted trays from San José Mogote (SJM) and Tierras Largas (TL). *a′*, top view of spout fragment, found while cleaning profile of Area C, SJM (San José phase levels). *a″*, side view of *a′*, showing incising. *a‴*, cross-section of *a′*. *b′*, side-view of spout fragment from Feature 160-south, Area D, TL, showing incising. *b″*, basal view of *b′*. *b‴*, top view of *b′*. (Both specimens San José phase.)

Figure 12.73. Top view and three-quarter view of the broken spout from a Leandro Gray spouted tray. The side has a panel of finely incised zigzag lines. Cleaning profile in Area C, San José Mogote (San José phase levels).

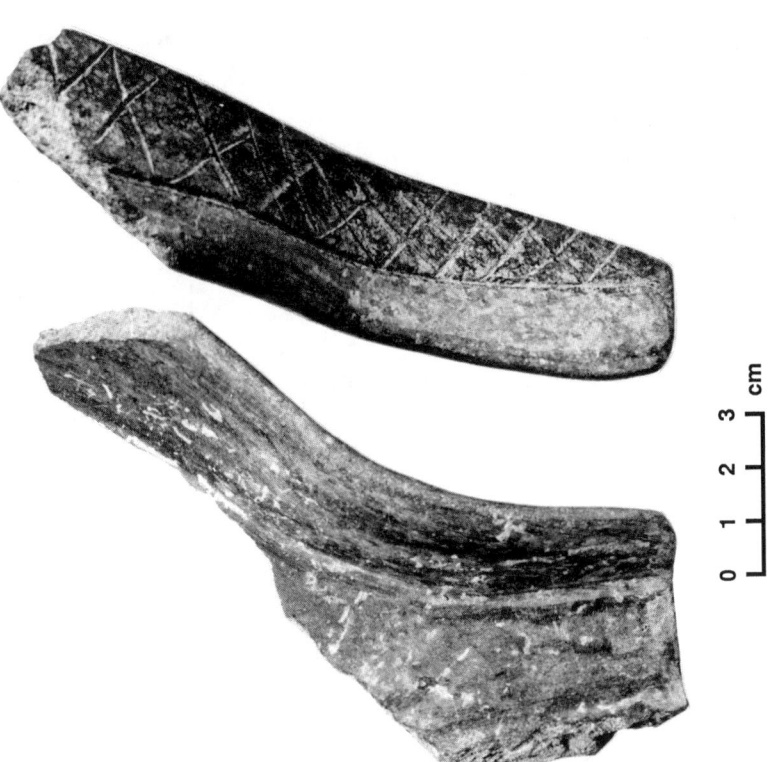

Figure 12.72. Top and side views of broken Leandro Gray spouted tray, Feature 150, Tierras Largas (San José phase). The side of the spout has a panel of deeply incised crosshatching.

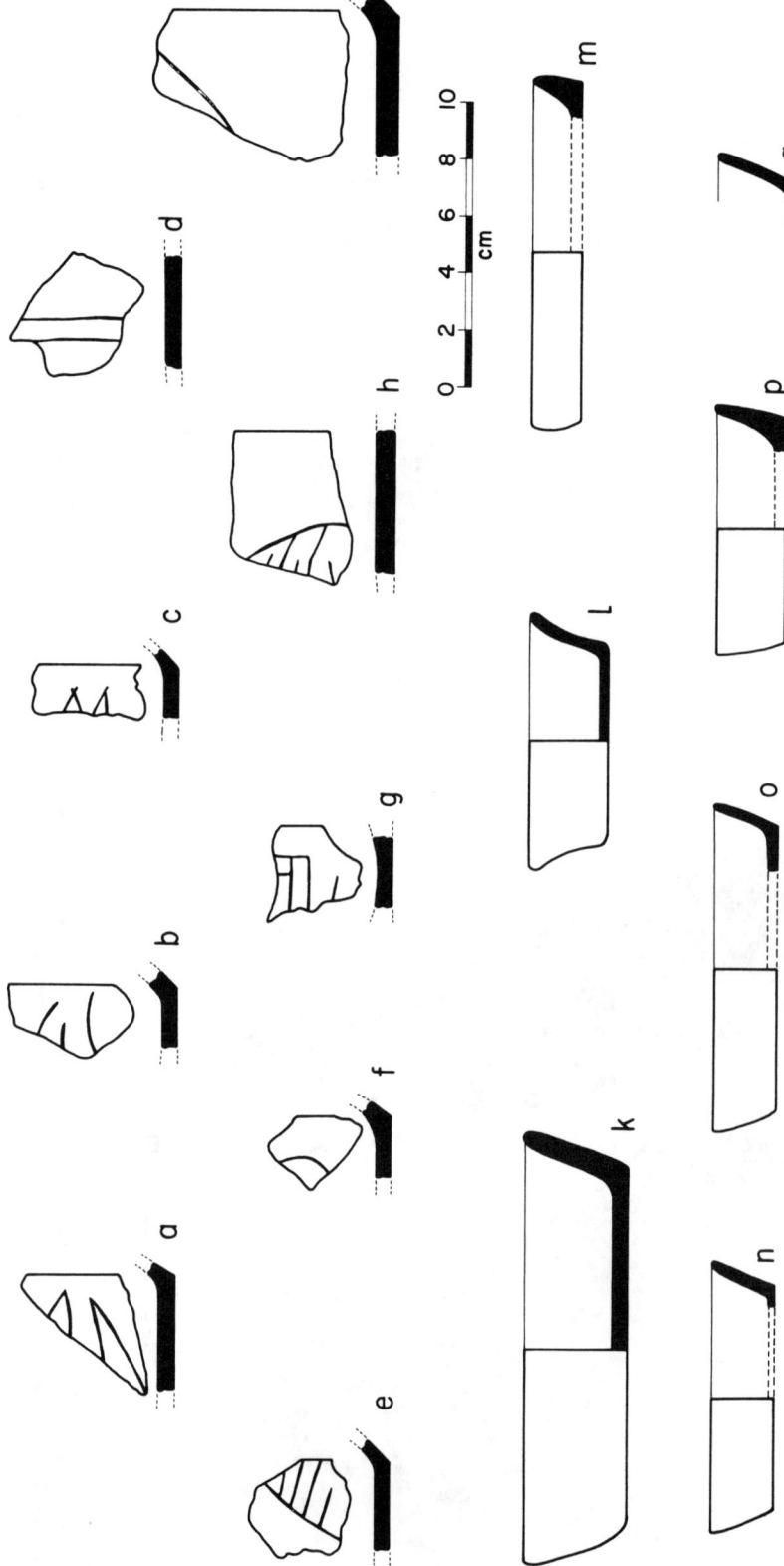

Figure 12.74. Leandro Gray vessels from San José Mogote (San José phase). *a–j,* sherds from flat-based bowls, showing "grater bowl" motifs incised on the upper surface (*a,* Zone D1 midden, Area A; *b, e, f,* Household Unit C2, Area A; *c, d, g, h,* Household Unit C3, Area A; *j,* Zone D2 midden, Area A). *k,* pigment dish, Vessel 1 of House 4, Area C (reconstruction from broken specimen piece-plotted on the house floor). *l,* pigment dish from below floor of House 6, Area C. This vessel had been used for both kaolin white slip and red hematite pigment, remains of which are slopped all over it. A Lupita Heavy Plain potter's bat (Fig. 12.123*l*) was found in association with this pigment dish, suggesting that a potter had stored the two vessels below the house floor. *m–q,* pigment dishes from Area A (*m,* Household Unit C3; *n, p,* Zone D1 midden; *o,* Zone D2 midden; *q,* Zone D3 midden).

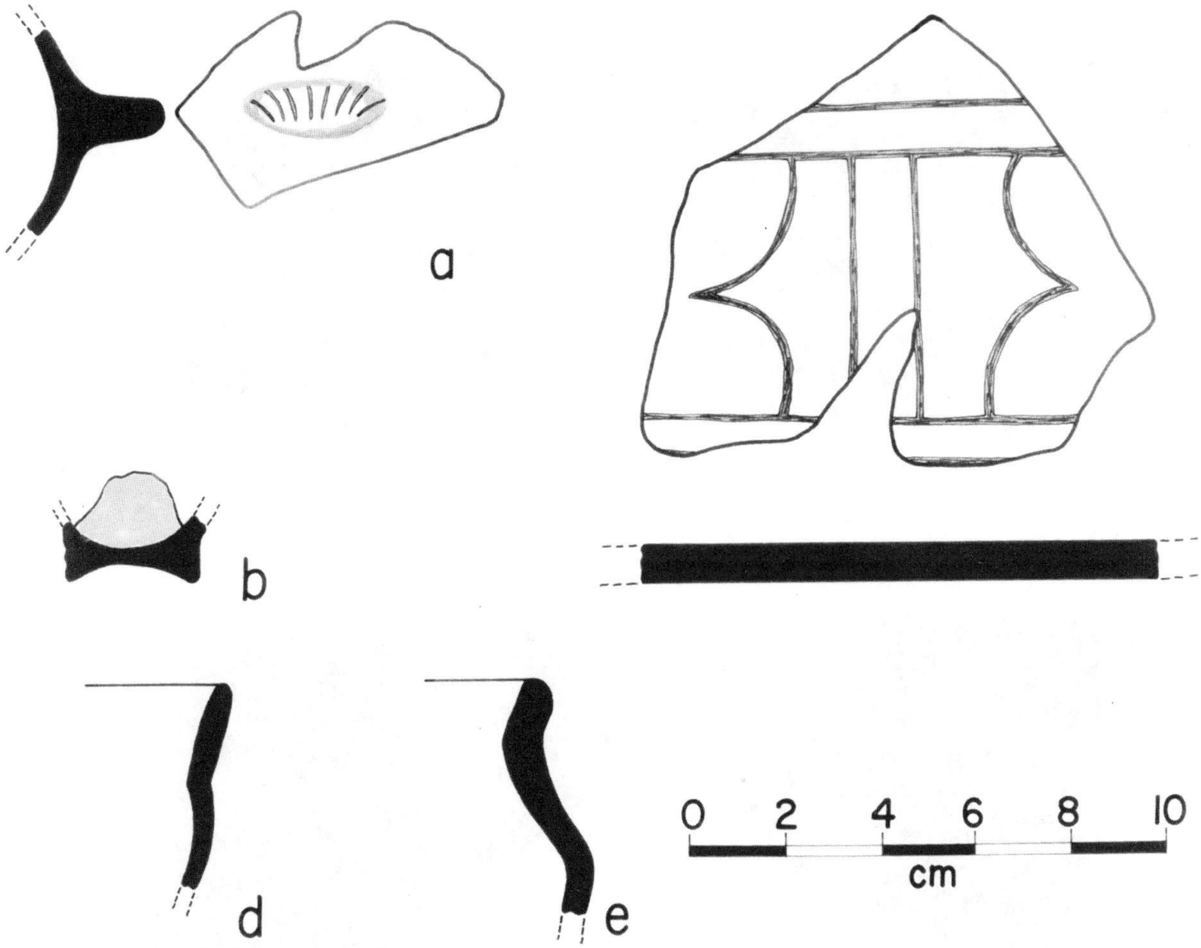

Figure 12.75. Leandro Gray vessels from San José Mogote (SJM) and Barrio del Rosario Huitzo. *a,* fragment of bird effigy vessel, Zone D2 midden, Area A, SJM. The incisions on the wing contain dry red pigment. *b,* probable fragment of multicompartment vessel, Household Unit C4, Area A, SJM (plan view). *c,* fragment of "grater bowl" base, cleaning profile, Area C, SJM (San José phase levels). *d,* fragment of composite silhouette bowl, Household Unit C4, Area A, SJM. *e,* fragment of composite silhouette bowl, Zone E1, Huitzo. (*e,* Guadalupe phase; *a-d,* San José phase.)

Figure 12.76. Sherd from a Leandro Gray effigy vessel, House 16, Area B, San José Mogote. This sherd appears to depict a duck whose bill curls down to form a strap handle. This San José phase specimen resembles duck effigies from the Basin of Mexico (width of sherd, 13.8 cm).

Figure 12.77. Leandro Gray sherds showing a variety of decorative techniques. All are from San José Mogote, Area C, and were found while straightening the profile at the level of the San José phase deposits. *a*, rim from tecomate or incurved-rim bowl, sculptured to resemble a cucurbit. *b*, bowl sherd with heavy three-dimensional sculpturing, overall design unknown. *c*, bowl with bolstered rim, burnished inside, left unburnished and carved outside. *d*, bowl similar to *c*, except that the rim bolster has been expanded to a ledge and decorated with deep rectangular punctations.

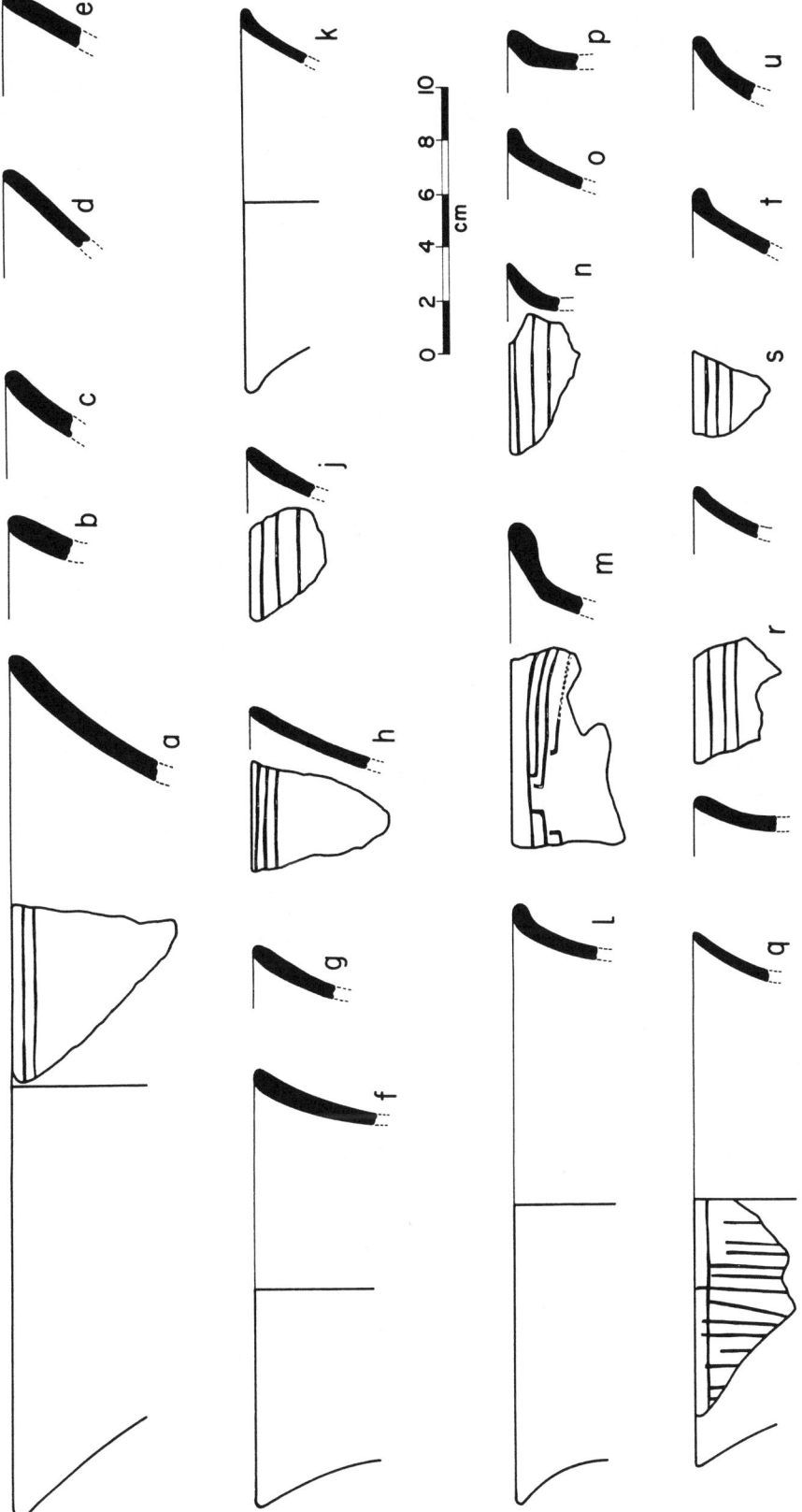

Figure 12.78. Leandro Gray bowls from San José Mogote (SJM) and Barrio del Rosario Huitzo. *a-j*, bowls with outcurved walls and plain direct rims, some with two to three incised parallel lines on the interior just below the rim. (*a, b*, Household Unit C2, Area A, SJM; *c-e*, Household Unit C1, Area A, SJM; *f-j*, Structure 4, Area A, Huitzo. All SJM specimens are San José phase; Huitzo specimens are from a Guadalupe phase provenience that could contain redeposited San José phase sherds.) *k-p*, bowls with outcurved walls and outturned rims, some with two to four incised parallel lines on the interior just below the rim; all from Guadalupe phase contexts. (*k, p*, Zone E1, Area A, Huitzo; *l, o*, Zone D, Area A, Huitzo; *m*, cutting profile, Area A, Huitzo, Guadalupe phase levels; *n*, Zone E2, Area A, Huitzo). *q-s*, bowls with slightly outcurved walls incised on the exterior, all from House 7, Area A, Huitzo (Guadalupe phase). *t, u*, outturned rims from bowls with exterior incising, Zone D, Area A, Huitzo (Guadalupe phase). Outcurved walls and outcurved or outturned rims were late attributes in Leandro Gray, with outturned rims largely restricted to the Guadalupe phase.

over 1.0 mm in diameter. In Payne's terms, most of the aplastic particles would be stopped by a 16-mesh geologist's screen. All those aplastic particles would have occurred naturally in the clay beds; none were added. By inspection, roughly 30–35% of the volume of the clay body is made up by this nonplastic material; its visible particles run from 0.1 to 1.0 mm, with most in the 0.5 mm range. Included are angular fragments of quartz, biotite mica, partially decomposed particles of feldspar and hornblende, and occasional fragments of garnet, all in a base of kaolinitic clay.

Firing Temperature

It was probably fired in a 720 to 760° C oxidizing atmosphere. Atoyac Yellow-white was fired at temperatures slightly higher than those used for Fidencio Coarse and Lupita Heavy Plain in order to set the white kaolin slip harder. This higher firing temperature (which reduces tolerance to thermal shock) was no disadvantage, since Atoyac Yellow-white was apparently never used for cooking and thus, was never subject to damaging heat.

Surface Treatment

Prior to slipping, the surface of the vessel was merely brushed to remove loose particles; otherwise, it remained rough. Over this surface, the white engobe (see below) was applied. When this had dried, Atoyac Yellow-white was very evenly burnished with a quartz pebble. Owing to the particle size and composition of the kaolinite, this burnishing has weathered to a dull matte finish in most samples; a few still retain a medium glossy appearance.

Application of White Engobe

Over the buff or reddish brown clay body of the vessel, the potters applied a true slip or engobe of nearly iron-free white kaolin. Some sherds have a slip so thick as to suggest that the vessel was dipped, or the engobe poured on (perhaps from a spouted tray). In other cases, a thinner slip seems to have been swabbed on, perhaps with a patch of animal fur. Perhaps the amount of white kaolin available determined whether the vessel was dipped or merely swabbed. The source of the kaolin was probably a local pegmatite dike or hydrothermal vent (see Simulating the Ware, below).

San José and Guadalupe phase samples of Atoyac Yellow-white show a considerable range of variation in the slip and in the amount of gross impurities. Payne notes that this variation could result from the use of different kaolin sources, since small pegmatite dikes with suitable raw material crop up at intervals over a great deal of the Oaxaca piedmont.

Color

The fired clay body usually shows a dark gray core (10 YR 4/1) sandwiched between layers that are reddish brown (2.5 YR 4/4; 5 YR 4/4) to weak red (10 R 4/3). The color of the engobe after firing ranges from light yellowish brown (10 YR 6/4) or very pale brown (10 YR 7/4) to light brownish gray (10 YR 6/2) in the Munsell system. An occasional sherd would pass for true creamy white, but in most cases there were too many iron impurities in the kaolin for it to be pure white.

Where the burnishing process has worn the slip down to a very thin layer and the clay body starts to show through, many sherds show the characteristic "rust-colored streaks" described by Coe (1961:64) for Conchas White-to-Buff.

Plastic Decoration

The most common plastic decoration on Atoyac Yellow-white was incising (*sgraffito*) done prior to firing, when the vessel was still damp but the surface had become somewhat dry. The incised lines cut through the slip and reveal the reddish brown clay body below it. Some incising was done with a sharp, smooth tool like a maguey spine; other incised lines may have been done with a flint or obsidian flake, which left a furrow with ragged edges but a smooth bottom. The instrument was pulled along the surface of the vessel, not pushed. Parallel lines with double-line-break motifs were the most common incised decoration.

A less common decoration was excising (*raspada*), also done when the vessel was leather-hard. Because of the light-colored engobe on Atoyac Yellow-white, one can frequently see that the design was outlined first with a maguey spine or sharp obsidian blade; then the slip and part of the surface of the clay body was removed, perhaps with a slat of cane or a chipped-stone tool. On a few vessels, it is clear that the excising did not follow the incised outline with complete fidelity. This same procedure may have been followed on Leandro Gray and San José Black-and-White, but because the surfaces of those wares are dark, the preliminary incising cannot be seen.

Representations of Earth or the were-jaguar were common excised motifs; often, dry red hematite powder (7.5 R 4/8) was rubbed into the excisions.

Simulation of the Ware

In 1970, Payne successfully simulated vessels of Atoyac Yellow-white by using (1) a clay body derived from weathered Precambrian gneiss, dug up from a piedmont spur near Tlacochahuaya in the Tlacolula region of the valley (Fig. 2.2c); (2) white engobe from a kaolin source that had formed as a hydrothermal (ancient hot spring) deposit in the volcanic tuff mountains between Mitla and San Lorenzo Albarradas; (3) a San José phase burnishing pebble of Matadamas chalcedony; and (4) a maguey spine, which perfectly duplicated the *sgraffito*. Payne fired the vessels in an electric kiln at 750° C.

Of all the raw materials involved, the most limited in availability was the engobe. In order for clay to fire white, it must be relatively free of iron. The hydrothermal vent that provided the white kaolin used by Payne was a relatively iron-free source. Other sources found by Payne included small pegmatite dikes intruding into the Mesozoic limestones of the valley. Perhaps the most iron-free white kaolin Payne found in his surveys, however, came from a source in the Valley of Nochixtlán, some 70 km northwest of Oaxaca City (Fig. 2.2e). While many of these small kaolin sources were suitable for white engobes, it is not clear whether any of them would have been suitable for the clay body of a ware like Xochiltepec White.

Vessel Forms

Bottles (Fig. 12.79b-d). This was one of the earliest forms to appear in Atoyac Yellow-white; it was already present during the transition from the Tierras Largas phase to the San José phase. At no time did bottles become common, and some of ours may even have been local imitations of imported Xochiltepec White bottles. A few of our examples had fluted bodies, perhaps in imitation of cucurbits. Atoyac Yellow-white bottles find their closest parallels in the Basin of Mexico.

Rim diameter: 5–7 cm
Height of neck: 7–9 cm
Diameter of body: Usually unknown (on one example, it is 15 cm).
Wall thickness: 4–6 mm
Decoration: Usually none, except for the vertical fluting mentioned above.

Bowls with Ocós-style grooved rim (Fig. 12.79a). A few bowl rims from the late Tierras Largas phase and early San José phase have a thickened rim (wedge-shaped in cross-section) whose upper surface bears a wide, shallow groove encircling the entire vessel. This attribute is reminiscent of specimens from La Victoria, Guatemala (Coe 1961: Fig. 18*j*, far right; Fig. 19*g*, far right). Wall thickness is 4–6 mm, while the thickened rim may be up to 12 mm thick. Other dimensions are unknown.

Flat-based bowls with outleaned walls (Figs. 12.80–12.82). As in the case of Leandro Gray, these "outleaned-wall bowls" were the most common vessel form in Atoyac Yellow-white. They were part of a continuum that ran from shallow bowls with walls outleaned at a 20–60° angle to deeper cylindrical bowls whose wall angles ranged from zero (vertical) to roughly 10°. Our term "outleaned-wall bowl" refers to those with walls in the 20–60° range. When decorated, such bowls had the design on the *interior*, indicating that the prehistoric potters also saw them as "open bowls."

Like their Leandro Gray counterparts, these bowls could be made in one of several ways. Some had evidently been press-molded inside or outside previous bowls. Others began as a circular slab of clay (the base) and had their walls built up by the addition of concentric rings of clay. The joints were smoothed with the fingers, then the whole vessel was brushed to remove rough particles. It was then coated with the white kaolin engobe. These bowls were evenly burnished once on all surfaces with a quartz pebble when leather-hard; when completely dry, they were burnished a second time on the interior (the side that would be most visible).

Rim diameter: At least half the measurable specimens have a rim diameter between 20 and 24 cm, with the mode at 22 cm. The range was from 12 to 32 cm, with a few rare examples as large as 40 cm.
Height: Normally one-fourth to one-third the rim diameter.
Basal diameter: Normally about two-thirds the rim diameter.
Wall thickness: Usually 5–9 mm
Volume: One complete bowl with a rim diameter of 12 cm held 310 ml, and would have accommodated an individual serving of food for one (young) person (it accompanied a child burial). Another with a rim diameter of 21 cm held 840 ml, and would have accommodated an individual serving for an adult male. Based on similar Leandro Gray specimens, those with rim diameters of 31 cm may have held up to 2.3 liters and probably accommodated enough food for several adults. Our statistics on rim diameters suggest that half these bowls were for individual adult servings, more than a quarter for nuclear family servings, and less than a quarter for children.
Decoration: Virtually none at the start of the San José phase. During later San José times, and well into the Guadalupe phase, incised lines (*sgraffito*) occur on about half the rim sherds. The usual pattern is for parallel lines to encircle the upper wall, interrupted at intervals (usually twice per vessel) by one variant or another of the double-line-break motif. The regularity of the lines suggests that potters guided the instrument (possibly a maguey spine or chipped stone flake) by running one finger along the rim of the vessel while incising.

Excised (*raspada*) designs are much less common on outleaned-wall bowls. The most frequent motifs are local versions of pan-Mesoamerican symbols for Earth, or the were-jaguar. A few bowls with outleaned walls contain "grater-bowl" or pseudo-*molcajete* designs on the inside of the base, but such designs are scarce in Oaxaca compared to some regions of Mesoamerica.

Flat-based bowls with vertical, or nearly vertical, walls (Figs. 12.83–12.90). Like their Leandro Gray counterparts, these "cylinders" had walls varying from vertical to within 10° of vertical. They appear to have been made by press-molding, either over a mold like the one shown in Figure 2.7 or over a previous cylinder. A layer of wood ash or dry clay may have been used to keep the mold and the new vessel from sticking together. After application of the engobe, cylinders were evenly burnished once over the entire vessel, then burnished a second time on the exterior. When incised, the bowls we have called "cylinders" were incised on the *exterior,* which suggests that the prehistoric potters also saw them as distinct from outleaned-wall bowls.

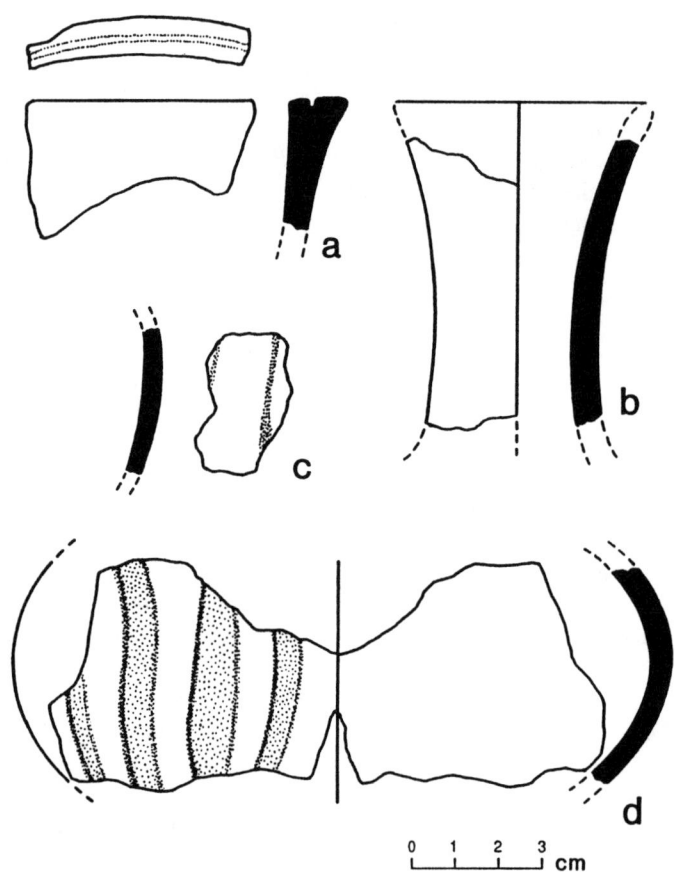

Figure 12.79. Some of the earliest vessel forms to appear in Atoyac Yellow-white. All examples are from San José Mogote. *a*, rim sherd from hemispherical bowl with thickened, flat-topped, eccentric rim, grooved on top like some Ocós and Tierras Largas phase specimens (Household Unit C3, Area A, San José phase). *b*, sherd from neck of bottle, Structure 5, Area C (late Tierras Largas phase); this sherd is literally our oldest example of Atoyac Yellow-white. *c, d*, body sherds from fluted bottles, Zone D3 midden, Area A (early San José phase).

Rim diameter: Two-thirds of the measurable cylinders have a rim diameter of 14–18 cm; occasional specimens are as small as 10 cm or as large as 30 cm.

Height: Normally about two-thirds the rim diameter.

Basal diameter: Normally about four-fifths the rim diameter.

Wall thickness: Usually 5–9 mm

Volume: Based on Leandro Gray specimens, those with a rim diameter of 10 cm would have held 450 ml each, and may have been for individual servings of food. One cylinder with a rim diameter of 19 cm held 1.6 liters, and thus may have provided servings for a nuclear family of 3–4 persons. Our rim diameter statistics suggest that more than two-thirds of all cylinders would have held enough for several adults.

Decoration: Very similar to that on outleaned-wall bowls, except that all decoration takes place on the exterior. Incised parallel lines encircle the vessel, usually near the rim but occasionally near the base as well. The most elaborate depictions of Earth or the were-jaguar—often combining excising with fine-line hachure—can be found on Atoyac Yellow-white cylinders.

Tecomates (Figs. 12.91–12.98). Atoyac Yellow-white tecomates resemble those from Chiapa de Corzo (Dixon 1959: Fig. 52) and the Isthmus of Tehuantepec (Zeitlin 1979). They run the gamut from thin-walled, medium-sized neckless jars to large, thick, "clunky" vessels with heavy plastic decoration. In profile, the rims expand in thickness as they near the mouth of the vessel, ending blunted or rounded off. These vessels appear to have been built up from concentric rings of clay.

Rim diameter: Most are 16–28 cm.

Body diameter: No complete specimens.

Height: Unknown

Decoration: Those that are decorated usually have a plain band at the rim, delimited by an incised line. Below this, the plastic decoration (which may be zoned or unzoned) includes plain, false, and interrupted rocker stamping; dentate stamping; punctation; incising; and other plastic techniques. The stamping or punctation could take place either before or after the slip was applied (usually the latter).

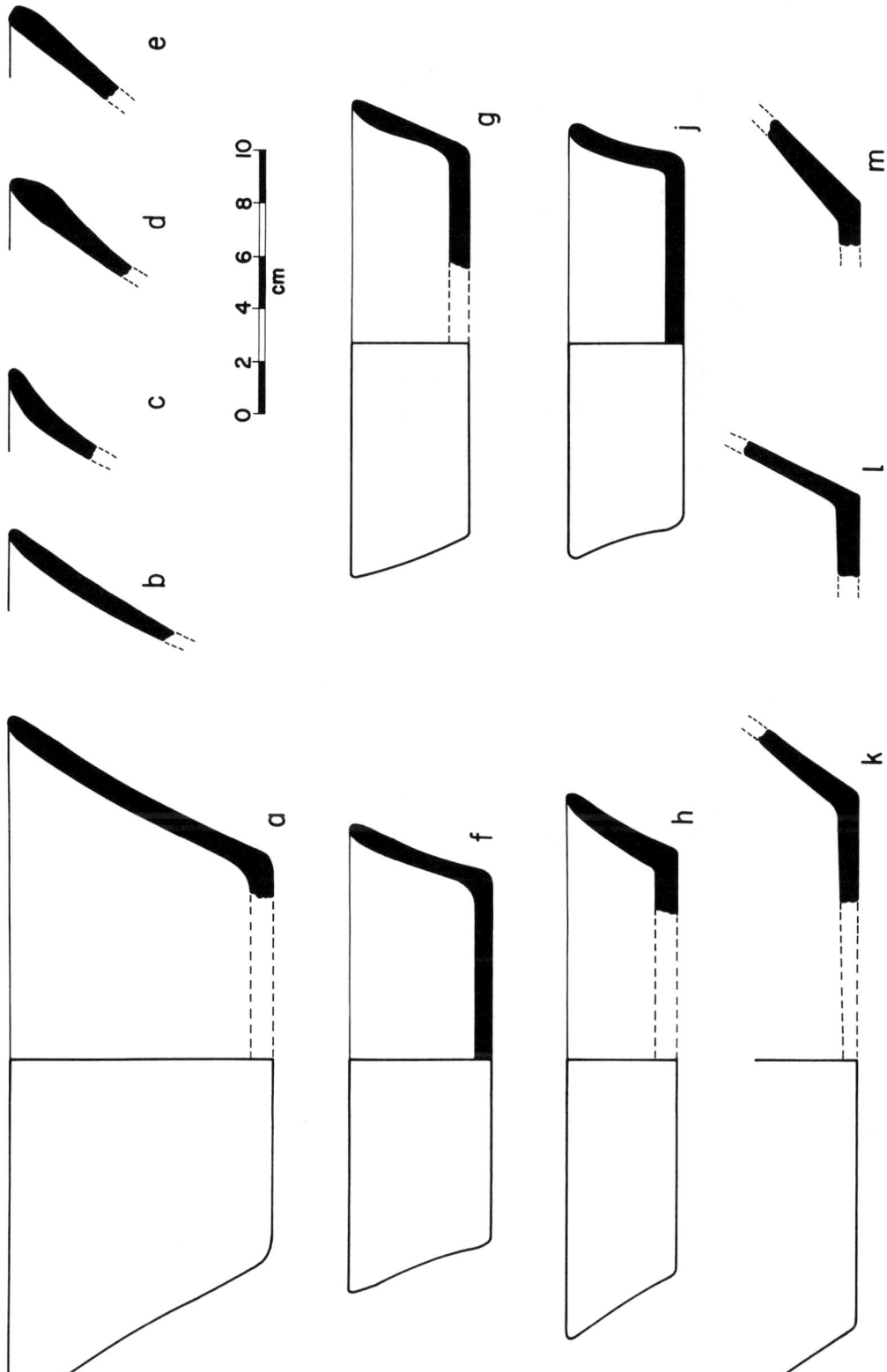

Figure 12.80. Atoyac Yellow-white bowls with flat base and outleaned or outcurved walls from San José Mogote (SJM), Tierras Largas (TL), and Barrio del Rosario Huitzo. Those from San José phase proveniences include a (Stage II of Structure 1, Area A, SJM); b (Household Unit C1, Area A, SJM); c (Zone D3 midden, Area A, SJM); d (Zone D1 midden, Area A, SJM); e (Household Unit C3, Area A, SJM); and m (Zone D2 midden, Area A, SJM). Examples that could be late San José phase include g, h, and l (all from between Stages II and III of Structure 1, Area A, SJM). Example k is from the fill of Structure 4 at Huitzo, an early Guadalupe phase provenience that may contain redeposited San José phase sherds. Both f and j are from Feature 112, TL, a Guadalupe phase provenience. In the chronological history of Atoyac Yellow-white, outleaned walls (h) tend to be earlier than outcurved walls (j).

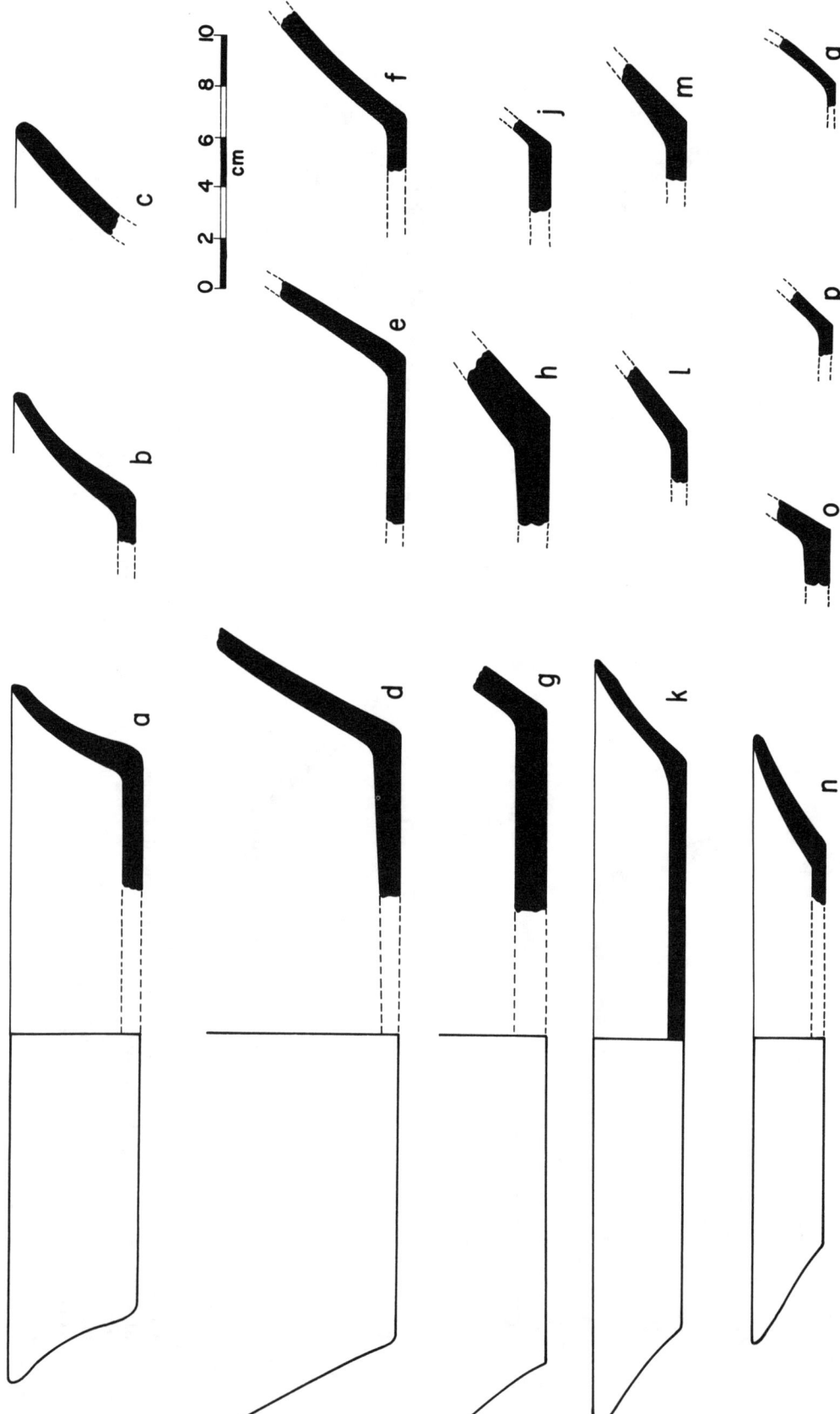

Figure 12.81. Atoyac Yellow-white bowls with flat base and outleaned or outcurved walls from San José Mogote (SJM) and Barrio del Rosario Huitzo. San José phase examples include *m* (Household Unit C2, Area A, SJM); *l* (Household Unit C3, Area A, SJM); *h* (Zone D1 midden, Area A, SJM); *c* (Zone D2 midden, Area A, SJM); *a* (Stage II of Structure 1, Area A, SJM). Examples that could be late San José phase include *b*, *e*, *k*, *n*, and *o* (all from between Stages II and III of Structure 1, Area A, SJM). Guadalupe phase examples include *g* (Zone E2, Area A, Huitzo) and *j* (Zone D, Area A, Huitzo). Specimens from early Guadalupe phase proveniences that could include redeposited San José phase sherds are *d* and *p* (Zone F3, Area A, Huitzo) and *f* and *q* (fill of Structure 4, Area A, Huitzo). As previously mentioned, outleaned walls (*d*, *e*) tend to be earlier than outcurved walls (*a*, *b*).

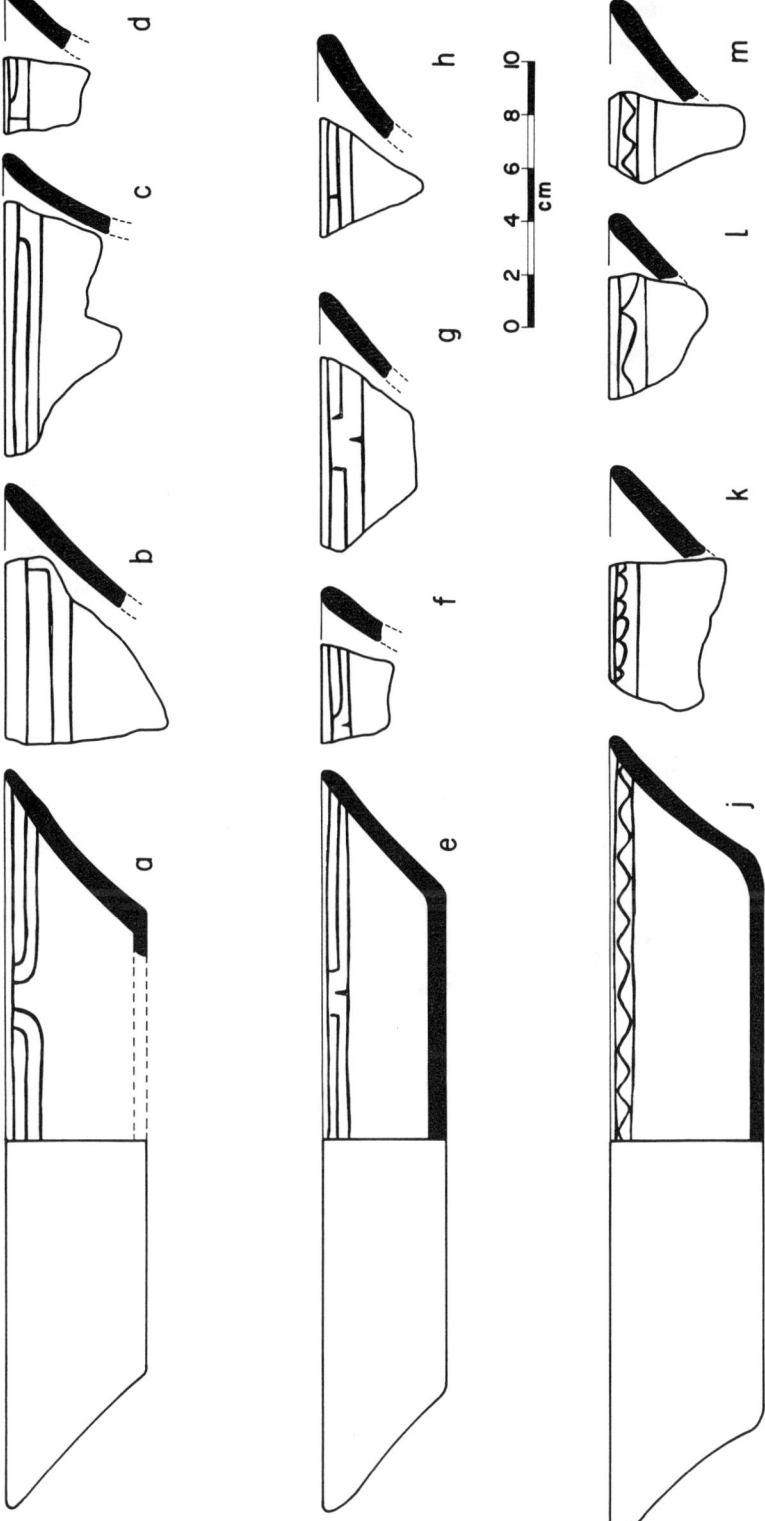

Figure 12.82. Atoyac Yellow-white bowls with outleaned walls and interior incising from San José Mogote (SJM) and Barrio del Rosario Huitzo. *a, e,* late San José phase examples from Stages II and III of Structure 1, Area A, SJM. *b-d, f-h,* early Guadalupe phase examples from Area A, Huitzo (*b,* Zone F2; *c, h,* fill of Structure 4; *d,* cleaning profile; *f,* Zone E2; *g,* Zone F3). *j-l,* bowls from Area A, Huitzo, showing Plog's Motif 35, a Guadalupe phase attribute (all from cutting the profile). *m,* bowl with Plog's Motif 38, also a Guadalupe phase attribute (Zone C4, Area A, Huitzo). Specimens *b, c, g,* and *h* are from early Guadalupe phase proveniences that could include redeposited San José phase sherds. *j-m* are all from Middle Formative deposits.

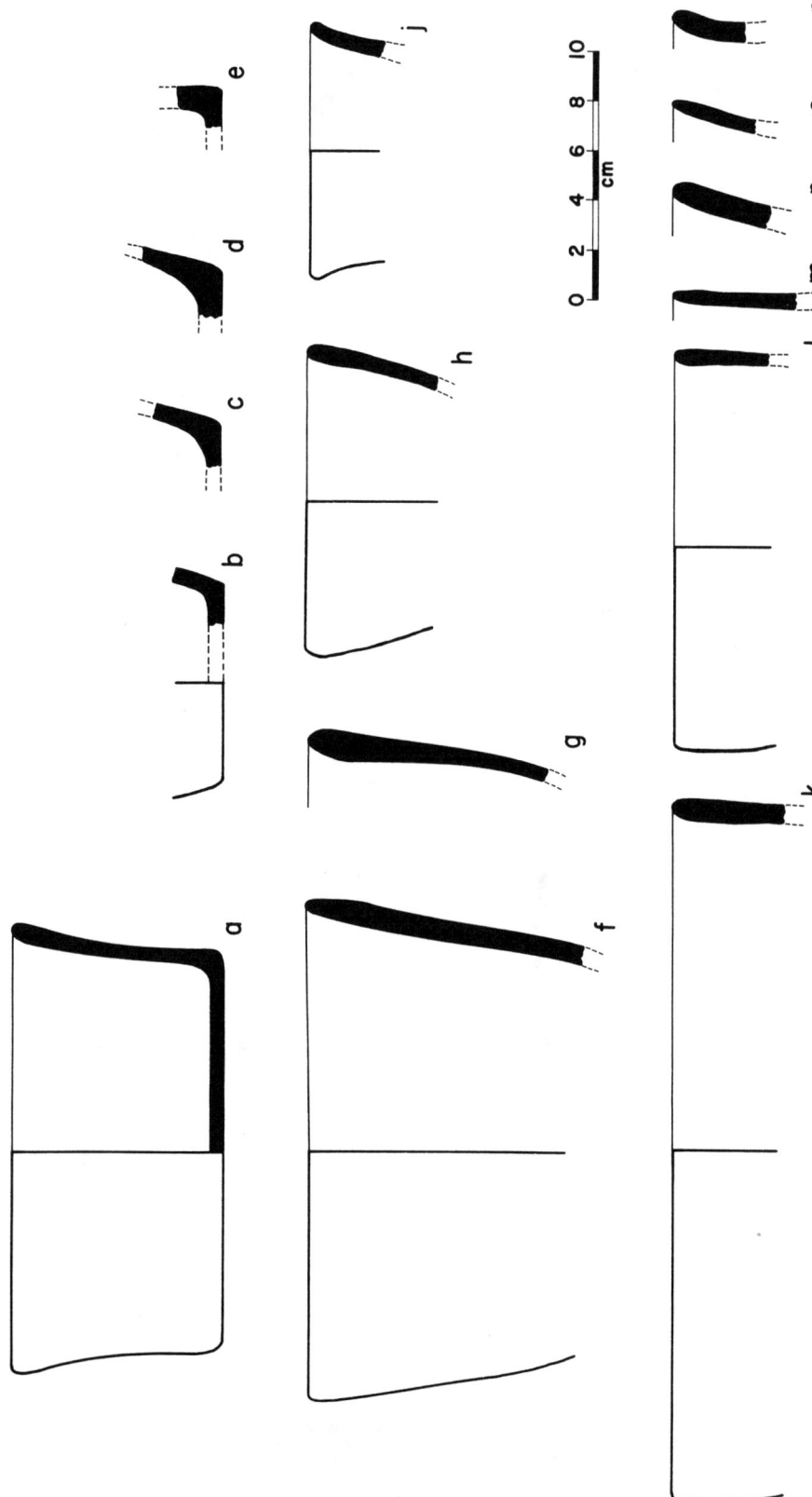

Figure 12.83. Atoyac Yellow-white cylinders or bowls with nearly vertical walls, undecorated, from San José Mogote (SJM) and Barrio del Rosario Huitzo. *a*, Vessel 1 from House 2, Area C, SJM (reconstructed from piece-plotted fragments). *b, c, e*, basal angle sherds, Area A, Huitzo (*b*, House 1; *c*, Zone F2; *e*, cleaning profile). *d*, basal angle sherd from Zone D2 midden, Area A, SJM. *f, g, h, n*, rim sherds from Area A of SJM (*h*, Household Unit C3; *f, g*, Household Unit C4; *n*, Zone D1 midden). *j, k, l, m, o, p*, rim sherds, Area A, Huitzo (*j*, fill of Structure 4; *k*, House 3; *m*, Zone E2; *l*, House 3; *m*, Zone F2; *o*, Zone F3; *p*, cleaning profile). *a, d, f, g, h*, and *n* are all San José phase examples. All other sherds are from Guadalupe phase proveniences, although *c, e, j, m, o*, and *p* are from proveniences that could have some redeposited San José phase sherds.

San José Phase 211

Figure 12.84. Atoyac Yellow-white cylinder with somewhat eroded slip. Vessel 7, Square C13, House 1, Area A, Tierras Largas (San José phase). This would be a typical medium-height cylinder for the phase.

Figure 12.85. Atoyac Yellow-white cylinder with somewhat eroded slip. Vessel 2 of Burial 4, Area A, Tierras Largas (San José phase). This shape would be typical of the phase; for a taller cylinder from the same burial, see Figure 12.86.

Figure 12.86. Atoyac Yellow-white cylinder with charcoal gray firing clouds. Two pairs of perforations for suspension can be seen about 3 cm below the rim. Vessel 3 of Burial 4, Area A, Tierras Largas (San José phase). This cylinder would be much taller than average for the phase; for a more typical cylinder from the same burial, see Figure 12.85.

Figure 12.87. Atoyac Yellow-white cylinder with three parallel incised lines just below the rim. Vessel 1 of Burial 12, San José Mogote (San José phase). This shape would be typical for one of the lower cylinders of the phase. This vessel has the usual white slip and parallel incised lines of Atoyac Yellow-white, but appears to have been made purely as a burial offering. The slip was applied in a hasty, streaky manner that is below the usual standard for this pottery type.

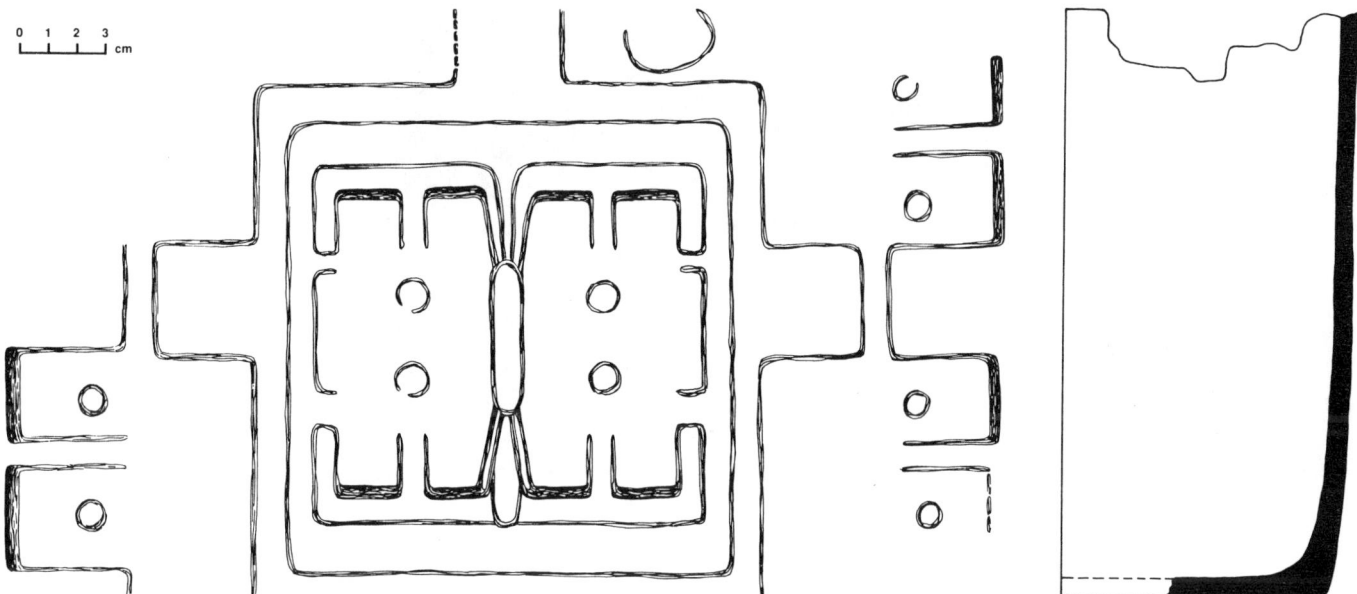

Figure 12.88. Atoyac Yellow-white cylinder from House 16, Area B, San José Mogote. At right is the cross-section of the vessel (basal diameter, 19 cm). At left is the rolled-out design excised on the outside of the cylinder (incomplete because of ancient damage). The design features a central trough, two circles and brackets to either side, downturned and upturned E's, all within a frame. Outside the inner frame is an outer frame with paired tabs projecting from it. This may be a depiction of Earth, with the central trough and circles symbolizing the center and the four world directions, respectively. The paired tabs of the outer frame may represent the cleft heads of were-jaguars, the open fissures into the Earth (late San José phase).

Figure 12.89. Fragments of Atoyac Yellow-white cylinder, incised on the exterior with Pyne's Motif 10 (were-jaguar) in fine-line hachure. This vessel has been deliberately smudged with carbon. Vessel 6, Square C13, House 1, Area A, Tierras Largas (San José phase).

Bowls with bolstered rim (Fig. 12.99). Like their Leandro Gray counterparts, these bowls have rims that have been externally bolstered by the addition of another concentric ring of clay. The thickness of the bolster varies between 8 and 32 mm. Bolstered-rim bowls in Volcán Burnished from Tlapacoya-Zohapilco (Niederberger 1987: Figs. 391, 395) resemble ours in both Atoyac Yellow-white and Leandro Gray.

    Rim diameter: 38–60 cm, with a mean of 46 cm.
    Height: Unknown (no complete examples).
    Wall thickness: 8–20 mm (except for the bolster).
    Decoration: While many of these bowls are completely slipped with the usual white engobe, perhaps a third are unslipped on the exterior below the bolstered rim. This unslipped, often rough exterior provides the background for excising and/or very wide-line incising. The repertoire of motifs is not the same as that seen on Leandro Gray bolstered-rim bowls; many of the motifs seem to be of local, rather than pan-Mesoamerican, significance. Occasional bolstered-rim bowls have three-dimensional designs modeled (or "sculptured") on them with added clay (Fig. 12.99*t*).

Jars with vertical necks (Fig. 12.100a-c, e, h-k). Like their Leandro Gray counterparts, these are jars with globular bodies and vertical (or nearly vertical) necks built up by means of concentric rings. The rim profiles are slightly tapered, or of the plain direct type. These jars are slipped over the whole exterior; the slip extends a few centimeters down inside the necks, but no farther.

    Rim diameter: 10–18 cm
    Height of neck: 6–10 cm
    Diameter of body: Unknown (no complete examples)

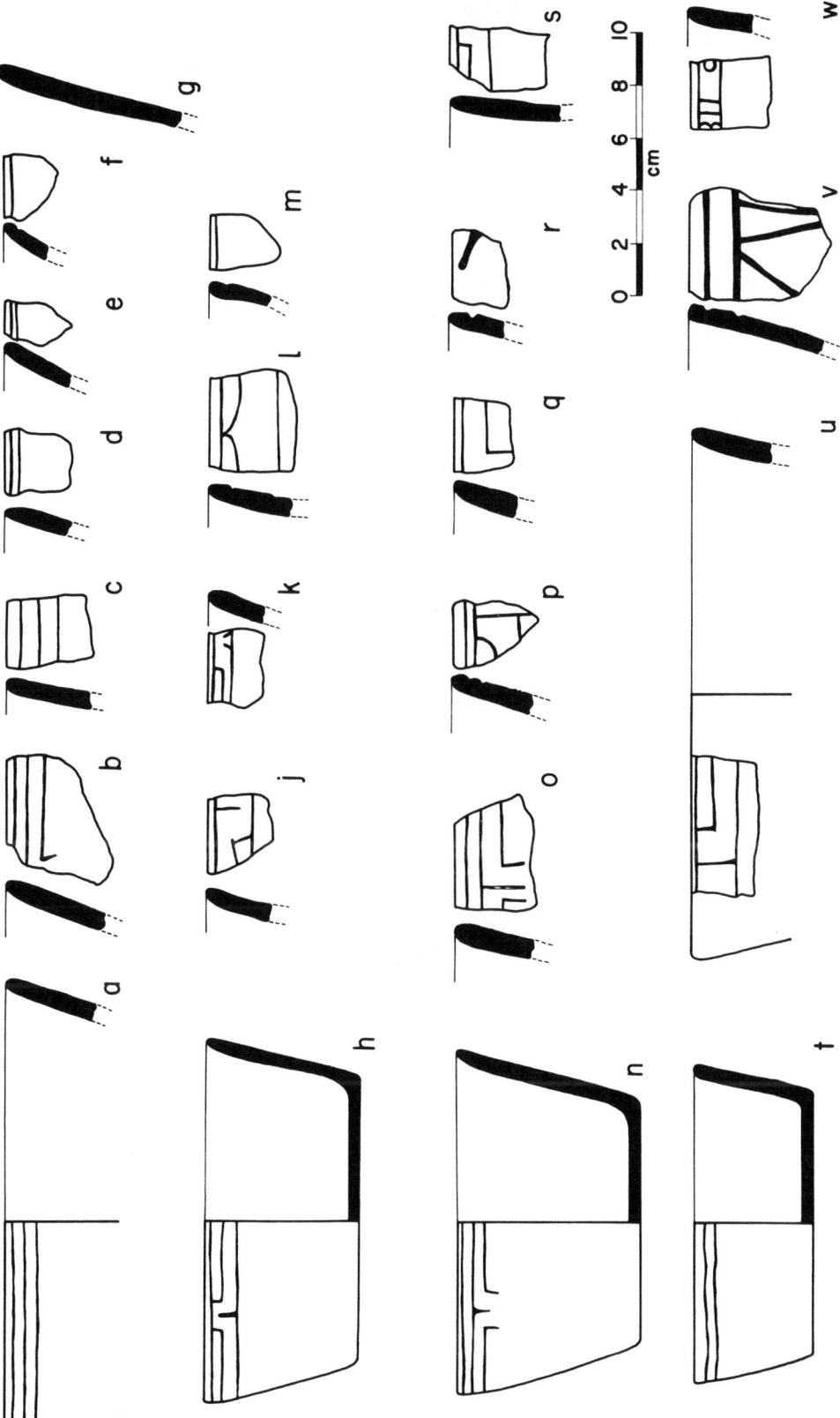

Figure 12.90. Atoyac Yellow-white cylinders or bowls with nearly vertical walls, decorated, from San José Mogote (SJM) and Barrio del Rosario Huitzo. *a, c, d,* rims with two to three parallel incised lines, Zone D, Area A, Huitzo. *b, e,* rims from Household Unit C1, Area A, SJM. *f,* Zone D2 midden, Area A, SJM. *g,* Household Unit C2, Area A, SJM. *h,* bowl found below House 6, Area C, SJM, showing Plog's Motif 4. *j-m,* rims with 1–3 incised lines, Area A, Huitzo (*j,* Zone E1; *k,* Zone F3; *l,* fill of Structure 4; *m,* cutting profile). *n,* bowl from contact between House 7 and Feature 25, Zone D2, Area C, SJM. *o,* rim from bowl with motif similar to *n,* surface, Area C, SJM. *p,* Household Unit C3, Area A, SJM. *q,* Zone F1, Area A, Huitzo. *r,* cylinder rim with excised design, cutting profile, Area A, Huitzo. *s,* Structure 4, Area A, Huitzo. *t,* bowl from Zone D, Area C, SJM, whose parallel incised lines encircle the vessel without any double-line-break. *u,* rim with Plog's Motif 10, Zone F1, Area A, Huitzo. *v,* rim with excised design, Zone D1, Area A, SJM. *w,* incised rim, Zone F3, Area A, Huitzo. Specimens *b, e-h, n, p, t,* and *v* are San José phase; specimens *k, l, q, s, u,* and *w* are from early Guadalupe phase proveniences that may contain redeposited San José phase sherds. Specimen *o* is undated. All other specimens are Guadalupe phase.

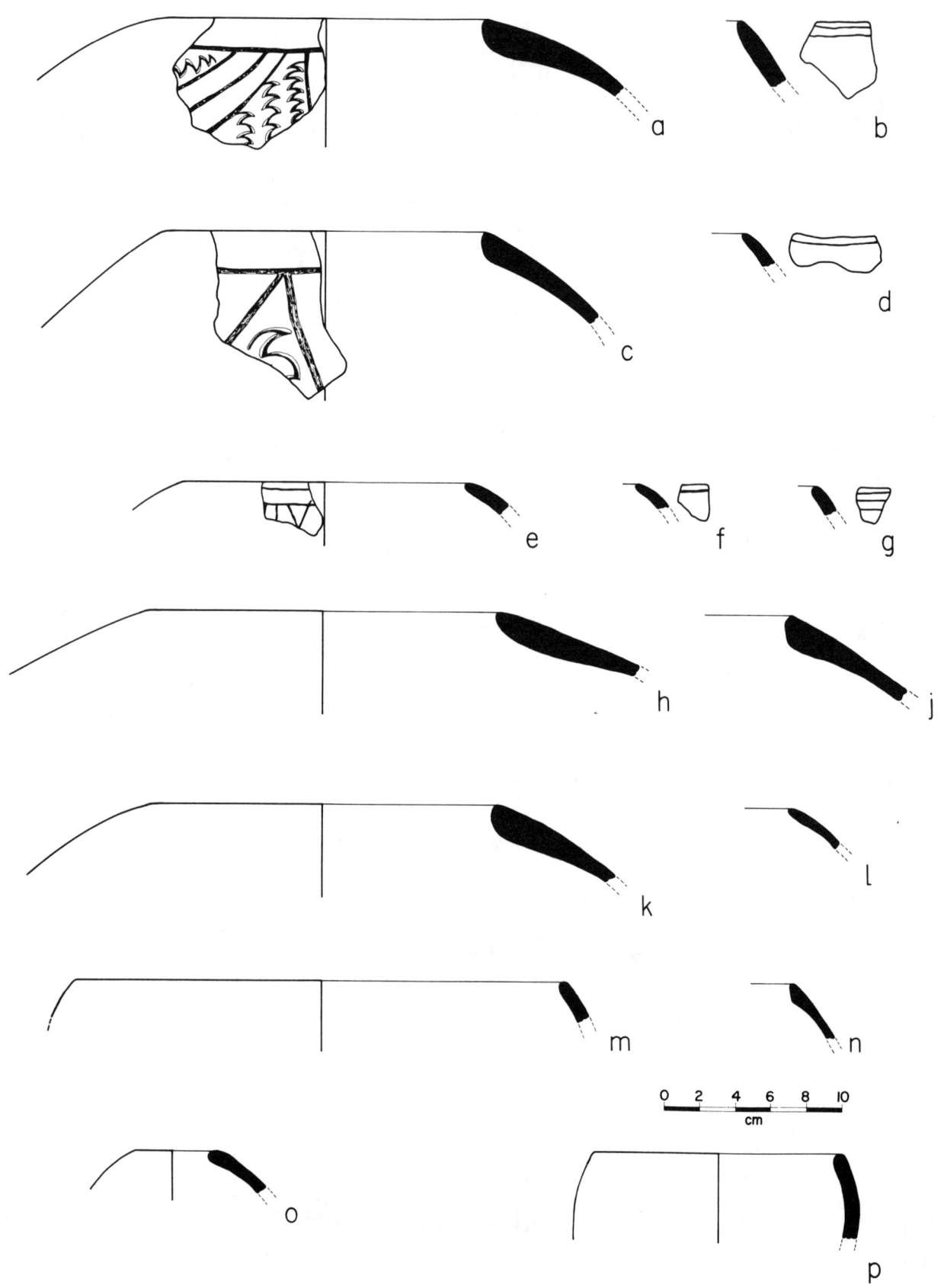

San José Phase

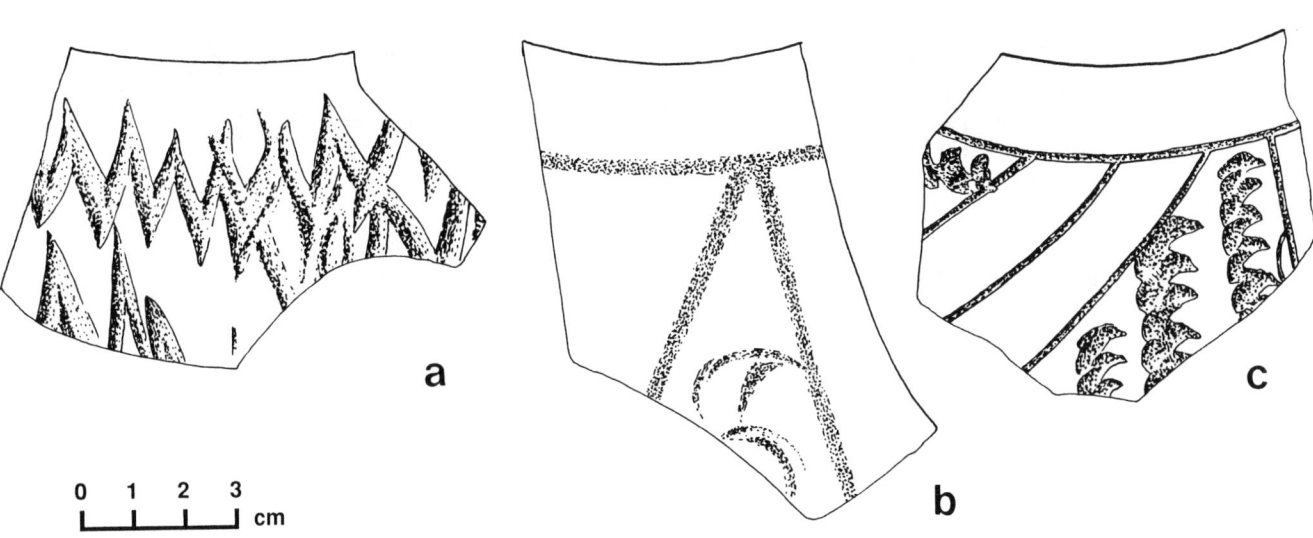

Figure 12.92. Atoyac Yellow-white tecomate rims with plastic decoration, all from Area A of San José Mogote. *a,* example of false rocker stamping, Stage II of Structure 1. *b,* example of zoned rocker stamping done with a large tool, Zone D2 midden. *c,* example of zoned rocker stamping in narrow rows done with a small tool (surface collection). All specimens would be typical of the San José phase.

Figure 12.91 (facing page). Atoyac Yellow-white tecomates and incurved-rim bowls from San José Mogote (SJM) and Barrio del Rosario Huitzo. *a,* tecomate with zoned false rocker stamping, surface, Area A, SJM. *b,* tecomate with incised band at rim, fill of Structure 4, Area A, Huitzo. *c,* tecomate with zoned false rocker stamping, Zone D2 midden, Area A, SJM. *d,* tecomate with incised band at rim, Zone D1 midden, Area A, SJM. *e,* tecomate with incised decoration, Zone F1, Area A, Huitzo. *f, g,* tecomates with incised bands at rim, both from Area A, Huitzo (*f,* Zone E1; *g,* Zone F3). *h,* Zone D3 midden, Area A, SJM. *j,* Zone D2 midden, Area A, SJM. *k,* surface, Area A, SJM. *l,* Zone D1 midden, Area A, SJM. *m,* House 7, Area A, Huitzo. *n,* Household Unit C4, Area A, SJM. *o,* small tecomate, Zone D, Area A, Huitzo. *p,* incurved-rim bowl, Zone F3, Area A, Huitzo. Specimens *c, d, h, j, l,* and *n* are San José phase. Specimens *a* and *k,* found on the surface, would also be typical of the San José phase. Specimens *b, e, g,* and *p* are from early Guadalupe phase proveniences that could contain redeposited San José phase sherds. Specimens *f, m,* and *o* are Guadalupe phase.

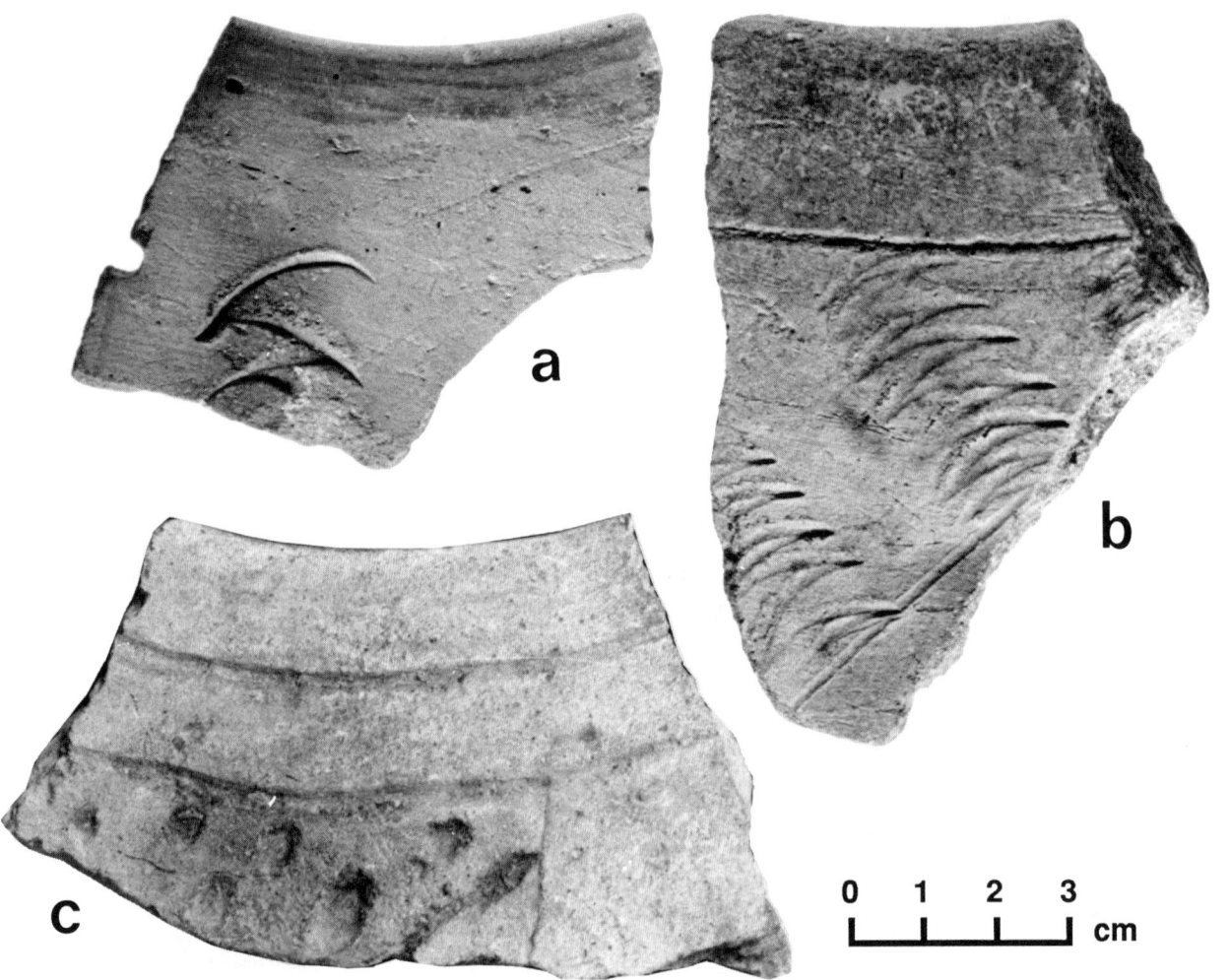

Figure 12.93. Atoyac Yellow-white tecomate sherds with plastic decoration, all from the San José phase. *a,* tecomate with plain rocker stamping, perforated for suspension (cleaning profile, Area A, San José Mogote). *b,* tecomate with plain rocker stamping in zones (cleaning profile, Area A, San José Mogote). *c,* tecomate with plain band at the rim and zoned punctation on the body (San Sebastián Abasolo, Test A, Zone D).

Wall thickness: Usually 5–9 mm

Decoration: Usually none. A few examples have a raised bulb on the neck like some Leandro Gray jars. The bulb appears to have been pushed through from the inside with the potter's thumb, and may be outlined or accompanied by incised lines. Similar jar necks with bulbs were found in Chiapa de Corzo I (Dixon 1959: Fig. 2*e*).

Oval bowls with pinched-in sides. As in other types of the Tierras Largas and San José phases, Atoyac Yellow-white has some hemispherical bowls whose rims have been pinched inward on opposite sides, perhaps in imitation of a gourd vessel that has been cross-sectioned through the stem scars.

Dimensions: Like those of hemispherical bowls (see below).

Hemispherical bowls (Fig. 12.101d-e). Never particularly common, these small bowls resemble earlier examples in Tierras Largas Burnished Plain. They grade into bowls with incurved rims (see below).

Rim diameter: 14–18 cm

Height: Usually between 40 and 60 percent of the rim diameter.

Wall thickness: 4–8 mm

Decoration: Rare. A few examples have incising on the exterior, like Ixta White examples from Tlapacoya-Zohapilco (Niederberger 1987: Fig. 506, top left).

Bowls with incurved rim (Figs. 12.92p; 12.101f-h). Very similar to the hemispherical bowls just described above, these bowls

Figure 12.94. Atoyac Yellow-white tecomate body sherd from Zone D1 midden, Area A, San José Mogote (San José phase). The horizontal scraped line near the bottom of the photograph indicates the point below which the tecomate is not decorated. Above that line, there are irregular zones of plain rocker stamping.

differ only in having a more restricted orifice. It is possible that by distinguishing them from hemispherical bowls, we have created a distinction that would have been meaningless to the Formative potter; we did so in case there might be some chronological differences between the two. It is also the case that these incurved-rim bowls resemble some Atoyac Yellow-white tecomates. However, they are so much smaller that we have kept them in a different category.

Dimensions: Similar to those of hemispherical bowls.

Spouted trays (Fig. 12.102b). These vessels appear to be virtually identical in shape and size to spouted trays in Leandro Gray. No complete examples were recovered. This is the kind of tray that could be used to pour white engobe onto other Atoyac Yellow-white vessels.

Pigment dishes (Fig. 12.102a). These small, ashtraylike vessels resemble their Leandro Gray counterparts. They retain traces of mineral pigment on the inside (usually red or yellow). Most are no more than 6–8 cm in diameter. As in the case of Leandro Gray, it is often impossible to tell rim sherds of pigment dishes from rim sherds of spouted trays when the latter do not include part of the spout.

Bowls with giant "macrorim" (Fig. 12.101m,n). These bowls differ from our vessel form "bolstered-rim" bowl by virtue of their huge size. They are large enough to have served as washtubs or dyeing vats, whereas bolstered-rim bowls are small enough to have held portions of food. Giant "macrorims" are notable for the very large size of their external bolster, which began as a series of added concentric rings of clay but was then shaped and

Figure 12.95. Atoyac Yellow-white tecomate body sherds from Zones D1 and D2 of the Area A midden, San José Mogote (San José phase). This plate shows only part of the variety in rocker stamping style and tool size that characterized this midden, used by numerous households producing shell ornaments and magnetite mirrors.

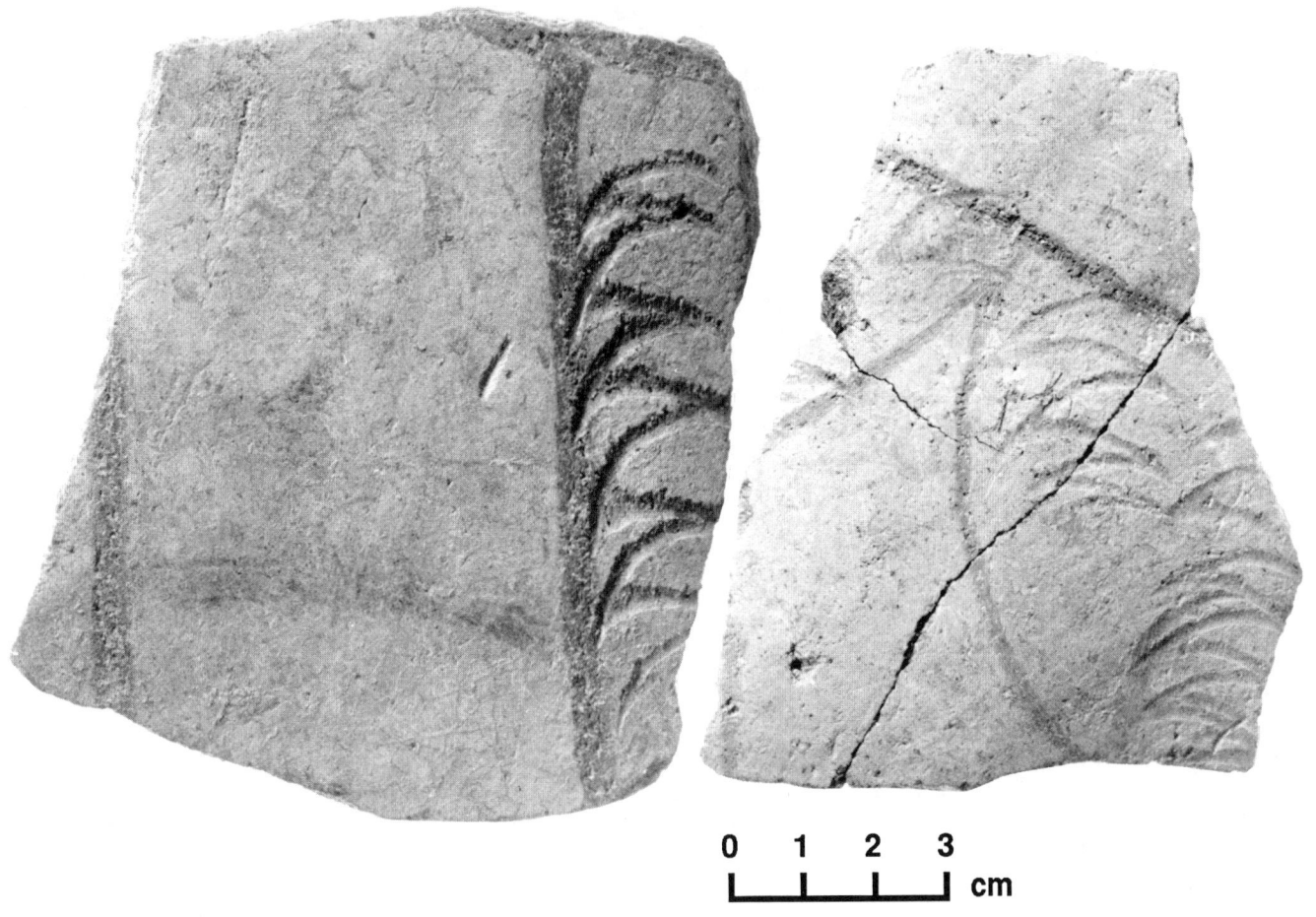

Figure 12.96. Body sherds from Atoyac Yellow-white tecomates with zoned rocker stamping, both from Area A, San José Mogote (San José phase). *Left,* Household Unit C4; *right,* Zone D1 midden.

modeled. Some rims reach a thickness of 4 cm or more and may be rounded, pointed, or squared-off in profile. Probably the rims were thickened in this way to provide a grip for picking up these heavy vessels.

Whatever the specific use of these large vessels, it may have been a widespread activity. Large bowls with similarly thickened rims occurred in Period I at Chiapa de Corzo (Dixon 1959: Fig. 3).

Rim diameter: 56–60 cm, with a few specimens even larger.
Height: Unknown (no complete specimens were found), but greater than 12 cm based on sizes of rim sherds.
Wall thickness (below the rim): 10–14 mm
Decoration: None

Jars with flaring rim (Fig. 12.100g). This vessel form is more typical of the Guadalupe phase, but rare examples occur in San José phase contexts.

Bowls with "grater bowl" base (Fig. 12.101j-l). These "pseudo-molcajete" bowls are rare in the San José phase, especially when one compares Oaxaca to the Basin of Mexico. They are somewhat more common in the Guadalupe phase.

Ceramic masks or effigy vessels (Fig. 12.103, top). Occasional fragments of what may be ceramic masks in Atoyac Yellow-white occur in San José phase deposits. Some are broken in ways that make it impossible to distinguish them from three-dimensional faces on effigy vessels.

SAN JOSE RED-ON-WHITE

General Description

A distinctive, often well-burnished bichrome ware, produced by the addition of a red hematite slip to selected areas of what

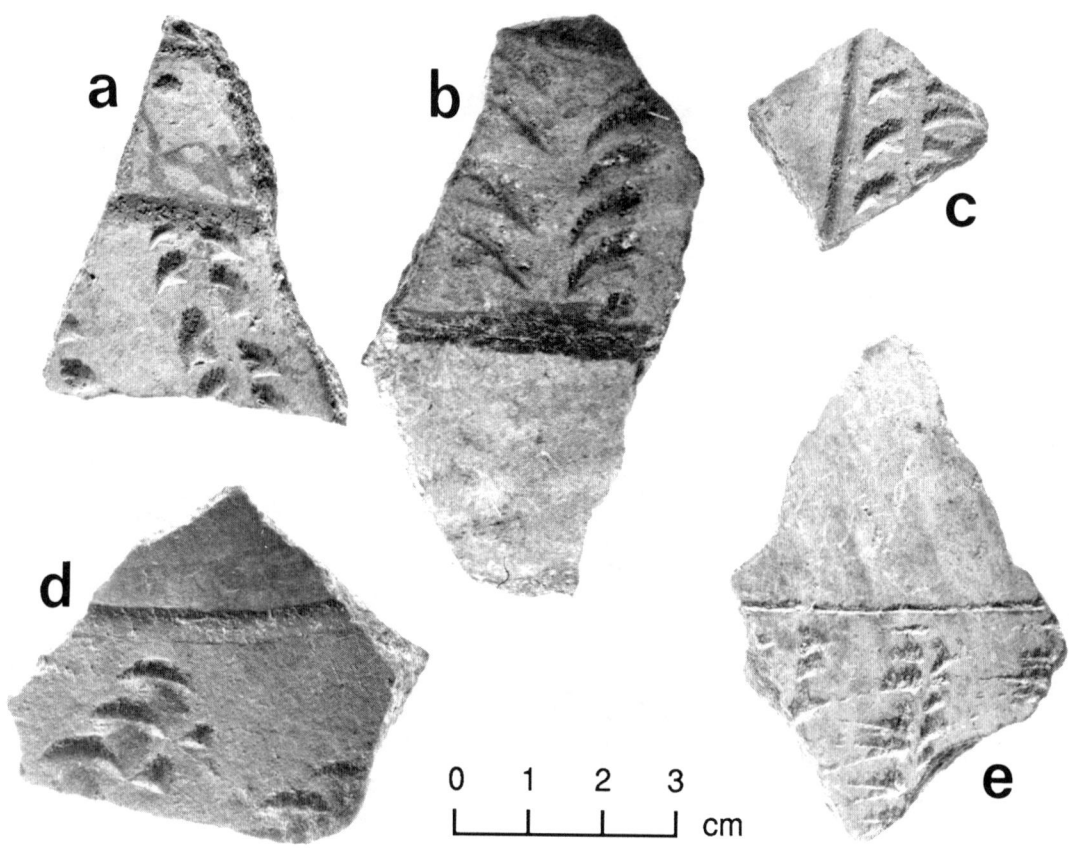

Figure 12.97. Atoyac Yellow-white tecomate body sherds with interrupted rocker stamping, Area A, San José Mogote (San José phase). Sherd *e* shows particularly clearly how the crescents of rocker stamping were later interrupted by streaks of burnishing. Sherds *a* and *c*, which are more typical examples, have only a single line of burnishing running vertically down the column of crescents. *a, d,* Zone D1 midden; *b, e,* Zone D2 midden; *c,* Household Unit C4.

would otherwise be Atoyac Yellow-white vessels. This type, a useful horizon marker for the San José phase, appeared in the form of bowls of various sizes and shapes, jars with necks, and tecomates. In the case of tecomates, a red band at the rim was often accompanied by red stripes that divided the body into white zones filled with rocker stamping.

Like Atoyac Yellow-white, San José Red-on-White was used for what seem to be serving or light storage vessels, never for cooking. Related red-on-white bichromes are so numerous at this time period that an overarching generic category would be useful. Pilli Red-on-White from the Basin of Mexico (Niederberger 1987: Figs. 461–464), Red-and-White Bichrome from Chiapa de Corzo (Dixon 1959:32–33), and Tilapa Red-on-White from the Chiapas-Guatemala Pacific Coast (Coe and Flannery 1967:38–40) are all related. There appears to be no comparable ware at San Lorenzo, Veracruz (Coe and Diehl 1980).

Chronological History

San José Red-on-White made its first sporadic appearance at the very end of the Tierras Largas phase, or during the transition from Tierras Largas to San José times. The few sherds known from such strata seem mostly to be hemispherical bowls. In other words, the common red-on-buff bowl of the Tierras Largas phase was joined by red-on-white bowls as soon as local potters began to use white kaolin engobes.

During the San José phase, this red-on-white bichrome occurred mainly as outleaned-wall bowls like those of the Cuadros phase at Salinas La Blanca, Guatemala; these amounted to more than half the diagnostic sherds. Other San José phase forms included tecomates, bolstered-rim bowls, and jars with vertical necks. Frequencies of San José Red-on-White peaked in the first half of the San José phase, then slowly declined.

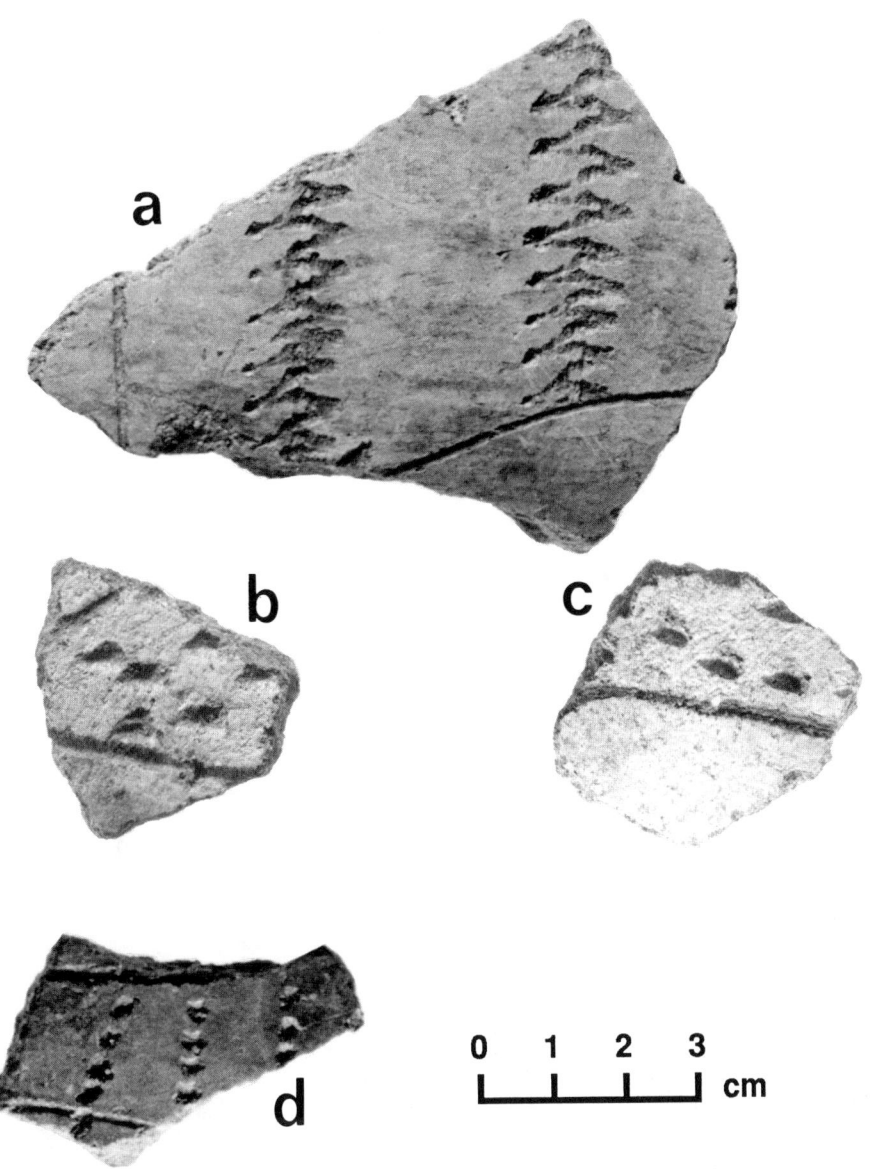

Figure 12.98. Atoyac Yellow-white tecomate body sherds with plastic decoration, all from San José Mogote (San José phase). *a,* sherd with zoned rocker stamping that appears to have been done with the edge of a marine shell (cleaning profile, Area C). *b, c,* zoned punctation on sherds from Area A (*b,* Household Unit C4; *c,* Household Unit C3). *d,* zoned dentate stamping (cleaning profile, Area C).

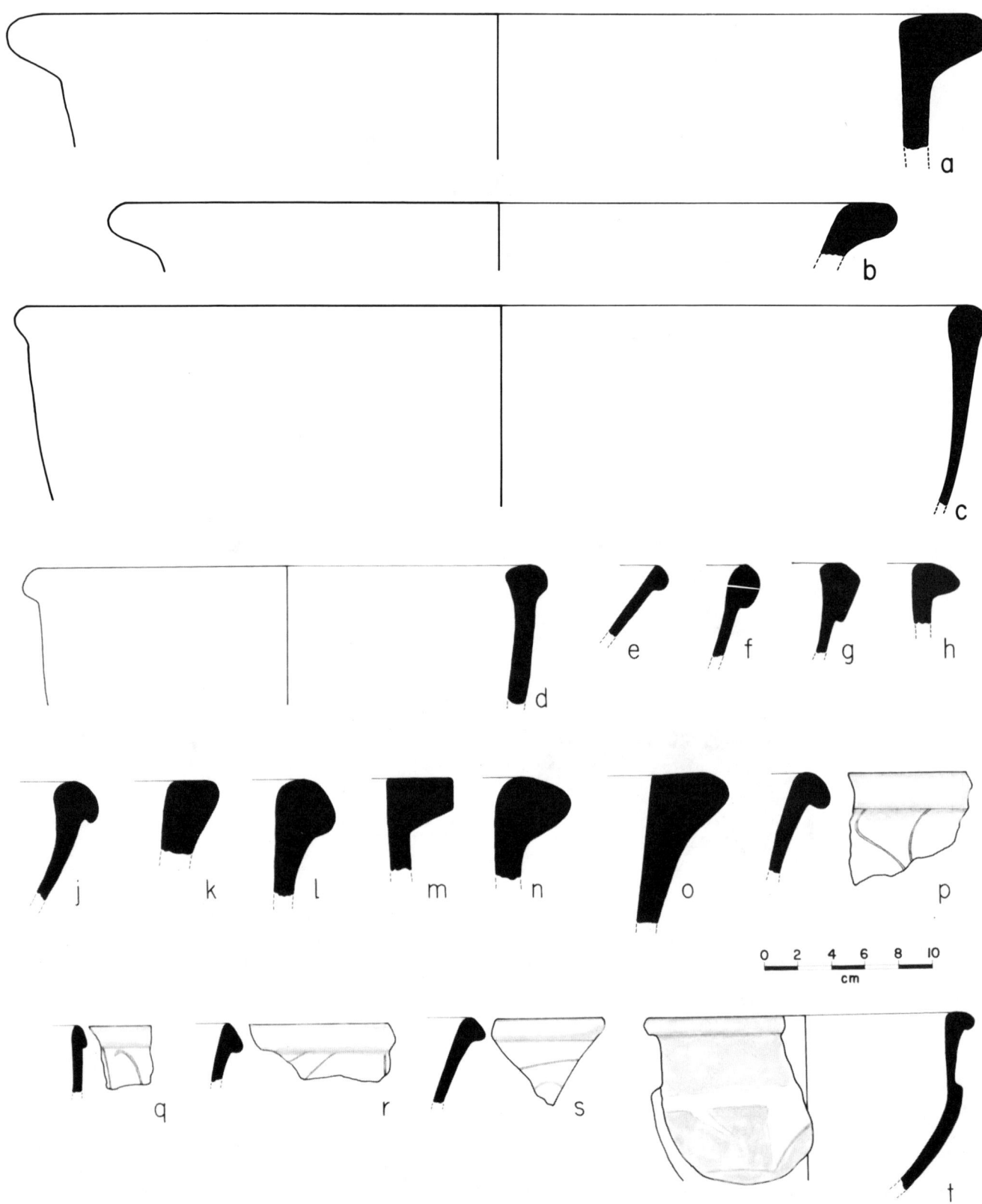

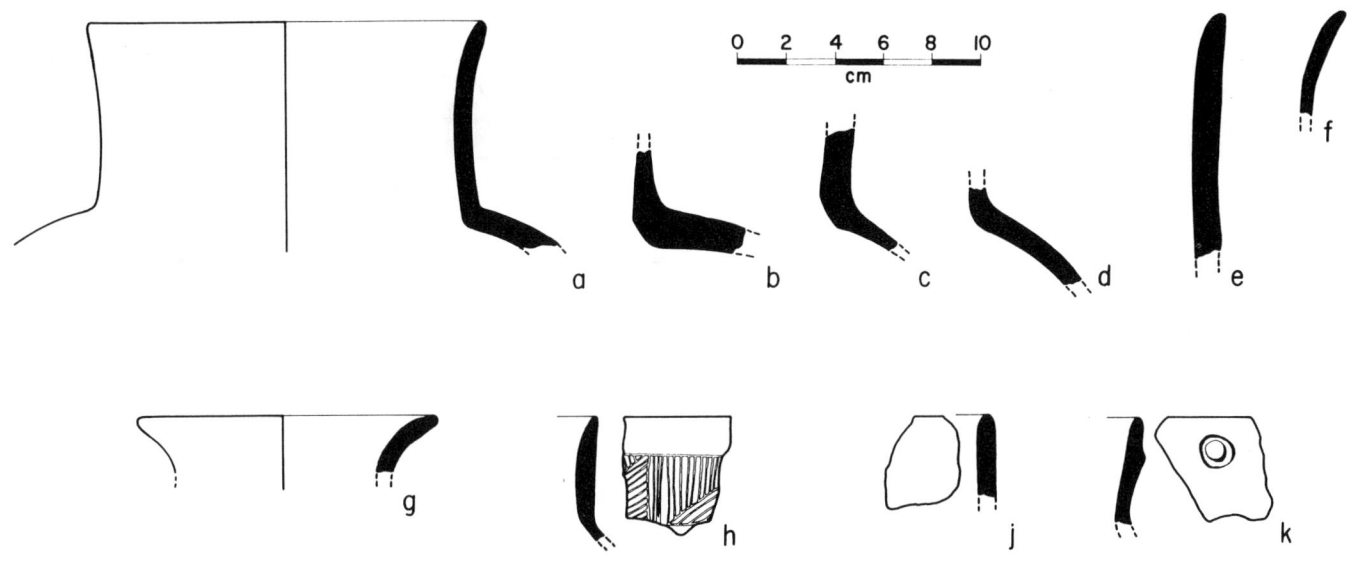

Figure 12.100. Atoyac Yellow-white jar necks from San José Mogote (SJM) and Barrio del Rosario Huitzo. *a*, vertical jar neck and shoulder from Stage II of Structure 1, Area A, SJM. *b-d*, jar shoulders (*b*, Household Unit C3, Area A, SJM; *c*, Household Unit C1, Area A, SJM; *d*, Zone F3, Area A, Huitzo). *e-f*, jar rims from Area A, SJM (*e*, Household Unit C3; *f*, Household Unit C1). *g*, flaring jar rim, totally slipped outside, slipped inside only to 2 cm below the rim (Zone F1, Area A, Huitzo). *h*, vertical jar rim with incised design on outside, Household Unit C3, Area A, SJM. *j*, vertical jar rim, totally slipped outside, slipped inside only to 1 cm below the rim (Zone D, Area A, Huitzo). *k*, vertical jar neck with raised bulb encircled by cane-end impression on exterior (Household Unit C3, Area A, SJM). All specimens from SJM are San José phase; *j* is Guadalupe phase. *d* and *g* are from Guadalupe phase proveniences that could contain redeposited San José phase sherds.

In the Guadalupe phase, red-on-white bichromes were virtually absent; a few sherds in early Guadalupe levels at Huitzo may simply be redeposited San José phase sherds.

Clay Body

The clay body is a residual piedmont clay identical in every way to that used for Atoyac Yellow-white.

Firing Temperature

It was probably fired at 720 to 760° C in an oxidizing atmosphere. The slightly higher firing temperature (relative to other San José phase types) served to set the kaolin engobe harder.

Surface Treatment and Slipping

The surface of the clay body was merely brushed to remove loose particles prior to the application of the first slip. Over this was applied the same, nearly iron-free kaolin engobe already described for Atoyac Yellow-white. Most sherds have an engobe so thick as to suggest that smaller vessels were dipped, or the kaolin poured on. However, in other cases (especially large tecomates), a thinner slip seems to have been swabbed on, perhaps with a piece of animal fur.

After this first white engobe had set—when it had turned dull and lost its wetness—a second slip was applied over it. This second slip was usually a red engobe composed of very finely ground hematite (sometimes specular) in a matrix of water and kaolin clay. Occasional vessels, however, indicate that in some cases the red coating may have been only a stain composed of water and ground hematite, with no added clay. (Larger vessels

Figure 12.99 (facing page). Atoyac Yellow-white bowls with bolstered rim from San José Mogote (SJM) and Barrio del Rosario Huitzo. *a-c*, large specimens, undecorated (*a*, Stage II of Structure 1, Area A, SJM; *b*, found while cutting profile, Area A, Huitzo; *c*, Zone D2 midden, Area A, SJM). *d*, medium-sized specimen, undecorated, Stage II of Structure 1, Area A, SJM. *e-h*, rims from Area A, SJM (*e, h*, Zone D2 midden; *f*, Zone D1 midden; *g*, Household Unit C3). *j*, rim of bowl similar to *c*, Zone D1 midden, Area A, SJM. *k-o*, very heavy rims, undecorated (*k* found while cutting profile, Area A, Huitzo; *l, o*, Zone D1 midden, Area A, SJM; *m*, Stages II-III, Structure 1, Area A, SJM; *n*, Household Unit C1, Area A, SJM). *p-s*, bowls with excising on exterior below bolstered rim, all from Area A, SJM (*p*, Zone D1 midden; *q-s*, Stages II-III, Structure 1). *t*, unusual bolstered rim bowl with sculptured motif on exterior, possibly a giant U motif (Zone D1 midden, Area A, SJM). Specimens *b* and *k* are from Guadalupe phase proveniences that could contain redeposited San José phase sherds. All other specimens are from San José phase contexts. Specimen *p* has red pigment rubbed on the exterior.

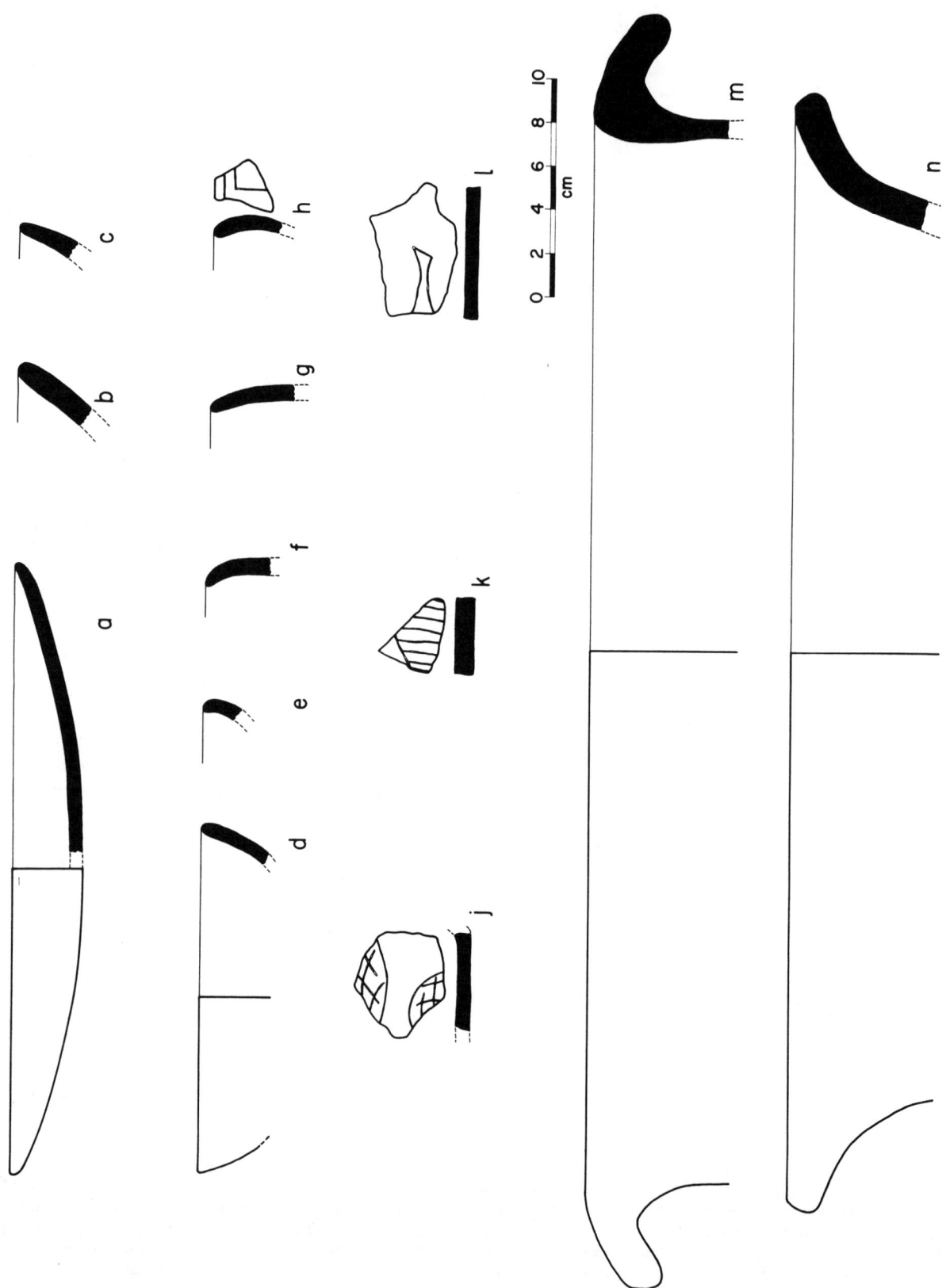

Figure 12.101. Miscellaneous vessel forms in Atoyac Yellow-white. *a-h* shows the variation in round-bottomed bowls, from extremely shallow (*a*) to hemispherical but open (*d-e*) and on to incurved-rim (*f-h*). All are plain except for *h*, which is incised on the exterior. San José phase specimens from Area A at San José Mogote include *f* (Household Unit C1); *h* (Household Unit C2); *g* (Household Unit C3); and *a* (Zone D1 midden). Guadalupe phase specimens from Area A at Huitzo include *b* (Zone E1) and *e* (Zone D). Specimens *c* and *d*, also from Area A at Huitzo, are from Guadalupe phase proveniences that could contain redeposited San José phase sherds (*c*, fill of Structure 4; *d*, found while cleaning profile). *j-l*, sherds from flat bowl bases incised in "grater bowl" style. *j* is a San José phase example from Household Unit C3, Area A, SJM. *k* and *l* are Guadalupe phase examples from Area A, Huitzo (*k*, Zone C4; *l*, Zone F2). *m* and *n* are large bowls with giant "macrorims," both from Household Unit C2, Area A, SJM (San José phase).

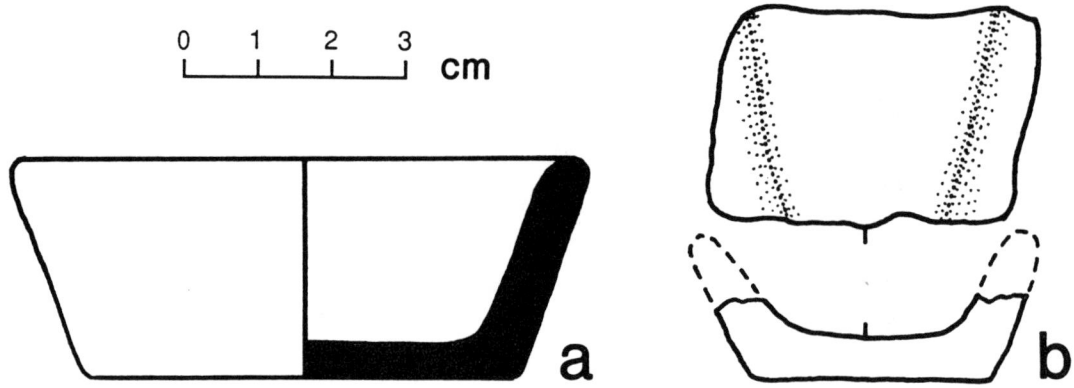

Figure 12.102. Atoyac Yellow-white vessels which, because of the traces of pigment found in them, are suspected of having been used as pigment dishes during the San José phase at San José Mogote. *a,* miniature bowl from Burial 11, Area C. *b,* top view and cross-section of spouted tray fragment, Household Unit C3, Area A.

may have been the usual recipients of the latter treatment. There seems to have been a correlation between a streaky white slip that had merely been swabbed on, and a watery red stain with no added clay.) Finally, after the red slip or stain had set, the vessel was burnished once with a quartz pebble.

Color

In sherd profiles, the clay body usually shows a very dark gray core (5 YR 3/1) sandwiched between reddish brown (2.5 YR 5/4) or very dusky red (10 R 2/2) layers. A smaller number of sherds, however, are reddish gray throughout.

As for vessel surfaces, the white engobe ranges from light yellowish brown (10 YR 6/4) to pinkish gray (7.5 YR 7/2) or light reddish brown (5 YR 6/4). The hematite slip ranges from weak red (7.5 R 4/4 or 10 R 4/4) to dark reddish brown (2.5 YR 3/4).

Plastic Decoration

The only vessels decorated in this ware were tecomates; they often showed rocker stamping or punctation (see below).

Simulation of the Ware

In 1970, Payne successfully simulated vessels of San José Red-on-White by using (1) a kaolinite clay body of weathered Precambrian gneiss from a piedmont spur near Tlacochahuaya in the Tlacolula region; (2) white engobe from a large kaolin source that had formed as a hydrothermal deposit in the volcanic tuff mountains east of Mitla; (3) a chunk of hematite ore from the Precambrian gneiss mountains near Valdeflores in the Valle Grande region, which he ground into red pigment in a mortar; and (4) a Precolumbian chert burnishing pebble.

By experimentation, Payne found that if the red slip was applied too soon (before the white slip had dried), the burnishing blurred the two slips together. On the other hand, if the red slip was applied too late (after the white was completely dry), the metallic hematite did not penetrate; it stayed on the surface and was crushed into gray streaks by the burnishing pebble, destroying the "specular red" effect. Thus, the timing of the application of the red slip or stain would have been a critical factor in the production of this pottery type.

Vessel Forms

Hemispherical bowls (Fig. 12.104a). The earliest form in which San José Red-on-Buff appeared, these vessels were clearly inspired by earlier hemispherical bowls in Avelina Red-on-Buff. They have a slightly flattened base and a direct or slightly tapered rim. Some of these bowls were slipped white, with a red band added at the rim; others were slipped all white on one side, all red on the other, with a red rim band on the white side.
  Rim diameter: 18–26 cm
  Height: About one-third the rim diameter.
  Wall thickness: 5–8 mm
  Plastic decoration: None

Bowls with incurved rim. These vessels are merely variants of the hemispherical bowl, distinguished by their more restricted orifice. Overall dimensions are like those of hemispherical bowls.

Oval bowls with pinched-in sides (Fig. 12.114m). These vessels are simply red-on-white versions of Avelina Red-on-Buff bowls with pinched-in sides. Overall dimensions are like those of their Avelina counterparts.

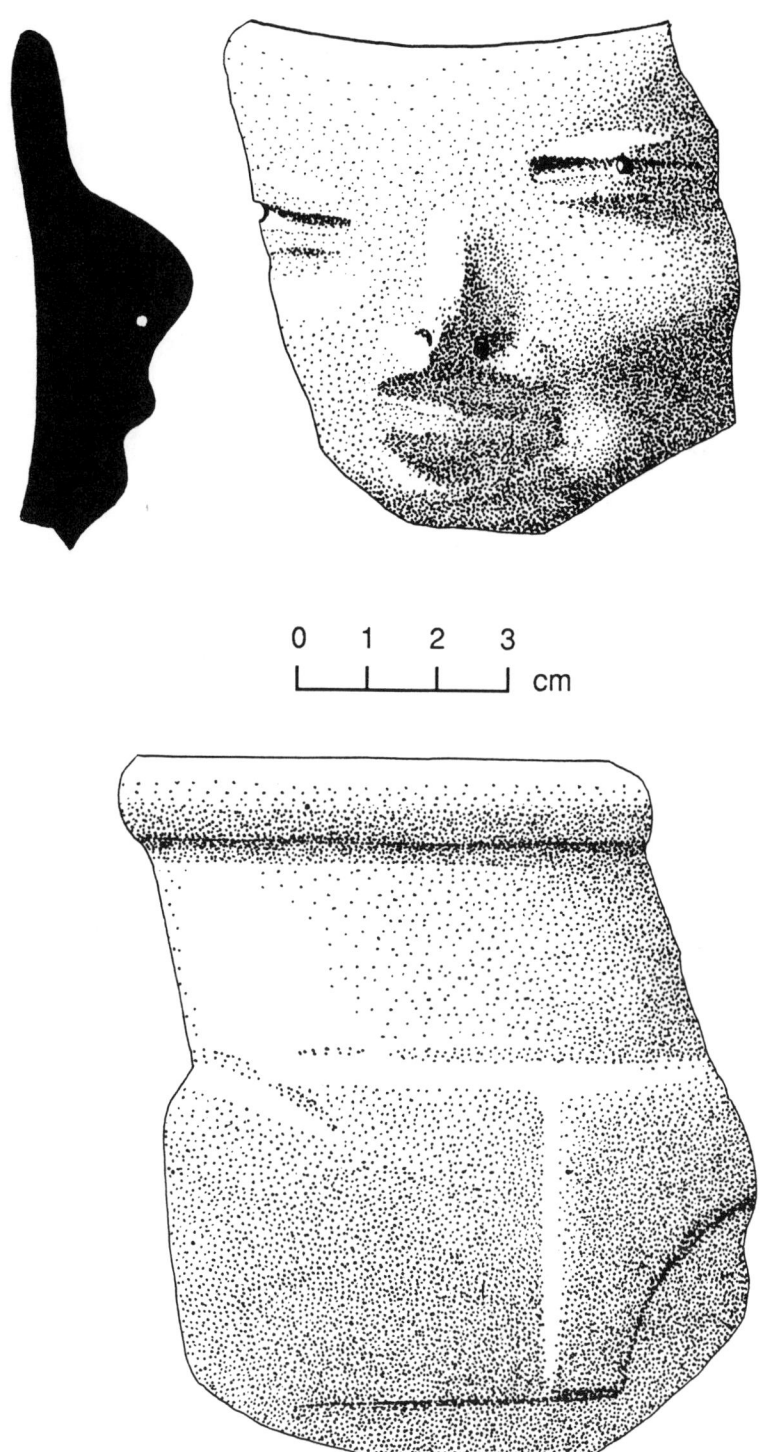

Figure 12.103. Atoyac Yellow-white ceramics with three-dimensional sculpturing. *Top*, rim of ceramic mask or effigy vessel with human face, perforated through the nasal septum and the pupils of the eyes. Household Unit C3, Area A, San José Mogote. *Bottom*, sherd from bowl with bolstered rim, sculptured on the outside with what may be part of a giant U-motif (see also Fig. 12.99*t*). Zone D1 midden, Area A, San José Mogote. (Both specimens are San José phase.)

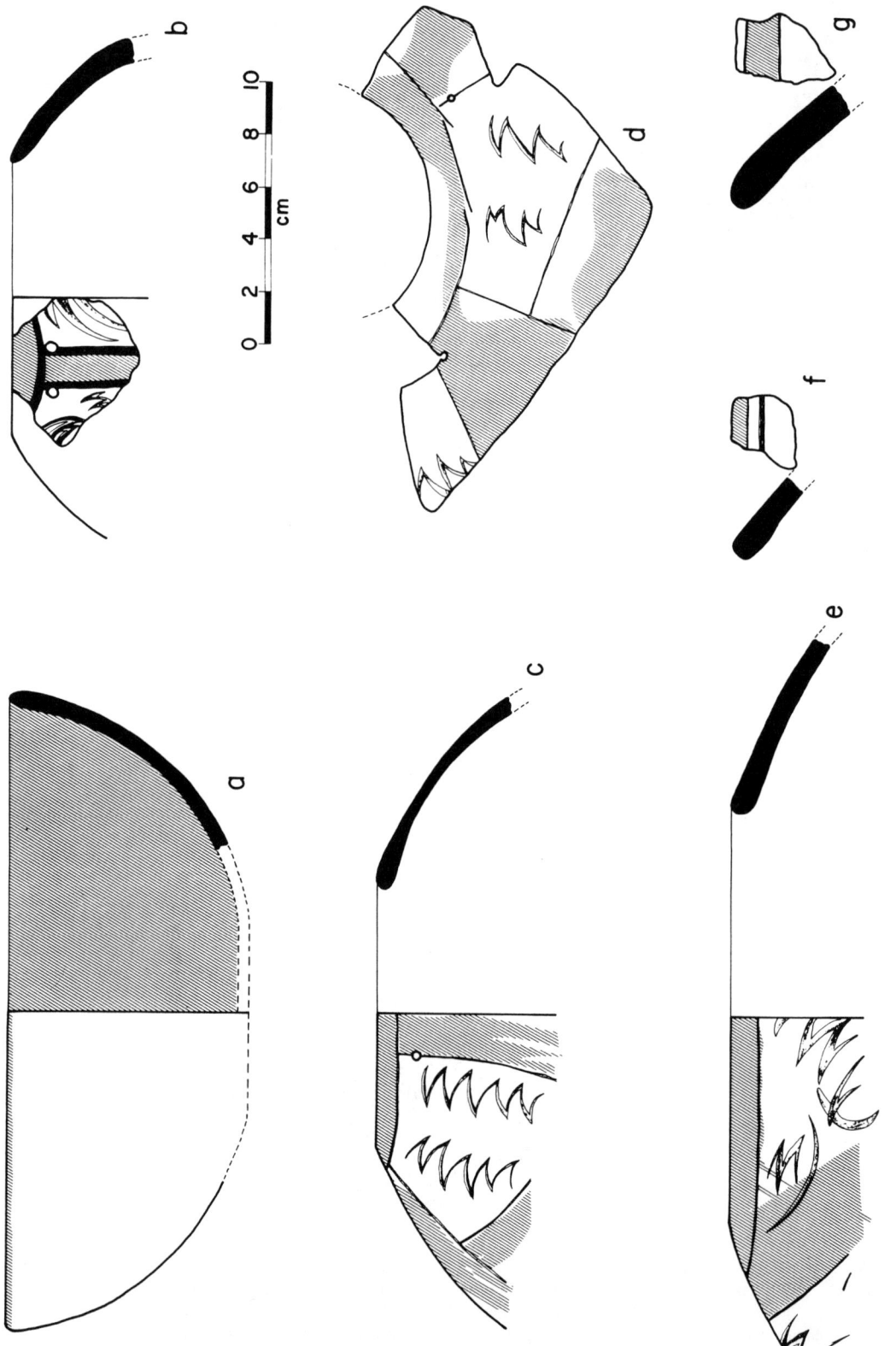

Figure 12.104. San José Red-on-White vessels, all from San José Mogote. *a*, hemispherical bowl, totally red inside, red rim on outside over white slip; Zone G, Area C (late Tierras Largas phase). *b*, tecomate with white-slipped zones of false rocker stamping, divided by red-slipped bands; perforated for suspension; Household Unit C3, Area A (San José phase). *c*, tecomate with white-slipped zones of false rocker stamping, divided by red-slipped bands; perforated for suspension; Stage I of Structure 1, Area A (San José phase). *d*, tecomate with white-slipped zones of false rocker stamping, divided by zones of sloppy red slip over white; perforated for suspension; Stage I of Structure 1, Area A (San José phase). *e*, tecomate with same description and provenience as *c*. *f, g*, tecomates with red band at rim over white slip, both San José phase examples from Area A, San José Mogote (*f*, Household Unit C4; *g*, Household Unit C1).

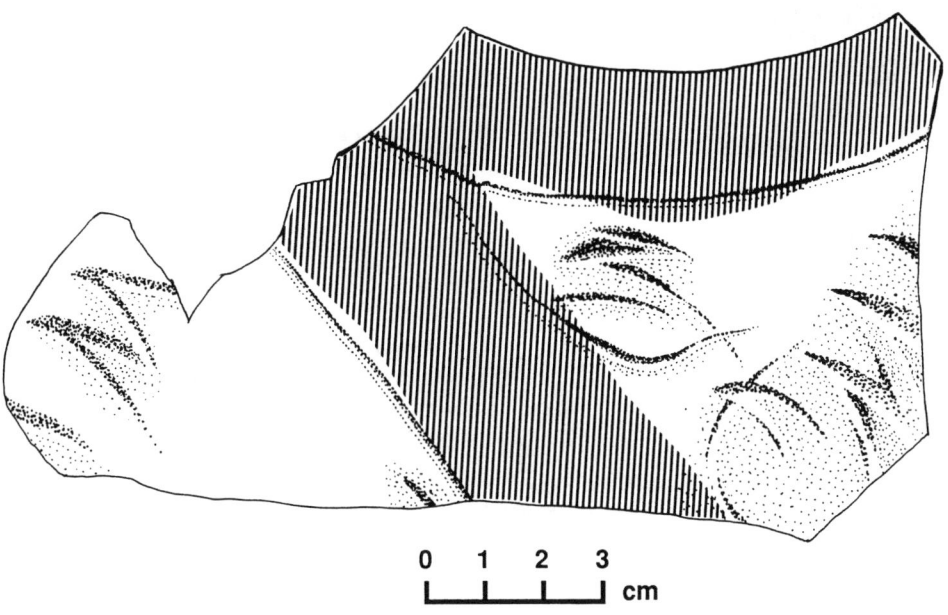

Figure 12.105. San José Red-on-White tecomate from puddled adobe cap of Stage I, Structure 1, Area A, San José Mogote (San José phase). This tecomate has a red band at the rim and additional red bands that separate zones of rocker stamping over a white slip.

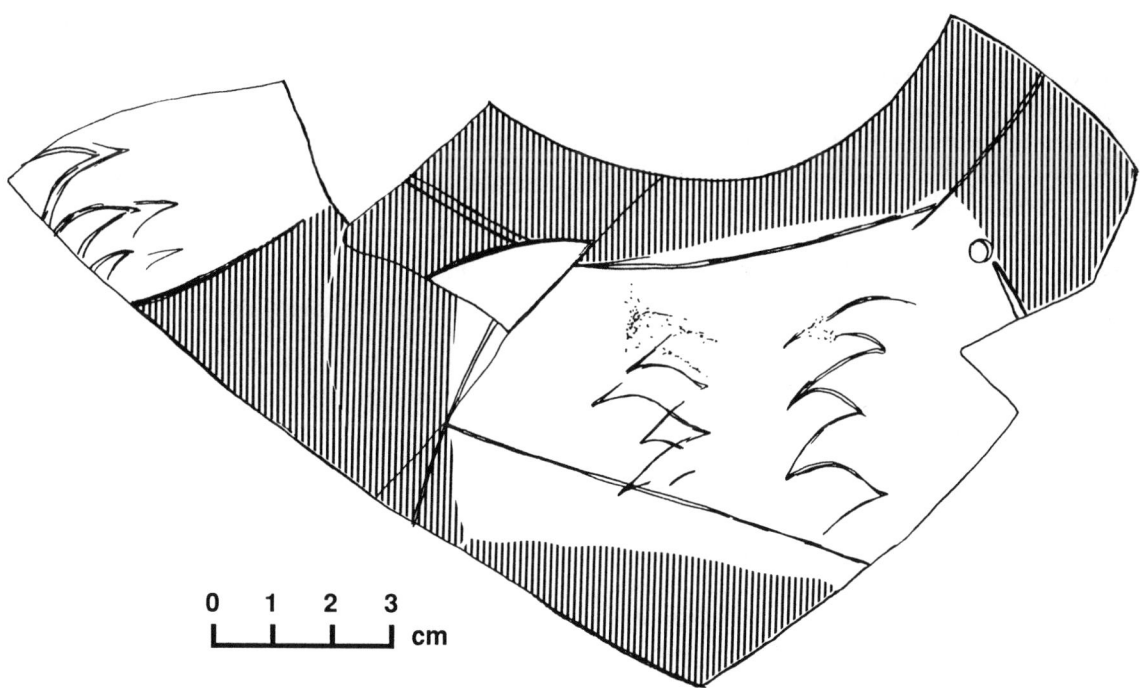

Figure 12.106. San José Red-on-White tecomate from puddled adobe cap of Stage I, Structure 1, Area A, San José Mogote (San José phase). This tecomate has a red band at the rim, and other red bands separating the white-slipped body into zones of very fine-line false rocker stamping; it has also been perforated for suspension.

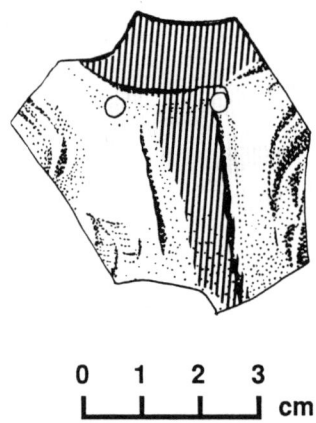

Figure 12.107. San José Red-on-White tecomate rim from Household Unit C3, Area A, San José Mogote (San José phase). This tecomate has a red band at the rim, additional red bands dividing it into zones of rocker stamping over white slip, and two perforations for suspension.

Tecomates (Figs. 12.104–12.111). These are large, globular neckless jars whose rims vary between rounded, blunt, and tapered-rounded in profile.

Rim diameter: 10–20 cm

Wall thickness: 5–9 mm

Other dimensions: Unknown (no complete specimens). The diameter of the body is estimated at 1.5–2.0 times the rim diameter.

Plastic decoration: All these tecomates have a band of red slip or stain at the rim, sometimes set off by incised lines done with an implement like a maguey spine or a chipped stone flake. Most have, in addition, red stripes dividing the body into irregular zones of different sizes. Often these zoning stripes are also set off by incised lines, although it is not unusual for the red slip to "slop over" the edges of the lines.

The zones that remained white were given plastic decorative treatment. This included (1) punctation, usually in the form of sloppy jabs; (2) true rocker stamping; (3) interrupted rocker stamping, in which the column of stamping was partially burnished smooth; and (4) false rocker stamping, in which zigzag incising (*sgraffito*) was used in imitation of actual stamping.

Jars (Fig. 12.112). Like their Atoyac Yellow-white counterparts, these jars were made by pounding a disc of clay into a cuplike shape to begin the base. Concentric rings of clay were then added to build up the globular body. The neck, which was usually vertical-walled, was built up with smaller concentric rings; after the rings had been pinched and smoothed together with wet fingers, both surfaces were scraped smooth with a piece of gourd or a rounded sherd. While many jars had direct vertical rims, a few had the rims flared outward slightly in the manner of Matadamas Red jars. The red slip or wash was usually applied to the rim or neck, with the body of the jar left white.

Rim diameter: 14–20 cm (based on a few measurable specimens).

Height of neck: 6–10 cm (estimated)

Wall thickness: 5–9 cm

Other dimensions: Unknown

Plastic decoration: None

Flat-based bowls with outleaned walls (Figs. 12.113a-d; 12.114a-f). This was the most common vessel form in San José Red-on-White. The methods of manufacture were the same as those described earlier for outleaned-wall bowls in Atoyac Yellow-white. Some bowls have a red band at the rim, with the lower wall left white; others have the lower wall slipped or stained red, with the rim left white. In addition, some bowls have a red band running around the inside of the base, or vertical red stripes on the walls. These striped bowls strongly resemble Tilapa Red-on-White bowls from Salinas La Blanca, Guatemala (Coe and Flannery 1967: Plate 13).

Rim diameter: Four-fifths of all specimens measured had a rim diameter between 20 and 26 cm, with the mode near 20 cm. The full range of rim diameters was 18–32 cm.

Height: Normally between one-fourth and one-third the rim diameter.

Basal diameter: Normally about two-thirds the rim diameter.

Plastic decoration: Limited to an occasional basal interior incised in "grater bowl" fashion.

Flat-based bowls with vertical (or nearly vertical) walls (Fig. 12.114k,l). These "cylinders" were similar to their counterparts in Atoyac Yellow-white, but were much rarer and had no plastic decoration. None were complete enough to measure. The red slip or stain was applied as a band at the rim, with the rest of the vessel left white.

Bowls with bolstered rim (Fig. 12.114g-j). These bowls had their rims externally bolstered with an additional concentric ring of clay, very much like their Atoyac Yellow-white and Leandro Gray counterparts. Some have a red band at the rim, with the rest of the vessel left white; others are slipped red on the inside and white on the outside. Some of the former are left rough and unslipped on the exterior, with the rough surface decorated by excising or wide-line incising.

Rim diameter: 30–34 cm

Height: Normally about one-fourth to one-third the rim diameter.

Wall thickness: 5–9 mm

Plastic decoration: Limited to excising or wide-line incising on those few vessels (mentioned above) that had been deliberately left rough and unslipped on the exterior below the rim. The motifs are generally local variants, rather than pan-Mesoamerican.

Bowls with outcurving walls (Fig 12.113e). This vessel form was rare in the San José phase and did not reach its peak until the Guadalupe phase (Middle Formative).

Figure 12.108. San José Red-on-White tecomate body sherds with rocker stamping in several styles. All sherds are San José phase examples from Area A of San José Mogote. The stamping technique varies from tightly spaced (*c*) to loosely spaced (*d*). *a*, Stage II of Structure 1; *b*, Household Unit C1; *c*, Household Unit C4; *d*, Household Unit C2.

LUPITA HEAVY PLAIN

General Description

This is an unslipped, unburnished utilitarian ware whose most common vessel form was a charcoal brazier or potstand with an annular base. Other forms include tecomates, outleaned-wall bowls, and saucerlike *platillos* which Payne believes may be potter's bats. While the charcoal braziers and *platillos* are unique to Lupita Heavy Plain, the bowls and tecomates look a lot like Atoyac Yellow-white bowls and tecomates that had simply never been slipped or burnished. Lupita Heavy Plain is not unique in this regard; Canoas Heavy Plain from the Tehuacán Valley (MacNeish, Peterson, and Flannery 1970:72) is an analogous type, and many of its vessels look like unslipped, unburnished versions of Canoas White.

Chronological History

It is possible that Lupita Heavy Plain made its first appearance in very late Tierras Largas phase times, or during the transition from Tierras Largas to San José; the occasional rare sherds that show up in such levels are mostly tecomate body sherds. On the other hand, this evidence should be considered with caution. Many tecomates with a red band at the rim, or with Matadamas Orange or Matadamas Red pigments on their upper bodies, would have had basal sherds or lower body sherds that were virtually indistinguishable from those of Lupita Heavy Plain.

Figure 12.109. San José Red-on-White tecomate body sherd with rocker stamping in a white zone. At the top of the sherd is a band of red slip delimiting the zone. Household Unit C4, Area A, San José Mogote (San José phase).

Figure 12.110. San José Red-on-White tecomate body sherd with interrupted rocker stamping in a white zone. San José Mogote, Area C, straightening profile at level of San José phase deposits.

Figure 12.111. San José Red-on-White tecomate body sherds with interrupted rocker stamping in white zones. The red band delimiting the zone can be seen on the left in each sherd. Zone D2 midden, Area A, San José Mogote (San José phase).

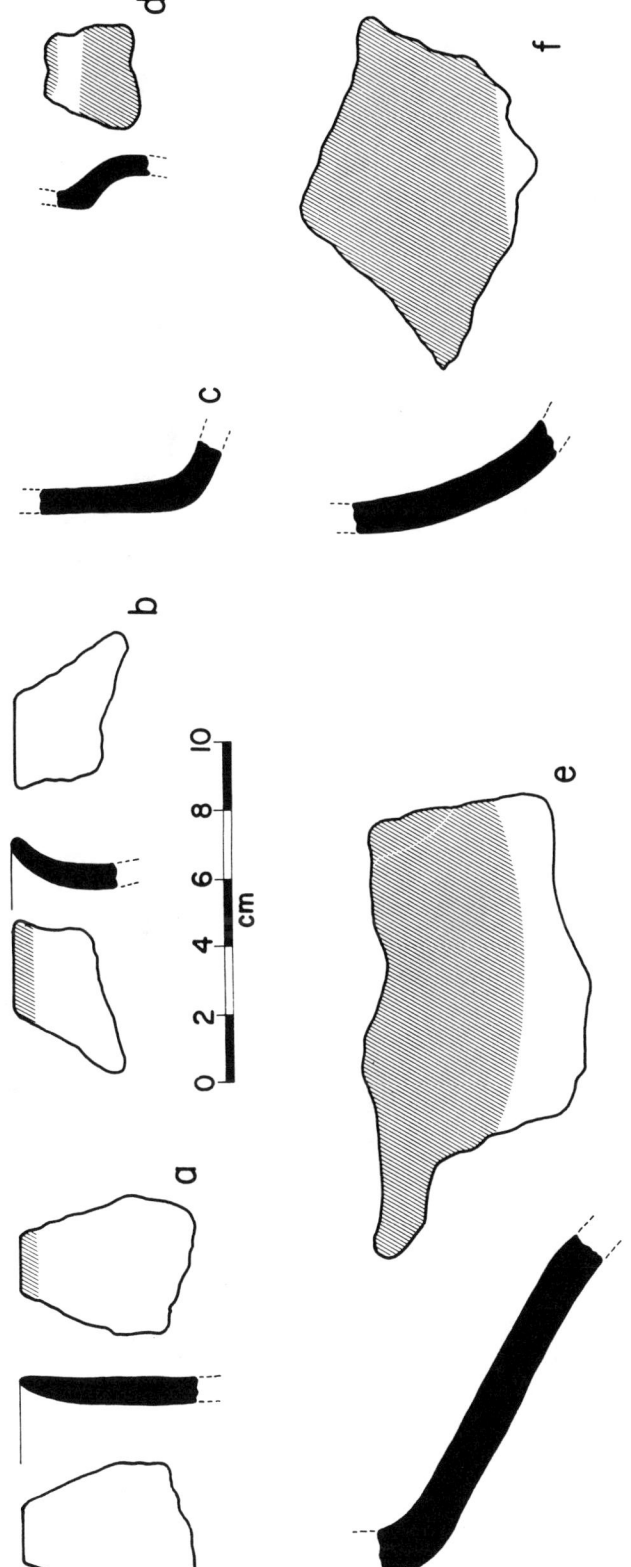

Figure 12.112. San José Red-on-White jar necks and shoulders, all from Area A at San José Mogote (San José phase). *a*, vertical jar neck with red rim band over white slip outside; white-slipped only on rim inside, left unslipped below (Zone D1 midden). *b*, flaring jar neck, white-slipped outside; red band on rim inside, left unslipped below (Zone D2 midden). *c*, jar neck, slipped red over white to shoulder; left white below (Zone D1 midden). *d*, jar shoulder, slipped red over white in bands (Zone D2 midden). *e, f*, jar shoulders slipped red over white as shown (Zone D3 midden).

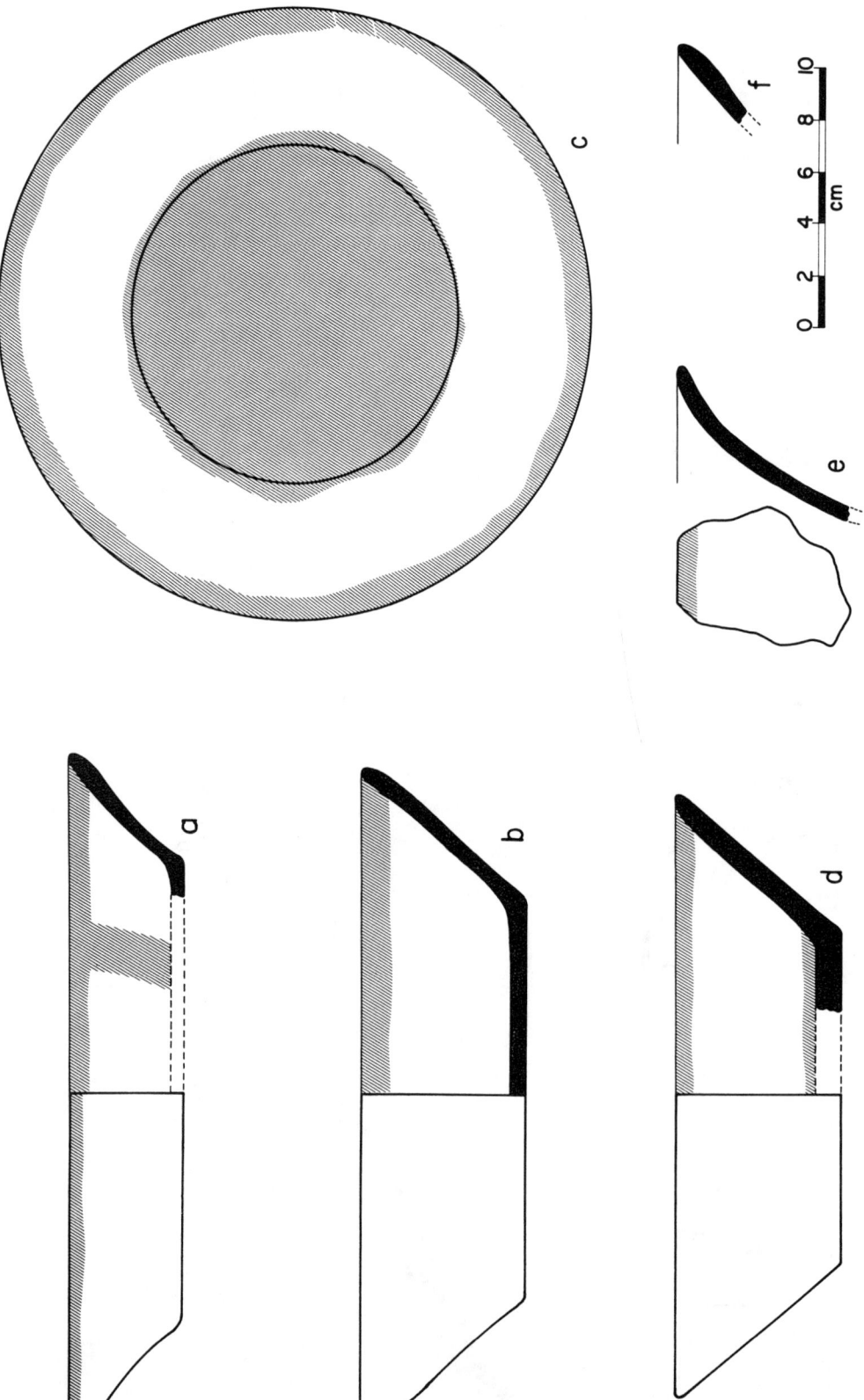

Figure 12.113. San José Red-on-White bowls from San José Mogote (SJM) and Barrio del Rosario Huitzo. *a*, outleaned-wall bowl with red band at rim inside and out, vertical red stripes inside, all over a white slip (Feature 37, Area C, SJM). *b*, outleaned-wall bowl with red band at rim over white slip inside, all white outside (Zone D1 midden, Area A, SJM). *c, d*, two bowls with red band at rim and red base inside, white everywhere else; *c* is an overhead view (Zone D3 midden, Area A, SJM). *e*, rim from bowl with outcurved wall, red band at rim over white slip inside (Zone F1, Area A, Huitzo). *f*, rim from bowl with inside wall slipped red, except for a 1-cm band at the rim that has been left white (Household Unit C3, Area A, SJM). *a–d, f*, San José phase; *e* is from a Guadalupe phase provenience that could contain redeposited San José phase sherds.

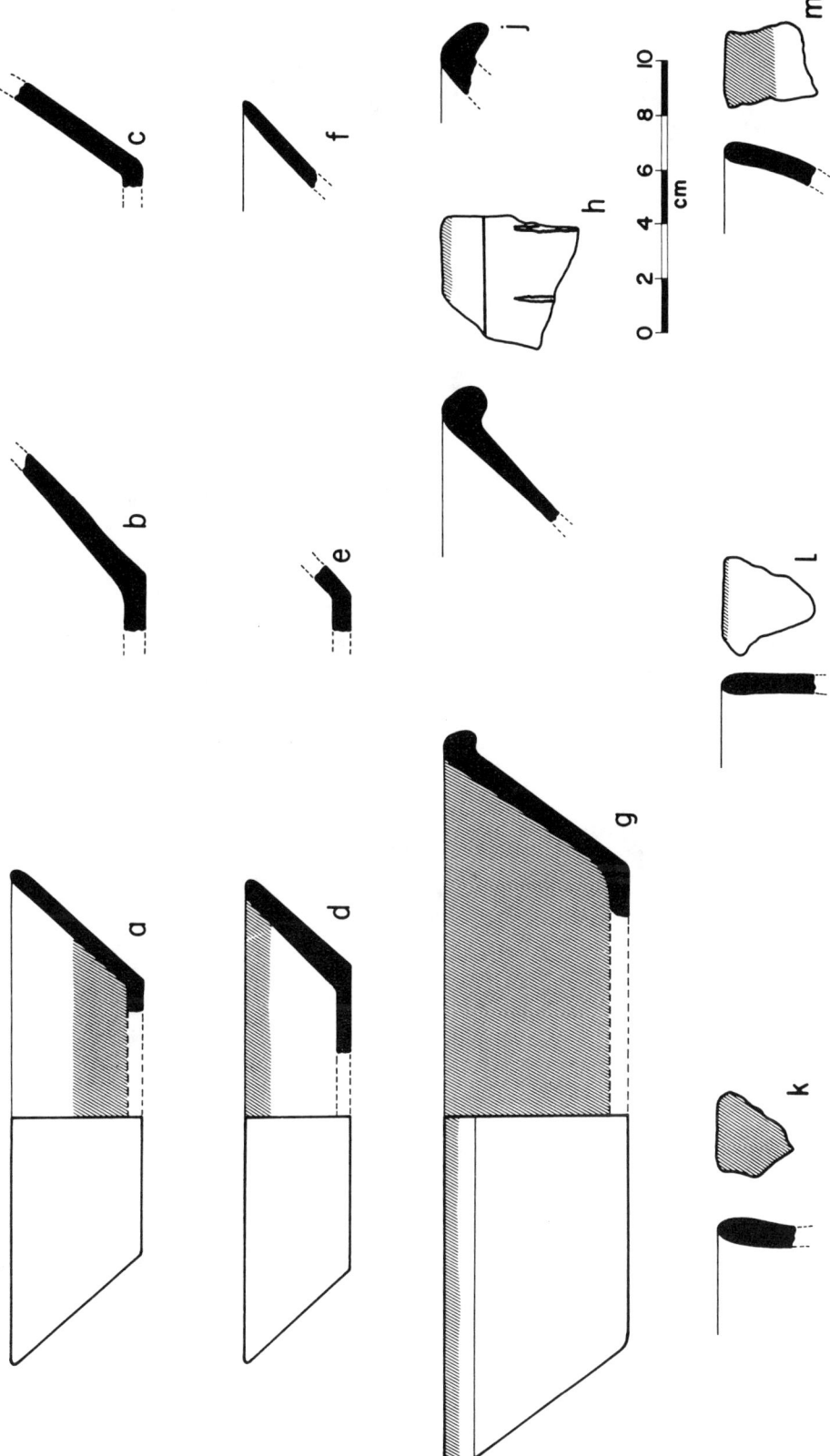

Figure 12.114. San José Red-on-White bowls from Area A of San José Mogote (San José phase). *a–f*, outleaned-wall bowls with red bands on the inside over a white slip. *a* and *f* have a wide red band at the base, while *c* and *e* have a narrow red band at the rim; *b* has a wide red band running around the middle. *d* and *f* have a narrow red band at the rim. *g–j*, bowls with bolstered rims. *g* is slipped solid red inside, and left white outside except for a red band on the rim. *h* and *j* are white-slipped inside, with a red band on the rim, and *h* has shallow grooves on the exterior. *k–l*, cylinders. *k* is solid red outside, and white with a red band at the rim inside; *l* is white with a red band at the rim inside and out. *m*, rim sherd from an oval bowl with pinched-in sides, white with a red band inside and out. *a*, *c*, and *f*, Household Unit C2; *d*, *g*, *j*, *k*, and *l*, Zone D1 midden; *h*, *m*, Zone D2 midden.

238　　　　　　　　　　　　　　　　　　　　　　　　*Early Formative Pottery of Oaxaca*

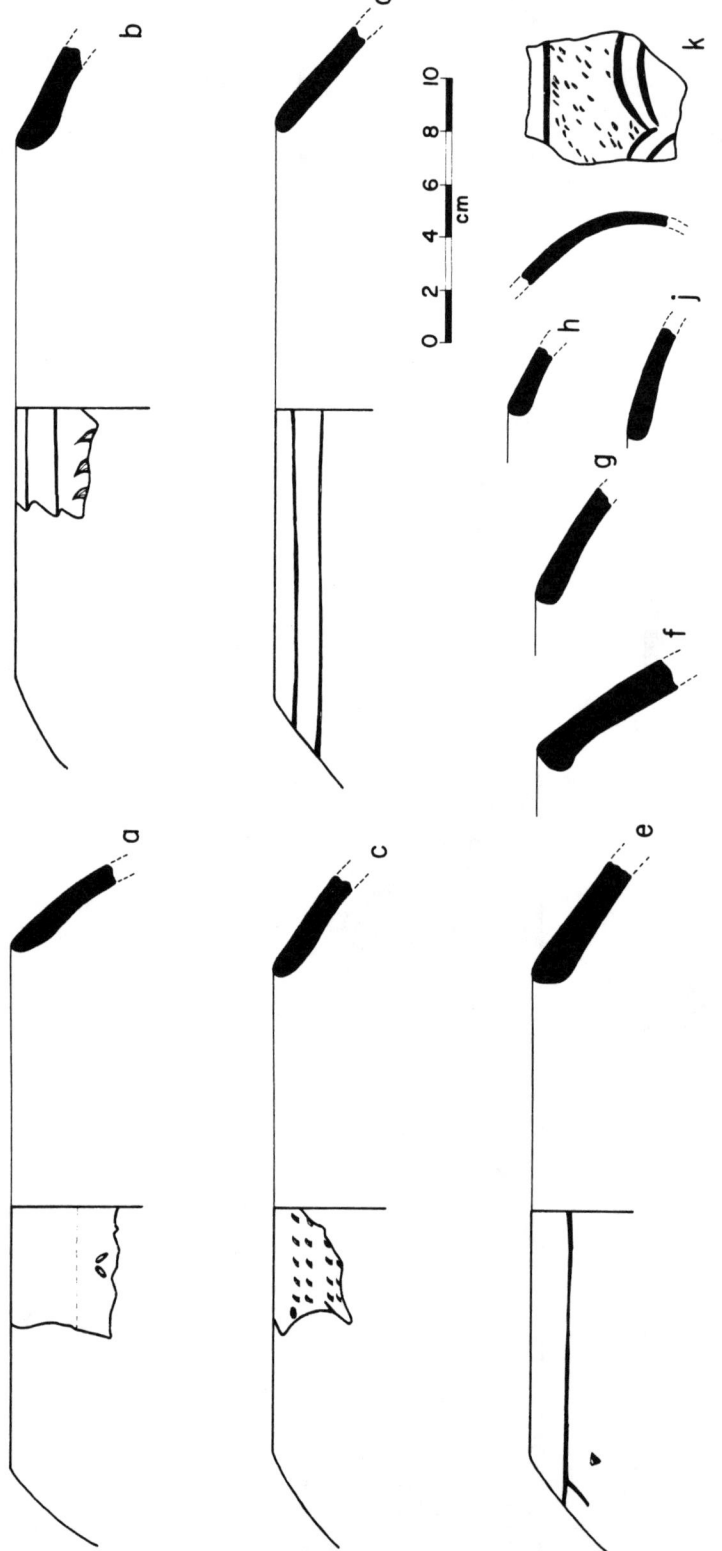

Figure 12.115. Lupita Heavy Plain tecomates from Area A at San José Mogote (San José phase). *a*, tecomate with burnished rim and punctate body, Household Unit C3. *b*, tecomate with burnished band between parallel incised lines at rim, rocker-stamped body; Zone D2 midden. *c*, tecomate with burnished rim, interrupted rocker stamping on body, perforated for suspension; Household Unit C4. *d*, tecomate with parallel incised lines at rim and plain body, Zone D3 midden. *e*, tecomate with burnished band at rim and punctate body, Zone D1 midden. *f, g*, tecomate rims, plain unburnished (*f*, Household Unit C1; *g*, Household Unit C3). *h*, tecomate with burnished rim and plain body, Zone D2 midden. *j*, tecomate rim, plain unburnished, Household Unit C3. *k*, tecomate body sherd with area of punctation (sloppy jab type) enclosed by incising, Household Unit C4.

San José Phase 239

Figure 12.117. Lupita Heavy Plain tecomate sherds with plastic decoration. *Top,* tecomate rim with plain rim outlined by incising, and paired jabs (or "pinches") on the body. *Bottom,* body sherd with zoned deep jabs. The horizontal incised line shows the point below which the tecomate was undecorated. San José Mogote, Area C, found while straightening the profile at the level of the San José phase deposits.

Figure 12.116. Lupita Heavy Plain tecomates with a plain band at the rim (outlined by deep grooves) and a plain body. Both are from Area A, San José Mogote (San José phase). *Left,* Zone D3 midden. *Right,* Zone D2 midden.

Figure 12.119. Lupita Heavy Plain tecomate body sherds decorated with sloppy jabs in zones. Household Unit C3, Area A, San José Mogote (San José phase).

Figure 12.118. Sherds from Lupita Heavy Plain tecomates with spaced pairs of jabs, all from Household Unit C3, Area A, San José Mogote (San José phase). The rim sherd at upper left has a burnished band at the rim, but no incising.

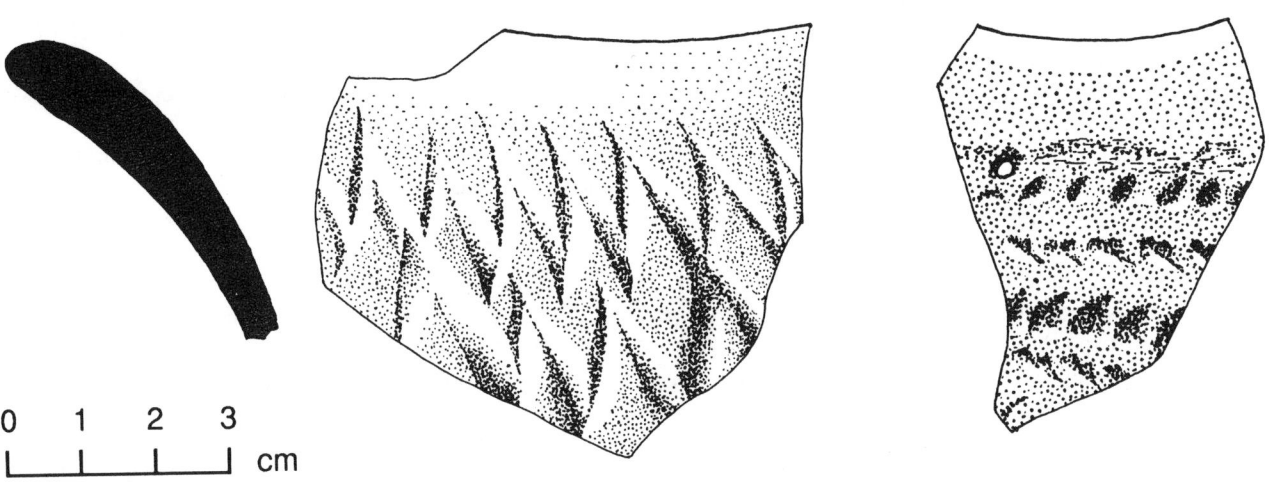

Figure 12.120. Lupita Heavy Plain tecomates with plastic decoration, both from Area A, San José Mogote (San José phase). *Left,* profile and exterior of rim sherd with false rocker stamping, fill of Stage II, Structure 1. *Right,* rim sherd with interrupted rocker stamping, perforated for suspension; Household Unit C4.

It was in the early San José phase that Lupita Heavy Plain appeared in the greatest variety of forms: braziers/potstands, tecomates, outleaned-wall bowls, pigment dishes, spouted trays, multicompartment vessels, *platillos,* and more. However, as mentioned above, at least some of the sherds we have classified as Lupita Heavy Plain could be from unslipped areas on other pottery types. In particular, small rocker stamped tecomate body sherds could be from vessels whose rims or zoning bands were pigmented and therefore got classified as some other type. This is always a problem when so many types are made on the same basic clay body.

The San José phase also witnessed both synchronic and diachronic variation in Lupita Heavy Plain. For example, during the early San José phase, the floors of charcoal braziers/potstands were uniformly plain. Late in the San José phase, some brazier/potstand floors began to show mat impressions; this was an attribute that increased through time, reaching its peak in the Middle Formative.

As for synchronic variation, it was seen most clearly in the distribution of the *platillos* we believe to have been potter's bats—the saucer-like *tournettes* on which a potter can rotate a new vessel he/she is making. Area A households and middens at San José Mogote had a number of these, while Area C households had fewer (Chapter 14). This difference cannot be chronological, since *platillos* existed from the earliest San José phase until Guadalupe times. One possibility, of course, is that more pottery-making was done in Area A than in Area C. However, a possibility that we consider even more likely is this: our excavations in Area C were usually limited to the house itself, while our excavations in Area A included a great deal of the work space in the adjacent dooryard. It is in those dooryards—where most pottery-making was presumably done—that most of the presumed potter's bats were discovered, which could account for the larger numbers in Area A.

We should note, however, that potter's bats were occasionally stored beneath a house floor, as in the case of House 6 in Area C (see Fig. 12.123*l*), where a potter's bat and a pigment dish were found beneath the floor.

During the Guadalupe phase, Lupita Heavy Plain lost a great deal of its variety in vessel forms. Potter's bats continued, but tecomates seem to have died out (in fact, the few tecomate sherds in Guadalupe levels at Huitzo could be redeposited San José phase examples). The bulk of all Lupita Heavy Plain vessels in Guadalupe levels were charcoal braziers/potstands, many with mat-impressed or basketry-impressed floors. Braziers were common in the Guadalupe phase because Guadalupe phase families, like San José phase families before them, cooked in braziers rather than having a hearth inside the house.

Lupita Heavy Plain was present but rare in early Rosario times, disappearing before the end of the phase.

Clay Body

The clay body is a residual piedmont clay resulting from the decomposition of Precambrian gneiss. It was used essentially as found, except perhaps for removal of the larger nonplastic particles. By inspection, roughly 30–35% of the volume of the body is aplastic material; the particles range from 0.25 to 5.0 mm in diameter, with most in the 1.0 mm size range. In Payne's terms, most aplastic particles in Lupita Heavy Plain would be stopped by an 8-mesh geologist's screen. Included are angular fragments of quartz, biotite mica, partially decomposed particles of feldspar and hornblende, and occasional fragments of garnet, all in a base of kaolinite clay. The clay may have been sieved or winnowed before use, but all the nonplastic particles are ones that would have occurred naturally in the clay beds; none appear to have been added.

Firing Temperature

The firing temperature was probably around 700 to 720° C in an oxidizing atmosphere. The purpose of firing at such a low temperature was to produce a ware that would resist thermal shock; this would have been particularly necessary in the case of the charcoal braziers, which might have been subjected to heat every day.

Color

In cross-section, sherds usually show a very dark gray core (2.5 YR N 3/0) sandwiched between pinkish gray outer layers (7.5 YR 6/2). Thinner sherds, which fired one even color throughout, are often reddish brown (5 YR 5/3).

The color of the surface varies from pinkish gray (7.5 YR 6/2) to weak red (10 R 5/2) to dark gray (2.5 YR N 4/0). However, many of the dark gray areas appear to be the result of the walls and floors of the charcoal braziers having been burned with glowing coals.

Surface Treatment

As a general rule, no slip, wash, or stain was ever added to Lupita Heavy Plain. (Fig. 12.123 does show one or two bowls onto which watery white pigment was striped, but they are unique specimens which don't fit any of our other types either.) Typical Lupita vessels have merely been smoothed with the fingers while wet, then finished with a piece of smooth vegetal material such as a section cut from maguey leaf.

Plastic Decoration

Only a few vessel forms in Lupita Heavy Plain ever received plastic decoration. Charcoal braziers/potstands sometimes had mats or baskets pressed into the floor of the vessel while the clay was still wet; in some cases, such impressions might even have been accidental rather than deliberate, as when a slab of clay for the floor of a brazier was rolled out on a mat. Tecomate bodies may show rocker stamping, dentate stamping, or punctation, but as mentioned above, our counts could include small sherds from unslipped areas on other types of tecomates.

Vessel Forms

Tecomates (Figs. 12.115–12.122; see also Fig. 12.130c). As in other wares, these neckless jars began as slabs of clay pounded into a cuplike shape for the base; concentric rings were then added to build up the globular body. Rim profiles are typically blunt or slightly rounded, and most tecomates in this type are of the large, "clunky" type.

Rim diameter: 15–25 cm
Height: Unknown (no complete examples).
Wall thickness: 8–12 mm
Decoration: While many of these tecomates were absolutely plain, some had a band at the rim. This band could be created merely by burnishing the first few centimeters below the rim, while leaving the rest of the vessel plain; alternatively, a band could be indicated by one or two incised lines that encircled the vessel just below the rim. Such simple rim decoration was typical of Lupita Heavy Plain (Fig. 12.116).

The body of the tecomate was most often left plain, but could be divided into zones by means of simple incised lines. These zones could be filled with plain rocker stamping, interrupted rocker stamping, false rocker stamping, dentate stamping, or punctation of various kinds. The various kinds of plastic decoration mirrored those on other San José phase types; indeed, some of the punctation resembled that on the shoulders of Fidencio Coarse jars (see Fig. 12.119). In other cases, tecomates had plastic decoration without zoning (Fig. 12.120).

Flat-based bowls with outleaned walls (Fig. 12.123a–k). Like their Atoyac Yellow-white counterparts, many of these vessels were press-molded inside or outside of previous bowls. Rim profiles are plain and blunt to slightly tapered. One imagines that these less-than-lovely bowls were used for a variety of mundane household tasks.

Rim diameter: 15–24 cm
Height: About 30% of the rim diameter.
Basal diameter: About 70% of the rim diameter.
Wall thickness: 6–10 mm
Decoration: Usually none. Two unusual sherds from the San José phase (Fig. 12.123a, f) have a wash of watery white pigment along the rim; it is not the kind of engobe seen on Atoyac Yellow-white. A few other bowl sherds, mostly from the lower wall, show fragmentary excised or incised decoration (Fig. 12.123b). Those sherds, however, might be from vessels that the potters originally intended to turn into other pottery types—vessels that for one reason or another never got slipped.

Figure 12.121. Lupita Heavy Plain tecomate body sherds, showing several styles of rocker stamping. All specimens are from Area A of San José Mogote (San José phase). *a,* Zone D3 midden. *b, c,* Household Unit C3.

Charcoal braziers and/or potstands (Figs. 12.124–12.129). San José phase houses, for the most part, did not have hearths. Cooking was done over prepared charcoal, usually made from pine but occasionally from oak, manzanita, or mesquite. The charcoal was heated in large, heavy braziers that consisted of a large basin set on an annular base. Since these braziers could be carried from place to place, they allowed cooking to be done anywhere in the household, indoors or outdoors.

When we first saw these vessels, we assumed that we were dealing simply with potstands—vessels that made it possible to keep large globular jars upright by providing a receptacle for their round bases. Similar vessels in Canoas Heavy Plain, called "supported pot stands," had previously been found in the Tehuacán Valley (MacNeish, Peterson, and Flannery 1970: Fig. 40), and we assumed that our vessels were similar. In fact, some of them may have been used that way. However, during a visit to Oaxaca our colleague Gareth W. Lowe pointed out to us that many of our "potstands" were burned on the interior in ways that indicated use as charcoal braziers. Not long after Lowe's visit, this idea was confirmed when we found several braziers with the charcoal still in them, overturned on house floors; House 2 of Area C, San José Mogote, is one example (see Fig. 14.7).

Construction of these braziers/potstands began with a circular slab of clay averaging 12 mm thick; this was to be the "floor" of the vessel, the horizontal surface on which the charcoal rested (and above that, the jar to be heated). Concentric rings of clay were then added to this slab in order to produce the annular base. Next, the slab was turned right side up and concentric rings were added to produce the flaring walls of the receptacle in which the charcoal (or jar base) would be held.

During the late San José phase and the succeeding Guadalupe phase, the upper or lower surface of the vessel floor might show

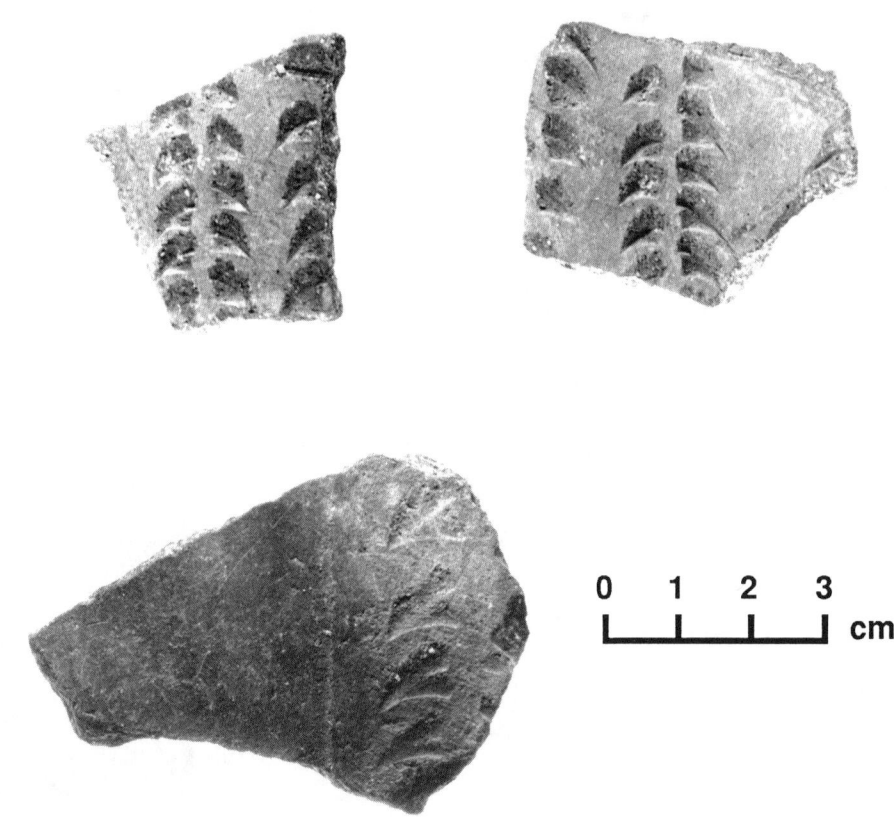

Figure 12.122. Lupita Heavy Plain tecomate body sherds with interrupted rocker stamping in zones. All specimens are from Area A of San José Mogote (San José phase). The sherd at upper left is from the Zone D3 midden; the other two are from the Zone D1 midden. Both the sherds in the top row show the way a vertical line of later burnishing has been used to interrupt the columns of rocker stamping crescents.

impressions of reed mats (*petates*), basketry, or coarse textiles made when the clay was still wet (Figs. 12.128–12.129). While we have considered these impressions to be "plastic decoration," they could originally have begun by accident, when the circular slab of clay that was to become the floor happened to be set on a mat. Whatever the case, the increase in frequency in such impressions over time suggests that they eventually came to be done deliberately.

Rim diameter: 40–60 cm, with most examples near the small end of the range.
Height: Usually about 50% of the rim diameter. One nearly complete specimen with a rim diameter of 52 cm has a height of 24 cm.
Basal diameter: Mostly 22–26 cm, with a few as large as 30 cm.
Wall thickness: 10–22 mm, with most specimens in the 12–16 mm range.

Volume: Most could easily have held 3–4 liters of wood charcoal.
Plastic decoration: Occasional mat impressions (or more rarely, basketry or coarse textile impressions) on the floor of the receptacle.

Platillos: possible potter's bats (Fig. 12.123l-p). These are low, saucer-shaped vessels, whose wear patterns suggested to Payne that they were *tournettes* or "potter's bats" for forming San José phase and Guadalupe phase pottery (see Chapter 2). When such small bats are turned slowly by hand, a pattern of concentric scratches appears on the base. Our specimens show such scratches.

Each *platillo* was made from a single circular pat of clay, probably pressed over the bottom of an inverted jar or hemispherical bowl to give it its shape. Most of the complete (or nearly complete) examples we discovered came not from

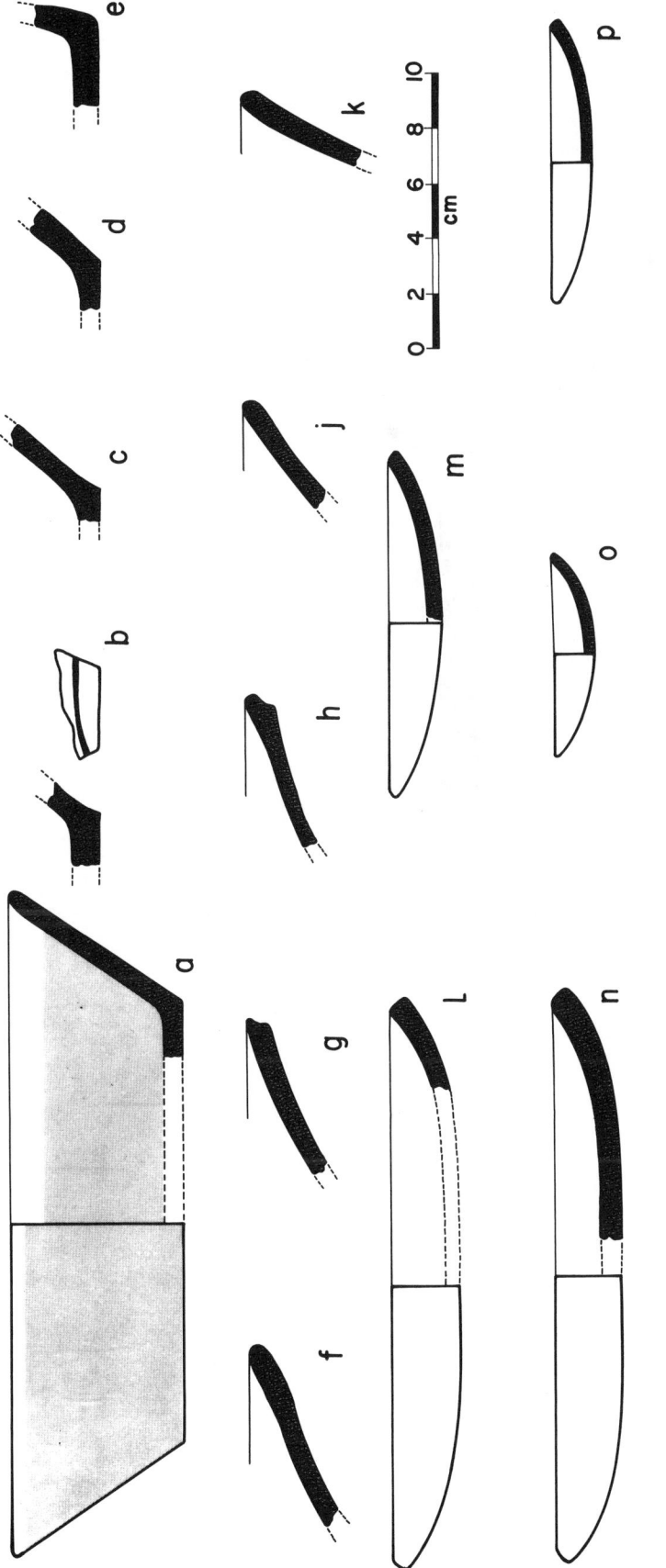

Figure 12.123. Lupita Heavy Plain bowls and *platillos* (probable potter's bats) from San José Mogote (SJM) and Tierras Largas. All specimens are San José phase. *a*, outleaned-wall bowl with unusual band of white wash at rim inside and out, Household Unit C4, Area A, SJM. *b*, basal angle sherd with excised line on outside, Zone D3 midden, Area A, SJM. *c–e*, basal angle sherds, plain (*c, d*, Zone D2 midden, Area A, SJM; *e*, Household Unit C3, Area A, SJM). *f*, rim of outleaned-wall bowl with unusual band of white wash at rim (like *a*), Zone D1 midden, Area A, SJM. *g–k*, rims from outleaned-wall bowls, plain (*g*, Zone D2 midden, Area A, SJM; *h, j*, Household Unit C4, Area A, SJM; *k*, Zone D1 midden, Area A, SJM). *l–p, platillos* or shallow dishes, believed to be *tournettes* or potter's bats. *l*, specimen found below House 6, Area C, SJM, in association with Leandro Gray pigment dish (Fig. 12.74*l*), in what may have been a potter's cache below the house floor. *m–p*, four specimens from House 1, Area A, Tierras Largas; this house seems to have been used as a work area after its abandonment.

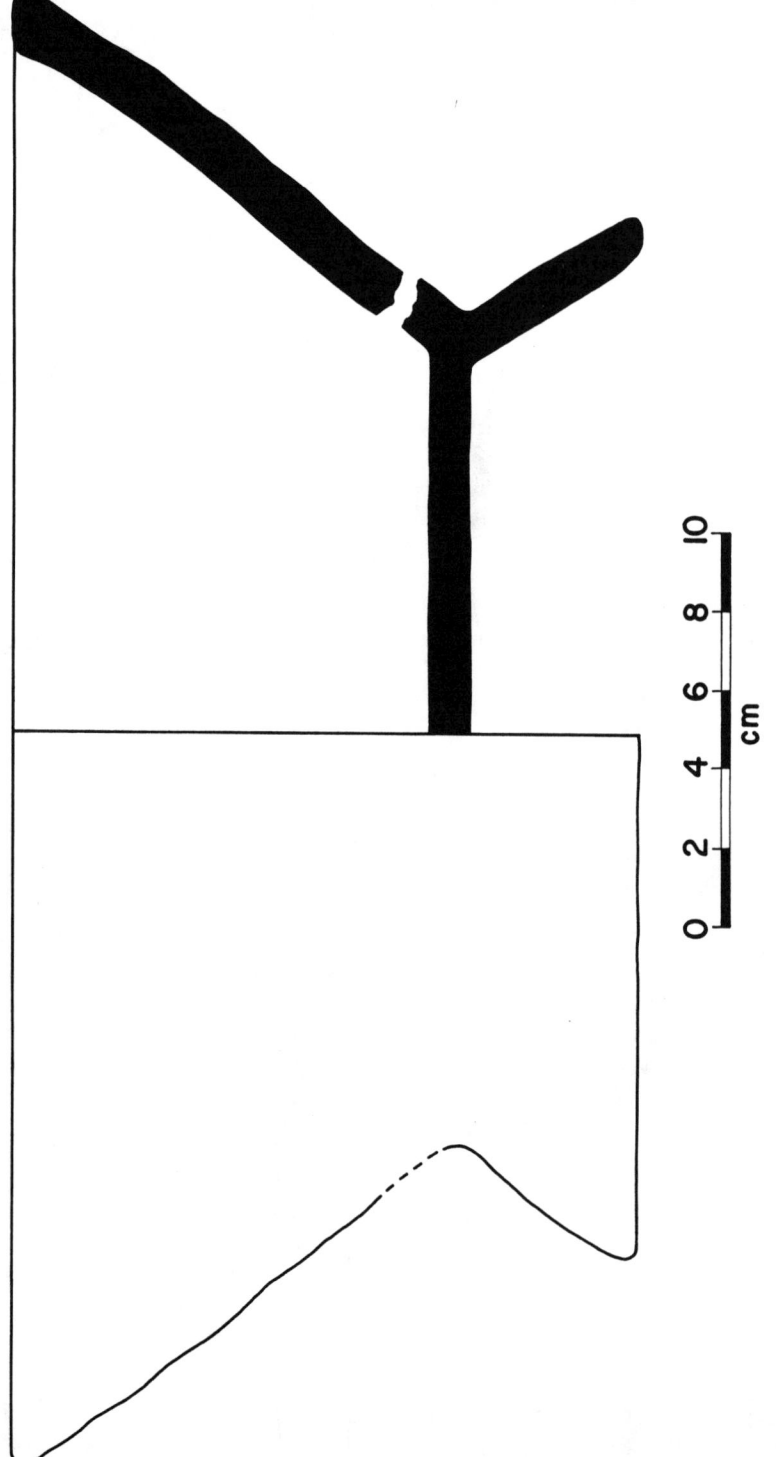

Figure 12.124. Lupita Heavy Plain charcoal brazier or potstand from below House 6, Area C, San José Mogote (San José phase).

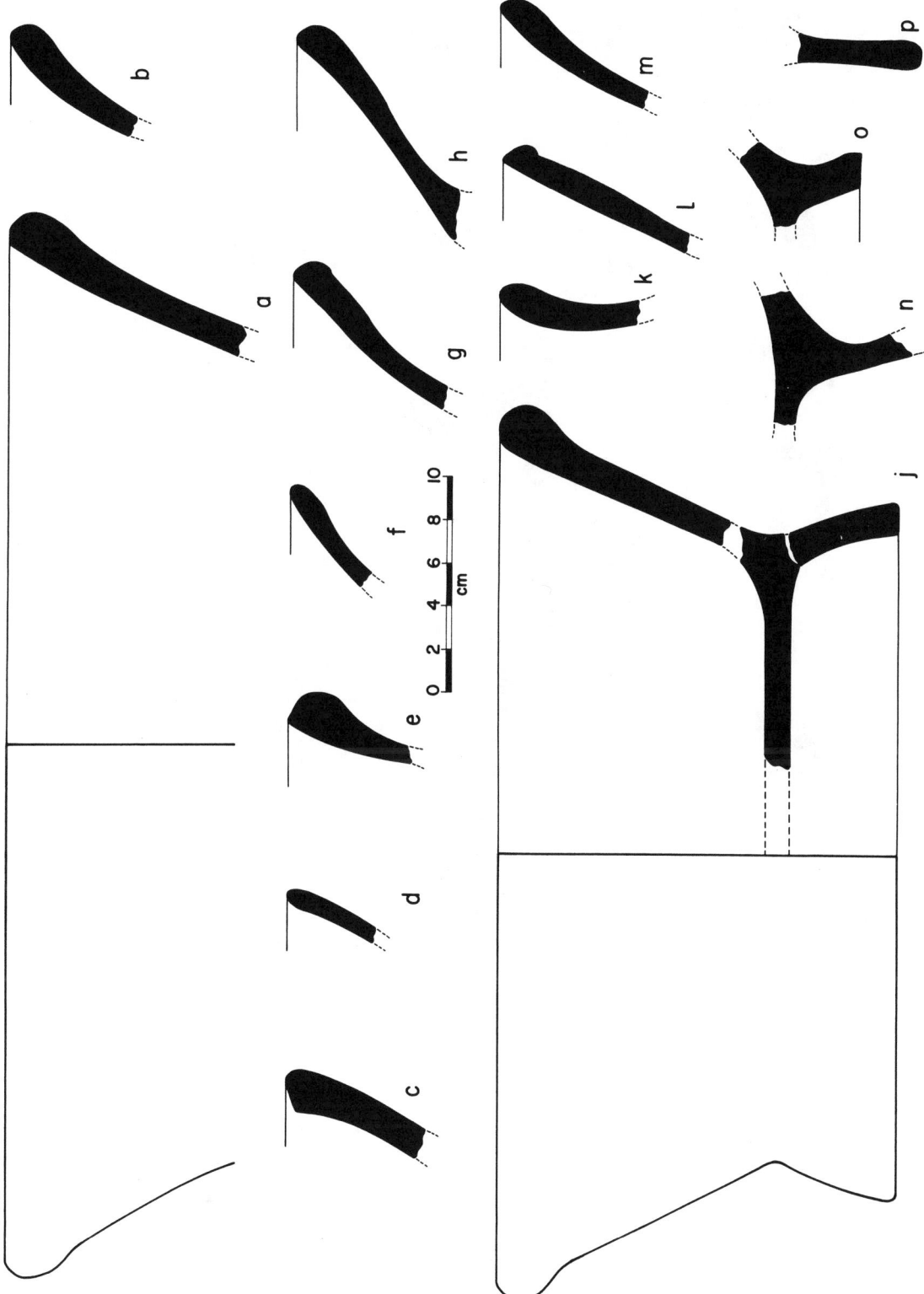

Figure 12.125. Lupita Heavy Plain charcoal braziers or potstands from San José Mogote (SJM) and Barrio del Rosario Huitzo. *a,* upper half of specimen from Zone C4, Area A, Huitzo. *b-h,* rim sherds (*b, e,* cutting profile, Area A, Huitzo; *c, g,* Zone D1 midden, Area A, SJM; *d,* Household Unit C3, Area A, SJM; *f,* Structure 4, Area A, Huitzo; *h,* Household Unit C4, Area A, SJM). *j,* Vessel 2, House 2, Area C, SJM (reconstructed from sherds piece-plotted on the house floor). *k-m,* rim sherds (*k,* House 7, Area A, Huitzo; *l,* Household Unit C4, Area A, SJM; *m,* cutting profile, Area A, Huitzo). *n-p,* basal sherds, all from Area A, SJM (*n,* Household Unit C4; *o,* Household Unit C2; *p,* Household Unit C3). Specimen *o* has an unusual band of red wash on the outside of the base. All specimens from SJM are San José phase. *f* is from an early Guadalupe phase provenience that could contain redeposited San José phase sherds. All other specimens from Huitzo are Guadalupe phase.

248 Early Formative Pottery of Oaxaca

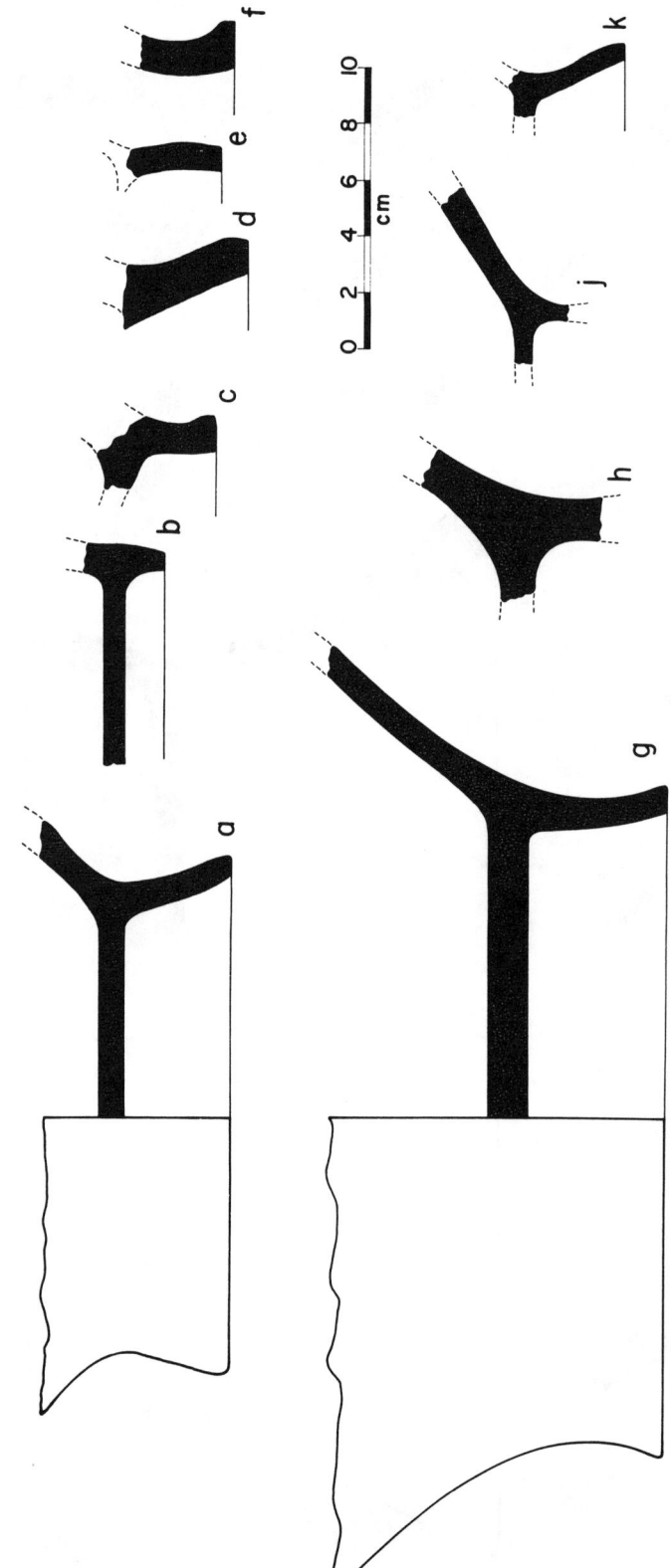

Figure 12.126. Lupita Heavy Plain charcoal braziers or potstands from San José Mogote (SJM) and Barrio del Rosario Huitzo. a, lower half of specimen found while cutting profile of Area C, SJM. b-f, basal sherds (b, Zone D, Area A, Huitzo; c, d, Household Unit C3, Area A, SJM; e, f, Zone E2, Area A, Huitzo). g, lower half of specimen found while cleaning profile, Zones F1-F3, Area A, Huitzo. h-k, basal sherds (h, j, cutting profile, Area A, Huitzo; k, Zone E1, Area A, Huitzo). All specimens from SJM are San José phase; g is from an early Guadalupe phase provenience that could contain redeposited San José phase sherds. All other specimens from Huitzo are Guadalupe phase.

San José Phase

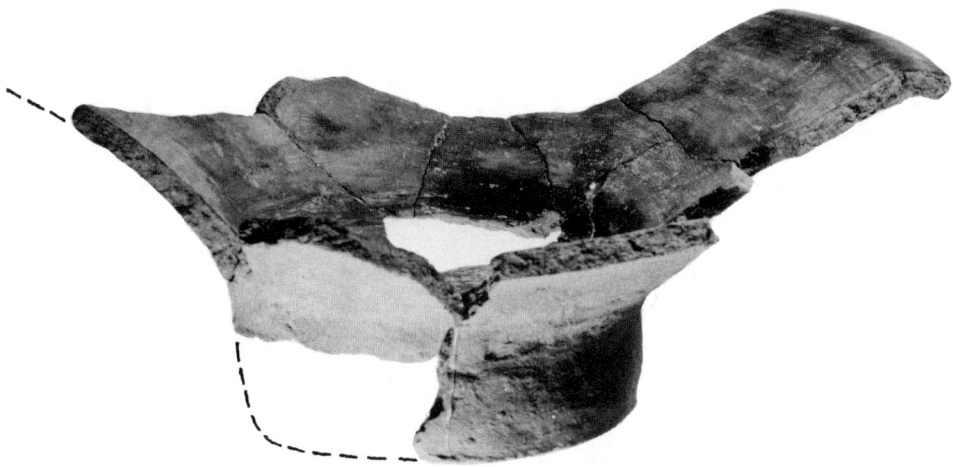

Figure 12.127. Broken Lupita Heavy Plain charcoal brazier or potstand (probably the former, judging from the dark stains on the interior). This vessel, which would once have had a basal diameter of 22 cm, preserves a rim-to-base cross-section. Vessel 8, Square C13, House 1, Area A, Tierras Largas (San José phase).

Figure 12.128. Fragment of Lupita Heavy Plain charcoal brazier or potstand with mat-impressed floor. Barrio del Rosario Huitzo, Area C; found while cleaning profile at level of Guadalupe phase deposits.

Figure 12.129. Lupita Heavy Plain charcoal brazier or potstand. On the right is a sherd from the floor of the vessel, showing the impression of a reed mat (*petate*) made while the clay was still damp. On the left is a plasticine impression made from the sherd, showing what the mat looked like. This sherd is from a level that, although dating to the Rosario phase, contained many redeposited sherds of the San José and Guadalupe phases. (San José Mogote, Mound 1, Zone C, overburden above Structure 19.)

middens, but from household units. House 1 at Tierras Largas alone produced at least three, and there were others in the dooryards of houses in Area A of San José Mogote. One (Fig. 12.123*l*) was stored below the floor of House 6 in Area C at the latter site, in association with a Leandro Gray pigment dish (Fig. 12.74*l*).

As described in Chapter 2, Formative potter's bats were probably rotated on inverted jars, just as they are today in villages like Atzompa (Fig. 2.3).

Rim diameter: 6–20 cm, with most in the 10–12 cm range.
Height: 1.5–3.0 cm
Wall thickness: 4–10 mm
Plastic decoration: None

Pigment dishes/spouted trays. We occasionally found small rim sherds that may be from either pigment dishes or spouted trays. They are so close in shape to pigment dishes/spouted trays in Atoyac Yellow-white that they may simply be unslipped versions of the latter.

Multicompartment vessels (Fig. 12.130). These vessels, sometimes referred to as "relish trays" because of their resemblance to the multicompartmental condiment holders used by some restaurants, have been found both at La Venta (Drucker 1952:122) and Chiapa de Corzo (Dixon 1959: Fig. 11*a*). Each vessel is like a small dish divided by low partitions into several round or rectangular compartments that could have held sauces, pigments, herbal seasoning, or some other material. They vary in height from 4 cm (Fig. 12.130*a*) to over 8 cm (Fig. 12.130*b*), but their full dimensions cannot be given, owing to a lack of complete specimens. Our best examples come from a midden in the vicinity of the magnetite-working households in Area A of San José Mogote. So far, no examples have come from truly "low status" households. It is possible that meals in medium-to-high-status households involved more use of sauces and/or condiments, and that multicompartment vessels were more common in such contexts.

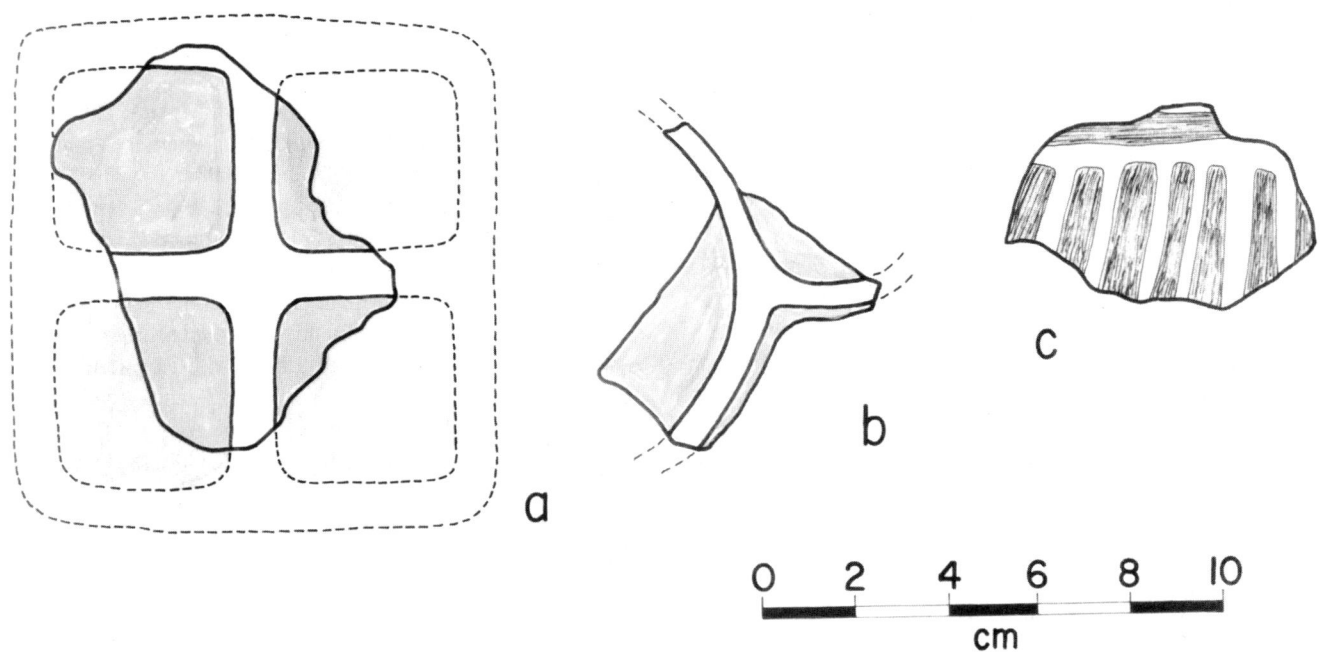

Figure 12.130. Unusual Lupita Heavy Plain vessels from Area A, San José Mogote (San José phase). *a,* top view of multicompartment vessel with rectangular compartments, Zone D2 midden (height, 4 cm). *b,* top view of multicompartment vessel with circular compartments, Zone D2 midden (height, > 8 cm). *c,* unusual tecomate (?) body sherd with deep sculpturing or fluting (recessed areas shaded), Household Unit C4.

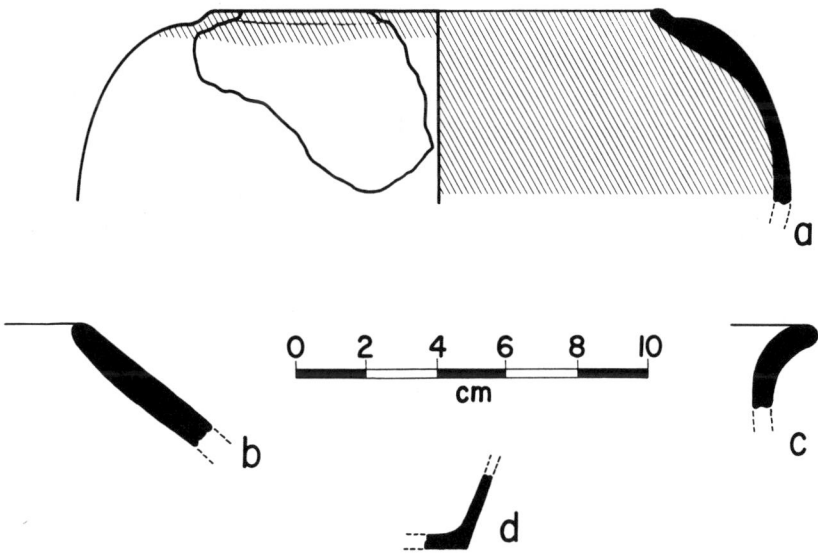

Figure 12.131. Vessels combining Atoyac Yellow-white and Matadamas Orange slips, from San José Mogote (SJM) and Tierras Largas (TL). *a,* tecomate with Atoyac Yellow-white slip outside, Matadamas Orange slip inside, plus a band of Matadamas Orange on the outside of the rim (over the white); found while cleaning profile of earliest San José phase levels, Area C, SJM. *b,* tecomate rim, white-slipped outside, orange-slipped inside; Household Unit C3, Area A, SJM. *c,* jar rim, white-slipped outside, orange-slipped inside; Household Unit C3, Area A, SJM. *d,* basal angle sherd from outleaned-wall bowl, white-slipped outside, orange-slipped inside; Feature 148, Area C, TL. (*d,* late Tierras Largas phase; *a-c,* San José phase.)

HYBRID TYPE: ATOYAC YELLOW-WHITE OUTSIDE, MATADAMAS ORANGE INSIDE

General Description

About the time that the kaolin engobe of Atoyac Yellow-white was introduced—and while Matadamas Orange pottery was still popular—some Formative Oaxaca potters tried combining attributes of both types. The vessel forms they used were borrowed either from Matadamas Orange (jars, small tecomates, and hemispherical bowls) or from Atoyac Yellow-white (large tecomates, incurved-rim bowls, and outleaned-wall bowls). What the potters usually did was swab kaolin white engobe on the exterior of the vessel, while coating the interior with orange-firing ferrous clay. Because this hybrid type was relatively short-lived, yet shows up at several sites, it constitutes a good horizon marker for the final moments of the Tierras Largas phase and the early part of the San José phase.

Chronological History

Vessels combining Atoyac Yellow-white and Matadamas Orange surfaces first appeared at the Tierras Largas phase/San José phase transition and lasted until middle San José times.

Physical Characteristics

The clay body and firing temperature of this type are identical to those of Atoyac Yellow-white; so are the surface color and treatment of the exterior. The surface color and treatment of the interior are identical to those of Matadamas Orange.

Vessel Forms

This hybrid type has no distinctive shape of its own; it merely borrows forms from the two types whose surface color it shares. Included among the various borrowed vessel forms are: tecomates (Fig. 12.131*a, b*); hemispherical bowls; bowls with incurved rims; flat-based bowls with outleaned walls (Fig. 12.131*d*); and jars (Fig. 12.131*c*).

SAN JOSE BLACK-AND-WHITE

General Description

All over Mesoamerica, at a time equivalent to the early San José phase, potters were experimenting with combinations of oxidation and reduction to produce vessels with patches or clouds of black and white. Here is another case where we badly need a generic category to incorporate all the named pottery types: Pampas Black-and-White from the Guatemalan Coast (Coe and Flannery 1967: Figs. 14–15); Suristmo Gloss Black-and-White Slipped from Tehuantepec (Zeitlin 1979: Figs. D-46 to D-49); San José Black-and-White from the Valley of Oaxaca (this volume); Tular Black-and-White and Perdida Black-and-White from southern Veracruz (Coe and Diehl 1980: Figs. 154–157); and Valle Bord Négatif from the Basin of Mexico (Niederberger 1987: Figs. 421–429). (We are uncertain whether White-rimmed Black from Morelos [Cyphers Guillén 1987: Fig. 13.33] should be included in this group, since it appears to be a standard white-rimmed black ware more properly compared with Coatepec White-rimmed Black of Tehuacán and Oaxaca; see below.)

Unlike the hard, well-made, white-rimmed black wares of later periods, the early black-and-white types listed in the paragraph above can be white with a black rim as often as they are black with a white rim. What they really feature are alternating, irregular patches of white and black that give the impression of light and dark clouds rolling across a stormy sky. This analogy is particularly apt because we consider many of the excised designs on San José Black-and-White to be stylized representations of Sky or lightning (Marcus 1989).

Vessel forms in San José Black-and-White are essentially the same as those in Atoyac Yellow-white, and the cream-colored kaolin engobe used was similar to that used on Atoyac vessels. Some cylindrical bowls share excised motifs with Leandro Gray, including the pan-Mesoamerican fire-serpent and crossed bands (St. Andrew's cross).

Chronological History

San José Black-and-White made its first appearance late in the Tierras Largas phase. The occasional sherds found in such levels seem to be from cylindrical bowls; unless those sherds were intrusive, they represent one of the earliest occurrences of cylinders in our sequence.

In the early San José phase, this black-and-white ware appeared in the form of excised cylinders, undecorated outleaned-wall bowls, bolstered-rim bowls, and bottles. By late San José phase times the bottles seem to have dropped out, but the three other vessel forms continued.

San José Black-and-White died out during the early Guadalupe phase, with outleaned-wall bowls being the last vessel form to disappear.

Clay Body

The clay body is a residual piedmont clay resulting from the decomposition of weathered Precambrian gneiss, essentially identical to that used for Atoyac Yellow-white.

Firing Temperature

The firing temperature was probably 700 to 720° C. San José Black-and-White was differentially subjected to strong reduction and neutral (or weakly oxidized) conditions in order to produce the characteristic color pattern.

Possible Methods of Differential Firing

In their descriptions of Pampas Black-and-White, an analogous pottery type from the Pacific Coast of Guatemala, Coe and Flannery (1967:33) suggested three alternative methods of firing that could have produced the ware's cloudy appearance. According to Payne, the method used to produce San José Black-and-White could have been any of those firing alternatives. We therefore repeat those alternatives here.

1. For a vessel with a white rim, black interior and black exterior: First, the entire vessel is fired so as to *oxidize* to white (or clear buff). Then, the inverted vessel is placed on a material like loose sand so that a portion of the rim is buried, with smudging material (possibly corncobs) inside and over it; it is fired for the second time in a reducing, smudging atmosphere which blackens all but the buried rim.

2. For the same kind of vessel, it is theoretically possible that the vessel is first smudged black all over, then buried upright in sand with only the rim protruding, and fired for a second time in an oxidizing atmosphere.

3. For a vessel with a white rim, black interior, white (or clear buff) exterior, the inverted vessel is placed over a second bowl which contains smudging material to ignite when fired. The exterior is fired in an oxidizing atmosphere, that portion of the interior enclosed by the second bowl being reduced to black; the slip inside the rim fires to white, the unslipped exterior to buff.

Color

In sherd cross-sections, the clay body fires very dark gray (7.5 YR N3/ to 10 YR 3/1); however, immediately below the white areas of the surface it may show patches of weak red (2.5 YR 4/2). The cloudy black areas of the surface range from true black (7.5 R N2/) to dark gray (7.5 YR N4/). The cloudy white areas vary from slightly off-white (10 YR 8/2) to light gray (2.5 Y 7/2) or very pale brown (10 YR 7/3).

Surface Treatment

After it was formed, the vessel was left rough, or at most, smoothed with a piece of gourd. Over this was applied the same white kaolin engobe used on Atoyac Yellow-white. The application of engobe varied from very even (when the vessel was dipped, or the slip poured on) to streaky (when it was swabbed on). The vessel was then burnished once with a quartz pebble when leather-hard, usually resulting in a dull gloss.

Plastic Decoration

Where present, plastic decoration usually consisted of carving or excising (*raspada*), done with an instrument like a slat of cane (*carrizo*). Often incising (*sgraffito*) was combined with excising. In some cases, it is possible to see that excised designs were sketched out in advance by light incising with a tool like a maguey spine. The designs often resemble those seen on Leandro Gray, but the range of motifs is not identical.

Addition of Dry Red Pigment

As in the case of Leandro Gray, dry red hematite powder was often rubbed into the roughened or excised areas on San José Black-and-White. The color of the pigment is close to 7.5 R 4/8 in the Munsell system. It is fugitive, and serves mainly to highlight the motif against the cloudy black-white background.

Vessel Forms

Flat-based bowls with vertical (or nearly vertical) walls (Figs. 12.132–12.134). These cylindrical bowls are close to Leandro Gray cylinders in overall shape and rim profile, but tend to be slightly smaller on average.
  Rim diameter: 6–30 cm
  Height: Usually about half the rim diameter.
  Wall thickness: 4–8 mm
  Plastic decoration: Excised motifs, or combinations of excising and incising, are common. The designs include fire-serpents, brackets, St. Andrew's crosses, and other pan-Mesoamerican motifs.

Flat-based bowls with outleaned walls (Fig. 12.135a-g). In shape, rim profile, and dimensions these are so similar to outleaned-wall bowls in Leandro Gray that the description and size ranges are not repeated here.
  Plastic decoration: Rare. A few examples may have excising or incising, but for the most part the sherds we recovered were too small to show the entire motif.

Bowls with bolstered-rim (Fig. 12.135h-k). These are so similar in shape, rim profile, and dimensions to bolstered-rim bowls in Leandro Gray that the description and size ranges are not repeated here.
  Plastic decoration: Rare. A few examples have incised lines on the bolstered rim. Interestingly, we found no examples with the exterior wall below the rim left unburnished and rough as a background for excising, as we did with Leandro Gray. Possibly the black-and-white clouds were considered decoration enough.

Bottles/jars with vertical necks (Fig. 12.135l). Occasional sherds of San José Black-and-White are from bottles or tall-necked jars. The sherds are often too small to enable us to distinguish between those two vessel shapes, so we have combined them on some ceramic charts. The example illustrated in Figure 12.135*l* had a rim diameter of 8 cm and would thus fall in our "jar" category. Few dimensions are available on the other bottle/jar sherds.

Effigy vessels (Fig. 12.136). We found occasional fragments of effigy vessels like the one shown in Figure 12.136. Most appear to represent birds, recalling some effigy vessels from the Basin of Mexico.

XOCHILTEPEC WHITE

General Description

This widely traded luxury ware is normally pure white or ivory clear through. In spite of comments by earlier workers, it is never slipped. Previous analysts were perhaps deceived by its very glossy surface, which was actually produced by double burnishing. Bottles, tecomates, collared tecomates, cylinders, fluted oval bowls with pinched-in sides, and composite silhouette bowls were all made in this type. Some vessels found in Oaxaca might have been imported from some Gulf Coast site like San Lorenzo, Veracruz. Others are so different as to suggest that there was a Oaxaca variety of the type as well as a San Lorenzo variety.

Xochiltepec White as an Export Ware

Excavating in Jocotal phase deposits of the Guatemalan Pacific Coast, Coe and Flannery (1967:60) found several sherds of a fine imported ware that was "white clear through." Not long afterward, in the Tehuacán Valley, MacNeish, Peterson, and Flannery (1970:84) recovered 44 sherds that were "snow-white from surface to surface." Ramón Piña Chan (pers. comm.) recognized these sherds as belonging to the type he had called "kaolin ware" at Tlatilco in the Basin of Mexico. He also recalled seeing similar pure white pottery in Morelos, an observation since confirmed by Cyphers Guillén (1987:210). Over the years it has become clear that this "kaolin" or "white-clear-through" pottery was widespread in Early and Middle Formative Mesoamerica, almost always rare and usually considered imported wherever it was found.

Finally, at San Lorenzo in Veracruz, Coe and Diehl (1980:152) decided to give this luxury ware a name: Xochiltepec White. They went on to suggest that it may have been made on the southern Gulf Coast, since suitable white kaolin clay "is available to potters today at La Chogostera, in the Coatzacoalcos Basin" and was probably the source used by the San Lorenzo potters (Coe and Diehl 1980:171). They also suggested that San Lorenzo may have been the source of imported "white-clear-through" pottery for many highland sites.

While we have no doubt that Xochiltepec White was exported by San Lorenzo to other parts of Mesoamerica (including Oaxaca), there are problems with any model of a single origin for "white-clear-through" or "kaolin" pottery. To begin with, there are alternative sources of pure white kaolin in the Nochixtlán Valley of Oaxaca (see Fig. 2.2e), in the mountains east of Mitla, in the Chalcatzingo region of Morelos (Grove 1987: Fig. 23.1), and in many other parts of Mesoamerica. Second, the descriptions of "white-clear-through" pottery and its vessel shapes are different from region to region.

"White-clear-through" sherds from Salinas La Blanca, Guatemala, were described as having a "bentonitic, untempered" clay body with "pumice spicules and glass fragments" (Coe and Flannery 1967:60). The shapes included a cylindrical bowl and a jar neck/annular base(?) sherd. Xochiltepec White sherds from San Lorenzo, on the other hand, were described as having a "pure white to ivory kaolin" clay body, and the shapes included tecomates, collared jars, and bottles (Coe and Diehl 1980:152, 171). What we have called Xochiltepec White at San José Mogote, Oaxaca, clearly comes from several different sources. Some vessels, probably imported, fit Coe and Diehl's description of Xochiltepec White at San Lorenzo. Other vessels, probably locally made, have a clay body derived from kaolinized feldspar, possibly from a vein or dike in the Oaxaca mountains.

Thus, at the moment, "Xochiltepec White" is a pan-Mesoamerican pottery type that almost certainly consists of several varieties: a San Lorenzo variety, a Guatemalan Coast variety, a Oaxaca Valley variety, and perhaps a Valley of Mexico variety. The San Lorenzo variety was certainly widely traded, but in areas like the Valley of Oaxaca it coexisted with locally made varieties. Gulf Coast specialists will surely be tempted to see these local varieties as imitations of the San Lorenzo variety, and some may well be just that. However, some other local varieties occur in vessel forms that do not appear at San Lorenzo at all.

We consider Xochiltepec White to be such an important example of pan-Mesoamerican trade ware that we would actively discourage the creation of separate local type names. Considering all these local ceramics to be varieties of one widespread type emphasizes an important phenomenon: important luxury wares tend to become imitated almost as soon as they appear. The mental template "Xochiltepec White," serving as a model of what luxury pottery should look like, is every bit as important as the raw material of which the actual vessels were made.

Finally, as we suggested earlier, we believe that Xochiltepec White may also have provided the model for Atoyac Yellow-white and other Early Formative white-slipped wares.

Chronological History

During the late Tierras Largas phase, Xochiltepec White was present in the vicinity of public buildings in Area C at San José Mogote. It took the form of bottles like those from the Chicharras phase at San Lorenzo; most were probably imported from outside the Valley of Oaxaca.

During the early San José phase, Xochiltepec White appeared mainly as bottles, tecomates, collared tecomates, and cylindrical bowls. In the second half of the phase these shapes continued, and were joined by outleaned-wall bowls. San José phase vessels included both imported varieties and what may be local varieties. The imported varieties resemble San Lorenzo phase specimens from Veracruz.

The vessel repertoire changed during the Guadalupe phase,

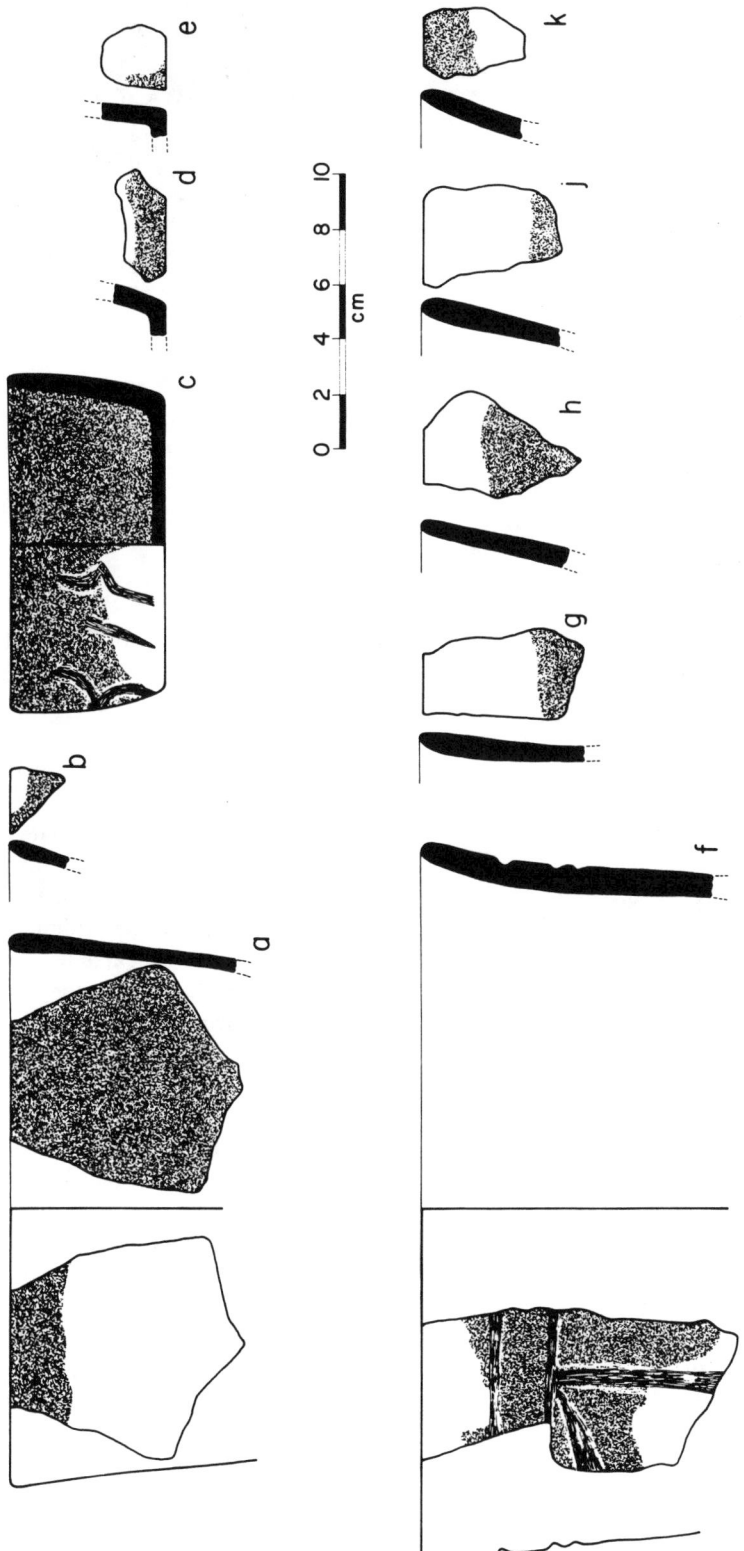

Figure 12.132. San José Black-and-White cylinders or bowls with nearly vertical walls, all from Area A, San José Mogote (San José phase). *a, b,* plain cylinders (*a,* Zone D3 midden; *b,* Zone D2 midden). *c,* low cylinder with Pyne's Motif 11 excised on the outside, Stage I of Structure 1. *d, e,* basal angle sherds (*d,* Zone D1 midden; *e,* Household Unit D2). *f,* tall cylinder with excising, Household Unit C3. *g–k,* rim sherds, plain (*g,* Household Unit C4; *h, j,* Zone D1 midden; *k,* Zone D2 midden).

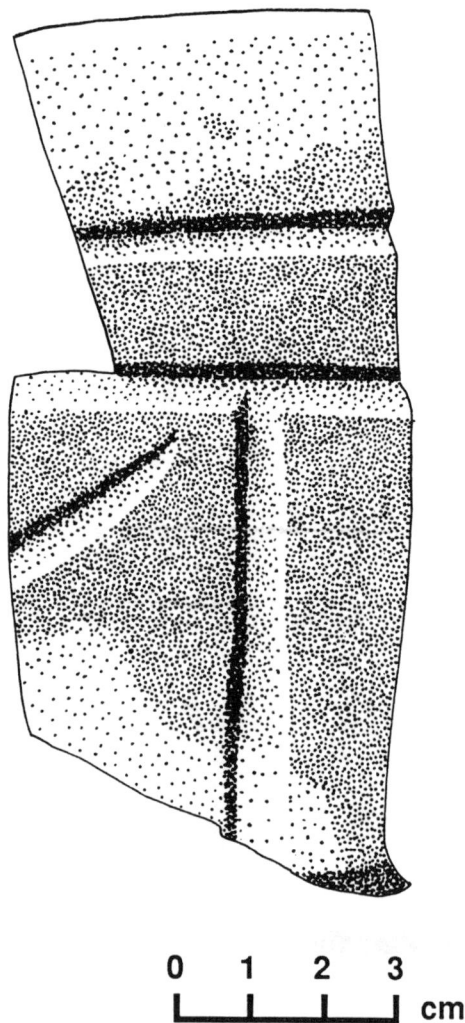

Figure 12.133. Rim sherd from San José Black-and-White cylinder with deep carving on the exterior. The stipple indicates the cloudlike patterns of black and white on the surface. This sherd is also shown in Figure 12.132*f*. Household Unit C3, Area A, San José Mogote (San José phase).

reflecting widespread stylistic preferences throughout Mexico. While cylinders and outleaned-wall bowls continued, there were new shapes such as fluted bowls with pinched-in sides, composite silhouette bowls, and bowls with flaring or outcurving walls. These Middle Formative vessels resemble specimens from the Tehuacán Valley rather than from Veracruz.

Xochiltepec White gradually disappeared during the course of the Guadalupe phase.

Clay Body

Of necessity, Xochiltepec White had to be made on an iron-free white kaolin clay. However, inspection of a wide range of samples convinced Payne that our vessels were coming from more than one source. One body was a fine-grained, kaolinized

Figure 12.134. San José Black-and-White low cylinder with deep excising. Motifs include the St. Andrew's cross (Pyne's Motif 7) and "music bracket" (Pyne's Motif 11). The photo shows the cloudy white areas near the rim, alternating with cloudy black areas. Found in the fill of Structure 1, Area A, San José Mogote (San José phase).

sedimentary clay, similar to that used as an engobe for Delia White (see below). Vessels made of this sedimentary kaolin were probably imported, perhaps even from San Lorenzo or some other site on the Gulf Coast.

Other vessels, however, seem to have been made from a kaolinized feldspar, probably from a vein or dike like those that supplied the engobe for Atoyac Yellow-white (see above). This variant was particularly common during the San José phase, and may have been locally made. At the very least, it was not made from the same material as the sedimentary kaolin variant. Thus, while the concept (or "mental template") behind Xochiltepec White was pan-Mesoamerican, the vessels and clays cannot be traced to a single source.

Firing Temperature

It was probably fired at 750 to 770° C, in a neutral to slightly oxidizing atmosphere. The neutral-fired vessels best fit the description "white-clear-through." This unusually high (for its time period) firing temperature would give the ware little resistance to thermal shock, but this was not a problem since it was never used for cooking.

Color

The clay body of vessels fired in a neutral atmosphere is virtually pure white (10 YR 8/2). The surface is generally this same color, but may have occasional gray patches where two vessels rested against each other in the firing rack (kiln?). The clay body of vessels fired in a slightly oxidizing atmosphere is more pinkish (5 YR 8/4, 7.5 YR 8/4). Such vessels have the more "ivory" surface described by Coe and Diehl (1980:171);

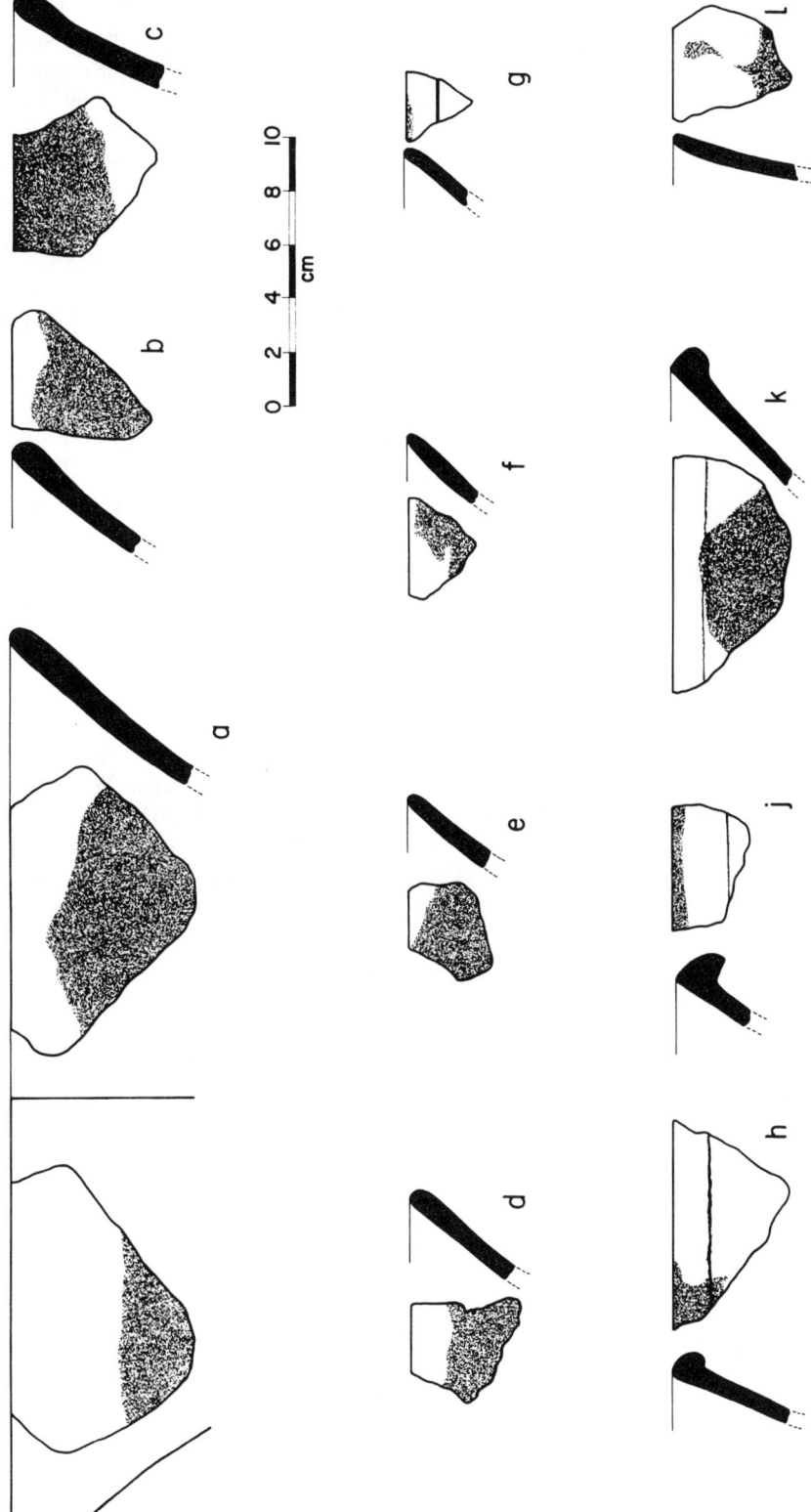

Figure 12.135. San José Black-and-White bowls, all from Area A, San José Mogote (San José phase). *a*, outleaned-wall bowl, Household Unit C3; *b-f*, rim sherds from outleaned-wall bowls, plain (*b*, Household Unit C4; *c*, Zone D2 midden; *d*, Zone D1 midden; *e, f*, Household Unit C2). *g*, outleaned-wall bowl rim with exterior incising, Zone D2 midden. *h-k*, bowls with bolstered rim (*h, k*, Household Unit C3; *j*, Household Unit C4). *l*, sherd from jar neck, unslipped on interior, Zone D2 midden.

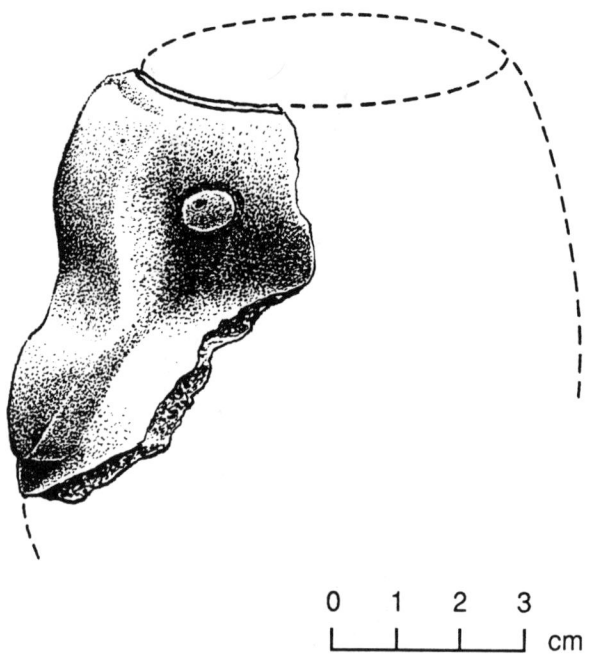

Figure 12.136. Fragment of effigy vessel in San José Black-and-White. The animal represented appears to be a coot (*Fulica* sp.) or some other waterfowl. Tierras Largas, House 1 (San José phase).

this color is called "very pale buff" (10 YR 8/4) in the Munsell system.

Surface Treatment

Vessels were usually double-burnished with a quartz pebble (once when leather-hard, a second time when virtually dry). This burnishing has brought the clay mineral to the surface, achieving a high gloss (and often producing the effect some analysts call a "self slip," which really involves no slip at all).

Plastic Decoration

Some bottles may have fluting or grooving on the body, sometimes in imitation of a cucurbit. Cylindrical bowls, while usually plain, may have excised pan-Mesoamerican designs similar to those on Leandro Gray. In a few cases, these carved areas have the same dry red (hematite) pigment rubbed into them as do some Leandro Gray designs.

Vessel Forms

Bottles (Fig. 12.137). This was probably the ideal, or model, that the makers of Atoyac Yellow-white bottles were trying to imitate. Probably no finer bottles were ever made in Formative Mesoamerica. The specimens we recovered are hard, very fine-grained, pure white, and rare, occurring mainly near public buildings of the late Tierras Largas phase and in the households of relatively well-to-do villagers of the San José phase. Necks of these bottles are tall, and the shoulders may have a sharp carination (Figs. 12.137b, 12.138). "Slender-necked bottles" in Xochiltepec White characterized the Chicharras phase at San Lorenzo (Coe and Diehl 1980:152) and are probably contemporaneous with our earliest specimens; we do not know whether they also had carinated shoulders.

Rim diameter: 3–4 cm
Height of neck: Estimated at 5–6 cm
Wall thickness: 4–8 mm
Plastic decoration: A few small sherds (not illustrated) are from bottles whose bodies were fluted, like the Atoyac Yellow-white specimens shown in Fig. 12.79c, d.

Tecomates with plain rims (Fig. 12.139a, b). These are simple, undecorated tecomates with rims that are gently rounded to slightly tapered in profile. Similar tecomates occur at San Lorenzo.

Rim diameter: 8–14 cm
Height: Unknown, but probably about two-thirds the rim diameter.
Wall thickness: 4–8 mm
Decoration: None

Tecomates with collared rims (Fig. 12.139c, d). This shape is virtually unique to Xochiltepec White, and would appear to be identical to that of Coe and Diehl's "collared jars with restricted orifices" from San Lorenzo (Coe and Diehl 1980:171, Fig. 146). Just at the point where the rim of a normal tecomate (or "restricted-orifice bowl") would end, the walls of these distinctive vessels change angle and rise steeply to form a high "collar" around the opening. This vessel is so unlike anything else in the San José phase that we suspect all our examples may be imports from the San Lorenzo area.

Rim diameter: 3.5–10 cm
Height: Unknown (too few examples).
Wall thickness: 6–10 mm
Decoration: None

Flat-based bowls with vertical (or nearly vertical) walls (Fig. 12.139e-h). This vessel is probably the ideal, or model, that the makers of Atoyac Yellow-white cylinders were trying to imitate. The walls of the vessel are almost perfectly vertical, but sometimes expand in thickness a few centimeters below the rim, eventually tapering to a rounded point. The juncture between wall and base forms a sharp right angle. Similar cylinders occur at San Lorenzo (Coe and Diehl 1980: Fig. 146i). However, the variety of clay bodies used for our Oaxaca specimens suggests that while some are imports, others are locally made.

Rim diameter: 12–18 cm
Height: Usually about two-thirds the rim diameter.
Wall thickness: 4–8 mm

Decoration: Rare. Limited to an occasional excised motif, like those on Atoyac Yellow-white or Leandro Gray.

Flat-based bowls with outleaned walls. These vessels are identical in shape to their Atoyac Yellow-white counterparts. So few were found that no range of measurements can really be given.

Oval bowls with pinched-in sides (Fig. 12.139j). This rare form is more typical of the Guadalupe phase than of earlier periods; no similar vessels are reported from San Lorenzo, and we suspect our examples were made from a highland kaolin source. One vessel, with flutes radiating out from each pinched-in "dimple," strongly resembles a Río Salado Gray bowl from the early Santa María phase in the Tehuacán Valley (MacNeish, Peterson, and Flannery 1970: Fig. 42, bottom row, middle specimen).

Bowls with composite silhouette (Fig. 12.139k). This is a very late form in Xochiltepec White, appearing at the transition from San José phase to Guadalupe phase. Such bowls have lower walls that are convex in cross-section, with the angle reversing and turning outward (like a cuspidor) just below the rim. Rims are blunt to gently rounded. A few examples are fluted in the manner of a squash-effigy bottle. We do not see any vessels like these illustrated from San Lorenzo, and suspect that the ones we found are from a highland kaolin source.

Rim diameter: 15–30 cm
Height: Usually about one-third of the rim diameter.
Wall thickness: 4–8 mm
Decoration: Rare; limited to occasional fluting.

Unusual vessel (Fig. 12.140). One unusual tecomate or incurved-rim bowl appears to be Xochiltepec White, but was found covered with red paint and decorated with post-firing scraping and incising. This enigmatic sherd is probably from an imported vessel.

DELFINA FINE GRAY

General Description

Delfina Fine Gray is a fine-grained, rock-hard gray ware with an almost metallic sheen. While it shares a number of shapes and excised motifs with Leandro Gray, it is much more of a luxury ware, and was widely exported to the rest of Mesoamerica (see below). Tlapacoya-Zohapilco in the Basin of Mexico, Las Canoas in the Tehuacán Valley, San Lorenzo in southern Veracruz, and Aquiles Serdán on the Chiapas coast all received shipments of Delfina Fine Gray. It was only the second pottery type in our sequence (after Ocós Black) to employ the sedimentary alluvial clays of the valley floor, which became so important later at Monte Albán.

Delfina Fine Gray as an Export Ware

Working at Tlapacoya, D.F., in the 1960s, Muriel Porter Weaver (1967:28–30) identified a pottery type that she called Tlapacoya Grey. The type occurred in the form of "bowls with straight vertical walls, flat base" and was identical to the shape we refer to as "flat-based bowls with vertical (or nearly vertical) walls" or simply "cylinders." The vessels are described as uniformly gray and burnished in such a way as to produce "a metallic sheen." The description sounds like Delfina Fine Gray, and both of the vessels she illustrates (Weaver 1967: Plate 11) could easily have come from Oaxaca. The one on the right looks very much like Delfina Fine Gray, while the one on the left could be either Delfina Fine Gray or Leandro Gray.

Weaver agreed with Piña Chan's earlier assessment of this ware as "foreign to the area"; to her it called to mind the gray ware of Monte Albán (Weaver 1967:28). She, therefore, had four thin sections prepared, two from known Monte Albán gray wares and two from Tlapacoya Grey. All four were examined by geologist Howel Williams, who was not told ahead of time the provenience of the sherds. Williams agreed that the Tlapacoya Grey sherds were not of Basin of Mexico origin, and might well be from the Valley of Oaxaca. Of one sherd, he remarked:

> If, as I think, the parent deposit is an ignimbrite, it must be of the poorly consolidated, *sillar* type, such as is to be found near the bottoms of some ignimbrite sheets near Mitla. [Weaver 1967:30]

Christine Niederberger later worked at Tlapacoya-Zohapilco. In the course of her work she defined a pottery type called Atoyac Fine Gray (Niederberger 1987:564). This type, occurring mainly as flat-based bowls with vertical (or nearly vertical) walls (*vases-gobelets*), is described as having a "metallic gray slip." If, as Niederberger suggests, her Atoyac Fine Gray is the same type as Weaver's Tlapacoya Grey, what she technically means is "self-slip." The metallic sheen on Tlapacoya Grey/Delfina Fine Gray is produced by burnishing that brings the fine clay to the surface, rather than by the addition of an engobe.

In 1970, Niederberger loaned us a small sample of Atoyac Fine Gray sherds so that Payne could examine them. He concluded that they were similar enough to Delfina Fine Gray to be considered the same type. Her curiosity aroused by Payne's and Weaver's analyses, Niederberger then had two thin sections prepared, one each from her Atoyac Fine Gray and our Delfina Fine Gray. These thin sections were studied by geologist Wayne Lambert (1972). According to Niederberger (1987:564), the Delfina Fine Gray sherd showed a higher proportion of metamorphic material than the Atoyac Fine Gray sherd, but the latter showed enough metamorphic material to indicate a "foreign origin" for the type.

We believe we know why the Atoyac Fine Gray and Delfina Fine Gray thin sections were "similar but not identical." To preface our explanation, let us look in some detail at Lambert's 1972 petrographic analysis.

260 Early Formative Pottery of Oaxaca

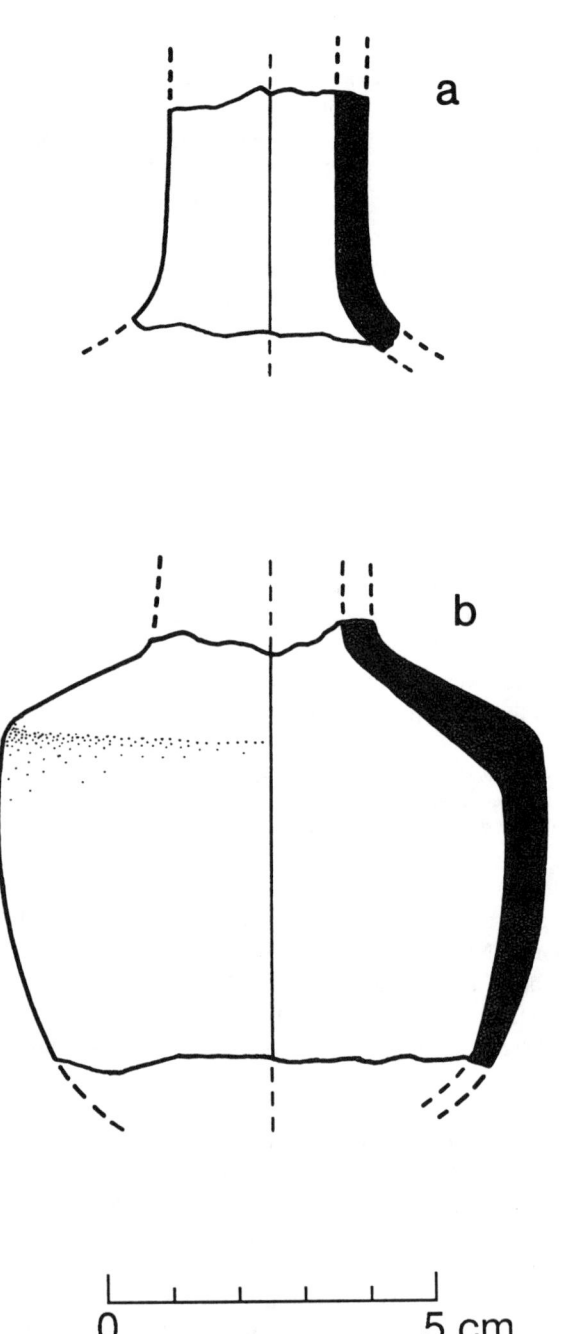

Figure 12.138. Xochiltepec White sherds from the shoulder of a carinated bottle (see also Fig. 12.137b). San José Mogote, Area C, Zone G (Tierras Largas phase).

Figure 12.137. Xochiltepec White bottle sherds from San José Mogote. *a,* bottle neck sherd, Household Unit C4, Area A (San José phase). *b,* sherd from shoulder of carinated bottle, Zone G, Area C (Tierras Largas phase).

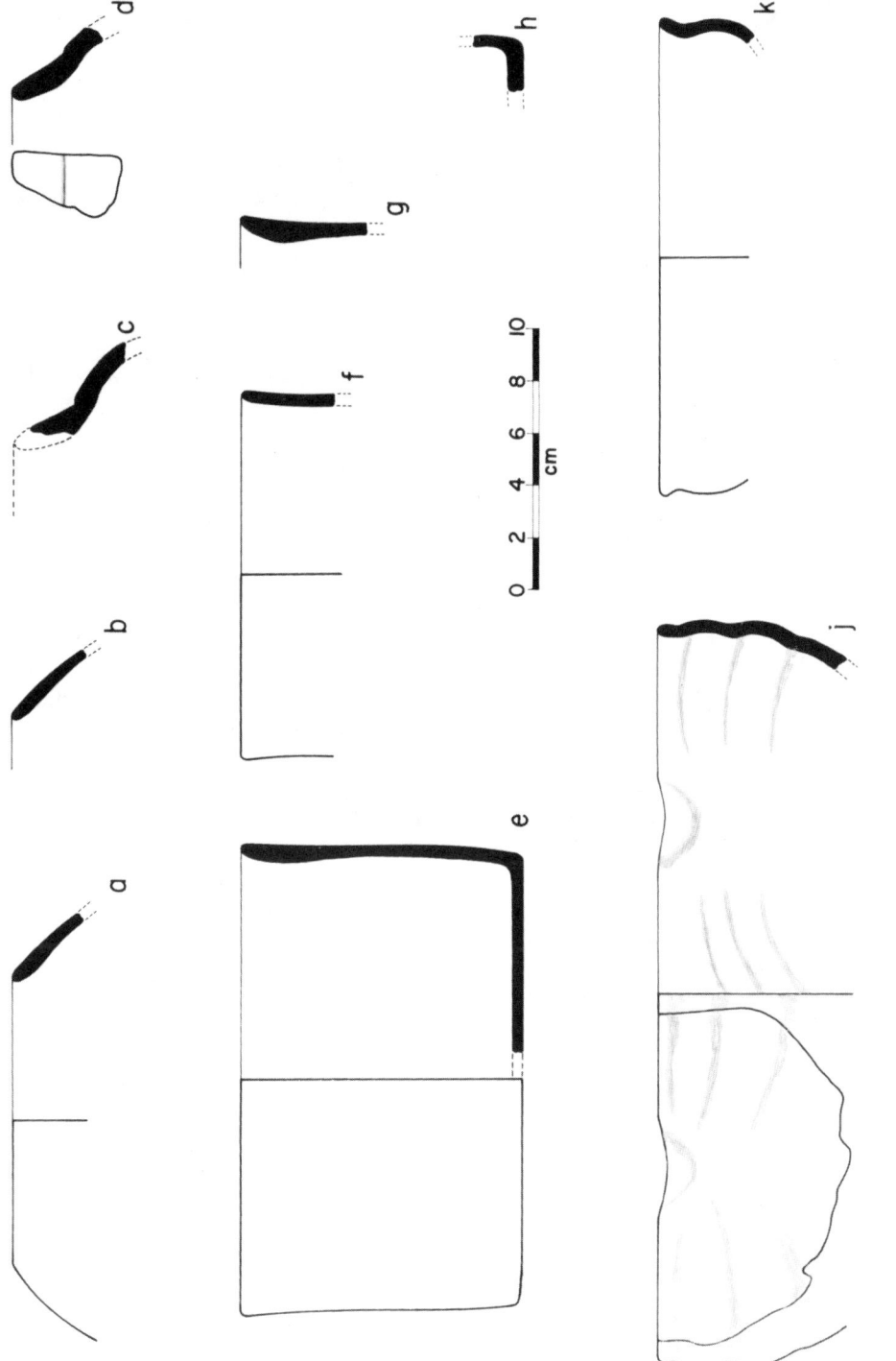

Figure 12.139. Xochiltepec White vessels from San José Mogote (SJM) and Barrio del Rosario Huitzo. *a, b,* tecomates with plain rim, Area A, SJM (*a,* Household Unit C4; *b,* Household Unit C3). *c, d,* tecomates with collared rim, Area A, SJM (*c,* Zone D2 midden; *d,* Household Unit C4). *e,* cylinder found while cleaning profile, Zone D, Area C, SJM. *f, g,* rims of cylinders similar to *e,* Area A, Huitzo (*f,* Zone F2; *g,* wall of Structure 1). *h,* basal angle sherd, Household Unit C3, Area A, SJM. *j,* oval bowl with pinched-in sides and squashlike fluting, Zone F3, Area A, Huitzo. *k,* bowl with composite silhouette, Zone F1, Area A, Huitzo. All specimens from SJM are San José phase; Huitzo specimens are from early Guadalupe phase proveniences that contain redeposited San José phase sherds.

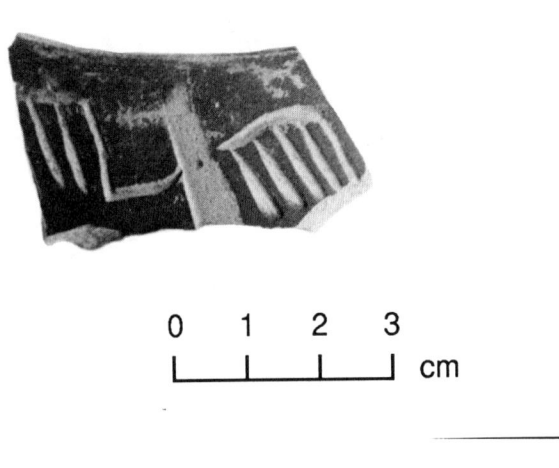

Figure 12.140. Sherd from an unusual tecomate or incurved-rim bowl. It appears to be a Xochiltepec White vessel covered with red paint, then decorated with post-firing scraping and incising. The scraping cuts through the red paint to expose the white clay body beneath. San José Mogote, Area C, found while cleaning profile at the level of the San José phase deposits.

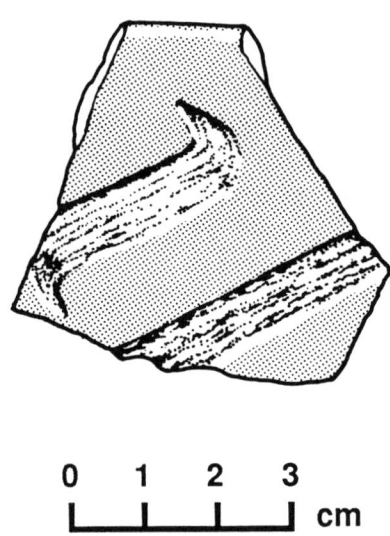

Figure 12.141. Delfina Fine Gray cylinder rim with excised design. This sherd was found at Las Canoas in the Tehuacán Valley, an Early Santa María phase site.

Of the two thin sections, Lambert says:

> [T]he two pottery fragments have some aplastic components in common, but each has additional components which are not present in the other. Materials derived from metamorphic rocks (metamorphic rock fragments, strained quartz, muscovite) are dominant in the Oaxaca fragment and make up at least half of the aplastic material in the Tlapacoya fragment. Materials derived from volcanic ash-fall or ash-flow deposits (glass and pumice fragments) are abundant in the Tlapacoya fragment but are virtually absent in the Oaxaca fragment. Carbonate grains, some in the form of shells, are present in the Oaxaca fragment but absent in the Tlapacoya fragment . . .
>
> The aplastic composition indicates that the two fragments are not identical but that they are related in some way. *Also, the composition suggests that either the aplastic material or the ceramic fragments were derived from the Oaxaca region.* Ash-fall and ash-flow deposits are present in the Tlapacoya area but metamorphic rocks are not. On the other hand, ash deposits, metamorphic rocks, and limestone (a possible source for the carbonate and shells) are present within a few kilometers of Oaxaca City. [Lambert 1972:3, italics ours]

We now wish we had given Niederberger ten sherds of Delfina Fine Gray for analysis, from several different parts of the valley. The fact is that even *within* the Valley of Oaxaca, not all Delfina Fine Gray vessels were made from the same clay body, since different parts of the valley had different parent geological material. Alluvial clay from the Cacaotepec region is very rich in metamorphic material, has a little carbonate from the local limestones, but contains fewer ash-flow minerals because it lies further from the Miocene volcanics. Alluvial clay from the Tlacolula region, on the other hand, would have much more volcanic ash and less metamorphic material, simply because of its location relative to *sillar*-type ignimbrites. The differences between Lambert's Delfina Fine Gray thin-section and his Atoyac Fine Gray thin section could simply mean that the two vessels were made in different regions of the Valley of Oaxaca. We therefore agree with Niederberger that her metallic gray cylinders are "foreign" and believe, on the basis of Payne's, Williams', and Lambert's analyses that at least some of them are Delfina Fine Gray cylinders from Oaxaca.

Moving south to the Tehuacán Valley, we can single out one rim sherd from an excised metallic gray cylinder found in Zone D1 of the site of Las Canoas (Fig. 12.141). In the early 1960s when the Tehuacán Formative pottery was being analyzed, this sherd was recognized as "foreign," but its place of origin was unknown. We now consider it to be Delfina Fine Gray.

Let us turn now to San Lorenzo on the southern Gulf Coast, where tropical soil acids frequently eat the surface off Formative sherds. "Coe has never seen potsherds with such sorry prospects for analysis, with such eroded and pitted surfaces . . . Because of this, it is often difficult to determine whether a vessel was slipped or not" (Coe and Diehl 1980:131). Because of this erosion, Coe and Diehl were forced to define some types, such as Calzadas Carved and Limón Carved-Incised, on the basis of their surviving plastic decoration rather than their vanished color and surface treatment. The result is that Calzadas Carved could include ceramics from several different sources, so long as they shared similar excised decoration.

In 1972 one of our Oaxaca project members, Nanette Pyne, had an opportunity to examine Coe's collection of Calzadas Carved pottery. Many of those sherds had excised depictions of the fire-serpent. Pyne instantly noted that while many of the motifs were specific to San Lorenzo, a smaller number (for example, Coe and Diehl 1980: Fig. 143*g, i*) were indistinguishable from motifs seen on Delfina Fine Gray and Leandro Gray in the Valley of Oaxaca. Those motifs were fresh in Pyne's memory because she was engaged in a study of San José phase design elements (Pyne 1976).

With Coe's permission, Pyne took small pieces off the 8 sherds that struck her as most "Oaxaca-like" and submitted them to Payne for microscopic analysis. One sherd, designated SL-B4–9-EC, showed "no apparent relationship" to Payne's Oaxaca type collection, but the other seven did. We can summarize Payne's results as follows (all sherd designations provided by Coe):

SL-B4–9-SUR: Very similar to Delfina Fine Gray, although it contains more particles of biotite mica than Payne's sherds of Delfina Fine Gray. Clearly from an alluvial valley floor clay like that used for Oaxaca's metallic gray ware.

SL-NW-M1–2c: Differs from Payne's type sample of Leandro Gray only in particle size. This is probably the result of the potter's selection of material from a different level of the same clay deposit.

SL-P-6e: Identical to SL-NW-M1–2c in both clay body composition and grain size.

SL-RNW-St-1p@: Made from the same clay body as Leandro Gray, although the nonplastic particles are a bit more coarse than Payne's type sample and the plastic (clay) content correspondingly lower. Despite this, the similarity in geologic origin is close.

SN-PNW-I-I1: Identical to Payne's control sample of Leandro Gray in both composition and firing conditions.

TE-R-72-G: Appears to be made from decomposed gneiss, probably deposited at a short distance from the parent material. The quartz grains are somewhat rounded, but the feldspar granules are small and somewhat more angular. (It could be of Oaxaca origin.)

SL-P-1c-X: Clay body probably from the alteration of pegmatite rocks, one with greater content of feldspars in the parent rock than is usual with gneiss-derived clays. (It could, however, be of Oaxaca origin.)

To summarize: Coe and Diehl's collection of Calzadas Carved evidently contains vessels from several different regions. Vessels made at San Lorenzo, which undoubtedly constitute the majority, evidently have "fine, quartzite sand" as their nonplastic material (Coe and Diehl 1980:162). A minority, however, appear to be imported vessels of Delfina Fine Gray and Leandro Gray, made on clay bodies like those in the Valley of Oaxaca. What seems most significant to us is that Pyne was apparently successful, six times out of seven, at picking out the Oaxaca sherds *based on their excised motifs*. What this suggests is that even though many of the motifs were pan-Mesoamerican, *each Formative region had its own distinct style of rendering them*. This association between style and clay body makes the identification of export wares more reliable.

Finally, let us consider what may be the southern limit for the importation of Delfina Fine Gray: Aquiles Serdán on the Pacific Coast of Chiapas. In 1970, we were shown a few sherds from this important site that appeared to us, and to Christine Niederberger, to be identical to Delfina Fine Gray of Oaxaca/Atoyac Fine Gray of Tlapacoya. The New World Archaeological Foundation kindly allowed us to take small fragments off these sherds so that Payne could examine them under the microscope. He reports that the Aquiles Serdán sherds had the same alluvial clay body as Delfina Fine Gray: part metamorphics, part volcanic ash flow, and close enough to be considered the same type.

The wide area over which this hard, metallic gray luxury ware was exchanged makes it one of Oaxaca's most important pottery types. Its popularity also helps to dispel the myth of a Formative Mesoamerica in which everything flowed from the Gulf Coast to the highlands. Delfina Fine Gray was exported as widely as Xochiltepec White, and one of the sites to which it was exported was San Lorenzo. This indigenous Oaxaca pottery was as well made as any ceramic type in early Formative Mesoamerica, and its success as an export ware may have increased the likelihood that burnished gray ware would go on to be featured in every subsequent period of Oaxaca prehistory.

Chronological History

Delfina Fine Gray is not presently known from the Tierras Largas phase, and even during the San José phase, it is known primarily from the large village of San José Mogote. Its scarcity at small hamlets suggests that it was considered a luxury ware, used mainly (if not exclusively) by families of moderate to high status.

Delfina Fine Gray comes very close to being restricted to the San José phase. Occasional sherds show up in Guadalupe phase deposits (and in contemporaneous levels in the Tehuacán Valley), but there is always the possibility that such sherds were redeposited. The type's chronological peak both as a local luxury ware and as an item of export establishes the contemporaneity of the San José phase in Oaxaca, the Ayotla phase at Tlapacoya, and the San Lorenzo phase in southern Veracruz. Its vessel forms are prototypical of the San José phase: cylinders (more than 50% of the diagnostic sherds), outleaned-wall bowls, bolstered-rim bowls, pigment dishes, bottles, and jars with vertical necks.

Clay Body

Delfina Fine Gray is made from a finely sorted, redeposited alluvial floodplain clay. The body is approximately half nonplastics and half clay minerals of a kaolinite-montmorillonite mixture, resulting from the disintegration of both Precambrian crystalline metamorphics and Miocene volcanic ash flows. All these materials have been transported some distance from the original parent formations and subjected to deoxidation by humic acids. All of the clay minerals have been broken down into extremely fine particles (ca. 2–3 millimicrons); the nonplastics vary in size, but are generally under 0.2 mm. Payne estimates that about a third of the nonplastic material remains on a 30-mesh screen, but

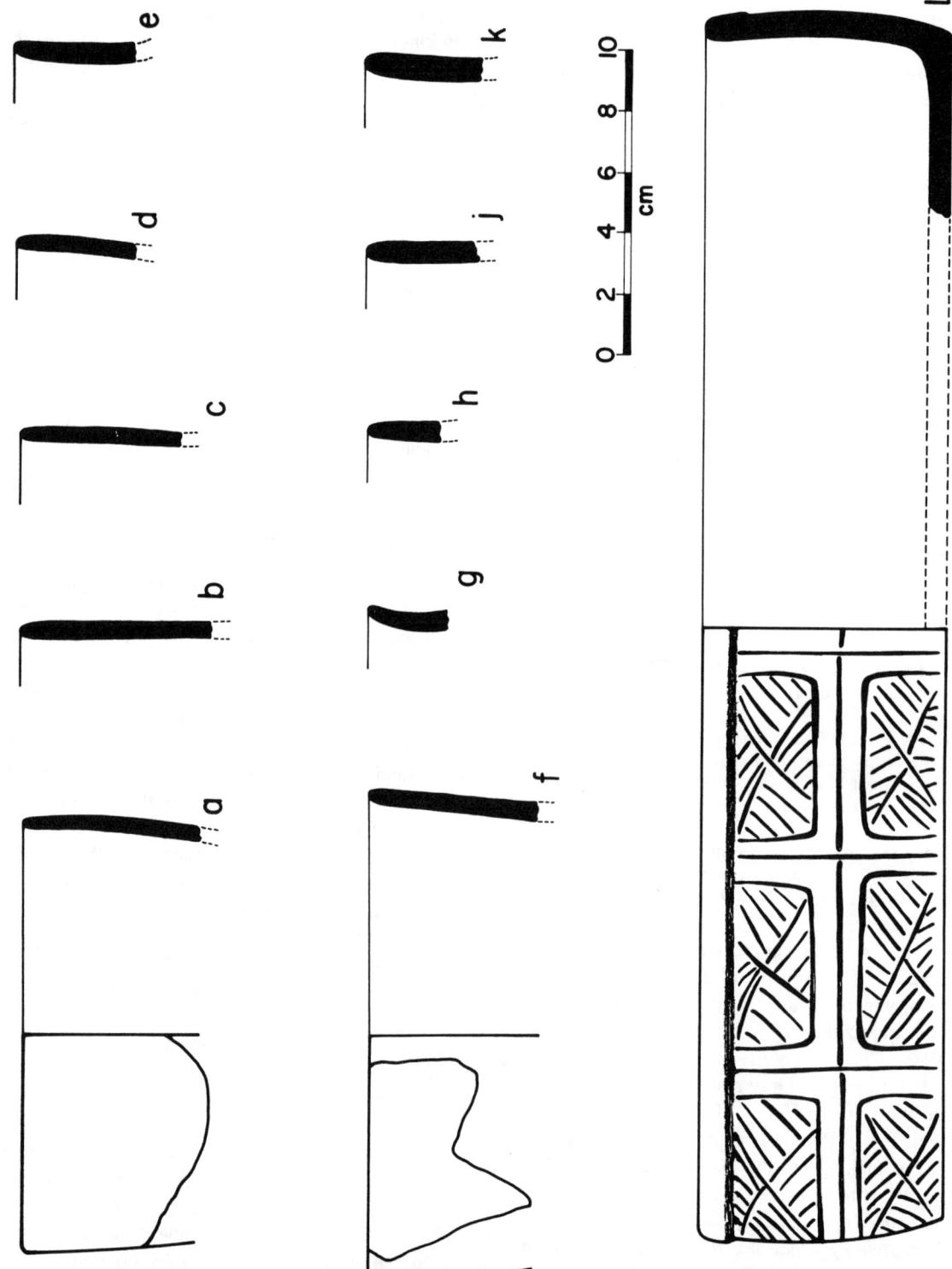

Figure 12.142. Delfina Fine Gray cylinders or bowls with nearly vertical walls, all from Area A of San José Mogote (San José phase). *a–k,* undecorated cylinders (*a, d, f,* Household Unit C4; *c, e,* Household Unit C3; *h,* Household Unit C2; *b, g, k,* Zone D1 midden). *l* is a low cylinder with a slightly bolstered rim, deeply incised on the outside, with two horizontal rows of cartouches inside rectangles. In each cartouche is the "mat" symbol (Pyne's Motif 4). *l* has been reconstructed from sherds found in Zones D1 and D2 of the Area A midden.

Figure 12.143. Delfina Fine Gray cylinder from the Zone D midden, Area A, San José Mogote (San José phase). The portion at the top was found in Zone D1, while the portion at the bottom was found in Zone D2. A reconstruction drawing of this vessel is shown in Figure 12.142*l*. It features "mat" symbols in cartouches.

passes through 18-mesh. The remaining two-thirds, principally ground silicates, grades down into sizes of 150–300 mesh.

One of the most common clay bodies used for Delfina Fine Gray resembles that from an alluvial deposit near Cacaotepec, whose major *visible* inclusions are quartz, amphiboles, pyroxines, and undissolved feldspar, presumably washed down to the valley floor from Precambrian metamorphics. This clay was probably used pretty much as found. Occasional clay bodies, however, have enough disintegrated volcanic tuff in them to suggest that the alluvial clay used came from closer to Oaxaca's Tertiary ignimbrites. This difference within Delfina Fine Gray probably accounts for the differences between Wayne Lambert's two thin sections (see above).

Firing Temperature

It was probably fired at 750° C or higher, in a reducing atmosphere. The result is a very hard ware with a definite "ring" when struck.

Color

The color of the clay body is an even, neutral gray throughout (7.5 R N6/ to 2.5 YR N6/). The color of the surface varies from gray (2.5 Y N5/ or 2.5 YR N6/) to light gray (2.5 Y N7/).

Surface Treatment

Delfina Fine Gray was smoothed with a piece of gourd or a rounded sherd, then burnished once, very carefully and evenly, with a quartz pebble when leather-hard. Because of the extremely fine grain of this ware, the clay minerals brought to the surface by burnishing produce a hard, almost metallic sheen. Some analysts would probably refer to this surface as a "self slip," but it does not involve the addition of an engobe or wash.

Plastic Decoration

Like Leandro Gray, this pottery type was decorated by excising (*raspada*), sometimes combined with incising (*sgraffito*). The designs are often pan-Mesoamerican, with the fire-serpent being particularly common; less frequent were fine-line hachure representations that may be were-jaguars. Coe and Diehl (1980:162) believe that excised designs in Calzadas Carved were cut out with an obsidian blade. While we cannot speak for their designs, Payne believes that ours in Oaxaca were *outlined* with an obsidian blade, but then had the strip of clay removed with something like a slat of cane (*carrizo*). This left the floor of the excision rough, so that dry red pigment could be rubbed into the design. Even if that method were used at San Lorenzo, it might not be possible to detect, given the extremely eroded condition of the sherds described by Coe and Diehl.

The Addition of Dry Red Pigment

Dry red hematite powder (7.5 R 4/8 in the Munsell system) was often rubbed into excised designs. In other cases, one whole section of the vessel might be roughened (either by *raspada* or extensive fine-line hachure) and then coated with dry red pigment, left to contrast with the otherwise metallic gray surface.

Vessel Forms

Flat-based bowls with vertical (or nearly vertical) walls (Fig. 12.142–12.146). These "cylinders" were the most common form in which Delfina Fine Gray was made, and by far the most common form in which it was exported. Many, like their Leandro Gray counterparts, had been press-molded over previous cylinders or actual molds. Rim profiles are usually direct and rounded, or slightly tapered; a few vessels flare slightly at the rim, like the later beakers in Delia White (see below). There is usually a very sharp angle made by the juncture between the flat base and the lower wall. Walls vary from absolutely vertical to slightly concave or slightly convex. Because excised designs may occur only once on a vessel, the high number of excised sherds we found suggests that most cylinders were decorated.
- *Rim diameter:* The normal range is 8–20 cm, with a mode of 15–16 cm. One unusual vessel had a diameter of 38 cm.
- *Height:* Normally 50–75% of the rim diameter, but in rare cases it may be as little as 25%.
- *Basal diameter:* Normally 80–99% of the rim diameter.
- *Wall thickness:* 4–8 mm
- *Volume:* Based on similarly-shaped Leandro Gray cylinders, the vast majority of these bowls would have held enough to serve several persons (or a small nuclear family) at one meal. Those with a rim diameter of 15–16 cm, for example, would have held about 1.5 liters, and even those as small as 14.5 cm (rim) by 10.5 cm (height) would have held 1.2 liters.
- *Plastic decoration:* Common. The designs are on the outside of the cylinder and involve excising, incising, fine-line incised hachure, or combinations of all three. Dry red pigment was frequently rubbed into the roughened, carved, or incised areas, and in some cases even deep excision was filled with red pigment to the level of the unmodified vessel surface. Motifs included fire-serpents, were-jaguars, "eye," or "sunburst" patterns, and many other designs reminiscent of Tlatilco, Tlapacoya, and Las Bocas in the central highlands. One unique vessel (Figs. 12.142*l*, 12.143) has a series of mat (*petate*) designs in cartouches, very similar to the "mat motifs" that accompany persons of authority in later Zapotec inscriptions and Mixtec codices (Marcus 1992).

Flat-based bowls with outleaned walls (Fig. 12.146g-k). This form is relatively rare and, in contrast to the cylinders described above, apparently never had plastic decoration. In shape and rim profile the vessels are like their Leandro Gray counterparts. They are highly burnished and very hard.
- *Rim diameter:* 20–30 cm
- *Height:* Normally one-fourth to one-third the rim diameter.
- *Wall thickness:* 4–8 mm
- *Plastic decoration:* None

Bowls with bolstered rim (Figs. 12.147a-d, 12.148). Like similar vessels in Leandro Gray, these bowls have the rim thickened by the addition of a concentric ring of clay. Since excised motifs may occur only once on a vessel, most bowls must have been decorated. Sometimes the exterior below the bolster is left rough and unburnished in preparation for *raspada* decoration, and frequently, dry red pigment is rubbed into the design, the roughened areas, or both.
- *Rim diameter:* 16–24 cm
- *Height:* Estimated at 30–40% of the rim diameter.
- *Wall thickness:* 6–9 cm, except near the thickened bolster.
- *Plastic decoration:* Frequent use of excising and incising (or a combination of the two) on the exterior below the bolstered rim. Common motifs are fire-serpents or crossed bands (St. Andrew's cross).

Bottles and/or jars with vertical necks (Fig. 12.147e-h). These vessels have globular bodies and relatively tall vertical (or nearly vertical) necks. Some sherds come from true bottles, while others are from vertical-necked jars such as those seen in Atoyac Yellow-white and Leandro Gray. We are presenting the two forms

Figure 12.144. Sherd from Delfina Fine Gray cylinder, decorated on the outside with "music brackets" and fine-line hachure. Dry red pigment has been rubbed into the incising. San José Mogote, Area A, Household Unit C2 (San José phase). A reconstruction of this vessel appears in Figure 12.146*e*.

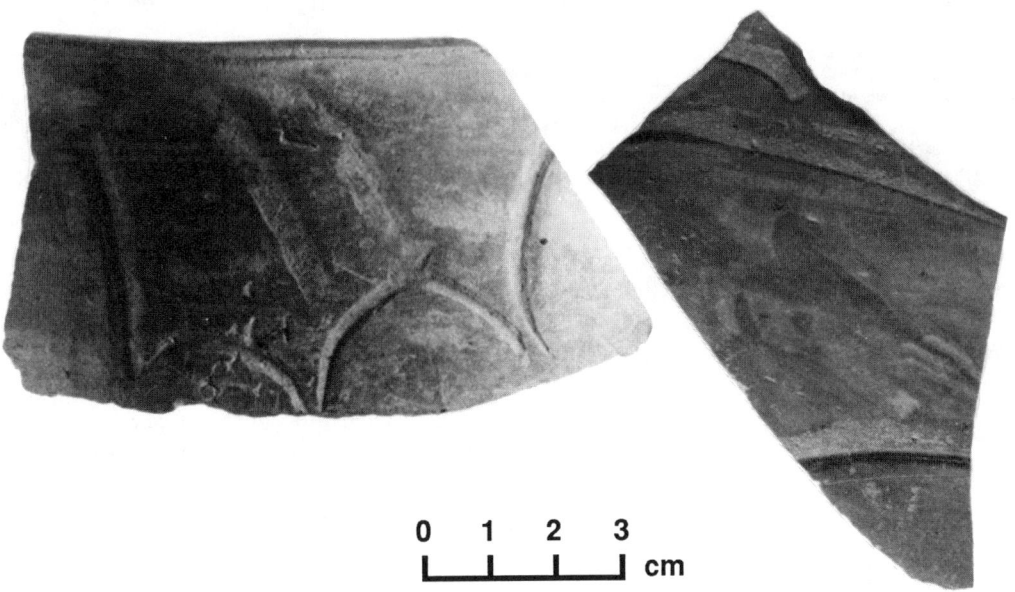

Figure 12.145. Delfina Fine Gray cylinder sherds found while straightening profile of Area C, San José Mogote, at the level of the San José phase deposits. *Left,* cylinder rim with an excised sunburst motif. (This vessel resembles the one shown in Fig. 12.146*c*.) *Right,* body sherd with what appears to be part of an excised fire-serpent motif.

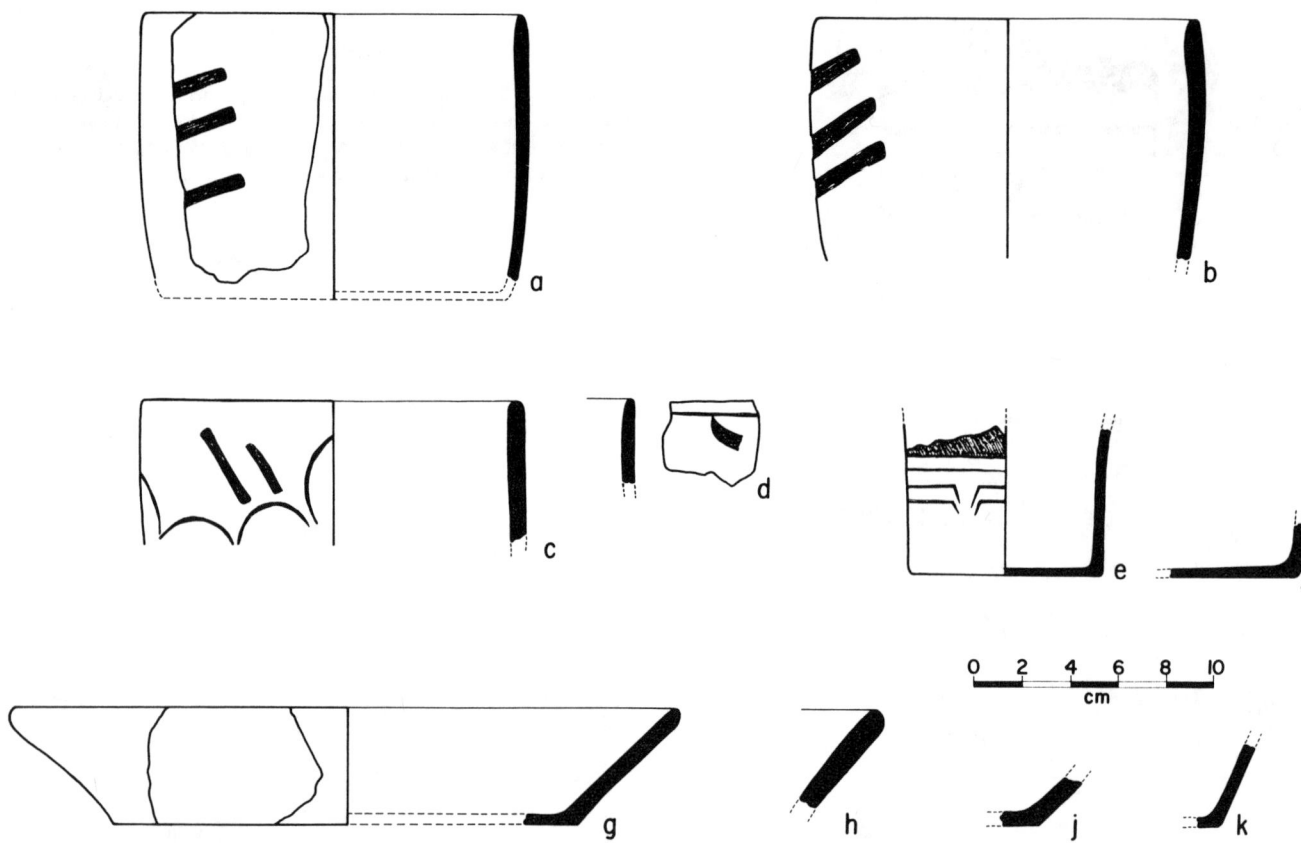

Figure 12.146. Delfina Fine Gray bowls of several kinds, all from San José Mogote (San José phase). *a, b,* cylinders with excised bands filled with dry red pigment, probably parts of fire-serpent motifs, Area A (*a,* Household Unit C2; *b,* Zone D1 midden). *c,* cylinder with excised bands inside sunburst motif, Zone D, Area C. *d,* cylinder rim with excising, Household Unit C1, Area A. *e,* cylinder base decorated with "music brackets" and fine hachure, filled with dry red pigment; Household Unit C2, Area A. *f,* plain cylinder base, Household Unit C3, Area A. *g-k,* outleaned-wall bowls, plain, Area A (*g, h, k,* Household Unit C4; *j,* Household Unit C2).

together because, in many cases, it was impossible to tell whether certain small sherds had come from a bottle or a jar.

Rim diameter: For jars, 12–18 cm; for bottles, not known, but estimated to be 3.5 to 7.0 cm.
Height of neck: Unknown due to a lack of restorable specimens.
Wall thickness: 4–9 mm
Plastic decoration: None

Pigment dishes (Fig. 12.147j). These are similar to Leandro Gray pigment dishes in general size and conformation, and like the latter, most have traces of red hematite on the inside. Why the San José phase villagers used such a fine ware for some of their pigment dishes is unknown, but it may be that the shiny surface helped prevent liquid from escaping into the vessel wall.

Rim diameter: 10 cm (one restorable example)
Height: 2.4 cm (one restorable example)
Wall thickness: 4–6 mm
Plastic decoration: None

SAN JOSE SPECULAR RED

General Description

This is a red-slipped ware used for bowls of various sizes and shapes, tecomates, and jars with necks. It is distinguished by its coarseness, relative to Avelina Red-on-Buff or Clementina Fine Red-on-Buff, and by the fact that it is completely covered with engobe, not simply striped. San José Specular Red is burnished, and shows characteristic silvery sparkles of crystalline hematite. Unlike Matadamas Red, which occurs in what are typical Tierras Largas phase shapes, this type occurs in typical San José phase shapes.

Chronological History

This type was virtually restricted to the San José phase.

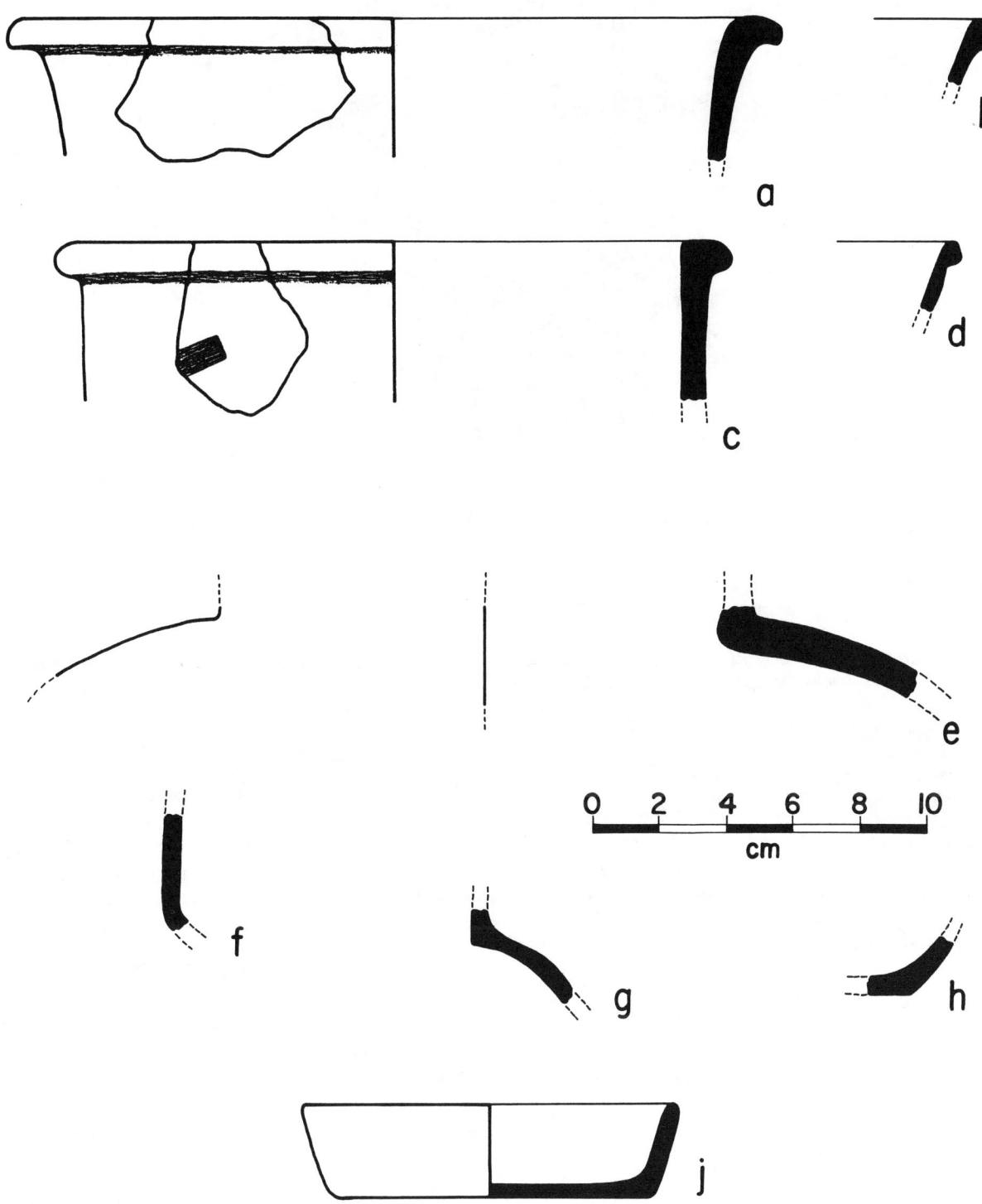

Figure 12.147. Delfina Fine Gray vessels from San José Mogote (San José phase). *a-d,* bolstered-rim bowls; *c* is excised, the others plain. (*a,* Zone D2 midden, Area A; *b,* Household Unit C3, Area A; *c,* Feature 141, Area C; *d,* Household Unit C3, Area A). *e,* shoulder of jar with vertical neck, Zone D1 midden, Area A. *f,* sherd from neck of bottle or vertical-necked jar, Household Unit C3, Area A. *g,* shoulder of bottle or jar, Zone D2 midden, Area A. *h,* basal angle sherd from bottle or jar (unsmoothed inside), Household Unit C3, Area A. *j,* pigment dish, Zone D2 midden, Area A.

Figure 12.148. Sherd from Delfina Fine Gray bolstered rim bowl, excised on the outside with a fire-serpent design (probably Pyne's Motif 1). Dry red pigment has been rubbed into the excisions. San José Mogote, Area C, cutting profile at level of San José phase deposits.

Clay Body

A residual piedmont clay, derived from the weathering and decomposition of Precambrian gneiss. It is so identical to the clay body used for Atoyac Yellow-white and San José Red-on-White, including grain size and nonplastic inclusions, that we simply refer the reader to our descriptions of those types.

Firing Temperature

It was probably fired at 700 to 720° C. Variations in the color of the clay body suggest that the firing atmosphere varied from weak oxidation to weak reduction.

Color

In cross-section, sherds vary in color from weakly oxidized reddish brown (5 YR 4/4) to weakly reduced black (7.5 YR 2/0) or dark gray (10 YR 3/1). The color of the red engobe varies from weak red (7.5 R 4/4) through red (7.5 R 4/6) to dark red (7.5 R 3/6) in the Munsell system; the sparkles of silvery hematite are clearest when the sherds are wet.

Surface Treatment

Vessels were smoothed with a piece of gourd or a rounded sherd prior to slipping. After the engobe had been applied and allowed to dry, the vessel was carefully and evenly burnished, once, with a quartz pebble.

The Red Engobe

The most important attribute of this type is an engobe of clay of the same type as the body, mixed with ground-up hematite ore. (*Barro colorado* is not usually sufficient to produce the "specular" effect because the hematite is too broken down.) Usually the engobe was applied over all of one surface of the vessel—the surface which, depending on the shape, would be the most easily seen. The application varies from thin (swabbed on with a piece of animal fur) to thick (either the slip was poured on, or the vessel was dipped). For details on how to achieve a specular red slip, see Simulating the Type, below.

Plastic Decoration

Plastic decoration was rare. Tecomates might have a plain band added to the rim by means of two heavily incised lines, done with something blunter than a maguey spine. The unslipped exteriors of bolstered-rim bowls might have excised designs like those seen on Leandro Gray bolstered-rim bowls. For the most part, however, San José Specular Red was undecorated.

Simulating the Type: Or, How to Achieve the Specular Red Effect

In 1970, we asked Payne to simulate San José Specular Red for us. He went first to the locality called "La Casahuatera" in the Cacaotepec piedmont where the Atzompa potters get their *barro áspero*; here he found a clay body similar to that of Atoyac Yellow-white. He went next to the small hamlet of La Bandita (an *agencia* of Valdeflores) in the extreme southern Valle Grande, where he had previously located hematite ore in the Precambrian gneiss hills. This ore was already mixed with enough clay so that when thoroughly ground in a mortar, it had all the necessary properties for an engobe. In cases where the clay content of the ore was not sufficient, it could be added.

During the process of grinding up the ore, the hematite crystals are reduced to particles small enough to pass through a 30-mesh screen. It is these highly reflectant particles that give the red pigment its specular appearance. Additional reflectant particles, also derived from the same ore, are biotite mica and hornblende, both of which can be seen in the engobe under a binocular microscope.

The timing of the application of the red engobe is crucial: it must be applied while the clay body is still sufficiently damp so that the particles of crystalline hematite (and other reflectant particles) will penetrate the body. When this is done, burnishing carried out soon afterward with a quartz pebble will arrange the cleavage planes of the minerals parallel to and on the surface, so as to produce the desired sparkling effect. If the engobe is applied after the body has dried, the reflectant minerals (including the hematite) will be crushed or smeared on the surface, and the specular effect will be lost.

After a bit of experimentation Payne's simulated vessels, fired at 720° C in an electric kiln, came out very much like San José Specular Red.

Vessel Forms

Flat-based bowls with outleaned walls (Fig. 12.149a–d). This was the most common shape in which San José Specular Red occurred. The bowls are generally slipped completely red on the interior and then burnished, with the exterior burnished but left unslipped (except for a frequent red band at the rim). In their shape, rim profile, and overall proportions these bowls are similar to those in Atoyac Yellow-white; none, however, are incised on the rim. Like Atoyac Yellow-white outleaned-wall bowls, they could either be press-molded or built up by concentric rings. Most San José Specular Red bowls are on the large side—in the 2–3 liter volume range—and thus, would have held enough for a nuclear family. The smaller bowls seen in Atoyac Yellow-white apparently were not duplicated in this red-slipped ware.

Rim diameter: 26–40 cm
Height: Normally one-quarter to one-third the rim diameter.
Wall thickness: 5–10 mm
Plastic decoration: Relatively rare. A few bowls have "grater-bowl" or pseudo-*molcajete* designs incised on the interior of the base (Fig. 12.149j).

Flat-based bowls with vertical (or nearly vertical) walls (Fig. 12.149h). The cylinder was not a common shape in specular red, but a few were found. The exterior of the vessel was usually slipped red and burnished, while the interior was burnished but left unslipped. No dimensions can be given owing to small sample size. A few examples were excised in the manner of Leandro Gray cylinders.

Flat-based bowls with bolstered rim (Figs. 12.149e–g; 12.150, bottom). These vessels are similar in shape, rim profile, and overall dimensions to bolstered-rim bowls in Atoyac Yellow-white and Leandro Gray. The bowls are slipped red over the whole interior, while the exterior was left unslipped except for a red band on the rim bolster; both surfaces are burnished.

Rim diameter: 14–24 cm
Height: Roughly one-third the rim diameter.
Wall thickness: 4–8 mm, except near the thickened rim.
Plastic decoration: Some bowls have simple excising or incising on the unslipped exterior of the vessel. The motifs are mostly parallel lines or crossed bands (St. Andrew's cross).

Tecomates (Figs. 12.149m–n, 12.150, 12.151). Our small sample of tecomates, usually slipped specular red and burnished over the whole exterior (Fig. 150, top), has rim diameters that range from as small as 6 cm to as large as 26 cm. Most rims are plain and direct, but one set of tecomates has the wall thickened at a point roughly 3–4 cm below the rim, an area from which it tapers in profile to a rounded point at the rim. Holes punched through the shoulder for suspension with cords are not uncommon.

Rim diameter: 6–26 cm
Body diameters: Unknown
Plastic decoration: The usual pattern for these tecomates is heavy incised lines forming a plain band at the rim, with a uniform red slip and no zones. One unique tecomate, however (Fig. 12.151), has a specular red rim and zoning bands, with rocker stamping in unslipped zones. While we have tentatively classified it as San José Specular Red, it may in fact be a "mistake": a potential San José Red-on-White tecomate that never got slipped white.

Jars (Fig. 12.149k, l). Owing to our small sample, it is difficult to give a complete description of these jars, which may have been inspired by earlier vessels in Matadamas Red. In general, they seem to be small, with globular bodies and relatively short, slightly flaring necks. The exterior is slipped specular red and burnished, while the interior is left plain except for a slipped and burnished red band at the rim. The range of dimensions is not known.

Bottles (not illustrated). A few sherds appear to be from bottles (or possibly jars with vertical necks). Most are too small to provide much information.

LA MINA WHITE

General Description

This pottery has a glossy, pure white to ivory white engobe over a fine-grained, brick red to orange-red clay body, often lateritic. This type occurs in southern Veracruz (where it may be native), and in highland Oaxaca and Puebla (where some or all of it may be imported). We suspect that it may have been traded even more widely, but has not always been reported.

La Mina White as an Export Ware

In the early Santa María phase levels of the Tehuacán Valley, MacNeish, Peterson, and Flannery (1970:84) discovered 31 sherds of an imported ware they called "White-slip Red-paste." This pottery had a "glossy white slip" on a "hard, finely tempered, brick-red" clay body. It soon became clear that this ware was similar, though not identical, to the pottery type Coe and Diehl (1980:154) were calling La Mina White at San Lorenzo, Veracruz. La Mina White is described as having "a thin white slip over an orange tan paste with medium coarse sand temper." Despite the fact that the clay body fired red in the Tehuacán case and orange in the San Lorenzo case, the shapes are similar.

In Oaxaca, we have recovered several hundred sherds resembling both the brick red variant seen in Tehuacán and the more orange variant seen in Veracruz. Separation of the two variants was made difficult because they sometimes grade into one another. It is not always clear whether the color difference is related to the clay body or to firing conditions. It is simply not yet known how many varieties of La Mina White there are, and where each was made.

Chronological History

La Mina White is known so far only from the San José phase. This is chronologically interesting, since it occurs both in the form of bottles like those of the Chicharras phase at San Lorenzo, and in the form of cylinders and tecomates like those of the San Lorenzo phase.

Clay Body

A residual piedmont clay, very fine grained, and in some cases somewhat lateritic. We believe that most of our specimens were made on lateritic clays foreign to the Valley of Oaxaca. However, some examples could be local imitations, made by winnowing or refining Oaxaca's gneiss-derived clays and firing them a uniform red. Among the fine particles (generally under 0.5 mm) are quartz, feldspar, biotite mica, and pyroxenes.

Firing Temperature

A temperature of at least 740 to 750° C (in an oxidizing atmosphere) would have been necessary to produce the pure white color of the kaolin engobe.

Color

The clay body of the brick red variant has fired to 2.5 YR 6/8 in the Munsell system. The kaolin engobe fires pure white to slightly off-white (10 YR 8/2 to 2.5 Y 8/2). Sherds of the orange variant come close to fitting the description of La Mina White given by Coe and Diehl (1980).

The White Engobe

A very high-quality, iron-free kaolin engobe was applied evenly over the whole vessel, either by dipping or pouring. The engobe, which is not unlike the pure white clay body used for Xochiltepec White, may have been refined by decanting. It could be the product of a thermal vent, or a fossil hot spring like that producing some of the kaolin clays Payne examined.

Surface Treatment

La Mina White was burnished (once) with a quartz pebble after the white engobe had dried sufficiently.

Plastic Decoration

No vessels had decoration of any kind.

Vessel Forms

Flat-based bowls with vertical (or nearly vertical) walls (Fig. 12.152a-d). These are similar to our cylinders in Atoyac Yellow-white, but also resemble some La Mina White vessels illustrated by Coe and Diehl (1980). Rim diameters range from 10–20 cm, and the wall thickness is usually 4–8 mm.

Tecomates/incurved rim bowls (Fig. 12.152e-f). Because of the small size of the sherds involved, it was not always possible to separate tecomates from bowls with incurved rims. At least a few of the incurved rim bowls evidently had flat bases (Fig. 12.152g). No average dimensions of the vessels could be given, but their wall thickness is usually 4–8 mm.

The shapes of these vessels are very much like the tecomates and incurved-rim bowls illustrated by Coe and Diehl (1980: Fig. 149) for La Mina White of the San Lorenzo phase.

Bottles (not illustrated). These bottles are very similar in shape to those illustrated by Coe and Diehl (1980: Fig. 125a) for La Mina White of the Chicharras phase at San Lorenzo.

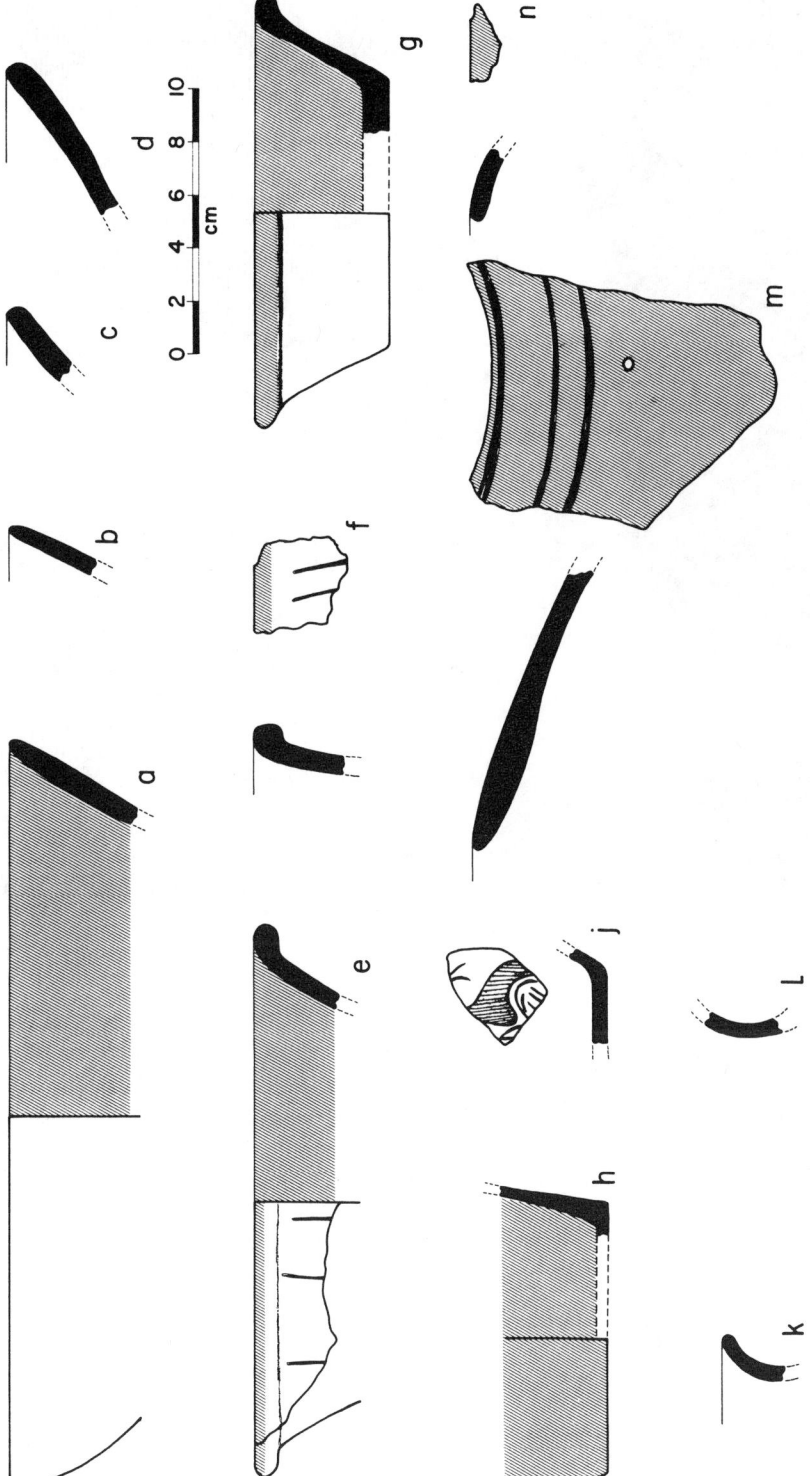

Figure 12.149. San José Specular Red vessels, all from San José Mogote (San José phase). *a-d*, outleaned-wall bowls, slipped totally red inside, burnished but unslipped outside (*a, c, d*, Zone D1 midden, Area A; *b*, Household Unit C2, Area A). *e-g*, bowls with bolstered rim. *e*, slipped totally red inside, outside left unslipped except for the top of the rim bolster, some incising on exterior (Stages II-III, Structure 1, Area A). *f*, similar to *e*, Household Unit C3, Area A. *g*, slipped red inside as far down as wall-base juncture, outside left unslipped except for bolstered rim, excised on interior of base (Household Unit C4, Area A). *h*, base of cylinder, slipped red inside and outside, Household Unit C3, Area A. *j*, flat base with "grater bowl" design, Household Unit C3, Area A. *k*, jar rim, slipped red outside; red band at rim 1 cm wide on inside; Household Unit C3, Area A. *l*, jar neck, slipped red on outside only, Zone D2 midden, Area A. *m*, tecomate rim with shallow grooves outlining a rim band; perforated for suspension; slipped red outside only (cleaning profile, Zones D and E, Area C; see also Fig. 12.150, top). *n*, tecomate rim, slipped red outside, Household Unit C2, Area A.

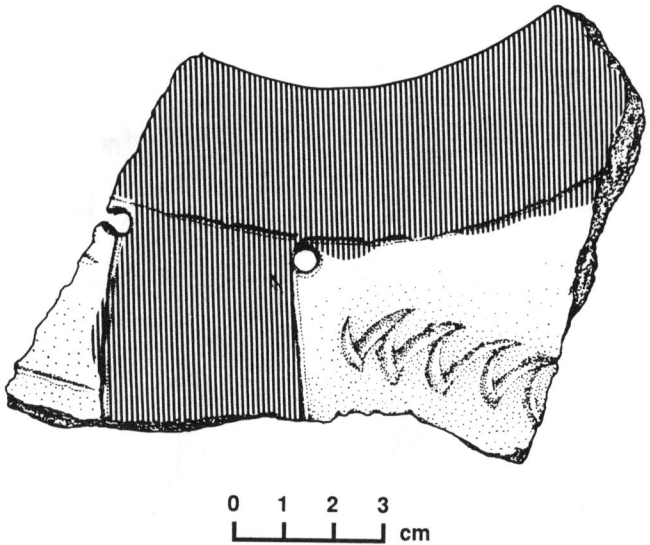

Figure 12.151. Unusual tecomate rim sherd, tentatively classified as San José Specular Red. Most San José Specular Red tecomates are slipped specular red over the whole exterior. This tecomate, however, has an incised band at the rim, and a body divided by incised bands into unslipped zones decorated with rocker stamping. The specular red slip that fills the rim band and the zone-dividing bands is indistinguishable from the slip on other San José Specular Red tecomates. There are two perforations near the rim band for suspension. While we have tentatively assigned this tecomate to San José Specular Red, it might represent a potter's mistake: a San José Red-on-White tecomate that for one reason or another never got slipped white. San José Mogote, Area C, Feature 41 (San José phase).

Figure 12.150. San José Specular Red sherds. *Top,* tecomate rim with shallow grooves outlining a rim band. The whole sherd is slipped specular red, and has been perforated for suspension. For profile drawing, see Figure 12.149*m*. *Bottom,* rim from bolstered-rim bowl slipped red on the inside, left unslipped on the outside except for the bolstered rim; incised on the unslipped exterior with what may be a variant of the "mat" motif. (Both sherds from San José Mogote, Area C, found while cleaning profile at the level of the San José phase deposits.)

COATEPEC WHITE-RIMMED BLACK

General Description

This is a very hard, fine-grained "white-rimmed black ware" with a metallic sheen, having a definite ring to it when struck. Originally defined in the Tehuacán Valley, this type turns out to have been widespread in Puebla and Oaxaca during the late Early Formative and most of the Middle Formative. So far, however, it has never proved to be abundant at any one site, and it is not yet clear how many centers of production were responsible for it.

Differences in its clay body and its range of vessel forms argue strongly that the type consists of several varieties, made in several different regions; yet vessels from those different regions superficially look very similar. Obviously, the "mental template" was more widespread than the clay body used.

Outleaned-wall bowls in Coatepec White-rimmed Black look very similar whether they come from Moyotzingo in northern Puebla (Jörg Aufdermauer's collections); Las Bocas in western Puebla (looters' backdirt); Tehuacán in southern Puebla (MacNeish's collections); Nochixtlán in northern Oaxaca (Ronald Spores' collections); or San José Mogote in central Oaxaca (our collections). They do not, however, closely resem-

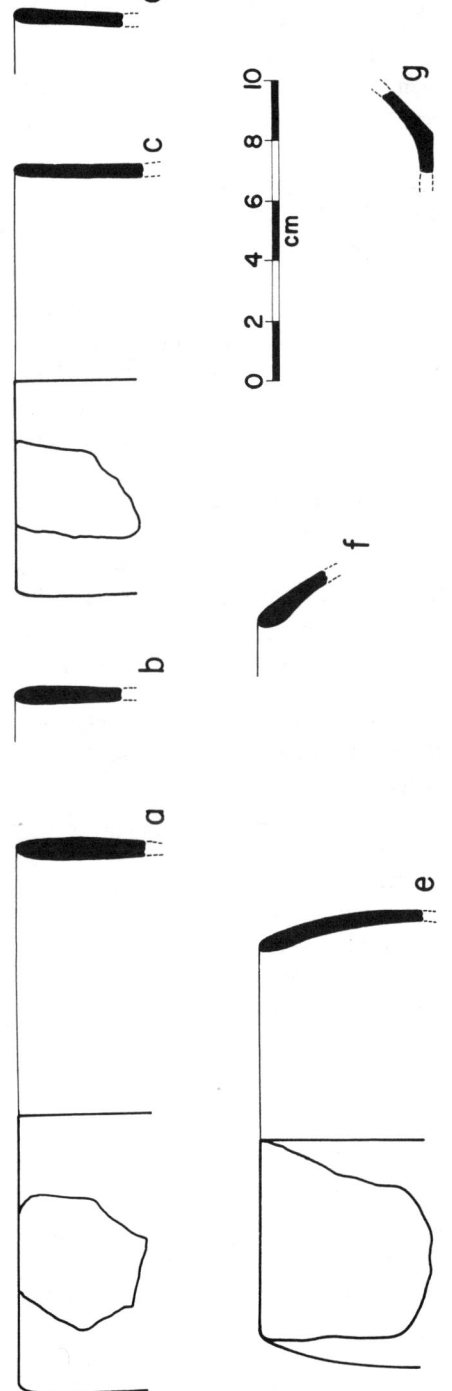

Figure 12.152. La Mina White vessels, all from Area A of San José Mogote (San José phase). *a–d*, rims of cylinders (*a–c*, Household Unit C4; *d*, Zone D2 midden). *e*, incurved-rim bowl, Zone D1 midden. *f*, tecomate or incurved-rim bowl, Household Unit C4. *g*, basal angle sherd from bowl, Household Unit C4.

ble any of the white-rimmed black wares from San Lorenzo on the Gulf Coast (Coe and Diehl 1980).

Chronological History

In Oaxaca, Coatepec White-rimmed Black occurs sporadically throughout the San José and Guadalupe phases. Never common, it appears more frequently at San José Mogote than at any of the smaller villages. It is virtually limited to outleaned-wall bowls and cylinders.

This contrasts with the Tehuacán Variety of the same type, which occurs in a much wider range of vessel forms (MacNeish, Peterson, and Flannery 1970: Fig. 64). The type is also much more common in Tehuacán, with almost 800 specimens recovered by excavation.

Clay Body: The Tehuacán Variety

The original definition of Coatepec White-rimmed Black (Tehuacán variety) is given in MacNeish, Peterson, and Flannery (1970:108). There the type is described as having a clay body, 11% of which is nonplastic particles 0.1–0.5 mm in diameter, and less than 5% of which is nonplastic particles under 0.1 mm in diameter. It is also described as having "a fine slip." We have found it necessary to modify this original definition because (1) Payne's analysis shows that it is "self-slipped," rather than slipped; and (2) it would have been impossible to manufacture the ware with a percentage of nonplastics as low as the Tehuacán report suggests. The problem is that the particle size is so fine that much of it is undetectable even under a binocular microscope.

The nonplastics in the Tehuacán Variety are described as quartz, quartzite, plagioclase (feldspar), biotite mica, muscovite mica, rhyolite and andesite (both volcanics), and volcanic glass. The amount of volcanic tuff in the clay makes it sound very much like the valley-floor alluvial clay used for the Oaxaca Variety, but the exact relationship between the two has not been geologically determined.

Clay Body: The Oaxaca Variety

The clay body is a finely sorted, redeposited alluvial (floodplain) clay that is virtually identical to the clay body used for Delfina Fine Gray (see above). It consists of a kaolinite-montmorillonite mixture ultimately derived from both the Tertiary volcanics and the Precambrian metamorphics, transported some distance from the parent formations, and subjected to de-oxidation by humic acids. About 50% of the volume of the body is nonplastic materials, but most are so fine-grained they cannot be seen even under an ordinary binocular microscope. (It is probably for that reason that Volume III of the Tehuacán reports underestimates the percentage of nonplastics.)

Coatepec White-rimmed Black could be simulated using the same alluvial floodplain clay employed in the making of Delfina Fine Gray. The main difference between the two is in the technique used to produce a black (reduced) wall with a white (oxidized) rim. Payne's reconstruction of how that was done is given below.

Firing Temperature

It was probably fired at 750° C or higher, in a reducing atmosphere. The result is a very hard ware with a definite ring when struck.

Color

In cross-section, sherd cores have usually been reduced to a uniform gray (7.5 YR N5/ to N7/), sandwiched between surfaces that are either black or white depending on where they are located on the vessel. The black color of the lower wall of the vessel is usually uniform, while the oxidized rim varies from white (7.5 YR N8/) to light gray (2.5 Y N7/) to buff or pink (7.5 YR 7/4).

Surface Treatment

This ware is not slipped, but the fineness of the clay particles brought to the surface during burnishing gives it the appearance of a "self slip." Coatepec White-rimmed Black was smoothed with a piece of gourd or a rounded sherd, then burnished (once) very evenly and well with a quartz pebble. Because of the fine grain of the clay body, the burnishing produces an almost metallic sheen like the one seen on Delfina Fine Gray.

Plastic Decoration

Plastic decoration is virtually nonexistent on Oaxaca specimens.

Production of the White-rimmed Black Effect

Examination of a number of Coatepec White-rimmed Black sherds under the binocular microscope revealed cases where particles of silty clay material still clung to parts of the white rim. These were particles that had been fired along with the vessel, then survived millennia in the soil and vigorous washing by an archaeologist. Payne tentatively suggests, therefore, that Coatepec White-rimmed Black was produced by coating the rim with something like a mixture of resin and silty clay. In the course of firing, this area would be protected from the reducing atmosphere of the furnace and remain a neutral white. After firing, it would be a simple matter to flake off the resin-clay mixture (although, as mentioned above, some traces of it remained). The principle involved is similar to the "resist" technique used later on Socorro Fine Gray of the Rosario phase, which preserves the burnish on the rim of the vessel. Note that this method of producing white-rimmed black is different from the alternatives proposed for San José Black-and-White (see above).

We do not know if this method was used on the Tehuacán Variety of Coatepec White-rimmed Black. However, one comment in Volume III of the Tehuacán reports raises this possibility. According to MacNeish, Peterson, and Flannery (1970:108–10), "The area fired white along the rim is usually irregular, but becomes an almost even band in late specimens." This "even band" is the rule, rather than the exception, in the Oaxaca Variety. Thus, it is possible that the "resist" technique was adopted late in the history of the Tehuacán Variety.

Vessel Forms

Flat-based bowls with outleaned walls (Figs. 12.153a–j, 12.154). This was the most common shape in the Oaxaca Variety. Rim profiles were extremely variable: plain and direct, tapered, and slightly expanded examples are all included in our sample.

Rim diameter: 22–32 cm, with a mode of about 26 cm.
Height: Usually one-fourth to one-third the rim diameter.
Basal diameter: Usually about two-thirds the rim diameter.
Wall thickness: 4–8 mm
Plastic decoration: None

Flat-based bowls with vertical (or nearly vertical) walls (Fig. 12.153k). This shape was relatively rare in Oaxaca. Rim profiles were usually direct and slightly rounded or blunted. Because of the small size of our sample, we are unable to give a range of dimensions; one cylinder had a rim diameter of 18 cm.

Plastic decoration: None

DELIA WHITE

General Description

A luxury white ware that appears mainly in one distinctive vessel form: tall beakers with a slightly flaring rim, made on an extremely fine clay body. The creamy, kaolin slip has the appearance of white automobile enamel applied evenly with a spray gun. The region(s) where Delia White was manufactured are not known. At least two different clay bodies can be recognized under the microscope, but the slip and form of the vessels are identical. At least one, and perhaps both, of the clay bodies could be foreign to the Valley of Oaxaca.

Chronological History

Delia White was not present in the early San José phase. It appeared sporadically in middle San José, but was always rare. In the late San José phase it increased slightly, sometimes appearing as burial offerings. However, it was never common in the Early Formative.

It was in the early Guadalupe phase that Delia White reached its peak frequency. This was especially true of the tall white beakers, which would have held enough liquid for one adult individual at one meal. Their presence around public buildings and relatively high-status households suggests that they were prized as luxury vessels, perhaps for beverages such as chocolate or pulque.

Delia White began to decline in frequency during the late Guadalupe phase. During the Rosario phase it was absent to rare, its place being taken by comparable beakers in Socorro Fine Gray.

Clay Body

The clay body used for Delia White is uniformly fine, in the neighborhood of 24 mesh. Under the microscope, Payne has distinguished two variants as follows.

Variant A. This was an alluvial clay redeposited at great distance from the parent formation, which seems to have been weathered crystalline (granitic) rock in an extreme state of decomposition. The feldspars are largely broken down, but scattered particles of pyroxenes and quartz and occasional fragments of biotite mica can be detected. Most particles are under 0.3 mm. It would not surprise us to learn that this clay was foreign to the Valley of Oaxaca.

Variant B. This is redeposited clay of lacustrine or aeolian origin, showing extremely fine division of principal ingredients. The parent material was weathered crystalline rock, but the clay body was deposited a great distance away. In addition, the body may have been further refined by decanting. Sparse grains of rounded quartz and rare feldspar can be detected, but most particles are under 0.3 mm. We know of no lacustrine settings in the Valley of Oaxaca that could have produced this clay body.

Firing Temperature

It was probably fired at 750 to 770° C, in an atmosphere that varied from full oxidation to weak reduction. (Apparently, little attention was paid to the oxidation-reduction contrast because the engobe was so iron-free that it stayed pure white in the above range of atmospheres.)

Color

In the case of Variant A, oxidized specimens show a clay body fired light brown (7.5 YR 6/4). Examples of Variant B, on the other hand, tend to have a clay body that fired light gray (10 YR 7/1). Weakly reduced specimens of Variant A also fired this color, which makes separation of the two variants difficult without microscopic analysis of every sherd.

These variations in clay body and firing atmosphere had no effect on the color of the kaolin engobe. Regardless of clay body, it varied only from pure white to slightly off-white (10 YR 8/2).

Surface Treatment

All vessels were carefully smoothed, perhaps with a piece of gourd, before slipping. After the engobe had dried, they were

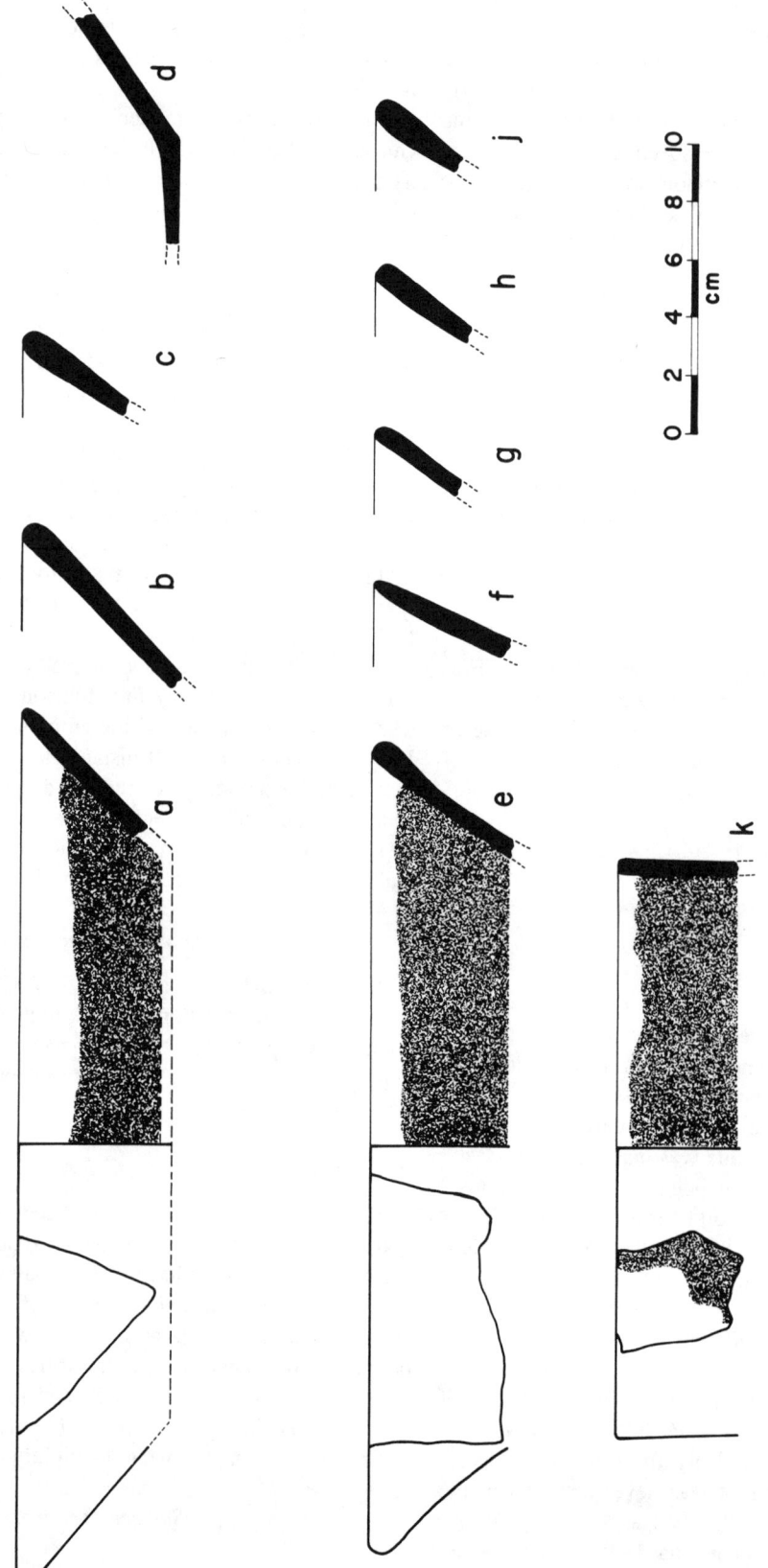

Figure 12.153. Coatepec White-rimmed Black bowls from San José Mogote (SJM), Tierras Largas (TL), and Barrio del Rosario Huitzo. a–c, rims of outleaned-wall bowls, Area A, SJM (a, Zone D2 midden; b, c, Zone D1 midden). d, basal angle sherd from outleaned-wall bowl, Household Unit C3, Area A, SJM. e–j, rims from outleaned-wall bowls (e, Zone E, Area C, SJM; f, Household Unit C3, Area A, SJM; g, House 3, Area A, Huitzo; h, Zone D1 midden, Area A, SJM; j, Feature 105, TL). k, cylinder rim, Zone D1 midden, Area C, SJM. (All specimens from SJM are San José phase; the specimens from TL and Huitzo are Guadalupe phase.)

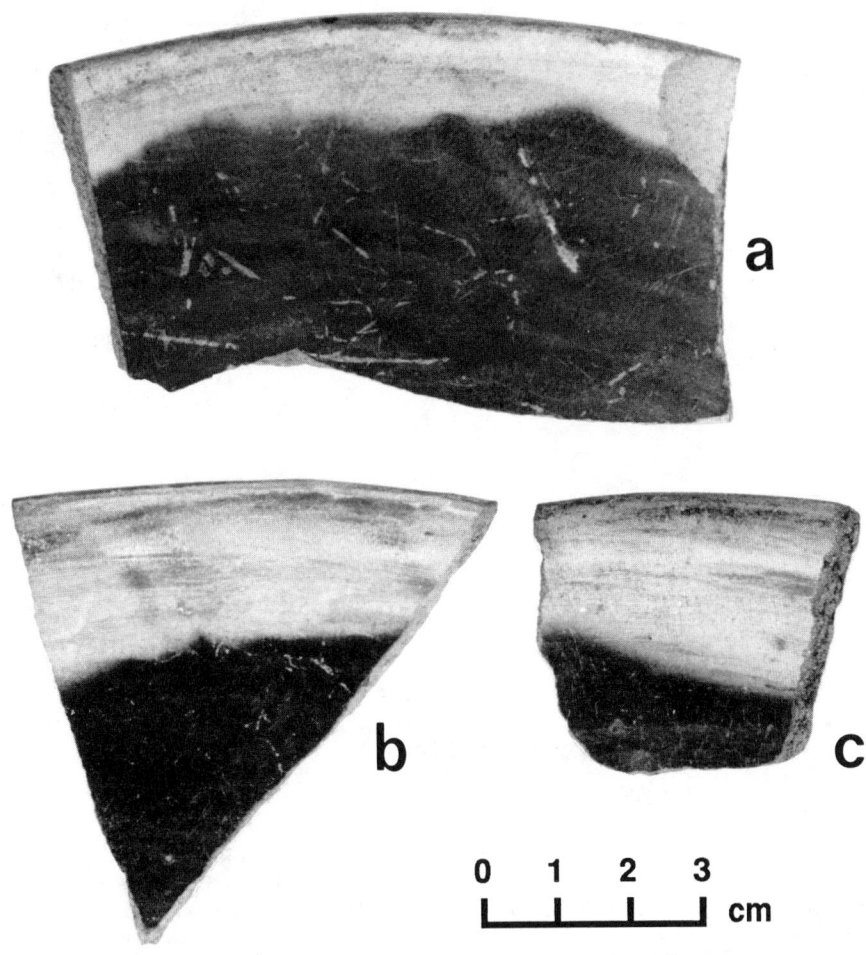

Figure 12.154. Coatepec White-rimmed Black outleaned-wall bowl rims from San José Mogote (San José phase). *a*, Zone E, Area C. *b*, Zone D2 midden, Area A. *c*, Zone D1 midden, Area A.

burnished (once) very evenly with a quartz pebble. The resultant surface has a slick, shiny appearance.

Application of the White Engobe

Delia White vessels were covered by a pure white, iron-free kaolin engobe, applied so evenly that the vessel must have been dipped, or the engobe poured on. Particularly in the case of the beakers, the vessels are small enough so it is not unlikely that they were dipped in engobe.

The source of this kaolin engobe is unknown. In contrast to earlier white wares, like Atoyac Yellow-white or Xochiltepec White, vessels in Delia White have the appearance of shiny white enamel, such as that used on automobiles or household appliances today. We have not yet seen beakers with an engobe like this in pottery collections from neighboring areas such as Tehuacán, Nochixtlán, the Isthmus of Tehuantepec, or the southern Gulf Coast.

Plastic Decoration

Plastic decoration is rare; usually limited to incising (*sgraffito*).

Vessel Forms

Tall beakers with slightly flaring rims (Figs. 12.155a-f, 12.156). This is by far the most common form in which Delia White appeared. Bases are flat to slightly convex. The vessel walls are tall, vertical for the lower two-thirds of the beaker, then gently flaring over the upper third. So far all complete (or nearly complete) beakers have been found in Guadalupe phase contexts.

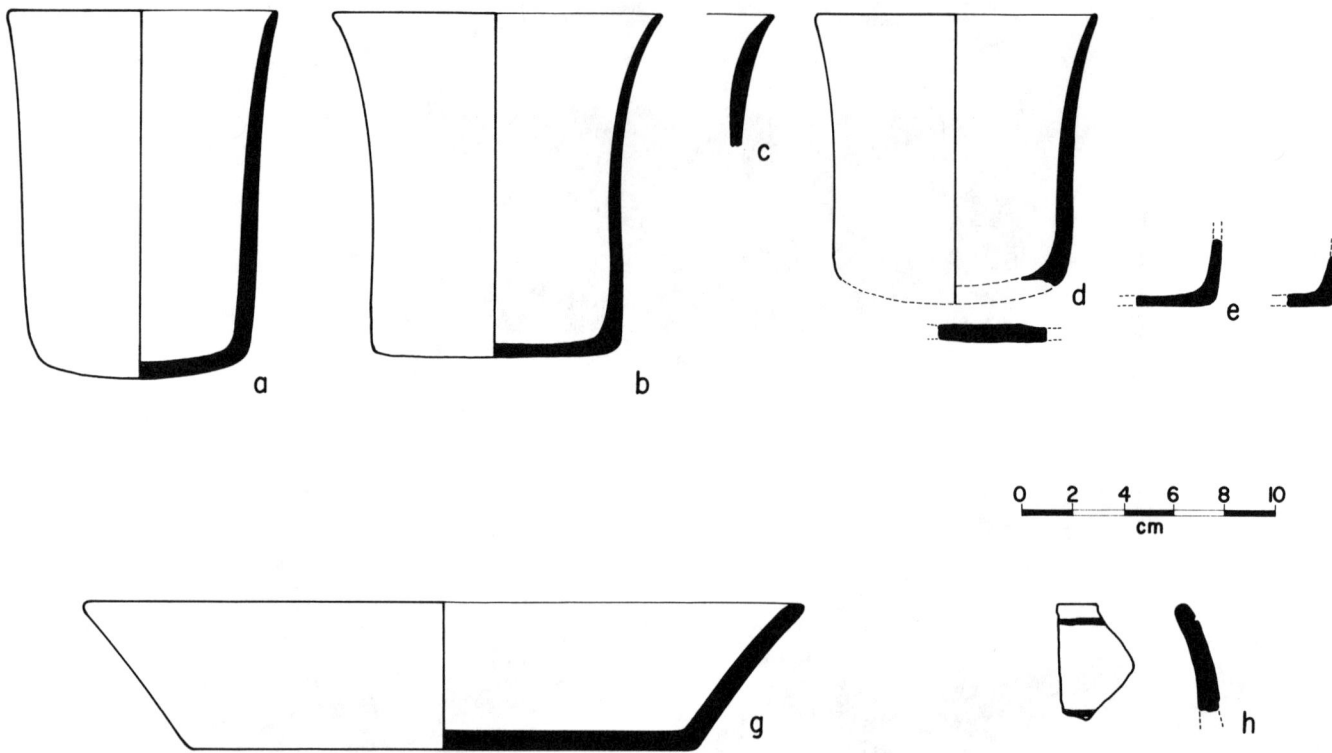

Figure 12.155. Delia White vessels from Tierras Largas (TL), San José Mogote (SJM), and Barrio del Rosario Huitzo. *a,* beaker, Variant A, Feature 58, TL (Guadalupe phase). *b,* beaker, Variant A; Vessel 1 of Feature 99, TL (Guadalupe phase). *c,* rim of beaker, Zone F3, Area A, Huitzo (an early Guadalupe phase provenience that could contain redeposited San José phase sherds). *d,* beaker, Variant B, fill of Structure 4, Area A, Huitzo (an early Guadalupe phase provenience that could contain redeposited San José phase sherds). *e, f,* bases of beakers from early Guadalupe phase proveniences at Huitzo that could contain redeposited San José phase sherds (*e,* fill of Structure 4, Area A; *f,* Zone F3, Area A). *g,* outleaned-wall bowl, Variant A, reconstructed from sherds scattered over the floor of House 4, Area C, SJM (San José phase). *h,* incurved-rim bowl with incised decoration, Zone E1, Area A, Huitzo (Guadalupe phase).

Barrio del Rosario Huitzo, Fábrica San José, Tierras Largas, and San José Mogote all had them, and we have seen fragments of them on the surface of other sites. Because these vessels would have held 600–800 cc of liquid, we suspect that they are for individual use, either in ritual contexts or by relatively high-status persons.

Rim diameter: Usually 9–12 cm
Height: Usually 10–14 cm, or roughly 1.0 to 1.3 times the rim diameter.
Basal diameter: Rarely more than 80% of the rim diameter.
Wall thickness: Usually 3–7 mm
Plastic decoration: None

Flat-based bowls with outleaned walls (Fig. 12.155g). This was perhaps the first vessel shape in which Delia White occurred; it is known as far back in time as House 4 in Area C at San José Mogote (relatively late in the San José phase). We have so few examples that no range of dimensions can be given.

Bowls with incurved rims (Fig. 12.155h). This is a rare form, similar in shape to incurved-rim bowls in Atoyac Yellow-white. One example from Huitzo has an incised line at the rim, perhaps made with a maguey spine.

Hemispherical bowls (Figs. 12.157, 12.158). One unique Delia White vessel, found with a late San José phase burial, is a large hemispherical bowl covered with a complex pattern of incised lines. The pattern looks like a series of step-fret motifs that may have evolved out of earlier double-line-break design elements. This vessel is so atypical that we doubt it was made in the Valley of Oaxaca.

OTHER FOREIGN POTTERY TYPES

We have described a number of pottery types that we believe originated in other regions of Mesoamerica, reaching Oaxaca as import wares. We pointed out that many of those pottery types

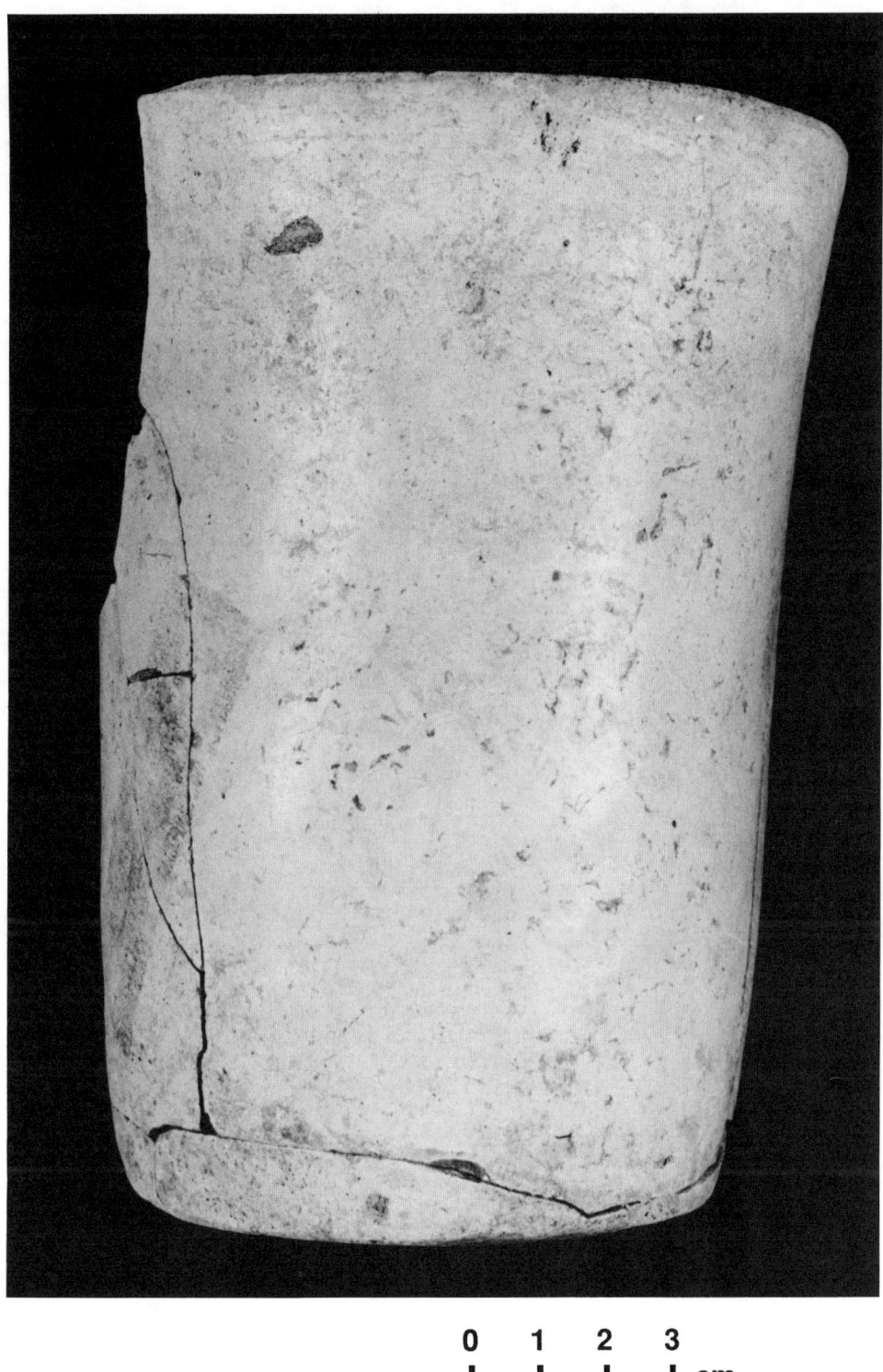

Figure 12.156. Delia White beaker, Variant A, from Feature 58, Tierras Largas (Guadalupe phase).

282 Early Formative Pottery of Oaxaca

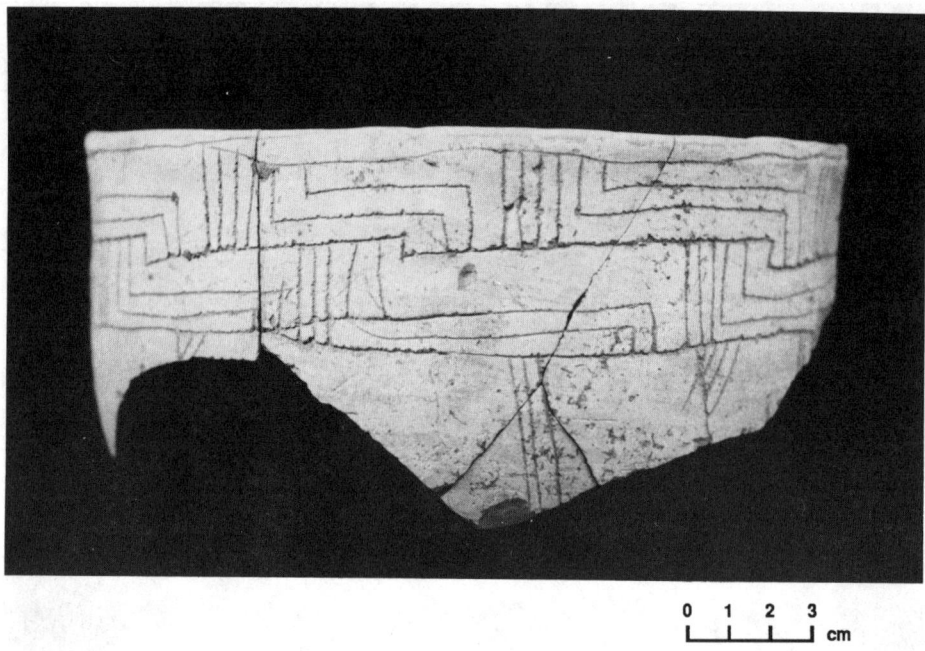

Figure 12.157. Delia White hemispherical bowl, Variant A, with elaborate incising. Burial 14, Area C, San José Mogote (late San José phase). For a reconstruction of this bowl, see Figure 12.158.

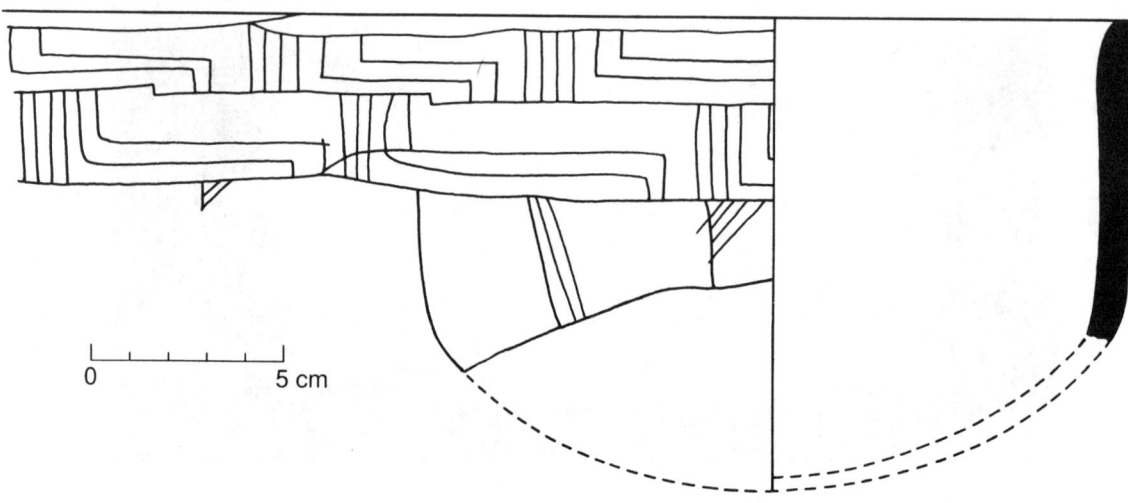

Figure 12.158. Reconstruction drawing of incised hemispherical bowl in Delia White shown in Figure 12.157. Burial 14, Area C, San José Mogote. Because Delia White is rarely incised, this late San José phase bowl is unusual and almost certainly imported from outside the Valley of Oaxaca.

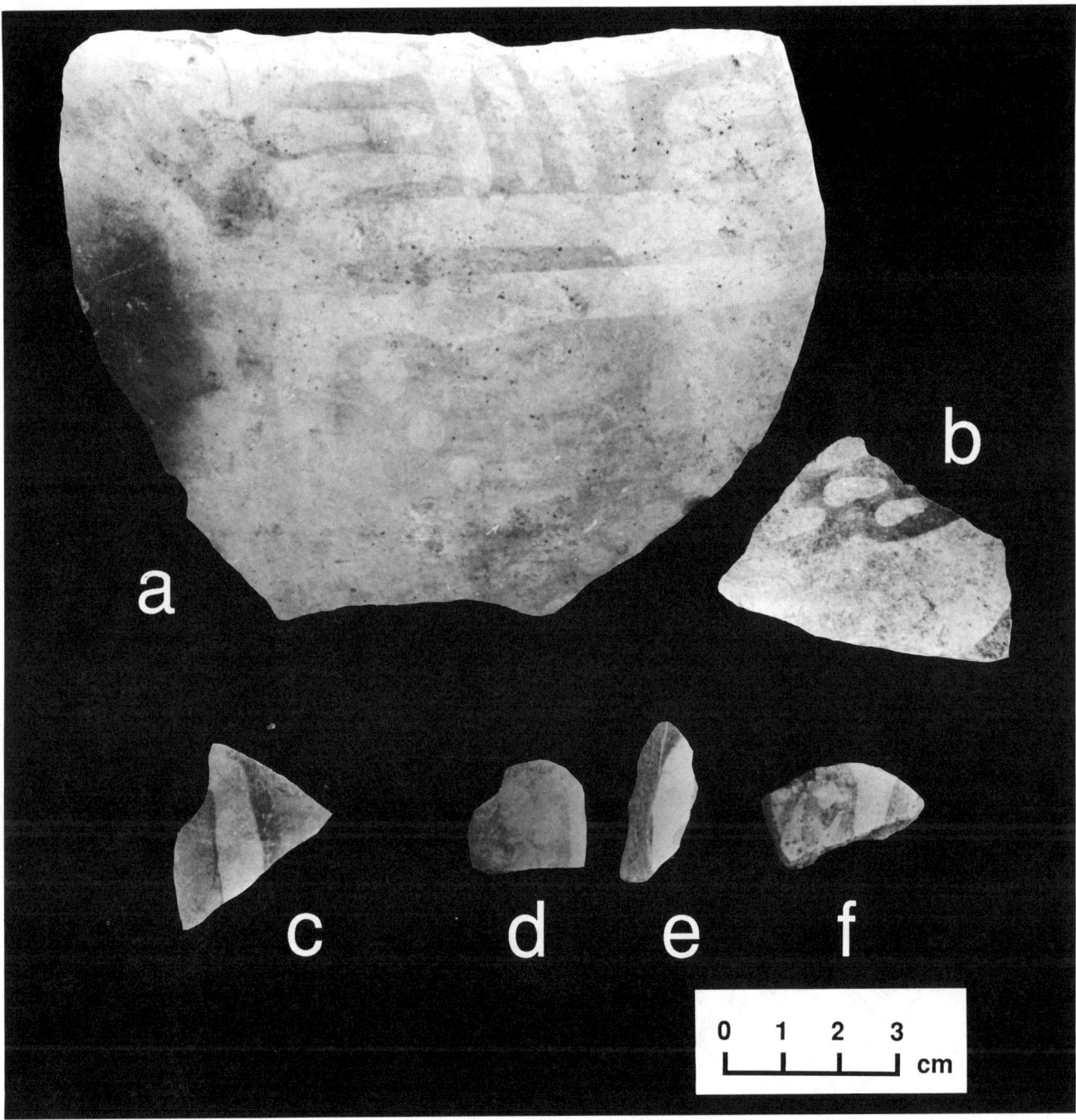

Figure 12.159. Paloma Negative sherds from Tlapacoya-Zohapilco, Basin of Mexico, and Area A of San José Mogote (SJM). *a*, large sherd from Zohapilco T IV A-6. *b*, small sherd from Zohapilco T IV A-7. *c*, small sherd from SJM, Area A, Household Unit C4. *d-f*, small sherds from SJM, Area A, Household Unit C1. *c-f* are all San José phase. (*a* and *b*, courtesy of Christine Niederberger.)

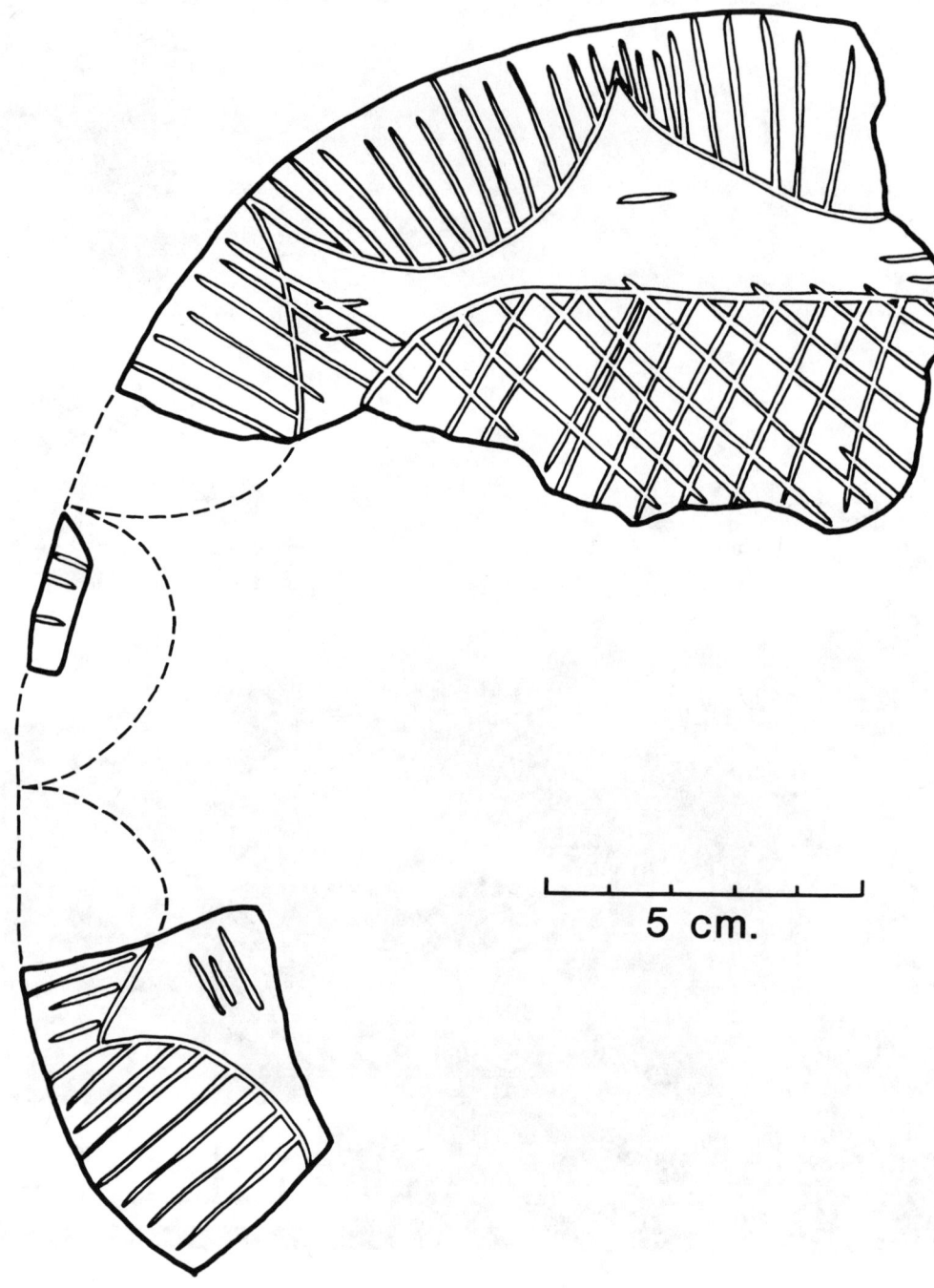

Figure 12.160. Fragments of probable Cesto White bowl with sunburst "grater bowl" design incised on the interior of the base. Vessel 6, House 16, Area B, San José Mogote (very late San José phase). This bowl is comparable to specimens from Tlapacoya-Zohapilco illustrated by Niederberger (1987: Figs. 482–484).

Figure 12.161. Guamuchal Brushed tecomate sherds from Area C, San José Mogote (San José phase). *Top,* tecomate rim with a raised, brushed band decorated by two rows of finger punches that include fingernail marks (Feature 27, Zone E). *Bottom,* tecomate sherd with raised brushed band (Feature 29, Zone E).

came to be imitated on local Oaxaca clays almost as soon as they arrived. Such types tend to occur with some regularity and usually appear at more than one Formative village.

There were, however, other foreign pottery types that occurred only sporadically, and seem never to have been locally imitated. These rarer foreign types showed up almost exclusively at San José Mogote, the largest village in the valley. This was the village that seems to have had the greatest contact with other regions of Mesoamerica.

Undoubtedly there were many gifts exchanged between highly ranked individuals at San José Mogote and highly ranked individuals in other regions, and some of the our foreign vessels may simply have been the containers in which those gifts arrived. Alternatively, some families at San José Mogote may have had "trade partners" in certain other regions with whom they exchanged products. Supporting the latter alternative is the fact that each of these rare foreign pottery types seems to show up in one specific residential ward at San José Mogote, and not in others. While this might be sampling error, it could also be synchronic variation (see Chapter 16).

PALOMA NEGATIVE

This Valley of Mexico type, defined by Niederberger (1987:554–57), occurs throughout the Ayotla phase and earliest Manantial phase at Tlapacoya-Zohapilco. It has distinctive patterns of dots, triangles, long and short lines, all done in whitish gray "resist" technique against a grayish brown background. Unmistakable sherds of this type appeared in Household Units C4 and C1 in Area A of San José Mogote (Fig. 12.159). The identification of Paloma Negative was confirmed by Niederberger herself.

CESTO WHITE

This Valley of Mexico type (Niederberger 1987:569–72) is most characteristic of the Manantial phase. The clay body is reddish brown; over this goes a white engobe reminiscent of that used for Atoyac Yellow-white. One of the most distinctive vessel forms is an outleaned-wall bowl with a hachured sunburstlike "grater bowl" design incised on the inside of the base (Niederberger 1987: Figs. 482–484). The incising exposes the brick red clay body, highlighting the design. Vessel 6, piece-plotted on the floor of House 16, Area B, San José Mogote, was such a "grater bowl" (Fig. 12.160). Since House 16 was a late San José phase provenience, correlation with the Manantial phase seems perfect (see Chapter 19).

MADERA BROWN?

House 16 of Area B, San José Mogote, also produced a sherd of what may be Madera Brown pottery from Morelos. David Grove, who defined Madera Brown at the site of La Juana/San Pablo in the Valley of Morelos, has examined our sherd and agrees that it "might" be Madera Brown (Grove, personal communication).

GUAMUCHAL BRUSHED

This type was originally found in Cuadros phase levels on the Pacific Coast of Guatemala and defined by Coe and Flannery (1967:28–30). More recently it was discovered by Pierre Agrinier at Mirador in western Chiapas (Agrinier 1989). The only vessel form in which Guamuchal Brushed occurs is a large tecomate with a raised, brushed band encircling the vessel just below the plain rim band (Coe and Flannery 1967: Plates 6–9). The brushed band may be further decorated by finger-punching, stepped jabs, herringbone gouges, and other plastic techniques. Several Guamuchal Brushed tecomate sherds were found in Features 27 and 29 of Area C, San José Mogote (Fig. 12.161). Several more were found in Feature 41, a pit associated with House 9 in Area C. Our identification of the type has been confirmed by Michael Coe. Since all three features were San José phase proveniences, the correlation with the Cuadros phase seems reasonable.

Synchronic Variation in Foreign Types

While one must always consider the possibility of sampling error, it appears that there are differences in the proveniences of foreign wares at San José Mogote that may be as interesting as the types themselves.

Area C, near the western edge of the village, gave us Guamuchal Brushed from Chiapas or western Guatemala. This residential ward also showed southern connections in some of its other ceramics.

Area B, in the south-central part of the village, gave us Cesto White from the Basin of Mexico and possibly Madera Brown from Morelos. The motifs on Atoyac Yellow-white pottery from Area B also showed similarities with Basin of Mexico motifs.

Area A, near the eastern edge of the village, gave us Paloma Negative from the southern Basin of Mexico. In this residential ward, the motifs in Leandro Gray and Delfina Fine Gray also showed similarities with vessels from Tlapacoya.

The localized occurrence of these rare foreign types contrasts with the more widespread occurrence of Ocós Black, Xochiltepec White, Coatepec White-rimmed Black, and Delia White. Several of these export wares seem to have been imitated with local raw materials as soon as they arrived, and some of the imitations are so good that they cannot be detected without expert microscopic examination. While never abundant, they could show up anywhere at San José Mogote.

Chapter 13

The Transition from Tierras Largas Phase to San José Phase: Midden Stratigraphy

Area C, near the western limits of the site of San José Mogote, provided us with the clearest stratigraphy for the transition from the Tierras Largas phase to the San José phase.

Area C falls within the jurisdiction of the *municipio* of Guadalupe Etla, rather than the *agencia* of San José Mogote. Here the piedmont spur on which the archaeological deposits lie begins to drop off westward toward the alluvial plain of the Atoyac River. The break in slope occurs on land belonging to Sr. Espiridión Hernández, whose *mojonera* (a deeply-set stone property marker) served as the "zero datum" for Area C (see Figs. 9.1 and 9.2).

Near Sr. Hernández's *mojonera,* the natural slope is broken by a large cut bank, produced early in the twentieth century when masses of earth were removed from the site to make adobes. All the adobe walls of the courtyards and dairy cattle pens below this cut bank are filled with Early Formative sherds. In the cut bank itself, there were up to 2.5 m of Formative deposits exposed when we first examined it in 1967. This cut bank lay 400 m due west of Area A, and promised to complement the data from the latter area.

In 1969, we decided to shave the Area C cut bank to a true vertical profile whose stratigraphy could be read. We began by shaving a 37.5 m section running almost due north–south (magnetic). These deposits proved so interesting that a crew of workers under James Schoenwetter continued profile cutting for an additional 36 m to the north, at which point bedrock appeared at a higher level and some of the earliest deposits were consequently absent. Meanwhile, a crew of workers under Flannery continued the profile 19.5 m to the south, at which point it intersected the Area B profile. This gave us a 93 m cross-section which we will call the Area C Master Profile (see Chapter 9).

While the whole 93 m profile was informative, the original 37.5 m section proved to be the most interesting. We therefore designated this segment a Control Section, which meant that all levels would be carefully excavated by small teams of experienced workers, all deposits would be screened, and all sherds would be saved no matter how small.

The stratigraphy of the Control Section of the Area C Master Profile was extremely complex, including midden deposits, pits and other features, burials, houses, and public buildings. With Sr. Hernández's *mojonera* serving as the datum point, both north–south and east–west, we set stakes along the top of the profile at one-meter intervals to establish the first set of 1 × 1 meter squares. These squares were to be labeled South 1 to South 38 (abbreviated S1-S38), with S1 running from 0.0 to 1.0 m south of the *mojonera* and S38 running from 37.0 to 38.0 south of the *mojonera*. We considered the earth we had removed while cutting the profile to have come from this initial set of squares, making the profile itself the east wall of Squares S1-S38. This allowed us to establish the grid shown in Figure 9.2 of Chapter 9, one in which numbers run N-S and letters of the alphabet run E-W. In other words, as we began systematic excavation of the shaved profile, we would be cutting into Squares S1A-S38A.

The entire profile was drawn before we began this systematic excavation. Numbers were assigned to every house, feature, public structure, and burial that could be seen in the profile. For example, the bones of Burials 1, 2, and 4 (Squares S27 and S29) could be seen sticking out of the profile long before they were excavated; the modern adobe makers had already cut off their western extremities. The sand floor of House 4 was already visible in cross-section in the east profile of Squares S15-S19. The cross-sections of Structures 3, 5, and 6, still enigmatic at that time, were already visible in the profile (see Chapter 11).

In this chapter, we will limit ourselves to the profiles of squares S15 through S33, which are shown in Figures 13.1–13.4. From earliest to latest, the relevant strata of the control section were as follows.

Features in Bedrock

Bedrock in Area C was soft white volcanic tuff (ignimbrite), riddled with postholes and storage pits of the Tierras Largas phase. Two of the pits in bedrock, Features 22 and 23, are included in our sherd counts for the Control Section (Table 13.1). Neither pit had a very large sample, but both were sealed beneath

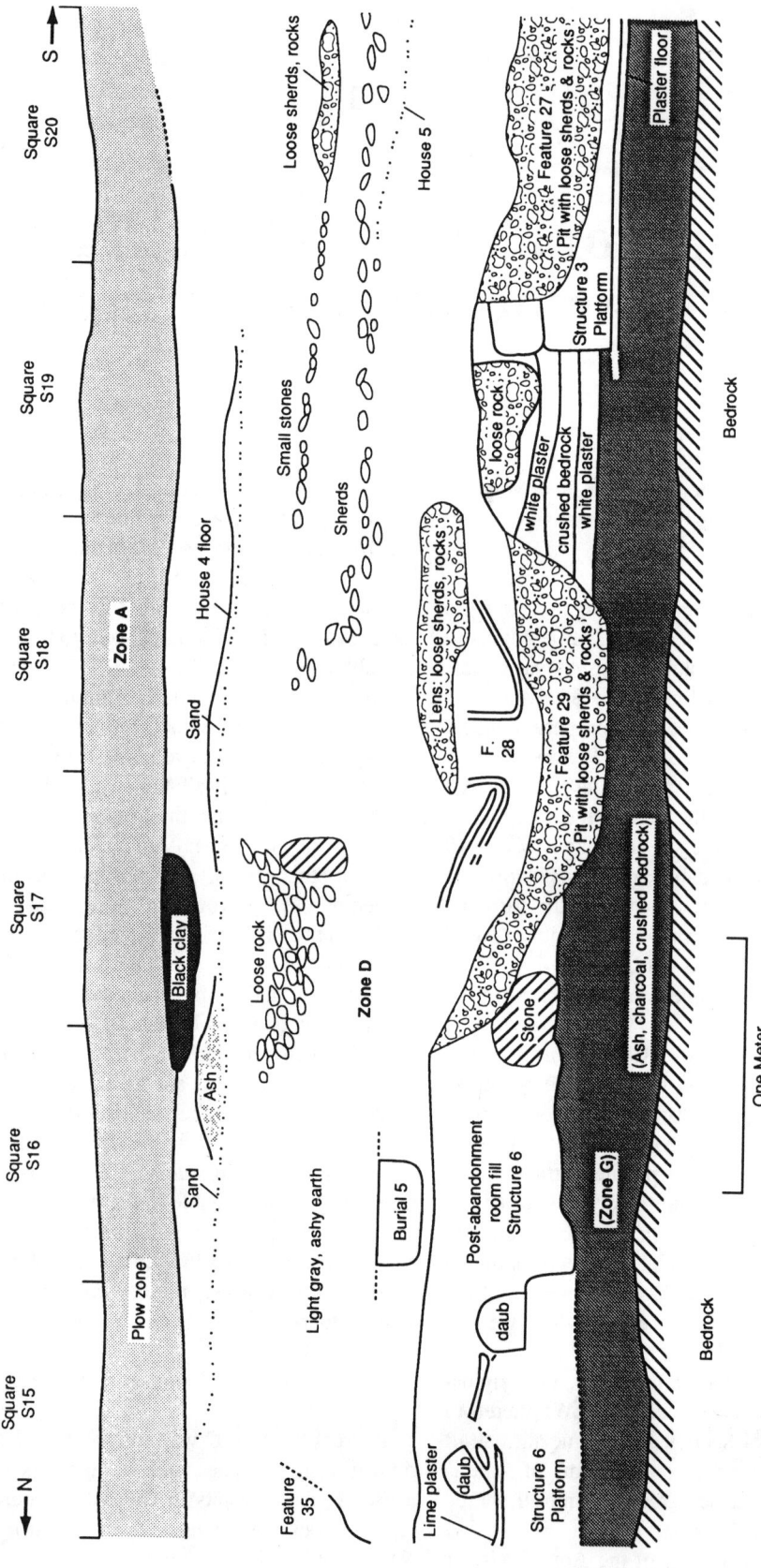

Figure 13.1. East profile of Squares S15–S20 of the Control Section, Area C Master Profile, San José Mogote.

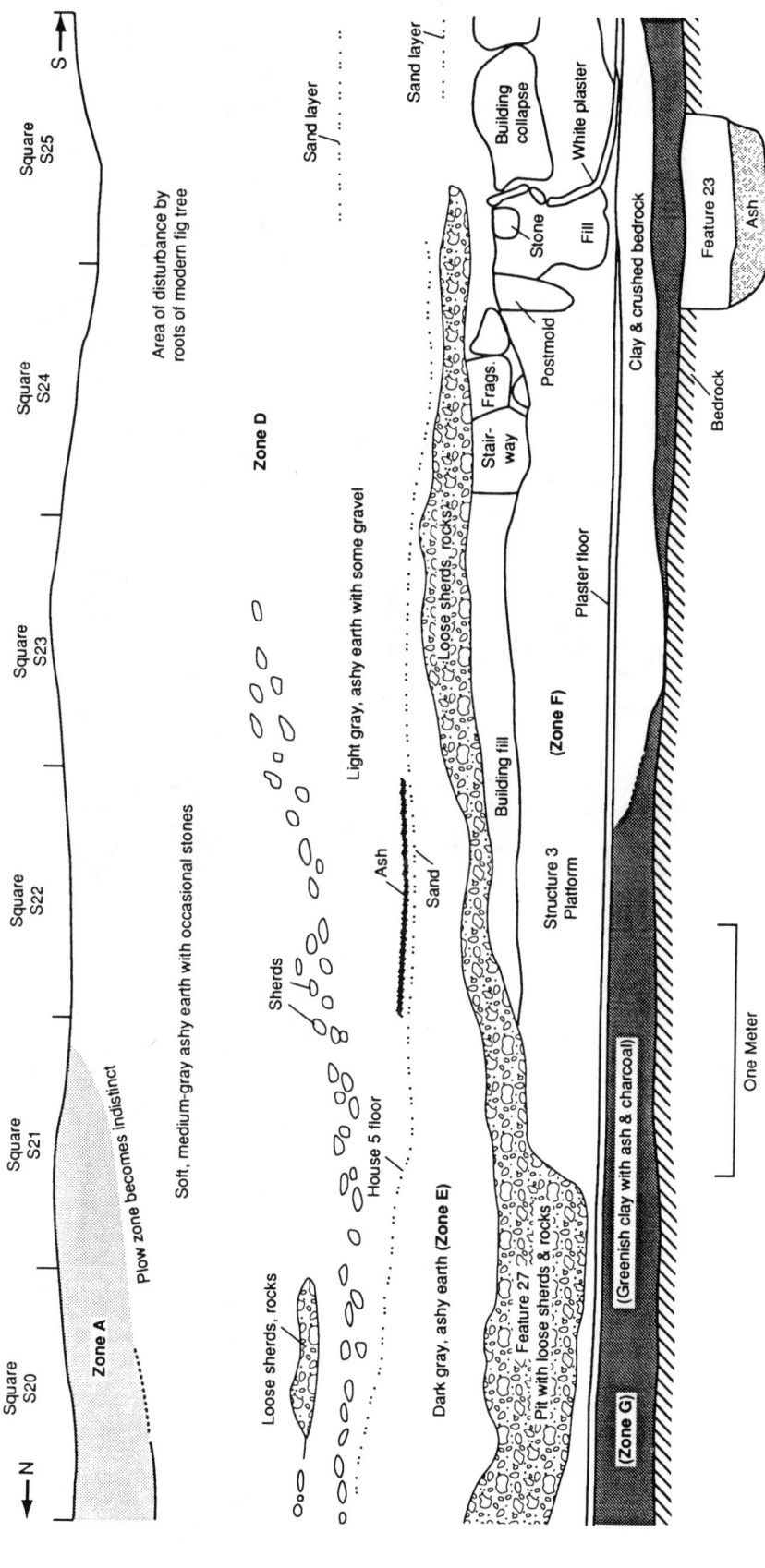

Figure 13.2. East profile of Squares S20–S25 of the Control Section, Area C Master Profile, San José Mogote.

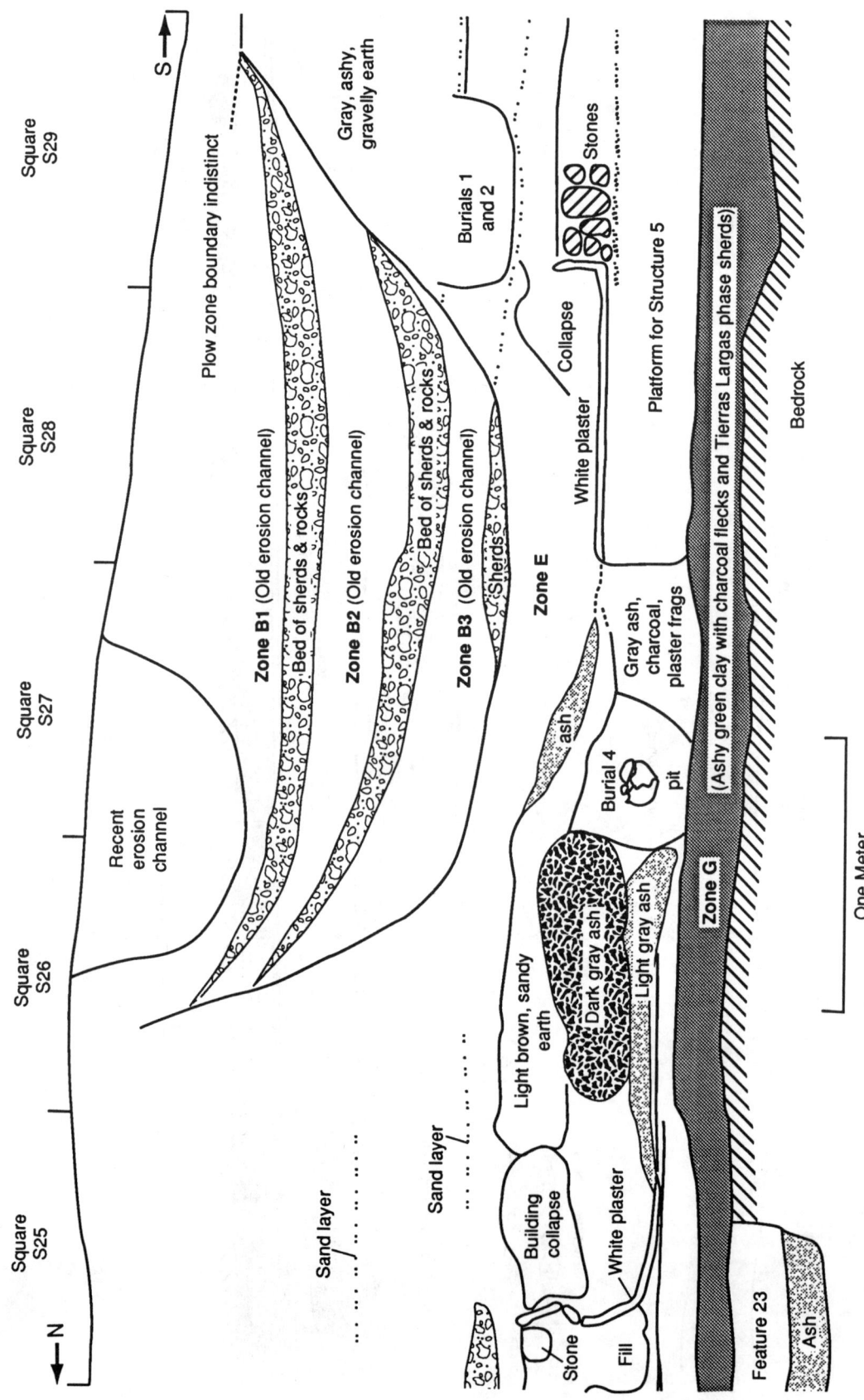

Figure 13.3. East profile of Squares S25–S29 of the Control Section, Area C Master Profile, San José Mogote.

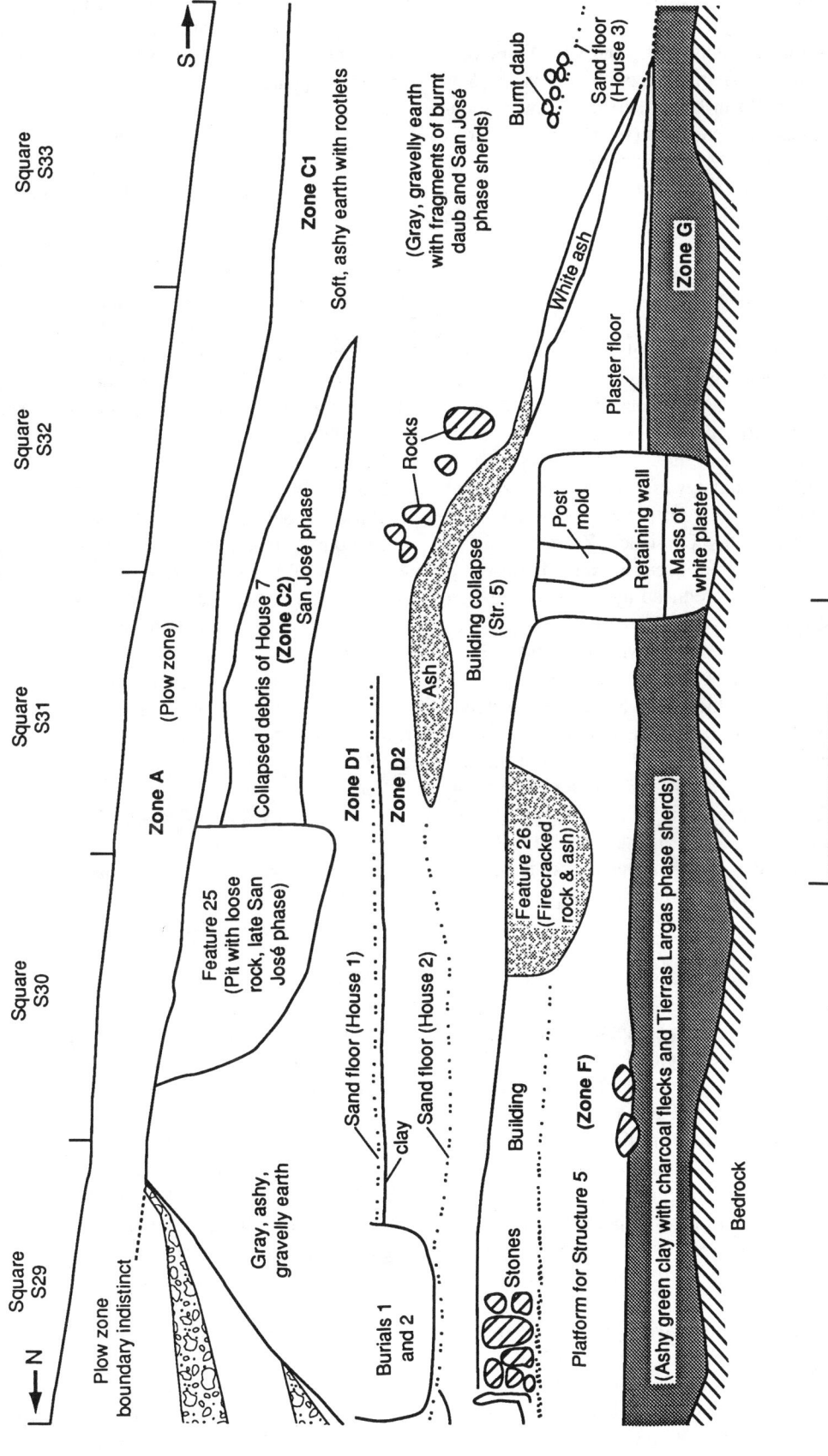

Figure 13.4. East profile of Squares S29–S33 of the Control Section, Area C Master Profile, San José Mogote.

Zone G; this made it unlikely that either would have intrusive sherds.

These features are shown in Figures 13.5 and 13.6. Our suspicion is that both date to late Tierras Largas times. When Yda Schreuder included Feature 23 in her Brainerd-Robinson seriation of Tierras Largas phase proveniences (see Chapter 10), it fit best between Features 75 and 142 of Household Unit LTL-1 at Tierras Largas. It will be remembered that these were judged to be the latest features in a late Tierras Largas phase household unit.

Zone G

Zone G was a thick layer of midden debris, charcoal flecks, discarded lime plaster, and the kind of greenish-black clay that sometimes forms above volcanic tuff bedrock. It directly overlay bedrock, but was not necessarily the level from which the postholes in bedrock had come. Some of those holes were from posts driven down from the public buildings of Zone F; others seemed to be from small residences whose construction might have preceded the laying down of the Zone G midden. Zone G itself, at least in this part of Area C, did not seem to contain houses. It appeared to be a barrio midden, produced by repeated dumping of household and construction debris over a period of time.

Our sample of Zone G sherds was drawn only from those 1 × 1 meter squares that were without later intrusive features. The sample totaled 1909 sherds, of which 1839 (96%) were of types that peaked in frequency during the Tierras Largas phase; only 38 (2%) were of types that went on to reach their peak in the San José phase. Our assessment of Zone G is that it dates to the late Tierras Largas phase. This assessment is strengthened by the fact that when Yda Schreuder added Zone G to her Brainerd-Robinson seriation of Tierras Largas phase proveniences, it fit best between Features 75 and 142 of Household Unit LTL-1 at Tierras Largas.

Zone F

The most distinctive feature of stratigraphic Zone F was a series of Tierras Largas phase public buildings. Three of those buildings—Structures 3, 5, and 6—are described and dated in Chapter 11. Our sample of sherds from Zone F did not come from any of those buildings; it was drawn from the areas intervening between them. The matrix in such areas consisted of midden debris mixed with thousands of tiny fragments of lime plaster and daub; the plaster and daub fragments were presumed to be decomposition products of buildings such as Structures 3, 5, and 6.

As Table 13.1 makes clear, Zone F also dated to the late Tierras Largas phase. Of the sample of 512 sherds, 471 (92%) were Tierras Largas phase diagnostics, while only 19 (4%) were of types that went on to reach their peak in the San José phase. Five of those sherds were of curious "hybrid types": one combined attributes of Atoyac Yellow-white and Matadamas Red, while four combined attributes of Clementina Fine Red-on-Buff and San José Red-on-White. Such "hybrids" appear to be short-lived experiments at combining old Tierras Largas phase slips with some of the new engobes that would eventually characterize the San José phase.

Zone E

Zone E was a diffuse layer of sherds and refuse from the San José phase, which overlay the razed public buildings of Zone F. It seemed to represent a period of leveling and filling prior to the construction of ordinary wattle-and-daub residences of the San José phase. Feature 27, an irregular borrow pit intrusive from Zone E into Zone F, yielded sherds of what appear to be Guamuchal Brushed tecomates from the region of Chiapas/Guatemala (see Fig. 12.161). Such sherds are characteristic of the Pac phase at Mirador, Chiapas (Agrinier 1989), and the Cuadros phase at Salinas La Blanca, Guatemala (Coe and Flannery 1967).

Zone E seemed to fall somewhere in the first half of the San José phase, but could not be assigned to the very beginning of the phase. Of our sample of 712 sherds (drawn only from squares with no intrusive features), 393 (55%) were San José phase diagnostics and 280 (39%) were of Tierras Largas phase types that lasted into the early San José phase. To be sure, some of the latter could have been redeposited from earlier levels, especially given the number of pits dug down from Zone E.

Zone E has the look of refuse from low-status households; 217 of the sherds (30%) were from Fidencio Coarse vessels, while types like Delfina Fine Gray and San José Black-and-White were absent.

Selected Features from Zone E

Several features, most of them pits, increased our understanding of Zone E in the Control Section of the Area C profile. Two of those pits were Features 27 and 29.

Feature 27, a rugged and irregular pit, or depression, filled with loose rock and sherds, began in Zone E and intruded into the ruins of Structure 3. Because its contents appeared to be debris swept into a borrow pit, they were not deemed worthy of statistical treatment. However, the contents were recorded because they provide us with a look at the kind of sherds lying around Area C at the time of the deposition of Zone E.

Included were abundant Tierras Largas Burnished Plain hemispherical bowls and jar body sherds (mostly with wiped or plain interiors); Avelina Red-on-Buff hemispherical bowls; Matadamas Red and Matadamas Orange body sherds; a jar slipped with both Matadamas Orange and Atoyac Yellow-white slips; Fidencio Coarse jar body sherds; Leandro Gray excised cylinders and outleaned-wall bowls; Atoyac Yellow-white cylinders, vertical-necked jars, rocker stamped tecomates, and smudged bolstered-rim bowls with excised fire-serpent motifs; body sherds from Lupita Heavy Plain rocker stamped tecomates; a few Lupita Heavy Plain charcoal braziers/potstands; numerous San José Red-on-White bowls; San José Black-and-White cylinders, bolstered-rim bowls, and zoned punctate tecomates; and fragments of typical San José figurines. Like Zone E, Feature 27 probably falls somewhere in the first half of the San José phase.

At least three sherds in Feature 27 were from types foreign to the Valley of Oaxaca. Two were Coatepec White-rimmed Black bowl rims. The third was a tecomate rim of what appeared to be Guamuchal Brushed (Fig. 12.161), an important type of the Pac phase of central Chiapas (Agrinier 1989) and the Cuadros phase of the Pacific Coast of Guatemala (Coe and Flannery 1967: Plates 6–9).

Feature 29 was a second ragged, irregular pit or depression filled with loose rock and sherds, only a meter north of Feature 27 and in the same Master Profile. It began in Zone E and intruded into the ruins of Structure 6.

The fill of Feature 29 resembled that of Zone E. Included were abundant Tierras Largas Burnished Plain jars and hemispherical bowls; Avelina Red-on-Buff hemispherical bowls; Clementina Fine Red-on-Buff hemispherical bowls; Matadamas Orange jars, bowls, and tecomates; abundant Fidencio Coarse jar body sherds; Leandro Gray cylinders with excised fire-serpent motifs; and a few Atoyac Yellow-white sherds, consisting mainly of undecorated body sherds.

Again, the most notable find in Feature 29 was a tecomate rim sherd identifiable as Guamuchal Brushed (Fig. 12.161). This second find of a Guamuchal Brushed sherd, combined with a third specimen found in Feature 41, provides us with good crossties between the Valley of Oaxaca and the Chiapas/Guatemala region. Within our Area C profile, Cuadros trade wares span the period from the beginning of Zone E (early San José phase) to the time of House 9, a residence with which Feature 41 is contemporaneous and probably associated (middle San José phase).

Zone D2

Zone D of the Control Section was a uniform stratum of tan or buff San José phase debris from the decomposition of dozens of whitewashed wattle-and-daub houses. It was up to 1.5 m thick in places, but really presented no strong color or texture differences that would have facilitated its subdivision. The sole exceptions to this uniformity were a series of sand-coated clay floors from houses, which were visible in the profile but did not run the full length of the Control Section.

More than a dozen of those houses were observed in the profile, and ten of them were numbered before excavation. Each was clearly recognizable because of the layer of clean sand on its floor, seen in cross-section where the house had been cut through by recent adobe makers. Selecting a block of one-meter squares that included a given house, we peeled off the overlying deposits, stopping 15 cm above the house floor. From here down, work proceeded by trowel, ice pick, paint brush, and whisk broom, with tools and restorable pottery vessels mapped *in situ* on the house floor. When these had been recorded and lifted, the house floor was sampled for pollen, then scraped and sprayed to bring out the color of the postmolds. Each of those postmolds was then mapped and cross-sectioned.

All houses had been truncated to some degree by the adobe-makers, but we excavated as many squares as were necessary to complete the surviving part of the house floor. Finally, all the earth from the floor was sieved through 6-mm mesh in case any small artifacts, bones, sherds, or flint chips had been missed during the course of excavation, and all ash deposits were saved for flotation.

Eight of the houses from Zone D are described, and their sherd assemblages listed, in Chapter 14. Those eight houses appear to span a considerable portion of the San José phase, beginning well back in the first half of the phase and ending late in the second half.

The stratigraphic level we have designated Zone D2 was the lower portion of Zone D (Fig. 13.4). The Zone D2 pottery sample shown in Table 13.1 was taken from below House 6, the earliest of the Zone D houses. It yielded 605 diagnostic sherds, which are listed in Table 13.1.

Of the 605 diagnostic sherds from Zone D2, 499 (82%) are San José phase diagnostics; only 86 (14%) belong to Tierras Largas phase types that lasted into early San José times. Fidencio Coarse is the most common type represented (278 sherds), while Leandro Gray is almost twice as numerous as Atoyac Yellow-white. We would assign Zone D2 to the first half of the San José phase, and consider it to represent midden debris from relatively low-status households.

Later Stratigraphic Levels

The later stratigraphic levels of the Control Section will not be considered in this volume, but are briefly described below. They will be discussed more fully in the final report on San José Mogote.

Zone C. This was a localized layer of soft earth that capped Zone D in places, and also belonged to the San José phase. In some squares, it had two facies: Zone C1, the upper part, which consisted of soft ashy earth and rootlets, and Zone C2, a lens of brown earth that turned out to be the collapsed remains of House 7. That house dated to late in the San José phase (Fig. 13.4).

It should be mentioned that Zone C of the Area C Master Profile yielded several artifacts that would not be out of place in the Basin of Mexico. Included were several Tlatilco-style roller stamps (Figs. 13.7, 13.8) and a *yuguito* or "miniature yoke" in polished black stone (Fig. 13.9). Such *yuguitos* are thought by some scholars to be stone representations of ballplayers' equipment, but their actual function is not yet determined.

Zone B. Zone B was a U-shaped area, 3.4 m wide, which turned out to be the cross-section of a filled-in arroyo (Fig. 13.3). The arroyo postdated the Formative period, but contained no Postclassic (Monte Albán IV and V) sherds. It had originally cut to a depth of 1.6 m below the surface, then later was filled in by stages. At depths of 0.8, 1.2, and 1.6 m there were lenses of

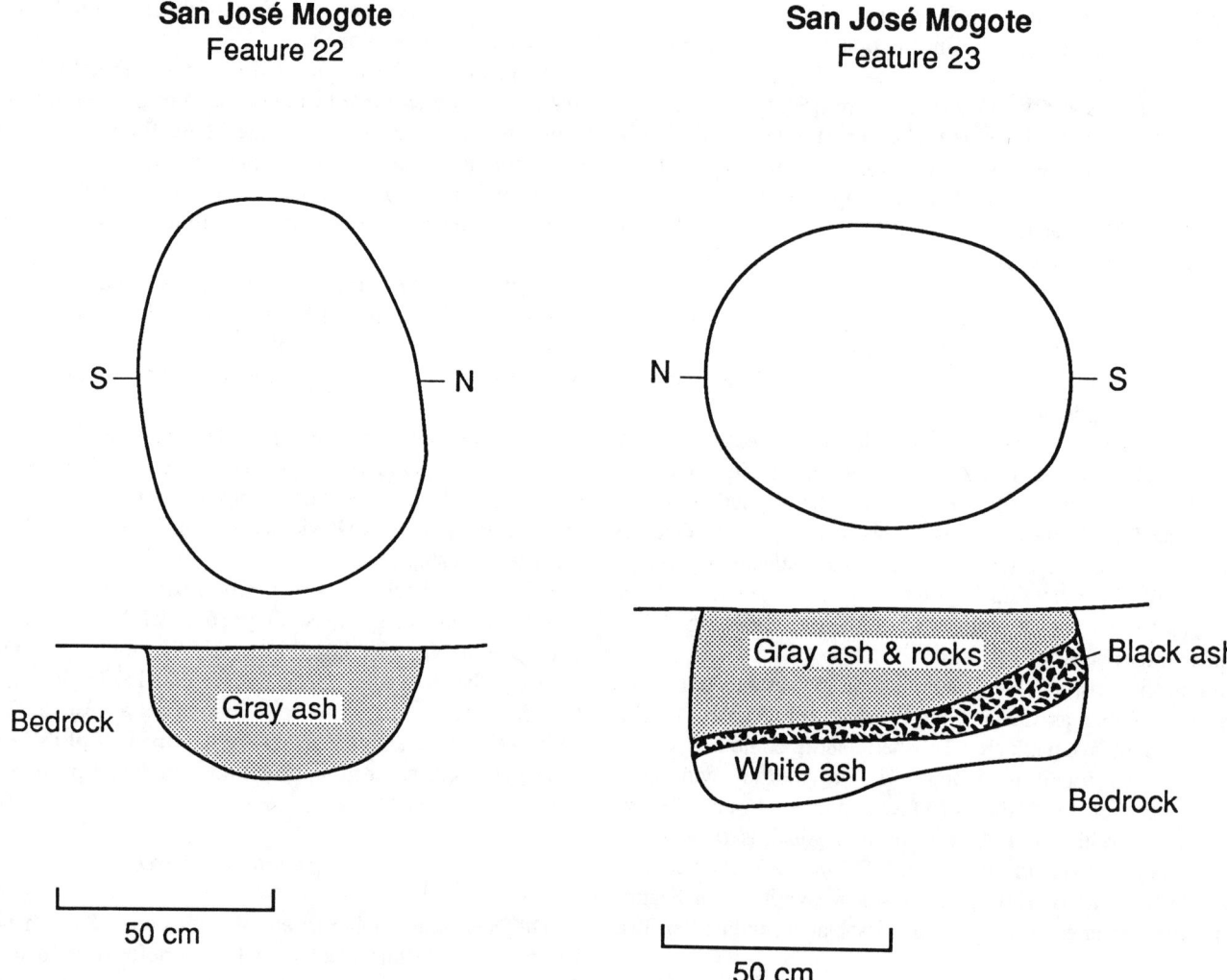

Figure 13.5. Feature 22, a pit dug into bedrock, Area C, San José Mogote (late Tierras Largas phase).

Figure 13.6. Feature 23, a pit dug into bedrock, Area C, San José Mogote (late Tierras Largas phase).

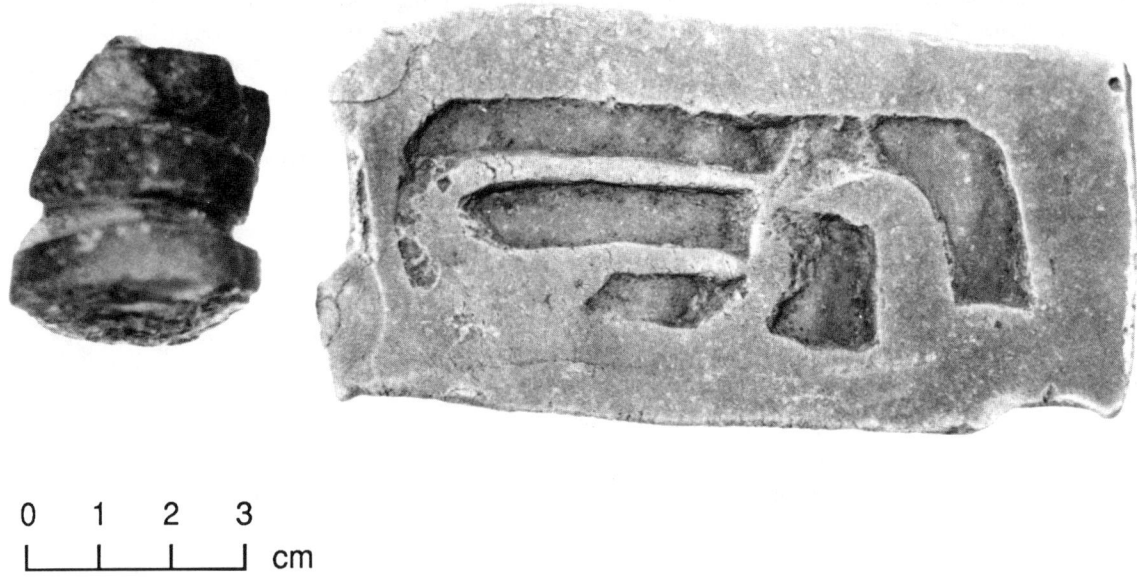

Figure 13.7. Tlatilco-style roller stamp from Zone C, Area C, San José Mogote (San José phase). *Left,* the seal itself (broken). *Right,* a plasticine impression of the rolled-out design, apparently a "paw-wing" motif.

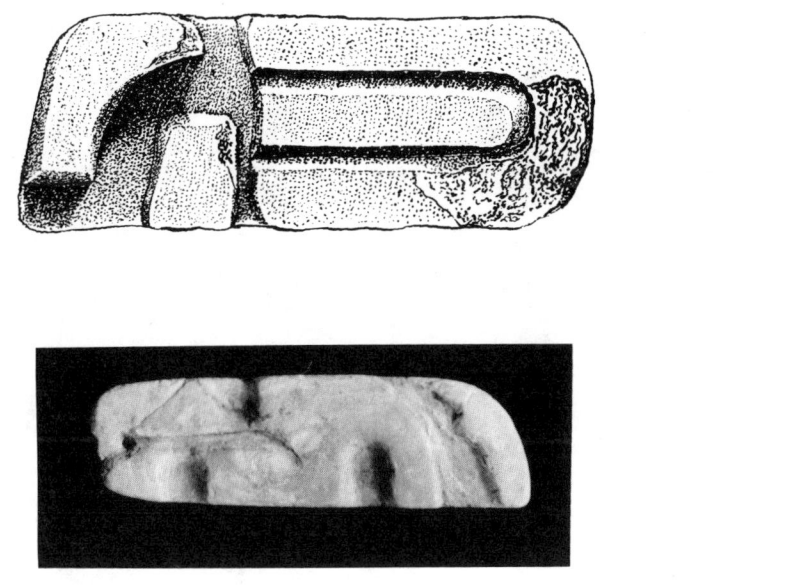

Figure 13.8. San José phase objects with variants of the "paw-wing" motif, both from Area C, San José Mogote. *Top,* artist's reconstruction of the rolled-out design on the Tlatilco-style roller stamp shown in Figure 13.7. *Bottom,* a pearl oyster ornament from the floor of House 9 (Square S17B). This shell ornament was apparently broken while being perforated (length, 3.5 cm).

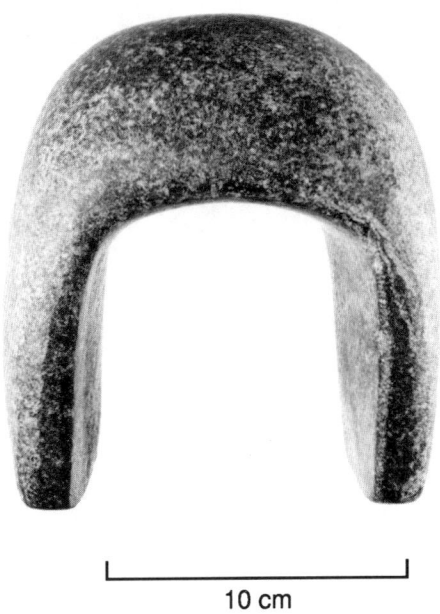

Figure 13.9. "Yuguito" of fine-grained black stone (San José phase). Square S2, Area C Master Profile, San José Mogote.

sherds and gravel from rapid erosion stages, separated by beds of finer silt and alluvium. The sherds in the gravel lenses were redeposited and water-worn, being a mixed collection of San José phase, Rosario phase, Monte Albán II, and Monte Albán III. Clearly, therefore, the filling in of the arroyo had taken place before the maize fields above and to the east had received their present scattering of Monte Albán V sherds. This arroyo was not visible until the profile had been shaved with sharp trowels; and as we carefully removed the lenses of channel fill, we contemplated the completely useless sequence that would have resulted had we chosen to place a test pit in that area without shaving the profile first.

Zone A was the plow zone; it had culturally mixed material.

TABLE 13.1
Sherds from the Control Section of Area C Master Profile, San José Mogote (Earliest Strata Only)

	Features		Zones			
	22	23	G	F	E	D2
TIERRAS LARGAS BURNISHED PLAIN						
Jar rims	-	-	51	12	11	2
Jar body sherds: pocked interior	8	14	445	85	33	9
Jar body sherds: wiped interior	2	13	237	56	42	12
Jar body sherds: plain interior	4	29	341	78	80	15
Jar shoulders: burnished interior	-	-	23	6	4	1
Hemispherical bowls: plain rims	1	-	32	12	7	3
Hemispherical bowls: notched/slashed rims	-	-	2	1	-	-
Hemispherical bowls: basal curves	-	2	23	5	4	-
Hemispherical bowls: body sherds	4	23	225	47	35	9
Outleaned-wall bowls: plain rims	1	-	1	1	-	-
Outleaned-wall bowls: plain flat bases	-	-	2	-	1	-
Outleaned-wall bowls: body sherds	-	-	1	1	-	-
Bottle neck sherds	-	-	-	-	-	1
Misc. unclassified rims (incl. miniatures)	-	-	2	-	1	-
Misc. unclassified bases (incl. miniatures)	-	-	1	1	-	1
Total	20	81	1386	305	218	53
TIERRAS LARGAS UNBURNISHED PLAIN						
Jar rims	-	-	3	-	-	-
Hemispherical bowls: plain rims	-	-	1	-	-	-
Miniature bowls, basal curves	-	-	3	-	-	-
Total	-	-	7	-	-	-
AVELINA RED-ON-BUFF						
Jar rims	-	-	-	4	1	-
Jar body sherds:						
pocked int., rectilinear design ext.	-	-	3	2	2	-
pocked int., curvilinear design ext.	-	-	2	2	1	-
wiped int., rectilinear design ext.	-	-	27	20	11	1
wiped int., curvilinear design ext.	-	-	11	9	4	-
plain int., rectilinear design ext.	-	-	8	5	3	1
plain int., curvilinear design ext.	-	-	7	3	2	1
Hemispherical bowl rims:						
red rim band only	1	4	20	11	2	2
rim band interior, all red exterior	-	-	23	9	1	-
rim band, exterior design	-	-	2	1	-	-
rim band ext., all red interior	-	-	4	1	-	-
rim band, interior design	-	-	3	3	-	-
all red, both sides	-	1	2	-	-	-
Hemispherical bowl body sherds:						
exterior all red, interior plain	-	-	35	15	2	1
exterior design, interior plain	-	-	13	7	-	-
exterior design, interior all red	-	-	1	-	-	-
exterior plain, interior all red	-	-	10	6	1	-
exterior plain, interior design	-	-	10	5	-	1
exterior design, interior design	-	-	1	-	-	-
Misc. bowl body sherds	1	-	-	1	1	-
Misc. unclassified rims (incl. miniatures)	-	-	2	-	-	-
Misc. unclassified bases (incl. miniatures)	-	-	1	-	-	-
Misc. unclassified body sherds (incl. miniatures)	-	-	6	-	-	-
Total	2	5	191	104	31	7
CLEMENTINA FINE RED-ON-BUFF						
Hemispherical bowl rims:						
red rim band	-	-	30	3	1	1
rim band interior, all red exterior	-	-	10	1	-	-
rim band exterior, all red interior	-	-	11	1	-	-
rim band, interior design	-	-	1	-	-	-

TABLE 13.1 (continued)

	Features		Zones			
	22	23	G	F	E	D2
all red, both sides	-	-	1	-	-	-
all red interior, design exterior	-	-	3	-	-	-
Hemispherical bowl body sherds:						
exterior all red, interior plain	-	-	18	2	-	1
exterior design, interior plain	-	-	4	-	-	-
exterior design, interior all red	-	-	1	-	-	-
exterior plain, interior all red	-	1	26	3	1	-
exterior plain, interior design	-	-	6	1	-	-
exterior all red, interior design	-	-	1	-	-	-
all red, both sides	-	-	1	-	-	-
exterior design, interior design	-	-	1	-	-	-
Misc. bowl body sherds	-	-	13	2	-	-
Hemispherical bowls, basal curves	-	-	1	-	-	-
Misc. unclass. rims (incl. miniatures)	-	-	2	1	-	-
Misc. unclass. body sherds (incl. miniatures)	-	-	4	1	1	1
Total	-	1	134	15	3	3
MATADAMAS RED						
Jar rims	-	-	15	4	1	1
Jar body sherds: pocked interior	-	-	13	4	-	-
Jar body sherds: wiped interior	-	-	47	15	-	1
Jar body sherds: plain interior	-	1	30	9	1	-
Jar shoulders: burnished interior	-	-	10	3	1	-
Bottle shoulders	-	-	1	-	-	-
Total	-	1	116	35	3	2
MATADAMAS ORANGE						
Jar rims	-	-	-	2	4	2
Jar body sherds: pocked interior	-	-	-	-	1	-
Jar body sherds: wiped interior	-	-	-	1	3	2
Jar body sherds: plain interior	-	1	-	1	4	5
Hemispherical bowls: plain rims	-	-	-	2	2	1
Hemispherical bowls: body sherds	-	-	-	1	2	1
Outleaned-wall bowls: plain rims	-	-	-	-	2	2
Outleaned-wall bowls: plain flat bases	-	-	-	1	3	2
Tecomate body sherds: rocker-stamping	-	-	1	-	-	1
Misc. unclass. body sherds	-	-	1	1	2	3
Total	-	1	2	9	23	19
OCOS BLACK						
Thin tecomates: zoned dentate stamping	-	-	2	-	-	-
Fluted cylinder: rim sherds	-	-	-	-	-	1
Misc. body sherds	-	-	1	3	2	1
Total	-	-	3	3	2	2
FIDENCIO COARSE						
Hemispherical bowls: plain rims	-	-	-	-	1	-
Tecomate rims	-	-	-	1	-	1
Jar rims: burnished	-	-	-	-	5	3
Jar rims: unburnished	-	-	-	-	1	3
Jar shoulders: sloppy jabs	-	-	-	-	2	1
Jar shoulders: neat punctation	-	-	-	-	1	2
Jar shoulders: paired jabs	-	-	-	-	2	3
Plain body sherds	-	-	-	2	205	265
Total	-	-	-	3	217	278
LEANDRO GRAY						
Bottle neck/rim sherds	-	-	2	-	-	-
Outleaned-wall bowls: plain rims	-	-	3	1	8	3

TABLE 13.1 (continued)

	Features		Zones			
	22	23	G	F	E	D2
Outleaned-wall bowls: plain flat bases	-	-	-	-	4	3
Outleaned-wall bowls: excised sherds	-	-	-	-	3	2
Cylinders: plain rims	-	-	-	-	3	8
Cylinders: plain flat bases	-	-	1	-	2	2
Cylinders: excised rims	-	-	-	-	3	1
Cylinders: excised body sherds	-	-	-	-	3	3
Bolstered-rim bowls: burnished exterior	-	-	-	-	2	1
Bolstered-rim bowls: ext. rough, excised	-	-	-	-	2	3
Vertical jar necks: plain	-	-	-	-	1	1
Pigment dishes/spouted trays: rims	-	-	-	-	2	1
Bowls with thickened, wedge-shaped rim	-	-	-	-	-	1
Misc. incised body sherds	-	-	-	-	3	2
Plain body sherds	-	-	2	1	35	62
Total	-	-	8	2	71	93
ATOYAC YELLOW-WHITE						
Outleaned-wall bowls: plain rims	-	-	1	-	4	2
Outleaned-wall bowls: plain flat bases	-	-	-	-	3	2
Outleaned-wall bowls: incised rims	-	-	-	-	-	8
Cylinders: plain rim	-	-	-	-	4	3
Cylinders: plain flat bases	-	-	1	-	1	3
Cylinders: incised rims	-	-	-	-	2	2
Cylinders: excised sherds	-	-	-	-	3	2
Cylinders: rocker stamped sherds	-	-	-	-	-	1
Tecomate body sherds: rocker stamping	-	-	-	1	1	3
Bolstered-rim bowls: ext. slipped	-	-	-	-	1	1
Bolstered-rim bowls: ext. unslip., excised	-	-	-	-	-	2
Vertical jar necks: plain	-	-	-	-	-	1
Incurved-rim bowls: incised rims	-	-	-	-	-	1
Misc. excised body sherds	-	-	-	-	2	3
Misc. incised body sherds	-	-	-	-	-	2
Plain body sherds	-	-	1	1	20	17
Total	-	-	3	2	41	53
"HYBRID" ATOYAC YELLOW-WHITE/MATADAMAS RED						
Outleaned-wall bowl rims:						
specular red interior, yellow-white ext.	-	-	-	1	-	-
Total	-	-	-	1	-	-
"HYBRID" CLEMENTINA/SAN JOSE RED-ON-WHITE						
Outleaned-wall bowl rims:						
specular red int., red-rimmed white ext.	-	-	-	2	-	-
specular red ext., red-rimmed white int.	-	-	-	2	-	-
Total	-	-	-	4	-	-
SAN JOSE RED-ON-WHITE						
Hemispherical bowls: rims	-	-	8	-	-	-
Tecomates with red band at rim: rims	-	-	-	-	-	1
Tecomate body sherds: red zoning stripe	-	-	-	-	2	1
Tecomate body sherds: zoned rocker-stamping	-	-	-	1	3	2
Tecomate body sherds: zoned punctation	-	-	-	-	-	2
Outleaned-wall bowls: red rim, white wall	-	-	1	-	6	2
Cylinders: white ext., red int.	-	-	-	-	1	-
Misc. body sherds	-	-	13	3	11	15
Total	-	-	22	4	23	23
LUPITA HEAVY PLAIN						
Tecomate body sherds: rocker-stamping	-	-	-	-	1	1
Tecomate body sherds: fingernail impressions	-	-	-	-	1	-
Outleaned-wall bowls: plain rims	-	-	-	-	1	2

TABLE 13.1 (continued)

	Features		Zones			
	22	23	G	F	E	D2
Bolstered-rim bowls: rims	-	-	-	-	-	1
Braziers/potstands: rims	-	-	-	-	4	3
Braziers/potstands: bases	-	-	-	-	2	3
Braziers/potstands: textile-impressed floors	-	-	-	-	-	1
Plain body sherds	-	-	-	-	7	11
Total	-	-	-	-	16	22
SAN JOSE BLACK-AND-WHITE						
Cylinder rims: plain	-	-	1	-	1	2
Cylinder rims: excised	-	-	-	-	2	1
Cylinder body sherds: incised	-	-	-	-	-	1
Outleaned-wall bowls: plain rims	-	-	-	-	1	1
Bolstered-rim bowls: rims	-	-	-	-	1	2
Misc. decorated body sherds	-	-	-	-	3	2
Plain body sherds	-	-	-	1	2	4
Total	-	-	1	1	10	13
XOCHILTEPEC WHITE						
Bottle shoulder: body sherds	-	-	4	1	-	-
Cylinder rims	-	-	-	-	2	3
Cylinder bases	-	-	-	-	1	1
Plain body sherds	-	-	-	1	2	1
Total	-	-	4	2	5	5
DELFINA FINE GRAY						
Cylinders: plain rims	-	-	-	-	1	2
Misc. body sherds	-	-	-	-	1	-
Total	-	-	-	-	2	2
SAN JOSE SPECULAR RED						
Outleaned-wall bowls: rims	-	-	-	-	1	2
Bolstered-rim bowls: ext. unslipped, excised	-	-	-	-	1	2
Tecomate body sherds: rocker-stamped	-	-	-	-	-	3
Jar shoulders: zoned punctation	-	-	-	-	3	-
Plain body sherds	-	-	-	-	1	1
Total	-	-	-	-	6	8
LA MINA WHITE						
Cylinder rims	-	-	-	-	1	-
Bottle neck/body sherds	-	-	-	-	-	2
Misc. body sherds	-	-	-	-	1	-
Total	-	-	-	-	2	2
POSSIBLE FOREIGN WARES						
Hemispherical bowls: orange/brown wash	-	-	-	-	1	-
Guamuchal Brushed tecomate rim	-	-	-	-	-	1
Total	-	-	-	-	1	1
UNCLASSIFIED SHERDS						
Rims	-	-	-	1	1	2
Body sherds	-	-	32	21	37	17
Total	-	-	32	22	38	19
GRAND TOTAL	22	89	1909	512	712	605

Chapter 14

Chronological Variation during the San José Phase: Household Sequences in Two Residential Wards

Our sample of San José phase households is large enough to provide examples of both kinds of variation mentioned in Chapter 5: synchronic and diachronic.

In this chapter we consider thirteen households (and an associated midden) from Areas A and C, two residential wards at San José Mogote. Both residential wards are ones in which representations of Sky, lightning, or the fire-serpent were abundant on pottery, and representations of Earth, earthquake, or the were-jaguar were rare to absent. The most noticeable differences among these houses, therefore, are diachronic rather than synchronic.

Area C provides us with a stratigraphic sequence of eight houses spanning most of the San José phase, plus one additional late San José phase house. Area A provides us with a stratigraphic sequence of four households spanning most of the San José phase, plus a barrio midden from the early San José phase. The midden and the thirteen houses are among our best San José phase proveniences.

In Chapters 15–17 we will shift to an examination of synchronic variation in San José phase households. At that time we will consider differences between high-status and low-status households, fire-serpent and were-jaguar households, and households from different districts of the Valley of Oaxaca.

Area A: Four Households and a Midden

The most prominent landmark at San José Mogote is Mound 1, known locally as "el Mogote del Cacique"; during Monte Albán II times, it formed the southern border of the site's Main Plaza. Area A of San José Mogote lies to the east of this mound, on a gentle slope that descends from Mound 1 toward a low-lying area of alluvial bottomland (see Fig. 9.1). A small dry arroyo runs west to east through the northern part of Area A; it was in the bank of this arroyo that we first discovered San José phase pottery.

At a point roughly 60 m east of the northeast corner of Mound 1, we shaved the south side of the arroyo to a vertical face with square-ended shovels and sharp trowels. The cultural stratigraphy was very clear, and several household units could be seen in cross-section. Even before excavation began, we could see that the arroyo had cut through a large midden lying on bedrock, a series of households, and some overlying artificial fill.

We laid out a 3 × 4 m area, oriented magnetic N-S and divided into twelve one-by-one-meter squares. Excavation of alternate squares began at the arroyo profile, so that each cultural stratum seen in the profile could be traced southward as we worked from the known to the unknown (see Fig. 18.7).

Where actual house floors or dooryard surfaces were present, they were treated as the units of excavation. Tools were mapped in place on the floors, which were then sprayed with a fine mist of water from a crop sprayer to bring out the color differences of the postholes. All postmolds, hearths, and pits were mapped, cross-sectioned, and excavated separately. Samples were taken for radiocarbon dating, pollen analysis, and flotation for carbonized seeds. Where true floors were not present, we followed the observed cultural stratigraphy, but when such strata were very thick we divided them into arbitrary subunits of 20 cm. All deposits, of whatever nature, were screened through 6-mm mesh after all the visible sherds, artifacts, animal bones, and wood charcoal had been removed. All house floors were excavated by trowel and whisk broom, while layers of construction fill were excavated with sharpened steel digging-bars, picks, shovels, and large sugar scoops.

From earliest to latest, the strata found were as follows (see Fig. 14.1).

Bedrock

Bedrock occurred at a depth of 2.2 to 2.4 m below the surface, and consisted of soft white volcanic tuff (ignimbrite). There were

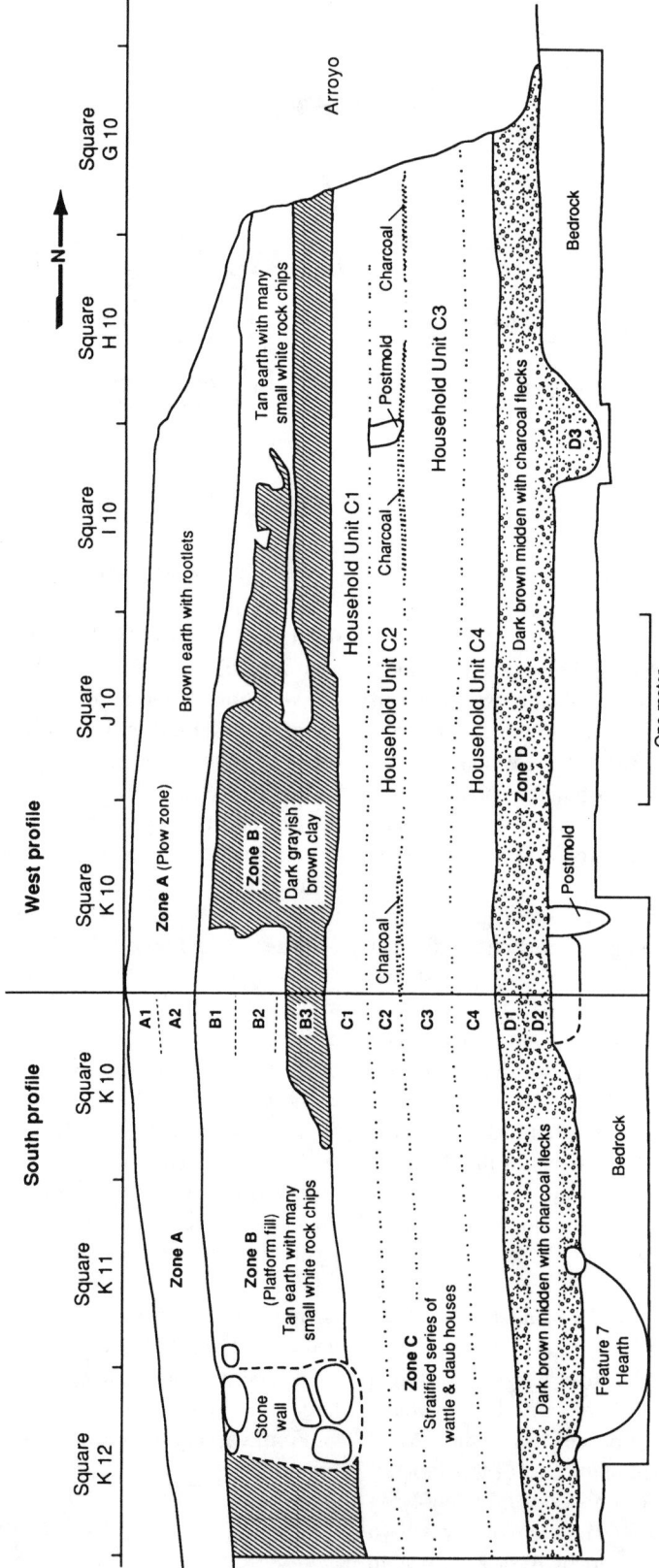

Figure 14.1. South and west profiles of Area A, San José Mogote, showing the stratigraphic relationship of Household Units C4–C1 and the Zone D midden.

postholes, pits, and even a hearth (Feature 7) dug into bedrock, but the houses once associated with them had been destroyed. This was disappointing, because the houses should have been early San José phase, or transitional from late Tierras Largas to early San José phase. No radiocarbon samples were available; even the hearth had only fine gray ash.

Zone D

Zone D was a dark brown midden with charcoal flecks, so thick and extensive that we believe it to have been a barrio midden for Area A. While there were no clear stratigraphic breaks within Zone D, it was so thick that we arbitrarily divided it into upper (D1), middle (D2), and lower (D3) levels just in case there had been changes in ceramics during the course of its deposition. The sherd contents of D1, D2, and D3 are given in Table 14.1. We would assign this pottery sample to the first half of the San José phase, and note its strong affiliations with the Ayotla phase in the southern Basin of Mexico and the Cuadros phase on the Chiapas-Guatemala Pacific Coast.

Zone C

Zone C comprised a series of four superimposed household units labeled (from top to bottom) C1, C2, C3, and C4. These households spanned most of the San José phase, from the first half of the period (C4) to late in the second half (C1). Unfortunately, no single house was completely exposed; in most cases, what we recovered was part of a house, plus part of the adjacent dooryard. This was not all bad, since there were often important features in the dooryard that did not occur in the house.

All the households in Zone C were engaged in the manufacture of magnetite mirrors and the cutting and drilling of *Spondylus* and pearl oyster shell into ornaments. One of the most common chert tools found in Area A was a small drill or perforator associated with shellworking (Parry 1987: Plates 7, 8). It was also the case that all Area A households were ones in which fire-serpents carved on Leandro Gray or Delfina Fine Gray pottery were dominant over were-jaguars on Atoyac Yellow-white pottery. (That was equally true of the Zone D midden.)

The sherds recovered from Household Units C4–C1 are given in Table 14.1. Perhaps the most interesting of the households were C3 and C2, which had large artifact samples and a number of features. They are shown in Figures 14.2–14.4.

Household Unit C3 (Fig. 14.2). An area of abundant daub fragments from a collapsed wattle-and-daub wall occurred along the western profile of our excavation, suggesting that there had been a house immediately to the west. Most of the area we exposed was a dooryard to the east of that house. Features excavated in that dooryard included a stone-bordered hearth (Feature 6); two recessed circular areas that may have been ritual features (Features 3 and 8); and a fire-reddened bell-shaped pit (Feature 2).

Feature 3 was a circle 120 cm in diameter, recessed 5 cm into the dooryard; it had been mud-plastered, given a light coating of lime whitewash, and painted red with specular hematite. There were some stones in its center that may, or may not, have been associated. Feature 8 was a similar recessed circle found some 3 m to the south; it also had been mud-plastered and whitewashed, but had been painted cream or yellow rather than red (Marcus 1989:187). Unfortunately, neither Feature 3 nor 8 contained more than a few redeposited sherds; they may have been ritual features.

One provenience that did have a modest sherd sample was Feature 2, a bell-shaped pit also in the dooryard of Household Unit C3. Feature 2 had originally been dug down from the level of the C3 dooryard. Its mouth was only 0.7 m in diameter, but at its full depth of 0.65 m it had expanded to 1.35 m. As can be seen in the cross-section drawing (Fig. 14.3), this pit had been heated to the point where its clay-lined walls turned red and were almost as hard as brick. In the bottom we discovered a layer of charcoal overlain by firecracked rock, in turn overlain by a layer of white ash. There were identifiable burnt cornstalks in the charcoal layer, suggesting that this was one type of fuel used.

We do not know the function of Feature 2. Obviously, it could have served as an earth oven, but for what food? Subterranean cooking of maguey hearts (*Agave potatorum*) has a long history in the Valley of Oaxaca (Flannery 1986), but maguey-roasting pits tend to be basin-shaped and require oak or manzanita fuel, not cornstalks.

At any rate, when the time came for Household Unit C2 to be laid out, Feature 2 had to be filled in and capped with a layer of clay. The sherds swept into it at that time essentially duplicated what we had found in Household Unit C3. They included Fidencio Coarse jar necks and body sherds; Leandro Gray outleaned-wall bowls, cylinders, and bolstered-rim bowls; Atoyac Yellow-white outleaned-wall bowls, cylinders, and bolstered-rim bowls; San José Red-on-White body sherds; Lupita Heavy Plain brazier/potstand fragments; San José Black-and-White outleaned-wall bowls; Delfina Fine Gray body sherds; and traces of Avelina Red-on-Buff and Tierras Largas Burnished Plain hemispherical bowls. These sherds add little to what we already knew about Unit C3.

Household Unit C2 (Fig. 14.4). Our excavation of C2 seems to have caught parts of two houses, separated by 1.5 m of dooryard. It is probable that both these buildings were part of the same household, as in the case of Houses 16 and 17 in Area B (Chapter 15). Normally, households in villages of the San José phase were separated by 20–30 m of open space. When buildings are this close together, we suspect we are dealing with a house plus a kitchen, or two houses from an extended family.

Both houses had partial stone foundations. The northernmost house, which filled almost half the excavated area, was represented by three large postmolds, a line of wall foundation stones, and scattered wattle-and-daub debris. Inside the house was a small storage pit (Feature 1) which began at the level of the floor, and may originally have had a stone lid. The southernmost house,

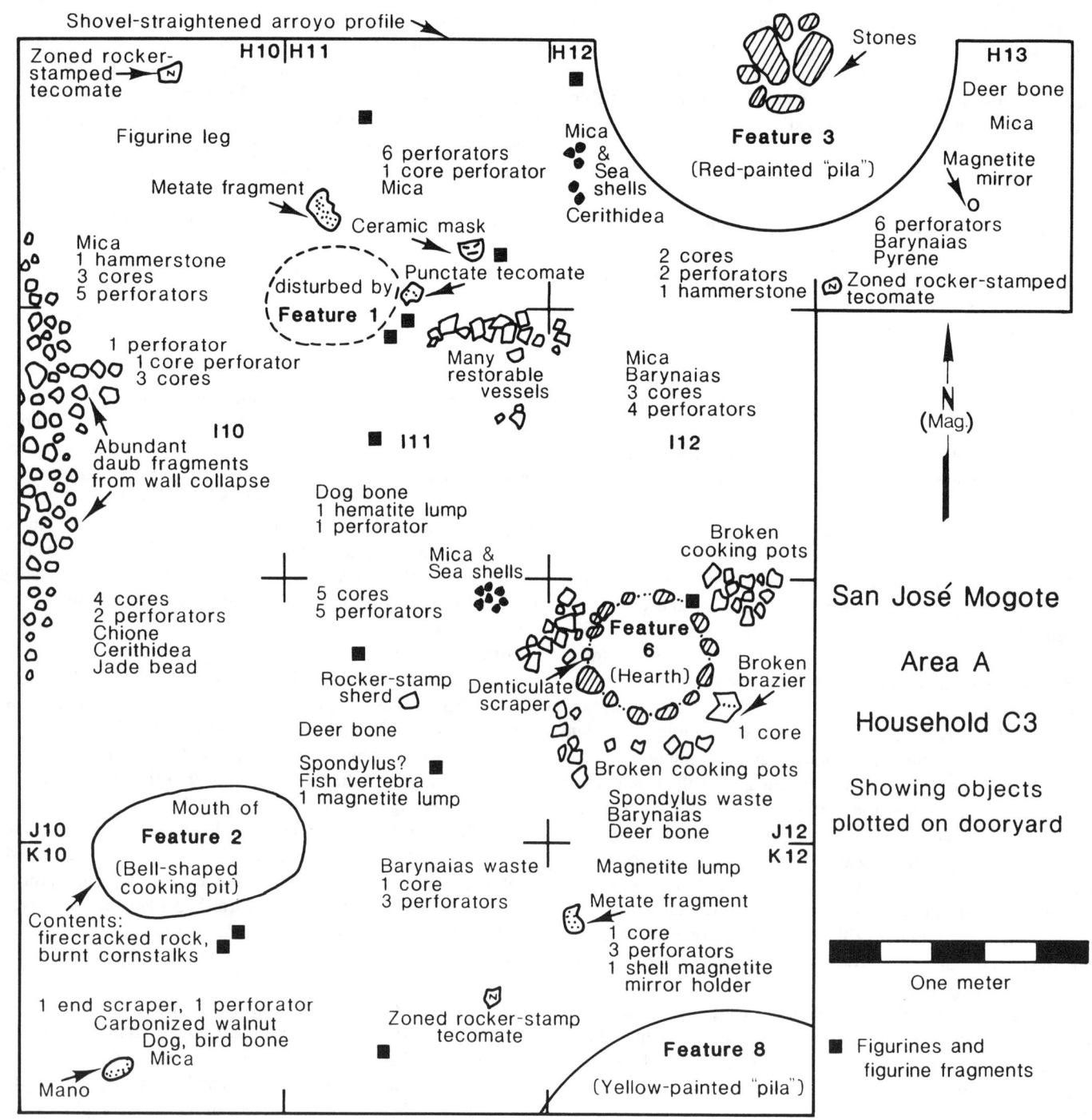

Figure 14.2. Plan of Household Unit C3, Area A, San José Mogote.

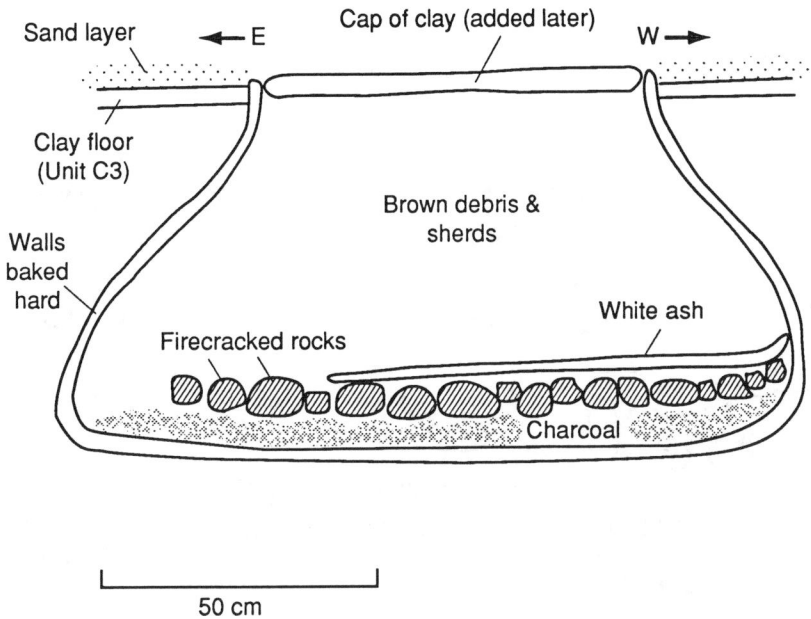

Figure 14.3. Cross-section of Feature 2, Household Unit C3, a bell-shaped pit used as an earth oven.

only one corner of which was found, had smaller postholes and no evidence of wattle-and-daub. This could mean that it was a cook shack, ramada, or roofed work area like House 16 of Area B. An outdoor hearth (Feature 4) was found in the dooryard immediately to the east.

Zone B

Some time after the abandonment of Household Unit C1, two large pyramidal platforms (Structures 1 and 2) were built in Area A. One of these, Structure 1, was built directly over Household Unit C1. Its construction involved the bringing in of hundreds of basketloads of earthen fill (see Figs. 18.7–18.8).

Zone B was a thick layer of the construction fill associated with Structure 1. As can be seen in the profile drawing (Fig. 14.1), Zone B had two facies: (1) dark grayish-brown clay and (2) tan earth with many small white rock chips. These two facies appeared to be different types of earth, brought in as fill by different work gangs. The dark grayish-brown clay appeared to have come from the low-lying alluvial bottomland immediately to the east of Area A. The tan earth with small rock chips appears to have come from a piedmont spur even farther to the east, on the other side of the railroad line that links Tehuacán and Oaxaca. Thus, it is possible that several residential groups were responsible for the construction of Structure 1, a public building dated in Chapter 18.

We divided Zone B into arbitrary levels B1, B2, and B3. Its sherds were all Early Formative in date, but because they came from redeposited fill, we did not use them for statistical purposes. At periodic intervals within this construction fill, we found boulder retaining walls whose purpose seemed to be to prevent the fill from slumping.

Zone A

Zone A was the plow zone, and its contents were mainly eroded sherds that looked like the result of slopewash.

Summary of Area A

Zones D3-D1 (midden) and Household Units C4-C1 yielded more than 30,000 sherds for analysis (Table 14.1). Zones B and A are not relevant to this report.

Eight Houses from Area C, San José Mogote

We have already described the Master Profile for Area C at San José Mogote, a vertically cut cross-section that ran magnetic

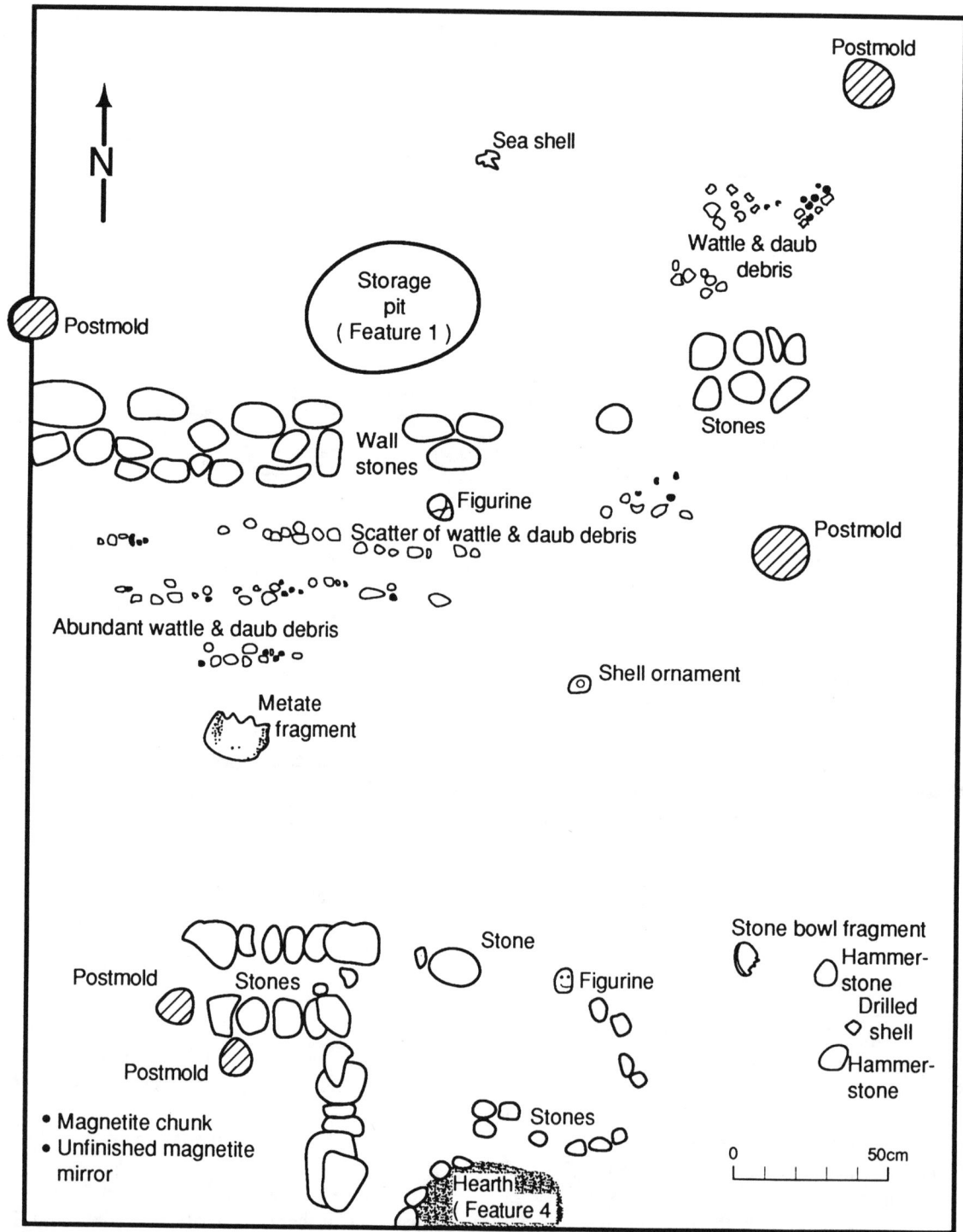

Figure 14.4. Plan of Household Unit C2, Area A, San José Mogote.

TABLE 14.1
Sherds from Midden Levels (D3-D1) and Household Units (C4-C1), Area A, San José Mogote

	Middens			Household Units			
	D3	D2	D1	C4	C3	C2	C1
TIERRAS LARGAS BURNISHED PLAIN							
Jar rims	2	5	2	1	7	4	7
Jar body sherds: pocked interior	-	1	13	3	9	8	2
Jar body sherds: wiped interior	14	42	58	30	54	38	31
Jar body sherds: plain interior	4	33	77	41	40	28	25
Jar shoulders: burnished interior	5	7	2	5	5	5	3
Hemispherical bowls: plain rims	2	12	33	18	29	15	13
Hemispherical bowls: notched/slashed rims	-	1	-	-	-	-	-
Hemispherical bowls: basal curves	-	-	2	-	1	1	1
Hemispherical bowls: body sherds	12	45	79	54	80	53	16
Outleaned-wall bowls: plain rims	-	-	2	3	-	-	-
Outleaned-wall bowls: thickened, grooved rim	-	-	-	-	-	-	1
Same as above + zoned dentate rocker st.	-	-	-	1	-	1	-
Outleaned-wall bowls: plain flat bases	-	-	2	-	-	-	-
Outleaned-wall bowls: dentate st. body sherds	-	-	1	-	-	-	-
Tecomates: zoned dentate st. rims	-	-	-	-	-	-	1
Tecomates: zoned dentate st. body sherds	-	1	-	-	3	-	-
Tecomates: rocker stamped body sherds	-	2	-	-	1	-	-
Tecomates: misc. incised body sherds	-	3	1	-	-	-	-
Misc. unclassified rims (incl. miniatures)	-	-	16	3	-	-	-
Misc. unclassified bases (incl. miniatures)	-	-	3	-	-	-	-
Misc. uncl. body sherds (incl. miniatures)	-	-	-	1	-	-	1
Total	39	152	291	160	229	153	101
AVELINA RED-ON-BUFF							
Jar shoulders: rectil. design ext.	-	-	-	-	-	1	-
Jar body sherds:							
pocked int., rectilinear design ext.	-	-	-	-	1	-	-
wiped int., rectilinear design ext.	-	3	4	2	2	4	3
wiped int., curvilinear design ext.	-	-	2	-	-	-	-
plain int., rectilinear design ext.	-	-	2	2	4	-	-
plain int, curvilinear design ext.	-	-	-	-	1	-	-
Hemispherical bowl rims:							
red rim band only	-	4	10	1	6	10	4
rim band interior, all red exterior	1	-	4	-	2	-	2
rim band exterior, all red interior	-	1	-	-	2	1	-
all red, interior and exterior	-	-	-	2	-	-	-
Hemispherical bowl body sherds:							
all red exterior, plain interior	-	-	3	3	6	-	-
design exterior, plain interior	-	-	-	1	-	1	-
plain exterior, all red interior	-	1	3	-	3	-	2
plain exterior, design interior	-	-	-	1	-	1	-
all red, interior and exterior	-	-	1	-	-	-	-
designs on interior and exterior	-	-	-	-	1	-	-
Hemispherical bowls: basal curve sherds	-	-	-	-	1	1	-
Misc. unclassified rims (incl. miniatures)	-	-	-	3	-	-	-
Misc. uncl. bases (incl. miniatures)	-	-	-	-	-	1	-
Total	1	9	29	15	29	20	11
CLEMENTINA FINE RED-ON-BUFF							
Hemispherical bowl rims:							
red rim band only	-	-	2	2	2	2	2
rim band interior, all red exterior	1	-	-	-	-	1	-
rim band interior, design exterior	-	-	-	-	-	-	1
rim band exterior, all red interior	-	1	-	-	2	-	-
rim band exterior, design interior	1	-	-	-	-	-	-
all red, interior and exterior	1	-	-	-	-	-	-
Hemispherical bowl body sherds:							
all red exterior, plain interior	-	-	-	4	-	2	-
design exterior, plain interior	-	-	-	2	-	-	-
plain exterior, all red interior	-	-	1	2	-	3	-
plain exterior, design interior	-	-	-	1	1	-	-
all red, interior and exterior	-	-	1	-	-	-	-
design exterior, design interior	2	-	-	-	-	-	-
Misc. unclass. rims (incl. miniatures)	-	1	-	-	-	-	-
Total	5	2	4	11	5	8	3

TABLE 14.1 (continued)

	Middens				Household Units		
	D3	D2	D1	C4	C3	C2	C1
MATADAMAS RED							
Jar rims	2	-	3	3	-	-	-
Jar body sherds: pocked interior	-	-	-	-	1	-	-
Jar body sherds: wiped interior	5	-	-	6	5	2	1
Jar body sherds: plain interior	-	-	2	3	2	1	-
Jar shoulders: burnished interior	-	1	1	-	1	-	2
Bottle body sherds	-	-	-	-	-	1	-
Tecomates: turned-up rim	-	-	-	-	-	-	1
Total	7	1	6	12	9	4	4
MATADAMAS ORANGE							
Jar rims	4	13	9	10	8	4	6
Jar body sherds: wiped interior	8	34	27	33	28	32	24
Jar body sherds: plain interior	15	28	59	26	38	26	26
Jar shoulders: burnished interior	-	-	-	1	2	2	1
Hemispherical bowls: plain rims	2	21	13	7	8	9	2
Hemispherical bowls: basal curves	1	-	1	-	1	-	-
Hemispherical bowls: body sherds	12	25	66	42	55	43	27
Outleaned-wall bowls: plain rims	-	2	4	1	3	-	-
Outleaned-wall bowls: rims, incised ext.	-	-	-	2	-	1	-
Outleaned-wall bowls: thickened rims	-	1	-	-	-	-	-
Outleaned-wall bowls: plain flat bases	1	1	4	2	4	-	1
Outleaned-wall bowls: incised basal sherds	-	-	1	-	-	-	-
Outleaned-wall bowls: zoned punct. bases	-	-	1	-	-	-	-
Tecomate rims: plain rocker stamping	1	-	-	-	-	-	-
Tecomate rims: dentate rocker stamping	-	-	-	-	1	-	-
Tecomate body sherds: plain rocker stamping	1	1	1	-	-	2	-
Tecomate body sherds: dentate rocker st.	-	1	-	-	-	-	-
Tecomate body sherds: misc. decorated	1	2	2	2	-	2	1
Misc. unclass. rims (incl. miniatures)	-	10	6	8	7	1	10
Misc. uncl. body sherds (incl. miniatures)	1	-	-	2	1	2	-
Total	47	139	194	136	156	124	98
OCOS BLACK							
Cylinder rims: plain	-	-	2	2	1	-	-
Cylinder rims: excised	-	-	1	-	-	-	-
Cylinder body sherds: excised	-	-	3	-	-	-	-
Cylinder bases: plain	-	3	1	2	-	-	2
Bottle neck sherds: plain	-	-	1	-	-	-	-
Bottle body sherds: plain	-	-	2	2	1	-	-
Bottle body sherds: incised	-	-	4	-	-	-	-
Outleaned-wall bowls: plain rims	-	-	-	-	-	-	2
Outleaned-wall bowls: plain flat bases	-	-	-	-	-	-	2
Plain body sherds	1	1	6	1	1	-	1
Total	1	4	20	7	3	-	7
FIDENCIO COARSE							
Hemispherical bowls: rims	-	7	3	12	5	9	-
Tecomate rims	-	1	-	-	2	-	-
Tecomate body sherds: finger punching	-	-	-	1	-	-	-
Tecomate body sherds: rocker stamping	-	-	-	-	2	-	-
Jar rims, burnished	5	18	63	31	34	10	2
Jar rims, unburnished	5	24	59	37	55	25	15
Jar shoulders: sloppy jabs	-	2	1	-	2	6	-
Jar shoulders: neat punctation	-	2	6	2	-	1	1
Jar shoulders: rows of slashes	-	1	-	-	1	-	-
Jar shoulders: long parallel lines	-	-	5	-	-	-	1
Jar shoulders: paired jabs	-	-	8	2	2	1	5
Jar shoulders: unident. designs	3	1	4	2	6	2	2
Plain body sherds	447	1419	3221	1869	3137	1715	1627
Total	460	1475	3370	1956	3246	1769	1653
LEANDRO GRAY							
Bottle body sherd, fluted	-	2	1	-	-	-	-
Bottle neck/rim sherds	-	2	-	1	-	1	-

TABLE 14.1 (continued)

	Middens			Household Units			
	D3	D2	D1	C4	C3	C2	C1
Outleaned-wall bowls: plain rims	14	61	102	93	146	85	49
Outleaned-wall bowls: plain flat bases	6	18	45	43	66	30	22
Outleaned-wall bowls: excised body sherds	3	13	43	10	19	3	3
Outleaned-wall bowls: incised rims	-	-	-	3	-	3	5
Cylinders: plain rims	1	24	48	72	45	37	23
Cylinders: plain flat bases	4	14	33	18	22	20	3
Cylinders: excised rims	1	12	28	20	23	7	2
Cylinders: excised body sherds	10	38	86	88	69	43	27
Bowl rims, too small to show shape	-	17	36	23	43	16	4
Tecomate rims (may incl. incurved-rim bowls)	-	2	10	3	7	1	4
Tecomate body sherds:							
zoned rocker stamping	-	-	-	1	-	-	-
zoned interrupted rocker stamping	-	-	-	-	2	-	1
dentate stamping	-	4	-	-	1	-	-
dentate rocker stamping	-	-	-	-	1	1	-
Bolstered-rim bowls: burnished exterior	1	5	10	9	17	5	3
Bolstered-rim bowls: ext. rough, excised	-	13	25	23	21	4	6
Vertical jar necks: plain	1	4	6	5	8	2	3
Vertical jar necks: decorated	-	-	-	-	2	-	-
Oval bowls with pinched-in sides: rims	-	-	-	1	-	-	-
Hemispherical bowls: rims	-	-	-	-	1	3	-
Bowls with gadrooned rim: rims	-	-	-	1	2	-	-
"Grater bowl" bases	-	1	3	-	4	9	-
Spouted trays: spout sherds	-	-	-	-	1	-	-
Pigment dishes/spouted trays: rim sherds	1	1	6	1	5	2	1
Multicompartment vessels	-	-	-	1	-	-	-
Bird effigy vessels	-	1	-	-	-	1	-
Misc. decorated body sherds	-	11	7	4	9	4	2
Plain body sherds	73	449	1036	740	1153	672	516
Total	115	692	1525	1160	1667	949	674
ATOYAC YELLOW-WHITE							
Bottles: body sherds, fluted	1	-	1	-	-	-	-
Bowls: Ocós-style grooved rims	1	-	-	-	-	-	-
Outleaned-wall bowls: plain rims	9	41	58	30	45	27	18
Outleaned-wall bowls: plain flat bases	3	15	22	26	35	28	4
Outleaned-wall bowls: excised body sherds	-	1	5	1	-	-	-
Outleaned-wall bowls: incised rims	-	-	-	1	9	14	13
Cylinders: plain rims	-	10	31	19	30	11	9
Cylinders: plain flat bases	5	5	19	10	11	10	8
Cylinders: incised rims	2	2	5	2	14	10	14
Cylinders: excised body sherds	-	3	22	5	2	-	1
Bowl rims: too small to show shape	2	19	29	18	21	21	22
Tecomate rims: plain	1	3	5	2	1	1	1
Tecomate body sherds:							
zoned rocker stamping	7	12	15	14	29	12	8
zoned interrupted rocker stamping	2	5	7	5	4	1	4
dentate stamping	-	-	1	-	-	-	-
zoned punctation	-	-	1	3	1	-	-
Bolstered-rim bowls: exterior slipped	1	7	14	5	9	4	-
Bolstered-rim bowls: ext. unslip., excised	-	2	5	8	-	1	-
Vertical jar necks, plain	1	3	7	8	8	-	3
Vertical jar necks, decorated	-	-	-	-	2	-	-
Oval bowls with pinched-in sides: rims	-	-	1	-	1	-	-
Hemispherical bowls: plain rims	-	-	10	-	-	-	-
Incurved-rim bowls: rims	-	-	-	2	3	1	2
"Grater bowl" bases	-	-	-	-	1	-	-
Spouted trays: spout sherds	-	-	-	-	1	-	-
Pigment dishes/spouted trays: rim sherds	-	-	-	-	-	-	-
Bowls with giant "macrorim": rims	-	-	-	-	-	2	1
Misc. decorated body sherds	-	8	12	12	19	13	6
Plain body sherds	145	461	857	591	826	514	562
Total	180	597	1127	762	1073	670	676
SAN JOSE RED-ON-WHITE							
Hemispherical bowls: rims w/ red band	-	-	5	-	-	-	-
Incurved-rim bowls: rims w/ red band	-	-	-	-	-	1	-

TABLE 14.1 (continued)

	Middens			Household Units			
	D3	D2	D1	C4	C3	C2	C1
Tecomates:							
rims with red band	-	-	1	1	1	-	1
body sherds w/ red zoning stripe	-	-	1	4	5	4	2
body sherds w/ zoned rocker stamping	-	1	2	2	8	4	2
body sherds w/ interrupted rocker stamp	6	2	1	2	2	-	-
Outleaned-wall bowls: red rim, white wall	9	21	55	37	22	17	13
Outleaned-wall bowls: white rim, red wall	-	-	-	2	3	-	-
Bolstered-rim bowls: rims	-	3	8	-	2	1	1
Misc. bowl bases	5	-	3	2	3	4	-
Jar necks	2	5	8	7	1	1	1
Oval bowls with pinched-in sides	-	1	-	-	-	-	-
"Grater bowl" bases	-	-	-	-	-	-	1
Plain body sherds	3	16	35	20	30	2	5
Total	25	49	119	77	77	34	26
LUPITA HEAVY PLAIN							
Tecomates:							
plain unburnished rims	-	1	-	-	2	-	1
zoned/burnished rim, plain body	1	1	-	-	-	-	-
burnished rim, rocker stamped body	-	1	-	1	1	-	-
burn. rim, interrupt. rocker stamp. body	-	-	1	1	-	-	-
burnished rim, punctate body	-	-	1	-	1	-	-
Tecomate body sherds:							
rocker stamping	5	2	12	3	7	7	1
interrupted rocker stamping	1	6	6	5	7	5	1
dentate stamping	-	1	-	-	-	-	-
punctation	-	-	-	7	5	-	-
miscellaneous decoration	-	-	-	1	1	-	7
Outleaned-wall bowls: plain rims	3	15	21	16	12	1	1
Outleaned-wall bowls: white wash on rim	-	-	1	1	-	-	-
Outleaned-wall bowls: plain flat bases	2	9	6	4	5	-	1
Bowl body sherds, excised	1	-	1	1	-	-	-
Bowl body sherds, incised	-	-	-	2	4	6	-
Pigment dishes/spouted trays: rim sherds	-	-	-	-	1	-	-
Multicompartment vessels	-	2	-	-	-	-	-
"Platillos" (potter's bats ?)	-	2	2	2	7	1	-
Braziers/potstands: rims	4	10	24	18	29	9	7
Braziers/potstands: bases	1	2	5	5	10	3	7
Braziers/potstands: plain floors	-	2	4	3	6	3	6
Misc. decorated sherds	1	9	-	1	6	1	-
Plain body sherds	6	47	48	50	97	31	7
Total	25	110	132	121	201	67	39
"HYBRID": ATOYAC YELLOW-WHITE OUTSIDE, MATADAMAS ORANGE INSIDE							
Bowl body sherds	7	3	9	4	8	3	4
Tecomate rims	-	-	-	-	1	-	-
Jar rims or shoulders	-	-	-	-	3	-	-
Jar or tecomate body sherds	-	-	-	-	3	-	-
Total	7	3	9	4	15	3	4
SAN JOSE BLACK-AND-WHITE							
Cylinders: plain rims	2	5	11	2	5	-	1
Cylinders: excised rims	-	-	1	1	2	-	-
Outleaned-wall bowls: plain rims	2	8	9	7	22	5	2
Outleaned-wall bowls: excised rims	-	1	-	-	-	-	-
Bowls with bolstered rim: rims	-	-	1	1	3	-	-
Miscellaneous bowl bases	-	-	3	1	2	1	-
Bottles/tall-necked jars: rims	-	2	-	-	1	-	-
Plain body sherds	10	30	65	24	16	13	11
Total	14	46	90	36	51	19	14
XOCHILTEPEC WHITE							
Bottle necks	-	-	-	1	-	-	-
Tecomates: collared rims	-	1	-	1	-	-	-
Tecomates: plain rims	-	-	-	2	3	-	-
Cylinders: plain rims	-	-	-	-	1	1	3

TABLE 14.1 (continued)

	Middens			Household Units			
	D3	D2	D1	C4	C3	C2	C1
Cylinders: plain bases	-	-	-	-	1	-	1
Spouted tray fragments ?	-	-	-	-	1	-	-
Plain body sherds	-	1	7	5	7	9	9
Total	-	2	7	9	13	10	13
DELFINA FINE GRAY							
Cylinder rims: plain	-	3	6	11	4	4	-
Cylinder rims: excised	-	-	6	2	1	3	2
Cylinder rims: 1 side rough.,red pigment	-	-	6	-	-	-	-
Cylinder bases: plain	-	-	14	1	2	3	-
Cylinder body sherds: excised and/or incised	-	1	2	3	3	2	3
Cylinder body sherds:1 side rough.,red pigm.	-	-	6	-	-	-	-
Outleaned-wall bowls: plain rims	-	-	1	2	-	-	-
Outleaned-wall bowls: plain flat bases	-	1	-	2	1	1	1
Bolstered-rim bowls: rims	-	1	-	-	-	-	-
Miniature bolstered-rim bowls: rims	-	-	-	-	2	-	-
Jars with vertical necks: neck/shoulder	-	2	5	-	-	-	-
Bottle necks	-	-	-	-	1	-	-
Pigment dishes: rims	-	2	-	-	-	-	-
Bowls with "mat" motif	-	3	4	-	-	-	-
Plain body sherds	6	12	25	22	29	14	10
Total	6	25	75	43	43	27	16
SAN JOSE SPECULAR RED							
Outleaned-wall bowls: plain rims	1	1	3	6	3	2	1
Cylinder rims: plain	1	-	-	-	2	-	-
Cylinder rims: excised	-	-	-	1	-	-	1
Bolstered-rim bowls: ext. unslip., excised	-	1	1	-	1	-	-
Bowl rims: too small to show shape	-	-	-	-	-	1	-
Tecomate rims	-	4	-	-	-	1	-
Jar necks	-	1	-	-	4	2	-
Bottle body sherds	-	-	-	-	1	-	-
"Grater bowl" bases	-	-	-	1	2	1	-
Plain body sherds	7	17	46	12	31	20	15
Total	9	24	50	20	44	27	17
LA MINA WHITE							
Cylinder rims	-	-	-	4	-	-	-
Tecomates/incurved-rim bowls: rims	-	-	2	1	-	-	-
Bottle neck sherds	-	-	-	-	1	-	-
Rims too small to show shape	-	-	1	-	-	-	-
Cylinders/bowls: flat basal sherds	-	-	-	1	-	-	-
Body sherds: incised	-	-	-	-	-	1	-
Body sherds: plain	1	2	22	8	9	5	2
Total	1	2	25	14	10	6	2
COATEPEC WHITE-RIMMED BLACK							
Outleaned-wall bowls: plain rims	-	1	3	-	1	-	-
Outleaned-wall bowls: plain flat bases	-	-	-	-	1	-	-
Cylinders: plain rims	-	-	1	-	-	-	-
Undecorated body sherds	-	-	-	1	2	-	-
Total	-	1	4	1	4	-	-
DELIA WHITE							
Plain body sherds	1	1	2	-	1	3	-
Total	1	1	2	-	1	3	-
PALOMA NEGATIVE							
Bowl body sherds	-	-	-	2	-	-	3
Total	-	-	-	2	-	-	3
UNCLASSIFIED SHERDS							
Rim sherds	-	20	21	17	17	13	14
Body sherds	47	102	97	74	105	87	98
Total	47	122	118	91	122	100	112
GRAND TOTAL	990	3456	7197	4637	6998	3993	3473

north-south for 93 meters along the western edge of the site. One section of that profile, approximately 37.5 m long, was selected as the Control Section because it contained so many interesting buildings and features, and the stratigraphy was unusually clear. Our excavation of Zones A-G in that Control Section was described in Chapter 13.

One of the most interesting levels in the control section was Zone D, a uniform layer of tan or buff San José phase debris from the decomposition of countless whitewashed wattle-and-daub houses. More than a dozen sand-coated floors from such houses could be seen in cross-section in the profile, and many of them were numbered at the time the profile was drawn (see Figs. 13.1–13.4).

Because of time limitations, we were only able to excavate nine of these floors. One sand-coated surface ("House 8") turned out not to belong to an actual residence; it was merely the eroded foundation for a once-plastered surface that had evidently surrounded Structure 7, a San José phase public building described in Chapter 18. The remaining eight sand-coated surfaces we excavated did turn out to be house floors. In order, from earliest to latest, they were House 6, House 5, House 2, House 11, House 9, House 1, House 10, and House 4.

This sequence of eight houses, whose sherd assemblages are given in Table 14.2, spans the lifetime of a residential ward in Area C of San José Mogote. That residential ward seems to have been one in which fire-serpents in Leandro Gray and Delfina Fine Gray pottery predominate over were-jaguars in Atoyac Yellow-white. Area C was a residential ward that had significant relationships both with the Basin of Mexico and with Chiapas/Guatemala. Tlatilco-style roller stamps and stone *yuguitos* are reminiscent of the former area (see Chapter 13), and Guamuchal Brushed tecomates indicate contact with the latter region (see Chapter 12).

The eight houses reported here span a considerable portion of the San José phase, from relatively early in the period until relatively late. They clearly do not span the *entire* phase, since Zone D was underlain by Zone E (early San José), and overlain by Zone C (late San José). However, comparisons with our midden stratigraphy suggest that House 6 was abandoned well into the second half of the phase.

Since these eight houses represent our largest sample of domestic architecture from a single Early Formative residential ward, brief descriptions of each house will be given here, as well as some photographs and drawings. In general, the Area C houses were 3–4 m wide and 5–6 m long. Some had four pine corner posts around 25–30 cm in diameter, and smaller posts elsewhere. Others had uniformly smaller posts. Houses differed as to whether or not the wattle-and-daub walls were weight bearing. For example, House 2 had a wattle wall set *outside* the large posts that supported the roof. In the case of other houses, the posts that bore the weight of the roof were incorporated into the wattle-and-daub wall itself.

There was at least one doorway, usually a meter wide, on one of the long sides of the house; it could be framed by posts or stones. House floors had often been worn to the point where they were slightly basin-shaped, and some had been resurfaced two or three times with new layers of clay and sand. Occasionally there might be a line of stones along one or more walls, often encircling the corner posts.

Walls of the Zone D houses were of reeds or canes (often *Phragmites*), known locally as *carrizo*. This material was also woven into mats (probably for sleeping on), which only occurred on certain parts of the floor. Over the wattle walls went a layer of mud that was smoothed and then whitewashed with a lime solution (often as thick as a pottery slip). Burned fragments show that house corners were square, and that the outer surface was occasionally burnished. The roof was apparently of thatch, and the burned grasses may have included *Phalaris*.

Bell-shaped pits, presumably for storage, accompanied many houses. Where it is possible to associate a pit with a house, we will discuss the contents of the pit. Cooking was apparently done in braziers of Lupita Heavy Plain pottery, and the commonly used fuel was pine, probably in the form of large chunks of prepared charcoal. On the downslope or leeward side of the house, the ash from these braziers might be dumped repeatedly until a midden accumulated, as in the case of House 2.

House 6

This house, of which only a remnant had survived, was the earliest and northernmost. It was built in an area where Zone D rested on bedrock, with no underlying Zones E-G. Feature 32, a large bell-shaped pit dug into bedrock some distance to the north, may have been in the dooryard of House 6 (Fig. 14.5). There were also a number of items associated with pottery making cached beneath the floor of House 6; included were a potter's bat (Fig. 12.123*l*) and a pigment dish for mixing engobe (Fig. 12.74*l*).

House 5

This house was probably built close to the time of House 2, but only a remnant was found.

House 2

This was one of our most interesting houses, even though its rear portion had been truncated by adobe makers. The intact eastern third of the house included a doorway, a partial line of stones marking the base of the wattle-and-daub wall, two corner postmolds, and a great many items (including restorable vessels) that could be piece-plotted on the floor (Figs. 14.6, 14.7).

House 2 was one whose weight-bearing posts were set well into the house, with the wattle-and-daub wall running around the outer periphery (Fig. 14.8). This pattern resembles several found by Wauchope (1938: Fig. 44) in the Maya area, where the wattle house wall may be like a screen that surrounds the house, but does not bear the weight of the roof.

Figure 14.5. Feature 32, a pit associated with House 6 of Area C, San José Mogote. Only the lower part of the pit, the part cut into bedrock, is shown in the photograph; the bell-shaped upper part, which was cut through soil, had been removed at this point.

The silica "ghost" of a reed mat, perhaps a *petate* for sleeping, was found in the northeast corner of House 2. In the doorway was a crushed Lupita Heavy Plain charcoal brazier, its ashy contents spilled. In the southeast corner of the house was an area where chert tools had been prepared from nodules and then used to cut and drill shell and mica. At least two pieces of chert had been turned into burnishing pebbles of the type used on Formative pottery. A fragment of a stone palette appeared to have been used to grind hematite powder into red pigment. Finally, banked up against the outside of the south wall of House 2 was a midden of gray ash. It appeared to be the same kind of gray ash that had been spilled from the Lupita Heavy Plain brazier in the doorway, and probably represented the dumping of several days' worth of brazier ash.

House 11

This remnant of a house was accompanied by three burials whose graves had been dug into a midden in the adjacent dooryard. One, an adult male (Burial 5) was accompanied by a Leandro Gray cylinder with an excised fire-serpent motif (Fig. 12.53). The other two burials were infants (Burials 10 and 11). One was accompanied by a mano, a miniature olla, a bead, and a drilled shell. The other was accompanied by a smaller cylinder, a hemispherical bowl, and the sherds of a large storage jar.

House 9

This house, only partly preserved, had mica- and shell-working areas on its floor; all items were piece-plotted. An unusually high number of pits were associated with this house, including Features 37, 38, 40, 40-east, and 41 (see below).

House 1

Only a remnant of this house was recovered.

Figure 14.6. Worker Juan Martínez exposes the floor of House 2, a San José phase residence, most of which had been destroyed by adobe makers before our arrival. In this view, looking south down the Area C profile, Martínez's feet are outside the slightly basin-shaped floor area, while his trowel is just inside. Visible are (1) a work area where chert was chipped and shell ornaments made, used for so long that a depression was worn in the floor; (2) an icepick stuck vertically in a postmold to mark its location; (3) a patch of ash, spilled in the doorway of the house when a Lupita Heavy Plain brazier overturned and broke; and (4) some of the stones in the base of the wattle-and-daub wall, forming the eastern limit of the house. For a drawing of the surviving remnant of this house, see Figure 14.7.

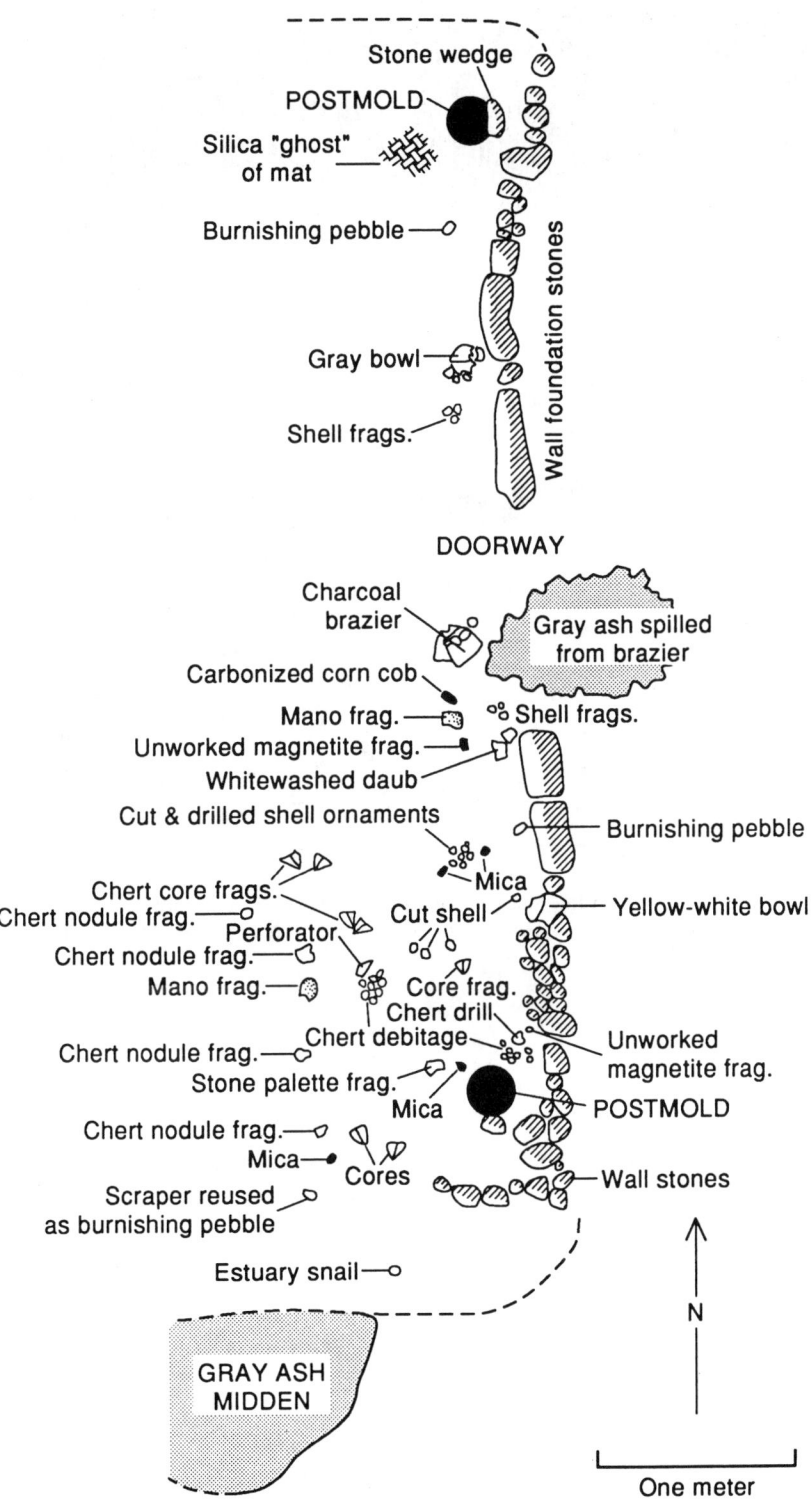

Figure 14.7. Plan of House 2, Area C, San José Mogote, showing objects piece-plotted on the floor. (For a photograph of this floor, see Fig. 14.6.)

Figure 14.8. Artist's reconstruction of House 2, Area C, San José Mogote. This view, from the west, shows that the wattle-and-daub wall lay outside the roof-support posts and was non-weight-bearing. There are other structures with similar construction elsewhere in Mesoamerica (see text). (Drawing by David Reynolds.)

House 10

This house had apparently been oriented roughly north-south, but was badly disturbed in places by later pit-digging and earth-moving activities.

House 4

This was a relatively well preserved house whose floor had been resurfaced several times (Fig. 14.9). A pit (Feature 35) was related to the most recent floor (Fig. 14.10). A number of postmolds were found along the eastern margin of the floor. In the southeast corner of the house lay an activity area where chert tools had been made from nodules and cores, then used to cut and drill shell ornaments. House 4, therefore, gave us a third example of a house with a shell-working area like those found in Houses 2 and 9. It also appeared that all three chert- and shell-working areas were in the southeast quadrants of their respective houses.

Features Related to the Area C Houses

Several deposits in Area C, mostly pits, were related to Houses 1 to 10. These deposits were not treated as control units, but their diagnostic sherds were noted. From earliest to latest, they were as follows:

1. *In a depression below House 6* were found nine fragments of Atoyac Yellow-white cylinders and outleaned-wall bowls; several San José Black-and-White cylinders with excised fire-serpent designs; Leandro Gray cylinders; Fidencio Coarse jars; Tierras Largas Burnished Plain hemispherical bowls; Matadamas Red and Matadamas Orange sherds; and at least four legs from "pretty lady" figurines. The impression is of debris from the first half of the San José phase, with many Tierras Largas phase types still present.

2. *Feature 32*, a large storage pit (Fig. 14.5), was part of House 6's household unit. The trash left behind in it included quantities of Tierras Largas Burnished Plain and Avelina Red-on-Buff, as well as San José Red-on-White bowls and tecomate body

sherds with rocker stamping. There were also fragments of large, hollow, white-slipped "dolls." The impression was of debris from early in the San José phase, with many Tierras Largas phase types still present.

3. *Feature 37* was a typical bell-shaped storage pit, partly intrusive into the remains of Structure 5. Its stratigraphic position showed that it had to have been deliberately filled in before House 2 could have been built over it. It should, thus, have contained a sample of types present before the construction of House 2. The sample included Fidencio Coarse jars and tecomates; a San José Red-on-White jar rim; Leandro Gray cylinders with excised fire-serpents; a sculptured-and-excised Leandro Gray bowl; an early Atoyac Yellow-white bowl with Tierras Largas-style rim slashes and zoned rocker stamping; an Ocós Black sherd; three Avelina Red-on-Buff hemispherical bowls; three Tierras Largas Burnished Plain hemispherical bowls; several Matadamas Red jars; and two figurine bodies, one of them white-slipped. The impression given was of debris from the first half of the San José phase.

4. *Features 40 and 40-east* bore the same relationship to House 9 that Feature 37 had borne to House 2; they were pits that had to be deliberately filled in before House 9 could be built over them. Feature 40-east was larger and less symmetrical, while Feature 40 was smaller and lay *within* 40-east—a kind of "pit within a pit."

Feature 40 had Leandro Gray cylinders with excised fire-serpents; Leandro Gray bolstered-rim bowls; Lupita Heavy Plain braziers/potstands and rocker stamped tecomates; Tierras Largas Burnished Plain jars and hemispherical bowls; and Avelina Red-on-Buff hemispherical bowls.

Feature 40-east had Leandro Gray cylinders; Atoyac Yellow-white tecomates with zoned punctation; Atoyac Yellow-white cylinders; San José Black-and-White sherds; Fidencio Coarse jars with paired jabs; Tierras Largas Burnished Plain hemispherical bowls, jars, and tecomates with fine dentate rocker stamping; some Avelina Red-on-Buff, including hemispherical bowls and an oval bowl with pinched-in sides; and Matadamas Orange jars. The impression given was of debris from the first half of the San José phase. Presumably, this material was present in the area when House 9 was built.

5. *Feature 41* was a bell-shaped pit contemporaneous with House 9, and possibly part of the same household unit. The small sample of sherds was most likely from somewhere in the middle of the San José phase. Perhaps its most interesting contents were two tecomate rims of what appears to be Guamuchal Brushed, a pottery type of the Chiapas/Guatemala region.

6. *Feature 38* was an ash-filled pit in the floor of House 9. The sherd sample was small and showed only types common in the house itself.

7. *Feature 35* was associated with House 4 (Figs 14.9, 14.10). House 4 had had its floor resurfaced several times; Feature 35 was an irregular concavity in the penultimate floor, deliberately filled in before the final floor was laid down. It contained fragments of Lupita Heavy Plain braziers/potstands with mat-impressed floors (a late San José phase attribute); Atoyac Yellow-white cylinders, outleaned-wall bowls, giant macrorims, and tecomates with interrupted rocker stamping; Leandro Gray cylinders with excised fire-serpents; San José Red-on-White outleaned-wall bowls and zoned rocker-stamped tecomates; Fidencio Coarse jars with zoned sloppy jabs; and fragments of white-slipped solid figurines. The impression given is of debris from the second half of the San José phase, with no Tierras Largas types included.

In retrospect, the features associated with San José phase households in Area C confirm our conclusion that the sequence of houses there spans much of the phase, from relatively early (House 6) to relatively late (House 4). No houses from either initial San José phase or terminal San José phase seem to have been present. As always, the reader should bear in mind our earlier caveats about the use of sherds from features.

Summary of Area C

Houses 6, 5, 2, 11, 9, 1, 10, and 4 yielded more than 2,000 sherds. The associated features yielded at least 2,000 more, but were not treated statistically.

318

Early Formative Pottery of Oaxaca

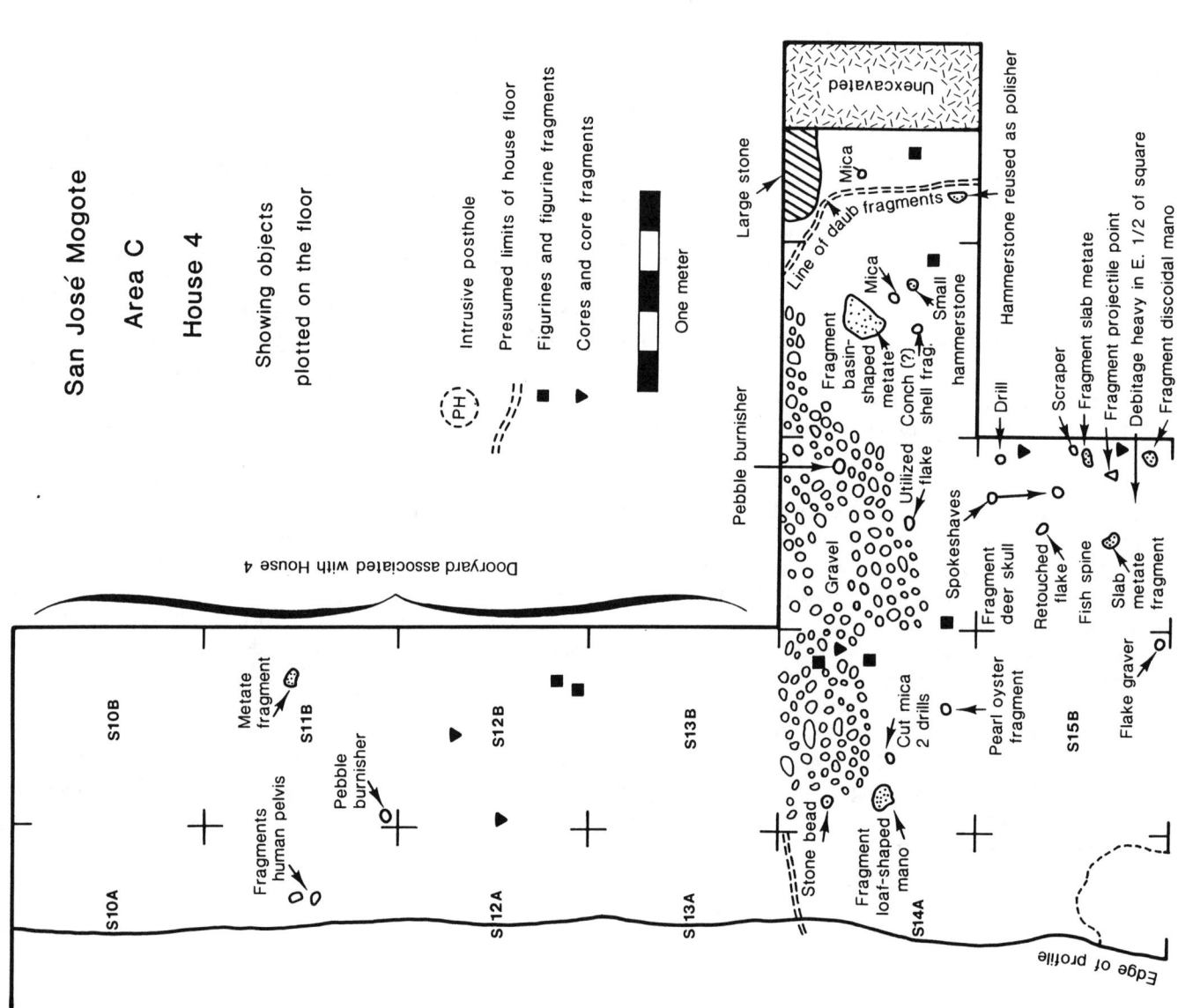

Chronological Variation during the San José

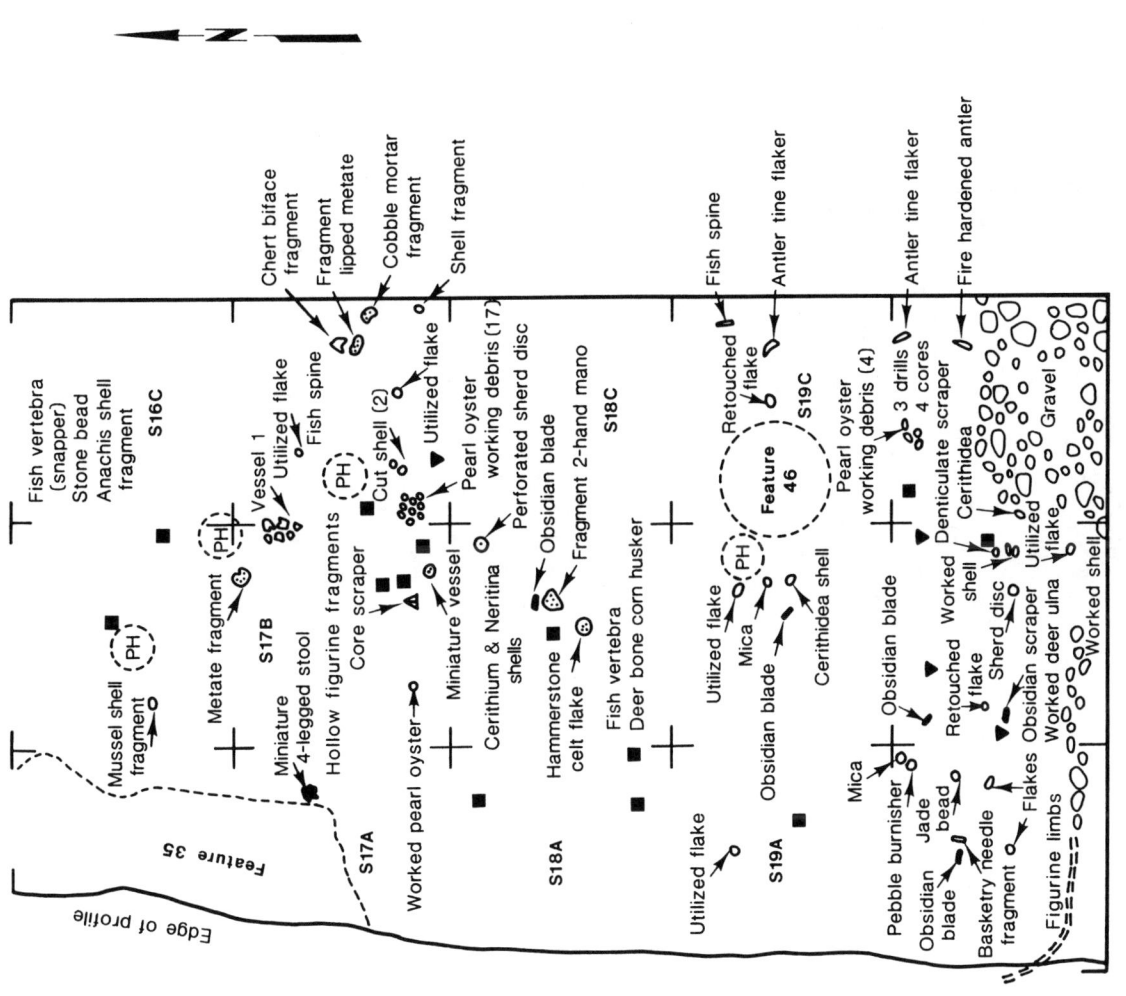

Figure 14.9. Plan of House 4, Area C, San José Mogote. (Redrawn from Marcus 1989: Fig. 8.17.)

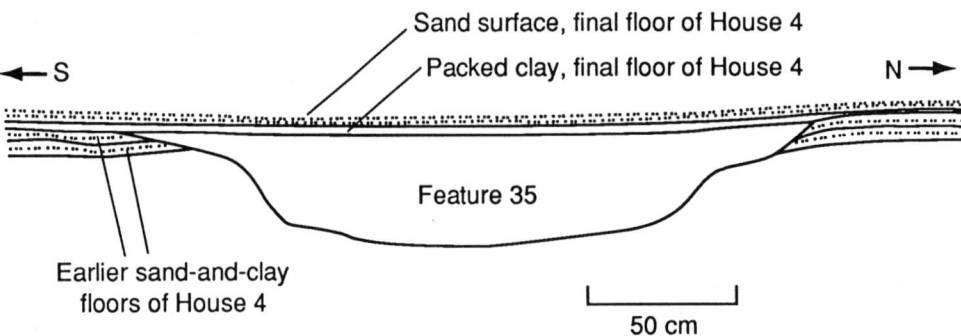

Figure 14.10. Cross-section of Feature 35, a subfloor depression in House 4, Area C, San José Mogote. The location of this feature is given in Figure 14.9.

TABLE 14.2
Sherds from Eight Houses in Area C, San José Mogote

	_____ Houses _____						
	6	5	2	9	1	10	4
TIERRAS LARGAS BURNISHED PLAIN							
Jar rims	2	-	7	16	-	4	5
Jar body sherds: pocked interior	1	-	-	-	-	-	-
Jar body sherds: wiped interior	-	-	-	-	-	-	1
Jar body sherds: plain interior	-	-	-	3	-	-	3
Jar shoulders: burnished interior	3	-	-	-	-	-	-
Hemispherical bowls: plain rims	2	2	12	28	9	4	29
Hemispherical bowls: basal curves	-	-	1	1	-	-	-
Hemispherical bowls: body sherds	-	-	4	2	1	-	3
Outleaned-wall bowls:							
plain rims	-	-	-	-	-	-	1
plain flat bases	-	-	2	-	-	-	-
dentate stamped body sherds	-	-	-	1	-	-	-
Tecomates: rocker stamp. body sherds	-	-	-	1	-	-	-
Tecomates: body sherds w/zoning line	-	-	5	1	-	-	-
Tecomates: misc. incised body sherds	-	-	-	-	-	-	1
Misc. unclassified rims	-	1	2	-	1	2	1
Misc. unclassified bases	1	-	2	3	-	1	2
Misc. unclassified body sherds	3	2	1	5	1	-	2
Total	12	5	36	61	12	11	48
TIERRAS LARGAS UNBURNISHED PLAIN							
Jar rims	-	-	-	-	-	-	3
Hemispherical bowls: plain rims	-	-	-	-	1	-	1
Total	-	-	-	-	1	-	4
AVELINA RED-ON-BUFF							
Jar rims	-	-	-	2	-	-	1
Jar body sherds:							
plain int., rectil. design ext.	-	-	1	1	-	-	1
Hemispherical bowl rims:							
red rim band only	2	-	6	4	3	2	5
rim band int., all red exterior	-	-	1	1	1	-	4
all red, exterior and interior	-	-	-	-	-	-	1
Hemispherical bowl body sherds:							
all red exterior, plain interior	1	-	1	1	-	-	-
plain exterior, all red interior	-	1	-	1	-	1	1
miscellaneous	2	1	2	2	1	1	2
Outleaned-wall bowl: red rim band	-	-	1	-	-	-	-
Misc. uncl. rims (incl. miniatures)	-	-	4	-	-	-	-
Total	5	2	16	12	5	4	15
CLEMENTINA FINE RED-ON-BUFF							
Hemispherical bowl rims:							
red rim band only	-	2	2	6	3	-	2
rim band interior, all red ext.	-	-	-	5	-	-	-
Hemispherical bowl body sherds:							
all red exterior, plain int.	-	-	1	1	-	-	-
plain exterior, all red int.	-	-	-	1	-	-	1
Misc. unclass. body sherds	2	-	1	1	-	-	2
Total	2	2	4	14	3	-	5
MATADAMAS RED							
Jar shoulders	-	-	-	1	-	-	-
Jar body sherds: wiped interior	1	-	2	1	-	-	1
Jar body sherds: plain interior	1	-	1	2	-	-	2
Total	2	-	3	4	-	-	3
MATADAMAS ORANGE							
Jar rims	-	-	2	-	1	1	6
Jar shoulders: burnished interior	-	-	-	-	-	-	1
Jar body sherds: plain interior	-	-	-	-	-	-	1
Hemispherical bowls: plain rims	-	-	-	-	-	-	6
Hemispherical bowls: basal curves	1	-	1	1	-	-	1
Hemispherical bowls: body sherds	2	1	3	3	1	1	2
Outleaned-wall bowls: plain rims	1	-	-	1	-	-	1

TABLE 14.2 (continued)

	Houses						
	6	5	2	9	1	10	4
Outleaned-wall bowls: plain flat bases	1	-	1	-	1	-	-
Tecomate body sherds: misc. decorated	1	-	1	1	-	-	1
Misc. unclassified rims	3	1	2	2	1	1	3
Misc. unclassified body sherds	5	1	4	6	2	-	7
Total	14	3	14	14	6	3	29
OCOS BLACK							
Plain body sherds	-	-	1	1	-	-	-
Total	-	-	1	1	-	-	-
FIDENCIO COARSE							
Tecomate rims	1	1	-	-	-	-	2
Tecomate body sherds: finger punching	-	-	-	1	-	-	-
Tecomate body sherds: rocker stamping	-	-	-	1	-	-	-
Jar rims: burnished	2	4	-	7	-	-	22
Jar rims: unburnished	7	3	-	3	-	7	8
Jar shoulders: sloppy jabs	-	-	-	1	1	1	2
Jar shoulders: neat punctations	-	-	-	1	-	-	1
Jar shoulders: incised band	-	-	-	-	-	-	2
Misc. body sherds	32	26	5	43	1	22	84
Total	42	34	5	57	2	30	121
LEANDRO GRAY							
Bottle neck/rim sherds	-	1	-	1	-	-	-
Outleaned-wall bowls:							
plain rims	8	3	8	15	1	1	33
plain flat bases	2	1	8	14	4	-	22
incised rims	-	-	1	-	-	-	1
excised rims	1	1	-	-	-	-	1
Cylinders: plain rims	5	4	4	14	8	4	39
Cylinders: plain flat bases	2	2	8	8	2	1	14
Cylinders: excised rims	1	1	2	8	-	-	8
Cylinders: excised body sherds	1	1	7	35	-	-	13
Cylinders: incised rims	-	1	2	4	-	-	6
Cylinders: incised body sherds	-	-	6	-	-	-	4
Cylinders: exterior roughened	-	-	-	-	-	-	2
Bowl rims, too small to show shape	1	-	1	2	-	-	3
Tecomate rims							
(may include incurved-rim bowls)	-	-	-	1	-	-	3
Tecomate body sherds: dentate stamp	-	-	-	1	-	-	-
Bolstered-rim bowls:							
burnished exterior	1	-	-	9	-	-	7
exterior rough, excised	1	-	-	3	-	-	1
Vertical jar necks: plain	-	1	1	1	-	-	6
Hemispherical bowls: rims	-	-	1	1	-	-	-
Bowls with gadrooned rims: rims	-	-	1	-	-	-	-
"Grater bowl" bases	-	-	-	2	-	-	1
Spouted trays: spout sherds	-	-	-	8	-	-	-
Pigment dishes/spouted trays: rims	1	-	-	1	-	-	-
Misc. uncl. rims (incl. miniatures)	-	-	-	1	-	-	-
Misc. body sherds	11	9	22	56	9	2	81
Total	35	25	72	185	24	8	245
ATOYAC YELLOW-WHITE							
Bowl: Ocós-style grooved rim	-	-	1	-	-	-	-
Outleaned-wall bowls:							
plain rims	8	7	17	32	6	1	26
plain flat bases	4	4	3	6	14	3	14
incised rims	9	11	2	-	12	1	11
excised body sherds	-	-	-	-	-	-	2
Cylinders: plain rims	6	2	18	16	6	-	21
Cylinders: plain flat bases	4	3	11	3	5	-	9
Cylinders: incised rims	2	2	11	-	4	2	15
Cylinders: excised sherds	-	-	-	3	-	-	3
Bowl rims: too small to show shape	2	1	3	5	1	1	8

TABLE 14.2 (continued)

	\multicolumn{7}{c}{Houses}						
	6	5	2	9	1	10	4
Tecomate rims: plain	1	-	-	2	-	-	-
Tecomate body sherds:							
zoned rocker stamping	-	-	3	5	14	1	3
dentate stamping	-	1	-	-	-	-	-
zoned punctation	-	-	2	5	-	-	2
Bolstered-rim bowls:							
exterior slipped	-	-	3	1	1	-	4
ext. unslipped, excised	-	-	-	-	-	-	3
Vertical jar necks: plain	1	-	1	1	-	-	1
Jars with outcurved rim: rims	-	-	1	1	2	2	2
Hemispherical bowls: rims	-	-	-	-	2	-	-
"Grater bowl" bases	-	-	-	-	8	-	-
Spouted trays: spout sherds	-	-	-	1	-	-	-
Bowls with giant "macrorim": rims	2	-	2	2	-	-	1
Squash effigy sherds	-	-	-	2	-	-	-
Misc. body sherds	11	13	21	30	37	4	53
Total	50	44	99	115	112	15	178
SAN JOSE RED-ON-WHITE							
Hemisph. bowls: rims w/red band	-	-	-	-	-	-	1
Incurved-rim bowls: rims w/red band	-	-	-	-	-	-	1
Tecomate rims: zoned rocker stamping	-	2	-	-	-	-	1
Tecomate body sherds:							
red zoning stripe	-	5	-	-	1	-	2
excised zoning line	-	-	2	-	-	-	-
rocker stamping	-	2	-	-	-	-	3
miscellaneous	-	-	-	-	-	-	1
Outleaned-wall bowls:							
red rim, white wall	1	5	1	-	-	-	8
Jar rims	-	-	-	4	1	-	2
Jar necks	-	-	-	1	-	-	-
Cylinder rims: red band at rim	-	-	2	-	-	-	-
Other	1	-	1	1	-	-	1
Misc. body sherds	-	3	2	2	-	-	6
Total	2	17	8	8	2	-	26
LUPITA HEAVY PLAIN							
Tecomates:							
plain, unburnished rims	1	-	-	-	-	-	-
zoned/burnished rims, plain body	-	-	-	-	-	-	2
burnished rims, rocker st. body	-	-	-	1	-	1	-
burnished rims, punctate body	-	-	-	3	-	-	-
Tecomate body sherds:							
misc. decoration	-	-	-	-	-	-	1
Outleaned-wall bowls:							
plain rims	-	-	-	3	-	-	5
plain flat bases	1	-	-	4	-	-	5
incised basal sherd	-	-	-	-	-	-	2
Pigment dishes/spouted trays: rims	-	-	-	1	-	-	-
Braziers/potstands: rims	12	2	*	4	-	-	10
Braziers/potstands: bases	1	5	-	2	-	-	12
Braziers/potstands: plain floors	1	1	-	-	-	-	6
Misc. body sherds	10	3	-	11	-	-	12
Total	26	11	*	29	-	1	55
"HYBRID": ATOYAC YELLOW-WHITE OUTSIDE, MATADAMAS ORANGE INSIDE							
Hemispherical bowl rim, incised ext	-	-	-	-	-	-	1
Incurved-rim bowls: rims	-	-	-	-	-	-	1
Small vessels: rims	-	-	-	1	-	-	-
Total	-	-	-	1	-	-	2
SAN JOSE BLACK-AND-WHITE							
Cylinders: plain rims	-	-	-	6	-	-	-
Cylinders: excised rims	-	-	-	2	1	-	-

TABLE 14.2 (continued)

	Houses						
	6	5	2	9	1	10	4
Outleaned-wall bowls: plain rims	-	-	1	1	-	-	-
Bowls with bolstered rim: rims	-	-	1	1	-	-	-
Misc. body sherds	-	-	-	5	-	-	-
Total	-	-	2	15	1	-	-
XOCHILTEPEC WHITE							
Bottles: shoulder or body sherds	-	-	-	-	-	-	1
Cylinders: plain rims	-	-	-	1	-	-	-
Outleaned-wall bowls: plain rims	-	-	-	1	-	1	-
Outleaned-wall bowls: basal sherds	-	-	-	-	-	-	1
Total	-	-	-	2	-	1	2
DELFINA FINE GRAY							
Cylinders: plain rims	-	-	2	-	-	-	7
Cylinders: plain bases	-	-	1	-	-	-	2
Outleaned-wall bowls: plain rims	1	-	1	1	-	-	1
Outleaned-wall bowls: plain bases	-	-	1	-	-	-	-
Bottle shoulder, rocker stamped	-	-	-	1	-	-	-
Incised body sherds	-	-	-	2	-	-	-
Total	1	-	5	4	-	-	10
SAN JOSE SPECULAR RED							
Outleaned-wall bowls: basal sherds	-	-	-	1	-	-	-
Bolstered-rim bowls:							
ext. unslipped, excised	-	-	-	1	-	-	-
Tecomates: plain rims	-	-	-	-	1	-	-
Tecomates: body sherds	-	-	-	-	-	-	1
Jar rims	-	-	-	4	-	-	-
Jar necks	-	-	-	-	-	-	2
Jar shoulders	-	-	-	3	-	-	-
Miscellaneous rims	-	-	-	-	-	-	1
Miscellaneous body sherds	1	-	2	1	-	3	1
Total	1	-	2	10	1	3	5
LA MINA WHITE							
Bottles: body sherds	-	-	-	1	-	-	-
Cylinders: plain rims	1	-	-	-	-	-	2
Total	1	-	-	1	-	-	2
COATEPEC WHITE-RIMMED BLACK							
Outleaned-wall bowls: rims	2	1	-	-	-	-	1
Total	2	1	-	-	-	-	1
DELIA WHITE							
Outleaned-wall bowls: rims	-	-	-	-	-	-	8
Outleaned-wall bowls: flat bases	-	-	-	-	-	-	8
Total	-	-	-	-	-	-	16
UNCLASSIFIED SHERDS							
Misc. rim sherds	-	-	1	2	2	6	2
Misc. body sherds	1	3	7	1	11	11	1
Total	1	3	8	3	13	17	3
GRAND TOTAL	196	147	275	536	182	93	770

* A restorable brazier (Vessel 2) was plotted *in situ* in House 2.

House 14, Area C

House 14 was found at a depth of 1.4–1.5 m in Squares S18F, S19F, S20F, S18G, S19G, and S20G of Area C at San José Mogote. Those squares lay 6–8 m east of the Master Profile. House 14 occurred in stratigraphic Zone C, just above the Zone C/Zone D contact. Stratigraphically, this places it in the late San José phase and makes it later than House 4 of the Control Section, which has already been described.

House 14 had undergone two floor resurfacings; our plan drawing (Fig. 14.11) was done at the level of the uppermost floor. Three postmolds from the east side of the house were found, as were traces of a second building that may have been an associated lean-to or ramada. To the east of House 14 was a dooryard, with an ashy gray midden banked up against the east side of the house. This midden actually produced most of the sherds associated with the House 14, since the uppermost house floor was relatively clean.

Several items confirm the late San José phase date of this household. Included are a Leandro Gray bowl with an outcurved rim; a series of Atoyac Yellow-white cylinders incised with Plog's Motifs 50, 58, and 68; and a brick red composite silhouette bowl (nonlocal). All these are items that went on to be important in the subsequent Guadalupe phase.

The sample of 157 sherds from the dooryard midden associated with House 14 is as follows:

TIERRAS LARGAS BURNISHED PLAIN
Jar rims	7
Hemispherical bowls: plain rims	7
Outleaned-wall bowls: plain rims	2
Tecomates: plain rims	1
Total	17

AVELINA RED-ON-BUFF
Jar rims: red band int., wide band ext.	1
Hemispherical bowl rims: red rim bands	3
Hemispherical bowl rims: rim band, red int.	1
Total	5

CLEMENTINA FINE RED-ON-BUFF
Hemispherical bowl rims: red rim bands	1
Total	1

MATADAMAS ORANGE
Jar rims	1
Outleaned-wall bowls: plain rim	1
Total	2

FIDENCIO COARSE
Jar rims: burnished	5
Jar rims: unburnished	6
Total	11

LEANDRO GRAY
Outleaned-wall bowls: plain rims	10
Cylinders: plain rims	13
Cylinders: plain flat bases	1
Cylinders: excised rims	3
(Note: excising includes Pyne's Motifs 1, 3, and 15/16)	
Cylinders: incised rims	3
Cylinders: incised body sherds	1
Cylinders: rocker stamped rims	1
Incurved-rim bowls: plain rims	2
Incurved-rim bowls: excised rims	1
Bolstered-rim bowls: burnished exterior	1
Bolstered-rim bowls: exterior rough, excised	2
Vertical jar necks: plain	1
Hemispherical bowls: punctate rims	1
Outcurved-rim bowls: incised rims	1
Total	41

ATOYAC YELLOW-WHITE
Outleaned-wall bowls: plain rims	6
Outleaned-wall bowls: plain flat bases	1
Outleaned-wall bowls: incised rims	18
Cylinders: plain rims	12
Cylinders: plain flat bases	2
Cylinders: incised rims	6
(Note: double-line-breaks include Plog's Motifs 50, 58, and 68)	
Cylinders: incised body sherds	1
Cylinders: excised sherds	2
Tecomate sherds: zoned rocker stamping	2
Bolstered-rim bowls: plain rims	6
Bolstered-rim bowls: exterior incised	2
Vertical jar necks: plain	1
Vertical jar necks/shoulders: incised	3
Incurved-rim bowls: plain rims	1
Incurved-rim bowls with fluted body	1
Total	64

SAN JOSE RED-ON-WHITE
Hemispherical bowls: rims w/red band	1
Tecomates: body sherds w/red zoning stripe	2
Outleaned-wall bowls: red rim, white wall	3
Total	6

LUPITA HEAVY PLAIN
Outleaned-wall bowls: plain rims	1
Braziers/potstands: rims	5
Total	6

DELFINA FINE GRAY
Cylinder rims: plain	1
Total	1

COATEPEC WHITE-RIMMED BLACK
Cylinders: plain rims 1
Total 1

POSSIBLE FOREIGN WARES
Rare white incurved-rim bowl 1
Brick red composite silhouette bowl 1
Total 2

GRAND TOTAL 157

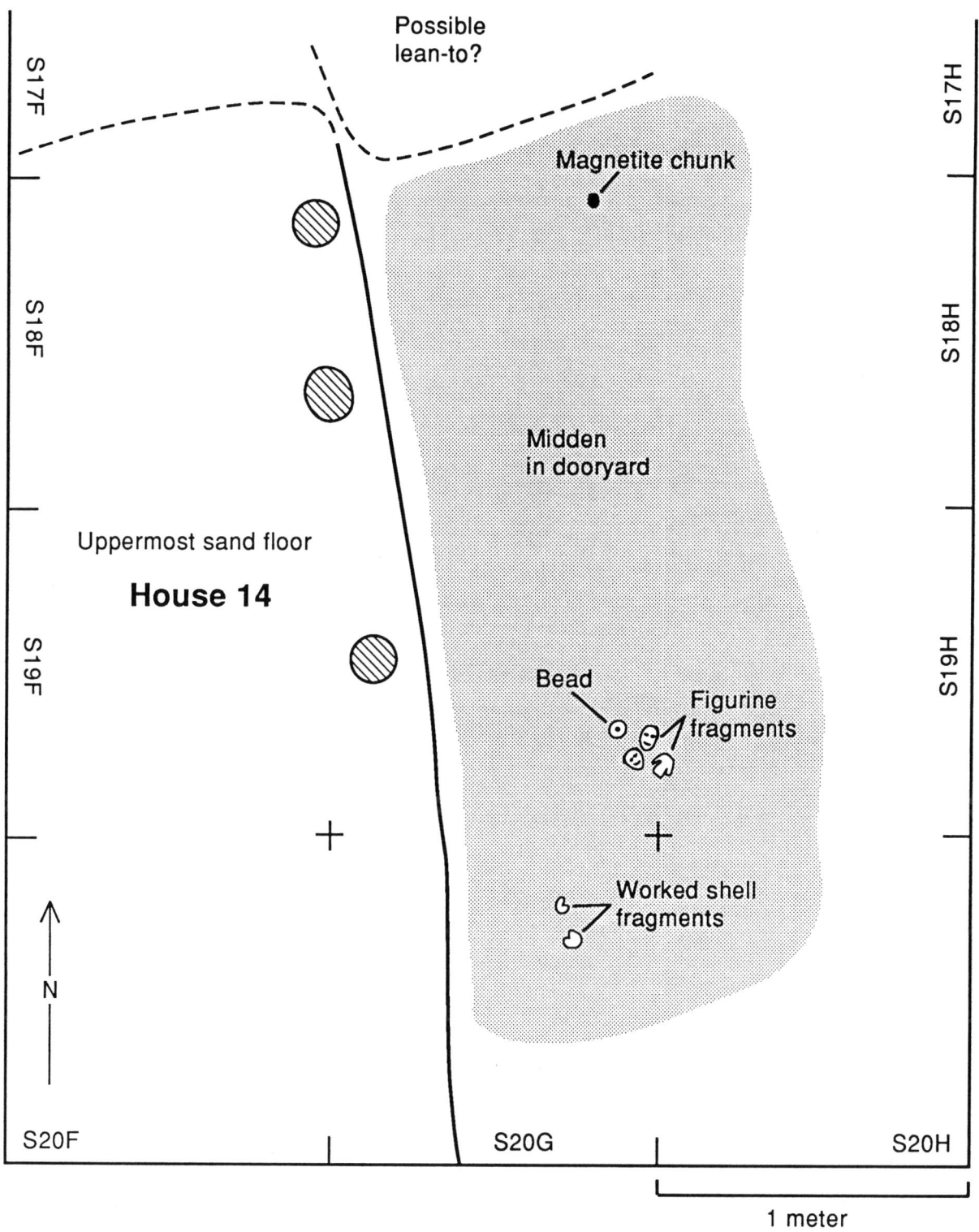

Figure 14.11. Plan of House 14, Area C, San José Mogote, showing objects piece-plotted in dooryard midden. (For a view of the two superimposed floors belonging to this house, see Fig. 4.24.)

Chapter 15

Synchronic Variation 1: Differences Between a High-Status Household and a Low-Status Household

As we noted in Chapter 5, not all variation in pottery assemblages is diachronic. Depending on circumstances, some of the variation between two assemblages can be synchronic, resulting from factors other than chronological difference.

In the case of the San José phase, at least three causes of synchronic variation come to mind. The first is the difference in pottery available to high-status families when compared to low-status families. The second is the difference between residential wards whose pottery featured fire-serpents and those whose pottery featured were-jaguars. The third is the difference between two villages separated by many kilometers, such as one in the Etla region and one in the Tlacolula region.

Examples of these three kinds of synchronic variation will be given in Chapters 15, 16, and 17. In this chapter we look at two households from San José Mogote: House 13, which we consider a relatively low-status residence, and Houses 16–17, which we consider two components of a relatively high-status residence.

The key word here is "relatively." As we have stated previously, we consider the San José phase to have been "a time of emerging status differences which took the form of a continuum from relatively higher to relatively lower status, without a division into true social classes such as characterized later periods of Zapotec prehistory" (Marcus 1989:165–68). Thus, the differences among households are differences of degree rather than differences of kind. The higher a family's status, the more likely they were to have had (1) a better-made, whitewashed house, or a two-structure household; (2) greater consumption of venison; (3) fancier or more highly decorated pottery, or more imported wares; (4) greater access to jade; and (5) greater access to *Spondylus,* pearl oyster, pearly freshwater mussel, and other ornamental raw materials from outside the Valley of Oaxaca. Magnetite and mica also figured in this continuum, but they were locally available rather than imported.

Houses 13 and 16–17 were selected in part because both seemed to have been occupied relatively late in the San José phase. Their rough contemporaneity therefore minimizes the effects of diachronic, or chronological, variation. We should stress that neither house falls near the limits of the status continuum; undoubtedly there were households of lower status than House 13, and households of higher status than Houses 16–17. We have chosen them because they are generally coeval, well enough preserved so that many details of their construction are known, and reasonably well supplied with artifacts that should reflect status differences.

House 13, San José Mogote: A Low-Status Household

Mound 1 at San José Mogote lies only 60 m west of the Area A residential ward (see Fig. 9.1). The core of this "mound" is a natural hill that was greatly modified during the Middle Formative and Protoclassic. During the San José phase the hill was still largely unmodified, although a few structures were built there. One of these was House 13 (Fig. 15.1).

Only the southern half of House 13 could be excavated, since the northern half had been disturbed by the foundations of Structure 14, a stone masonry building whose earliest building stage was Middle Formative. The house would have been roughly 3 × 5 m with a doorway on the west. This doorway, presumed to be in the middle of one of the long sides, was framed with stones. In contrast to House 2 of Area C (see Figs. 14.7–14.8), at least some of House 13's postmolds (nos. 2, 3, 4, 6, and 9) were set along the outer margins of the floor, indicating that the wattle-and-daub walls were weight-bearing. A few postmolds (nos. 5, 7, and 8) occurred farther inside the house; it is not known whether they were from posts added later, or from posts providing extra support for the south end of the roof. All postmolds were relatively small (15–16 cm in diameter) and one (no. 2) contained a stone wedge, presumably added when the post became loose. One post (no. 1) helped frame the doorway.

House 13 was relatively poorly made. Its daub was roughly

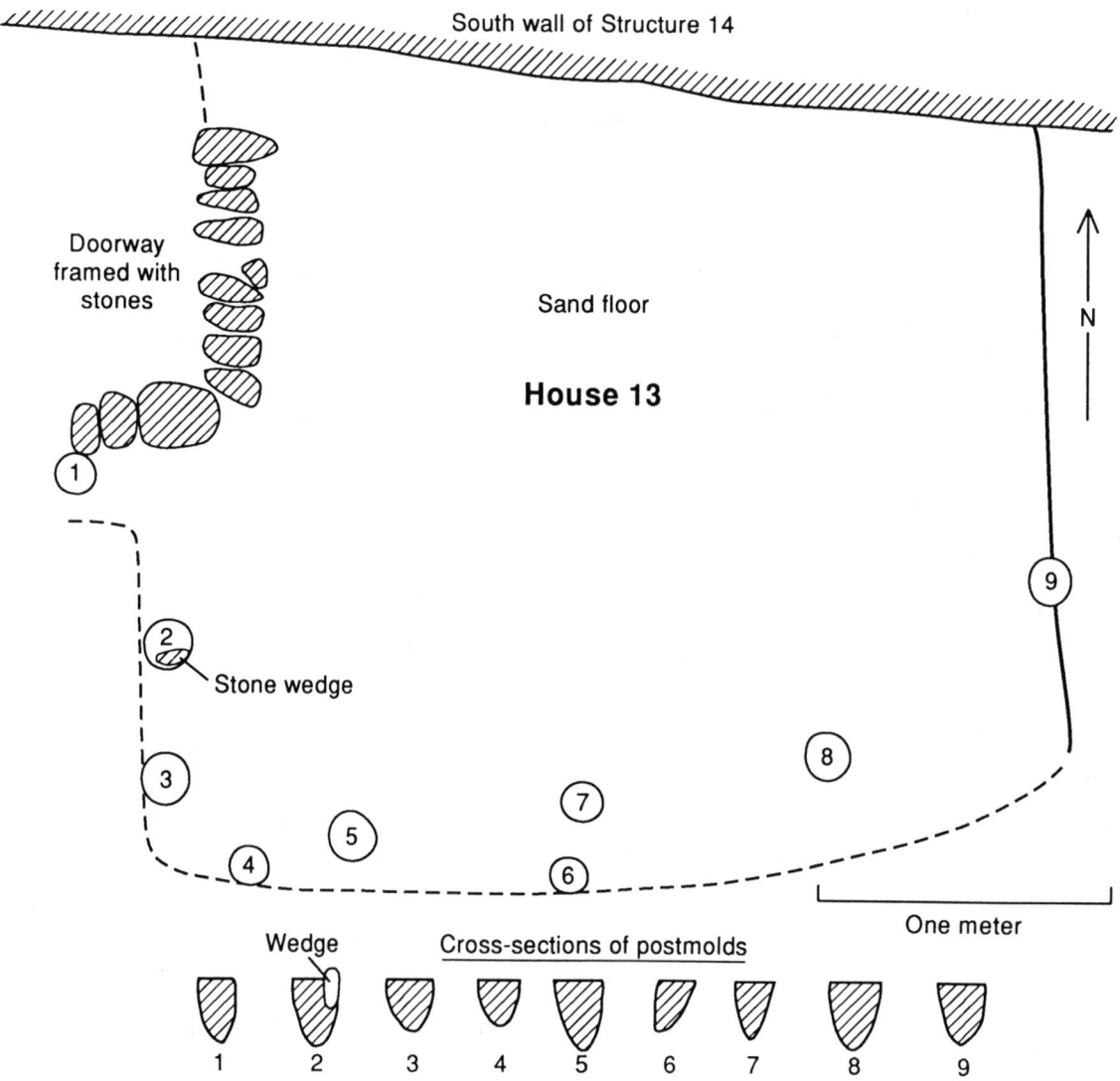

Figure 15.1. Plan view of House 13, Mound 1, San José Mogote (San José phase). Postmolds are shown as numbered circles; the corresponding cross-sections are shown at the bottom of the illustration.

the same buff color as Tierras Largas Burnished Plain, having been given an outer coating of slightly finer clay but no whitewash. Its corners were also slightly rounded rather than nicely squared, another trait of lower status houses. Our artist's reconstruction of the house (Fig. 15.2) assumes that the disturbed half was a mirror image of the well-preserved half.

Items left behind on the floor also indicated that House 13 was the home of a relatively low-status family. There was less deer bone, for example, than in the usual whitewashed house with well-made square corners. Small bone needles for sewing were found, but none of the longer basketry needles found in Houses 16–17 (see below). There was also no jade found in the house, although a small fragment (0.3 g) was found not far above the floor debris.

The occupants of the house seem to have been modest producers of *Spondylus* and freshwater mussel ornaments, and consumers of pearl oyster ornaments made elsewhere. There were six fragments of magnetite in the house, perhaps indicating that during the San José phase, Mound 1 should be considered part of Area A, where so many magnetite mirrors were made. However, chipped stone associated with the house was very meager by the standards of Area A houses. The one craft item in highest frequency in House 13 was mica, numerous small fragments of which were piece-plotted by Marcus. These fragments may be debris from the cutting up of mica sheets, perhaps as decoration for costumes or masks.

As will be clear from the list given below, the pottery of House 13 was relatively undecorated, compared with collections from

Figure 15.2. Artist's reconstruction of House 13, as it might have looked during occupation. (Drawing by David Reynolds.)

higher status households. The range of double-line-break motifs on Atoyac Yellow-white was limited, running mainly to Plog's Motifs 23 and 54. Designs on Leandro Gray were also limited, with only one case of Pyne's Motif 1 (fire-serpent) and two cases of Motif 16 (fine-line chevrons). The presence of a fire-serpent motif strengthens our suspicion that House 13 was related to Area A, whose pottery also featured Sky or fire-serpent designs.

Several vessel forms suggest a relatively late San José phase date for House 13. They include a Leandro Gray bowl with a slightly everted rim; an Atoyac Yellow-white bowl with an everted rim; a Lupita Heavy Plain brazier with a basketry-impressed (rather than mat-impressed) floor; and a restorable Atoyac Yellow-white composite silhouette bowl with exterior incising (Vessel 3). All those attributes went on to become more common in the Guadalupe phase.

Vessel 3 was actually found in a household midden just outside House 13. Inside the house were fragments of Vessels 1 (a Leandro Gray outleaned-wall bowl) and 2 (an Atoyac Yellow-white effigy vessel of some kind).

In addition, the presence of Delia White and Coatepec White-rimmed Black sherds in House 13 strengthens our impression of a late San José phase date. The scarcity of San José Red-on-White leads to the same conclusion.

While House 13 had most of the pottery types seen in late San José times, it had only a few sherds of such luxury wares as Delfina Fine Gray, Xochiltepec White, and Delia White. This would be in keeping with a family of relatively low status. We did find one possible sherd of an imported ware that has not been securely identified.

The 353 sherds from House 13 were as follows:

TIERRAS LARGAS BURNISHED PLAIN
Hemispherical bowls: plain rims	11
Outleaned-wall bowls: plain rims	1
Tecomates: plain rims	1
Miscellaneous body sherds	5
Total	18

AVELINA RED-ON-BUFF
Jar shoulders: burnished, design exterior	1
Hemispherical bowl rims: red rim band only	1
Total	2

CLEMENTINA FINE RED-ON-BUFF
Hemispherical bowl rims: red rim band only	1
Total	1

MATADAMAS RED
- Jar rims — 1
- Misc. body sherds — 3
- Total — 4

MATADAMAS ORANGE
- Jar rims — 4
- Hemispherical bowls: plain rims — 4
- Misc. body sherds — 8
- Total — 16

OCOS BLACK
- Bottle neck/shoulder sherds — 1
- Bolstered-rim bowls: rims — 1
- Total — 2

FIDENCIO COARSE
- Jar rims: unburnished — 3
- Tecomate rims — 1
- Tecomate body sherds: interrupted rocker stamping — 2
- Misc. body sherds — 83
- Total — 89

LEANDRO GRAY
- Outleaned-wall bowls: plain rims — 19
- Outleaned-wall bowls: plain flat bases — 4
- Outleaned-wall bowls: incised rims — 2
- Cylinders: plain rims — 9
- Cylinders: plain flat bases — 4
- Cylinders: excised rims (Pyne's Motif 1) — 1
- Cylinders: incised rims (Pyne's Motif 16) — 2
- Bowl rims, too small to show shape — 4
- Tecomate body sherds: zoned dentate stamp — 1
- Incurved-rim bowls: plain rims — 3
- Bolstered-rim bowls: excised exterior — 1
- Vertical jar necks: plain — 2
- Oval bowls with pinched-in sides: rims — 1
- Pigment dishes/spouted trays: rim sherds — 2
- Bowls with thickened, wedge-shaped rim — 1
- Bowls with slightly everted rim — 1
- Misc. decorated body sherds — 3
- Misc. undecorated body sherds — 17
- Total — 77

ATOYAC YELLOW-WHITE
- Outleaned-wall bowls: plain rims — 9
- Outleaned-wall bowls: plain flat bases — 9
- Outleaned-wall bowls: incised rims — 12
- Cylinders: plain rims — 10
- Cylinders: plain flat bases — 5
- Cylinders: incised rims — 5
- Cylinders: incised body sherds — 1
- Tecomate body sherds: zoned rocker stamp — 1
- Vertical jar necks: plain — 1
- Bowls with giant "macrorim": rims — 1
- Bowls with everted rim — 1
- Misc. undecorated body sherds — 23
- Total — 78

SAN JOSE RED-ON-WHITE
- Hemispherical bowls: rims — 1
- Total — 1

LUPITA HEAVY PLAIN
- Braziers/potstands: rims — 7
- Braziers/potstands: bases — 4
- Braziers/potstands: plain floors — 3
- Braziers/potstands: basketry-impressed floor — 1
- Misc. body sherds — 4
- Total — 19

SAN JOSE BLACK-AND-WHITE
- Cylinder rims: plain — 1
- Cylinder bases: plain — 1
- Outleaned-wall bowls: plain flat bases — 1
- Total — 3

XOCHILTEPEC WHITE
- Cylinder rims: plain — 1
- Cylinder bases: plain — 1
- Cylinder body sherds — 1
- Total — 3

DELFINA FINE GRAY
- Cylinder bases: plain — 1
- Cylinder body sherds: plain — 1
- Cylinder rims: incised — 1
- Total — 3

COATEPEC WHITE-RIMMED BLACK
- Outleaned-wall bowls: plain rims — 1
- Total — 1

DELIA WHITE
- Plain body sherds — 2
- Total — 2

POSSIBLE FOREIGN WARE
- Madera Brown from Morelos? — 1
- Total — 1

UNCLASSIFIED SHERDS — 33

GRAND TOTAL — 353

Houses 16–17, San José Mogote: A High-Status Late San José Phase Household

In Area B of San José Mogote (Fig. 9.1), almost on the border between the lands of Guadalupe Etla and those of the *agencia* of San José, there stands a vertical cut bank left by adobe makers and by the excavation of a modern dooryard or *solar*. This vertical bank runs 99.5 m west until it passes the Master Profile of Area C (see Chapter 13). In 1969 we turned this cut bank into a vertical profile by shaving it with square-ended shovels, sharpened digging bars, and sharp trowels. The westernmost 70 m of the profile were drawn in 1969 and proved rather uninviting; they included the area of artificial fill shown earlier in Figure 4.9, Chapter 4.

In 1974, however, we re-shaved and drew the easternmost 29.5 m of the profile with more satisfying results. This part of the Area B profile rises in altitude as it runs east, eventually passing over an area of piedmont spur whose soft bedrock was perfect for the carving out of residential terraces. Immediately the profile became more interesting in this area, showing house floors, pits, hearths, and rain-runoff canals in cross-section.

We chose a five-meter section of the eastern Area B profile to investigate (Fig. 15.3). By 1974, we had, under certain conditions, shifted from 1 × 1 m squares to 2 × 2 m squares to allow us more flexibility. If we were digging through large areas of slopewash or construction fill in which there was no point in piece-plotting objects, we stayed with the 2 × 2 m squares. When we found an Early Formative house, or some other area where piece-plotting was required, we simply divided each 2 × 2 m square into four 1 × 1 m squares. Thus, a 2 × 2 m square called N1E6 would become 4 smaller squares called "N1E6 northwest," "N1E6 southwest," and so on. In the five-meter-wide area shown in Figure 15.3, Zone A (the plow zone) was removed by 2 × 2 m squares, while the House 17 floor was excavated by 1 × 1 m squares. This area was first excavated by John W. Rick in 1974 and continued by Marcus in 1978.

What the Area B excavation showed was a large, flat residential terrace, deliberately leveled by San José phase villagers who had cut into the soft volcanic tuff bedrock using hard metamorphic celts. This terrace had had a complex history. The first occupants had excavated a number of small canals and a large cistern (Feature 58) into bedrock (Fig. 15.4). The canals clearly appeared to have diverted rain runoff away from houses; some of this water evidently wound up in the cistern, which even had an overflow canal in case it filled to the brim. While there were many postholes of all sizes in the bedrock of the terrace, the pattern was confusing because they had come down from several different depths and belonged to more than one set of houses.

Stratigraphically above these bedrock features and postholes were the floors of Houses 16 and 17. While both of these buildings were called "houses" in the field, it eventually became clear that only one—House 17—was an actual wattle-and-daub house. House 16 was a lean-to, shed, or roofed work area of some kind, perhaps connected to House 17 as shown in the Figure 15.5 reconstruction drawing. Its posts were small and few in number, and it had no evidence of daub fallen from collapsing walls.

Figure 15.6 shows a plan view of this household unit, with House 16 to the north and House 17 to the south.

House 17

House 17, a whitewashed wattle-and-daub residence truncated by the Area B profile, lay to the south of a ridge of bedrock "backdirt" from one of the canals shown in Figure 15.4. Its surviving floor had a light scatter of tools which we piece-plotted, including a biface roughout reused as a chopper, and several chert cores. Also found were cooking and storage vessels. Cached below the floor were two artifacts of metamorphic rock that appeared to be tools for planing and smoothing wood (Marcus 1989:183–184).

House 16

House 16, a structure used as a work area of some kind, lay to the north of the canal "backdirt." It contained a hearth (Feature 62) and a larger, keyhole-shaped firepit, apparently for heat-treating chert (Feature 61). The presence of this firepit was not surprising, because one of this household's main activities was the manufacture of bifaces from heat-treated chert (Parry 1987:98). Other crafts suggested by debris on the floor include basketry making and pearl oyster ornament manufacture (Marcus 1989:184). In addition, a lightly baked clay mold for making cylindrical bowls was found associated with Feature 62 (see Fig. 2.7).

Smashed on the floor of House 16 were numerous restorable vessels in Atoyac Yellow-white, and a possible Cesto White vessel from the Basin of Mexico (see Fig. 12.160). In keeping with the rest of the ceramics from this household, representations of Earth or the were-jaguar were dominant on these ceramics. This seemed to be true of other households in Area B as well.

Evidence for High Status

Although both House 13 and Houses 16–17 belonged to late San José phase households, there were numerous differences between them. House 17 was of better construction, with a thick coating of whitewash almost approaching a slip. Houses 16–17 had more deer bone, more evidence of *Spondylus* and pearl oyster shell, and more exotic items such as ceramic masks, stingray spines, fish spines, and drum otoliths. This household's occupants were heavily involved in craft activities such as pottery making, sewing, basketry making, and chert biface production. They had also invested a great deal of time in hacking the sloping bedrock of Area B into a series of stepped terraces suitable for large households. On the other hand, they seem to have been less involved in the cutting of mica sheets than were the occupants of House 13.

One of the occupants of House 17, a middle-aged woman

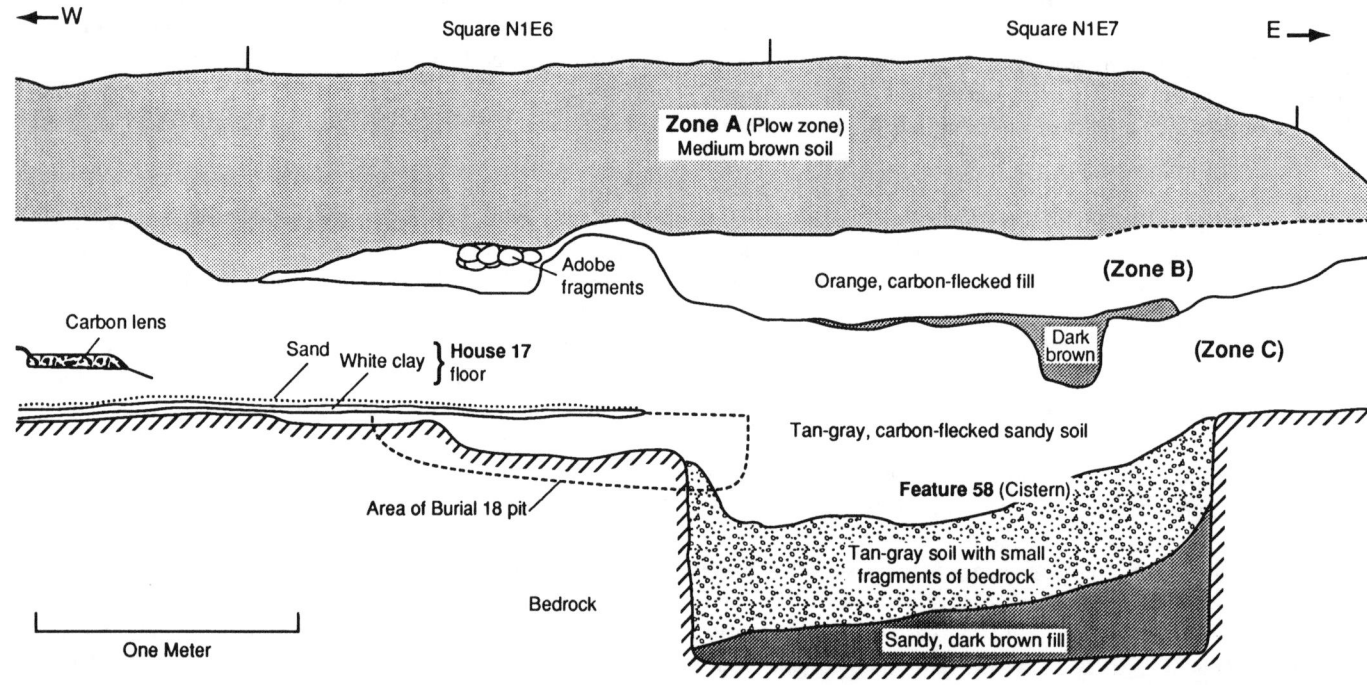

Figure 15.3. A 5-m section of the Area B profile, San José Mogote, before excavation began. This drawing reveals the cross-sectioned floor of House 17.

(Burial 18), had been buried beneath the floor in a pit extending into bedrock (Fig. 15.4). She was accompanied by two jade earspools and three jade beads, the largest amount of jade found with any San José phase burial thus far. In addition, an even finer jade earspool was found on the floor of House 16. In short, whatever the criteria used, Houses 16–17 emerge as the residence of a higher status family when compared with House 13.

Let us now look at the pottery assemblages from House 17 and House 16, commenting both on the vessels that suggest a late San José phase date and on those that suggest relatively high status for the household. The 170 sherds from House 17 are as follows:

TIERRAS LARGAS BURNISHED PLAIN
Jar rims	2
Jar body sherds: plain interior	5
Hemispherical bowls: plain rims	6
Hemispherical bowls: plain body sherds	10
Outleaned-wall bowls: plain rims	1
Total	24

AVELINA RED-ON-BUFF
Hemispherical bowl rims: red rim band only	1
Total	1

CLEMENTINA FINE RED-ON-BUFF
Hemispherical bowl rims:	
red rim band only	1
all red interior, design exterior	1
Total	2

MATADAMAS RED
Jar rims	3
Jar body sherds: plain interior	2
Total	5

FIDENCIO COARSE
Jar rims: unburnished	1
Plain body sherds	8
Total	9

LEANDRO GRAY
Outleaned-wall bowls: plain rims	5
Outleaned-wall bowls: plain flat bases	2
Outleaned-wall bowls: incised rims	1
Cylinders: plain rims	2
Cylinders: plain flat bases	1
Cylinders: incised body sherds	1
Incurved-rim bowl: excised rim	1

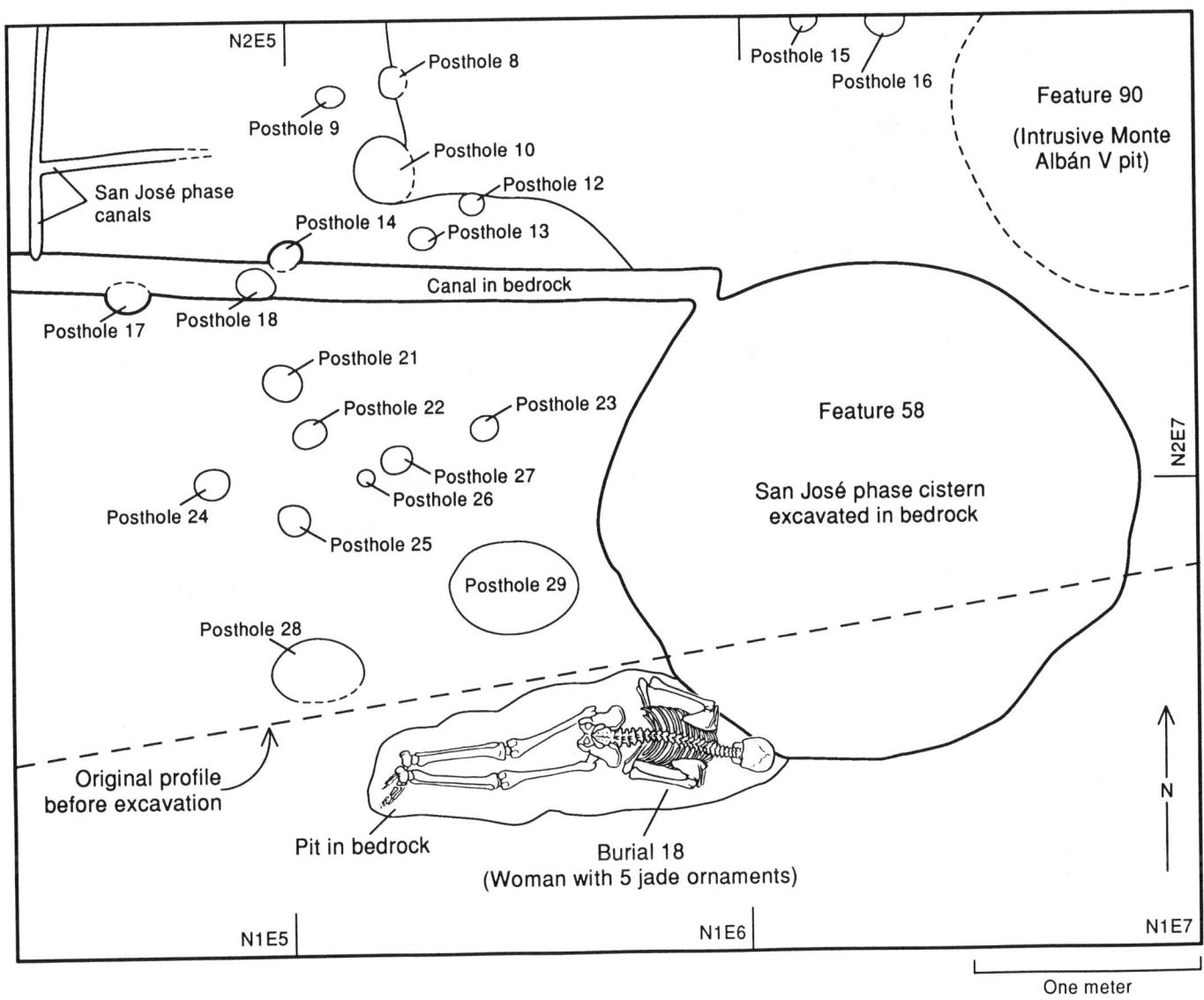

Figure 15.4. Plan view of bedrock in Area B of San José Mogote, showing postholes, rain-runoff canals, a cistern (Feature 58), and a burial (Burial 18). The dashed line indicates the original profile shown in Figure 15.3.

Pigment dishes/spouted trays: rim sherds	1
Plain body sherds	29
Total	43

ATOYAC YELLOW-WHITE

Outleaned-wall bowls: plain rims	3
Outleaned-wall bowls: plain flat bases	1
Outleaned-wall bowls: incised rims	6
Cylinders: plain rims	3
Cylinders: plain flat bases	1
Cylinders: incised rims	4
Tecomate body sherds: zoning line	1
Vertical jar necks: plain	2
Hemispherical bowls: plain bases	1
Incurved-rim bowls: incised rims	1
Spouted trays: spout sherds, incised	1
Bowls with giant "macrorim": rims	1
Plain body sherds	52
Total	77

LUPITA HEAVY PLAIN

Outleaned-wall bowls: plain rims	1
Braziers/potstands: rims	1
Total	2

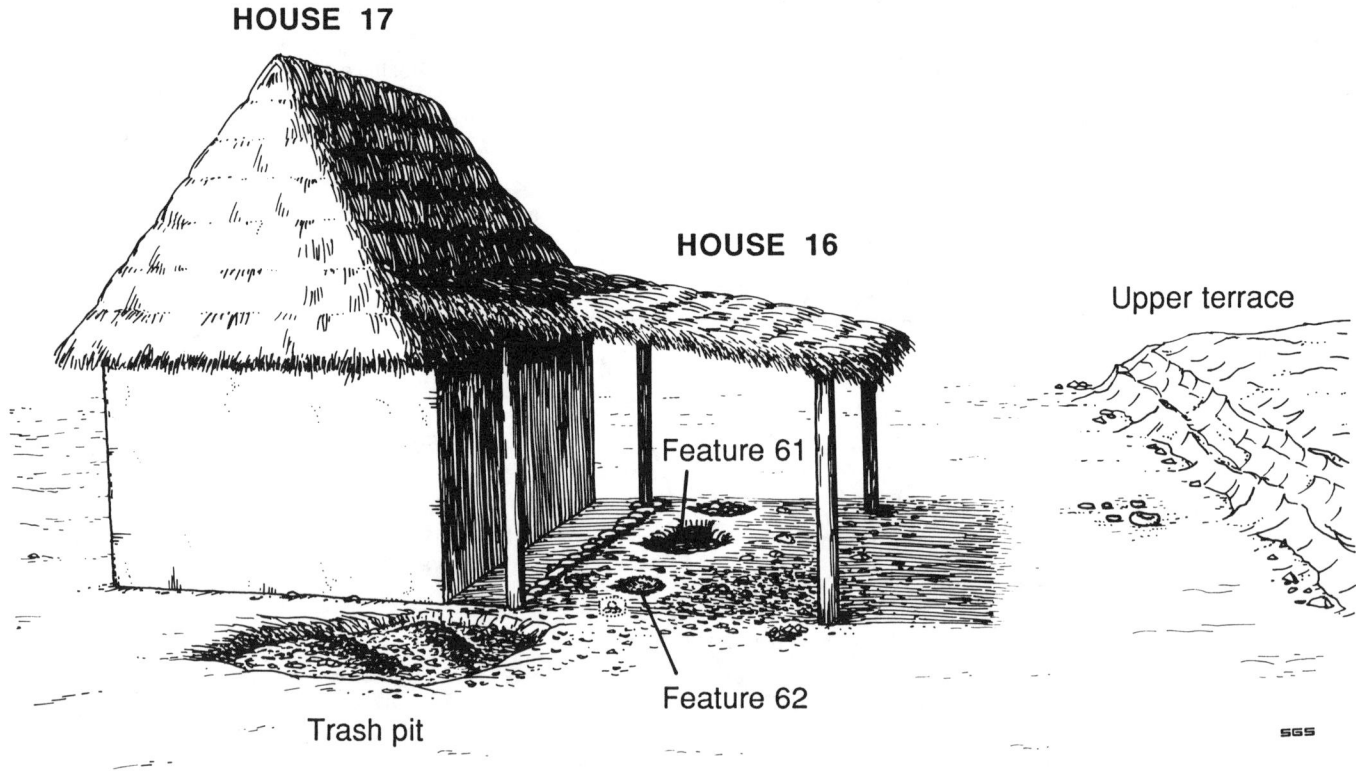

Figure 15.5. Artist's reconstruction of House 17 (left) and its attached shed or lean-to, "House 16" (right). Also shown are many of the features seen in Figure 15.6.

SAN JOSE BLACK-AND-WHITE	
Outleaned-wall bowls: plain rims	1
Total	1
XOCHILTEPEC WHITE	
Vertical jar necks, plain	1
Total	1
SAN JOSE SPECULAR RED	
Jar necks	3
Body sherds	2
Total	5
GRAND TOTAL	170

Addendum

Vessel 1, a restorable Fidencio Coarse tecomate, was plotted *in situ* in Square N2E6. It was undecorated except for a sloppy red wash and had not been perforated for suspension. Rim diameter: 15 cm.

One of the first things we notice is that House 17 has almost no sherds of Fidencio Coarse (9) compared to Atoyac Yellow-white (77). This suggests that cooking (and other tasks involving coarse jars) was probably done in House 16, the lean-to, rather than in House 17. Strengthening this suggestion is the fact that House 16 has 107 sherds of Fidencio Coarse (see below).

This raises the possibility that some high-status household units consisted of several structures, with one reserved for domestic tasks such as cooking. If this was so, the relative absence or abundance of Fidencio Coarse in any one structure may not be chronologically useful. Rather, it may reflect functional differences between structures, and hence point to synchronic variation between households of high and low status.

House 17 also has a number of characteristics suggesting a late San José phase date. These include (1) a dominance of outleaned-wall bowls over cylinders (three to two) in both Leandro Gray and Atoyac Yellow-white, and (2) an absence of San José Red-on-White.

Now let us turn to House 16, the lean-to, shed, or roofed work area of this household. Its sample of 607 sherds was as follows:

TIERRAS LARGAS BURNISHED PLAIN	
Jar rims	4
Jar body sherds: plain interior	8
Hemispherical bowls: plain rims	3
Hemispherical bowls: body sherds	6

Outleaned-wall bowls: plain rims	2
Outleaned-wall bowls: incised rims	1
Total	24

AVELINA RED-ON-BUFF

Hemispherical bowl rims: red rim band only	1
Jar/tecomate body sherds:	
plain interior, design exterior	1
Total	2

CLEMENTINA FINE RED-ON-BUFF

Hemispherical bowl rims: red rim band only	1
Total	1

MATADAMAS RED

Jar rims	2
Body sherds	3
Total	5

MATADAMAS ORANGE

Jar rims	2
Body sherds	2
Total	4

FIDENCIO COARSE

Tecomate rims:	
plain rim band, dentate stamp. body	3
plain rim band, neat punctation body	1
Jar rims, burnished	2
Jar rims, unburnished	14
Miscellaneous bowl rims	1
Plain body sherds	86
Total	107

LEANDRO GRAY

Outleaned-wall bowls: plain rims	5
Outleaned-wall bowls: plain flat bases	2
Outleaned-wall bowls: incised rims	5
Outleaned-wall bowls: slightly everted rim	3
Cylinders: plain rims	12
Cylinders: plain flat bases	3
Cylinders: body sherd with Pyne's Motif 17	1
Tecomate rims:	
1 incised line at rim	1
2 incised lines at rim, zoned false rocker st.	1
Bolstered-rim bowls: burnished exterior	2
Vertical jar necks: plain	4
Oval bowls with pinched-in sides: rims	1
Pigment dishes w/red pigment: rims	1
Effigy vessels: duck's bill handle	1
Fragment of strap handle	1
Plain body sherds	43
Total	86

ATOYAC YELLOW-WHITE

Outleaned-wall bowls:	
plain rims	11
plain flat bases	8
incised rims	40
wide evert. rim, incised and	
excised (Chalcatzingo-style)	4
Cylinders: plain rims	14
Cylinders: plain flat bases	8
Cylinders: incised rims	35
Tecomate rims: plain	1
Tecomate body sherds: zoned rocker stamp	2
Vertical jar necks: plain direct rims	5
Vertical jar necks: slightly everted rims	2
Jar shoulders	2
Incurved-rim bowls: plain rims	2
Incurved-rim bowls: incised rims	5
Incurved-rim bowls: incised/pattern burnished	1
"Grater bowl" bases	1
Bowls with giant "macrorim": rims	2
Bowls with eccentric tabs/bumps on rim	5
Squash effigy vessel sherds	1
Bowls, completely slipped int.;	
rim slipped ext., lower exterior wall	
left rough, excised	1
Strap handle fragments	1
Plain body sherds	162
Total	313

SAN JOSE RED-ON-WHITE

Tecomates:	
rims with red band	5
body sherds w/zoned rocker stamping	2
Outleaned-wall bowls: red rim, white wall	1
Total	8

LUPITA HEAVY PLAIN

Outleaned-wall bowls: rims	2
Outleaned-wall bowls: plain flat bases	1
Jar rims	2
Braziers/potstands: rims	2
Braziers/potstands: bases	3
Plain body sherds	5
Total	15

SAN JOSE BLACK-AND-WHITE

Cylinders: plain rims	2
Outleaned-wall bowls: plain rims	3
Tecomates: plain rims	2
Bowl with bolstered rim: rims	1
Plain body sherds	3
Total	11

XOCHILTEPEC WHITE

    Cylinders: incised horizontal and vertical lines   2
    Hemispherical bowls: incising, hachure   1
    Outleaned-wall bowls: plain rims   1
    Outleaned-wall bowls: incised rims   1
  Total   5

DELFINA FINE GRAY

    Cylinder rims: incised   1
  Total   1

DELIA WHITE

    Beaker rim   1
  Total   1

FOREIGN WARES

    Madera Brown from Morelos?
        Hemispherical bowls: plain rims   1
    Coatepec White from Tehuacán
        Cylinders: incised rims   1
        Cylinders: plain flat bases   1
    Cesto White from Basin of Mexico
        "Grater bowl"   *
  Total   3

UNCLASSIFIED SHERDS

    Body sherds   21
  Total   21

GRAND TOTAL   607

* A partially restorable vessel (see Vessel 6, Addendum) was plotted *in situ*.

Addendum

In addition to the sherds already listed above, six whole or partially restorable vessels were plotted *in situ* in House 16. They were as follows:

Vessels 1 and 2, although plotted at separate locations within Square N3E6, eventually turned out to be two parts of the same Atoyac Yellow-white cylinder. Because it was incised with our most iconographically complete version of Earth, it is described in Chapter 12 and illustrated in Figure 12.88.

Vessel 3, plotted in Square N2E6, was an Atoyac Yellow-white cylinder with three incised lines at the rim and a triple-line-break with a freestanding element (Plog's Motif 4).

Vessel 4, plotted in Square N2E6, was an Atoyac Yellow-white cylinder with two incised lines at the rim and a standard double-line break (Plog's Motif 50).

Vessel 5, plotted in Square N2E5, was a Lupita Heavy Plain outleaned-wall bowl.

Vessel 6 amounts to half a vessel, pieced together from 17 sherds scattered over the floor of House 16. It was instantly recognizable as a foreign piece—a bowl with a sunburstlike "grater bowl" pattern incised on the interior of the base (see Fig. 12.160). The vessel is slipped white over a reddish clay body; neither the clay, nor the slip, nor the design appear local. We have tentatively assigned Vessel 6 to Cesto White, a common type of the Manantial phase at Tlapacoya-Zohapilco in the Basin of Mexico; Niederberger (1987: Fig. 482) illustrates several bowls with similar designs. (Some Conchas White-to-Buff "grater bowls" from La Victoria on the Guatemalan Pacific coast have similar designs [Coe 1961: Fig. 26], but they have long tripod supports and their clay body and slip are not similar to Vessel 6.)

Vessel 7, found in a hearth in Square N3E5, was an undecorated Fidencio Coarse jar with the usual sloppy red wash on its neck and shoulders.

In addition to the vessels plotted inside Houses 16 and 17, two other vessels were plotted outside on the volcanic tuff terrace that formed part of the same household unit. One was an Atoyac Yellow-white shallow vertical-walled dish (or "low cylinder") found in Square N6E6. The other was a small Delia White cylinder found in N5E6.

Looking over the list of sherds and plotted vessels from House 16, one sees a number of pieces that argue for a late San José phase date. Many of those pieces have attributes that went on to be even more important in the Middle Formative.

For example, we found four sherds from an Atoyac Yellow-white outleaned-wall bowl with a wide, everted rim that is both excised and incised, in the style of Amatzinac White from Chalcatzingo (Cyphers Guillén 1987: Fig. 13.26). This style of decoration on everted rims is most common in the Cantera phase at Chalcatzingo, suggesting a placement late in the San José phase. (We should stress that these sherds, shown in Fig. 16.5*p*, are the *only* such sherds in our entire collection, which otherwise shows very few ties to Chalcatzingo.)

Other evidence for a late San José phase placement includes Atoyac Yellow-white bowls with eccentric tabs or bumps on the rim; a fragment of strap handle; and at least two sherds of Coatepec White, an import ware whose major popularity occurred in the Guadalupe phase. Coatepec White, well known in the Tehuacán Valley (MacNeish, Peterson, and Flannery 1970: Figs. 62, 63), will be described later in our volume on Middle Formative pottery.

Atoyac Yellow-white (313 sherds) greatly outnumbers Leandro Gray (86 sherds) in House 16. This, too, could be taken to indicate a late San José phase date. However, in this case we are dealing with synchronic variation as well, because Houses 16–17 belong to a residential ward featuring the were-jaguar rather than the fire-serpent. In such residential wards, Atoyac Yellow-white tends to predominate, since it was the medium for most were-jaguar motifs. This aspect of synchronic variation will be covered in Chapter 16.

Finally, it is characteristic of high-status households that they contain more imported foreign wares than low-status households; House 16 had several. Included are the Coatepec White sherds already mentioned, which are probably from Tehuacán. We also recovered an apparent Cesto White "grater bowl" from the Basin of Mexico (see above); a possible Madera Brown sherd from

Morelos; and some nonlocal Xochiltepec White, possibly from the Gulf Coast.

Conclusion

Houses 13 and 16–17 illustrate some of the synchronic differences between a low-status household and a high-status household.

House 13, consisting of one poorly made house, had only a few sherds of luxury wares such as Delfina Fine Gray, Xochiltepec White, and Delia White; it, in fact, had very little pottery imported from other regions. Since it belonged to a residential ward emphasizing Sky or fire-serpent motifs, it had virtually as many sherds of Leandro Gray (77) as Atoyac Yellow-white (78). Its most numerous type of pottery, however, was Fidencio Coarse (89 sherds), a coarse utility ware common in low-status households.

Houses 16–17, a household consisting of one well-made house and a roofed work area, had many more examples of imported wares from other regions (Gulf Coast, Tehuacán, Morelos/Basin of Mexico). Because it belonged to a residential ward emphasizing Earth or were-jaguar motifs, it had almost four times as much Atoyac Yellow-white as Leandro Gray. The distribution of Fidencio Coarse pottery is also interesting; 107 sherds of this utilitarian ware were found in the roofed work area (kitchen?), while only nine were found in the well-made house. Such functional differences may be typical of the various structures within a multistructural high-status household.

Both households had ceramic attributes that indicate a late San José phase date, including vessel forms and attributes that increased during the Middle Formative. However, the real warning of this chapter is that many ceramic differences between structures have nothing to do with chronology. Differences that could be synchronic include the percentages of foreign wares, the relative frequencies of Fidencio Coarse, and the proportion of Leandro Gray to Atoyac Yellow-white.

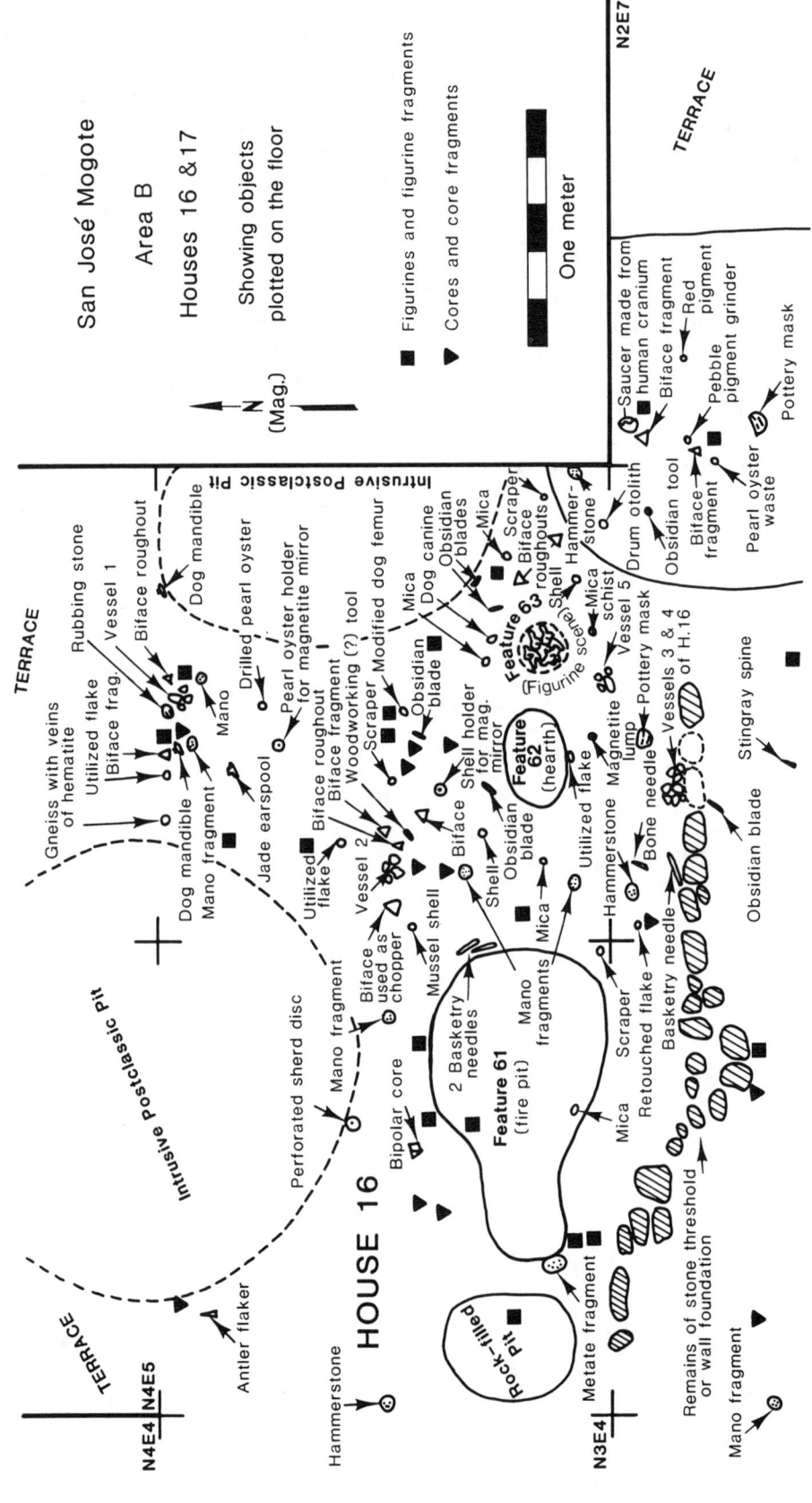

Synchronic Variation 1

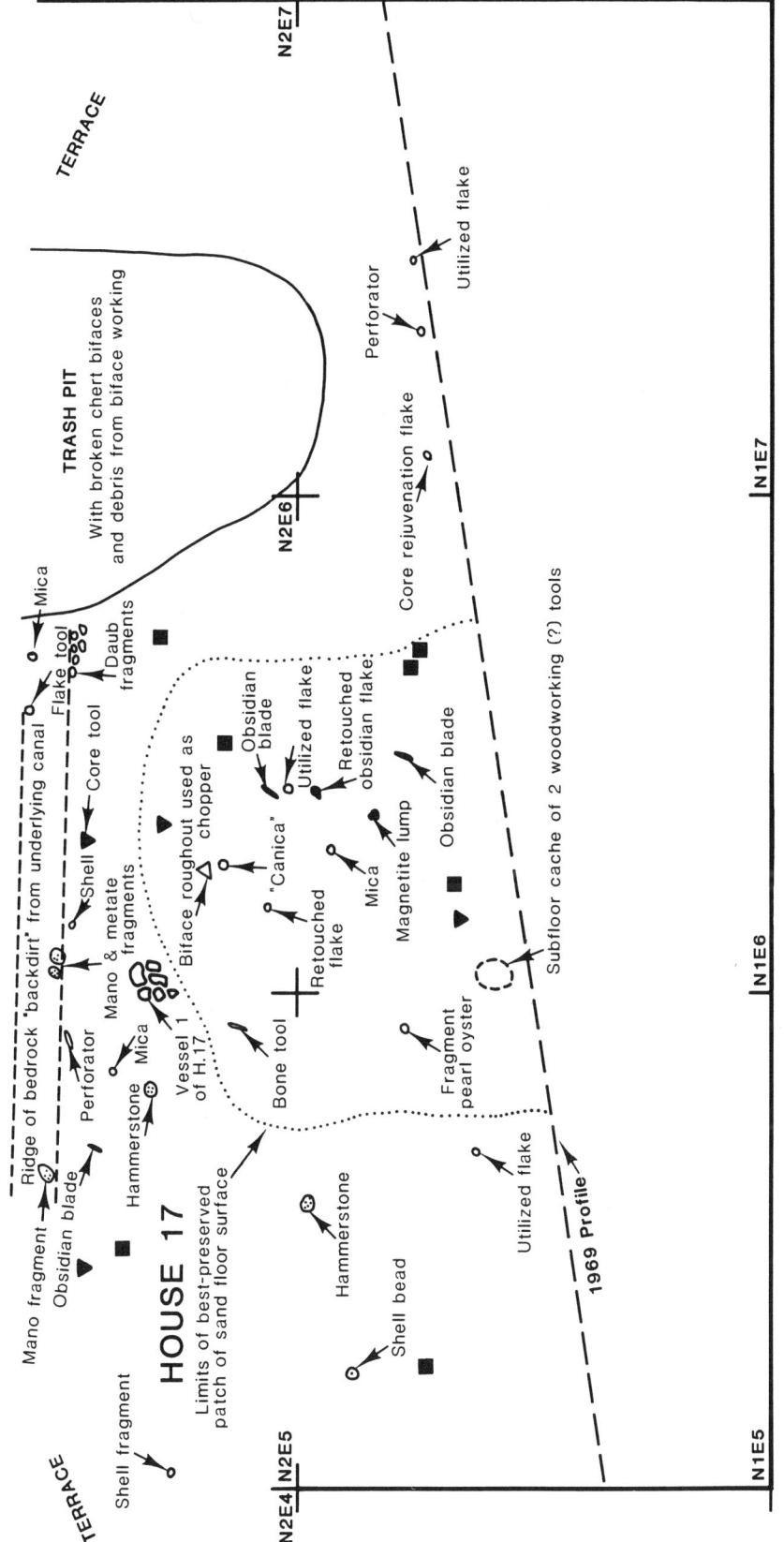

Figure 15.6. Plan view of Houses 16 and 17, Area B, San José Mogote (San José phase). All relevant features are shown, as well as objects piece-plotted *in situ*. (Redrawn from Marcus 1989: Fig. 8.19.)

Chapter 16

Synchronic Variation 2: Differences Between Residential Wards at the Same Village

In Chapter 12 we discussed Pyne's evidence that two groups of free-standing motifs, the so-called fire-serpent and were-jaguar, were more strongly associated with residential groupings than with public buildings (Pyne 1976). Their distribution was almost mutually exclusive, households with high frequencies of fire-serpents having a negative statistical association with were-jaguars, and vice versa. These associations cannot be dismissed as chronological (diachronic) variation, since they can be shown to persist throughout the entire San José phase.

Elsewhere Marcus has argued that the fire-serpent represents Sky or Lightning, while the were-jaguar represents Earth (Marcus 1989:170–174). The mutually exclusive distribution of these two motifs by residential ward could mean that groups of families occupying the same part of the village wished to emphasize their association with one of two great world divisions, Earth and Sky, or the supernatural beings associated with those divisions.

The partitioning of large sites such as San José Mogote into were-jaguar or fire-serpent barrios is one of our best examples of *synchronic* variation in ceramics. Pyne's (1976) contingency tables present the statistical data in convenient form, but some of our colleagues have expressed a desire to see illustrations of some of the actual motifs from a fire-serpent household and a were-jaguar household. We agree that nothing makes the point more effectively than seeing the actual sets of motifs. In this chapter, therefore, we look in more detail at the inventories of free-standing motifs and double-line-breaks from Areas A and B at San José Mogote, two contrasting residential wards.

Household Units C4-C1, Area A

The four household units in Area A of San José Mogote show a high degree of association with fire-serpent motifs (Pyne 1976; see also Chapter 14). Those four households (C4-C1) yielded a total of 1,369 diagnostic sherds of Leandro Gray (there were also 3,081 undecorated Leandro Gray body sherds). Some 279 of the diagnostic sherds were from excised cylinders, while 35 were from excised outleaned-wall bowls. The same four households produced 54 diagnostic sherds of Delfina Fine Gray (there were also 75 undecorated Delfina Fine Gray body sherds). Perhaps 19 of the diagnostic sherds were from cylinders that had excising and/or incising.

Those 333 decorated gray ware sherds were the primary medium for fire-serpent motifs (Table 16.1). Figures 16.1 and 16.2 illustrate representative examples of Leandro Gray and Delfina Fine Gray sherds with such decoration.

Let us now turn to the Atoyac Yellow-white sherds from Household Units C4-C1. Those four households yielded 688 yellow-white diagnostics (there were also 2,493 undecorated Atoyac Yellow-white body sherds). Some 40 of the diagnostics were incised cylinder rims, while 37 were incised outleaned-wall bowl rims. Those 77 incised rims were the main medium for double-line-break motifs, which (as we argued in Chapter 12) seem to have evolved from stylized were-jaguars.

To be sure, not every incised yellow-white sherd had a double-line-break motif. Since those motifs occur only one or two times on each vessel, many sherds simply show incised lines encircling the rim. Figure 16.3 shows all the motifs that could be identified. Note that one of those is the so-called "mat" motif (Fig. 16.3d), and two (Fig. 16.3g, h) are simply areas of hachure. That leaves only 3 actual double-line-breaks found on cylinders, and two found on outleaned-wall bowls (Fig. 16.3a, b, c, e, f).

Of the double-line-breaks occurring on cylinders, 16.3a occurs eight times, 16.3b once, and 16.3c once. Of those occurring on outleaned-wall bowls, 16.3e occurs only once, and 16.3f only once. These are very low frequencies for households with so many hundreds of Atoyac Yellow-white sherds. Such frequencies show that although Atoyac Yellow-white was very common in the Area A households, representations of the were-jaguar were not. Chronological factors cannot be invoked to explain away this scarcity of double-line-breaks, since we have higher frequencies of such motifs in both earlier and later deposits elsewhere on the site.

It is significant that these Area A households also produced nine Atoyac Yellow-white sherds with excising. Many of these

TABLE 16.1
Occurrence of Sherds with Pyne's Motifs, Area A, San José Mogote

Motif No.	Household Units			
	C4	C3	C2	C1
1	12	13	4	3
2	2	7	3	2
3, 4, 5	-	6	4	3
6, 7	2	2	2	-
8, 9	1	-	3	-
10	1	-	-	1
11	-	3	1	1
12, 13, 14	-	-	-	-
15	1	-	2	-
16	2	-	-	1
17	4	-	-	-
18	1	1	1	3

SOURCE: Pyne 1976: Table 9.12.

Motifs 1-7 are versions of the fire-serpent; Motifs 8-14 are versions of the were-jaguar; and Motifs 15-18 are of local significance only (all motifs shown in Figs. 12.5-12.16, Chapter 12).

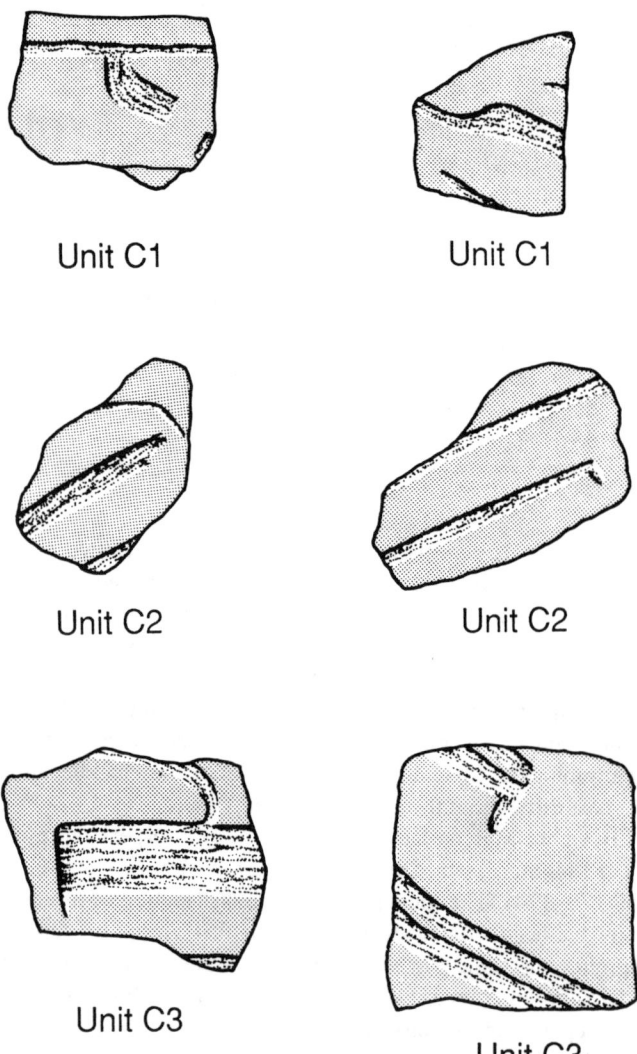

Figure 16.1. Excised Leandro Gray sherds from Household Units C4-C1, Area A, San José Mogote (San José phase). All seem to show some variant of the fire-serpent.

had fire-serpent motifs (Fig. 16.2, bottom), a design usually found on gray ware. Thus, the fire-serpent associations of Area A extend even to white ware.

Houses 16–17, Area B

Now let us turn to Houses 16–17 of Area B, components of a household unit whose association was with the were-jaguar. Houses 16 and 17 yielded 129 sherds of Leandro Gray; 57 of these were diagnostics and 72 were undecorated body sherds (Chapter 15). Out of the 57 diagnostic sherds, only one was excised—a surprisingly low figure. Just as significant is the fact that House 16 produced only one sherd of Delfina Fine Gray, while House 17 produced none.

If we turn next to Figure 16.4, which shows the decorated gray ware sherds from House 16, we learn yet another significant fact: not a single representation of the fire-serpent can be found. In Leandro Gray, the lone design on a cylinder is Pyne's Motif 17, "nested chevrons" (Fig. 16.4, top); the lone design on an outleaned-wall bowl is a variant of the double-line-break motif (Fig. 16.5b). Just as significant is the fact that the only decorated Delfina Fine Gray cylinder from House 16 has an incised design that appears to represent Earth (Fig. 16.4c). Thus, even the gray wares of Houses 16–17 do not carry representations of the fire-serpent; they carry double-line-breaks and complex Earth motifs usually found on yellow-white pottery.

The association with Earth or the were-jaguar becomes even clearer when we examine the Atoyac Yellow-white pottery of Houses 16–17. Those two houses yielded 390 yellow-white sherds; 176 of these were diagnostics, while 214 were undecorated body sherds. Of the 176 diagnostics, 39 were incised cylinder rims; 46 were incised outleaned-wall bowl rims; and 7 were incised incurved-rim bowls. Immediately we note that although Houses 16–17 had only a fourth as many Atoyac Yellow-white diagnostics as Household Units C4-C1, they provide us with more incised outleaned-wall bowl rims and virtually the same number of incised cylinder rims.

In addition, House 16 produced a much greater variety of double-line-breaks and Earth or were-jaguar motifs than did Household Units C4-C1 (Fig. 16.5). The motifs on Atoyac Yellow-white cylinders include not only familiar double-line-breaks (Fig. 16.5a-d), but also more elaborate depictions of the four world directions (Fig. 16.5f) and the were-jaguar's cleft skull and eyebrows (Fig. 16.5e). Outleaned-wall bowls bore at least eight versions of the double-line-break (Fig. 16.5h-o). One incurved-rim bowl had an incised motif showing Earth with its four world quadrants (Fig. 16.5g). Overall, the impression is of a household in which associations with Earth or the were-jaguar are very strong.

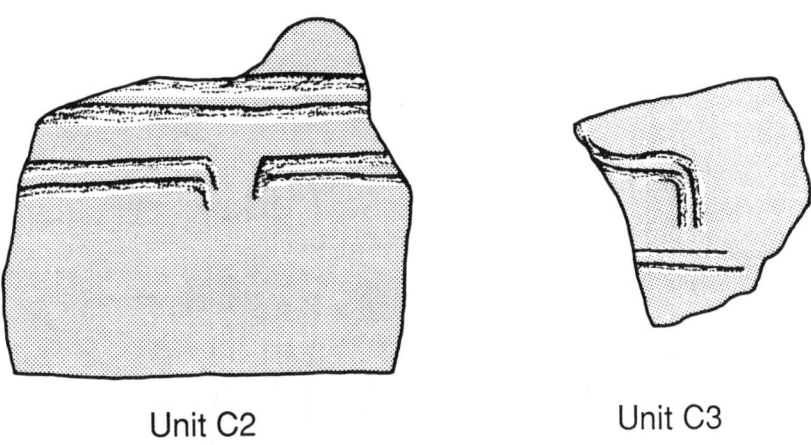

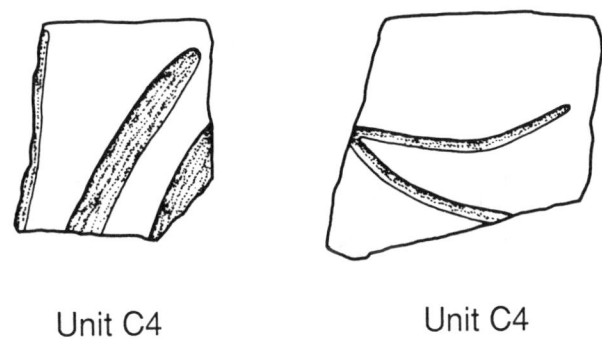

Figure 16.2. Excised Delfina Fine Gray and Atoyac Yellow-white sherds from Household Units C4-C1, Area A, San José Mogote (San José phase). All seem to show some variant of the fire-serpent.

One unusual Atoyac Yellow-white vessel from House 16 deserves comment (Fig. 16.5*p*). It is an outleaned-wall bowl with a wide, everted rim, the latter showing a double-line-break that combines incising (*sgraffito*) with excising (*raspada*). Such decoration, which is extremely rare in Oaxaca, recalls some incised-and-excised Amatzinac White bowls from Chalcatzingo, Morelos (Cyphers Guillén 1987: Fig. 13.26).

Finally, let us turn to the restorable vessels that were plotted *in situ* in House 16 (see Chapter 15). Vessels 1 and 2 of House 16, although plotted at separate locations within Square N3E6, turned out to be two parts of the same Atoyac Yellow-white cylinder (see Fig. 12.88). This vessel, already published by Marcus (1989: Fig. 8.15), has what appears to be an elaborate depiction of Earth on its exterior. Central to the design is a frame with a central bar or "trough"; there are two circles and a bracket to either side, and motifs like downturned and upturned E's that complete the frame. Surrounding the central frame is a border that, when complete, seems to have featured four stylized werejaguars; the cleft in the were-jaguar's skull is suggested in each case by the gap between paired tabs with circles in them. What we may see here is the center of the earth surrounded by four were-jaguars representing the four Mesoamerican world quarters (Parsons 1936:313). It is our most iconographically complete version of Earth, and coupled with the virtual absence of fire-serpents from Area B, it identifies the area as a were-jaguar barrio.

346   *Early Formative Pottery of Oaxaca*

Incised and excised designs on Leandro Gray

1. Design on cylinder:

a.

2. Design on outleaned-wall bowl:

b.

Incised designs on Delfina Fine Gray

1. Design on cylinder:

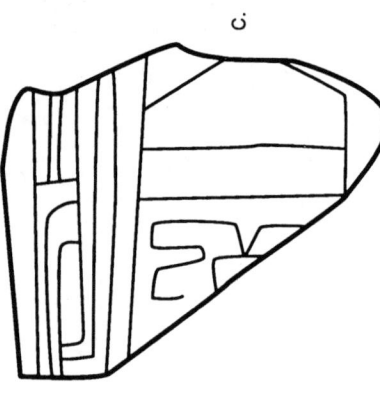
c.

Figure 16.4. Decorated Leandro Gray and Delfina Fine Gray sherds from House 16, Area B, San José Mogote (San José phase). Almost no trace of the fire-serpent can be found in the sample from this household.

1. Designs on cylinders:

a.
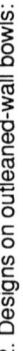

b.

c.

d.

2. Designs on outleaned-wall bowls:

e.
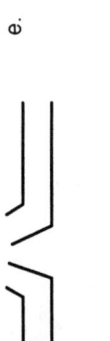

f.
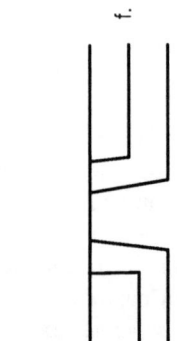

g.

h.

Figure 16.3. Incised design elements on Atoyac Yellow-white vessels from Household Units C4-C1, Area A, San José Mogote (San José phase). Double-line-breaks were scarce in these households.

1. Designs on cylinders:

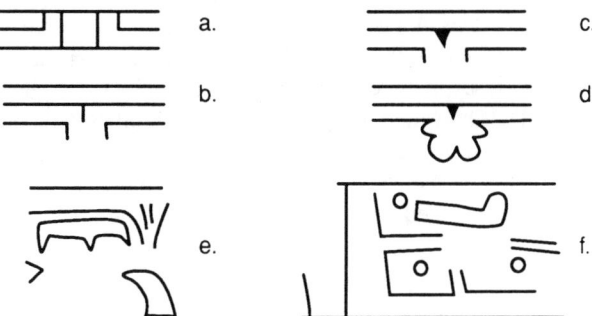

2. Design on incurved-rim bowl:

3. Designs on outleaned-wall bowls:

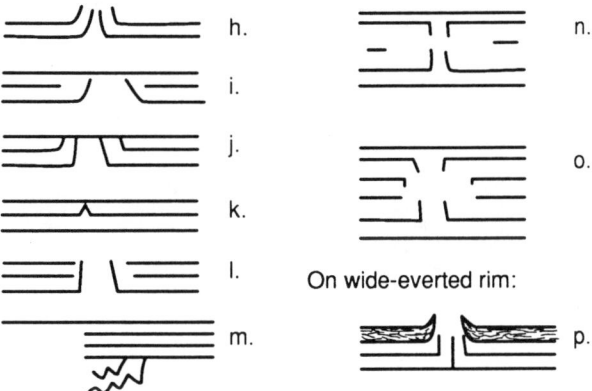

Figure 16.5. Incised design elements or larger motifs on Atoyac Yellow-white vessels from House 16, Area B, San José Mogote (San José phase). Double-line-breaks were many and varied in this household, as were motifs depicting Earth or the were-jaguar.

Conclusion

A comparison of household units in Areas A and B of San José Mogote reinforces the pattern discovered by Pyne in 1976. As a general rule, potters of the San José phase carved fire-serpent motifs on Leandro Gray and Delfina Fine Gray, while reserving double-line-breaks or were-jaguar motifs for Atoyac Yellow-white. Such was the almost mutually exclusive distribution of those two motifs, however, that it resulted in exceptions to that general rule.

The occupants of Houses 16–17 produced many elaborate depictions of Earth or the were-jaguar on yellow-white pottery, and put such motifs even on their gray ware. Households C4-C1, on the other hand, produced many depictions of Sky or the fire-serpent on Leandro Gray and Delfina Fine Gray, and put such motifs even on their yellow-white pottery. Houses 16–17 had a great variety of double-line-breaks on Atoyac Yellow-white; Households C4-C1 had only a few such motifs on yellow-white pottery, presumably because the double-line-break evolved from the were-jaguar.

This demonstrable synchronic variation between residential wards sounds a warning to all archaeologists who are tempted to use design elements to establish fine-grained chronologies: not all variation in motifs is chronological.

Chapter 17

Synchronic Variation 3: Differences Between Villages 30 km Apart

In addition to the synchronic variation brought out in Chapters 15 and 16, there were also differences in pottery assemblage between villages located in different parts of the Valley of Oaxaca. In this chapter we look at the San José phase ceramics from the site of San Sebastián Abasolo in the eastern valley or Tlacolula region (see Fig. 1.1). We first present the midden stratigraphy from Operation A at Abasolo; second, we look at the sherd sample from a late San José phase house there. The Abasolo pottery collections can then be compared with the ones from Areas A and C of San José Mogote, which have already been presented in Chapter 14.

One of the most obvious sources of synchronic variation between contemporaneous sites is the fact that not all communities had access to the same raw materials for pottery making. The residual piedmont clays that formed above Precambrian gneiss in the Cacaotepec region—readily accessible to the villagers of San José Mogote and Tierras Largas—were more than a day's round trip from Abasolo. Abasolo's nearest source of such clays would have been the southern piedmont of the Tlacolula subvalley; included in that region are the clays used today by the potters of San Marcos Tlapazola (see Fig. 2.9). It is also the case that transported valley-floor alluvial clays of the Abasolo area are likely to contain more volcanic tuff than those near Cacaotepec, since ignimbrites are such a major part of the rock formations along the northern margin of the Tlacolula subvalley.

Such differences in available raw materials did not necessarily result in contemporaneous villages making different pottery types in the *cultural* sense. It appears that San José Mogote and Abasolo shared most of the usual "mental templates." However, even when two villages attempted to make the same types of pottery, the resulting ceramics could show slight differences based on the different raw materials used. For example, Atoyac Yellow-white sherds from Abasolo and San José Mogote look superficially similar, because a similar kaolin engobe (possibly even from the same source) was used. When one looks at the underlying clay body, however, it does not always have the same appearance. Simply put, the Abasolo clay body looks more like that used by today's San Marcos potters, while the San José Mogote clay body looks more like that used by today's Atzompa potters.

It is differences like these—differences imposed by the local geology—that make us place so much importance on the *cultural* aspects of our pottery types. If we can see that two Formative villages were both striving to make their Atoyac Yellow-white look the same, we are unlikely to split it into two types just because the potters didn't have access to the same raw material. After all, a San Nicolás projectile point is still a San Nicolás point, whether it was made on chert from Matadamas or silicified tuff from the Mitla Fortress (Hole 1986).

Different villages, however, also showed differences in workmanship that were probably cultural rather than imposed by raw material. For example, Delfina Fine Gray from San José Mogote appears to be more highly burnished and better made than most of the Delfina Fine Gray from Abasolo. We hesitate to make too much of this, because so much of the Abasolo pottery has been buried below the subsurface water table and has suffered deterioration, particularly to the surface finish. It is equally likely, however, that San José Mogote had more skilled potters than Abasolo, simply because it was a major chiefly center and Delfina Fine Gray was one of its principal export wares. In Table 17.1 we have tentatively separated Delfina Fine Gray into two varieties—a "standard" variety like that seen at San José Mogote and Tierras Largas, and an "Abasolo" variety which is less expertly made.

Perhaps the most significant difference between San José Mogote and Abasolo, as we point out below, is the fact that Abasolo has a pottery type that we have never found at San José Mogote. As yet unnamed because of our small sample size, this "local fine white ware" sometimes occurs in squash effigy shapes that remind us of Middle Formative types in other regions, such as the Tehuacán Valley (MacNeish, Peterson, and Flannery 1970: Fig. 42, row 7, center). This fact led us to reexamine some of our Guadalupe phase collections from the Etla region, to see if this fine white ware occurred there as well; it did not. Thus,

Abasolo's unnamed white ware would seem to be a Tlacolula-area phenomenon. Unfortunately, we did not have access to Michael Whalen's collections from Tomaltepec (Whalen 1981) because they had already been turned over to I.N.A.H. We therefore cannot say whether the ware's distribution extends that far to the west of Abasolo.

Midden Stratigraphy of Operation A at Abasolo

San Sebastián Abasolo is a village in the Tlacolula arm of the Valley of Oaxaca, 30 km southeast of San José Mogote. Its Formative deposits go back at least to the San José phase. In spite of the intervening distance, Plog's study of design elements on Atoyac Yellow-white suggests that Abasolo shared more elements with San José Mogote than would have been predicted by the gravity model (Plog 1976:270). In addition, the areas we excavated at Abasolo seem to show the same affinity toward Sky/Lightning or fire-serpent motifs as Areas A and C of San José Mogote (Pyne 1976; Flannery and Marcus 1976b; Marcus 1989). Indeed, one of the most gratifying aspects of the San José phase deposits at Abasolo is that they showed us that our Early Formative typology should work for the entire valley.

As mentioned above, the San José phase deposits yielded a local fine white ware that we have not yet recovered from any of our Etla sites. This local fine white ware was made on a cream-to-buff fine clay body whose nonplastic particles are so small as to be invisible to the naked eye. The clay body appears to be from some alluvial source or ancient thermal spring deposit, rather than from any of the residual piedmont sources with which we are familiar. The vessels were also given a cream to white kaolin engobe.

Unfortunately, most of the early sherds at Abasolo had spent long periods below the subsurface water table. The result is that the white engobe on this type is badly eroded; in fact, some specimens had almost no surface remaining. Before we give it a final name and description, we will need to see more of this pottery from better-preserved deposits.

Common shapes in this local fine white ware include hemispherical bowls fluted to resemble cucurbits. There are also plain hemispherical bowls or incurved-rim bowls. All can be distinguished from vessels of Xochiltepec White, which also occur at Abasolo.

Occasionally, the Abasolo potters put a standard Atoyac Yellow-white engobe on the cream-to-buff fine clay body normally used for the local white ware. This procedure created another ware not seen at San José Mogote.

Figure 17.1 shows the south profile of Operation A at Abasolo, the excavated area that yielded the most interesting series of San José phase middens. Sherd counts for each level are given in Table 17.1. From earliest to latest, the strata discovered were as follows:

Zone F

Here were sterile layers of gravel and coarse sand, apparently antedating occupation.

Zone E

This was a layer of yellow clay, with some San José phase remains.

Zone D

A probable barrio midden of the San José phase, Zone D was so thick that we arbitrarily divided it into upper (D1) and lower (D2) halves even though there were no natural breaks in it. Two funnel-shaped "walk-in" wells of the San José phase, Features 3 and 6, passed through this midden. Both antedated Zone D and reached down below the 1969 subsurface water table. In the bottom of each well was a smashed jar, probably Fidencio Coarse but terribly eroded. These were presumably jars that had been lost in the process of drawing water from the wells.

House 1

This was a house floor and a lens of collapsed wattle-and-daub debris overlying Zone D. It is dealt with separately below.

Zone C

Zone C was another barrio midden of the San José phase, so thick that we arbitrarily divided it into upper (C1) and lower (C2) halves even though there was no natural break within it. Three San José phase infants (Burials 1, 2, and 4) had been buried in this midden. Burials 1 and 4 were accompanied by Leandro Gray vessels, some of which had excised fire-serpent motifs (see Figs. 12.49–12.51). Burial 2 had two small tecomates, one of them a cucurbit effigy (see Fig. 12.60). Some of these burial offerings intruded into House 1 (Fig. 17.1).

House 2

This was a remnant of Rosario phase house that overlay Zone C.

Zone B

This was a layer of greasy black alluvium, dating to the transition from Monte Albán IV to Monte Albán V (Postclassic). A "walk-in" well (Feature 1) was associated; owing to extremely muddy conditions, our excavations never reached the lowest point of the well.

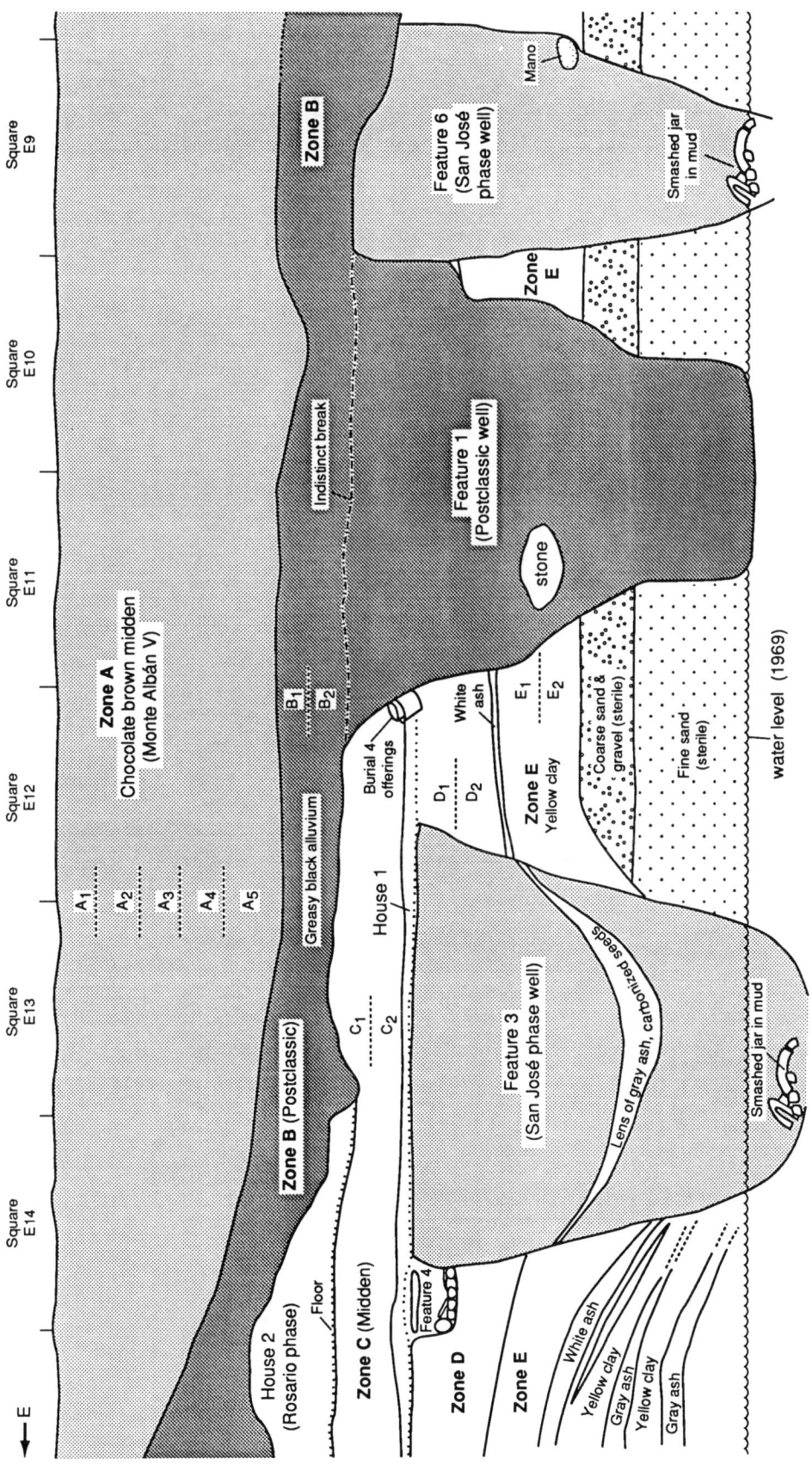

Figure 17.1. The south profile of Operation A at San Sebastián Abasolo.

TABLE 17.1
Sherds from the Lower Strata of Operation A, San Sebastián Abasolo

	\multicolumn{6}{c}{Stratigraphic Zones}					
	E2	E1	D2	D1	C2	C1
TIERRAS LARGAS BURNISHED PLAIN						
Jar rims	-	-	-	3	2	-
Jar body sherds: plain interior	3	-	-	5	6	-
Hemispherical bowls: plain rims	-	-	2	-	-	-
Hemispherical bowls: body sherds	-	-	2	-	-	-
Total	3	-	4	8	8	-
AVELINA RED-ON-BUFF						
Hemisph. bowl rims: red rim band only	1	1	-	-	-	-
Misc. bowl body sherds (eroded)	1	3	-	-	-	-
Incurved-rim bowl: incised rim	*1	-	*1	-	-	-
*(from same vessel)						
Total	3	4	1	-	-	-
MATADAMAS RED						
Jar shoulders: burnished interior	-	-	1	-	-	-
Total	-	-	1	-	-	-
MATADAMAS ORANGE						
Jar rims	-	-	6	8	6	3
Jar shoulders	3	-	-	12	-	2
Hemispherical bowls: plain rims	-	-	3	10	1	2
Outleaned-wall bowls: plain rims	-	-	-	1	-	-
Misc. body sherds	5	3	11	35	12	11
Total	8	3	20	66	19	18
FIDENCIO COARSE						
Hemispherical bowls: rims	-	-	1	-	-	-
Incurved-rim bowls: rims	-	-	2	-	-	-
Tecomate rims	-	-	1	-	-	-
Jar rims (eroded)	-	1	3	3	8	3
Jar shoulders: sloppy jabs	-	1	-	-	-	1
Jar shoulders: neat punctation	-	-	-	1	-	1
Jar shoulders: unident. designs	-	-	1	-	1	1
Possible strap handle	-	-	1	-	-	-
Body sherds (eroded)	6	8	17	9	12	21
Total	6	10	26	13	21	27
LEANDRO GRAY						
Outleaned-wall bowls:						
plain rims	-	2	2	3	4	1
plain flat bases	-	-	1	1	3	1
incised rims	-	-	1	1	-	-
Cylinders:						
plain rims	-	-	3	8	3	17
plain flat bases	-	-	1	2	3	13
excised rims	-	-	-	1	-	2
excised body sherds	-	-	-	-	1	10
excised basal angle sherds	-	-	-	-	-	5
incised body sherds	-	-	2	-	-	-
body sherds w/incising & excising	-	-	-	-	-	1
Bowl rims: too small to show shape	-	-	-	-	-	4
Tecomates: plain rims	-	-	-	-	-	4
Incurved-rim bowls: incised rims	-	-	-	-	3	1
Vertical jar necks/shoulders	-	-	-	1	-	-
Hemispherical bowls: plain rims	-	-	-	1	-	-
Plain body sherds (eroded)	3	3	18	27	31	85
Total	3	5	28	45	48	144
ATOYAC YELLOW-WHITE						
Outleaned-wall bowls:						
plain rims	-	1	8	5	5	-
plain flat bases	-	3	2	3	1	-
incised rims	-	1	4	4	6	2
Cylinders: plain rims	-	-	2	3	3	5
Cylinders: plain flat bases	-	-	1	3	1	5

TABLE 17.1 (continued)

	Stratigraphic Zones					
	E2	E1	D2	D1	C2	C1
Cylinders: excised body sherds	-	-	-	-	1	-
Cylinders: incised rims	-	1	2	2	2	2
Cylinders: slightly flaring rims	-	-	1	-	2	4
Tecomate rims	-	-	-	2	1	-
Tecomate body sherds:						
zoned rocker stamp	-	-	1	-	1	5
zoned punctation	-	-	2	2	-	-
Bolstered-rim bowls: slipped ext.	-	-	-	1	1	-
Vertical jar necks/shoulders	1	-	2	-	1	1
Hemispherical bowls: plain rims	-	-	-	1	-	-
Incurved-rim bowls: plain rims	-	-	-	1	1	-
"Grater bowl" bases	-	-	1	-	-	-
Bowls with giant "macrorim": rims	-	-	1	-	-	-
Jars with flaring necks: rims	-	-	-	-	-	1
Fragment of strap handle	-	-	-	1	-	-
Plain body sherds (eroded)	3	9	43	45	42	48
Total	4	15	70	73	68	73
SAN JOSE RED-ON-WHITE						
Hemispherical bowls:						
rims with red band only	-	-	-	-	1	8
Incurved-rim bowls:						
rims with red band only	-	-	1	-	-	-
Tecomates:						
body sherds w/red zoning stripe	-	-	1	-	-	-
Outleaned-wall bowls:						
red rim, white wall	-	-	2	2	1	1
white rim, red wall	-	-	-	-	-	1
Jar necks/shoulders	-	-	1	-	-	1
Misc. body sherds (eroded)	-	-	2	2	1	2
Total	-	-	7	4	3	13
LUPITA HEAVY PLAIN						
Tecomate body sherds:						
interrupt. rocker stamp	-	-	1	-	-	-
Hemispherical bowls: plain rims	-	-	-	1	-	-
Braziers/potstands: rims	-	-	2	4	2	8
Braziers/potstands: bases	-	-	2	1	1	-
Braziers/potstands: plain floors	-	-	-	1	1	1
Misc. body sherds (eroded)	-	-	-	1	-	1
Total	-	-	5	8	4	10
"HYBRID TYPE": ATOYAC YELLOW-WHITE OUTSIDE, MATADAMAS ORANGE INSIDE						
Bowl body sherds	-	-	-	-	-	1
Total	-	-	-	-	-	1
SAN JOSE BLACK-AND-WHITE						
Cylinders: plain rims	-	-	-	-	1	1
Cylinders: plain flat bases	-	-	-	-	1	-
Total	-	-	-	-	2	1
XOCHILTEPEC WHITE						
Incurved-rim bowls: plain rims	-	-	-	2	-	-
Cylinders: plain rims	-	-	-	-	-	1
Cylinders: plain flat bases	-	-	1	-	-	-
Total	-	-	1	2	-	1
DELFINA FINE GRAY (STANDARD VARIETY)						
Cylinders: plain rims	-	-	2	-	-	-
Outleaned-wall bowls:						
plain rims	-	-	1	-	-	-
plain flat bases	-	-	1	-	-	-
Total	-	-	4	-	-	-
DELFINA FINE GRAY (ABASOLO VARIETY)						
Cylinders: plain rims	-	-	-	-	1	-
Cylinders: plain body sherds	-	-	-	-	-	1

TABLE 17.1 (continued)

	Stratigraphic Zones					
	E2	E1	D2	D1	C2	C1
Outleaned-wall bowls:						
plain flat bases	-	-	-	-	1	-
Jar rims	-	-	-	-	1	-
Bowls with outcurving wall:						
rims	-	-	-	1	-	-
flat bases	-	-	-	1	-	-
Total	-	-	-	2	3	1
SAN JOSE SPECULAR RED						
Vertical jar necks/rims	-	-	-	2	-	-
Total	-	-	-	2	-	-
LA MINA WHITE						
Cylinders: plain rims	-	-	-	-	-	1
Tecomates/incurved-rim bowls: rims	-	-	-	1	-	-
Body sherds: plain	-	-	-	-	-	1
Total	-	-	-	1	-	2
LOCAL FINE WHITE WARE						
Hemispherical bowls: plain rims	-	-	2	-	-	-
Fluted hemisph. bowls: rims	-	-	1	-	-	-
Fluted hemisph. bowls: body sherds	-	-	2	-	-	-
Vessels with convex walls:						
basal sherds	-	-	2	-	-	-
Cylinders:						
plain rims	-	-	-	-	1	-
slightly flaring rims	-	-	-	-	4	-
Outleaned-wall bowls:						
plain rims	-	-	-	-	1	-
plain flat bases	-	-	-	-	2	-
Squash effigy bowls: rims	-	-	-	5	-	5
Squash effigy bowls: body sherds	-	-	-	2	1	3
Total	-	-	7	7	9	8
LOCAL FINE WHITE CLAY BODY WITH ATOYAC YELLOW-WHITE SLIP						
Small outleaned-wall bowls	-	-	-	1	-	-
Cylinder with slightly flaring rim	-	-	1	-	-	-
Total	-	-	1	1	-	-
ABERRANT DELIA WHITE (DELIA SLIP OVER CINNAMON/BRICK RED CLAY BODY)?						
Beaker rim (eroded)	-	-	1	-	-	-
Total	-	-	1	-	-	-
POSSIBLE FOREIGN WARES						
Bowl with convex base, unident. orange clay body	-	-	-	-	1	-
Body sherds, unident. orange clay body	-	-	-	1	-	-
Total	-	-	-	1	1	-
UNCLASSIFIED SHERDS						
Misc. rim sherds (eroded)	-	-	1	2	2	6
Misc. body sherds (eroded)	2	3	7	15	17	31
Total	2	3	8	17	19	37
GRAND TOTAL	29	40	184	250	205	336

Zone A

This was a chocolate brown midden dating to Monte Albán V (late Postclassic).

House 1 of Abasolo

As the profile of Operation A at Abasolo indicates (Fig. 17.1), House 1 was sandwiched between Zone D1 and Zone C2. Feature 3, a San José phase well associated with Zone D1, had to be completely filled in before the floor of House 1 could be laid down.

The most interesting feature of House 1 was an apparent cooking pit set in the floor. Called Feature 4, this was a bag-shaped pit 45 cm in diameter and 25 cm deep. Its bottom had firecracked rocks and sherds, and its upper fill was white ash with charcoal flecks. At a later stage in the life of the house, this pit was covered over by the sand from a floor resurfacing.

After the abandonment of House 1, it was covered over by Zone C, the apparent barrio midden already described.

The sherd sample from House 1 is given below. We would assign it a position very late in the San José phase, like most of the San José phase deposits at Abasolo.

Our sample of 77 sherds from House 1 is as follows:

MATADAMAS ORANGE
    Jar rims   2
    Jar shoulders: burnished interior   2
    Misc. body sherds   4
    Total   8

FIDENCIO COARSE
    Jar rim: unburnished   1
    Jar shoulders   1
    Misc. body sherds   5
    Total   7

LEANDRO GRAY
    Cylinder rims: incised (Pyne's Motif 15)   1
    Misc. bowl bases   1
    Total   2

ATOYAC YELLOW-WHITE
    Outleaned-wall bowls: plain flat bases   2
    Outleaned-wall bowls: incised rims   2
    Cylinders: plain rims   1
    Cylinders: plain flat bases   2
    Tecomate body sherds: plain   3
    Tecomate body sherds: zoned rocker stamp   1
    Hemispherical bowls: rims   1
    Bowl with slightly flaring rim   1
    Plain body sherds   5
    Total   18

SAN JOSE RED-ON-WHITE
    Outleaned-wall bowls: red rim, white wall   2
    Total   2

SAN JOSE BLACK-AND-WHITE
    Body sherds   1
    Total   1

SAN JOSE SPECULAR RED
    Body sherds   1
    Total   1

LOCAL FINE WHITE WARE
    Outleaned-wall bowl: slightly everted rim   1
    Possible beaker/cylinder sherds   1
    Total   2

UNCLASSIFIED SHERDS
    Undecorated jar body sherds   33
    Very eroded body sherds   3

GRAND TOTAL   77

Chapter 18

Dating San José Phase Public Buildings

Some major changes in the construction of public buildings took place during the San José phase. At the start of the phase, the only public buildings for which we have any evidence are similar to the Tierras Largas phase structures described in Chapter 11—small, lime-plastered one-room buildings on low rectangular platforms. Such buildings appear in at least two areas of San José Mogote; some were built in Area C, on the western edge of the site, and at least one was built on Mound 1 near Area A. In this chapter we will date Structure 7, one of the San José phase public buildings from Area C.

By the middle of the phase, there had been an increase in the diversity of structures. In the case of some, it is not clear what kind of building—public or residential—we are dealing with. Such is the case with Structure 16 of Area A, a one-room building on a meter-high puddled adobe platform. We will date Structure 16 in this chapter, but we can only provide a tentative function for it.

Finally, by the late San José phase, public architecture had become truly monumental. Adobes that were oval to circular in plan and planoconvex in cross-section made their first appearance; so did dry-laid stone masonry. Public buildings were now placed on large pyramidal platforms constructed of earthen fill rising in several tiers, faced with stones, and accompanied by simple stairways. Structures 1 and 2 of Area A, also dated in this chapter, are examples of that kind of architecture.

Structure 7, Area C

Structure 7—a lime-plastered, one-room public building of the San José phase—shares a number of features with earlier Tierras Largas phase public buildings like Structures 3, 5, and 6 (Chapter 11). Like those earlier structures, it was oriented roughly 8° west of true north, and had a floor sunk about 20 cm below the surface of the platform on which it stood (Figs. 18.1–18.4). A series of pine posts, 16 cm in diameter and spaced 70–100 cm apart, ran around the edges of the floor.

Near the northeast corner of the floor, James Schoenwetter (who excavated the structure) found a number of silica "ghosts" of reed mats (*petates*) overlying the plaster floor (Fig. 18.1).

We see two possible explanations for these mat fragments. On the one hand, the building could have had a mat-covered floor. On the other hand, the mat fragments could represent parts of the roof that had collapsed on the floor after abandonment.

Structure 7 differed from its Tierras Largas counterparts mainly in the color of its lime plaster. Rather than being pure white, it was identical in color to the slip on Atoyac Yellow-white pottery: cream, yellowish, or white-to-buff, and highly burnished.

Structure 7 was best preserved in its northeast corner, and deteriorated steadily as it ran southwest. The plastered surface of the floor was preserved up to 2.0–2.5 m from the northeast corner, then eroded away. Beneath it were a series of layers that showed us how the floor had been built (Fig. 18.4). First, the builders had laid down a layer of coarse sand like that on the floors of ordinary San José phase residences. Over this went a layer of hard-packed clay about 1 cm thick. Over that went a thin layer of very fine, winnowed orange sand. The yellow-white lime plaster was laid down on this layer of fine sand.

As the floor of Structure 7 ran west and south, these various layers disappeared one by one through erosion. First went the plaster; then the fine orange sand; then the packed clay. Eventually, 4 m from the northeast corner, only the underlying layer of coarse sand remained. This was the first part of the structure found, and it so resembled a standard house floor that we tentatively labeled it "House 8." Only after Schoenwetter had traced it to the northeast corner, and the overlying layers had appeared, did we realize that it was merely the subfloor sand of a plastered public building. At this point, "House 8" was eliminated as a label and replaced with "Structure 7."

The following questions and answers will lead the reader through our reasoning in dating Structure 7.

1. What stratigraphic units preceded the building of Structure 7?

Answer: According to the Harris Matrix established for Area C, Structure 7 postdates House 1, whose ceramics have been listed in Chapter 14. House 1 falls somewhere near the middle of our sequence of San José phase houses from Area C.

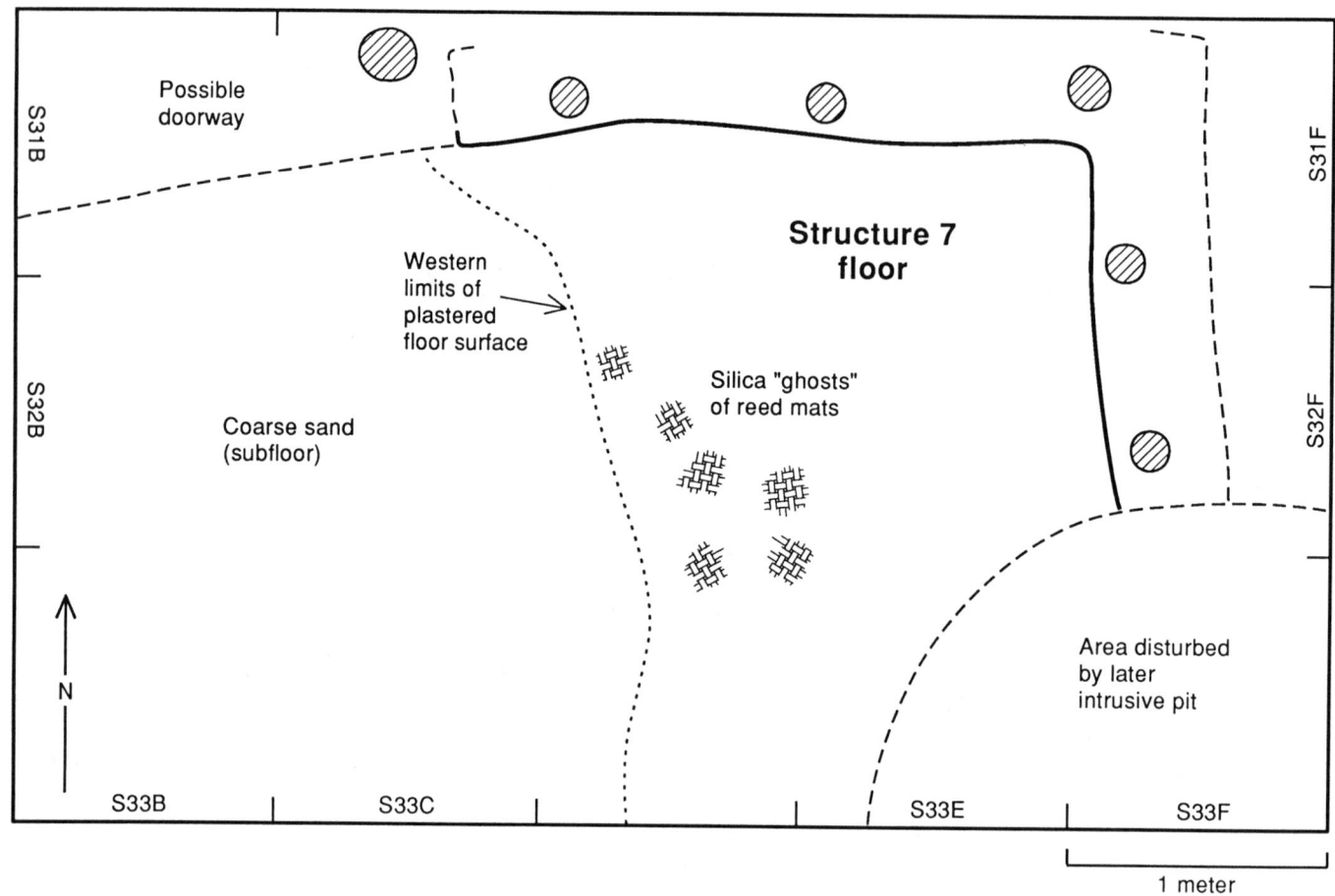

Figure 18.1. Partial plan of Structure 7, Area C, San José Mogote, a San José phase public building. Like the Tierras Largas phase public buildings shown in Chapter 11, this was a one-room building on a low platform (see Fig. 4.7 for a view of such a building when broken down). Figure 18.2 gives a view of Structure 7 from the east; Figure 18.3 is a photograph giving almost the same perspective as this drawing. Structure 7 can be located within Area C by comparing the 1 × 1 m square designations to Figure 9.2 of Chapter 9.

2. Were any sherds incorporated into the construction material of Structure 7?

Answer: None were visible in the profile of the platform, which consisted mainly of crushed bedrock, clay, earth, and sand. We chose not to take apart the platform of Structure 7, because at that time it was one of our few San José phase public buildings, and we preferred to preserve it for future reference.

3. Were there sherds lying on the floor of Structure 7?

Answer: Yes, in various contexts. First, there was a small sample of sherds lying on the intact plaster floor in the northeast corner. Since these sherds lay among pieces of fallen plaster from the upper walls of the building, they are probably postabandonment debris rather than *in situ* materials. Second, there was a larger sample of sherds from the coarse sand layer that constituted the lowest stage of the floor. Since the upper layers of the floor were eroded away at this point, these sherds are not "trapped below the plaster surface"; they, too, could be postabandonment debris.

Let us look first at the smaller sample, those sherds from the intact plastered surface. Those 67 sherds were as follows:

TIERRAS LARGAS BURNISHED PLAIN
    Hemispherical bowls: plain rims   3
    Hemispherical bowls: body sherds   10

AVELINA RED-ON-BUFF
    Jar shoulders: rectilinear design exterior   3

MATADAMAS ORANGE
    Hemispherical bowls: plain rims   2

FIDENCIO COARSE
    Jar rims, unburnished   2

Figure 18.2. The northeast corner of Structure 7, seen from the east. The north arrow rests on the recessed floor of the building. On the right can be seen two of the postmolds of the north wall, embedded in a surviving portion of the building's platform. (Reference to Fig. 4.7 helps to clarify Fig. 18.2.)

Jar body sherds	7
LEANDRO GRAY	
Outleaned-wall bowls: plain rims	3
Cylinders: plain rims	2
Cylinders: excised rims	2
Cylinders: excised body sherds	5
ATOYAC YELLOW-WHITE	
Outleaned-wall bowls: plain rims	3
Outleaned-wall bowls: incised rims	3
Cylinders: plain rims	5
Cylinders: incised rims	3
SAN JOSE RED-ON-WHITE	
Outleaned-wall bowls: red rim, white body	2
Tecomate body sherds: zoned rocker stamp	2

UNCLASSIFIED SHERDS	
Worn body sherds	10
GRAND TOTAL	67

We turn now to the larger sample (255 sherds) from the coarse sand layer exposed by erosion. The sherds from this sample were as follows:

TIERRAS LARGAS BURNISHED PLAIN	
Jar rims	1
Hemispherical bowls: plain rims	3
Tecomate body sherds: incised zoning lines	3
Miscellaneous unclassified rims	1
TIERRAS LARGAS UNBURNISHED PLAIN	
Miscellaneous body sherds	2

Figure 18.3. The northeast corner of Structure 7 seen from the south, showing the recessed floor, the vertical faces of the north and east walls, and several postmolds. James Schoenwetter places his left hand against the north wall. At this point, the surviving patch of plaster floor had been cut through to expose the various subfloor levels shown in Figure 18.4. Schoenwetter's feet rest on the surface left after removal of the lowermost coarse sand. What appears to be a raised bench (some 10 cm east of his left hand) is actually a remnant of the original floor, complete even to the uppermost lime plaster. The dark stain on the profile is not a feature; it represents moisture that leaked from the severed root of a modern tree.

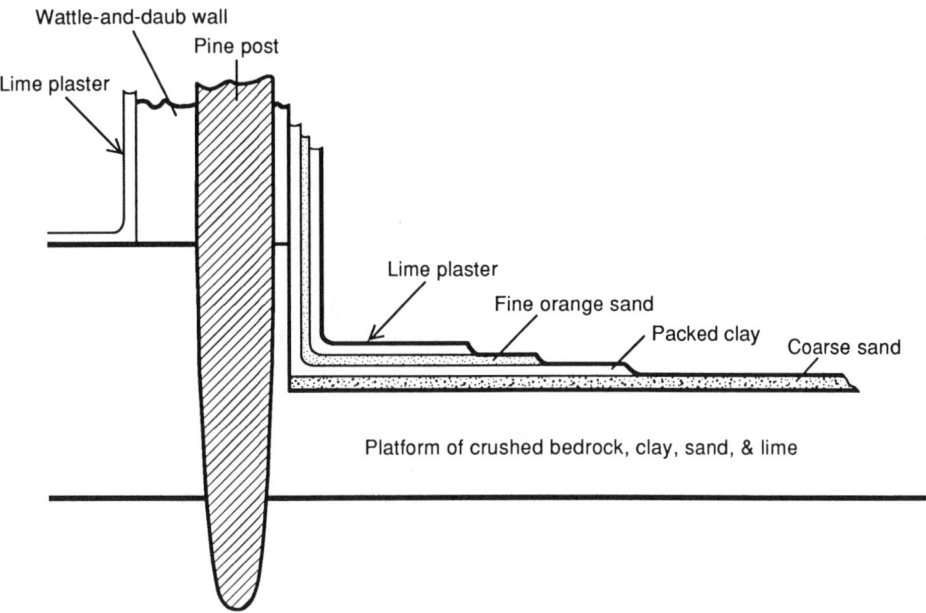

Figure 18.4. Cross-section drawing of the surviving remnant of Structure 7, San José Mogote, showing the various layers of construction. First came a series of pine posts, which gave the building its outline. Around this was built a platform of crushed bedrock, clay, sand, and lime; above this, the walls of the building were of wattle-and-daub (see Fig. 4.6). The area that was to be the floor of the building was left recessed 20 cm or more below the upper surface of the platform. The floor was built up of successive layers of coarse sand, hard packed clay, and fine orange sand. Over this went a layer of white lime plaster that covered the platform and the building. Each stage of construction offered opportunities for diagnostic sherds to become trapped in the various layers of the building.

AVELINA RED-ON-BUFF
   Hemispherical bowl rims:
      red rim band only   4
      rim band interior, all red exterior   2
      rim band exterior, all red interior   1
   Misc. unclassified rims (incl. miniatures)   4

CLEMENTINA FINE RED-ON-BUFF
   Hemispherical bowl rims: red rim band only   2

MATADAMAS ORANGE
   Jar rims   1
   Hemispherical bowls: plain rims   3

FIDENCIO COARSE
   Tecomate rims   1
   Tecomate body sherds: finger-punching   1
   Jar rims: burnished   8
   Jar rims: unburnished   3
   Jar shoulders: sloppy jabs   1
   Jar shoulders: rows of slashes   1
   Jar shoulders: long parallel lines   1
   Jar shoulders: incised band   1

   Jar body sherds   11

LEANDRO GRAY
   Bottle rim/neck sherd   1
   Outleaned-wall bowls: plain rims   8
   Outleaned-wall bowls: plain flat bases   6
   Cylinders: plain rims   8
   Cylinders: plain flat bases   5
   Cylinders: excised rims   1
   Cylinders: excised body sherds   4
   Cylinders: incised rims   3
   Cylinders: incised body sherds   7
   Outleaned-wall bowls: incised rims   3
   "Grater bowl" bases   2
   Pigment dishes/spouted trays: rim sherds   1
   Jar shoulders: rocker stamping   1
   Miniature vessels: rims   4
   Misc. incised body sherds   1
   Plain body sherds   12

ATOYAC YELLOW-WHITE
   Outleaned-wall bowls: plain rims   8
   Outleaned-wall bowls: plain flat bases   11

Outleaned-wall bowls: incised rims	9
Cylinders: plain rims	8
Cylinders: plain flat bases	11
Cylinders: incised rims	12
Tecomate body sherds: zoned rocker stamp	3
Hemispherical bowls: rims	1
Incurved-rim bowls: plain rims	3
"Grater bowl" bases	1
Pigment dishes/spouted trays: rim sherds	5
Jars with flaring rims	1
Misc. body sherds	15

SAN JOSE RED-ON-WHITE

Hemispherical bowls: rims with red band	3
Tecomate body sherds: zoned rocker stamp	4

LUPITA HEAVY PLAIN

Tecomates: burnished rim, rocker stamp. body	2
Outleaned-wall bowls: plain rims	1
Outleaned-wall bowls: plain flat bases	1
Pigment dishes/spouted trays: rim sherds	1
Braziers/potstands: rims	2
Braziers/potstands: bases	4
Braziers/potstands: plain floors	1
Misc. body sherds	8

SAN JOSE BLACK-AND-WHITE

Cylinders: plain rims	1

XOCHILTEPEC WHITE

Banded-rim tecomates: rims	1
Cylinders: plain flat bases	1

DELFINA FINE GRAY

Incised body sherds	1

UNCLASSIFIED SHERDS

Worn body sherds	14

GRAND TOTAL	255

4. What stratigraphic unit followed the abandonment of Structure 7?

Answer: According to the Harris Matrix established for Area C, Structure 7 predates House 7 (Zone C2), a residence of the second half of the San José phase (see Chapter 13).

Structure 16, Area A

Occasionally, excavations in Formative villages yield structures that are unique or so incompletely preserved that one hesitates to assign them a function. Such is the case with Structure 16 in Area A of San José Mogote, a building partly destroyed when Structure 2 was built. The only other building that in any way resembles Structure 16 at San José Mogote is Structure 11 at Santo Domingo Tomaltepec (Whalen 1981:38–43). We will therefore begin with a description of the latter building.

Structure 11 at Tomaltepec was a puddled adobe platform measuring roughly 4 m × 6 m and standing 1 m high. Its long axis was oriented 16–17° east of true north. No evidence of a stairway was found, but that might be because heavy overburden prevented the clearing of all sides of the structure.

The platform was built upon a layer of larger foundation stones, followed by alternating layers of adobe—sometimes puddled and sometimes in the form of small planoconvex adobes—and fist-sized stones set in a puddled adobe matrix (Whalen 1981:38). This could be one of the earliest uses of "bun-shaped" adobes in Formative Oaxaca. The exact placement of Structure 11 within the San José phase is not clear; it was built stratigraphically above an early San José phase household (ESJ-1), and therefore cannot date to the beginning of the phase. At the moment we have little evidence for the use of adobes before late San José phase times, and are therefore not sure exactly how early their use began.

One of the most interesting features of Structure 11 was a large, clay-plastered cell, possibly for storage, positioned so as to lie below the floor of any structure placed on the platform. This cell was several meters on a side and more than half a meter deep, with well-defined vertical walls. The function of the cell cannot be determined, since it was filled with postabandonment debris when discovered. This debris was "trash scraped up from the immediate area of the structure" and appeared to be ordinary household trash (sherds, grinding stones, carbonized seeds, chipped stone tools, animal bones, etc.).

Whalen was uncertain—as are we—whether to consider Structure 11 a "house platform" or a "large-scale storage facility." On the one hand, it did not have the typical orientation of a public building. On the other hand, it seems unlikely that an ordinary residence would have had such a large area of its floor taken up with a plastered storage cell. We also have no other examples of ordinary residences on such platforms. Tentatively, therefore, we consider Structure 11 to be a special-purpose building of some kind.

Now let us turn to Structure 16, Area A, San José Mogote (Fig. 18.5). It was discovered stratigraphically below the surface of Structure 2 during our excavations into the latter (see below). Structure 16 appears to have been built at the level of Household Unit C3 of Area A, whose sherd assemblage has already been listed in Chapter 14. Later, when Structure 2 was built, Structure 16 was badly damaged and then buried under many basketloads of earthen fill.

Structure 16 was a puddled adobe platform about 1 m high, oriented roughly 21° east of true north. It measured 3.45 m north-south; its east-west dimension could not be recovered because it had been truncated by the builders of Structure 2. Like Structure 11 at Tomaltepec, Structure 16 had been built of alternating layers of puddled adobe clay, occasional stones, and bits of what

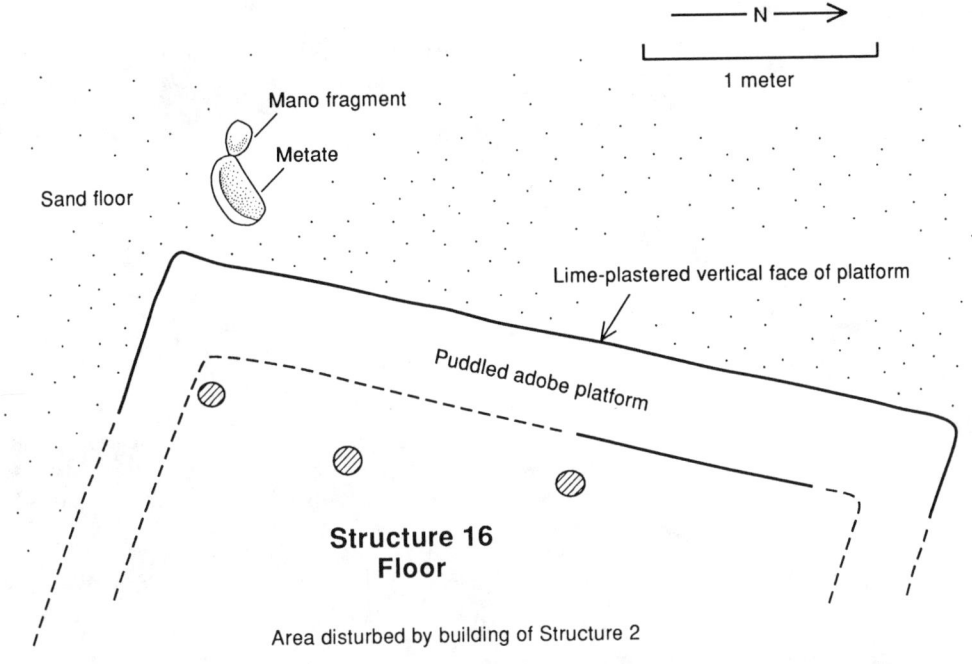

Figure 18.5. Plan view of Structure 16, Area A, San José Mogote, a one-room building on a puddled adobe platform surrounded by a sand floor. This building was partly destroyed by the later construction of Structure 2 (Fig. 18.7), which both covered Structure 16 and incorporated it within its fill.

may have been burnt daub or adobe fragments. Its nearly vertical west face (Fig. 18.6) had been given a coating of adobe clay followed by a solution of lime resembling whitewash.

Atop Structure 16 was a level floor of stamped clay with a light coating of sand. Because this floor began 25–40 cm in from the edge of the platform, its north-south dimension was only 2.85 m. Three postmolds from an apparent one-room building were found along the west edge of this floor. Each was 10–12 cm in diameter. In other words, the available evidence suggests that Structure 16 was the platform for a small one-room building of pole and thatch with a floor of stamped clay.

In the portion of Structure 16 that had been destroyed by the builders of Structure 2, we found traces of a lime-plastered cell (again, possibly for storage) not unlike the one recovered by Whalen in Structure 11 at Tomaltepec. However, because of extensive destruction, it was not possible to recover the dimensions of this plastered cell. We were simply left with the impression that our Structure 16 might have been another example of the kind of "special purpose" building exemplified by Structure 11 at Tomaltepec. What its special purpose might have been, we do not know.

Surrounding Structure 16 on the south and west was a level floor of stamped earth with an overlying layer of fine sand from the Atoyac River. A mano, a metate, and a sample of 37 sherds were found lying on this floor near the base of the platform.

1. What age was the sand floor at the base of Structure 16?

Answer: The sample of 37 sherds appears to be pure San José phase, which is not surprising given the position of the floor at roughly the level of Household Unit C3 of Area A. The sherds were as follows:

TIERRAS LARGAS BURNISHED PLAIN	
Jar body sherds: plain interior	1
Jar shoulders: burnished interior	1
Hemispherical bowls: plain rims	2
Hemispherical bowls: body sherds	1
CLEMENTINA FINE RED-ON-BUFF	
Hemispherical bowl rims: red rim band only	1
MATADAMAS RED	
Misc. body sherds	2
MATADAMAS ORANGE	
Hemispherical bowls: plain rims	1
Hemispherical bowls: body sherds	2
Jar/tecomate body sherds	1

Figure 18.6. Two workers expose the nearly vertical west face of the puddled adobe platform supporting Structure 16. Because of the height of this platform, the building must have had a stairway on one of its destroyed sides.

FIDENCIO COARSE	
Jar body sherd	1
LEANDRO GRAY	
Outleaned-wall bowls: plain rims	2
Cylinders: plain rims	1
Cylinders: lower half unslipped, excised	1
Jar/bottle body sherds: excised	1
Misc. decorated body sherds	1
Plain body sherds	3
ATOYAC YELLOW-WHITE	
Outleaned-wall bowls: incised rims	1
Cylinders: incised rims	1
"HYBRID TYPE": ATOYAC YELLOW-WHITE OUTSIDE, MATADAMAS ORANGE INSIDE	
Bowl body sherds	2
XOCHILTEPEC WHITE	
Outleaned-wall bowls: plain rims	1

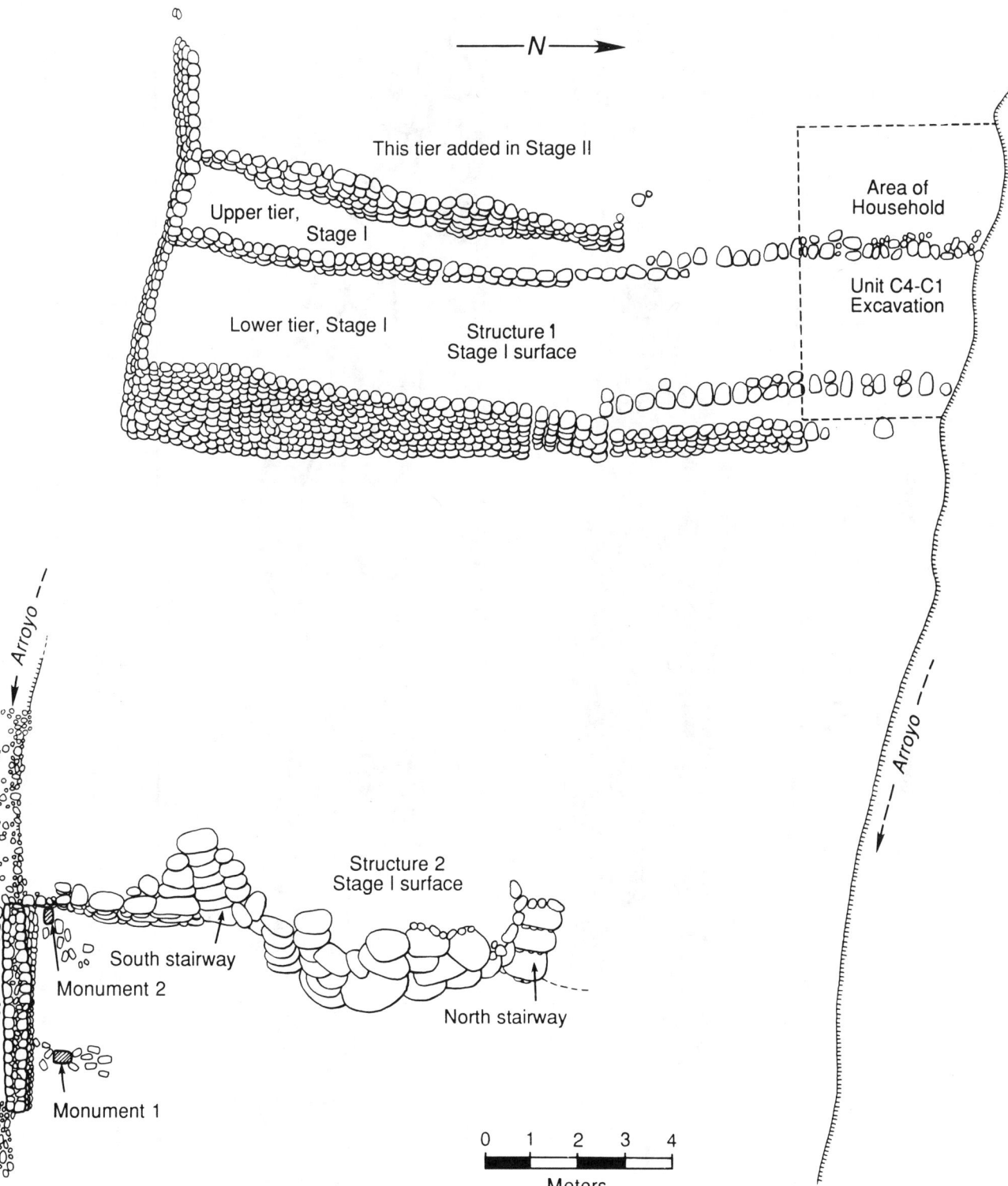

Figure 18.7. Plan view of Structures 1 and 2, Area A, San José Mogote (San José phase). Household Units C4-C1 antedated these structures and were eventually buried beneath them. Those households were exposed in the bank of the arroyo running along the north edge of Structure 1, and eventually were uncovered by excavations in the area surrounded by dashed lines.

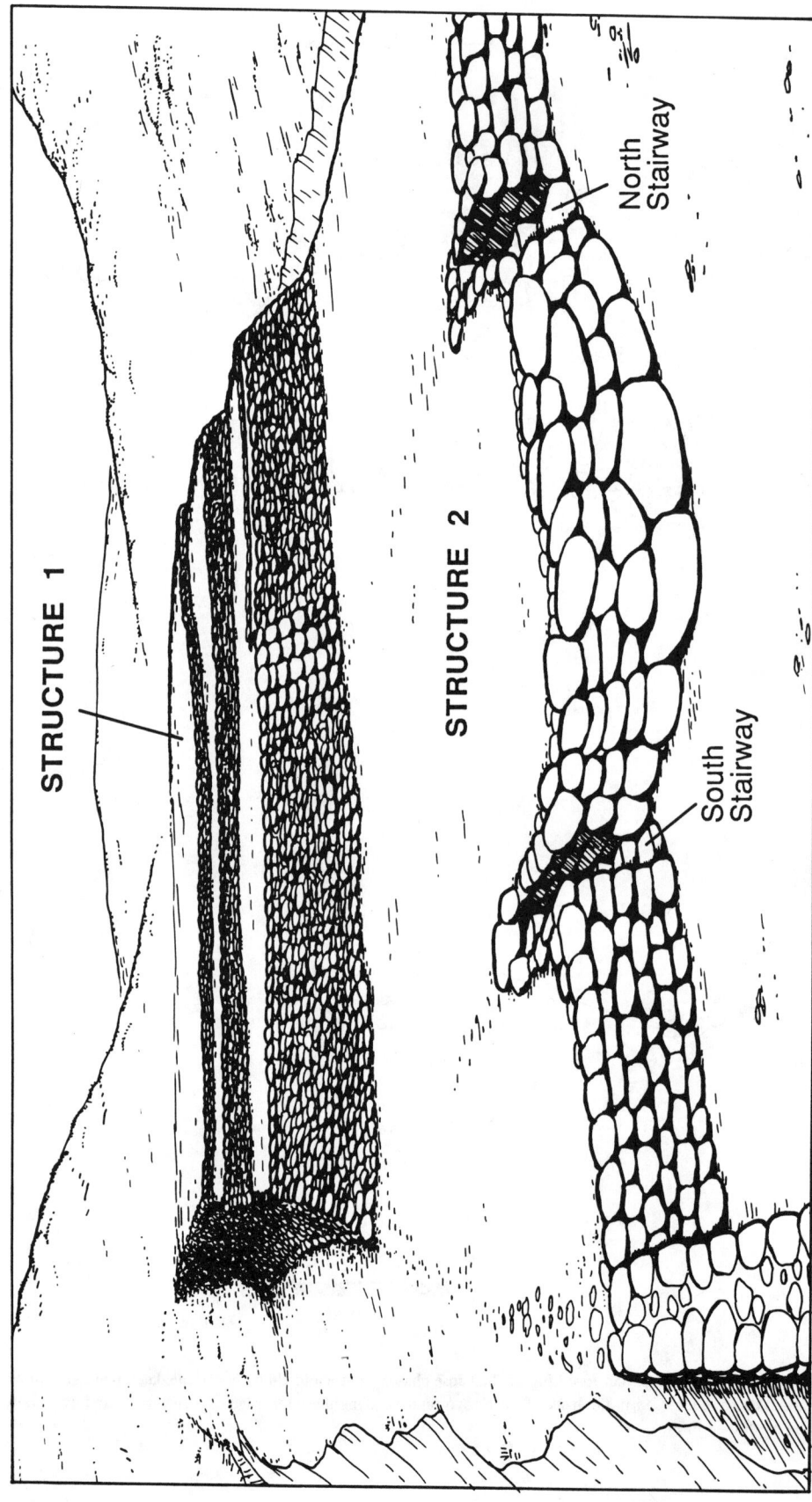

Figure 18.8. Artist's reconstruction of Structures 1 and 2, San José Mogote, as they might have looked late in the San José phase. Not shown are the wattle-and-daub public buildings that once stood atop them but were eventually eroded away, leaving only traces of clay floors. (Drawing by David Reynolds.)

18.7–18.8). Each appeared to be the pyramidal platform for a public building, and there were reasons to believe that both structures were part of the same architectural complex. Both were contoured to a gentle slope coming down off the piedmont spur on which most of the later ceremonial architecture of San José Mogote was built. This slope ran generally west to east, between shallow arroyos. These arroyos defined the north and south limits of Structures 1 and 2; since the arroyos lay 18 m apart, neither structure could extend more than 18 m north to south.

Each platform was different, a rough-and-ready structure that was adapted to the slope without much concern for bilateral symmetry or straightness of walls. It is likely that the public buildings atop the platforms were more carefully constructed and symmetrical, but owing to the slope of the land they had been largely eroded away. All that remained were a few patches of hard-packed, almost burnished, puddled-adobe floor surfaces to indicate where the buildings had been.

Let us begin with Structure 2, the easternmost part of the complex. It stands 1.0 m high, and may once have run the full 18 m north-south between the two arroyos. Its irregular eastern edge was faced with boulders, some of them local and some of them brought in from as far as 5 km away. Specifically, the facing included limestone from the Matadamas quarries (see Fig. 3.1) and travertine from Fábrica San José (Drennan 1976a). Two carved stones, one depicting a feline and the other a raptorial bird, had fallen out of a nearby east-west wall (Fig. 18.9).

The east face of Structure 2 contained our earliest stone stairways. Each was so narrow (60–75 cm) that it could only have accommodated one person at a time. Called the North and South Stairways, they were inset into the wall and consisted of three to seven stones serving as steps (Fig. 18.10).

Anyone ascending the North or South Stairway of Structure 2 apparently reached a level platform surface with a clay floor. Buried beneath this floor were the remains of Structure 16, the enigmatic building on a puddled adobe platform which has been described above. Structure 16 was damaged when Structure 2 was built, and its surviving remnant was surrounded by basketloads of earthen fill. Some of this fill contained planoconvex adobes—one of our earliest examples of this form of architecture, which reached its peak during the Guadalupe phase.

Some 9–11 m west of the boulder-lined face of Structure 2, we find the base of the east wall of Structure 1 (Fig. 18.11). Structure 1 was a pyramidal platform faced with stones, originally at least 18 m wide north-south, and running east-west for more than 9 m until its traces were lost. The lower stage of the platform (designated Stage I) had a lower tier 1.5 m high and an upper tier 0.5 m high. At a slightly later date, another tier (Stage II) had been added; now badly destroyed, it may once have contributed another 0.5 m to the height of Structure 1. A final cap of clay (Stage III), which probably constituted the last enlargement of the structure, was almost too eroded to detect.

Buried beneath the surface of Structure 1 was the sequence of household units (C4 through C1) already described in Chapter 14. In that locality, the earthen fill of Structure 1 (Stage I) consti-

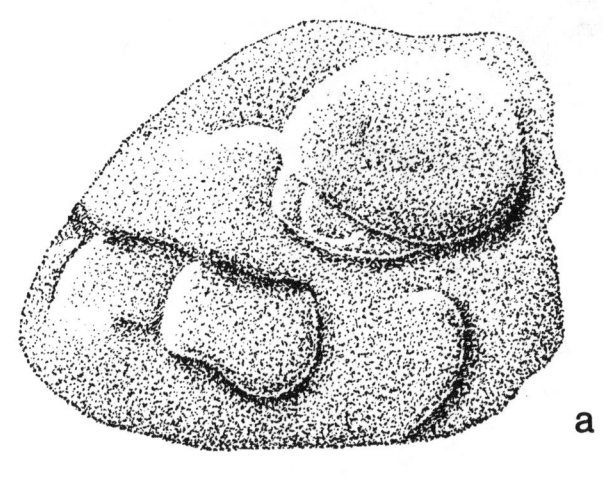

Figure 18.9. Monuments 1 and 2, two carved stones associated with Structure 2, San José Mogote. *a*, Monument 1, a possible feline. *b*, Monument 2, a possible raptorial bird. (For the location of these monuments, which had fallen from a wall, see Fig. 18.7.)

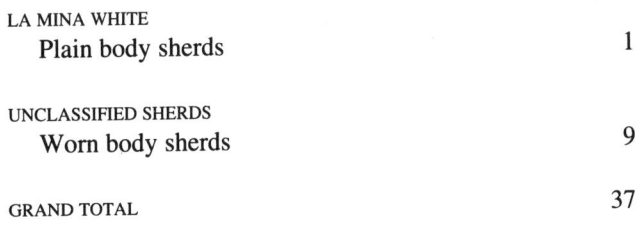

2. *What was the nature of the postabandonment material above Structure 16?*

Answer: Hundreds of basketloads of earth had been heaped over Structure 16 during the construction of Structure 2 (see below). The sherds in these basketloads of fill were all San José phase or earlier.

Structures 1 and 2, Area A

Two of the most impressive buildings of the San José phase were Structures 1 and 2 in Area A, San José Mogote (Figs.

Figure 18.10. The south stairway of Structure 2 (see Fig. 18.7 for location).

Figure 18.11. Structure 1 as it appeared when initially discovered (view from the southeast).

tuted stratigraphic Zone B above Household Unit C1. Simple retaining walls of fieldstones had been laid down over the collapsed remains of the C1 house; then basketloads of blackish-gray alluvial clay from a low-lying area east of the piedmont spur had been dumped in the gaps between the retaining walls. Finally, the sloping walls of the pyramidal platform were covered with stones, all apparently of local material.

Let us now proceed to the dating of Structures 1 and 2.

1. What stratigraphic units preceded the building of Structures 1 and 2?

Answer: Household Units C4-C1 all lay stratigraphically below the surface of Structure 1. The ceramics of Household Unit C1, the most recent of these residential units, have already been given in Table 14.1, Chapter 14. Structure 16 lay stratigraphically below Structure 2; its associated sherds have already been given (above).

2. Did any other levels intervene between Household Unit C1 and the surface of Structure 1?

Answer: Yes. To level the area and fill in all the depressions, the builders brought in hundreds of basketloads of black to blackish-gray alluvial clay from a low-lying area just east of the piedmont spur on which Households C4-C1 had been built. This alluvial clay was also used as fill behind the sloping stone-masonry walls of Structures 1 and 2.

3. Were there any sherds in this black alluvial clay?

Answer: Yes. The clay was designated stratigraphic Zone B, and it did contain sherds. However, they were not very helpful, because they appeared to be sherds that had washed down from the piedmont spur into the low-lying area to the east. In general, they duplicated the San José phase ceramics already found in Household Units C4-C1; however, many were extremely waterworn and eroded.

4. What remained of the surface of Structures 1 and 2?

Answer: Because Structures 1 and 2 occupied a slope coming down from the piedmont spur toward the valley floor, they had been badly treated by erosion over the centuries. However, in August of 1974, Marcus discovered one intact patch of the original puddled adobe floor (or platform surface) that had run east from the base of Structure 1 to the stairways of Structure 2. The center of this patch lay 2 m east of the base of Structure 1, and 11.8 m north of its southern limits. Where the floor rested on sterile clay over bedrock (near the base of Structure 1), it consisted only of a 2-cm-thick layer of puddled adobe clay, smoothed on top and possibly whitewashed with a solution of lime and water. Where it crossed depressions or irregularities in Zone B, it was occasionally supported by round, planoconvex ("bun-shaped") adobes. This was one of the earliest appearances of true adobes in our sequence.

5. Were there any sherds lying on this surviving patch of floor or platform surface?

Answer: Yes, there were 52 sherds lying on it, as follows:

TIERRAS LARGAS BURNISHED PLAIN
    Hemispherical bowls: plain rims   1
    Outleaned-wall bowls: plain rims   1

MATADAMAS ORANGE
    Jar neck/shoulder sherds   2

FIDENCIO COARSE
    Jar rims: unburnished   2
    Jar shoulders: plain   2

LEANDRO GRAY
    Outleaned-wall bowls: plain rims   2
    Outleaned-wall bowls: plain flat bases   1
    Outleaned-wall bowls: incised rims   1
    Cylinders: plain rims   1
    Cylinders: plain flat bases   2
    Cylinders: decorated rims   1
    Cylinders: decorated body sherds   1
    Jar/tecomate body sherds   10

ATOYAC YELLOW-WHITE
    Outleaned-wall bowls: plain rims   6
    Outleaned-wall bowls: plain flat bases   1
    Outleaned-wall bowls: incised rims   1
    Cylinders: plain rims   2
    Cylinders: plain flat bases   1
    Vertical jar necks: plain   1
    Jars with outcurved rim   1

SAN JOSE RED-ON-WHITE
    Outleaned-wall bowl: red rim, white wall   1
    Jar neck   1

SAN JOSE SPECULAR RED
    Jar necks   2

UNCLASSIFIED SHERDS
    Worn body sherds   8

GRAND TOTAL   52

6. Could the 52 sherds lying on the puddled-adobe floor be considered in situ*?*

Answer: Probably not. They were accompanied by the same kind of debris one finds in and around ordinary residences in Area A (obsidian, chert, mica, marine shell), and Structures 1 and 2 are clearly not "ordinary residences." Therefore, the 52 sherds probably represent postabandonment debris.

7. What other postabandonment debris was found in the area of Structures 1 and 2?

Answer: Banked up against the sloping, stone-masonry faces of Structures 1 and 2 were masses of postoccupational debris, all of which had to be removed in order to expose the structures. A great deal of this debris appeared to be featureless slopewash, mainly black and blackish gray clay that had eroded out of Stages II and III of Structure 1. Within this slopewash, however, were lenses of uneroded sherds that appeared to represent postabandonment trash dumping. Because they were protected by the soft slopewash around them, these lenses occasionally produced some nice rim sherds for illustration (see, for example, Figs. 12.104–12.108). While none of these postabandonment deposits were deemed worthy of statistical treatment, they were informative for the following reason: not one sherd found in them would have been out of place in the Zone D3-D1 midden or Household Units C4-C1 of Area A.

8. What stratigraphic level overlay the postabandonment debris above Structures 1 and 2?

Answer: Zone A. This was the plow zone of Area A, and consisted mainly of slopewash from Mound 1 (on the west) and Mound 2 (on the north). Zone A was not very useful; its contents included a little bit of everything found in Area A, plus sherds of Monte Albán II (Protoclassic) that had washed down from public buildings on Mounds 1 and 2. Also present were small Tierras Largas phase sherds—almost certainly eroded out of the Monte Albán II buildings, whose construction fill included basketloads of earth dug up from earlier deposits.

Zone A, therefore, included sherds of two phases—Tierras Largas and Monte Albán II—no *in situ* evidence of which was found below the surface in Area A. This is instructive, since Zone A is the surface survey layer. So much for the notion that surface collections are a direct reflection of what is under the ground.

Conclusion

Structures 1 and 2 were built after the abandonment of Household Unit C1 of Area A. Their use as the pyramidal platforms for public buildings ceased at a time when San José phase sherds were still the most recent ceramics available to be incorporated into the postabandonment debris. Not a single Guadalupe phase pottery type (Socorro Fine Gray, Josefina Fine Gray, Guadalupe Burnished Brown, etc.) can be associated with either structure. Thus, Structures 1 and 2 may even have been abandoned prior to the occupation of Houses 16–17 in Area B. Our dating: some time in the second half of the San José phase.

Chapter 19

Ceramic Crossties and Early Formative Radiocarbon Dates

By now the alert reader will have noticed two unusual features of this ceramic report. Not a single radiocarbon date, or absolute date of any kind, has so far been mentioned. Nor has the word "Olmec" been used.

As will become clear in this chapter and the next, both omissions were deliberate. We believe that over-reliance on radiocarbon dates—which have repeatedly let us down—greatly undermines archaeologists' traditional skills at correlating regional sequences by systematic comparison of ceramic types, attributes, and motifs. We further believe that the term "Olmec" has been so overextended, and the influence of the southern Gulf Coast so overemphasized, that it has prejudiced our efforts to determine which Formative regions are in fact most closely related. In Chapters 19 and 20, we take the position that (1) ceramic crossties should take precedence over radiocarbon dates, and (2) we cannot assume *a priori* that we know where any of Early Formative Mesoamerica's horizon markers originated. Our conclusions differ from orthodoxy in several ways.

In this chapter, we give our radiocarbon dates in the manner recommended by the journal *Radiocarbon*—uncalibrated, using the 5568-year half-life, and subtracting the midpoint of the assay from A.D. 1950. Following current conventions, we report such dates with the lower case "b.c." rather than "B.C.," to indicate that the date is in radiocarbon years rather than "real time." The key to the three radiocarbon labs used is as follows:

M—University of Michigan
SI—Smithsonian Institution
GX—Geochron Laboratories

Problems with Radiocarbon Dating

Fifty years ago, an archaeologist trying to correlate two sequences of village farming cultures from neighboring regions would have used the attributes of the ceramics to establish contemporaneity. When he found that the two sites shared identical complexes of vessel shape, clay body, surface color, and decoration he would declare them contemporaneous.

With the announcement of radiocarbon dating in 1949, archaeologists were seduced by the notion of absolute chronological correlation. "People said, 'Now the shackles of imprecise chronology have been struck from our wrists,'" Robert Braidwood used to joke. People soon found out better. When Braidwood himself got back his radiocarbon dates from Jarmo, Iraq, he could only describe the results as "whimsical." Jarmo was a village occupied for probably no more than 500 years, its range of dates expected to fall somewhere between 6750 and 6000 b.c. Its twelve (uncalibrated) radiocarbon determinations, however, spanned an impossible six-thousand-year period from 9280 b.c. ± 300 to 3310 b.c. ± 450 (Braidwood, Howe et al. 1960:159).

Decades later, Norman Hammond, excavating at Cuello in Belize, defined a phase named Swasey. Based on ceramic crossties with other regions, Swasey should have dated to roughly 900–700 b.c. Inexplicably, Hammond's radiocarbon determinations spanned the years from 3190 b.c. ± 445 to 230 b.c. ± 70 (Hammond 1977, Hammond et al. 1977). In a recent overview of the problem, Andrews and Hammond (1990) have placed the Swasey ceramics in the Middle Formative period, relying on ceramic crossties rather than the anomalous dates.

Why were the Jarmo and Cuello dates so far off? We will probably never know, but they represent only two examples out of hundreds that should warn us not to let radiocarbon dates overrule our common sense. Archaeologists tend to believe radiocarbon dates because they are produced by men in white lab coats. They would do well to remember, however, that those same men in white lab coats once told us that the half-life of ^{14}C was 5,568 years. Later, they changed that to 5,730 years. More recently, they have confessed to us that one of the original basic assumptions of radiocarbon dating is, in fact, wrong: the amount of radioactivity in the earth's atmosphere has *not* remained constant throughout the centuries, but has oscillated (Stuiver and Quay 1980).

Over the last thirty years, many archaeologists have come to rely less and less on detailed ceramic crossties and more and more on radiocarbon dates. In view of the known problems and uncertainties of radiocarbon dating, we now feel that this trend should be reversed. In this book, we give priority to ceramic crossties, and regard even our own radiocarbon dates with skepticism.

We also believe that there has been a trend, over time, to use radiocarbon dates in ways that were never intended by the physicists who produced them. Every radiocarbon determination consists of a range with a midpoint and a standard deviation. A radiocarbon assay of 1000 b.c. ± 200 simply means that the chances are two out of three (66.7%) that the "true" date falls somewhere between 1200 and 800 b.c. That means that there is one chance in three (33.3%) that the "true" date falls outside that range. If one wants better odds, one can double the standard deviation: there is a 95% chance that the "true" date falls between 1400 and 600 b.c.

In the example above, we have put the word "true" in quotation marks to remind ourselves of an important fact: radiocarbon assays do not really measure the age of a piece of charcoal, but its level of radioactivity. Since we now know that the amount of radioactivity in the earth's atmosphere has oscillated, our notions about the relationship between radioactivity and the "true" age of the charcoal may be overly optimistic.

We do not suggest that archaeologists stop running radiocarbon dates, merely that they use them more cautiously than they have. For example, we do not believe that radiocarbon dates can be used to produce a "staggered" chronology for the Formative as Tolstoy (1989b and pers. comm.) has recently tried to do. What Tolstoy has done is to look at radiocarbon dates from all over Mesoamerica—dates collected with different levels of care, often from dubious contexts, and run by many different laboratories—and used the midpoints to infer that a certain type of pottery might have originated in one area at Time A, spread to a second area by Time A + 50 years, and from there spread on to a third area by Time A + 100 years.

There are so many problems with this inference that we hardly know which one to discuss first. To begin with, most excavators have not told us the context of the charcoal they collected: was it on a floor, in a midden, or redeposited in mound fill? Second, they have usually not told us whether the provenience falls early or late in the phase. Third, they have usually not told us what kind of plant the charcoal came from: was it a maize stalk less than a year old, or a baldcypress tree 500 years old? Fourth, we know that even though there should not be differences among radiocarbon labs, there are; some labs tend to give "older" dates than others (see below).

Fifth, of course, there is nothing sacred about the midpoint of a radiocarbon assay. If the date from our midden is 1250 b.c. ± 150, and the date from your midden is 1200 b.c. ± 150, is our midden 50 years older than yours? Hardly. Our "one-sigma" range (one standard deviation) is 1400–1100 b.c., while yours is 1350–1050 b.c. In radiocarbon terms, the two dates are essentially the same; in fact, the "true" date of your midden could even be older than the "true" date of ours.

Beyond the obvious problems of radiocarbon chronology, we have additional reasons for not believing in staggered chronologies. Ethnohistoric documents (Torquemada 1975–1979, 4:320–21 [Book 14, Chapter 1] and Clavijero 1974:212 [Book 7, Chapter 12]) tell us that Motecuhzoma the Younger regularly ate fish brought from the Gulf of Mexico to Tenochtitlán, a distance of 80 leagues by the shortest route. The fish, brought by runners, were still fresh when they reached him. How rapid was foot transportation in ancient Mexico? Morley (1937, Vol. 2:233–34) has estimated that a man with a burden of 25–35 kg could travel 4.5 km per hour. Hammond (1978), discussing the overland cacao route between the Maya highlands and lowlands, estimates that a trader could cover 32 km per day. This means that a trip of 320 km might take only ten days, a trip of 640 km only twenty days. Even a longer trip, such as one from Teotihuacán to Kaminaljuyú (1000 km), might have taken only a month or so.

Our point is that once a new type of ceramic arose in Mesoamerica—assuming that it was appealing or attractive to people in other regions—we need not assume that it took twenty-five, or fifty, or even a hundred years to reach those areas. Nor do we believe that people in the Valley of Oaxaca, for example, were imitating pottery made fifty years previously in some other area. We do not picture San José phase villagers saying to San Lorenzo phase villagers, "Let us have some of that good old Chicharras phase pottery, if you still have any lying around." When we see identical ceramics in the Basin of Mexico, Oaxaca, and Chiapa de Corzo, we believe that all the deposits are essentially contemporaneous. If the radiocarbon dates do not show this, it is just one more example of why radiocarbon dates should be taken with a grain of salt.

The format for this chapter is as follows. For each of our ceramic phases, we discuss the crossties with contemporaneous phases in other regions. On the basis of those crossties, we give the dates (in uncalibrated radiocarbon years) that we expected for our material. We then look at all the radiocarbon dates we actually obtained on material of that phase (once again, in uncalibrated radiocarbon years).

For each date, we discuss the context of the charcoal sample. We believe that this discussion of context is particularly important, since it can shed light on why a date we obtained might have diverged from the date expected. We lament the fact that so few of our colleagues give us similar insights into the context of their charcoal samples, because we suspect it could explain at least part of the differences between their dates and ours.

The Espiridión Complex

The only collection of sherds that resembles our Espiridión material is the Purrón complex from the Tehuacán Valley. Johnson and MacNeish (1972) assign their Purrón material to the period 2300–1500 b.c. When one examines the radiocarbon assays closely, however, one finds that the oldest actual Purrón date is 1925 b.c. ± 131. The estimate of 2300 b.c. was derived by "splitting the difference" between the youngest Abejas phase date and the oldest Purrón complex date.

Since no actual Tierras Largas phase date has exceeded 1400 b.c. (see below), and no actual Purrón date has exceeded 1925 b.c., our expectation is that the Espiridión complex should fall somewhere between 1900 and 1400 b.c. In fact, as we explained in Chapter 7, the high frequency of Tierras Largas Burnished Plain leads us to equate our Espiridión collection with very late Purrón, perhaps no earlier than 1600–1500 b.c.

Unfortunately, we recovered insufficient charcoal from our Espiridión deposits to provide a radiocarbon date.

The Tierras Largas Phase

Tierras Largas is the first phase of our sequence to show widespread resemblances to the pottery of other areas. It is related to a whole series of ceramic complexes in highland areas between the Basin of Mexico and the Valley of Oaxaca. It is, perhaps, our Avelina Red-on-Buff and Clementina Fine Red-on-Buff that find their greatest parallels in other pottery assemblages, but Tierras Largas Burnished Plain bowls with dentate rocker stamping are good horizon markers as well.

Close ties with Tierras Largas can be seen in Area K203 at Yucuita in the Nochixtlán Valley (Spores 1972, 1983). Excavations there produced analogs for Tierras Largas Burnished Plain and Avelina Red-on-Buff; a radiocarbon date of 1300 b.c. ± 180 (GX-2187) was associated.

Strong resemblances can also be seen in the Early Ajalpan phase of the Tehuacán Valley (MacNeish, Peterson, and Flannery 1970). In Chapter 8, we have already noted how similar hemispherical bowls and bottles of Coatepec Red-on-Buff and Ajalpan Fine Red are to Tierras Largas phase specimens. This Early Ajalpan material dates to 1500–1200 b.c.

Given the close ties between Oaxaca, Tehuacán, and Nochixtlán, it is no surprise that the Cañada de Cuicatlán also has Early Ajalpan/Tierras Largas material. Rancho Dolores Ortíz near San Pedro Chicozapotes, excavated by Adriana Alaniz (pers. comm.), has fine red bottles and red-on-buff bowls of this period.

Farther to the north, Tierras Largas material finds parallels in the Nevada phase of Tlapacoya-Zohapilco in the Basin of Mexico. Niederberger (1987: Fig. 466) illustrates Pilli Red-on-Buff bowls identical to our Avelina specimens. She even has oval bowls with pinched-in sides in this type (ibid.: Figs. 511–512). Niederberger assigns dates of 1350–1250 b.c. to the Nevada phase.

While the Basin of Mexico/Tehuacán/Oaxaca connections are clear on the Tierras Largas horizon, Morelos is somewhat different. Cuautla Red-Slipped of the Amate phase (1500–1100 b.c.) seems to be the Morelos equivalent of Avelina Red-on-Buff, but the range of shapes is not very similar (Cyphers Guillén 1987:203).

Once we move south of the Oaxaca highlands, there is a noticeable dropoff in similarity to our ceramics. John Clark has correctly diagrammed this situation in Figure 8 of a recent article (Clark 1991:24). He assigns the Oaxaca-Puebla highlands to a "red-on-buff" style horizon, while the southern Gulf Coast, Isthmus of Tehuantepec, and Pacific Coast of Chiapas are assigned to a "Locona interaction sphere." That interaction sphere would include the Locona phase sites of the Chiapas coast (1350–1250 b.c.), the Lagunita phase sites of the Tehuantepec area (Zeitlin 1979), and the Ojochi-Chicharras phase sites of Veracruz-Tabasco (Coe and Diehl 1980).

In the Isthmian lowlands near Juchitán, Oaxaca, the "red-on-buff" and "Locona" interaction spheres overlap. There the site of Laguna Zope shares both the red-on-buff bowls of the Oaxaca highlands and the tecomates of the Chiapas coast. Red-rimmed and red-slipped hemispherical bowls in Suristmo Red-on-Buff Gloss-Burnished resemble our Avelina and Clementina examples (Zeitlin 1979:74 and Fig. D-16*a, b*). Suristmo Buff Gloss-Burnished, which amounts to 30 percent of the Lagunita phase sherds, is compared by Zeitlin (1979:57) to Tierras Largas Burnished Plain. The jars and flat-based bowls (ibid.: Fig. D-12*a*) and tecomates (ibid.: Figs. D-10, D-11*a*) in this ware do resemble Tierras Largas Burnished Plain; however, hemispherical bowls like ours are absent.

As we move farther south down the Chiapas coast, similarities with Oaxaca dwindle. Bayo Plain–polished ware of the Barra phase at Altamira has some dimple-based bowls reminiscent of Tierras Largas Burnished Plain, but the resemblance is not very close (Lowe 1975). A few rims of Cotán Grooved Red (ibid.: middle of Fig. 13) resemble Tierras Largas specimens, but most are not similar. Radiocarbon dates reported by Lowe are 1410 b.c. ± 225 and 1350 b.c. ± 160, in the Early Ajalpan range.

One of the key pottery types of the Pacific Coast of Chiapas, of course, is Ocós Black, which seems to have reached Oaxaca in the late Tierras Largas and early San José phases as an import. Since an Ocós phase site is now known from the Grijalva Depression (Gareth Lowe, pers. comm.), it is possible that our imported Ocós Black is not from as far away as the Pacific Coast. Clark (1991:15) would now date the Ocós phase to 1250–1150 b.c., which gives us reason to expect a date of roughly 1200 b.c. for the Tierras Largas/San José transition. The relationship of Ocós Black to Suristmo Black Burnished of Laguna Zope (Zeitlin 1979:132) is not clear.

Interestingly, we see few ties between Tierras Largas and the southern Gulf Coast. Coe and Diehl (1980:137) compare Camaño Coarse of the Ojochi phase at San Lorenzo with Ajalpan Coarse; this would, in turn, relate it indirectly to Tierras Largas Burnished Plain. Tecomates in Camaño Coarse are similar to Tierras Largas Burnished Plain specimens, but hemispherical bowls like ours are missing. Ojochi does, however, have hemispherical bowls in other coarse buff wares.

An interesting chronological question is raised by John Clark and Michael Blake's new work on the Pacific Coast of Chiapas. Coe and Diehl (1980:137) "guess-date" the Ojochi phase to 1500–1350 b.c., and add: "Ojochi is a country-cousin version of the far more sophisticated Ocós phase of Guatemalan Soconusco ... and must be contemporary with it." But Clark and Blake now date Ocós to 1250–1150 b.c. (uncalibrated; see Clark 1991:15). While we cannot resolve the disparity between these two estimates, the later dates for Ocós would fit better with our recovery of Ocós Black in late Tierras Largas/early San José phase contexts (see above).

There are a few more possible ties between Oaxaca and the Gulf Coast at this time level. Small, fluted, incurved-rim bowls like those in Centavito Red of the Ojochi phase (Coe and Diehl 1980: Fig. 107*l*, *m*) occur in the Tierras Largas phase, but they appear in Tierras Largas Burnished Plain and Ocós Black rather than in red ware. Xochiltepec White of the Chicharras phase (ibid: Fig. 112) looks identical to Xochiltepec White of the late Tierras Largas and early San José phases—as might be expected, if it were traded from the Gulf Coast to Oaxaca. Aguatepec Thick bolstered-rim bowls of the Chicharras phase (ibid.: Fig. 130), thought by Coe and Diehl (1980:156) to have been gray before they eroded, look like Leandro Gray specimens. Tatagapa Red rocker stamped tecomates (ibid.: Fig. 132*a-e*) are analogous to some San José Specular Red tecomates. Obviously, all of these ties between Chicharras and early San José suggest to us that Coe and Diehl (1980:150) are on the right track when they suggest a date of 1250–1150 b.c. for Chicharras.

Based on all the ceramic crossties mentioned above, what might our *expected* date for the Tierras Largas phase be? We might expect it to begin by 1400 or 1350 b.c. and last until 1200 or 1150 b.c. Now let us look at the actual ^{14}C dates.

Dates from San José Mogote

Three charcoal samples from Area C of San José Mogote were run by the University of Michigan. Results were as follows:

M-2330 (Area C, Feature 23)	1330 b.c. ± 180
M-2372 (Area C, fill of Structure 5)	1320 b.c. ± 160
M-2331 (Area C, Zone G, Master Profile)	1170 b.c. ± 150

All these proveniences have been discussed in earlier chapters of this volume. None date to the beginning of the Tierras Largas phase, but all could contain redeposited charcoal from the first half of the Tierras Largas phase. Feature 23 was a pit in bedrock, sealed below Zone G of the Master Profile. Its date fits our expectations. Structure 5 was a late Tierras Largas phase public building, and the charcoal sample was trapped below plaster debris from the collapse of its walls. Its date fits our expectations. Zone G was a layer of midden dating to the second half of the Tierras Largas phase. The midpoint of M-2331 is perhaps 80 years younger than our expectations, but its one-sigma range (1320–1020 b.c.) brackets our expected date of about 1250 b.c. These three dates from San José Mogote would seem to be supported by the date of 1300 b.c. ± 180 on Tierras Largas-like ceramics from Yucuita, Oaxaca (see above).

Dates from the Tierras Largas Site

Three charcoal samples from the site of Tierras Largas, found with sherds considered by Winter (1972) to be late Tierras Largas phase in date, have also been run by Michigan. These dates are more problematic than those from San José Mogote, since none fit our expectations. They are as follows:

M-2353 (Feature 116, Household Unit LTL-1)	1080 b.c. ± 150
M-2352 (Sample Square 1995)	1070 b.c. ± 150
M-2351 (Sample Square 1995)	1010 b.c. ± 150

None of these charcoal samples were associated with any of the sherd collections used in this volume; indeed, only Winter has seen the sherds with which they were found. M-2353 comes from a bell-shaped pit associated with LTL-1, a household unit described in Chapter 10. However, it was not one of the bell-shaped pits selected by Winter as having an adequate sherd sample for Schreuder's seriation. As we pointed out in Chapter 4, when one uses material from storage pits, there is always the danger that one is getting later items swept into the pit at the time it was filled. A pit dug in late Tierras Largas times could be filled during the early San José phase.

M-2351 and M-2352 are even more problematic, since both come from a test square dug as part of Winter's random sampling program (Winter 1976). Such squares were usually shallow, since bedrock was not far below the plow zone at Tierras Largas. Once again, we cannot rule out the possibility of early San José phase charcoal lying in contact with late Tierras Largas phase sherds. Indeed, as our ceramic charts show, all of the common pottery types of the Tierras Largas phase—Tierras Largas Burnished Plain, Avelina Red-on-Buff, Clementina Fine Red-on-Buff, Matadamas Red, and Matadamas Orange—lasted into the early San José phase. Thus, a small sample of such pottery could not be used to guarantee a Tierras Largas phase date.

In other words, because none of the Tierras Largas charcoal samples were sealed in deeply buried deposits the way the three samples from Area C of San José Mogote were, we believe they should be regarded with caution. To be sure, when one considers their entire one-sigma range, it does reach back to the presumed late Tierras Largas/early San José phase transition:

M-2353	1230–930 b.c.
M-2352	1220–920 b.c.
M-2351	1160–860 b.c.

Our expectation, based on crossties with other regions, is that the San José phase should begin by 1200 or 1150 b.c. Adding one standard deviation to the midpoint does push these dates back to 1230–1160 b.c., around the time of our suspected Tierras Largas/San José transition. However, given the context of the charcoal, there are so many reasons why these three dates might fail to meet our expectations that it would be unproductive to speculate further.

The San José Phase

With the beginning of the San José phase, the Valley of Oaxaca shows at least some ceramic crossties with virtually every region of Mesoamerica. From the Basin of Mexico to Copán, Honduras, the pan-Mesoamerican motifs carved and incised on pottery are so widespread that one can literally see Mesoamerica emerge for the first time as a culture area. Interestingly, however, it is often the largest and most important sites in each region that share the most crossties; many types, modes, and attributes seem to have passed the smaller hamlets by.

This tendency for the largest sites to share more of the trade wares and exotic attributes suggests that an emerging elite was involved in the spread of many ceramic characters. It also means that Oaxaca's main ties were no longer simply with the regions nearest to it, such as Nochixtlán, Tehuacán, and the Cuicatlán Cañada. To a significant extent, the ties between San José Mogote and the larger sites of the southern Basin of Mexico seem to have been stronger than would have been predicted on the basis of distance.

Ties with the Basin of Mexico

Strong ties become evident when one compares the San José phase pottery of San José Mogote with the Ayotla phase pottery of Tlapacoya-Zohapilco (Niederberger 1987). Flat-based bowls with outleaned walls in Niederberger's Volcán Burnished, excised with fire serpents (ibid.: Fig. 382), are almost identical to our Leandro Gray examples. Niederberger's *vase-gobelet* is identical to our cylinder, and the excised Volcán Burnished example she illustrates (ibid.: Fig. 395) is indistinguishable from ours. The Volcán cylinder shown in her Figure 398, with the upper third burnished and the lower two-thirds left rough and excised, is identical to Leandro Gray examples. Moreover, her excised bolstered-rim bowls in Volcán Burnished (ibid.: Fig. 391) resemble vessels from the Tomaltepec cemetery in Oaxaca (Whalen 1981); they link the Ayotla and early San José phases.

Another of Niederberger's types, Tortuga Burnished, resembles our material. The Tortuga outleaned-wall bowl with an excised double-line-break illustrated in her Figure 386 is like San José phase specimens. So is the dimple-based hemispherical bowl in the same type, illustrated in her Figure 406.

Niederberger's type Valle Negative Rim (ibid.: Fig. 422) is very much like San José Black-and-White. The carved black-and-white cylinder she illustrates in her Figure 429(2) is especially similar to ours. Our collections have both her carved St. Andrew's cross motif, and the incised version she calls "cat's whiskers" (ibid.: Fig. 432).

The Coapexco Beige cylinder with a fire-serpent motif, shown in Niederberger's Figure 436 (right), resembles many of our Leandro Gray cylinders.

Flat-based bowls with outleaned walls in Pilli Red-on-White (Niederberger 1987: Fig. 461, right) resemble San José Red-on-White. So do her red-on-white hemispherical bowls (ibid.: Fig. 463).

Cesto White bowls with flat bases, outleaned walls, and *sgraffito* double-line breaks from Zohapilco (ibid.: Figs. 474–476) are very similar to Atoyac Yellow-white specimens, even to the details of the motifs (Fig. 19.1). One difference is that Niederberger's variety of "grater bowl" bases is greater than ours (ibid.: Figs. 482–490), although there is significant overlap (Fig. 19.2). Like Atoyac Yellow-white, Cesto White increases in frequency over time, becoming more common in Niederberger's Manantial phase (= late San José) than it was in her Ayotla phase (= early San José).

Finally, there are actual cases of imported wares. As we showed in Chapter 12, genuine specimens of Niederberger's Paloma Negative and Cesto White types reached San José Mogote during the San José phase (the former during early San José/Ayotla times, the latter during late San José/Manantial times). In turn, Delfina Fine Gray and Leandro Gray were exported to Tlapacoya, winding up in Weaver's "Tlapacoya Grey" type and Niederberger's "Atoyac Fine Gray" type (Weaver 1967; Niederberger 1987: Figs. 469–471). Given the amount of interaction between San José Mogote and Tlapacoya-Zohapilco, it is no surprise that Niederberger's spouted trays (ibid.:560) and carinated or fluted bottles with tall necks (ibid.:540–42) look just like our Leandro Gray specimens.

San José Mogote also shows strong ties with Tlatilco (Porter 1953, Piña Chan 1958, Tolstoy 1989a). Porter illustrates flat-based bowls with outleaned walls, bottles, tecomates, incurved-rim bowls, rocker-stamped vessels, spouted trays, solid cylindrical clay stamps, pottery masks, and stone "yuguitos," all of which resemble San José phase specimens. Indeed, we can point to the following illustrations in Porter (1953) that recall San José specimens. Her Figure 14 (left) shows a vessel with annular base like our Lupita Heavy Plain braziers. Her Plate 6I shows a black bottle with "sunburst" motif similar to our Ocós Black specimens. Her Plate 6E, F shows flat-based bowls excised on the outside with the fire-serpent and St. Andrew's cross that are similar to Leandro Gray examples. Her Plate 6D shows a flat-based bowl excised on the interior like Leandro Gray vessels from the Zone D midden in Area A, San José Mogote. Her Plate 6C shows fine-line hachure and "mat" motifs on cylinders similar to ours. Her Plate 7A, B shows fluted bottles similar to ours. Her Plate 11E shows a bolstered-rim bowl very much like ours. Her Plate 11F shows a zoned rocker stamped tecomate like our San José phase specimens. Many Leandro Gray cylinders are identical to the vessel she shows in her Plate 11H. Finally, Porter illustrates cylinder stamps (Plate 13A, B), pottery masks (Plate 13D), and stone "yuguitos" (Plate 13G, H) that are very similar to San José phase specimens.

Piña Chan (1958) also illustrates white-slipped cylinders (Lám. 37), bolstered-rim bowls (Lám. 36), cylinders with excised St. Andrew's crosses (Lám. 41), fluted bottles (Lám. 44), and spouted trays (Lám. 45) from Tlatilco that are very close to San José phase examples. Tolstoy (1989a) confirms the presence

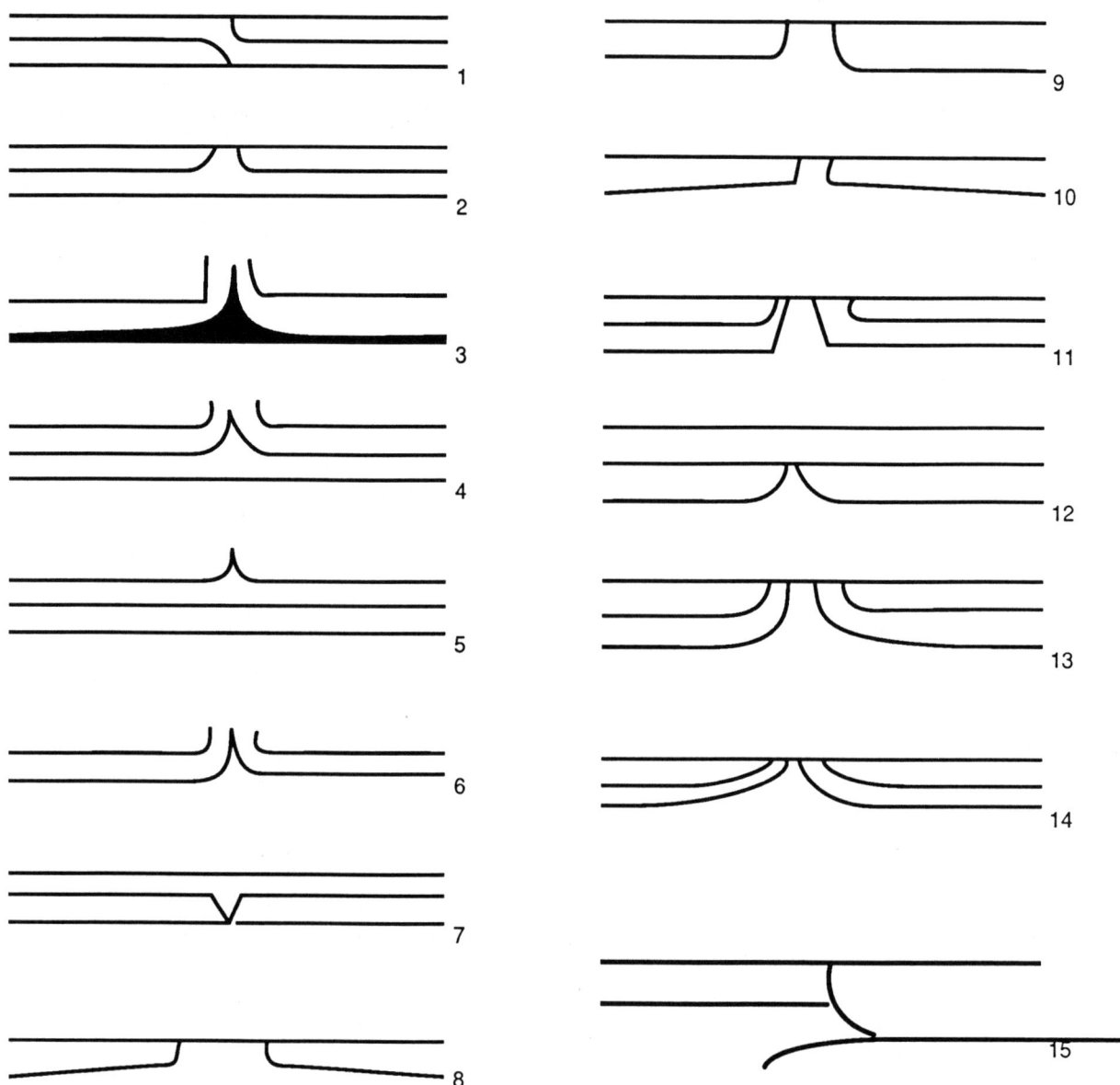

Figure 19.1. Double- and triple-line-break motifs on Cesto White and Pilli White vessels from Tlapacoya-Zohapilco, Basin of Mexico (redrawn from Niederberger 1987: Figs. 475–476). These motifs show very strong similarities to the double- and triple-line-break design elements on Atoyac Yellow-white vessels from the Valley of Oaxaca (see Figs. 12.19–12.21).

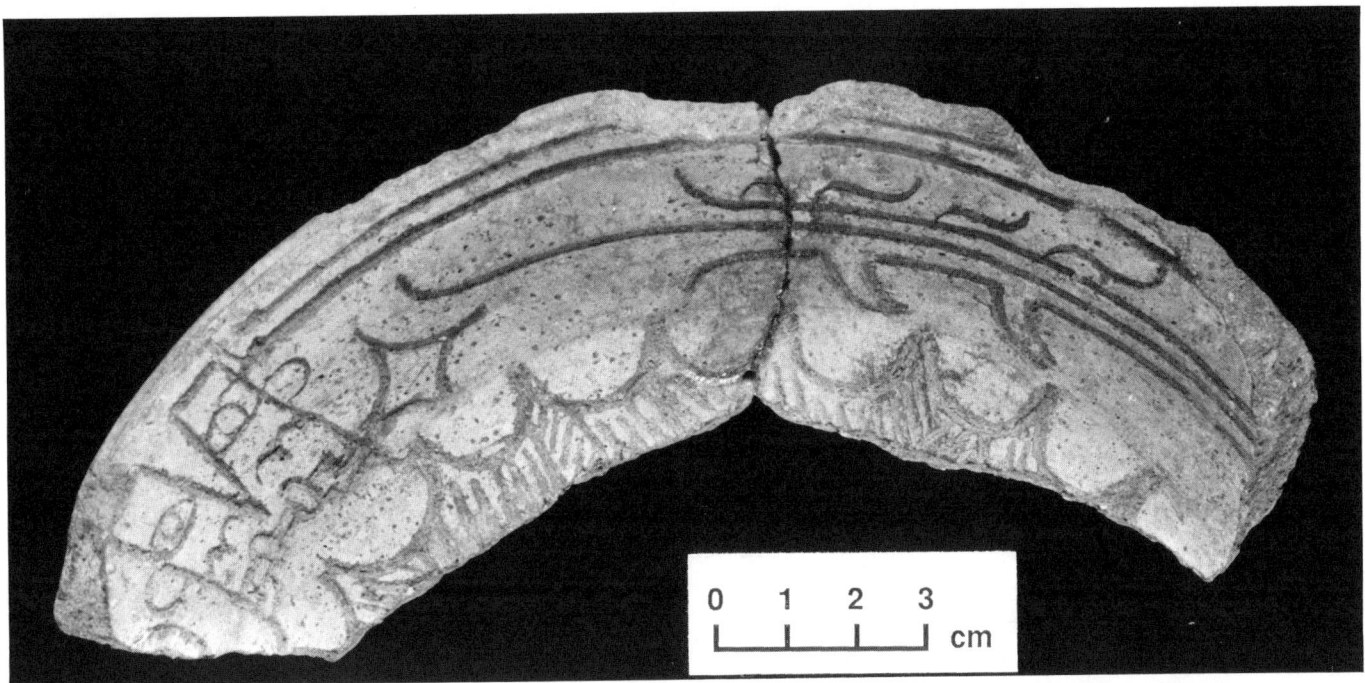

Figure 19.2. Portion of Cesto White bowl from Tlapacoya-Zohapilco, Basin of Mexico. While the sunburst "grater bowl" design incised on the base would be out of place in the Valley of Oaxaca, the cleft-head representation of Earth (far left) shows strong similarity to Atoyac Yellow-white examples (see Fig. 12.13). (Photo courtesy of Christine Niederberger.)

of all these items at Tlatilco, and adds the fact that Coapexco has Niederberger's Valle Negative Rim, Volcán Burnished, and Tortuga Burnished, three pottery types with strong resemblances to San José phase material.

We have devoted a great deal of space to these Oaxaca/Basin of Mexico crossties for a reason. It is with the large southern Basin of Mexico sites, whose pottery we have just described, that San José Mogote finds its strongest similarities. No other region comes close. San José Mogote shares more in the way of vessel shape, surface color, plastic decoration, and overall style with Tlapacoya and Tlatilco than it does with many sites that lie geographically closer to the Valley of Oaxaca.

Contrasts with Morelos

To appreciate just how similar San José ceramics are to those of Tlapacoya and Tlatilco, we need only compare them to the pottery of Chalcatzingo in Morelos (Cyphers Guillén 1987). Although Morelos is no farther away from Oaxaca than is the Basin of Mexico, its ceramics are unexpectedly—perhaps even astonishingly—different.

The relevant period for Chalcatzingo would be the Barranca phase, perhaps 1100–700 b.c. in uncalibrated radiocarbon years. We know that Barranca is broadly contemporaneous with the San José phase because Amatzinac White (Cyphers Guillén 1987:211) is clearly analogous to Atoyac Yellow-white, but its vessel forms and incised designs are strikingly different. Even its double- and triple-line break motifs are unique (see Fig. 19.3). This is fascinating in light of how similar the incised double- and triple-line-breaks of Cesto White from Tlapacoya-Zohapilco are to San José phase counterparts (compare Figs. 19.1 and 12.19–12.21). Even more different is the excised rim decoration on Amatzinac White in the subsequent phase, Cantera, which resembles nothing from the Valleys of Oaxaca or Mexico (see Cyphers Guillén 1987: Fig. 13.26).

To be sure, one can find a few parallels with Oaxaca. Chalcatzingo's Carved Gray, which begins prior to the Barranca phase but continues into it, has bolstered-rim bowls like those in Leandro Gray (ibid.: Fig. 13.8a). Tenango Brown "annular base braziers" from Chalcatzingo (ibid.: Fig. 13.32p) resemble Lupita Heavy Plain braziers. Chalcatzingo's White-Rimmed Black (ibid.: Fig. 13.33) looks like Coatepec White-Rimmed Black, a type linking Tehuacán and Oaxaca. And Cyphers Guillén's "kaolin" ware (ibid.: 210 and Fig. 13.9) is almost certainly Xochiltepec White, an export ware linking Oaxaca and San Lorenzo. Far more impressive, however, is how *different* Chalcatzingo's pottery looks from our San José phase collections—especially given how similar our material is to that from the southern Basin of Mexico.

Ties with Southern Puebla

It is easy to find resemblances between the late Ajalpan phase of the Tehuacán Valley and the San José phase of the Valley of

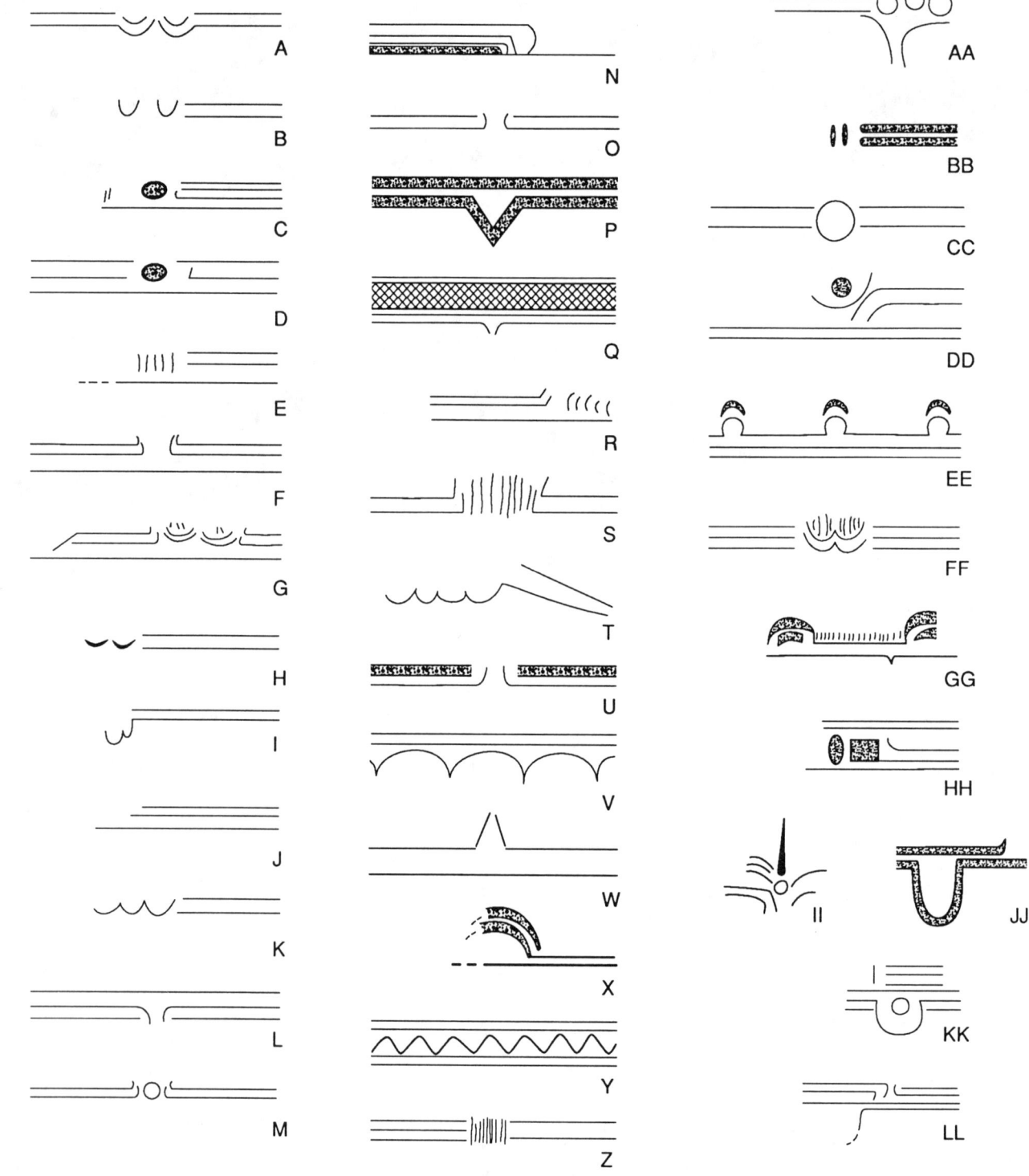

Figure 19.3. Double- and triple-line-break motifs on Amatzinac White pottery from Chalcatzingo, Morelos (redrawn from Cyphers Guillén 1987: Fig. 13.23). While a few of these design elements (e.g., F, L, O, W) resemble those on Atoyac Yellow-white bowls of the San José phase (Figs. 12.19–12.21), the vast majority are strikingly different. Two motifs (Q, Y) are not unlike Guadalupe phase specimens from Huitzo.

Oaxaca. Our Atoyac Yellow-white is like Tehuacán's Canoas White (MacNeish, Peterson, and Flannery 1970); our Fidencio Coarse is like Río Salado Coarse; our Lupita Heavy Plain is like Canoas Heavy Plain. But these are the kinds of resemblances in general utilitarian wares that one might expect to see in two areas separated by only 150 km. What is so far missing in Tehuacán are the flamboyant shapes, the bichromes, and the hundreds of pan-Mesoamerican motifs. One sherd of imported Delfina Fine Gray with an excised fire-serpent showed up at Las Canoas in Tehuacán (see Fig. 12.141), and it stood out like a sore thumb. So strikingly absent from the Tehuacán ceramics is any explosion of pan-Mesoamerican motifs that Coe and Diehl (1980:169) have even proposed that there might be a hiatus in the Tehuacán sequence between 1150 and 900 b.c.

There is, however, another possibility—that the pan-Mesoamerican motifs tend to show up at certain sites and not others. In the Nochixtlán Valley, for example, they show up at Etlatongo but not (so far) at Yucuita (Ronald Spores, pers. comm.). Spores' Reyes White shows ties with Canoas White of Tehuacán and Atoyac Yellow-white of Oaxaca, but at Yucuita, at least, it does not seem to feature carved cylinders and bolstered-rim bowls with fire-serpents and were-jaguars like those of Etlatongo. We therefore suspect that the pan-Mesoamerican complex we see so clearly at Tlapacoya, Tlatilco, San Lorenzo, and San José Mogote may be primarily a phenomenon of large villages with emerging elites; it may not show up as strongly at smaller villages, where social inequality was not yet as well expressed.

Ties with the Gulf Coast

One region where social inequality was presumably well developed was San Lorenzo in southern Veracruz (Coe and Diehl 1980). There the San Lorenzo phase (1150–900 b.c.) shares a number of features with the San José phase.

One of the pottery types showing the greatest similarity to our material is Calzadas Carved (Coe and Diehl 1980:162). The flat-based bowls, the bolstered-rim bowls, and the bowls left partly burnished/partly rough are very like Leandro Gray and Delfina Fine Gray examples. Indeed, as pointed out in Chapter 12, Coe's collections of Calzadas Carved include at least half a dozen sherds of Delfina or Leandro bowls made on Oaxaca clay bodies. When eroded, they would be hard to detect in such a collection; Nanette Pyne was able to pick them out because of slight differences in the repertoire of carved fire-serpent motifs between Oaxaca and southern Veracruz.

Interestingly—in spite of the similarities between Leandro Gray, Delfina Fine Gray, and Calzadas Carved—the Valley of Oaxaca has produced nothing resembling San Lorenzo's Limón Carved-Incised (Coe and Diehl 1980:171).

Xochiltepec White of the San Lorenzo phase (ibid.: Fig. 146) looks very much like the Xochiltepec White imported into the Valley of Oaxaca during the San José phase. Not surprisingly, more of this import ware showed up at San José Mogote than at smaller villages.

Other links to San Lorenzo, however, are more vague. Perdida Black-and-White flat-based bowls (Coe and Diehl 1980: Fig. 129) resemble our earliest San José Black-and-White, but our bowls are much more likely to be carved than are theirs. Aguatepec Thick bolstered-rim bowls of the San Lorenzo phase (ibid.: Fig. 153) look like Leandro Gray examples. Tatagapa Red rocker-stamped tecomates of both the Chicharras phase (ibid.: Fig. 132a-e) and the San Lorenzo phase (ibid.: Fig. 159c-f) look like San José Specular Red examples. Camaño Coarse punctate tecomates (ibid.: Fig. 135h) resemble Lupita Heavy Plain specimens. Mojonera Black of the San Lorenzo phase (ibid.: Fig. 151) has a slight resemblance to our Ocós Black. None of these resemblances, however, are as close as those between Tlapacoya-Zohapilco and San José Mogote. And the moment San Lorenzo enters the Nacaste phase (900–700 b.c.), its similarities to Oaxaca fade rapidly.

Relations to the South

When we turn our attention south toward the Isthmus of Tehuantepec, we see the same pattern we saw to the north; relationships with certain major centers are very strong, while relationships with smaller sites are more vague or generalized.

San José Mogote's relationships with the large sites of Mirador and Chiapa de Corzo in the Central Depression of Chiapas are very strong. During its Pac phase (1100–900 b.c.), Mirador shares both Calzadas Carved and Limón Carved-Incised with San Lorenzo (Agrinier 1989). It also shares Guamuchal Brushed, Tilapa Red-on-White, Pampas Black-and-White, and several other types with Salinas La Blanca and the Pacific Coast of Chiapas (ibid.). Our earlier chapters have already documented the importation of Guamuchal Brushed to San José Mogote, the strong resemblance of San José Red-on-White to Tilapa Red-on-White, the strong resemblance of San José Black-and-White to Pampas Black-and-White, and the link between Calzadas Carved and our Delfina and Leandro gray wares. What the presence of Guamuchal Brushed at Mirador means is that we may not need to look as far as the Guatemalan coast to find a source for the brushed tecomates imported to Area C of San José Mogote.

Chiapa de Corzo reaffirms the ties between Oaxaca and the Grijalva Depression. Of the six most common vessel shapes of Chiapa I (Dixon 1959: Fig. 1), only one (the everted-rim bowl) would not be typical of the San José phase. Dixon's Figure 52 shows tecomates with paired jabs, rocker stamping, and simple rim banding identical to those seen on tecomates in Lupita Heavy Plain and Fidencio Coarse. In our type descriptions, we have already noted such San José/Chiapa I similarities as incised white ware, giant macrorims, multicompartment vessels, and many other shared features.

Since the site of Laguna Zope, near Juchitán, lies between Chiapa de Corzo and San José Mogote, we might expect it to show similarities to both sites (Zeitlin 1979). These expectations are met. However, like many sites of the Tehuacán and Nochixtlán Valleys, Laguna Zope seems to lack the flamboyant explosion of pan-Mesoamerican motifs. Resemblances to San José are strongest during Zeitlin's Golfo phase (1100–800 b.c.). Suristmo White-slipped (Zeitlin 1979:160) resembles Atoyac Yellow-white, while Suristmo Red-on-White Slipped (ibid.: 181) resembles San José Red-on-White. Interestingly, while there are some depictions of the fire-serpent in the Golfo phase, they occur on white-slipped bowls (ibid.: Fig. D-43b), rather than on gray ware—the opposite of the pattern at San José Mogote.

To continue our comparisons, Suristmo Black-and-White Slipped of the Golfo phase strongly resembles San José Black-and-White; it occurs in tecomates, flat-based bowls, and bolstered-rim bowls (ibid.: Figs. D-46 to D-48). Both black-and-white pottery and white-slipped pottery have a long history at Laguna Zope, perhaps rivaling their antiquity at San Lorenzo and antedating their appearance in the Valley of Oaxaca.

Finally, Suristmo Buff Wiped tecomates of the Golfo phase (ibid.: Figs. D-6 to D-8) resemble Lupita Heavy Plain specimens, and Suristmo Buff Burnished annular based pot rests (ibid.: Fig. D-22d, e) look like Lupita Heavy Plain braziers/potstands.

Moving south to the Pacific Coast of Chiapas and Guatemala, our San José phase collections find parallels in the Cuadros phase at Salinas La Blanca (Coe and Flannery 1967). As we have pointed out earlier, Conchas White-to-Buff of the Cuadros phase resembles Atoyac Yellow-white; Pampas Black-and-White resembles San José Black-and-White; Tilapa Red-on-White resembles San José Red-on-White; and Guamuchal Brushed was actually imported into San José Mogote. In addition, Teófilo Punctate (ibid.: Plate 12) has areas of zoned slashes, sloppy jabs, neat jabs, punctations, and other plastic decorative attributes that show up on the shoulders of our Fidencio Coarse jars. However, now that we know that many of these types also occur at Mirador in western Chiapas, we are uncertain whether we should look to the Pacific Coast, the Grijalva Depression, or both regions for the source of our southern import wares.

How far to the south can we find ties to our San José phase material? A Gordon phase cemetery at Copán, Honduras, recently unearthed by Fash (1982), features cylinders and out-leaned-wall bowls carved with some of the same pan-Mesoamerican motifs we see at Tlapacoya and San José Mogote.

Expected Dates for the San José Phase

Having examined the ceramic crossties, we are now in a position to propose a date for the San José phase. The usual consensus among Mesoamericanists is that the florescence of pan-Mesoamerican motifs such as the fire-serpent and were-jaguar occurred between 1200 and 900 b.c. (Tolstoy 1989b).

The regional phases defined by individual investigators oscillate around this 300-year period. Coe and Diehl (1980) give 1150–900 b.c. for the San Lorenzo phase. Niederberger (1987) places her Ayotla phase at 1250–1000 b.c., somewhat earlier than San Lorenzo. Grove (1987) places his Barranca phase at 1100–700 b.c., slightly later. Agrinier's (1989) Pac phase is given as 1100–900 b.c.; Zeitlin's (1979) Golfo phase is 1100–800 b.c. Clark (1991) has now assigned the Cherla and Cuadros phases of the Pacific Coast to the time span 1150–900 b.c. We believe that it would be a mistake to place much emphasis on the slight ^{14}C differences among these phases. The differences are about what we would expect, given all the known problems with archaeological charcoal and the variations among radiocarbon laboratories.

Our expectation is that the San José phase should begin somewhere between 1200 and 1150 b.c. and end somewhere between 900 and 850 b.c. (uncalibrated).

Dates from the Zone D Midden, Area A, San José Mogote

We have no radiocarbon dates for the start of the San José phase, unless one considers the three already-discussed ^{14}C dates from the site of Tierras Largas to fall at the Tierras Largas/San José phase transition (see above). Four charcoal samples from the Zone D midden of Area A, San José Mogote, probably belong to the first half of the San José phase. They are as follows:

SI-466 (Zone D1)	1050 b.c. ± 120
GX-785 (Zone D1)	975 b.c. ± 85
SI-467 (Zone D2)	860 b.c. ± 120
M-2104 (Zone D3)	720 b.c. ± 200

Expected dates for this midden were 1150–1000 b.c. The Zone D1 dates meet this expectation. SI-466 seems perfect, while GX-785 looks only 25 years too recent; its one-sigma range covers the expected period easily.

The dates from Zones D2 and D3 are clearly too recent (especially since they came from lower strata within the midden). For what it's worth, adding one standard deviation pushes SI-467 back to 980 b.c. and M-2104 back to 920 b.c.

Dates from Household Units, Area A, San José Mogote

Five charcoal samples from household units in Area A, stratigraphically above the Zone D midden, were also run. They were as follows:

SI-462 (Household Unit C1)	690 b.c. ± 120
SI-463 (Household Unit C2)	780 b.c. ± 120
SI-464 (Household Unit C3)	1170 b.c. ± 120
GX-875 (Feature 2 [Unit C3])	930 b.c. ± 95
SI-465 (Household Unit C4)	980 b.c. ± 120

Our expectation was that these four household units might fall between 1100 and 900 b.c. The three dates from Units C3 and C4 meet our expectations; GX-875 and SI-465 are within our predicted range, while SI-464 is a mere 70 years older than expected (less than one standard deviation).

The dates from Units C1 and C2, however, are too young,

especially SI-462. Adding one standard deviation to SI-463 pushes it back to 900 b.c., a plausible date given the results of GX-875. However, adding one sigma to SI-462 only pushes it back to 810 b.c. This date is unacceptable because it falls in the Middle Formative Guadalupe phase. The ceramic assemblages from Units C2 and C1 indicate that they are relatively close in time to Unit C3; it is doubtful that more than 50 years separated each household unit from the one below it.

Thus, of the nine radiocarbon assays from Area A of San José Mogote, we consider five to be good; three to be fair; and only one (SI-462) to be bad, in terms of our expectations.

Dates from Area C, San José Mogote

Only two charcoal samples from Area C of San José Mogote have been run. They are as follows:

    M-2355 (Zone E, Master Profile)   660 b.c. ± 150
    M-2354 (Feature 24)   890 b.c. ± 150

Our expected date for both these proveniences was 1100–1000 b.c., based on ceramic crossties with other regions. Neither date meets our expectations, with M-2355 falling well into the Middle Formative Rosario phase. This is an impossible date, since at least ten indisputable San José phase houses lay stratigraphically above Zone E.

The date on Feature 24 (M-2354), on the other hand, is not too bad. Adding one standard deviation to it pushes the date back to 1040 b.c., within our expected range.

Dates from San Sebastián Abasolo

Three charcoal samples from San Sebastián Abasolo were associated with San José phase material. However, Abasolo is located in an area of the Valley of Oaxaca that seems never to have gone through a Guadalupe phase like the one we found in the Etla region. We anticipated, therefore, that the Abasolo area might have had a kind of "epi-San José" that lasted to 850–800 b.c. or even later.

One problem with charcoal samples from Abasolo is that the San José phase levels have all, at one time or another, been below the ground water table. The ground water in the vicinity of Abasolo has dissolved carbonates in it, some of it from old limestones and some from recent travertines. The effects of this ground water on charcoal submerged for centuries is unknown.

The three samples run were as follows:

    M-2358 (Feature 3)   650 b.c. ± 150
    M-2371 (Feature 3)   780 b.c. ± 150
    M-2357 (Zone D, Operation A)   730 b.c. ± 200

Our expected dates for these proveniences fall somewhere late in the San José phase—generally later than 950 b.c., and possibly as late as 800 b.c. if our suspicions about an "epi-San José" phenomenon are confirmed. The midpoints of all three dates seem too recent, but all three also have large standard deviations. If one adds one sigma to M-2357, it pushes the Zone D2 date back to 930 b.c.—not bad for a level expected to date to 950–850 b.c. Similarly, if one adds one sigma to M-2371, it pushes the filling-in of Feature 3 (a well) back to 930 b.c.

The other date for Feature 3 (M-2358) seems too recent even for an "epi-San José." Adding one standard deviation to the midpoint pushes it back to 800 b.c., barely within the limits of what we consider plausible.

Our evaluation of these Abasolo dates is that, while they could be used to support the notion of an "epi-San José" phase lasting until 800 b.c. in the eastern Valley of Oaxaca, we recommend waiting until we have run some charcoal samples that have not been submerged below the water table.

The San José-Guadalupe Transition in the Etla Region

In his review of radiocarbon dates from the Oaxaca region, Drennan (1983b:365) points out that the "only two reasonable dates" for the transition from the San José phase to the Guadalupe phase are M-2102 (850 b.c. ± 150) and GX-1296 (840 b.c. ± 160). If this is the case—and we believe that it is—then the San José phase in the Etla region must have ended by 900 or 850 b.c. This seems plausible on the basis of our ceramic crossties with other parts of Mesoamerica. It also leaves open the possibility of a longer San José phase in those parts of the valley where no true Guadalupe ceramic complex ever appeared.

Sample M-2012 affords us the opportunity to reinforce our earlier observations about differences between radiocarbon laboratories. Let us return for a moment to Figure 4.8 of Chapter 4, the profile drawing of Area A at Barrio del Rosario Huitzo. In the lower right corner of the drawing, in Zone F3, appears a dark-shaded object labeled "carbon from burnt post." This heavy post was part of a public building of the early Guadalupe phase. So much charcoal was available that we divided the sample into two identical halves. Half went to the University of Michigan radiocarbon lab; half went to Geochron Labs. The results were as follows:

    M-2102 (pine post, Zone F3)   850 b.c. ± 150
    GX-1126 (pine post, Zone F3)   1400 b.c. ± 140

Note that M-2102 fits our expectation for an early Guadalupe provenience, 850 b.c. On the other hand, GX-1126 falls in the early Tierras Largas phase! If the post had been made of baldcypress, which can live up to a thousand years, we might be able to explain away this discrepancy by arguing that the Geochron sample had come from the inner rings, while the Michigan sample came from the outer rings. But ethnobotanist Richard Ford has identified this post as pine, and from a tree hardly likely to have lived 550 years.

Conclusion

We recommend that archaeologists revive the age-old technique of correlating sites by ceramic crossties. When two sites have identical ceramics, it is likely that they are contemporaneous. When your radiocarbon assays contradict the ceramic crossties, we suggest that you defer to the crossties; they are probably more reliable. There are still so many problems with radiocarbon dating that archaeologists need to consider not only their own radiocarbon assays, but also those of every other archaeologist working on the same ceramic horizon.

On those grounds, we propose the following dates (in uncalibrated radiocarbon years) for our Early Formative phases. We believe that our Espiridión complex falls somewhere between 1900 and 1400 b.c., and perhaps no earlier than 1600–1500 b.c. We believe that our Tierras Largas phase begins by 1400 or 1350 b.c. and lasts until 1200 or 1150 b.c. We believe that our San José phase begins by 1200 or 1150 b.c. and lasts until 900 or 850 b.c. in the Etla and central regions of the Valley of Oaxaca. In those regions, the transition to a Guadalupe phase was evidently complete by 850 b.c. In the extreme eastern and southern parts of the valley, where we have so far found little evidence for a Guadalupe ceramic complex, a kind of "epi-San José" may have lasted until 850–800 b.c., or even slightly later.

Chapter 20

The Olmec and the Valley of Oaxaca: A Revision

In October of 1967, a conference on the Olmec was held at Dumbarton Oaks in Washington, D.C. Michael D. Coe, who only a year earlier had begun work at San Lorenzo in Veracruz, presented a paper (Coe 1968). Flannery, who only a year earlier had begun work in the Valley of Oaxaca, also presented a paper (Flannery 1968). A paper by David Grove, who only a year earlier had begun work in Morelos, was added to the symposium volume (Grove 1968). Perspective on the Gulf Coast was added by some of the pioneers of Olmec archaeology, researchers such as Matthew Stirling (1968) and Robert Heizer (1968).

To understand the papers given at the conference, one has to consider what was known in 1967. Drucker, Heizer, and Squier (1959) had laid out before us the wonders of Complex A at La Venta, a series of public buildings and monuments oriented 8° west of true north. Their radiocarbon dates had shown it to be Middle Formative in date. Coe's new radiocarbon dates suggested that "Olmec culture," including the carving of colossal heads, might go back to the Early Formative (1200–900 b.c.). All other Formative sites seemed to pale by comparison, although it was becoming clear that many had "ties" to the Gulf Coast. These ties took the form of shared ceramics, and in particular, shared design motifs such as the were-jaguar and fire-serpent.

Little was known about the Early Formative in other regions of Mexico. To be sure, Coe (1961) had discovered the flamboyant Ocós culture of Soconusco, but it was distinctly non-Olmec. Early Formative had been found at Chiapa de Corzo (Dixon 1959), but it came from the lower levels of deep soundings below the more spectacular Late Formative deposits at the site. Tehuacán was known to have Early Formative (MacNeish 1964), but it was thought to be unspectacular. Tlatilco in the Basin of Mexico was known to have "stylistic ties" to the Olmec, but it would be three more years before Tolstoy and Paradis (1970) revised the Formative chronology of the Basin to show that this "Olmec-looking" material was Early Formative. Christine Niederberger had not yet carried out her excavation at the Zohapilco sector of Tlapacoya, which would push back the Basin of Mexico sequence still further (Niederberger 1987).

The result is that the audience at Dumbarton Oaks heard a lot about the "Olmec Heartland" or "Metropolitan Olmec" (i.e., the southern Gulf Coast) versus the "Colonial Olmec" or "Provincial Olmec" (i.e., every other part of Mesoamerica). They were told that the Basin of Mexico was too high and too cold to have developed as precociously as the Gulf Coast did; the Valleys of Oaxaca and Tehuacán were too arid, inevitably lagging behind the Olmec Heartland. The model was one of an Olmec "mother culture" that eventually civilized the rest of Mesoamerica. It was not clear whether this civilizing had been done by conquest, by religious missionary work, by the establishment of colonies outside the Heartland, or by economic imperialism. All that seemed certain was that the backward, marginal cultures of highland Mesoamerica would never have become civilized had the Olmec not colonized or acculturated them.

One dissenting voice at the Dumbarton Oaks conference was Flannery (1968:79–80), who refused to see the Valley of Oaxaca as having been invaded by Olmec armies or proselytized by Olmec missionaries. Even then, with only limited settlement pattern survey data available, it was clear that the population density of the Mexican highlands was too high for us to imagine it as a vacuum waiting to be filled. How, then, to explain the similarity of excised designs on Oaxaca's Leandro Gray and San Lorenzo's Calzadas Carved? How to explain the shared fire-serpents, were-jaguars, U-motifs, St. Andrew's crosses, and "paw-wing" motifs?

What Flannery proposed was a model for interaction between Oaxaca and the Olmec that was based on ethnographic analogy. The analogy was provided by Leach's (1954) classic description of highland Burma, where more sophisticated valley-dwelling Shan were supplied with jade by Kachin hill tribes; and by McClellan's (1953) description of the Pacific Northwest, where the more highly ranked Tlingit were supplied with furs by their Athabascan neighbors. In both cases, the less sophisticated group who supplied the resource began to emulate the behavior, symbolism, and status trappings of their more sophisticated neighbors. Some Kachin tribes became "Hill Shan"; some Athabascans became "Inland Tlingit." It happened without conquest, without colonization, and without religious proselytizing, although there was often a movement of brides from the more sophisticated group to the less sophisticated.

In this analogy, the San José phase villagers were seen as suppliers of such goods as magnetite mirrors to the more sophisticated Olmec. This part of the model, at least, is confirmed by trace element analysis of two mirrors from San Lorenzo that were made on Valley of Oaxaca magnetite (Pires-Ferreira 1975). On the basis of this interaction, the villagers of the Valley of Oaxaca were thought to have picked up many aspects of Olmec behavior—carving were-jaguars and fire-serpents on their pottery, building adobe mounds, orienting their public buildings 8° west of true north, and so on. It was even considered possible that Olmec women might have married high-ranking men at San José Mogote. This possibility was supported by the discovery of young women, such as Burial 1 of San José Mogote, whose cranial deformation differed from the usual Early Formative Oaxaca style.

To be sure, Flannery did not see the Oaxaca villagers as having been converted by Olmec contact into a rank society. On the contrary, he argued that only those highland societies which *already had an emerging elite* would have had an interest in the Olmec. "The areas most likely to form exchange systems with, and truly emulate the behavior and symbolism of, the Olmec were not the least developed regions of the highlands, but the most developed—areas of high agricultural and demographic potential like the Valleys of Oaxaca, Mexico, Morelos, and Puebla, for example" (Flannery 1968:106).

Thus, in 1967, we had at least two contrasting views on the relationship between highland Mexico and the Gulf Coast. One held that an Olmec "mother culture," spreading out of the lowlands, had civilized the highlands through colonization, conquest, or missionization. The other held that rank societies had evolved independently in the highlands, but that none of them were quite as highly evolved as the Olmec. In the latter view, highland societies supplied the Olmec with exotic raw materials and borrowed a lot of Olmec iconography. This view gave the societies of the highlands credit for developing to a rank society level on their own, but it was still—as pointed out recently by Love (1991:73)—an "Olmec-centric" view. It still assumed that the "advanced and sophisticated Olmec had an unmistakable impact on their less advanced and less sophisticated highland neighbors" (Flannery 1968:79).

A quarter of a century has passed since the Dumbarton Oaks Conference on the Olmec. In those twenty-five years, a lot of research has been brought to completion and a lot of ideas have changed. Coe and Diehl (1980) have brought out the San Lorenzo report. Grove (1987) has brought out his work at Chalcatzingo in Morelos. The first fifteen years of work on San José Mogote are now in the process of being written up. And there has been another conference on the Olmec, this time at the School of American Research in Santa Fe (Sharer and Grove [eds.] 1989). Not unexpectedly, all this new research requires some major revisions to Flannery's 1968 model.

Perhaps the most significant difference between the 1968 Dumbarton Oaks volume and the 1989 Santa Fe volume is that most Formative specialists no longer see the Olmec as a "mother culture." Rather, to borrow Norman Hammond's (1989) phrase, they see the various regional developments of 1200–900 b.c. as "sister cultures" whose interaction accelerated the evolution of complex society everywhere in Mesoamerica.

This new view is only partly the result of excavations in Oaxaca, Morelos, Soconusco, and the Basin of Mexico, which has shown those regions to be less "underdeveloped" than once thought. It is also partly the result of Coe and Diehl's excavations at San Lorenzo, which make "the Gulf Coast societies no longer seem as precocious as once thought" (Love 1991:73). Love goes on to say:

> Stripped of their privileged status as more complex and as the nexus of stylistic generation, the Gulf Coast societies now appear to be only one part of a group of early complex societies that participated in a network of shared style, iconography, and symbology. We are now free to place less emphasis on the chronological interpretation of style, with its focus on the origins and geographical distribution of style, and examine the way style operates in a social context. [Love 1991:73]

This revised view of the Olmec immediately calls into question the application of the term "Olmec" to everything and anything artistically interesting in Early Formative Mesoamerica. As Grove (1989:9) points out in the Santa Fe volume, over the years the term Olmec "has come to mean just about anything anyone wishes it to. The term has now passed far beyond the original definition of a Gulf coast archaeological culture, to also encompass certain types or classes of artifacts found outside of that region ('Olmec jades,' 'Olmec roller seals,' 'Olmec baby-face figurines') . . . 'Olmec motifs' . . . and an 'Olmec art style' represented by the same symbols or motifs."

To this we would add that many of the artifacts Grove mentions are more abundant *outside* the Gulf Coast than within it. For example, large hollow "baby-face" figurines and roller stamps are far more common in the Basin of Mexico than at San Lorenzo or La Venta. It is difficult to imagine why artifacts more typical of Tlatilco, Tlapacoya, or Las Bocas than the Gulf Coast should be called "Olmec."

"Is it not misleading," Grove (1989:10) goes on to say, "to label non-Gulf coast artifacts as 'Olmec'? To do so obscures their actual function or meaning within any regional society because it preordains an interpretation that their importance was somehow linked to the Gulf coast Olmec. Several archaeologists have informed me that they realize such artifacts are not Olmec but continue to use the term because it is a 'convenient' descriptive adjective."

Grove (ibid.) proposes substituting a more culturally neutral term, such as "X Complex," which does not imply that all such artifacts and motifs originated in one area. This is not the first time that such a term has been proposed. The problem has always been gaining widespread acceptance for such a label, and no one has ever been able to explain why certain terms catch on with archaeologists and others do not.

In a very important passage, Grove (1989:11) goes on to show that many of the pan-Mesoamerican motifs discussed in Chapter

12 of this volume are treated differently at San Lorenzo, Tlatilco, Las Bocas, Tlapacoya, Chalcatzingo, and San José Mogote. The repertoire of motifs is different at each site, the vessel forms on which they are executed are different, and the surface colors with which they are associated are different. Grove might well have added that certain motifs do not occur at San Lorenzo at all, which is why Nanette Pyne was able to pick imported Delfina Fine Gray sherds from Oaxaca out of Coe's Calzadas Carved collections (see Chapter 12).

Grove (1989:13–14) concludes:

> Those of us believing in regional cultural developments "independent" of the Gulf coast are not trivializing the Gulf coast achievements nor insisting that interaction did not take place . . . However, for decades now a few "Olmec" potsherds or figurine fragments have provided easy "answers" to explain complex sociopolitical developments outside of the Gulf coast . . . [We] cannot afford at this time to use the same term for artifacts and art motifs which we also use to name an archaeological culture. Those terms *do* create implications of "source" and "influences," whether intended . . . or not.

In light of this new perspective on the Early Formative, we shall provide in the remainder of this chapter a revision of Flannery's 1968 paper, "The Olmec and the Valley of Oaxaca," bringing it more in line with the discoveries of the last 25 years.

How Our Ideas Have Changed

1) In 1967, it was widely believed that the Olmec were Mesoamerica's first complex society. That view is no longer universally held. New work on the Pacific Coast of Chiapas has now led Clark (1991) and Blake (1991) to claim that that region might have reached a "chiefdom" or rank society level of sociopolitical development prior to 1200 b.c.

It is more difficult than most archaeologists think to provide a convincing argument for early rank society. Just having large mounds or well-made buildings is not enough. It must be shown that differences in rank were inherited, not merely achieved, and it must be shown that public works were directed by an elite rather than resulting from community collaboration. While all the facts are not yet in, it would not surprise us to learn that there were minimal chiefdoms in Soconusco by the Ocós phase. There is no suggestion that the Gulf Coast had achieved rank society that early; Coe and Diehl (1980:137) acknowledge that fact when they describe their Ojochi phase as "a country-cousin version of the far more sophisticated Ocós phase of Guatemalan Soconusco."

2) In 1967, the best-known example of a ceremonial complex oriented 8° west of north was La Venta. When we found a Guadalupe phase building—Structure 3 of Huitzo—oriented the same way, we considered it possible that the Middle Formative people of Oaxaca had been influenced by their Gulf Coast contemporaries (Flannery 1968).

Two years later, however, we began to find public buildings of the Tierras Largas phase oriented 8° west of north. Those buildings were pre-Olmec, and associated with radiocarbon dates falling between 1400 and 1300 b.c. (see Chapter 19). All were set on low platforms and coated with lime plaster. No comparable buildings, and no comparable use of lime plaster, have been documented for the Gulf Coast at 1400–1300 b.c. At the present state of our knowledge, we would have to say that both the 8° orientation and the use of stucco were earlier in Oaxaca than on the Gulf Coast.

Moreover, even in later periods of the Formative, Oaxaca's architecture seems more advanced than that of the Gulf Coast. Bun-shaped adobes are apparently earlier in Oaxaca than on the Gulf; so too is stone masonry, including stairways like those on Structure 2 of San José Mogote (see Fig. 18.10). Both areas had rectangular adobes in the Middle Formative, but the Rosario phase of Oaxaca also had stone masonry platforms made of multiton limestone blocks (Flannery and Marcus 1976a, 1983a).

Finally, it is now clear that much of Middle Formative La Venta was contemporaneous with Period Ia of Monte Albán, which began by 500 b.c. There is no doubt that La Venta is an impressive site, but Monte Albán was an even more spectacular stone masonry urban center from the moment of its founding. Thus, there would seem to be no reason to attribute Oaxaca's precocious public architecture to "Olmec influence."

3) In 1967, it was assumed that something called "the Olmec style" had originated on the Gulf Coast. Any hints of such style in the highlands were therefore attributed to emanations from the Gulf. Some archaeologists even attempted to use the midpoints of radiocarbon dates to document an alleged slow diffusion of various pottery motifs from lowlands to highlands.

We now believe that, on the contrary, excised motifs such as the fire-serpent and were-jaguar appeared essentially simultaneously on the Gulf, in the Basin of Mexico, in Oaxaca, and in Chiapas. Coe and Diehl (1980) have selected 1150 b.c. for the start of the San Lorenzo phase, essentially the same beginning we have selected for the San José phase. Only Niederberger (1987) has selected an earlier date for the excised motifs, by beginning her Ayotla phase at 1250 b.c. Such differences in chronology seem to us merely to reflect the differences between radiocarbon labs and conditions of charcoal deposition.

Where did all these motifs begin? The fact is that there is no one region where all of them are found. San Lorenzo does not have the full range of fire-serpent or were-jaguar motifs, nor does Tlapacoya, nor does San José Mogote; rather, each site has its own repertoire. Moreover, there are certain motifs that are ten times as common at Tlapacoya-Zohapilco or San José Mogote as they are at San Lorenzo or La Venta. To call such motifs "Olmec" makes no sense to us.

Grove (1989) has suggested that much of the iconography of the period 1200–900 b.c. may simply be the first representation, in ceramics, of symbols whose origin goes back to an earlier time. They may not represent the sudden inventions of one regional culture, but rather a body of cosmological and iconographic material shared by the common ancestors of many Formative societies. Indeed, there have been prior suggestions that the motifs themselves might have existed earlier in a different medium. Forty years ago, Muriel Porter (1953:36) described the style of excising seen on Tlatilco vessels as "massive and slow in feeling and design, suggesting that it might originally have been a motif applied to vessels of stone or wood" (or, one might add, to pyro-engraved gourds).

We agree with Grove that the pan-Mesoamerican motifs of 1200–900 b.c. are more likely to reflect the common ancestry of Formative cultures than the differential brilliance of one culture. The ideas behind them may have been there for centuries prior to their first appearance on pottery, and the use of excising may indeed reflect the transfer of designs from wood or gourds to ceramics.

4) In 1967, the Gulf Coast was regarded as precocious; it was argued that river levee agriculture there had been extraordinarily productive, leading to high populations and rapid social evolution. The Basin of Mexico, on the other hand, was considered "too high" and "too cold" for successful early agriculture. Its frosts, its high altitude, and its relative aridity were thought to have slowed the development of agriculture, population, and social complexity. This predisposed us to think of Gulf Coast influences on Oaxaca.

Today that contrast seems overdrawn. For one thing, settlement pattern surveys have shown both the Basin of Mexico and the Valley of Oaxaca to have had impressive Early Formative populations, rivaling or even exceeding those of the Southern Gulf. For example, surveys by Kowalewski et al. (1989) have revealed at least 40 San José phase settlements in the Valley of Oaxaca, with an estimated population of nearly 2,000 persons. For the equivalent period in the Basin of Mexico ("Early Horizon Phase II"), the known sites include two large villages, one small village, twelve hamlets, and two indeterminate occupations, with an estimated total population of 4,000 to 5,000 persons (Sanders, Parsons, and Santley 1979:183). As Kowalewski et al. (1989:67) point out, "this would be about two or three times the total population of the Valley of Oaxaca, but because the Basin of Mexico is much larger, the densities are roughly equivalent."

Not only do these surveys reveal the Basin of Mexico to be far from the backward, agriculturally marginal region it was once thought to be, they show it to have had a considerable Early Formative population. Three of the Basin sites—Tlatilco, Coapexco, and Tlapacoya—are among the largest population concentrations of their time period in Mesoamerica. Moreover, the intersite comparisons we carried out in Chapter 19 now indicate that San José phase pottery is much more like the pottery of Tlapacoya-Zohapilco and Tlatilco than it is like the pottery of San Lorenzo. It seems to have been the southern Basin of Mexico—*not* the southern Gulf Coast—with which the Early Formative villagers of the Valley of Oaxaca interacted most closely.

Moreover, it is now clear that some of the most developed and sophisticated versions of Early Formative motifs occurred in the Basin of Mexico. Let us look at the depictions of the were-jaguar in Figure 20.1, both of which come from Tlapacoya. These are not simple, provincial imitations of motifs that were more elaborate in some "Olmec Heartland"; they rival or exceed in sophistication anything pictured by Coe and Diehl (1980) from San Lorenzo. The same could be said of the large, hollow, white-slipped "baby face" dolls so typical of Tlatilco, Las Bocas, and Tlapacoya; they are clearly a highland product, one that is represented at San Lorenzo only by occasional fragments. We therefore conclude that there is a substantial body of Early Formative material, including both artifacts and ceramic motifs, that should be considered more properly "Central Mexican" than "Olmec." This body of material more strongly influenced San José Mogote than did anything from San Lorenzo.

5) The current revision of our thinking is not based solely on new data that show the highlands to have been more advanced than we formerly thought. It is also based on Coe and Diehl's San Lorenzo report, which shows the Early Formative Olmec not to have been as far ahead of their highland neighbors as we expected. Palangana phase San Lorenzo is thought to have had a series of mounds laid out in imitation of Complex A at La Venta, but that mound series was a Middle Formative accomplishment. When we move back to the Chicharras and San Lorenzo phases, we find no lime-plastered public buildings, no adobe platforms, no stone masonry like that of Oaxaca. A great many of the earthen mounds at the site, which we had anticipated would be early, apparently date to the Late Classic Villa Alta phase. Perhaps most surprising is the discovery that the highest-ranking Olmec who ever lived at San Lorenzo probably lived in a thatched-roof, wattle-and-daub house, just like everyone at Tlapacoya or San José Mogote.

Indeed, the biggest difference between San Lorenzo and its highland contemporaries was its corpus of stone monuments, including the famous colossal heads. These monuments are properly called "Olmec," because they do not occur outside the Olmec region. They are magnificent, but they are no larger nor more spectacular than the colossal sculptures of Easter Island, which we know were produced by a chiefdom (Bahn and Flenley 1992). By themselves, they do not elevate Olmec culture to a level of sociopolitical complexity higher than that of chiefdoms in the Basin of Mexico, Morelos, or Oaxaca. By themselves, they cannot make us forget that San Lorenzo was essentially a large village of wattle-and-daub structures, some of them probably on low earthen mounds. San Lorenzo invested its human labor in basalt monuments while San José Mogote invested in stone masonry platforms, adobes, and lime plaster.

If Olmec influence had really provided the impetus for cultural evolution in the highlands, we would expect to see highland imitations of San Lorenzo's monuments. There are sources of volcanic rock near Tlapacoya and Tlatilco that could have been used; they weren't. San José Mogote had access to the same soft volcanic tuffs from which the palaces of Mitla were carved; they could have been used for colossal heads, but weren't. The only

tures had their own list of priorities and were not simply imitating Olmec prototypes.

A Revised Model for 1994

Our 1994 position, therefore, is that Early Formative Mesoamerica did not have a *cultura madre;* to borrow Hammond's (1989) phrase, it consisted of many *culturas hermanas.* We suspect that the dichotomy of Earth and Sky proposed by Marcus (1989) is very ancient and widespread, and that even the iconography of were-jaguar (= Earth and Earthquake) and fire-serpent (= Sky and Lightning) may have antedated 1200 b.c. We base this conclusion on the fact that both supernatural beings are seen in highly stylized form at the moment of their first appearance on pottery. The fact that they occur in excised (or incised-excised) technique may mean that the motifs were transferred to pottery from wooden vessels or gourds. We believe that this transfer to pottery took place essentially simultaneously over the entire area from the Basin of Mexico to Copán, reaching its peak between 1150 and 900 b.c. We believe that its rapid and widespread dispersal resulted from the much higher level of interregional interaction that accompanied the rise of rank society in Mesoamerica. At the same time, we note that each region had its own design repertoire, which only partially overlapped with those of other regions.

We still support some aspects of Flannery's 1968 paper on the Olmec and the Valley of Oaxaca. For example, we still believe that the Shan/Kachin and Tlingit/Athabascan cases provide useful models for the interaction of neighboring cultures when one group is more sophisticated than the other. However, we no longer believe that the Olmec were significantly more sophisticated than the Valley of Oaxaca cultures; indeed, in areas such as public architecture, the Valley of Oaxaca appears to have been more sophisticated than the Olmec. We also still believe that the circulation of exotic raw materials used in status paraphernalia—jade, magnetite, pearl oyster, *Spondylus,* and other items—was one of the most important mechanisms linking all regions of Formative Mesoamerica and providing conduits for new ideas, new motifs, and even exchanges of brides. However, we no longer believe that the Gulf Coast was the region San José Mogote most closely interacted with; we would now assign that role to the Basin of Mexico.

We still believe that Mesoamerica's Early Formative cultures were in close contact with each other, and that neighboring elites made gifts of exotic items to each other. However, we now believe that we overestimated the amount of imitation, and underestimated the amount of competition, between Early Formative chiefdoms. At the level of rank society, the latter is typically an impetus for the accomplishment of great things.

Suggestions for the Future

Like the majority of the authors in the 1989 Santa Fe volume, we suggest that archaeologists restrict the term "Olmec" to the

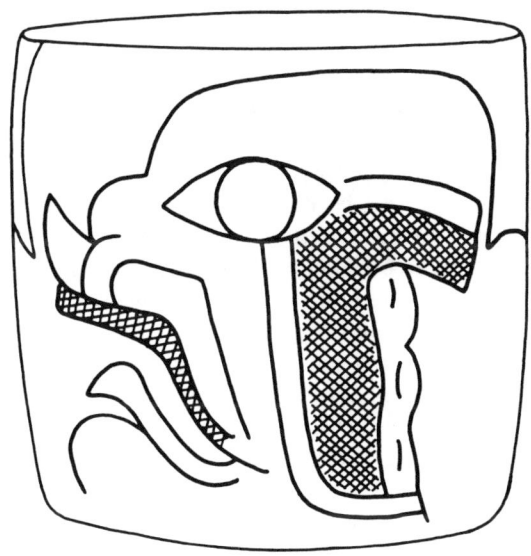

Figure 20.1. Depictions of Earth, or the were-jaguar, on white-slipped vessels from Tlapacoya, Basin of Mexico. Iconographically, these vessels are as sophisticated as (or more sophisticated than) any found at San Lorenzo on the Gulf Coast. (Redrawn from Niederberger 1987: Figs. 439 and 449.)

two stone monuments of the San José phase are non-Olmec in style (see Fig. 18.9). Chalcatzingo carved magnificent scenes on the living rock in Middle Formative times, but none of its products are like San Lorenzo's sculpture-in-the-round. All of these highland cultures *could* have carved colossal heads, had they wanted to. The fact that they didn't even try—not even to the extent of crude imitations—should tell us that highland cul-

southern Gulf Coast. San Lorenzo, La Venta, and Tres Zapotes are Olmec; Tlatilco, Tlapacoya-Zohapilco, San José Mogote, Las Bocas, Etlatongo, and Chalcatzingo are not. Colossal basalt heads are Olmec; hollow, white-slipped "baby face" dolls and roller stamps are not. We also suggest the elimination of terms such as "Olmec Heartland," "Metropolitan Olmec," and "Colonial Olmec," because they imply the presence of an empire where none existed. The southern Gulf Coast was not so much the "heartland" of the Olmec as the *only* land of the Olmec.

As for the widespread were-jaguars, fire-serpents, U-motifs, St. Andrew's crosses, and other designs of the period 1200–900 b.c., we propose that they simply be called "pan-Mesoamerican motifs," as they are in this volume. Some motifs are largely associated with the Basin of Mexico, others with Oaxaca, still others with the Gulf Coast. The ideas behind them are probably very ancient and widespread, and no region shows us more than a small percent of the inventory. Moreover, as Grove (1989) points out, their associations are different from region to region. In Oaxaca, excised fire-serpents are associated with men's burials (Flannery and Marcus 1976b). In the Basin of Mexico, they are associated with women's burials (Tolstoy 1989a).

Finally, what name can we give to the period 1200–900 b.c.? If we can't call it "Olmec," what can we call it? Jiménez Moreno (1966) proposed the term *Tenocelome,* but it failed to catch on. Grove (1989) has used "X Complex," but it is not yet clear whether or not it will catch on. As we have said, no one has been able to predict why certain names catch on with archaeologists and others don't.

One term that does seem to be gaining in acceptance is "Early Horizon." This is a designation borrowed from Andean archaeologists (Uhle 1913; Rowe 1960, 1962). In Peru, the term has been used to identify the first period in the archaeological sequence in which a genuine "horizon style" can be said to have swept over the ceramics of the entire culture area.

More and more Mesoamericanists are using this term, but doing so inappropriately by Peruvian standards. In Mesoamerica, the term is usually applied to the entire Early Formative, from 1900 to 900 b.c. This is inappropriate, because there was no "horizon style" in Mesoamerica prior to 1200 or 1150 b.c. For example, between 1400 and 1150 b.c., as pointed out by Clark (1991: Fig. 8), Mexico was divided into "red-on-buff" vs. "Locona interaction sphere" ceramic provinces.

If Mesoamericanists are willing to restrict the term "Early Horizon" to the period between 1200/1150 b.c. and 900/850 b.c., we would find it an acceptable label. During that period, pan-Mesoamerican motifs excised on pottery, differentially fired black-and-white wares, and rocker stamped tecomates do indeed combine to give us a genuine "style horizon" stretching from Tlatilco to Copán.

The term "Early Horizon," however, should not be extended beyond those temporal limits. There is much greater regionalism before 1200 b.c. and after 850 b.c. Purrón, Espiridión, Tierras Largas, Barra, Ocós, Ojochi, Nevada, and other pre-1200 b.c. cultures should simply continue to be called "Early Formative" (or by analogy with Peru, "Initial Period"). Guadalupe, Nacaste, Conchas I, and other post–850 b.c. cultures simply should continue to be called "Middle Formative."

No one doubts that the Olmec of the southern Gulf Coast made major contributions to the art and iconography of this "Early Horizon." They were the creators of the colossal basalt head, and their Middle Formative descendants went on to create parabolic hematite mirrors and massive offerings of jade and serpentine celts. The Early Horizon Olmec were not, however, the creators of lime plaster, adobe architecture, stone masonry, well irrigation, canal irrigation, check dams, and architectural terracing. Those accomplishments, and many others, we owe to regions outside the southern Gulf. We need to understand those regions, and our understanding has been hampered by models in which the Olmec, acting like an urban Mesopotamian state, civilize everybody else.

Of all the areas slighted by such models, it is perhaps the Basin of Mexico that has been most unfairly treated. It is now clear that it could not have been the high, cold, marginal area it was once portrayed to be. Some 4,000 to 5,000 people, most of them living in the southern Basin, produced some of the best and most sophisticated ceramics of the Early Horizon. They created many of the artifacts and motifs we most associate with that horizon, and they exerted more influence on areas like the Valley of Oaxaca than the Olmec ever did. We believe that more extensive work at places like Tlapacoya and Tlatilco might well produce public buildings like those of the Tierras Largas and San José phases. Indeed, we will be surprised and disappointed if such buildings do not show up.

Chapter 21

Resumen en Español

por Sonia Guillén

Este volumen presenta un análisis de los tipos de cerámica del horizonte Formativo Temprano en el Valle de Oaxaca. Las épocas son: *complejo Espiridión* (1900–1400 a.C.), *fase Tierras Largas* (1400–1150 a.C.), y *fase San José* (1150–850 a.C.). El primer capítulo elabora sobre el contenido de este libro.

El Capítulo 2 fue escrito por el ceramólogo William O. Payne. Su trabajo identifica las fuentes de materia prima (barro, engobes, pigmentos) en la geología del valle. Además, Payne presenta lo que se conoce sobre la fabricación de cerámica en la época Formativa en Oaxaca: el uso del molde y del platillo (*tournette*), y el método de cocción sobre la superficie del terreno. En el Capítulo 3 se examina la manera como se elabora la cerámica en cuatro aldeas tradicionales del valle—San Marcos, Coyotepec, Ocotlán, y Atzompa—señalándose varias técnicas que probablemente han sobrevivido desde la época Formativa.

El Capítulo 4 examina los procesos de formación de los sitios Formativos del Valle de Oaxaca y la manera como esos procesos afectan la calidad de las colecciones de tiestos. Se toman en cuenta los depósitos de (1) la casa; (2) el solar de la casa; (3) el pozo tronco-cónico; (4) el pequeño basural del barrio; (5) el gran basural del pueblo; (6) el relleno del edificio público; y (7) el relleno del arroyo intrusivo. Este volumen pone énfasis solamente en aquellas colecciones de tiestos provenientes de depósitos o contextos primarios, es decir, en las colecciones que no han sido redepositadas.

En el Capítulo 5 se discute la idea que toda variación en las muestras de cerámica representa diferencias cronológicas (diacrónicas). En los sitios Formativos de Oaxaca existe abundante variación sincrónica entre muestras contemporáneas—por ejemplo, en las diferencias entre la cerámica de familias de alto y bajo rango; las diferencias entre barrios de la misma aldea grande; y las diferencias entre aldeas de la región de Etla y aldeas de la región de Tlacolula. Esa variación sincrónica es investigada en los Capítulos 15, 16, y 17.

El Capítulo 6 presenta la tipología escogida para el presente estudio. Uno de los objetivos fue correlacionar la cerámica oaxaqueña con colecciones Formativas de la Cuenca de México; de los valles de Tehuacán, Morelos y Nochixtlán; del Istmo de Tehuantepec; de la Costa del Golfo; de la Cuenca del Río Grijalva; y de la Costa de Soconusco. La tipología escogida facilita comparaciones con los estudios hechos en todas estas regiones; desafortunadamente, no corresponde con la tipología empleada en Monte Albán por Caso, Bernal y Acosta (1967). En un futuro estudio del Formativo Medio los autores tratarán de vincular las dos tipologías divergentes.

El Capítulo 7 presenta la descripción del complejo Espiridión, es decir, la cerámica más antigua que se conoce hasta ahora en el Valle de Oaxaca. Esta cerámica está relacionada con el complejo Purrón del Valle de Tehuacán (MacNeish, Peterson, y Flannery 1970). Las vasijas son ollas muy sencillas y cajetes hemisféricos sin decoración ni pintura; toda la cerámica es de color natural: café claro o bayo, a veces con manchas oscuras causadas durante la cocción. Se han distinguido tres tipos: Purrón Plain (ollas muy sencillas y burdas, un tipo encontrado por MacNeish en Tehuacán); Espiridión Thin (cajetes hemisféricos muy delgados, casi imitando a una jícara); y Tierras Largas Burnished Plain (ollas y cajetes hemisféricos ligeramente bruñidos, un tipo que es más frecuente en la fase Tierras Largas). Existe además una pequeña mascarita o cabeza de una figurilla que representa un felino—hasta ahora el objeto de "arte" más antiguo del valle. Se considera posible que la mayoría de formas del complejo Espiridión sean imitaciones (en barro) de vasijas de jícara de la época precerámica. Casi toda la colección de cerámica del complejo Espiridión se encontró en el piso de Casa 20 del sitio de San José Mogote (Etla), una pequeña choza de carrizo y barro (bajareque).

En el Capítulo 8 se presentan los tipos de cerámica de la fase Tierras Largas. El Tierras Largas Burnished Plain (de color bayo natural ligeramente bruñido) obtiene su máxima popularidad durante esta fase, que se inicia entre 1400 y 1350 a.C. y termina entre 1200 y 1150 a.C. Una variedad no bruñida (*Tierras Largas Unburnished Plain*) es menos común y puede constar de vasijas no terminadas o malamente hechas. Las formas son ollas, cajetes hemisféricos, cajetes de fondo plano y paredes inclinadas, y tecomates. La decoración, sumamente rara, se limita a pequeñas picaduras o ocasional "rocker stamp."

Dos tipos de esta época son rojo-sobre-bayo. Avelina Red-on-Buff es el más común y aparece en forma de ollas o cajetes hemisféricos. El barro es similar al de Tierras Largas Burnished Plain, pero las vasijas tienen rayas o diseños geométricos en pintura roja (hematita). El tipo Clementina Fine Red-on-Buff es menos común y aparece como una versión más fina de Avelina; a veces aparece en forma de botella.

Esta fase incluye otros tipos tales como Matadamas Red (principalmente ollas con un engobe de color rojo oscuro, a veces con pequeños cristales de hematita metálica), y Matadamas Orange (ollas y tecomates con un engobe naranja, a veces con "rocker stamp" o "dentate stamp").

Finalmente aparece un tipo de cerámica negra bien pulida, en los sitios más grandes y importantes de esta época. Parece ser el tipo Ocós Black, originalmente descubierto por Coe (1961) en la zona de Chiapas/Guatemala. Se presenta en forma de cajete, tecomate, o botella; mientras algunos ejemplares son hechos con barro oaxaqueño, otros pueden ser importados de otras regiones.

El Capítulo 9 examina el Area C en el extremo oeste de sitio de San José Mogote, donde una estratigrafía muy detallada documenta la transición entre el complejo Espiridión y la fase Tierras Largas. Además, el Area C presenta una estratigrafía de capas de basural y varias casas de carrizo y barro de la fase Tierras Largas. En el Capítulo 10 se presenta una muestra de cuatro unidades domésticas y elementos domésticos de la misma fase—tres en el sitio de Tierras Largas y uno en el Area B de San José Mogote. Para todas las unidades se proporcionan porcentajes de la cerámica de cada tipo. En el Capítulo 11 se presenta la cerámica de tres edificios públicos de la fase Tierras Largas, las Estructuras 3, 5, y 6 de San José Mogote. Los Capítulos 9–11 comparan muestras de tiestos provenientes de tres contextos: basural, unidad doméstica, y edificio público.

El Capítulo 12 introduce la fase San José, que se inicia entre 1200 y 1150 a.C. y termina entre 900 y 850 a.C. Pertenece a un horizonte que muestra el estilo multiregional que anteriores generaciones de arqueólogos han llamado "Olmeca," un estilo que por varias razones preferimos llamar "pan-Mesoamericano" (véase el Capítulo 20). Se ven representaciones de las entidades "Tierra" (simbolizada por el "hombre-jaguar") y "Cielo" (simbolizado por la "serpiente de fuego" o "dragón del cielo"). Además, aparece por primera vez el motivo inciso que Coe (1961) llamó "double-line-break," aparentemente una simplificación de "Tierra/hombre-jaguar." Se presentan en el Capítulo 12 los inventarios completos de todos estos diseños, al menos en sus variantes o versiones oaxaqueñas.

La cerámica de la fase San José es muy llamativo por sus colores, su decoración, sus formas, y su abundante variación. Existen muchos tipos, y éstos se presentan en el Capítulo 12. Fidencio Coarse (un tipo utilitario algo tosco) aparece principalmente en forma de grandes ollas con un baño de color ladrillo. Estas piezas a veces son decoradas con zonas de picadura; tiestos de esas ollas forman gran parte de las muestras de basural de esta época.

Leandro Gray (un tipo gris oscuro bien pulido) es uno de los tipos más diagnósticos de la fase San José. Aparece en forma de vasos o cajetes cilíndricos, y platos o cajetes de fondo plano y paredes inclinadas, frecuentemente decorados con la "serpiente de fuego" en forma raspada. Además hay botellas, ollas con cuello cilíndrico, cajetes con borde reforzado, tecomates, platos vertederas, y vasijas efigies.

Atoyac Yellow-white es otro tipo importante de esta fase; tiene un engobe de kaolín (blanco amarilloso) sobre un barro café o bayo. Aparece en casi las mismas formas que se encuentran en Leandro Gray: cajetes cilíndricos, cajetes de fondo plano y paredes inclinadas, botellas, ollas con cuello cilíndrico, cajetes con borde reforzado, platos vertederas, tecomates, etc. Pero los cajetes en Atoyac Yellow-white tienen una frecuencia mayor de diseños "hombre-jaguar" o líneas incisas con "double-line-break." Además son más comunes en este tipo los tecomates con "rocker stamp" o picadura en zonas.

En esta fase abundan otros tipos de cerámica. San José Red-on-White tiene el mismo engobe blanco amarilloso que hemos visto en Atoyac Yellow-white, pero con rayas o zonas de engobe rojo encima. Aparece principalmente en forma de tecomate o cajete de fondo plano. Lupita Heavy Plain es un tipo tosco, de color bayo natural, que normalmente se encuentra en forma de brasero con soporte anular.

Un tipo "híbrido" muy curioso, más abundante en los comienzos de la fase, consiste en cajetes con engobe blanco amarilloso (tipo Atoyac Yellow-white) en el exterior y un engobe anaranjado (tipo Matadamas Orange) en el interior.

San José Black-and-White pertenece a la categoría de cerámica que en otras regiones de Mesoamérica se llama "white-rimmed black ware." El alfarero varió la oxidación y la reducción durante el proceso de cocción en tal forma que las vasijas (principalmente cajetes) muestran zonas nubladas de negro alternando con blanco.

La fase San José también incluye tipos especiales de cerámica que viajaban por las redes de intercambio entre las regiones. Uno de estos tipos es Xochiltepec White, un tipo originalmente definido por Coe y Diehl (1980). Igual que la cerámica llamada "kaolín" en Tlatilco (Piña Chan 1958), Xochiltepec White es de color blanco puro adentro y afuera. En el Valle de Oaxaca aparecen dos o tres variedades, algunas probablemente de origen local (hay depósitos de kaolín en la sierra de Mitla). Otro tipo importado es La Mina White (Coe y Diehl 1980), distinguido por su engobe de kaolín blanco sobre un barro color ladrillo.

Un tipo importante de origen oaxaqueño es Delfina Fine Gray, hecho con barro fino aluvial. Aparece en forma de vasos, cajetes cilíndricos, y cajetes de fondo plano y paredes divergentes; frecuentemente la decoración es un motivo raspado de la "serpiente de fuego." La superficie de las vasijas Delfina Fine Gray ha sido tan bruñida que da al investigador la impresión de ser un esmalte metálico de color gris claro. Este tipo fue exportado de Oaxaca a muchos otros sitios, por ejemplo Tlapacoya-Zohapilco en la Cuenca de México; San Lorenzo, Veracruz; Aquiles Serdán, Chiapas; y Las Canoas, Valle de Tehuacán.

El tipo San José Specular Red no es muy común; tiene un engobe rojo con cristales de hematita sobre un barro café. Aparece en forma de tecomates y cajetes.

Casi al final de la fase San José aparecen dos tipos que siguen aumentando en frecuencia durante el Formativo Medio. Uno de esos tipos es Coatepec White-rimmed Black, identificado por primera vez en el Valle de Tehuacán (MacNeish, Peterson, y Flannery 1970). Aparece en forma de cajetes de fondo plano y paredes divergentes, hecho con un barro fino y cocido muy duro, de color negro con un borde blanco producido por excelente control de oxidación y reducción. Otro tipo de San José tardío (y del Formativo Medio) es Delia White, utilizado casi exclusivamente en copas blancas muy elegantes. Existen al menos dos variedades de barro dentro de este tipo, ambas probablemente de otras regiones. Estas variedades tienen en común un engobe bien pulido que casi parece un esmalte blanco.

Finalmente, durante la fase San José se encuentran otros cuatro tipos de cerámica importada de otras regiones de Mesoamérica: Paloma Negative y Cesto White (Cuenca de México), Guamuchal Brushed (de Chiapas o Guatemala), y un tipo que puede ser Madera Brown de Morelos. Estos tipos extranjeros aparecen en distintos barrios, indicando su participación variable en las redes de intercambio.

En el Capítulo 13 se presenta la estratigrafía de una porción de Area C, San José Mogote, donde una serie de capas de basural documentan la transición de la fase Tierras Largas a la fase San José. Allí los porcentajes de tiestos de cada tipo de cerámica pueden ser utilizados para definir la fase.

En el Capítulo 14 se examina la variación cronológica (diacrónica) durante la fase San José. En el Area A de San José Mogote hay una secuencia de cuatro unidades domésticas y un basural que abarcan gran parte de la fase. En el Area C del mismo sitio hay una secuencia de ocho casas de carrizo y barro (con elementos asociados) que también abarcan gran parte de la fase. Una novena casa en la misma área (Casa 14) representa la parte final de la fase. Se examinan los tiestos de cada casa, elemento, o basural para entender los cambios de porcentajes dentro de la fase.

Habiendo estudiado la variación diacrónica en la fase San José, en los siguientes tres capítulos comenzamos a examinar la variación sincrónica dentro de la misma fase. En el Capítulo 15, por ejemplo, se compara la Casa 13 de San José Mogote (una unidad doméstica de bajo rango social) con las Casas 16–17 del mismo sitio (una unidad doméstica de alto rango social).

La unidad de bajo rango consta de una sola choza con muy pocos tiestos de tipos lujosos como Delfina Fine Gray y Xochiltepec White; el tipo más abundante es Fidencio Coarse, principalmente ollas toscas. En cambio, la unidad de alto rango consta de dos estructuras, una casa y una ramada o "cocina." La "cocina" contenía 10 veces más tiestos de Fidencio Coarse que la casa; la unidad, en general, tenía más cerámica importada de la Cuenca de México/Morelos, Tehuacán, y la costa del Golfo. La diferencia no puede ser cronológica, porque todos los atributos de la cerámica soportan una fecha dentro de la fase San José tardío. En el caso de la unidad doméstica del alto rango, se ve muy claro que para entender los porcentajes de tipos, un simple pozo no es suficiente; uno tiene que excavar toda la unidad.

El Capítulo 16 muestra la diferencia sincrónica entre las Areas A y B de San José Mogote, dos barrios residenciales separados por 250 metros. Los alfareros del Area A dan más énfasis a la "serpiente de fuego," un motivo muy abundante en la cerámica gris (Leandro Gray, Delfina Fine Gray); los de Area B dan más énfasis al "hombre-jaguar," un motivo muy abundante en la cerámica blanca (Atoyac Yellow-white). Estas variaciones en motivos afectan los porcentajes de la cerámica, siendo la gris más abundante en el Area A, y la blanca más abundante en el Area B. Esta diferencia sincrónica es independiente de la variación diacrónica; todos los atributos cronológicos ya establecidos en los Capítulos 13–14 muestran la contemporaneidad de los dos barrios.

El Capítulo 17 examina la diferencia entre dos sitios contemporáneos separados por 30 kilómetros: San José Mogote (Etla) y San Sebastián Abasolo (Tlacolula). En los dos sitios la estratigrafía muestra la misma secuencia básica en términos de atributos cronológicos. Sin embargo, Abasolo tiene un tipo de cerámica blanca fina que no aparece en San José Mogote, y San José Mogote tiene varios tipos importados que no aparecen en Abasolo. Además, las vasijas de Delfina Fine Gray de la zona de Abasolo no muestran la calidad observada en San José Mogote, y aparentemente fueron hechas con barros diferentes. Así, la secuencia básica de fases que hemos definido aparentemente sirve para todo el Valle de Oaxaca; sin embargo, ningún sitio muestra toda la variación que existe en cada fase.

En el Capítulo 18 se utiliza la secuencia de cerámica para fechar cuatro edificios públicos de la fase San José: las Estructuras 1, 2, 7, y 16 de San José Mogote.

En el Capítulo 19 se presenta el inventario de los fechados de carbono 14 para los sitios oaxaqueños. Se examinan no solamente las fechas, sino también los problemas de contexto arqueológico en el caso de varias muestras. Además se dan los inventarios de tipos y atributos que han servido para ligar la cerámica oaxaqueña a la de otras regiones durante el Formativo Temprano.

Finalmente, en el Capítulo 20 se discute el significado del término "olmeca" en vista de todos los nuevos descubrimientos en los últimos 20 años, tanto en Oaxaca como en Mesoamérica en general. Esos descubrimientos han derribado la idea de un "imperio olmeca" basado en el Golfo de México, subyugando a los valles serranos por conquista, colonización, o influencia cultural. En vez de una "cultura madre" en Veracruz-Tabasco, tenemos una serie de "culturas hermanas" en la Cuenca de México, Morelos, Puebla, Oaxaca, Guerrero, Chiapas, y el Golfo.

En el caso de Oaxaca, edificios públicos acabados con estuco y con una orientación de ocho grados al oeste del norte aparecen en la fase Tierras Largas, mucho antes que en San Lorenzo o en La Venta. Durante la fase San José, la arquitectura pública sigue siendo más sofisticada que en el Golfo, y se puede comprobar (por análisis espectroscópico) que vasijas Delfina Fine Gray y espejos de magnetita oaxaqueña fueron importados a San Lorenzo (Pires-Ferreira 1975). En vez de la cultura más avanzada de su época, la cultura olmeca del Golfo parece ser una sociedad de "jefatura" entre muchas. Como evidencia de ello, durante la fase San José la cerámica oaxaqueña fue más influida por la Cuenca de México (Tlapacoya-Zohapilco, Tlatilco) que por San Lorenzo.

En este volumen concluimos que el término "olmeca" se debe restringir a las culturas del Golfo (ver Grove 1989). Los motivos "hombre-jaguar," "serpiente de fuego," etc. no son "olmecas" sino "pan-Mesoamericanos." Los mejores ejemplos de estos motivos en cerámica vienen de la parte sur de la Cuenca de México, no de Golfo; el repertorio de motivos de la cerámica de San Lorenzo es mucho más limitado. Llamar "olmeca" a una pieza de Tlapacoya, de Chalcatzingo, de San José Mogote, o de Chiapas es fomentar un mito—el mito de una costa desarrollada y un altiplano subdesarrollado—en el cual nadie cree hoy en día.

Bibliography

Agrinier, Pierre
1989 Mirador-Plumajillo, Chiapas, y sus relaciones con cuatro sitios del horizonte olmeca en Veracruz, Chiapas y la costa de Guatemala. *Arqueología* 2:19–36.

Alaniz, Adriana
1975 Note in *Boletín*, no. 2. (Mayo). Oaxaca, Mexico: Centro Regional de Oaxaca, Instituto Nacional de Antropología e Historia.

Andrews, E. Wyllys, V, and Norman Hammond
1990 Redefinition of the Swasey phase at Cuello, Belize. *American Antiquity* 54:570–84.

Arkell, Anthony J.
1960 The origin of black-topped red pottery. *Journal of Egyptian Archaeology* 46:105–6.

Bahn, Paul, and John Flenley
1992 *Easter Island, Earth Island*. London: Thames and Hudson.

Beals, Ralph L.
1973 *Ethnology of the Western Mixe*. New York: Cooper Square Publishers.

Blake, T. Michael
1991 An emerging Early Formative chiefdom at Paso de la Amada, Chiapas, Mexico. In *The Formation of Complex Society in Southeastern Mesoamerica*, edited by William R. Fowler, Jr., pp. 27–46. Boca Raton: CRC Press.

Braidwood, Robert J., Bruce Howe et al.
1960 *Prehistoric Investigations in Iraqi Kurdistan*. Studies in Ancient Oriental Civilization no. 31. Chicago: Oriental Institute, University of Chicago.

Brainerd, George W.
1951 The place of chronological ordering in archaeological analysis. *American Antiquity* 16:301–13.

Brush, Charles F.
1965 Pox Pottery: earliest identified Mexican ceramics. *Science* 149:194–95.

Caso, Alfonso, Ignacio Bernal, and Jorge R. Acosta
1967 *La Cerámica de Monte Albán*. Memorias del Instituto Nacional de Antropología e Historia no. 13. Mexico.

Childe, V. Gordon
1958 *The Dawn of European Civilization* (6th ed., rev.). New York: Alfred A. Knopf.

Clark, John E.
1991 The beginnings of Mesoamerica: *apologia* for the Soconusco Early Formative. In *The Formation of Complex Society in Southeastern Mesoamerica*, edited by William R. Fowler, Jr., pp. 13–26. Boca Raton: CRC Press.

Clark, John E., and T. Michael Blake
1989 El origen de la civilización en Mesoamérica: los Olmecas y Mokaya del Soconusco de Chiapas, Mexico. In *Preclásico o Formativo: Avances y Perspectivas,* edited by M. Carmona, pp. 385–405. Mexico: Museo Nacional de Antropología.

Clavijero, Francisco Javier
1974 *Historia Antigua de México*. Mexico: Editorial Porrúa.

Coe, Michael D.
1961 *La Victoria: An Early Site on the Pacific Coast of Guatemala*. Papers of the Peabody Museum of Archaeology and Ethnology, Harvard University, vol. 53. Cambridge, Massachusetts.
1965 The Olmec style and its distribution. In *Handbook of Middle American Indians*, vol. 3, edited by Gordon R. Willey, pp. 739–75. Austin: University of Texas Press.
1968 San Lorenzo and the Olmec civilization. In *Dumbarton Oaks Conference on the Olmec,* edited by Elizabeth P. Benson, pp. 41–71. Washington, D.C.: Dumbarton Oaks Research Library and Collection.

Coe, Michael D., and Richard A. Diehl
1980 *In the Land of the Olmec*, vol. 1: *The Archaeology of San Lorenzo Tenochtitlán*. Austin: University of Texas Press.

Coe, Michael D., and Kent V. Flannery
1967 *Early Cultures and Human Ecology in South Coastal Guatemala*. Smithsonian Contributions to Anthropology, vol. 3. Washington, D.C.

Córdova, Juan de
[1578] *Vocabulario en lengua zapoteca*. Mexico: Pedro Charte y Antonio Ricardo.
1942

Covarrubias, Miguel
1957 *Indian Art of Mexico and Central America*. New York: Alfred A Knopf.

Cushing, Frank H.
1886 A study of Pueblo pottery as illustrative of Zuni culture growth, 4th Annual Report. *Bureau of American Ethnology, 1882–1883*, pp. 467–621. Washington, D.C.

Cutler, Hugh C., and Thomas W. Whitaker
1967 Cucurbits from the Tehuacán Caves. In *Prehistory of the Tehuacán Valley,* vol. 1: *Environment and Subsistence,* edited by Douglas S. Byers, pp. 212–19. Austin: University of Texas Press.

Cyphers Guillén, Ann
1987 Ceramics. In *Ancient Chalcatzingo,* edited by David C. Grove, pp. 200–51. Austin: University of Texas Press.

DeCicco, Gabriel
1969 The Chatino. In *Handbook of Middle American Indians,* vol. 7: *Ethnology,* edited by Evon Z. Vogt, pp. 360–66. Austin: University of Texas Press.

Dixon, Keith A.
1959 *Ceramics from Two Preclassic Periods at Chiapa de Corzo, Chiapas, Mexico.* Papers of the New World Archaeological Foundation no. 5. Orinda, California.

Dodge, Ernest S.
1943 *Gourd Growers of the South Seas: An Introduction to the Study of the Lagenaria Gourd In The Culture Of The Polynesians.* Ethnographical Series no. 2. Boston: The Gourd Society of America. Salem: Peabody Museum.

Drennan, Robert D.
1976a *Fábrica San José and Middle Formative Society in the Valley of Oaxaca.* Prehistory and Human Ecology of the Valley of Oaxaca, Vol. 4, edited by Kent V. Flannery. Memoirs of the Museum of Anthropology, University of Michigan no. 8. Ann Arbor.
1976b A refinement of chronological seriation using nonmetric multidimensional scaling. *American Antiquity* 41(3):290–302.
1983a Ritual and ceremonial development at the early village level. In *The Cloud People: Divergent Evolution of the Zapotec and Mixtec Civilizations,* edited by Kent V. Flannery and Joyce Marcus, pp. 46–50. New York: Academic Press.
1983b Appendix: Radiocarbon dates from the Oaxaca region. In *The Cloud People: Divergent Evolution of the Zapotec and Mixtec Civilizations,* edited by Kent V. Flannery and Joyce Marcus, pp. 363–70. New York: Academic Press.

Drucker, Philip
1952 *La Venta, Tabasco: A Study of Olmec Ceramics and Art.* Bureau of American Ethnology Bulletin no. 153. Washington, D.C.: Smithsonian Institution.

Drucker, Philip, Robert F. Heizer, and Robert J. Squier
1959 *Excavations at La Venta, Tabasco, 1955.* Bureau of American Ethnology Bulletin no. 170. Washington, D.C.: Smithsonian Institution.

Fash, William L., Jr.
1982 A Middle Formative cemetery from Copán, Honduras. Paper delivered at the annual meeting of the American Anthropological Association, Washington, D.C.

Flannery, Kent V.
1968 The Olmec and the Valley of Oaxaca: a model for inter-regional interaction in Formative times. In *Dumbarton Oaks Conference on the Olmec,* edited by Elizabeth P. Benson, pp. 79–117. Washington, D.C.:Dumbarton Oaks Research Library and Collection.
1972 The origins of the village as a settlement type in Mesoamerica and the Near East: a comparative study. In *Man, Settlement, and Urbanism,* edited by Peter J. Ucko, Ruth Tringham, and Geoffrey W. Dimbleby, pp. 23–53. London: Gerald Duckworth and Co.

1976a Excavating deep communities by transect samples. In *The Early Mesoamerican Village,* edited by Kent V. Flannery, pp. 68–72. New York: Academic Press.
1976b Two possible village subdivisions: the courtyard group and the residential ward. In *The Early Mesoamerican Village,* edited by Kent V. Flannery, pp. 72–75. New York: Academic Press.
1983 The Tierras Largas phase and the analytical units of the early Oaxacan village. In *The Cloud People: Divergent Evolution of the Zapotec and Mixtec Civilizations,* edited by Kent V. Flannery and Joyce Marcus, pp. 43–45. New York: Academic Press.

Flannery, Kent V. (editor)
1976 *The Early Mesoamerican Village.* New York: Academic Press.
1986 *Guilá Naquitz: Archaic Foraging and Early Agriculture in Oaxaca, Mexico.* Orlando: Academic Press.

Flannery, Kent V., and Joyce Marcus
1976a The evolution of the public building in Formative Oaxaca. In *Cultural Change and Continuity: Essays in Honor of James Bennett Griffin,* edited by Charles Cleland, pp. 205–21. New York: Academic Press.
1976b Formative Oaxaca and the Zapotec cosmos. *American Scientist* 64:374–83.
1983a The Rosario phase and the origins of Monte Albán I. In *The Cloud People: Divergent Evolution of the Zapotec and Mixtec Civilizations,* edited by Kent V. Flannery and Joyce Marcus, pp. 74–77. New York: Academic Press.
1983b Urban Mitla and its rural hinterland. In *The Cloud People: Divergent Evolution of the Zapotec and Mixtec Civilizations,* edited by Kent V. Flannery and Joyce Marcus, pp. 295–300. New York: Academic Press.

Flannery, Kent V., and Joyce Marcus (editors)
1983 *The Cloud People: Divergent Evolution of the Zapotec and Mixtec Civilizations.* New York: Academic Press.

Flannery, Kent V. et al.
1970 *Preliminary Archaeological Investigations in the Valley of Oaxaca, Mexico, 1966 through 1969: Report to the Instituto Nacional de Antropología e Historia and the National Science Foundation.* Mimeographed. Ann Arbor: University of Michigan Museum of Anthropology.

Foster, George
1955 *Contemporary Pottery Techniques in Southern and Central Mexico.* Middle American Research Institute, Tulane University, Publication 22. New Orleans.

Furst, Jill L.
1978 *Codex Vindobonensis Mexicanus I: A Commentary.* Institute for Mesoamerican Studies, Publication No. 4. Albany: State University of New York at Albany.

Gifford, James C.
1960 The type-variety method of ceramic classification as an indicator of cultural phenomena. *American Antiquity* 25 (3): 341–347.
1976 *Prehistoric Pottery Analysis and the Ceramics of Barton Ramie in the Belize Valley.* Memoirs of the Peabody Museum of Archaeology and Ethnology, Harvard University no. 18. Cambridge, Massachusetts.

Green, Dee F., and Gareth W. Lowe
1967 *Altamira and Padre Piedra, Early Preclassic Sites in Chiapas, Mexico.* Papers of the New World Archaeological Foundation no. 20. Provo, Utah: Brigham Young University.

Grove, David C.
1968 The Pre-classic Olmec in central Mexico: site distribution and inferences. In *Dumbarton Oaks Conference on the Olmec,* edited by Elizabeth P. Benson, pp. 179–85. Washington, D.C.: Dumbarton Oaks Research Library and Collection.
1989 Olmec: what's in a name? In *Regional Perspectives on the Olmec,* edited by Robert J. Sharer and David C. Grove, pp. 8–14. Cambridge: Cambridge University Press.

Grove, David C. (editor)
1987 *Ancient Chalcatzingo.* Austin: University of Texas Press.

Hall, D. W., G. A. Haswell, and T. A. Oxley
1956 *Underground Storage of Grain.* British Colonial Office, Pest Information Laboratory, Department of Scientific and Industrial Research. London: H.M. Stationery Office.

Hammond, Norman
1977 The Early Formative in the Maya lowlands. In *Social Process in Maya Prehistory: Studies in Honour of Sir Eric Thompson,* edited by Norman Hammond, pp. 77–101. London: Academic Press.
1978 Cacao and Cobaneros: an overland trade route between the Maya highlands and lowlands. In *Mesoamerican Communication Routes and Cultural Contacts,* edited by Thomas Lee, Jr. and Carlos Navarrete. Papers of the New World Archaeological Foundation 40:19–25. Provo, Utah.
1989 Cultura Hermana: Reappraising the Olmec. *Quarterly Review of Archaeology* 9(4):1–4.

Hammond, Norman et al.
1977 Maya Formative phase radiocarbon dates from Belize. *Nature* 267:608–10.

Heizer, Robert F.
1968 New observations on La Venta. In *Dumbarton Oaks Conference on the Olmec,* edited by Elizabeth P. Benson, pp. 9–40. Washington, D.C.: Dumbarton Oaks Research Library and Collection.

Hendry, Jean Clare
1957 *Atzompa: A Pottery Producing Village of Southern Mexico.* Ph.D. dissertation, Cornell University. University Microfilms, Ann Arbor.

Hole, Frank
1986 Chipped-stone tools. In *Guilá Naquitz: Archaic Foraging and Early Agriculture in Oaxaca, Mexico,* edited by Kent V. Flannery, pp. 97–139. Orlando: Academic Press.

Hole, Frank, Kent V. Flannery, and James A. Neely
1969 *Prehistory and Human Ecology of the Deh Luran Plain.* Memoirs of the Museum of Anthropology, University of Michigan no. 1. Ann Arbor.

Holmes, W. H.
1903 *Aboriginal Pottery of the Eastern United States.* 20th Annual Report of the Bureau of American Ethnology, 1898–1899. Washington, D.C.: Bureau of American Ethnology.

Jiménez Moreno, Wigberto
1966 Mesoamerica before the Toltecs. In *Ancient Oaxaca,* edited by John Paddock, pp. 1–82. Stanford: Stanford University Press.

Johnson, Frederick, and Richard S. MacNeish
1972 Chronometric dating. In *The Prehistory of the Tehuacan Valley,* vol. 4: *Chronology and Irrigation,* edited by Frederick Johnson, pp. 3–55. Austin: University of Texas Press.

Kirkby, Michael J., Anne V. Whyte, and Kent V. Flannery
1986 The physical environment of the Guilá Naquitz cave group. In *Guilá Naquitz: Archaic Foraging and Early Agriculture in Oaxaca, Mexico,* edited by Kent V. Flannery, pp. 43–61. Orlando: Academic Press.

Kowalewski, Stephen A., Gary M. Feinman, Laura Finsten, Richard E. Blanton, and Linda M. Nicholas
1989 *Monte Albán's Hinterland, Part II: Prehispanic Settlement Patterns in Tlacolula, Etla, and Ocotlán, the Valley of Oaxaca, Mexico.* Memoirs of the Museum of Anthropology, University of Michigan no. 23. Ann Arbor.

Lambert, Wayne
1972 *Petrographic Study of Thin Sections L-3346 (Atoyac Gris Fin Ceramic Type, Tlapacoya) and L-3345 (Delfina Fine Gray Ceramic Type, Oaxaca).* Report sent jointly to Christine Niederberger and Kent V. Flannery.

Leach, Edmund R.
1954 *Political Systems of Highland Burma.* London: G. Bell & Sons.

Lorenzo, José Luis
1960 Aspectos físicos del valle de Oaxaca. *Revista Mexicana de Estudios Antropológicos* 16:49–63.

Love, Michael W.
1991 Style and social complexity in Formative Mesoamerica. In *The Formation of Complex Society in Southeastern Mesoamerica,* edited by William R. Fowler, Jr., pp. 47–76. Boca Raton: CRC Press.

Lowe, Gareth W.
1975 *The Early Preclassic Barra Phase of Altamira, Chiapas: A Review with New Data.* Papers of the New World Archaeological Foundation no. 38. Provo, Utah: Brigham Young University.

MacNeish, Richard S.
1964 Ancient Mesoamerican civilization. *Science* 143:531–37.

MacNeish, Richard S., Frederick A. Peterson, and Kent V. Flannery
1970 *The Prehistory of the Tehuacán Valley,* vol. 3: *Ceramics.* Austin: University of Texas Press.

Marcus, Joyce
1982 Field Notes, Cerro Azul Project, Cañete, Perú (unpublished).
1983 The Espiridión Complex and the origins of the Oaxacan Formative. In *The Cloud People: Divergent Evolution of the Zapotec and Mixtec Civilizations,* edited by Kent V. Flannery and Joyce Marcus, pp. 42–43. New York: Academic Press.
1989 Zapotec chiefdoms and the nature of Formative religions. In *Regional Perspectives on the Olmec,* edited by Robert J. Sharer and David C. Grove, pp. 148–97. Cambridge: Cambridge University Press.
1992 *Mesoamerican Writing Systems: Propaganda, Myth, and History in Four Ancient Civilizations.* Princeton, New Jersey: Princeton University Press.
n.d. Cerro Azul: a Late Intermediate community in the Cañete Valley, Peru. In preparation.

Marcus, Joyce, and Kent V. Flannery
1978 Ethnoscience of the sixteenth-century Valley Zapotec. In *The Nature and Status of Ethnobotany,* edited by Richard I. Ford. Anthropological Papers of the Museum of Anthropology, University of Michigan no. 67, pp. 51–79. Ann Arbor.

n.d. Ancient Zapotec ritual and religion: an application of the direct historical approach. In *The Ancient Mind,* edited by Colin Renfrew and Ezra B. W. Zubrow. Cambridge: Cambridge University Press. In press.

McClellan, Catharine
1953 The Inland Tlingit. In *Asia and North America: Transpacific Contacts.* Memoirs of the Society for American Archaeology 9:47–52. Salt Lake City.

Morley, Sylvanus G.
1937 *Inscriptions of Peten.* 5 volumes. Carnegie Institution of Washington Publication 437. Washington, D.C.

Munsell Color Company
1954 *Munsell Soil Color Charts* (1954 edition). Baltimore: Munsell Color Co.

Niederberger, Christine
1987 Paleopaysages et archéologie pre-urbaine du Bassin de Mexico, vol. II. *Etudes Mesoamericaines,* vol. XI. México, D.F.: Centre d'Etudes Mexicaines et Centramericaines.

Parry, William
1987 *Chipped Stone Tools in Formative Oaxaca, Mexico: Their Procurement, Production and Use.* Memoirs of the Museum of Anthropology, University of Michigan no. 20. Ann Arbor.

Parsons, Elsie Clews
1936 *Mitla: Town of the Souls.* Chicago: University of Chicago Press.

Piña Chan, Román
1958 Tlatilco (Segunda Parte). *Serie Investigaciones* 2. México, D.F.: Instituto Nacional de Antropología e Historia.

Pires-Ferreira, Jane W.
1975 *Formative Mesoamerican Exchange Networks, with Special Reference to the Valley of Oaxaca.* Memoirs of the Museum of Anthropology, University of Michigan no. 7. Ann Arbor.
1976 Shell and iron-ore mirror exchange in Formative Mesoamerica, with comments on other commodities. In *The Early Mesoamerican Village,* edited by Kent V. Flannery, pp. 311–28. New York: Academic Press.

Plog, Stephen
1976 The measurement of prehistoric interaction between communities. In *The Early Mesoamerican Village,* edited by Kent V. Flannery, pp. 255–72. New York: Academic Press.
n.d. *The Measurement of Prehistoric Human Interaction.* Undergraduate Honors Thesis in Anthropology, University of Michigan, Ann Arbor.

Porter, Muriel Noé
1953 *Tlatilco and the Pre-classic Cultures of the New World.* Viking Fund Publications in Anthropology no. 19. New York: Wenner-Gren Foundation for Anthropological Research.

Pyne, Nanette
1976 The fire-serpent and were-jaguar in Formative Oaxaca: a contingency table analysis. In *The Early Mesoamerican Village,* edited by Kent V. Flannery, pp. 272–80. New York: Academic Press.

Reichel-Dolmatoff, Gerardo
1965 *Colombia.* New York: Frederick Praeger.

Rice, Prudence
1987 *Pottery Analysis: A Sourcebook.* Chicago: University of Chicago Press.

Robinson, W. S.
1951 A method for chronologically ordering archaeological deposits. *American Antiquity* 16:293–301.

Rouse, Irving
1960 The classification of artifacts in archaeology. *American Antiquity* 25(3):313–23.

Rowe, John H.
1960 Cultural unity and diversification in Peruvian archaeology. In *Men and Cultures: Selected Papers of the Fifth International Congress of Anthropological and Ethnological Sciences,* pp. 627–31. Philadelphia.
1962 Stages and periods in archaeological interpretation. *Southwestern Journal of Anthropology* 18(1):40–54.

Sabloff, Jeremy A., and Robert E. Smith
1969 The importance of both analytic and taxonomic classification in the type-variety system. *American Antiquity* 34(3):278–85.
1972 Ceramic wares in the Maya area: a clarification of an aspect of the type-variety system and presentation of a formal model for comparative use. *Estudios de Cultura Maya* 8:97–115.

Sanders, William T., Jeffrey R. Parsons, and Robert S. Santley
1979 *The Basin of Mexico: Ecological Processes in the Evolution of a Civilization.* New York: Academic Press.

Schiffer, Michael B.
1976 *Behavioral Archaeology.* New York: Academic Press.
1987 *Formation Processes of the Archaeological Record.* Albuquerque: University of New Mexico Press.

Sharer, Robert J., and David C. Grove (editors)
1989 *Regional Perspectives on the Olmec.* Cambridge: Cambridge University Press.

Shepard, Anna O.
1963 Beginnings of ceramic industrialization: an example from the Oaxaca Valley. *Notes from a Ceramic Laboratory 2.* Washington, D.C.: Carnegie Institution of Washington.

Sinopoli, Carla M.
1991 *Approaches to Archaeological Ceramics.* New York: Plenum Press.

Smith, Robert E., Gordon R. Willey, and James C. Gifford
1960 The type-variety concept as a basis for the analysis of Maya pottery. *American Antiquity* 25(3):330–40.

Spores, Ronald
1972 *An Archaeological Settlement Survey of the Nochixtlán Valley, Oaxaca.* Vanderbilt University Publications in Anthropology no. 1. Nashville, Tennessee.
1983 Origins of the village in the Mixteca (Early Cruz phase). In *The Cloud People: Divergent Evolution of the Zapotec and Mixtec Civilizations,* edited by Kent V. Flannery and Joyce Marcus, p. 46. New York: Academic Press.

Stirling, Matthew W.
1968 Early history of the Olmec Problem. In *Dumbarton Oaks Conference on the Olmec,* edited by Elizabeth P. Benson, pp. 1–8. Washington, D.C.: Dumbarton Oaks Research Library and Collection.

Stolmaker, Charlotte
1973 *Cultural, Social and Economic Change in Santa María Atzompa.* Ph.D. dissertation, University of California at Los Angeles. University Microfilms, Ann Arbor.

Stuiver, Minze, and Paul D. Quay
1980 Changes in atmospheric Carbon-14 attributed to a variable sun. *Science* 207:11–19.

Tello, Julio C.
1960 *Chavín: Cultura Matriz de la Civilización Andina* (con revisión de Toribio Mejía Xesspe). Lima, Peru: Imprenta de la Universidad de San Marcos.

Tolstoy, Paul
1989a Coapexco and Tlatilco: sites with Olmec materials in the Basin of Mexico. In *Regional Perspectives on the Olmec,* edited by Robert J. Sharer and David C. Grove, pp. 85–121. New York: Cambridge University Press.
1989b Western Mesoamerica and the Olmec. In *Regional Perspectives on the Olmec,* edited by Robert J. Sharer and David C. Grove, pp. 275–302. New York: Cambridge University Press.

Tolstoy, Paul, and Louise I. Paradis
1970 Early and Middle Preclassic culture in the Basin of Mexico. *Science* 167:344–51.

Torquemada, Juan de
1975– *Monarquía Indiana.* 6 volumes. Mexico: Universidad Nacional
1979 Autonóma de México.

Uhle, Max
1913 Zur chronologie der alten culturen von Ica. *Journal de la Société des Américanistes de Paris,* n.s., v. 10:341–67. Paris.

Wauchope, Robert
1938 *Modern Maya Houses: A Study of Their Archaeological Significance.* Carnegie Institution of Washington, Publication 502. Washington, D.C.

Weaver, Muriel Porter
1967 *Tlapacoya Pottery in the Museum Collection.* Indian Notes and Monographs, Miscellaneous Series no. 56. New York: Museum of the American Indian, Heye Foundation.

Whalen, Michael E.
1981 *Excavations at Santo Domingo Tomaltepec: Evolution of a Formative Community in the Valley of Oaxaca, Mexico.* Memoirs of the Museum of Anthropology, University of Michigan no. 12. Ann Arbor.
1986 Sources of the Guilá Naquitz chipped stone. In *Guilá Naquitz: Archaic Foraging and Early Agriculture in Oaxaca, Mexico,* edited by Kent V. Flannery, pp. 141–46. Orlando: Academic Press.

Whitaker, Thomas W., and Hugh C. Cutler
1986 Cucurbits from Preceramic levels at Guilá Naquitz. In *Guilá Naquitz: Archaic Foraging and Early Agriculture in Oaxaca, Mexico,* edited by Kent V. Flannery, pp. 275–79. Orlando: Academic Press.

Willey, Gordon R., and Charles R. McGimsey
1954 *The Monagrillo Culture of Panama.* Papers of the Peabody Museum of Archaeology and Ethnology, Harvard University, vol. 49, no. 2. Cambridge, Massachusetts.

Willey, Gordon R., T. Patrick Culbert, and Richard E. W. Adams
1967 Maya lowland ceramics: a report from the 1965 Guatemala City conference. *American Antiquity* 32(3):289–315.

Wilson, Eddie
1945 *Gourd in Folk Literature.* Ethnographical Series no. 3. Boston: The New England Gourd Society.

Winter, Marcus C.
1972 *Tierras Largas: A Formative Community in the Valley of Oaxaca, Mexico.* Unpublished Ph.D. dissertation, University of Arizona. Tucson.
1976 Excavating a shallow community by random sampling quadrats. In *The Early Mesoamerican Village,* edited by Kent V. Flannery, pp. 62–67. New York: Academic Press.

Winter, Marcus C., and William O. Payne
1976 Hornos para cerámica hallados en Monte Albán. *Boletín del Instituto Nacional de Antropología e Historia* 16:37–40.

Young, David
1966 *Pottery Making in Santa María Atzompa.* Manuscript, Stanford University Field School.

Young, T. Cuyler, Jr.
1969 *Excavations at Godin Tepe: First Progress Report.* Royal Ontario Museum Art and Archaeology, Occasional Paper no. 17. Toronto.

Young, T. Cuyler, Jr., and Louis D. Levine
1974 *Excavations of the Godin Project: Second Progress Report.* Royal Ontario Museum Art and Archaeology, Occasional Paper no. 26. Toronto.

Zeitlin, Robert N.
1979 *Prehistoric Long-Distance Exchange on the Southern Isthmus of Tehuantepec, Mexico,* vol. II: *The Pottery of Laguna Zope.* Unpublished Ph.D. dissertation, Yale University. New Haven, Connecticut.

Zeuner, Frederick E.
1954 *Dating the Past.* London: Methuen.